THE EXPEDITIONS OF
John Charles Frémont

John Charles Frémont as he looked about 1849. From a print in
Walter Colton's *Three Years in California* (New York, 1850).

THE EXPEDITIONS OF
John Charles
Frémont

VOLUME 2
The Bear Flag Revolt
and the Court-Martial

EDITED BY

MARY LEE SPENCE AND DONALD JACKSON

560417

UNIVERSITY OF ILLINOIS PRESS

URBANA, CHICAGO, AND LONDON

THE EXPEDITIONS OF
John Charles Frémont

ADVISORY COMMITTEE

Herman R. Friis
Robert W. Johannsen

ACKNOWLEDGMENTS

As in Volume 1, we find it impossible to thank by name the many scholars and librarians who have given us assistance in preparing the present volume. We do wish to acknowledge, however, the continuing support of the National Historical Publications Commission, the Research Board of the University of Illinois, and the staff of the University of Illinois Press. We are grateful to Miss Jessie Fremont, Washington, D.C., the granddaughter of John Charles and Jessie Benton Frémont, for permission to use family papers.

During the preparation of the work, two distinguished members of our Advisory Committee died: Allan Nevins and Dale L. Morgan. Each was enthusiastic about the project, and each brought his own kind of expertise to our aid on many occasions.

The role of Donald Jackson has been secondary in the preparation of this volume. He has served mainly as an advisor, while the research and writing has been done by Mary Lee Spence.

M.L.S.

D.J.

CONTENTS

The Bear Flag Revolt and the Conquest of California

xi

THE ARREST AND COURT-MARTIAL OF FRÉMONT

ILLUSTRATIONS

INTRODUCTION

When John C. Frémont angrily resigned from the Army in the spring of 1848, telling botanist John Torrey that he hoped the government would continue to finance his scientific exploration even though he was now a civilian, he was looking back upon three years of tumult, intrigue, and bitterness. Those three years are spanned by the documents in this volume.

The period 1845-48 seemed to bring into focus the restlessness of American emigrants, with Oregon, Texas, and the Mexican borderlands all added to the Union. For Frémont they were pivotal years. Once again he had turned his talents to the exploration of the Far West, this time mixing political activity with scientific observation. His defiance of the military authority of Stephen Watts Kearny in California brought the exhausting experience of a court-martial, and later historians, among them Hubert Howe Bancroft and Bernard DeVoto, would label him a filibuster and adventurer, calling into question not only his conduct as an officer but also his character and honesty of purpose.[1] Harvard historian and philosopher Josiah Royce cast no epithets, but he charged Frémont with bringing a needless war into California and creating an estrangement between Mexicans and Americans which all his subsequent generosity and kindness could not eradicate. "From the Bear Flag Affair," wrote Royce, "we can date the beginning of the degradation, the ruin, and the oppression of the California people by our own."[2]

It may be that publication of these documents, including the transcript of the long court-martial proceedings in a supplementary volume, will provide further insight into California affairs, although clear-cut answers do not always appear. There are knotty questions about secret instructions or lack of instructions. Many documents

---

[1] BANCROFT, 5:85–100; DE VOTO, 197–201, 222–29, 470–77.
[2] ROYCE [1], 50–162 and particularly 111–12.

have not survived; those which have are sometimes contradictory and, perhaps deliberately, obscure in wording.

No one should try to understand the California of 1845–48, and the men who played leading roles there, without a thorough reading of the court-martial proceedings. It is hard to escape the conclusion that some historians of the period have not done so. One can admire Frémont's intrepidity as an explorer and his expertness as a geographer without particularly liking his ambition, his vanity, and his reliance upon his father-in-law for professional advancement. One can say, and many do, that John Charles and Jessie were a team of myth makers and empire builders. Yet the documents, when they are not aggravatingly silent, speak constantly to the point that in the California episode Frémont was as often right as wrong. And even a cursory investigation of the court-martial record produces one undeniable conclusion: neither side in the controversy acquitted itself with distinction.

What is required first, for an understanding of the whole matter, is a glance at the mood of the country, at Frémont's orders, and at the nature of the third expedition itself. Early in 1845 Congress had voted to annex Texas, that vast domain seized from a weak Mexico by hardy American settlers. Already a handful of venturesome Americans had established themselves in California; thousands of pioneers were wheeling along the Oregon Trail toward the green Willamette Valley; soon the Mormon Saints would establish their new Zion in the Great Basin of Utah.

Claimed by both the United States and England, the Oregon country had been opened to settlement under the 1827 Treaty of Joint Occupation, an extension of the earlier agreement of 1818. Not unexpectedly, American homeseekers won the battle of the census and soon came to predominate, their growing numbers along the Willamette demanding the establishment of a stable government by the United States. Although the British minister in Washington had rejected President James K. Polk's offer to divide the country at the forty-ninth parallel, Polk, in his annual message to Congress at the end of 1845, asked for power to abrogate the Treaty of Joint Occupation and extend protection of American law over settlers in the Oregon country. Not until June 1846 did the formal British offer to settle on the forty-ninth parallel reach Washington, but even this did not dispel all distrust of the British. Several months later Thomas Hart Benton received a letter from Frémont describing an attack upon him in Oregon by Klamath Indians supplied with tomahawks and iron arrowheads by the British, and suggesting that Secretary of State James Buchanan's attention be called to the fact that the Indians were "friendly" to the English and "unfriendly" to the Americans. Frémont's letter in a sense typified the fear of Great Britain, which had smoldered since the days of the Revolution and the War of 1812 and which had been rekindled and fanned by events of the 1830s and 1840s.

Had not England, for diplomatic, economic, and humanitarian reasons, flirted with an independent Texas? Was it not a rumor—or more than a rumor—that Britain had designs on California? It is clear now that such a rumor was unfounded, for the British government steadfastly opposed expansion into California, partly because it feared war with the United States and partly because its "Little England" policy discouraged further expansion of the empire in that period. But it is what government officials believe that determines action, and President Polk made his fear of the British occupation of California one of the cornerstones of his foreign policy.

Yet his and the country's mood was more positive on the subject of California. If Polk had been elected on a platform calling for the "re-annexation of Texas and the re-occupation of Oregon," implicit was an observable if less blatant interest in the Pacific Coast south of the Oregon line. There the tallow and hide trade had diminished in importance, but not before its Yankee agents and shipmasters had helped focus American attention on the balmy climate and economic potential of California. Along with a handful of serious settlers and a variety of mere travelers, they gave broad publicity to this land where vast estates were available almost for a pittance and economic opportunity was unlimited. In response, a steady trickle of emigrants was coming overland in the early forties. By 1846 Larkin estimated that three-fourths of the 1,000 or 1,200 foreigners living in California were Americans.

As these newcomers descended the western slopes of the Sierra, they could not fail to recognize the potential for political as well as material conquest. Through the years the native *Californios* had evolved their own pastoral and easy way of life—one indifferent to social change and disrespectful of a government administered from distant Mexico City. Distance and intermittent turmoil, both in the mother country and in California, made for near chaos during much of the 1830s. An able governor, José Figueroa, died in 1835, and then came a decade of internal strife typified by official corruption and petty revolt. When Governor Manuel Micheltorena and his tough *cholo* army were sent packing in 1845, all semblance of Mexican control went with them. Americans, not all men of impeccable motives, quickly grasped the implications. With a little effort, might not the Texas story be repeated on the shores of the Pacific? Were not American frontiersmen destined to extend their brand of civilization from sea to sea, engulfing more static societies in the process?

Certainly President Polk was not averse, provided he had the majority of his constituents behind him. But he also saw the need to avoid open conflict with Mexico and not to alienate the pro-American faction of the *Californios*. His efforts to purchase California rebuffed before they had hardly commenced, he turned to intrigue, always with a wary eye on the British. Thus, at about the time of Frémont's departure from the Missouri frontier, Commodore John D. Sloat was instructed to seize San Francisco and other Pacific ports if he should determine "with certainty" that Mexico had declared war against the United States. In October of the same year Sloat was ordered to take control of California "in the event of actual hostilities" between the Mexican and American governments, to communicate frequently with the U.S. consul at Monterey, and to divine as nearly as possible the designs of the English and the French in that region.[3] On the same day that Sloat's October orders were cut, the U.S. consul at Monterey, Thomas Oliver Larkin, was appointed a confidential agent and instructed to "exert the greatest vigilance in discovering and defeating any attempts which may be made by Foreign Governments to acquire a control" over California. He would not attempt to make her a state, Buchanan informed Larkin, but "if the People should desire to unite their destiny with ours, they would be received as brethren, whenever this can be done, without affording Mexico just cause of complaint."[4]

In the written orders under which Frémont mounted his third expedition, no mention was made of his entering California. His instructions were, in fact, very narrow. The chief of the Bureau of Topographical Engineers directed him to "strike the Arkansas as

---

[3] George Bancroft to John D. Sloat, 24 June and 17 Oct. 1845, CAL. HIS. SOC. DOCS., 2:164–65.

[4] Buchanan to Larkin, 17 Oct. 1845, LARKIN, 4:44–47.

soon as practicable, survey the Red River without our boundary line, noting particularly the navigable properties of each," and "determine as near as practicable the points at which the boundary line of the U.S. the 100th degree of longitude west of Greenwich strikes the Arkansas, and the Red River." It was important that the headwaters of the Arkansas be accurately determined, but long journeys should not be taken to determine isolated geographical points. In short, Frémont was to direct his efforts "to the geography of localities within reasonable distance of Bent's Fort and of the streams which run east from the Rocky Mountains." Later instructions permitted him to increase the size of his party, to detach a subgroup to explore the southern Rockies, and to pay some attention to the military aspects of the country. But a letter dated 14 May 1845 may be taken as an indication that the chief of the Topographical Bureau understood that Frémont's explorations would be more extensive than outlined by the official orders. He directed Frémont to have Lieut. James W. Abert return with his detachment to the United States as soon as practicable "in order that expenses of the expedition may be reduced, and funds be left to meet the events of your own efforts for more distant discoveries."

But there is still no mention of California, and when Frémont wrote in his *Memoirs* that it was decided "to extend the survey west and southwest to the examination of the great ranges of the Cascade Mountains and the Sierra Nevada, so as to ascertain the lines of communication through the mountains to the ocean in that latitude," he was either recalling oral instructions or justifying a *fait accompli*. The former seems more likely.[5] Officials registered no surprise when news reached Washington that Frémont was in California. In fact, a few days after the expedition left Westport on 26 June, the *Western Expositor,* a newspaper published in Independence, Missouri, reported that the main division of the expedition under Frémont would winter among the American settlements of Upper California and would then "pass round by the lower route . . . crossing the Colorado below the 'great kennion,' and return to the Arkansas by the waters of the Gila and St. Juan. . . ."[6]

Upon reaching California, Frémont wrote his wife that he in-

<hr />

[5] Three letters of J. J. Abert to Frémont, 12 Feb., 10 April, and 14 May 1845, in our Vol. 1; excerpt from the *Memoirs,* as Doc. No. 1, this volume.

[6] *Western Expositor* as quoted by *Missouri Republican,* 21 July 1845.

tended to "make a short journey up the eastern branch of the Sacramento, and go from the Tlamath [Klamath] Lake into the Wahlamath [Willamette] valley, through a pass alluded to in my report; in this way making the road into Oregon far shorter, and a *good* road in place of the present very bad one down the Columbia. When I shall have made this short exploration, I shall have explored from the beginning to end this road to Oregon." Probably Frémont intended to return to California after the "short exploration" and go home by the southern route. He later said he had obtained permission from the Mexican authorities not only to winter in the valley of the San Joaquin but "to continue his explorations south to the region of the Rio Colorado, and of the Rio Gila." After his initial difficulties with commanding general José Castro in California, he apparently gave up the idea of returning by the southern route, as perhaps outlined by his verbal instructions, for he wrote to Jessie, "Our government will not require me to return by the southern route against the will of this [the Mexican] government; I shall therefore return by the heads of the Missouri, going through a pass of which your father knows."

The season was late for scientific exploring when Frémont, then a brevet captain, actually got the expedition under way from St. Louis. He had not been able to leave Washington until the middle of May, the delay caused by work on his "second report." That publication was to win him a secure place in the nation's history and, after his promotion, according to Mrs. Frémont, make him "the most talked of and admired lieutenant-colonel in the army."

After reaching Bent's Fort in August 1845, Frémont detached part of his men under the command of Lieutenant Abert to move south into New Mexico through Raton Pass, then east through the Texas Panhandle and Oklahoma, following the course of the Canadian River to its confluence with the Arkansas at Fort Gibson. In the meantime, having been joined by Kit Carson, Richard Owens, and temporarily by mountain man Bill Williams, the main party ascended the Arkansas to its sources, crossed the Colorado River to the upper White (where Joseph R. Walker was added as a guide), and followed that down to the Green. Crossing the Green, the expedition proceeded west to Great Salt Lake and spent a number of days mapping the southern shore before undertaking the journey across the harsh Salt Desert. Water was scarce, but it was autumn, the party was mounted, some of its travel was at night, and it

reached the spring at the base of Pilot's Peak without undue difficulty. After a day's rest the men took up their march again on 1
November and wound their way westward through the short ranges
of the Great Basin, arriving at Mound Springs on 5 November. To
gain the maximum amount of cartographical information before
snow blocked the passes in the Sierra, Frémont there divided his
party. He took fifteen men across Nevada on a diagonal line; the
larger group, commanded by Theodore Talbot, guided by Walker,
and including topographer Edward M. Kern, he sent due west to
the Humboldt with instructions to follow that stream to its "sink."
They were then to turn south to reach the designated reunion point,
Walker Lake, at the eastern base of the Sierra.

When this rendezvous was made, Frémont divided the party
again, and with fifteen men he rode north to cross the mountains
via Donner Pass, reaching Sutter's Fort on 10 December. Gathering
supplies, he started southward on 13 December to meet the other
division of his party, which was to enter the San Joaquin Valley by
way of Walker Pass and wait for him on Kings River. But this
Talbot-Walker-Kern detachment mistakenly camped and waited on
the Kern, and so Frémont, unable to locate them, returned to Sutter's. It was not until mid-February that the entire party of approximately sixty men, many of whom had been with him on former
expeditions, reunited at William Fisher's Laguna farm, thirteen
miles south of Pueblo de San Jose.

In the meantime Frémont had obtained passports from Sutter
for himself and eight of his men and had gone to Yerba Buena,
where he was entertained by William Leidesdorff, the American
vice-consul. Leidesdorff accompanied him to Monterey to visit with
Consul Larkin, with whom Frémont undoubtedly discussed the
political situation in California and the increasing tide of American
emigration. He personally called upon the Mexican commanding
general to explain that he was engaged in surveying the nearest
route from the United States to the Pacific Ocean, and that members
of his party were citizens, not soldiers.[7] The British consul formally

---

[7] Frémont may have even written a letter to inform General Castro of his
motives in coming to California. Such a letter has never been found, but to
a copy of his own letter to the prefect of the Second District Larkin has added
a note: "The General was at his own request officially informed by Captain
Fremont of his motives in coming here, which motives were accepted by

protested Frémont's presence in California to the secretary of the departmental government. This may have inspired an inquiry from the prefect about the object of Frémont's mission, to which Larkin replied that the explorer, who had left his men on the frontiers of the Second Department, had come "to Monterey to obtain clothing, and funds to purchase animals and provisions, and when his men are recruited, intends to continue his journey to the Oregon Territory."[8] The impression was certainly given by the consul that the men were to winter and recoup on the frontiers. Frémont seems likewise to have given that impression to the Mexican authorities.

Once the men reunited near Pueblo de San Jose, Frémont resumed the work of the expedition—moving toward the towns and coast—apparently waiting on the season for operations in the north. He was encamped at William E. P. Hartnell's rancho, about twenty-five miles from Monterey, when on 5 March General Castro peremptorily ordered him to leave the department. Instead of complying, Frémont retired to a peak in the Gabilan Mountains and erected a log fort with the intention of fighting to the last man if attacked— or so he wrote Larkin. Below, at the Mission San Juan Bautista, the Mexicans began mustering and preparing artillery for an assault. Realizing that conflict would cause trouble for resident Americans as well as interrupt business, Larkin suggested that if it were inconvenient for Frémont to leave California, he come to an arrangement with the general and prefect to continue his camp "at some greater distance." "Your camping so near Town has caused much excitement." The consul also wrote "To the Commander of any American Ship of War in San Blas or Mazatlán" requesting that a sloop of war be sent to Monterey. He said he was informed by General Castro that positive orders had been received from Mexico to drive Frémont from the country.[9] Frémont found it prudent and convenient to withdraw to the north.

On 17 April Archibald H. Gillespie arrived in Monterey harbor. Next day he delivered to Larkin the Secretary of State's 17 October

---

Gen. Castro in not answering the letter" (LARKIN, 4:186–87). Most historians have considered both the application and the permission to be oral. For an example, see ROYCE [1], 115.

[8] POSNER, 107–8; Larkin to Manuel de Jesús Castro, 29 Jan. 1846, LARKIN, 4:186–87. Later the British Foreign Office rebuked James A. Forbes for his formal protest against Frémont's entry into California.

[9] Letter dated 9 March 1846, LARKIN, 4:243–44.

1845 dispatch, which he had committed to memory and destroyed before reaching Vera Cruz but now wrote out again. By this dispatch Larkin was appointed a "Confidential Agent in California" and was informed that Gillespie, in whom the president placed "entire confidence," was to cooperate as a confidential agent to help Larkin carry out his instructions.

President Polk had confidentially instructed Gillespie about his mission to California on 30 October 1845, a few days after an interview in which he attempted to secure Senator Benton's support for his Oregon policy. During the Polk-Benton interview the conversation turned to the subject of Frémont's presence in California.[10] A few days later, and evidently after some discussion with Secretary of State Buchanan, Benton wrote a letter to his son-in-law and included the packet of family letters which the State Department decided to have Gillespie carry to California.[11]

Gillespie, dubbed by Marti as the "Messenger of Destiny," did not stay long in Monterey but hurried on to San Francisco with a note from Larkin introducing him to Leidesdorff as "a Gentleman well worthy of Attention."[12] While there he received from the hands of a hard-riding courier a dispatch from Larkin dated 23 April, stating that Capt. John B. Montgomery of the *Portsmouth* had arrived at Monterey and was of the opinion that Commodore Sloat "may by the next mail (Six or eight days) have a declaration on the part of the United States against Mexico in which case, we shall see him in a few days to take the Country." The letter also contained an expression of the consul's opinion to prominent Californians, Castro and Mariano G. Vallejo among them, that the U.S. flag might fly in California in thirty days. "The former says, for his own plans, War is preferable to peace, as by War, affairs will

---

[10] POLK, 1:67–72, 83–84.

[11] Since most of the Benton family letters carried to California by Gillespie had originally been designated for the regular mails across Mexico, the historian John A. Hussey concludes that they could have contained no secret instructions for Frémont (HUSSEY [3]). However, many confidential letters were sent through the regular mails in care of mercantile firms. Gillespie sent his dispatches to the Secretary of the Navy in such a manner, and Commodore Sloat specifically requested that the Navy Department fold dispatches like ordinary mercantile letters, enclose them in a non-yellow envelope, and send them to a mercantile firm in Mazatlán (Sloat to Bancroft, 6 May 1846, DNA-45, Pacific Squadron, Commodore Sloat's Cruise, 1844–46).

[12] Larkin to Leidesdorff, 19 April 1846, HAWGOOD [1], 54.

at once be brought to a close, and each one know his doom. I [Larkin] answered, without War he could make certain Officers and secure to himself, and his friends, fame, honour, permanent employ and pay." The Oregon question, Larkin wrote, was unsettled, and Commodore Robert F. Stockton had not arrived.[13] While Gillespie was at Yerba Buena, the captain of the port was heard to say that the subprefect had received a courier on 24 April advising him of the expected war with Mexico. Leidesdorff and Gillespie shared information, and the vice-consul considered the rumors of war as "glorious news for Capt. Freemont."[14]

Gillespie dashed on to Sutter's Fort and 500 miles farther into the Oregon wilderness in pursuit of Frémont. What was his mission? To deliver a common letter of introduction and a packet of family letters? To obtain further information on conditions in California? To recall Frémont to California? Hardly the first or second. Letters could have been forwarded by a courier; Larkin, Leidesdorff, and others were better informed about intrigues, politics, and possible change in California than was Frémont.

In the spring of 1846 the general impression among Californians and American settlers on the Sacramento was that Gillespie had gone to Oregon to recall Frémont. Two months after that dramatic meeting in Oregon, Talbot wrote his mother, "About the 25th of April we started for Oregon, but had only reached the Klamet Lake when Lt. Gillespie of the U.S. Marines overtook us with orders directly from the United States for us to return to California."[15] This may have been what Frémont told his men. Yet in a letter written to Benton at the same time, Frémont implied that his return to the Sacramento was purely voluntary—prompted in part by snow in the mountains. Curiously there had been no mention of snow in an earlier letter to Benton.

It seems evident that President Polk wanted Frémont in California. A garrison would be needed even if Larkin were able to work out a program for the peaceful takeover of the country. Or, if hostilities came and the Navy took the ports, a small army would be an asset in holding fast. It is entirely possible that Polk verbally and confidentially instructed Gillespie to order Frémont and his

---

[13] Larkin to Gillespie, 23 April 1846, LARKIN, 4:340–41.
[14] Leidesdorff to Larkin, 25 April 1846, LARKIN, 4:348.
[15] Letter dated 24 July 1846 (DLC—Talbot Papers).

armed *voyageurs* to be on hand in California to help seize it when news of American hostilities arrived. Historian Richard Stenberg goes even further and insists that in view of his disingenuous and aggressive policy toward Mexico, it would not have been out of character for Polk to have given Frémont, through Gillespie, "encouraging discretionary authority covertly to incite the Americans in California to revolt or to provoke the Mexican authorities to attack him, acting in this as though on his own authority and carefully concealing Polk's hand."[16] Stenberg does not even accept Polk's denial in his diary in 1848 that "Col. Fremont had the authority to make the revolution,"[17] and Glenn W. Price's study of the Polk-Stockton intrigue in Texas would tend to support Stenberg's charge that Polk was often insincere.[18]

Less than a month after the return of the Army and Marine officers to the Sacramento Valley, the Bear Flag Revolt was in full swing. Undoubtedly emboldened by Frémont's presence, some of the rough and ready members of the *aguardiente* set saw themselves cast in the role of American patriots and were impelled to drastic action, to the distress of more substantial men like Larkin and Sutter. Early in June 1846, under Ezekiel Merritt, this group stole a large band of horses belonging to the Mexican army and then, with Merritt and William B. Ide leading the way, captured Mariano G. Vallejo's Sonoma garrison and raised the Bear Flag over the new "California Republic." Undoubtedly neither the Bear Flaggers nor the *Californios* against whom they directed their uprising knew that since 13 May an official state of war had existed between Mexico and the United States—a long-smoldering affair touched into flame by events along the Rio Grande.

Both Frémont and Gillespie were being credited by Californians as well as Americans with "springing" the Bear Flag Revolt and "fanning it on in a private manner."[19] Frémont wrote Benton that on 6 June he had made his decision about the course he would pursue and had immediately coordinated his operations with the "foreigners" inhabiting the valley. Even earlier—on 24 May—Gillespie had written Larkin: "I send this message to get such news as you

---

[16] STENBERG, 219.

[17] POLK, 3:395.

[18] See PRICE.

[19] Larkin to Buchanan, 18 June 1846, 30 June and 25 Aug. 1847, LARKIN, 5:41–44, 6:225–27, 291–92.

have & to give us some information in relation to the vessels of war —where they are & whether the Congress [with Stockton] has arrived."[20] Frémont is obviously included in the "us," and even at this early date the officers seem to have decided upon their course of action. Statements of peaceful intent and plans to return at once to the United States that appear in various letters to and from Frémont in May and June are likely mere facade. Some historians do believe that Frémont may have been included in Polk's program for California but had no secret instructions to start a revolution.[21] Possibly he assumed a role for himself. George Tays concludes that after his return to Sutter's Fort, Frémont decided to revenge himself for the Gabilan incident, and in a real sense the explorer's 25 July letter lends color to this charge. And historians have interpreted (but erroneously) a spring 1847 letter by his wife as asserting that Frémont was revenging a personal insult.[22] Although a bold and cool man, would he have dared to act so rashly merely to satisfy an injury to his vanity without some intimation from his government that such action was desirable or at least tolerable?

Another writer on California affairs, Ernest A. Wiltsee, thinks that the Polk administration wanted an undercover revolt to prevent a foreign fleet from landing and taking possession before American naval commanders could act.[23] In fact, Commodore Sloat was slow to raise the flag in California and probably did so only because of the Bear Flag Revolt and Frémont's successful operations on shore. On 31 May 1846 Sloat had received word of American victories at Palo Alto and Resaca de la Palma, and on 5 June of the capture of Matamoros. Even so, he still did not feel justified under his existing orders in taking possession of any part of California. Not until 7 June, after receiving word of the blockade of the east coast of Mexico, did he leave Mazatlán in the *Savannah,* reaching Monterey on 2 July. Although briefed by Larkin, he did not formulate a final plan

---

[20] LARKIN, 4:393–94.

[21] HUSSEY [3]; TAYS [2].

[22] Jessie B. Frémont had letters from her husband dated as late as 1 Oct. 1846, when she assured botanist John Torrey that her husband had no sympathy for the Mexican War. "Fighting is not his aim," she added, "& though he threw all his energy into the affair last July & August yet it was as if revenging a private insult for he knew nothing of the war" (21 March 1847, NNNBG—Torrey Correspondence).

[23] WILTSEE [2].

of action until 5 July, when the *Portsmouth*'s launch brought letters from Montgomery to Larkin and William Mervine, commander of the *Cyane*, detailing Frémont's action in conjunction with the Bears. Certainly Sloat had been in no hurry to seize California and would later be reprimanded by the Secretary of the Navy for his inactivity.[24]

Unfortunately, Benton's "somewhat enigmatical" letter to Frémont, bearing the late October 1845 date, has never been found. He refered to it in a letter to Buchanan in July 1848 and, some seven years later at Frémont's request, stated positively that "to save the administration from responsibility for what might happen, I [Benton], at their request, wrote the letter on which he [Frémont] acted."[25] Frémont was still trying to obtain reimbursements for his California expenditures, and in support of his application he made a statement of his comprehension of the communications brought by Gillespie:

Taken together, the character of these dispatches & the place and circumstances of their delivery answered to me for positive instructions from the head of the government & was received by me with the most unbounded satisfaction. I prepared to execute them entirely as a matter of course & determined to give them their broadest interpretation & to put to the fullest use every means in my power—men, money & arms—in securing to our country the territory of California, and while I regarded this communication to differ in nothing but its secret nature from regular instructions, I comprehended that I was expected to act as upon my own responsibility, leaving to the government to support me in such way & at such time as might be judged expedient. It is very probable that in the freedom of such responsibility I did more, & more promptly, than had been expected.[26]

In 1848 in his deposition before a subcommittee of the Military Affairs Committee of the Senate, he had been more restrained, although his pecuniary interest was still there. "This officer [Gillespie]

---

[24] Bancroft to Sloat, 13 Aug. 1846, *California Claims,* Senate Report 75, p. 71, 30th Cong., 1st sess., Serial 512.

[25] Benton to Buchanan, 15 July 1848 (PHi—Buchanan Papers); statement of Benton, 30 July 1855 (KyLoF—James Guthrie Papers). To Buchanan Benton had written, "My letter which accompanied yours, and what was said to Mr. Larkin (in the like case) led him to believe that he was to be *liberal* as well as active, discreet and zealous in accomplishing a great object."

[26] Frémont's description of his California expedition, 1845 (KyLoF—Guthrie Papers).

informed me that he had been directed by the Secretary of State to find me, and to acquaint me with his instructions, which had for their principal objects to ascertain the disposition of the Californian people, to conciliate their feelings in favor of the United States, and to find out, with a design of counteracting, the designs of the British government upon that country." Gillespie testified that he had shown Frémont a copy of Buchanan's 17 October dispatch to Larkin.[27] Gillespie likewise testified that when questioned by Commodore Sloat in the harbor of Monterey by what authority he was acting, Frémont replied that he had "acted upon his own authority, and not from orders of the government," which is what he had intimated to Benton in the 25 July 1846 letter. However, in July 1848 Benton wrote the Secretary of State seeking compensation from the contingent Foreign Intercourse Fund for Frémont because of his services in California. Buchanan indicated that he could not legally reimburse Frémont from that source and suggested an application to Congress—whereupon Benton and Frémont dropped the whole subject, apparently unwilling to lend support to the charge that he had been sent by the government to excite revolt in California in time of peace.[28]

The other major incident of Frémont's California venture of 1845–47, one that made him a still more controversial figure, was his refusal as lieutenant colonel to obey an order issued by his alleged superior officer, Brig. Gen. Stephen Watts Kearny. This quarrel also involved Commodore Robert F. Stockton, and for an understanding of its nature, at least a brief sketch of the conquest of California is essential (though the documents themselves provide richer detail).

The Stars and Stripes replaced the Bear Flag at Sonoma on 9 July 1846, and the three-week-old "Young California"[29] came to an end. On the invitation of Sloat, Frémont moved from Sutter's Fort to cooperate with the naval forces in holding the country already conquered and in chastising the Indians. Soon after his arrival Sloat resigned, and the peppery Stockton took command of the American naval forces in the Pacific. Stockton launched a vigorous campaign

[27] *California Claims,* Senate Report 75, p. 33.
[28] Benton to Buchanan, 15 and 20 July 1848 (PHi—Buchanan Papers).
[29] Leidesdorff's expression; see his 19 June 1846 letter to Larkin in LARKIN, 5:54–57.

to establish control over southern California. Frémont's battalion was taken into naval service, Frémont receiving an appointment as commander with the rank of major, and Gillespie a captaincy. Stockton likewise issued commissions to other officers of the battalion and sent Frémont south to San Diego, while he and Larkin, who still hoped to win over the Californians by peaceful means, sailed for San Pedro, the port for Los Angeles. There, disheartened by their failures to organize first an effective force of resistance and then a truce, Governor Pío Pico and General Castro fled the capital rather than surrender, and American forces joined to enter the City of the Angels unopposed.

Stockton wrote President Polk and the Secretary of the Navy that as soon as he could "safely do so," he would appoint Frémont governor and Gillespie secretary of the conquered territory. Such intentions were also communicated to Frémont, whom he appointed military commandant.

Early in September Stockton sailed north to Monterey and San Francisco. A few days later Frémont went by land to the Sacramento to augment the strength of the California Battalion and to recruit a thousand men for Stockton, who had visions of landing troops at Acapulco and marching overland to clasp hands with Gen. Zachary Taylor at the gates of Mexico City. Gillespie was left with fifty men to garrison Los Angeles, but scarcely two weeks after Frémont's departure the Angeleños rose in rebellion and forced Gillespie to withdraw from the city and embark on the merchant ship *Vandalia* in San Pedro harbor.

When Stockton heard of the disaster, he recalled Frémont from the Sacramento, sent Mervine south on the U.S.S. *Savannah* to give aid, and soon sailed himself on the *Congress*. Gillespie and Mervine rallied for an attack on Los Angeles but were repulsed, and even the arrival of Stockton made little difference in the military situation. All of southern California slipped back into the hands of the Californians. The Americans were able to reoccupy San Diego, but it was some time before they dislodged the Mexicans from the hilltops and procured the cattle and horses necessary to equip a land force to march against Los Angeles.

In the meantime Frémont and his force had boarded the *Sterling* with the intention of supporting Stockton in the south, but they learned from a passing vessel that the Californians had driven the stock into the interior. Without horses, Frémont hesitated. Then, using the discretionary authority Stockton had given him, he hauled back to Monterey, there to gather supplies and men, sending agents to the Sacramento to recruit newly arrived emigrants and even Indians.

At the end of November his battalion took up the line of march for Los Angeles. A few days later the conqueror of New Mexico, Stephen Watts Kearny, entered California from the east at the head of approximately a hundred dragoons. He had sent the major part of his Army of the West back to Santa Fe after getting word from Kit Carson near Socorro on the Rio Grande that the fighting in California was over. He must also have learned at this time that Frémont was to be governor of California.[30] Kearny came with orders issued in June, authorizing him to establish temporary civil governments over areas his army conquered in New Mexico and California and giving him command of volunteers sent to or organized in California. But as he neared Warner's rancho, he became aware of the precarious conditions in California. He dispatched an English rancher, Edward Stokes, to San Diego with a message for Stockton, who responded by sending reinforcements under Gillespie. These reached him on 5 December, and on the following morning in a cold rain, Kearny's tired, poorly organized force attacked at the Indian pueblo of San Pasqual and were defeated by the Californians, who not only outmanuevered the Americans but were devastating in the use of their long, deadly lances. Kearny immediately appealed to San Diego for aid, then moved to a more defensible position ten miles away. Only after a second plea to Stockton did a large relief party arrive before dawn on 11 December.[31]

---

[30] Under date of 6 Oct. 1846, Capt. Abraham R. Johnston recorded in his journal the meeting of Kearny's forces with Carson and mentioned the probability that Frémont was military and civil governor of California (House Exec. Doc. 41, p. 572, 30th Cong., 1st sess., Serial 517). William H. Emory, another officer with Kearny, made no mention of Frémont in his journal, and Benton charged that Emory expunged and rewrote his journal after Kearny's controversy with Frémont over the governorship.

[31] Kearny's supporters maintained that Stockton rejected the first appeal for aid, which was carried into San Diego by Alexander Godey, Thomas H. Burgess, and another. As the party returned to Kearny on Mule Hill, it was captured by the Californians but presumably was able to cache Stockton's letter in a tree. Later the Kearny forces exchanged a Mexican prisoner for Burgess, who reported that the commodore had refused to send reinforcements

Later, in his court-martial defense, Frémont would make much of Kearny's inability to move into San Diego without aid from Stockton. Kearny came not to conquer but to secure the fruits of conquest after others had done the work, insisted Frémont. Since he had been unable to take over California, his instructions from the Secretary of War were no longer applicable. Others conversant with the history of the war would sustain this view. A naval chaplain, one of the editors of the *Californian,* could write, "It is requiring too much of us . . . to claim our assent to the allegation that California has been conquered through the achievements of the army."[32]

Soon after Kearny reached San Diego, the sparring for supremacy of command commenced, although, in the joint expedition mounted against Los Angeles, Stockton seems to have been in general command with Kearny acting as his aide and commanding troops in the field. From the Mission San Juan Capistrano on 5 January Stockton issued a proclamation offering a general amnesty to all Californians except the leader of the revolt, José María Flores, on condition that he be given up as a prisoner. The Californians would not negotiate on these terms, lost the two battles of San Gabriel and the Mesa, and, after Flores had fled, turned north and surrendered to Frémont at the Mission San Fernando. Although he undoubtedly knew of the presence of his superior officer a few miles away at Los Angeles, Frémont granted generous terms and sent the treaty to Stockton by his aide William H. Russell, whom he also instructed to inquire carefully about who was in command in Los Angeles.[33] Russell reported that although Kearny seemed to be the better friend to the young explorer, Stockton was exercising the functions of civil and military governor, and that the general's having discharged

---

(GRIFFIN [1], 21:337). Stockton, Frémont, and their supporters denied this violently, Stockton insisting that as soon as the Godey party had arrived in San Diego, preparations were immediately begun to send a party to relieve Kearny. The cached letter was not found by Kearny's men and may have been taken by Gen. Andrés Pico's California force (CLARKE, 225).

[32] COLTON, 17 July 1847.

[33] BANCROFT, 5:387. The assistant surgeon with Kearny's dragoons, John S. Griffin, wrote in his diary, "The fact is, it is said that the Californians would not have negociated with Stockton on any terms, in consequence of the proclamation he sent them from the Mission of St. John's." He also noted, "We took the wind out of Fremonts sails by capturing the Puebla—and whipping the enemy on the 8th and 9th, but he has shown himself the better politician by negotiating first with the enemy" (GRIFFIN [1], 22:44).

certain duties implied an acknowledgment of the commodore's supremacy.

When Frémont entered Los Angeles, he went first to the quarters assigned to him by Stockton, then reported in person to Stockton, and afterward called on Kearny. Within two days of Frémont's arrival the conflict between the Army and the Navy over the interpretation of instructions from their respective departments came out into the open. Kearny considered Frémont's 13 January 1847 letter a report of the California Battalion to him, but at the court-martial Frémont contended the letter was written after receiving four friendly letters from Kearny. The general ordered that no change be made in the organization of the California Battalion without his approval and objected to Stockton's proposed institution of a civil government in California. Stockton responded by reiterating that Kearny's instructions had been negated by events before his arrival, intimated that he would ask the president for his recall, and suspended Kearny from command of the U.S. forces in Los Angeles other than the dragoons. On his part, Frémont refused to acknowledge the general's authority over him; noted that until Kearny and Stockton adjusted between themselves the question of rank, he would have "to report and receive orders, as heretofore, from the Commodore"; and accepted Stockton's commission as governor. At his court-martial he maintained that the question of rank between Stockton and Kearny was being tried in his person.

Kearny left Los Angeles on 18 January, having informed Stockton that he "would remain silent for the present" in order to prevent "collision between us & possibly civil war in consequence of it," leaving with the commodore the "great responsibility" of doing that for which he had no authority. At this time, despite his contentions, Kearny seems to have had real doubts about his own authority. In the cabinet consideration of the case following Frémont's court-martial, Secretary of State Buchanan would apply the word "pusillanimity" to Kearny, noting that "if he believed he had the authority, he yielded it to Com. Stockton & did not enforce it." To this the Secretary of War took exception and said that since Kearny had not the troops to command obedience, "he had acted with great forbearance & propriety."[34] The Mormon Battalion, 350 strong, ar-

---

[34] POLK, 3:336–38.

rived in California before Kearny left San Diego, but apparently the general did not seriously consider using the weary soldiers to force Frémont's obedience.

Stockton likewise left Los Angeles, and Frémont remained in relatively unperturbed governorship for several weeks, although lack of money was a recurring problem. On his way to San Francisco Kearny consulted with Commodore W. Branford Shubrick in Monterey and became aware of the Navy Department's 12 July instructions directing Sloat, or his successor, to organize a civil government when California was conquered. Although both Stockton and Frémont were unaware of these instructions when they defied Kearny in Los Angeles, they nevertheless bear out the explorer's contention in his court-martial that Washington had sent faulty orders. These 12 July instructions placing the civil administration in the hands of the naval commander postdated Kearny's own instructions, but Shubrick made no attempt to exercise any civil authority, and he and Kearny decided to await more explicit instructions from Washington. These arrived in San Francisco on 13 February—the very day Kearny's ship entered the bay. By a letter from Gen. Winfield Scott and a copy of a letter from the Secretary of the Navy, Kearny learned that the president wanted the supreme army authority to exercise the administrative functions of government. His uncertainty over his authority was ended, but he had not the grace to communicate these instructions to Frémont. However, in a letter to Frémont asking that the naval officers serving with the California Battalion be returned to the squadron, Shubrick wrote that he was instructed that Kearny was the commanding officer and invested with the administrative functions of government over the people and the territory.

When Kearny returned to Monterey, he sent his adjutant south with orders for Frémont to muster the California volunteers into the service of the United States and to bring the archives to Monterey. The battalion was at San Gabriel. Perhaps hoping that still later instructions and presidential approval of his appointment as governor would reach California, Frémont unwisely delayed. His secretary of state, William H. Russell, wrote to Philip St. George Cooke, whom Kearny had made commander in the Southern District, that the men refused to be mustered into service and that the governor deemed it unsafe to disband them, since rumors were rife of a threatened insurrection. Giving orders to Richard Owens not to surrender the arms and munitions to any corps, Frémont made a sensational ride to Monterey to see Kearny, allegedly to warn of impending trouble in the south and to see if Kearny would assume the debts Frémont had incurred as governor. But Kearny testified at the court-martial that he never knew the object of Frémont's visit and that it had been the cause of some speculation among others. The interview only added fuel to the fire of their controversy, though Frémont did agree to obey Kearny's orders. His wish to resign from the Army was summarily rejected.

Soon after Frémont departed to implement orders, Col. Richard B. Mason—who was to succeed Kearny as military governor of California—was sent south to inspect the troops and to give further instructions to Frémont. From the outset relations between the two officers were strained, and they ended with Frémont challenging the conservative Virginian to a duel. On Mason's request it was postponed until the officers could reach Monterey. In the interval Kearny and Commodore James Biddle learned of the impending affair of honor; the former forbade it, and the latter pled with Mason for a postponement, all of which caused Benton to charge later that Kearny and Biddle had conspired to extricate Mason from a difficult situation. The spectacle of an internecine fight between high-ranking Army officers, one of whom was a former governor and one of whom was to be governor, would have done nothing to promote U.S. interests in California.

After completing his military duties in the south, Frémont lingered on in Los Angeles. Kearny arrived there on 10 May, and the explorer requested permission to take a party of men to Mexico to join his regiment. Kearny had informed Frémont early in March that he was at liberty to leave California as soon as he had complied with orders, since the general-in-chief of the Army had directed that he not be detained against his wishes "a moment longer than the necessities of the service may require." Kearny refused this request and three subsequent applications by Frémont to leave the party and journey home. Obviously Frémont's conduct since March had so irritated the general that he had reverted to an earlier decision, made in January, to place him under arrest at a feasible time.

Kearny reviewed the troops in Monterey and ordered Frémont to surrender the topographical instruments. Frémont would later imply that it had been Kearny's intention to stop his topographical pursuits by requiring that he turn over his surveying instruments, but it is doubtful that the explorer, so agitated by his own problems, would have been able to accomplish much in the scientific field. One geographer indicts him for not being able to give Charles Preuss more constructive ideas about the country he crossed on the homeward journey in 1847, but he cites it as an example of Frémont's dependence upon his topographers.[35] On 31 May the march for home began via the Sacramento. In time the party passed the scene of the Donner tragedy of the preceding winter, and Kearny ordered Maj. Thomas Swords to bury the grisly remains.[36]

Long before Kearny and Frémont reached St. Louis, Lieut. William H. Emory had arrived in Washington with Kearny's version of his conflict with Stockton and Frémont; the Carson-Talbot-Beale party and William H. Russell brought the Frémont version. Benton was enraged by the appearance in the newspapers of letters and articles containing such statements as: "Com. Stockton's despatches are full of false representations," Kearny "routed the enemy [at San Pasqual], and chased him some miles," "Stockton rudely refused to grant his [Kearny's] requisition [for horses and men]," "General Kearny commanded the troops in both battles [8 and 9 January]," "After the battle of the 9th January, Andreas Pico . . . having twice broken his parole, and expecting no quarter from General Kearny, went off with a small portion of the enemy's force and effected a treaty with Colonel Fremont, securing to himself immunity from his crimes," and "Col. Fremont, angry that his request [for the governorship] was not at once complied with, withdrew his troops from Gen. Kearny's command without authority, went to Com. Stockton, and solicited from *him* the appointment of Governor."

Benton attributed many of these statements to Emory, whom he charged had been sent home to "magnify Kearny and the Army of the West as the conqueror of California," "to deny and face down the truth" about the defeat at San Pasqual, and "to vilify and undermine the reputations" of Stockton and Frémont. He demanded of the Adjutant General that Frémont be recalled and tried by court-martial to clear his name, if he were not already ordered home for arrest and trial. After Frémont's arrival Benton urged President

---

[35] C. I. WHEAT, 3:58.
[36] TURNER, 129. There were claims later that Frémont—not Kearny—had taken the trouble to collect and bury the bodies.

Polk to order either a court of inquiry or a court-martial, not only for Frémont's sake but also so that the government might be fully informed about what had happened in California. The irate senator was determined that his son-in-law be tried not *eventually* on Kearny's charge of mutiny and documents alone but *immediately* on all the unofficial charges and insinuations against him, even in newspapers if he could manage to have them included, but in this he was unsuccessful. President Polk hoped to avoid a court-martial, but Benton was determined to see his son-in-law "justified and exalted" and his persecutors "covered with shame and confusion." Months later, as Frémont's trial neared an end, his first benefactor, Joel R. Poinsett, noted that Frémont's "scrape" would do him little harm and that Kearny had been "inconsistent" in his accounts of the interviews with Frémont, but the former Secretary of War felt that Frémont would have fared better had not his counsel tried to glorify his services.[37]

Given wide coverage by the press, the trial commenced on 2 November at the Washington Arsenal in the District of Columbia. The charges were mutiny, with eleven specifications; disobedience of the lawful command of his superior officer, with seven specifications; and conduct to the prejudice of good order and military discipline, with five specifications. And many of the same specifications were used to support the three different offenses against the military code, a proceeding which Frémont thought was highly irregular.

As Kearny was chief witness for the prosecution, Frémont attempted to show the vindictive temper of the general toward him, to impeach his motives, to exhibit his defective and equivocating memory, and to discredit him as a witness before the court. Impartial observers might agree that he succeeded to a remarkable degree, but in the judgment of the court Kearny's honor and character remained "unimpeached." The tactic of trying to discredit the witness permitted the defense a wide latitude in questioning, but only a few of its many subjects and facets can be noted here.

Frémont cited as an exhibition of his punitive temper Kearny's failure to report to the War Department the recovery of the how-

---

[37] Poinsett to Gouverneur Kemble, 4 Jan. 1848, calendared in HEILMAN & LEVIN, no. 571.

itzer which had been lost at San Pasqual,[38] and as evidence of his failing memory the general's inability to remember that it was Christopher Carson who brought to his headquarters Frémont's 17 January letter. He implied that there was something lacking in Kearny's credibility when the latter testified that he knew not the nature of the reorganization which Stockton and Frémont contemplated making in the California Battalion or even that Gillespie's company had been part of the battalion. Frémont accused the general of attempting to keep Gillespie and other witnesses away from the trial and of drawing up questions for his own interrogation. Furthermore, he charged the prosecution with deliberately not calling William H. Emory as a witness, thus forcing the defense to do so and thereby sacrificing Frémont's right to cross-examine; the court could not and would not allow him to impeach his own witness. Emory was considered a key witness because he had delivered the order to Frémont forbidding any reorganization in the California Battalion without the approval of Kearny, and he was also the reputed source of much of the distorted newspaper information being given to the public on California affairs.

Although much of it was shaken during cross-examination, Kearny's testimony cast Frémont in the role of bargaining for the governorship, in effect ascribing a base and sordid motive for the offense of mutiny. Undoubtedly Frémont did desire the governorship and was put in an embarrassing position when offered the appointment by both Stockton and Kearny. Kearny also inferred that Frémont had destroyed documents, but when pressed to explain, he had to admit that this was merely his way of saying that he no longer possessed the originals and that he did not intend to imply that Frémont had "designedly" disposed of official papers.

Stockton was the principal witness for the defense, but unfortunately for Frémont, much of his testimony had little bearing on the charges, and there is some evidence that Stockton and Kearny had come to a *rapprochement* on the eve of the commodore's testi-

---

[38] On Frémont's arrival in Los Angeles on 14 Jan. Kearny's assistant surgeon had written in his diary, "We saw the howitzer we lost at San Pasqual —the only regret I had in seeing this was that the Enemy should have delivered it up, before we had an opportunity to take it, or some other piece from the Mexicans" (GRIFFIN [1], 22:41).

mony. Kearny wrote his brother-in-law, naval Lieut. William Radford, whom Commodore Biddle had permitted to come home from California with Kearny, that "the difficulty between Commodore S(tockton) and myself has been adjusted. I wrote to him asking if he alluded to me in his letter of November 3rd to the editors of the 'Republican.' He replied he did not. We have since that time twice met in the street and we salute each other. He says the affair between us is amicably and honorably adjusted to both parties. Colonel Benton will be very disappointed in the testimony of Commodore S as I think when he hears it. I have been led to believe that it will be much more against the defense than in its favor."[39] Stockton may not have been suborned, but was he supporting Frémont come "bondage or stripes," as the commodore himself had written earlier? Gillespie learned of the settlement of the misunderstanding between Stockton and Kearny and also seems to have moved toward the general's camp.

Finding Frémont guilty on all charges and specifications, the court sentenced him to be dismissed from the Army. Because of his distinguished public service and the peculiar circumstances of the case, seven of the thirteen members recommended him to the clemency of the president. Polk spent long hours reading the proceedings of the trial and sought the advice of his cabinet officials. He noted in his diary that he "was not satisfied that the proof in the case constituted 'mutiny'" but thought "the proof established disobedience of orders & conduct to the prejudice of good order and military discipline." He therefore decided to approve the sentence of the court-martial but cancel the punishment.[40] But when Frémont received the order to resume his sword and report to duty, he sub-

---

[39] For this and several additional documents indicating that Stockton and Kearny had come to an agreement, see CLARKE, 358–61. These sources show that Stockton's letter to the editor of the *Missouri Republican* had contained insinuations derogatory to Kearny and noted that those who misrepresented the command in California were guilty of falsehood and would "not go unwhipped of justice." Later on, being approached by an acquaintance of Kearny's, the commodore was willing to say that the letter could have no reference to Kearny, if the latter would admit that Stockton had been commander-in-chief on the march from San Diego to Los Angeles. This Kearny was willing to do, and there was a satisfactory exchange of letters between the two officers.

[40] POLK, 3:336–38.

mitted his resignation from the service, refusing to admit in any way the justice of the decision against him.

So bitter was the trial, and so savage and vindictive was Benton in his long Senate speech[41] opposing the nomination of Kearny for the brevet of major general, that it is difficult to give credence to a story that circulated in the newspapers shortly after the death of Kearny in St. Louis on 31 October 1848. This was to the effect that Mrs. Frémont had proposed to Mrs. Kearny a reconciliation between their husbands. The message, so the story goes, was not delivered because Mrs. Kearny did not want to disturb her dying husband. In a card in the *National Intelligencer* Benton emphatically denied that "any message of any kind" had been sent by the Frémonts and charged Emory with originating the false story. And Emory does indeed seem to have been the medium through which the story reached the Baltimore *Patriot*.[42] Kearny's brother-in-law, John D. Radford, took note of the reconciliation story as it appeared in the *Herald of Religious Liberty* and denied the deliverance of a message, adding, "Surgeon Wheaton of the Army brought such a message as coming from Col. Brant: it was delivered to Mrs. Kearny by him and there it rested."[43] Col. Joshua B. Brant was an acquaintance of Kearny. He was married to Benton's niece, and when Frémont returned from California under arrest, he received his callers at Brant's St. Louis residence.

However much friends might have desired it, it is doubtful that the Frémonts would have initiated a reconciliation. Frémont was out of the Army, and even the most blatant opportunist would have nothing to gain by such a move. In her old age Mrs. Frémont was still convinced that Kearny had perjured himself at her husband's court-martial. By that time, too, she was able to write a dramatic

---

[41] Appendix to the *Congressional Globe,* July 1848, 30th Cong., 1st sess., pp. 977–1040.

[42] See the "cards" of Benton and Emory in the *National Intelligencer,* 13 and 14 Dec. 1848; unsigned draft of a letter (probably by Davidge, a Senate clerk to the Claims Committee) to the editors of the *National Intelligencer;* and J. Hooker to Emory, 22 Dec. 1848 (CtY—W. H. Emory Papers). In his letter Hooker affirmed making a statement that "a verbal message was delivered to Mrs. Kearny in the name of Mrs. Fremont" to the effect that "Mr. & Mrs. Fremont had buried & ceased to cherish all bitterness of feeling towards him [Kearny]."

[43] Printed in CLARKE, 385–86.

but highly unlikely account of an overture of reconciliation. "General Kearny who lived in St. Louis sent his physician old Dr. Beaumont, to ask me to come and see him, he was dying, and would like to ask my forgiveness. I told Dr. Beaumont I could not go, I could not forgive him. There was a little grave between us I could not cross."[44]

Frémont's appearances at his general court-martial had no sooner ended when he urged upon Congress the wisdom and justice of paying the debts incurred in the conquest and governance of California during the turbulent years of 1846 and 1847, for which a sufficient amount of naval funds had not been available. These so-called California Claims, which were to plague Frémont and Congress for many years, were owed to four groups of people. The first set of claimants was Californians who had had their property seized by the Bear Flaggers. The second was both Californians and Americans who had furnished supplies, sometimes unwillingly, to the California Battalion, and for the most part had been given only receipts. The third was largely businessmen who had advanced Frémont money, often at high rates of interest, during his governorship. And the fourth was the volunteers who had received receipts—not money—for their services. The government was morally bound to make a speedy payment of all these claims before hardship forced the small claimant to part with his "promise" at a fraction of its value.

In fact, the existence of the unpaid claims was diminishing Frémont's popularity and causing great anxiety in California. A public meeting in San Fancisco in June 1847 protested against the possibility of his being returned to California as governor and appointed a Committee of Eight to prepare and produce "reliable instances of his misconduct." The protest was occasioned by a petition which had been circulated first in the south and then in the north asking President Polk to appoint Frémont governor, and support for the petition was being obtained by hints that the explorer's return would speed a settlement of the debts. The *Californian* took note

---

[44] Pp. 70, 80, of Jessie B. Frémont's unpublished memoirs (CU-B). NEVINS, 342, CLARKE, 383, and DE VOTO, 482, take note of her story. "A little grave" is a reference to the death of Benton Frémont on 6 Oct. 1848, less than three months after his birth. The mother attributed the poor health of her baby to the ordeal she underwent during her husband's court-martial.

of the disenchantment with Frémont, but it wanted to know how Commodore Biddle and General Kearny, who claimed to be the superior officers, could take from Stockton and Frémont in the name of the United States the country and government property, at the same time refusing to pay debts accruing on account of the war. "We have never been able to ascertain the difference between the man who wrongfully takes property and he who wrongfully *keeps* it."[45]

Frémont's memorial was referred to the Senate Military Affairs Committee, and its subcommittee, of which Benton was a member, took testimony on the necessity, nature, and amount of the indebtedness which had been incurred. Early in March Senator Lewis Cass introduced a bill appropriating $700,000 and naming Frémont and two other battalion officers—paymaster Pierson B. Reading and commissary officer Samuel J. Hensley—commissioners to adjudicate the claims. After a hard struggle the bill finally passed the Senate, but in the House, one week before adjournment, a substitute bill was reported, reducing the appropriation to $500,000 and appointing more nonpartisan commissioners. "It was very plainly seen," Gillespie wrote Abel Stearns, "that Frémont had made up a little family party, which did not suit the judgment of disinterested persons. It was generally understood that I was to have been one of the Commissioners; but I have been informed, I was considered too independent & not sufficiently agreeable, consequently was left out."

Whether Gillespie was "left out" because he was "too independent" of the Benton-Frémont forces or for some other reason is not clear. Emory wrote Jefferson Davis that he had some letters from Gillespie that told a different story on California than the one Gillespie told before the subcommittee of the Senate Military Affairs Committee, when the prospect of being a commissioner, with its consequent remuneration, was "glittering in the eyes of the deponent."[46] But it was clear that the letters of Col. Jonathan D. Stevenson and Governor Richard B. Mason, setting forth some of Frémont's financial

[45] *California Star,* 19 June 1847; *Californian,* 12 June 1847. William Garner wrote that William H. Russell employed a shoemaker to circulate the petition (GARNER, 184–85).

[46] *Congressional Globe,* 1847–48, 30th Cong., 1st sess., pp. 423, 604–8, 627–31, 676–78, 685, 696–98, 700–708, 1064; *Report on Bill Regarding California Claims,* House Report 817, 30th Cong., 1st sess., Serial 527; Emory to Davis, 14 May 1848 (ICHi).

transactions in Los Angeles and making it appear that he intended to defraud the government, were doing their work. The House adjourned with the intention of considering the California Claims at the next session, but nothing was heard of the subject for four years.

Frémont did not write a full scientific report of his third expedition as he had for the first and second, but he supervised the drawing of a map of Oregon and Upper California by Charles Preuss and produced a short *Geographical Memoir,* to be published in Vol. 3, to accompany that map. The plants he collected were again placed at the disposal of John Torrey, for the botanist and explorer hoped eventually to make arrangements with the government for the publication of a general account of the botany of California. When this prospect dimmed, Torrey described ten of the genera in *Plantæ Frémontianæ,* published in 1853 in the *Smithsonian Contributions to Knowledge,* each subject illustrated by a plate drawn by Isaac Sprague, an unrivaled botanical artist. The little botanical memoir, which is also to be published in Vol. 3, is limited in scope, although Frémont had sent back hundreds of species of plants from both Bent's Fort and San Francisco. Those from the Pacific Coast came by the *Erie,* and Torrey wrote a fellow scientist, Jacob Whitman Bailey, a description of how they had been packed. "There were two huge cases—filled with the tin cases." They were "soldered up after being filled with plants—then guarded by a strong frame of wood, & finally sowed up in a green cowhide." Torrey was already looking forward to the fourth expedition and the plants which might come into his hands.[47]

No doubt his early California experiences, and especially the ordeal of the court-martial—a "Dreyfus" case, Jessie later called it—were frustrating to the ambitious young explorer, but Frémont bore his setbacks well. At the beginning of the 1845 expedition the artist Alfred S. Waugh had found him "a pale intellectual looking young man, modest and unassuming, seemingly more accustomed to the refinements and luxuries of life, than to the toils and dangers of the wilderness." Waugh had expected "a man of herculean frame" but found one "small in stature and delicately formed,—voice low and musical, and of manners bland and gentlemanly. . . . He had no outward indications of the mountain traveller about him; all was

---

[47] Torrey to Bailey, 1 July 1848 (Museum of Science, the Library, Science Park, Boston—J. W. Bailey Papers).

quiet, well bred, and retireing. His conversation was modest, instructive and unpretending, with a grace and suavity that irresistably won all who approached him. Yet in his eye, you saw something which shewed contempt of danger and proclaimed him a man to be obeyed under all circumstances."[48] The events of 1847–48 had added a touch of bitterness to Frémont's character, and he suffered another defeat and humiliation in the failure of Congress to appropriate money for continuing his topographical surveys beyond the Mississippi. But there was a tenacity and a resiliency about him that would not be denied: soon he was seeking private backing for a railroad survey from St. Louis to California, and late October found him setting out once more for the Pacific Coast.

EDITORIAL PROCEDURES

THE DOCUMENTS

The original text is followed as closely as the demands of typography will permit, with several departures based on common sense and the current practice of scholars. In the matter of capitalization the original is followed, unless the writer's intention is not clear, in which case we resort to modern usage. Occasionally, in the interests of clarity, a long, involved sentence is broken into two sentences. Missing periods at the ends of sentences are supplied, dashes terminating sentences are supplanted by periods, and superfluous dashes after periods are omitted. In abbreviations, raised letters are brought down and a period supplied if modern usage calls for one. Words underscored in manuscript are italicized. The complimentary closing is run in with the preceding paragraph, and a comma is used if no other end punctuation is present. The acute accent mark on the *e* in Frémont is supplied when it appears in the document and omitted where it does not appear, but it is used in all of our own headings and references to Frémont. Procedures for dealing with missing or illegible words, conjectural readings, etc. are shown in the list of symbols, pp. li–lii. When in doubt about how to proceed in a trivial matter, we have silently followed modern practice; if the question is more important, the situation is explained in a note.

---

[48] WAUGH, 15.

Because Jessie B. Frémont wrote and signed so many of her husband's letters, we have felt that there should be some indication of this to the reader. Our solution to the problem is set forth in the list of symbols.

When a related document or letter is used—that is, not one directly to or from Frémont—extraneous portions are deleted, and the deletion is indicated by a symbol. The present volume contains more related documents than did Vol. 1, since we have tried not only to avoid repeated summaries but to give precision of meaning, particularly in the development of the controversy between Stephen Watts Kearny and Frémont. Some of the letters of Thomas H. Benton and William C. Jones are really Frémont documents; the two were his lawyers at the time of his court-martial.

The financial vouchers covering this period are too numerous and complex to continue the policy of printing them all. Consequently, only selected vouchers, requests, claims, and receipts are included, in order to show how the war in California was being financed or to document an interesting bit of history, such as the inclusion of the "Tularie" Indians in the California Battalion.

Many of the vouchers, receipts, and other papers relating to the settlement of the California Claims as well as the detailed proceedings and decisions of the California Claims Board are in the Records of the Office of the Quartermaster General in the National Archives. Useful printed summaries of the claims and decisions of the board are the reports of the Secretary of War to the Senate, especially Senate Exec. Doc. 63, 34th Cong., 1st sess., Serial 821. Service vouchers for men of the third expedition are in the Records of the United States General Accounting Office, particularly the microfilm collection known as T-135.

Because Frémont collected in and wrote extensively on natural history, mainly botany, on his first two western expeditions, we gave those matters a good deal of attention in Vol. 1. Plants mentioned in the present volume, either by binomial or common names, may usually be identified by referring to the index of Vol. 1.

Because the proceedings of the 1847–48 court-martial are quite long, they are presented as a separately bound supplement.

The Notes

The first manuscript indicated is the one from which the transcription has been made; other copies, if known, are listed next. If endorsements or addresses are routine, their presence is merely noted, but if they contribute useful information, they are quoted in full. For example, see the endorsement on the letter of Thomas H. Benton to Roger Jones, 22 August 1847, Doc. No. 208, concerning Benton's letter to have Frémont ordered home from California for arrest and trial.

Material taken from printed texts is so indicated (printed, LARKIN, 4:239–41), but no attempt is made to record other printed versions.

Unless previously done in Vol. 1, senders, receivers, and persons referred to in the manuscripts are briefly identified at first mention. For senders and receivers, this identification is made in the first paragraph of the notes and no reference number is used. The reader can easily find the identification of an individual by locating in the index the page on which he is first mentioned.

With the exception of Hubert Howe Bancroft's *Register of Pioneer Inhabitants of California, 1542–1848,* no source is cited for the kind of biographical information to be found in standard directories, genealogies, and similar aids.

Names of authors in SMALL CAPITALS are citations to sources listed in the bibliography on pp. 491–501. This device enables us to keep many long titles and other impedimenta out of the notes. In the case of two or more works by the same author, a number is assigned, as in ROGERS [1]. When a published work is being discussed, not merely cited, we often list it fully by author and title in the notes.

To avoid the constant repetition of the Frémont names, we have freely used the initials JCF and JBF for John Charles and Jessie.

SYMBOLS

DNA-92	Records of the Office of the Quartermaster General, California Claims Board, 1847–55
DNA-94	Records of the Adjutant General's Office
DNA-107	Records of the Office of the Secretary of War
DNA-153	Records of the Judge Advocate General's Office
DNA-217	Records of the United States General Accounting Office (T-135 denotes a collection of microfilm documents in this Record Group.)
DNA-393	Records of United States Continental Army Commands

OTHER SYMBOLS AND EDITORIAL AIDS

AD	Autograph document
ADS	Autograph document, signed
ADS-JBF	John C. Frémont document with text and signature in Jessie B. Frémont's hand
AL	Autograph letter
ALS	Autograph letter, signed
ALS-JBF	John C. Frémont letter with text and signature in Jessie B. Frémont's hand
D	Document
DS	Document, signed
DS-JBF	Document, Frémont's name signed by Jessie
f/w	Filed with
JBF	Jessie Benton Frémont
JCF	John Charles Frémont
Lbk	Letterbook copy
LR	Letter received
LS	Letter sent
RC	Receiver's copy
RG	Record Group
SC	Sender's copy
[ ]	Word or phrase supplied or corrected. Editorial remarks within text are italicized and enclosed in square brackets.
[?]	Conjectural reading or conjectural identification of an addressee
[. . .]	A word or two missing or illegible. Longer omissions are specified in footnotes.
< >	Word or phrase deleted from manuscript, usually by sender. The words are set in italics.
. . . .	Unrelated matter deleted by the editor. The symbol stands alone, centered on a separate line.

The 1845 Expedition and the Clash with the Californians

1. Excerpt from the *Memoirs*

[26 May–16 Aug. 1845]

Concurrently with the Report upon the second expedition the plans and scope of a third one had been matured. It was decided that it should be directed to that section of the Rocky Mountains which gives rise to the Arkansas River, the Rio Grande del Norte of the Gulf of Mexico, and the Rio Colorado of the Gulf of California; to complete the examination of the Great Salt Lake and its interesting region; and to extend the survey west and southwest to the examination of the great ranges of the Cascade Mountains and the Sierra Nevada, so as to ascertain the lines of communication through the mountains to the ocean in that latitude. And in arranging this expedition, the eventualities of war were taken into consideration.[1]

The geographical examinations proposed to be made were in great part in Mexican territory. This was the situation: Texas was gone[2] and California was breaking off by reason of distance; the now increasing American emigration was sure to seek its better climate. Oregon was still in dispute; nothing was settled except the fact of a disputed boundary; and the chance of a rupture with Great Britain lent also its contingencies.

Mexico, at war with the United States, would inevitably favor English protection for California. English citizens were claiming payment for loans and indemnity for losses. Our relations with England were already clouded, and in the event of war with Mexico, if not anticipated by us, an English fleet would certainly take possession of the Bay of San Francisco.

For use in such a contingency the only available force was our squadron in the North Pacific, and the measures for carrying out the design of the President fell to the Navy Department. During the year such precautionary measures as were practicable were taken, especially by the vigilant Secretary of the Navy, Mr. [George] Bancroft, whose orders continuously evince comprehending foresight and insistence. Imbued with the philosophy of history, his mind was alive to the bearing of the actual conditions, and he knew how sometimes skill and sometimes bold action determine the advantages of a political situation; and in this his great desire was to secure for the United States the important one that hung in the balance. In the government at Washington he was the active principle, having the activity of brain and keen perception that the occasion demanded. With him Mr. Benton had friendly personal relations of long standing.

As affairs resolved themselves, California stood out as the chief subject in the impending war; and with Mr. Benton and other governing men at Washington it became a firm resolve to hold it for the United States. To them it seemed reasonably sure that California would eventually fall to England or to the United States and that the eventuality was near. This was talked over fully during the time of preparation for the third expedition, and the contingencies anticipated and weighed. The relations between the three countries made a chief subject of interest about which our thoughts settled as the probability of war grew into certainty. For me, no distinct course or definite instruction could be laid down, but the probabilities were made known to me as well as what to do when they became facts. The distance was too great for timely communication; but failing this I was given discretion to act. The instructions early sent, and repeatedly insisted upon, to the officer commanding our Pacific squadron, gave specific orders to be strictly followed in the event of war. But these frequent discussions among the men who controlled the action of the Government, gave to me the advantage of knowing more thoroughly what were its present wishes, and its intentions in the event of war. And so it came that as soon as war was sure between Mexico and ourselves, Lieutenant [Archibald H.] Gillespie was despatched with instructions; and with letters which, if intercepted when crossing Mexico, would convey no meaning to others while to me they would be clear.[3] Plans and expressions relating to the future home in California were known by me to be intended as relating to its occupation by the United States.

Mrs. Frémont was to have accompanied me to the frontier, but the dangerous illness of Mrs. Benton kept her home. I went off with only Jacob and Chinook, who had been recalled from Philadelphia, and was glad to go back to his people.[4]

The Quaker family had been interested in him and careful to give him such rudiments of practical knowledge as he might be able to put to good use. But he was twenty years old when he left the Columbia with me; intelligent, with set character formed among the habits of Indian life, as ineradicable from Indian manhood as his love of free range from a wild horse. How far his brief education was likely to influence his life was made strikingly clear to us when on the evening he reached Washington he exhibited the parting gifts which he had received from his friends. Among these was a large Bible which had been made attractive in his eyes by its ornamentation. "Chinook been a Quaker all winter"—"Here," he added, with the short Indian laugh of pleasure, "Chinook put here name all wife, and all horse."

The knowledge which his eyes had taken in would be useful among his people. He was the son of a chief, and the stories he could tell of his life among the whites would add to his importance; and the kind treatment he had received would dispose himself and them to be friendly to the Americans.

The Indian boys [Juan and Gregorio] who had spent a happy winter in Kentucky met me at Saint Louis, bringing with them Sacramento,[5] aggressively well.

On the frontier I formed a camp where my party was quickly organized.[6] For this expedition ampler means had been provided, and in view of uncertain conditions the force suitably increased. In addition to the usual outfit of arms I had procured about a dozen rifles, the best that could be found; with the object of setting them up as prizes for the best marksmen, to be shot for during the journey. Many of my old men joined me. And I had again Godey.

The animals I had left on pasture were in fine condition; hardened by the previous journey and thoroughly rested they were well fitted to endure a campaign. From the Delaware nation twelve men had been chosen to go with me. These were known to be good hunters and brave men and two of them were chiefs, Swanok and Sagundai.[7] Mr. Preuss was not with me at this time; but was now in assured employment and preferred in his comfortable home to rest from the hardships of the last journey. In his place Mr. Edward M. Kern, of Philadelphia, went with me as topographer. He was besides an accomplished artist; his skill in sketching from nature and in accurately drawing and coloring birds and plants made him a valuable accession to the expedition. Lieutenants Abert and Peck had been attached to my command, and also with me were Mr. James McDowell, a nephew of Mrs. Benton, and Mr. Theodore Talbot, whose health had been restored by the previous journey.

It was getting late in the year. The principal object of the expedition lay in and beyond the Rocky Mountains, and for these reasons no time could be given to examinations of the prairie region. The line of travel was directed chiefly to pass over such country as would afford good camping-grounds; where water and grass, and wood and abundant game would best contribute to maintain the health of the men and the strength of the animals.[8] Along the route we met the usual prairie incidents of Indians and large game, which furnished always wholesome excitement. In those days these broke pleasantly in upon the silence and uniformity of the prairie and made a good school for the men. On the high plains we encountered a Cheyenne village which was out on a hunt. The men came to meet us on the plain, riding abreast and their drums sounding. They were in all their bravery, and the formidable line was imposing, and looked threatening to those of our people who were without experience in an Indian country. Men, tried and fearless in accustomed dangers, are often at the first encounter nervous in those that are unfamiliar. But the Cheyennes were friendly, and we on our side were too strong for any exhibition of hostility or rudeness; and so we gave the usual present in exchange for friendly conduct and good wishes.

We had lost an animal which in the night strayed off from the band, and early on the march next morning Basil [Lajeunesse], with a companion, had been sent out to look for it. He did not get in at night nor in the morning. I therefore remained encamped and with a small party went in turn to look for him. After a search of an hour or two we discovered them halted, and apparently scanning the horizon around, in some uncertainty where to look for us. We were down in a swale in the ground about three hundred yards away, and so out of sight that we had not been seen. We thought to try them, and quickly throwing off the greater part of our clothes we raised an Indian yell and charged. But there was no hesitation with them. They were off their horses in an instant and their levelled pieces brought us to an abrupt halt and a hearty laugh which we all enjoyed in having found them safe and well.

Returning to camp our first experiment suggested another. The camp lay in a sort of broad gully below the level of the prairie. It was midday and the people were careless and more occupied by getting the dinner than with Indians. Riding quietly down to the hollow which gave an easy approach we charged them with the usual yell. Our charge gave them a good lesson, though it lasted but a moment. It was like charging into a beehive; there were so many men in the camp ready with their rifles that it was very un-safe to keep up our Indian character beyond the moment of the charge. Still, like all excitements, it stirred the blood pleasantly for the moment.

On the second of August we reached Bent's Fort, on the Arkansas River.[9] This was our real point of departure. It was desirable to make a survey of the prairie region to the southward, embracing the Canadian and other rivers. I accordingly formed a detached party, in charge of which I placed Lieutenants Abert and Peck, Lieutenant Abert being in chief command. Including these officers, the command consisted of thirty-three men, and I had the good fortune to secure my friend Mr. Fitzpatrick for their guide.[10] I had endeavored to obtain the services of an Indian who knew well the country, and was a man of great influence, especially among the Camanches, but no offer that I could make him would induce him to go.[11] It happened that the Fort was well provisioned, and from its supplies we were able to furnish the party with a good outfit. This consisted principally of coffee and sugar for two months, several boxes of macaroni, and a quantity of rice, together with four fanegas[12] of Mexican flour. In addition they took with them eight steers brought up on the prairie and therefore easy to drive. They were furnished with four large circular tents, and as the face of the country which was covered by the projected survey was not much broken, four wagons were added for their outfit and camp equipage.[13] This outfit may appear luxurious for the prairie, but provisions go fast where thirty healthy men taking just the right quantity of exercise are to be fed three times a day.

Mr. Hatcher, who was a good hunter, was to accompany them as far as Bent's Post on the Canadian.[14]

On the 12th Mr. Fitzpatrick took leave of me and joined the party. On the same day Lieutenant Abert changed his encampment preparatory to making his start, and on the 14th the two officers came to take leave of me.

It is well to say here that on the journey to Bent's Fort I had been much prepossessed in their favor. They had shown themselves well qualified for such an expedition which as of course was entirely new to them. In this journey they have given evidence of the prudence and good judgment which enabled them to carry through successfully the expedition entrusted to their care.

The next day I sent Lieutenant Abert his instructions, which were to survey the Canadian from its source to its junction with the Arkansas, taking in his way the Purgatory River, and the heads of the Washita; and on the 16th he commenced his journey down the Arkansas.[15]

MEMOIRS, 422–26.

1. For the orders under which JCF mounted his third western expedition, see three letters of J. J. Abert to Frémont, 12 Feb., 10 April, and 14 May 1845, printed in Vol. 1; for a discussion of these orders, see the introduction to this volume.

It is well to remember that the *Memoirs,* not published until 1887, gave JCF the advantage of hindsight but deny the reader the immediacy of a contemporary document. We quote from this work extensively because JCF did not keep a journal on the 1845 expedition. That it frequently becomes a self-serving document, no one can deny.

2. On 1 March 1845 President Tyler had already signed the joint resolution passed by Congress for the admission of Texas as a state, and all that remained was to procure Texas's assent.

3. For a discussion of JCF's contention that he had been given discretion—even secret instructions—to act in California, see Doc. No. 22 and the introduction.

4. Except for the 15 Aug. 1845 order to James W. Abert (Doc. No. 2), no letters from JCF have been unearthed for a seven-month period—from the communique to Archibald Campbell of 22 May 1845 (printed in Vol. 1) until the letter to Jessie of 24 Jan. 1846. But the letters of participants, such as Theodore Talbot and Edward Kern, supply interesting bits of information.

On his way to St. Louis with Jacob Dodson and Kino, another Negro servant in the Benton household, JCF stopped to visit Benton at his farm in Kentucky. Meanwhile Talbot and William Chinook pressed on down the Ohio River to Cape Girardeau and then up the Mississippi to St. Louis, where, with the assistance of Robert Campbell, Talbot began buying "the thousand things required for the expedition." JCF arrived in St. Louis on 30 May and immediately began the task of engaging the men to accompany him. Talbot wrote a graphic description of this process to his sister Mary on 4 June:

> You ought to have witnessed the scene which we had here on Monday. Capt. Fremont it seems gave notice to those who wished to accompany him, through the papers, saying that if they collected at the Planters Warehouse (one of the largest houses in the City of that kind) that he would explain the objects, duties, pay, &c. of the Expedition. Long before the appointed hour the house was filled and Capt. Fremont found it necessary to adjourn to an open square. I walked round to the place of meeting about this time with Mr. Bent to see what was going on. The whole street and open space was crowded. We could easily trace the Captain's motions by the denser nucleus which moved hither and thither. They broke the fences down and the Captain finally used a wagon as his rostrum but it was impossible for him to make himself heard. Each one being unwilling to allow his neighbor the advantage of having a word with or even being seen by Fremont. So it was a grand tustle. Fremont at last took refuge in a hotel. This house is absolutely besieged they rush into his bedroom and all Jacob's strength & vigilance has been inadequate to keep them out. The Captains last expedient is to have himself locked up and the key taken off, this plan has been highly successful though rather inconvenient for Jacob has once or twice left him in duress rather longer than he desired.

Talbot thought JCF had in general selected excellent personnel, but he noted that "several however who will not render him much service have been thrust upon him in spite of him through the influence of their friends" and hoped that these might be replaced with good men on the Arkansas at Bent's or the Pueblo.

5. JCF's saddle horse, a gift from John A. Sutter in 1844.

6. On 5 June JCF rode the twenty miles from St. Louis to St. Charles, where he took a steamboat for Westport Landing. He then encamped on the prairies six or seven miles west of Westport to superintend the making of tents and the reduction of chaos to order. Talbot remained in St. Louis, sending out men and equipment, until 10 June, when he also left for the frontier. Incessant rain hampered organization, but on 23 June the camp moved several miles farther from Westport to "get away from civilization and Brandy," as Edward Kern expressed it. Talbot had been sent to Fort Leavenworth on 21 June for some needed articles, but he returned in time to move with the camp an additional five or six miles on 25 June and to see from ten to fourteen men, perhaps dissatisfied with strict discipline, leave the expedition. According to Isaac Cooper, who went with the party as far as Bent's Fort, no one except JCF was to keep a journal or other memoranda. On 26 June the expedition, still hampered by rain, began its slow but regular progress west. On 1 July two artists, Alfred S. Waugh and John B. Tisdale, overtook JCF and renewed their pleas, reinforced with letters of recommendation, to go with the expedition, but they were refused. They turned back on 4 July, as did the two or three ox carts which had been carrying camp equipment. Isaac Cooper noted that the usual order of the train was the captain and the campmaster, followed by the carriage with the "square black roof" carrying the captain's baggage and instruments, and then the

9

four wagons, one of which was drawn by a six-mule team. The wagons were followed by loose horses and mules, kept within certain bounds by several horsemen. Next came a long train of men on horseback leading pack mules, individually or by twos and threes. For details on the organization of the expedition and the division of the camp into ten messes, see Talbot to Mary Talbot, 9 June 1845, to Adelaide Talbot, 15, 18, and 25 June, 3 July 1845 (DLC—Talbot Papers); Edward Kern to Richard Kern, [19] June [1845] (CSmH); MS journal of Isaac Cooper, 1846 (CCS); I. COOPER, 9:71–73, 146–48, 221–22, 290–93, 366–68; *National Intelligencer,* 17 Oct. 1845.

7. Some of the Delawares took a shortcut from Westport and met the expedition at Bent's Fort. Isaac Cooper mentions this fact, as does Talbot in a 16 Aug. letter. Actually there seem to have been only nine Delawares, one of whom was a small boy, a kind of page or equerry. In a certificate dated 21 March 1857, printed in *Memorial of the Delaware Indians,* Senate Doc. 16, p. 159, 58th Cong., 1st sess., Serial 4563, JCF names eight: James Swanuck [Swanok, Swanick, Sewanik], James Sagundai [Saghundai, Secondi, Secondai], James Connor [Conner], Delaware Charley, Wetowka [Wetowah, Wetowa], Crane, Solomon Everett, and Bob Skirkett. James Swanuck was the son of the principal chief of the Delawares. The chief was erroneously reported as having been killed the previous summer by the Cheyennes. Sagundai was the uncle of the young Swanuck (CARTER [2]).

8. The expedition followed the Santa Fe Trail as far as the Pawnee fork of the Arkansas River, then up the Pawnee to its head and over to the Smoky Hill fork of the Kansas River. Traveling west on JCF's 1844 eastbound route, it reached the Arkansas River about twenty-five miles below Bent's Fort (Talbot to Adelaide Talbot, 10 and 16 Aug. 1845, DLC—Talbot Papers).

9. Talbot wrote, "We were welcomed by Mr. St. Vrain one of the elder partners of the Company & Mr. Geo. Bent who we saw last year with several others that we had met before" (Talbot to Adelaide Talbot, 16 Aug. 1845, DLC—Talbot Papers). The *National Intelligencer,* 10 Sept. 1845, notes that a letter had been received in Washington from JCF, dated 2 Aug. from Bent's Fort, but did not give its contents; apparently the letter is no longer extant.

10. Thomas Fitzpatrick was piloting Col. Stephen Watts Kearny and five companies of the 1st Dragoons, who were returning east to Fort Leavenworth from an expedition into the Indian country as far as South Pass on the Oregon Trail. Kearny had passed Bent's Fort two or three days before JCF arrived, and the latter now sent a courier to obtain the services of Fitzpatrick as a guide for Abert's detachment and to deliver the mail which he had brought "from the settlements" for the troops (report of Lieut. William B. Franklin to Kearny, 5 Nov. 1845, pp. 56–57, DNA–77, LR, "F").

11. The Indian whom JCF originally tried to obtain as guide for Abert's detachment was Tahkaibuhl, a Kiowa (ABERT [1], 2).

12. A *fanega* today is approximately 1.6 bushels. During the Santa Fe Trail period it was measured as 140 pounds, or approximately two bushels (TWITCHELL, 2:133n). According to Abert, his expedition was given eight *fanegas* of flour.

13. Abert thus "inherited" the wagons of the expedition, and JCF proceeded west without these encumbrances.

14. Virginia-born John L. Hatcher (ca. 1812–97) was one of the most able and trusted of the hunters and traders employed by William Bent. In 1859

he settled in the Sonoma Valley in California but some eight years later moved to Oregon, where he bought a farm in Linn County (CARTER [3]).

15. The *Journal of Lt. J. W. Abert, from Bent's Fort to St. Louis, in 1845,* Senate Exec. Doc. 438, 29th Cong., 1st sess., Serial 477, is a report of this detachment of JCF's expedition. A new edition of this journal, which appeared in 1970, omits many of the engravings illustrating the congressional document, but it contains watercolors from Abert's 1845 sketchbook. See ABERT [2].

2. Frémont to James W. Abert

BENT'S FORT, Arkansaw River
August 15th, 1845

SIR

In conformity to instructions from the Department directing an extension of our surveys along the base of the southern Rocky Mountains, you will immediately after the reception of these orders proceed to the mouth of the *Purgatoire* (Las Animas) branch of the Arkansaw,[1] and agreeably to the directions which you have already received in greater detail, continue up that stream to a point where it is intersected by the wagonroad to Santa Fe—crossing the *Raton,* a spur of the Rocky Mountains, by way of this road and striking the Red River (Canadian) of the Arkansaw a few miles below its issue from the mountains, you will ascend the stream to that place, and after having carefully determined your position, survey that river thence so far down as Fort Ceran, a trading post recently established by Mr. Bent.[2]

Leaving this post by way of Arrow Creek[3] your farther route will be southwardly through the broken country at the foot of the Rocky Mountains, crossing successively the Elk branch[4] of the Canadian and the Buffalo and Cut Nose Creeks[5] of the Great Red River. The points on these streams intersected by your line you will of course determine in position, making, if necessary on account of weather, some delay at the head of Cut Nose Creek, which you are directed strictly to consider the southern limit of your exploration.

You will thence descend to the junction of this stream with the Buffalo River, a point which you are also required to determine astronomically. Continuing your road down the latter river so far as a locality called the "Sand Hills" you will leave the waters of

Red River and cross northwardly to the Canadian Fork of the Arkansaw River.

The continuation of your route will now be down the Canadian Fork, and you will give particular attention, among your astronomical positions, to the determination of the mouth of Wolf River and the junction of the Canadian Fork with the Arkansaw River. Proceeding from this point immediately to the neighboring town of Van Buren [in Arkansas] you will be governed by the state of the season in your route to the city of St. Louis, where your party will be discharged, and paid by Mr. Robert Campbell, who has been provided with the necessary funds. A statement of their accounts will accompany this letter.

For the execution of these duties you will be furnished with a party of thirty-three men. Lieut. Peck will be attached to the party as your assistant, and Mr. Thomas Fitzpatrick will accompany you as guide.

The few astronomical positions which are here indicated to you are those only which are to be regarded among the more important and you will neglect no opportunity to multiply them along your line of travel, endeavoring as frequently as possible to control your chronometer by lunar distances, as I am unable to furnish you with instruments for other observations. It would be well to make a little delay for the determination of some marked position on your line in the neighborhood of the boundary between the United States and Mexico.

Should you find at St. Louis, no instructions for the disposition of the public property, I would recommend you to leave this to the discretion of Mr. Campbell until farther orders from the Chief of the Topographical Bureau.

It is expected that you will so regulate your travel as to reach the city of St. Louis within the present year, and so far as will be consistent with this end, the above instructions are to be considered absolute, and admitting of no departure except where they may be rendered entirely impracticable by the nature of the country. Very Respectfully Sir, Your Obedient Servant,

J. C. Frémont
Bt. Capt. Topl. Engrs.

Lieut. James Abert
Topl. Engineers
Fort William, Arkansaw River

LS, RC (DNA-77, LR). Endorsed: "Order from Capt. Fremont directing a Survey of the Cañadian River, August 15, 1845."

1. Purgatoire, later corrupted to "Picketwire," was the French name for the Purgatory; Las Animas was the early Spanish name for the same stream, a shortening of El Rio de las Animas Perdidas en Purgatorio.

2. Probably the trading post established in the winter of 1843–44 on Bent's Creek in northeastern Hutchinson County, Tex. It seems not to have been used very much by the Bents after 1845.

3. Probably the present White Deer Creek.

4. Apparently the present Red Deer Creek near Pampa, Tex.

5. Buffalo and Cut Nose creeks were Indian names for heads of the Washita (ABERT [1], 6). The Washita, often called the False Washita, rises on the Llano Estacado east of present Miami, Tex., and roughly parallels the Canadian, some ten to twenty miles below that river, until it turns south. It continues a southern course until it empties into the Red River at the Preston Bend above Denison, Tex. The Canadian flows eastward to the Arkansas.

3. Excerpt from the *Memoirs*

[16 Aug. 1845–24 Jan. 1846]

With Lieutenant Abert also went Mr. James McDowell, who decided to avail himself of the survey to return for the reason that his work would not be carried into the winter, while my journey to the Pacific was expected to be of long duration.

From the Fort I sent an express to Carson at a rancho, or stock farm, which with his friend Richard Owens[1] he had established on the Cimarron, a tributary to the Arkansas River. But he had promised that in the event I should need him, he would join me. And I knew that he would not fail to come. My messenger found him busy starting the congenial work of making up a stock ranch. There was no time to be lost, and he did not hesitate. He sold everything at a sacrifice, farm and cattle; and not only came himself but brought his friend Owens to join the party. This was like Carson, prompt, self-sacrificing, and true. I received them both with great satisfaction.

That Owens was a good man it is enough to say that he and Carson were friends. Cool, brave, and of good judgment; a good hunter and good shot; experienced in mountain life; he was an acquisition, and proved valuable throughout the campaign.

Godey had proved himself during the preceding journey, which had brought out his distinguishing qualities of resolute and aggressive courage. Quick in deciding and prompt in acting he had also the French *élan* and their gayety of courage.

"Gai, gai, avançons nous."
["Gaily, gaily, let us go along."]

I mention him here because the three men come fitly together, and because of the peculiar qualities which gave them in the highest degree efficiency for the service in which they were engaged.

The three, under Napoleon, might have become Marshals, chosen as he chose men. Carson, of great courage; quick and complete perception, taking in at a glance the advantages as well as the chances for defeat; Godey, insensible to danger, of perfect coolness and stubborn resolution; Owens, equal in courage to the others, and in coolness equal to Godey, had the *coup-d'ôeil* of a chess-player, covering the whole field with a glance that sees the best move. His dark-hazel eye was the marked feature of his face, large and flat and far-sighted.

Godey was a Creole Frenchman of Saint Louis, of medium height with black eyes and silky curling black hair which was his pride. In all situations he had that care of his person which good looks encourage. Once when with us in Washington, he was at a concert; immediately behind him sat the wife of the French Minister, Madame Pageot, who, with the lady by her, was admiring his hair, which was really beautiful, "but," she said, *"C'est une perruque."* They were speaking unguardedly in French. Godey had no idea of having his hair disparaged and with the prompt coolness with which he would have repelled any other indignity turned instantly to say, *"Pardon, Madame, c'est bien a moi."* The ladies were silenced as suddenly as the touch on a tree trunk silences a katydid.

On the 16th of August I left Bent's Fort with a well-appointed compact party of sixty; mostly experienced and self-reliant men, equal to any emergency likely to occur and willing to meet it.

On the 20th of August we encamped on the Arkansas at the mouth of the *Fontaine qui Bouit* River. I had with me good instruments for astronomical observations, among them a portable transit instrument. This I set up, and established here one of the four principal positions on which depend the longitudes of the region embraced in the expeditions. The longitude was determined by moon culminations and the latitude by sextant observations of Polaris and stars in the south.

The resulting longitude at this position is 104° 42′ 41″. The latitude 38° 15′ 18″.

On the 26th we encamped at the mouth of the Great Canyon [the eastern end of the Royal Gorge] and next morning leaving the [Arkansas] river passed in our way over a bench of the mountains which the trappers believed to be the place where [Zebulon] Pike was taken prisoner by the Mexicans. But this side of the river was within our territory. He supposed himself to be on the Arkansas when he was taken prisoner on the Rio del Norte, where he had built a stockade.[2]

Crossing various forks of the [Arkansas] river we finally, on September 2d, reached and continued up the main branch, having on our right the naked rock ridge of the mountain, and encamped at night on the head-waters of the Arkansas in Mexican territory; in latitude 39° 20′ 38″, longitude 106° 27′ 15″.

This was pleasant travelling. The weather now was delightful and the country beautiful. Fresh and green, aspen groves and pine woods and clear rushing water, cool streams sparkling over rocky beds.

In a pine grove at the head of the river we came to our delightful surprise upon a small herd of buffalo, which were enjoying themselves in the shade and fresh grass and water.[3] It was now very rare that these animals were found so far west, and this made for us a most pleasant and welcome incident, as it was long now since we had parted from the buffalo. This must have been a stray herd which had found its way into the upper mountains and they had remained for a long time undisturbed. Sometimes in severe winters deer find their way into the highest parts of the wooded mountains, and remain there, keeping fat and sheltered in the aspen groves which furnish them food. Probably this little herd of buffalo had done the same. The Utah [Ute] Pass was several days′ journey to the southeast, and this part of the mountain [i.e., the Rocky Mountains] was out of the way of ordinary travel.

Here along in these mountains was one of the pleasantest grounds in the journey. Game was plenty; deer and elk. We were some days after on the mountain slopes, where a lovely view extended across a broad valley to the opposite ridges. It was so fine a view that Kern sketched it. In looking over the country I had ridden off a mile or two from the party, keeping along the heights to enjoy the air and views, when I came upon a small band of buffalo, doubtless part of the herd which we had found in the pines at the top of the mountain. The ground was rough, but we had a fine race. I had closed up and was about to fire when the pistol which I held raised went off, and the ball passed so close to my head that I reined up in surprise. My holster pistols were a hair-trigger pair, and old companions which I liked for that, and because they were true as a rifle. *"Sacré bon coup,"* Basil said of them once when he saw the head of a quail cut off at long range. This time it was my own head. It is in this way that men have been sometimes lost in the mountains and never found. They lie like the trunk of a fallen tree worn by the snow and rain until the tall, rank grass covers and hides them. My trail would not have been taken in time and it would have been by the merest chance that any hunter would have passed the spot.

One of the Delawares had killed a fat buffalo cow. This singular meeting with the buffalo was our last; and they were probably the last stragglers that ever reached the western slope of the mountains. This was the general opinion of our people, whose experience would be likely to make it correct. The places where I have described them made then the broadest range of the buffalo from east to west, and make a fair exhibit of the abounding animal life of the country.

Passing that night of the 4th on Piny River, an affluent of Grand River, of the Colorado of the Gulf of California, we encamped the next day on the same river at "Williams Fishery," in longitude 106° 44′ 21″, latitude 39° 39′ 12″. We caught here a singular fish, which was called buffalo-fish from a hump on the back, rising straight up immediately behind the head.

Between fishermen and hunters the camp was abundantly supplied in all this part of our journey. These wood-clothed ranges, with their abundant game and healthful air, we have seen described as "impenetrable deserts whose rugged inaccessibility barred all passage, amid whose parched sterility unfortunate travelers were exposed to death from thirst and hunger."

The character of the mountain country has been so fully given in the previous journeys, that it does not need to be longer dwelt upon here.[4] On the 2d of October I encamped on a branch of the Timpanogos [Provo] River, and on the 10th reached the shore of the lake [Utah] and its outlet at the mouth of Hugh's Creek [Jordan River?], on the 12th. The geographical features of the country were carefully sketched; and astronomical observations, for which the continued fine weather favored us, were made on the different affluents to the Grand and Green River forks of the Great Colorado. The next day we encamped at a creek on the shores of the Great Salt Lake, where I made the second principal station for longitude. These observations resulted in longitude 112° 06′ 08″, and latitude 40° 45′ 53″.

It will be remarked that our journey from the head of the Arkansas River had been continuously in Mexican territory, as was all of the Salt Lake valley. Two weeks were spent in this valley and on its tributary streams, during which we were occupied in fixing the positions of various points, and extending our examination into and around the lake.

The rocky shores of its islands were whitened by the spray which leaves salt on everything it touches, and a covering like ice forms over the water which the waves throw among the rocks. This seems to be the dry season when the waters recede; and the shores of the lake, especially on the south side, are whitened with incrustations of fine white salt. The shallow arms of the lake, under a slight covering of briny water, present beds of salt extending for miles. Plants and bushes blown by the winds upon these fields are entirely incrusted with crystallized salt. The stem of a small twig, less than the size of a goose-quill, from the southeastern shore, showed a formation of more than an inch thick of crystallized salt. The fresh water received by the lake is great in quantity, from the many fresh-water streams flowing into it, but they seem to have no perceptible effect. We could find in it no fish, or animal life of any kind, the larvae which were accumulated in beds on the shore being found to belong to winged insects. On the contrary, the upper lake— the Timpanogos—which discharges into this by a stream about thirty-five miles long, is fresh water, and affords large trout and other fish in great numbers. These constitute the food of the Indians during the fishing season.

The mineral or rock salt is found in beds of great thickness at the heads of a stream in the mountains to the eastward behind the lakes. These strata probably underlie the bed of the Great Lake, and constitute the deposit from which it obtains its salt. It was found by us in the place marked by Humboldt on his map of New Spain as derived from the journal of the missionary Father Escalante, who towards the close of the last century attempted to penetrate the unknown country from Santa Fé of New Mexico to Monterey of

California.[5] But he does not seem to have got further in his adventurous journey—and this at that time was far—than the south end of the Timpanogos. Southeast of this lake is the chain of the Wahsatch Mountains, which make in that part the rim of the Great Basin. In this mountain, at the place where Humboldt has written *"Montagnes de sel Gemme"* (Rock Salt Mountain), the strata of salt are found in thick beds of red clay, at the heads of a small stream tributary to the Utah or Timpanogos Lake on its southeasterly side.

There is at the southern end of the lake a large peninsular island, which the Indians informed me could at this low stage of the water be reached on horseback. Accordingly on the 18th I took with me Carson and a few men and rode from our encampment near the southeastern shore across the shallows to the island—almost peninsular at this low stage of the waters—on the way the water nowhere reaching above the saddle-girths. The floor of the lake was a sheet of salt resembling softening ice, into which the horses' feet sunk to the fetlocks. On the island we found grass and water and several bands of antelope. Some of these were killed, and, in memory of the grateful supply of food they furnished, I gave their name to the island. An observation of the meridian altitude of the sun, taken on the summit of the peak of the island, gave for its latitude 40° 58′ 48″.

Returning to the shore we found at the camp an old Utah Indian. Seeing what game we had brought in he promptly informed us that the antelope which we had been killing were his—that *all* the antelope on that island belonged to him—that they were all he had to live upon, and that we must pay him for the meat which we had brought away. He was very serious with us and gravely reproached me for the wrong which we had done him. Pleased with his readiness, I had a bale unpacked and gave him a present—some red cloth, a knife, and tobacco, with which he declared himself abundantly satisfied for this trespass on his game preserve. With each article laid down, his nods and gutturals expressed the satisfaction he felt at the success of his imaginary claim. We could see, as far as an Indian's face lets expression be seen, that he was thinking, "I went to the White Chief who killed my antelope, and made him pay for it." There is nothing new under the sun.

The climate of this lake country does not present the rigorous winter due to its elevation and mountainous structure. Observations made during our stay here show that around the southern shore of the lake, latitude 40° 30′ to 41°, for two weeks in the month of October, from the 13th to the 27th, the mean temperature was 40° at sunrise, 70° at noon, and 54° at sunset; ranging at sunrise from 28° to 57°; at noon, from 62° to 76°; at four in the afternoon, from 58° to 69°; and at sunset, from 47° to 57°.

Until the middle of the month the weather remained fair and very pleasant. On the 15th it began to rain in occasional showers which whitened with snow the tops of the mountains on the southeast side of the lake valley. Flowers were in bloom during all the month. About the 18th, when we visited the large island in the south of the lake, *helianthus* [sunflower], several species of *aster, erodium cicutarium* [filaree], and several other plants were in fresh and full bloom; the grass of the second growth was coming up finely, and vegetation generally betokened the lengthened summer of the climate.

The 16th, 17th, and 18th were stormy with rain; heavy at night; the peaks of the Bear River range and tops of mountains covered with snow. On the 18th the sky cleared with weather like that of late spring, and continued mild and clear until the end of the month, when the fine weather was again interrupted by a day or two of rain. No snow showed within 2000 feet above the level of the valley.

On the 23rd I encamped at a spring in a valley opening on the southern shore of the lake. On the way, near the shore, we came to a small run flowing into the lake, where an Indian was down on his hands and knees, drinking water. Going there also to drink, we were surprised to find it salt. The water was clear, and its coolness indicated that it came from not far below the surface.[6]

On the 25th we moved camp to a valley near the southwestern shore about fifty miles from the station creek [JCF's Station Creek, now City Creek], and in longitude 113° 05′ 09″, latitude 40° 38′ 17″.[7]

At this point we were to leave the lake. From my neighboring mountain height looking westward, the view extended over ranges which occupied apparently the whole visible surface—nothing but mountains, and in winter-time a forbidding prospect. Afterwards, as we advanced, we found the lengthening horizon continued the same prospect until it stretched over the waters of the Pacific. Looking across over the crests of these ridges, which nearly all run north and south, was like looking lengthwise along the teeth of a saw.

Some days here [in Skull Valley] were occupied in deciding upon the direction to be taken for the onward journey. The route I wished to take lay over a flat plain covered with sage-brush. The country looked dry and of my own men none knew anything of it; neither Walker[8] nor Carson. The Indian declared to us that no one had ever been known to cross the plain, which was desert; so far as any of them had ventured no water had been found. It was probably for this reason Father Escalante had turned back. Men who have travelled over this country in later years are familiar with the stony, black, unfertile mountains, that so often discouraged and brought them disappointment. Nearly upon the line of our intended travel, and at the farther edge of the desert, apparently fifty to sixty miles away, was a peak-shaped mountain. This looked to me to be fertile, and it seemed safe to make an attempt to reach it. By some persuasion and the offer of a tempting reward, I had induced one of the local Indians to go as guide on the way to the mountain; willing to profit by any side knowledge of the ground, or water-hole that the rains might have left, and about which the Indians always know in their hunts through the sage after small game.

I arranged that Carson, [Auguste] Archambeau[lt], and [Lucien B.] Maxwell should set out at night, taking with them a man having charge of a pack-mule with water and provisions, and make for the mountain. I to follow with the party the next day and make one camp out into the desert.[9] They to make a signal by smoke in case water should be found.

The next afternoon, when the sun was yet two hours high, with the animals rested and well watered, I started out on the plain. As we advanced this was found destitute of any vegetation except sage-bushes, and absolutely bare and smooth as if water had been standing upon it. The animals being fresh I stretched far out into the plain. Travelling along in the night, after a few hours' march, my Indian lost his courage and grew so much alarmed that his knees really gave way under him and he wabbled about like a drunken man. He was not a true Utah, but rather of the Pi-utes, a Digger of the upper class, and he was becoming demoralized at being taken so far from his *gite*. Seeing that he could be of no possible use I gave him his promised reward and let him go. He was so happy in his release that he bounded off like a hare through the sage-brush, fearful that I might still keep him.

Sometime before morning I made camp in the sage-brush, lighting fires to signal Carson's party.[10] Before daybreak Archambeau rode in; the jingling of his spurs a welcome sound indicating as it did that he brought good tidings. They had found at the peak water and grass, and wood abundant. The gearing up was quickly done and in the afternoon we reached the foot of the mountain, where a cheerful little stream broke out and lost itself in the valley. The animals were quickly turned loose, there being no risk of their straying from the grass and water. To the friendly mountain I gave the name of Pilot Peak. From my observation this oasis is in the latitude 41° 00′ 28″ longitude 114° 11′ 09″. Some time afterward, when our crossing of the desert became known, an emigrant caravan was taken by this route, which then became known as *The Hastings Cut-off.*[11]

We gave the animals a day's rest here. The crossing of the desert had been a little strain upon them; many of them being grain-fed horses, unused to travelling on grass. These cannot stand being over-fatigued, soon reaching the stage which is called in the language of the country *resté;* from which they cannot recover without time, and must be left on the trail. With a mule it is very different. He may be *resté* at night, but give him plenty of good grass and water and he is ready for service in the morning.[12]

On the 1st of November we resumed our journey. The ridges which occupied the basin and which lay across our route are short, being the links which form the ranges; and between their overlapping points were easy passes by which the valleys connect. This is their regular structure.

Through these passes we wound our way and in the evening encamped at a spring in the head of a ravine which my observations put in longitude 114° 26′ 22″, latitude 40° 43′ 29″,[13] and the next day I made camp at a spring to which I gave the name of Whitton, one of my men who discovered it.[14]

In advancing, the country was always carefully examined, so far as the eye could form any judgment upon it; and from the early morning start the men were spread over it to search for a camping-place which with water should give the best grass.

The winter was now approaching and I had good reason to know what the snow would be in the Great Sierra. It was imprudent to linger long in the examination of the Great Basin. In order therefore to use to the best advantage the interval of good weather I decided to divide my party and run two separate lines across the Basin.

On the evening of the 8th I encamped on a small stream which I called Crane's Branch after one of my Delaware hunters. Crane was a good judge of country with a quick eye exercised in hunting. He was one of the men I liked to have near me. He was usually serious and dignified even for an Indian, who are naturally grave men. The objects which furnish ideas to the mind of an Indian are very few and mostly what he sees within a limited range. Within this, the game and other natural objects which come before his eyes; and outside of it, the enemies whom he goes to fight and scalp, if he can. These make his two sets of ideas. Nearer to the whites, other subjects force their way in confused shape through the barriers of an unknown language, but these are quite outside of the usual Indian understanding. The subjects belonging to their manner of life they hesitate to talk about with the whites; this and the difference of language make them reserved to us. With me the Delawares were now making the grand tour.

Crane's Branch led into a larger stream that was one of two forks forming a river to which I gave the name of Humboldt.[15] I am given by himself the honor of being the first to place his great name on the map of the continent.

Both the river and mountain to which I gave his name are conspicuous objects; the river stretching across the Basin to the foot of the Sierra Nevada, and the mountain standing out in greater bulk and length than its neighbors, and being one of those which I have named fertile mountains, having on it abundant water and grass, and woods.

Years after in travelling through that country I was glad to find that river and mountain held his name, not only on the maps, but in usage by the people.

I now divided the party, giving to Mr. Kern the charge of the main body with instructions to follow down and survey the Humboldt River and its valley to their termination in what was called "the Sink."[16] This is a broad level bottom of fertile land; probably once the bed of the lake when over all this region, at a time not very remote, the waters were higher. When I passed there two years later it was covered with grass and several varieties of clover. Thence to continue on along the eastern foot of the Sierra to a lake to which

I have given the name of Walker, who was to be his guide on this survey. I had engaged Mr. Walker for guide in this part of the region to be explored, with which, and the southern part of the "California Mountain" he was well acquainted. The place of meeting for the two parties was to be the lake [i.e., Walker Lake].

This party would have a secure line of travel in following the river, which would furnish grass and water for the entire journey and so keep the greater number of the animals in as good condition as the season admitted.

To accompany myself I selected ten men, among whom were some of the Delawares.[17] I took leave of the main party and set out on a line westward directly across the Basin, the look of the country inducing me to turn somewhat to the south.

We lost no time in pressing forward; but the tortuous course rendered unavoidable by the necessity of using just such passes as the mountains gave, and in searching for grass and water, greatly lengthened our road. Still it gave me knowledge of the country. The early morning began the day's work by the usual careful study of the ground ahead for indications to the best line of travel, and so soon as they were ready the hunters started out to the right and left, scouring the country as we advanced. When anything worthy of note was discovered a shot was fired, or the horseman would make a few short turns backward and forward as a signal that something requiring attention had been found.

We succeeded in finding always good camping-grounds, usually availing ourselves of the Indian trails which skirted the foot of the ridges. When well marked showing use, these never failed to lead to water and the larger the trail the more abundant the water. This we always found at the edge of the mountains, generally in some ravine, and quickly sinking into the ground; never reaching the valley except in seasons of rain. Doubtless artesian wells would find it and make fertile these valleys, which now are dry and barren.

Travelling along the foot of a mountain on one of these trails we discovered a light smoke rising from a ravine, and riding quietly up, found a single Indian standing before a little sage-brush fire over which was hanging a small earthen pot, filled with sage-brush squirrels. Another bunch of squirrels lay near it and close by were his bow and arrows. He was deep in a brown study, thinking perhaps of some game-trail which he had seen and intended to follow that afternoon, and did not see or hear us until we were directly upon him, his absorbed thoughts and the sides of the ravine cutting off sounds. Escape for him was not possible and he tried to seem pleased, but his convulsive start and wild look around showed that he thought his end had come. And so it would—abruptly—had the Delawares been alone. With a deprecating smile he offered part of his *pot-au-feu* and his bunch of squirrels. I reassured him with a friendly shake of the hand and a trifling gift. He was a good-looking young man, well made, as these Indians usually are, and naked as a worm.

The Delawares lingered as we turned away, but I would not let them remain. Anyhow they regarded our journey as a kind of war-path and no matter what kind of path he is upon a Delaware is always ready to take a scalp when he is in a country where there are strange Indians. We had gone but a short distance when I found they had brought away his bow and arrows, but I had them taken immediately back. These were well made; the bow strong, and made still stronger with sinews, and the arrows were all headed with obsidian worked in the usual spear shape by patient labor, and nearly as sharp as steel. The Delawares took them back willingly when I reminded them that they had exposed the poor fellow to almost certain starvation by depriving him at the beginning of winter of his only means to procure food.

At one of our camps on the foot-slopes of a ridge we found again springs of boiling water; but a little way distant from the spring of cold water which supplied us.

A day or two after we saw mountain sheep for the first time in crossing the Basin. None were killed, but that afternoon Carson killed an antelope. That day we travelled late, making for the point of a wooded mountain where we had expected to find water, but on reaching it found only the dry bed of a creek where there was sometimes running water. It was too late to go farther and I turned up the creek bed, taking the chance to find it above as the mountain looked promising. Well up, towards the top of the mountain, nearly two thousand feet above the plain, we came upon a spring where the little basin afforded enough for careful use. A bench of the mountain near by made a good camping-ground, for the November nights were cool and newly-fallen snow already marked out the higher ridges of the mountains. With grass abundant, and pine wood and cedars to keep up the night fires, we were well provided for.

Sagundai who had first found the spring saw fresh tracks made in the sand by a woman's naked foot, and the spring had been recently cleaned out. But he saw no other indications of human life. We had made our supper on the antelope and were lying around the fire, and the men taking their great comfort in smoking. A good supper and a pipe make for them a comfortable ending no matter how hard the day has been. Carson who was lying on his back with his pipe in his mouth, his hands under his head and his feet to the fire, suddenly exclaimed, half rising and pointing to the other side of the fire, "Good God! look there!" In the blaze of the fire, peering over her skinny, crooked hands, which shaded her eyes from the glare, was standing an old woman apparently eighty years of age, nearly naked, her grizzly hair hanging down over her face and shoulders. She had thought it a camp of her people and had already begun to talk and gesticulate, when her open mouth was paralyzed with fright, as she saw the faces of the whites. She turned to escape, but the men had gathered about her and brought her around to the fire. Hunger and cold soon dispelled fear and she made us understand that she had been left by her people at the spring to die, because she was very old and could gather no more seeds and was no longer good for anything. She told us she had nothing to eat and was very hungry. We gave her immediately about a quarter of the antelope, thinking she would roast it by our fire, but no sooner did she get it in her hand than she darted off into the darkness. Some one ran after her with a brand of fire, but calling after her brought no answer. In the morning, her fresh tracks at the spring showed that she had been there for water during the night. Starvation had driven her to us, but her natural fear drove her away as quickly, so soon as she had secured something to eat. Before we started we left for her at the spring a little supply from what food we had. This, with what she could gather from the nut-pine trees on the mountain, together with our fire which she could easily keep up, would probably prolong her life even after the snows came. The nut-pines and cedars extend their branches out to the ground and in one of their thickets, as I have often proved, these make a comfortable shelter against the most violent snow-storms.

This was Sagundai's Spring. The names of my camps here along become the record of the rivalry of the men in finding good camps. It became the recurring interest of each day to prove their judgment of country as well as their skill as hunters.

25

The region here along had a special interest for me and our progress was slow for the two following days. We had now reached a low valley line that extends along the eastern foot of the ridges which constitute the Sierra Nevada. Into this low ground the rivers from the Sierra as well as from the Basin gather into a series of lakes extending south towards the head of the Gulf of California. I had a reason for carefully examining this part of the Basin, but the time needed for it would interfere with other objects and the winter was at hand.

The place appointed for meeting the main party was on the eastward shore of Walker's Lake near the point where the river to which I had given the same name empties into it. Making our way along the foot of the mountain towards our rendezvous we had reached one of the lakes where at this season the scattered Indians of the neighborhood were gathering to fish. Turning a point on the lake shore the party of Indians some twelve or fourteen in number came abruptly into view. They were advancing along in Indian file, one following the other, their heads bent forward and eyes fixed on the ground. As our party met them the Indians did not turn their heads nor raise their eyes from the ground. Their conduct indicated unfriendliness, but, habituated to the uncertainties of savage life, we too fell readily into their humor, and passed on our way without word or halt. Even to us it was a strange meeting.

It was the solitary occasion where I met with such an instance of sullen and defiant hostility among Indians and where they neither sought nor avoided conflict. I judged that they either regarded us as intruders, or that they had received some recent injury from the whites who were now beginning to enter California, and which they wished but feared to avenge.

In this region the condition of the Indian is nearly akin to that of the lower animals. Here they are really *wild men*. In this wild state the Indian lives to get food. This is his business. The superfluous part of his life, that portion which can be otherwise employed, is devoted to some kind of warfare. From this lowest condition, where he is found as the simplest element of existence, up to the highest in which he is found on this continent, it is the same thing. In the Great Basin, where nearly naked he travelled on foot and lived in the sage-brush, I found him in the most elementary form; the men living alone; the women living alone, but all after food. Sometimes one man cooking by his solitary fire in the sage-brush which was his home, his bow and arrows and bunch of squirrels by his side; sometimes on the shore of a lake or river where food was more abundant a little band of men might be found occupied in fishing; miles away a few women would be met gathering seeds and insects, or huddled up in a shelter of sage-brush to keep off the snow. And the same on the mountains or prairies where the wild Indians were found in their highest condition, where they had horses and lived in lodges. The labor of their lives was to get something to eat. The occupation of the women was in gleaning from the earth everything of vegetable or insect life; the occupation of the men was to kill every animal they could for food and every man of every other tribe for pleasure. And, in every attempt to civilize, these are the two lines upon which he is to be met.

On the 24th we encamped at our rendezvous on the lake where beds of rushes made good pasturage for our animals.[18] Three days afterward the main party arrived.[19] They were all in good health, and had met with no serious accident. But the scarcity of game had made itself felt, and we were now all nearly out of provisions. It was now almost midwinter, and the open weather could not be expected to last.

In this journey across the Basin, between latitudes 41° and 38°, during the month of November from the 5th to the 25th, the mean temperature was 29° at sunrise and 40° at sunset, ranging at noon between 41° and 60°. There was a snow-storm between the 4th and 7th, snow falling principally at night, and the sun occasionally breaking out in the day. The lower hills and valleys were covered only a few inches deep with snow, which the sun carried off in a few hours after the storm was over. The weather continued uninterruptedly clear and beautiful until the close of the month. But though the skies were clear it was colder now that we had come within the influence of the main Sierra.

I was in the neighborhood of the passage which I had forced across it a year before, and I had it on my mind. Heavy snows might be daily expected to block up the passes, and I considered that in this event it would be hopeless to attempt a crossing with the material of the whole party.

I therefore decided again to divide it, sending the main body under Kern to continue southward along the lake line and pass around the Point of the California Mountain into the head of the San Joaquin valley. There, as already described, the great Sierra

27

comes down nearly to the plain, making a Point, as in the smaller links, and making open and easy passes where there is never or rarely snow. As before, Walker, who was familiar with the southern part of Upper California, was made the guide of the party; and, after considering the advantages of different places, it was agreed that the place of meeting for the two parties should be at a little lake in the valley of a river called the Lake Fork of the Tularé Lake [Kings River].

With a selected party of fifteen, among whom were some of my best men, including several Delawares, I was to attempt the crossing of the mountain in order to get through to Sutter's Fort before the snow began to fall. At the fort I could obtain the necessary supplies for the relief of the main party.

Leaving them in good order, and cheerful at the prospect of escaping from the winter into the beautiful "California Valley," as it was then called, we separated, and I took up my route for the river which flows into Pyramid Lake, and which on my last journey I had named Salmon-Trout [Truckee] River.

I now entered a region which hardship had made familiar to me, and I was not compelled to feel my way, but used every hour of the day to press forward towards the Pass at the head of this river.

On the 1st of December I struck it above the lower cañon, and on the evening of the 4th camped at its head on the east side of the pass in the Sierra Nevada. Our effort had been to reach the pass before a heavy fall of snow, and we had succeeded. All night we watched the sky, ready to attempt the passage with the first indication of falling snow; but the sky continued clear. On our way up, the fine weather which we had left at the foot of the mountain continued to favor us, and when we reached the pass the only snow showing was on the peaks of the mountains.[20]

At three in the afternoon the temperature was 46°; at sunset, 34°. The observations of the night gave for the longitude of the pass, 120° 15′ 20″, and for the latitude, 39° 17′ 12″. Early the next morning we climbed the rocky ridge which faces the eastern side, and at sunrise were on the crest of the divide, 7200 [7,135] feet above the sea; the sky perfectly clear, and the temperature 22°. There was no snow in the pass, but already it showed apparently deep on higher ridges and mountain-tops. The emigrant road now passed here following down a fork of Bear River, which leads from the pass into the Sacramento valley. Finding this a rugged way, I turned to the south and encamped in a mountain-meadow where the grass was fresh and green. We had made good our passage of the mountain and entered now among the grand vegetation of the California valley. Even if the snow should now begin to fall, we could outstrip it into the valley, where the winter king already shrunk from the warm breath of spring.

The route the next day led over good travelling ground; gaining a broad leading ridge we travelled along through the silence of a noble pine forest where many of the trees were of great height and uncommon size. The tall red columns standing closely on the clear ground, the filtered, flickering sunshine from their summits far overhead, gave the dim religious light of cathedral aisles, opening out on every side, one after the other, as we advanced. Later, in early spring, these forest grounds are covered with a blue carpet of forget-me-nots.

The pines of the European forests would hide their diminished heads amidst these great columns of the Sierra. A species of cedar (*Thuya gigantea*) occurred often of extraordinary bulk and height. *Pinus Lambertiani* [sugar pine] was one of the most frequent trees, distinguished among cone-bearing tribes by the length of its cones, which are sometimes sixteen or eighteen inches long. The Indians eat the inner part of the burr, and I noticed large heaps of them where they had been collected.

Leaving the higher ridges we gained the smoother spurs and descended about 4000 feet, the face of the country rapidly changing as we went down. The country became low and rolling; pines began to disappear, and varieties of oak, principally an evergreen resembling live oak, became the predominating forest growth. The oaks bear great quantities of acorns, which are the principal food of all the wild Indians; it is their bread-fruit tree. At a village of a few huts which we came upon there was a large supply of these acorns; eight or ten cribs of wicker-work containing about twenty bushels each. The sweetest and best acorns, somewhat resembling Italian chestnuts in taste, are obtained from a large tree belonging to the division of white oaks, distinguished by the length of its acorn, which is commonly an inch and a half and sometimes two inches. This long acorn characterizes the tree, which is a new species and is accordingly specified by Dr. Torrey as *Quercus longiglanda* (Torr. and Frem.)—long-acorn oak. This tree is very abundant and generally forms the groves on the bottom-lands of the streams; standing apart with a green undergrowth of grass which gives the appearance of cultivated parks. It is a noble forest tree, sixty to eighty feet high with a summit of wide-spreading branches, and frequently attains a diameter of six feet; the largest that we measured reached eleven feet. The evergreen oaks generally have a low growth with long branches and spreading tops.

At our encampment on the evening of the 8th, on a stream which I named Hamilton's Creek,[21] we had come down to an elevation of 500 feet above the sea. The temperature at sunset was 48°, the sky clear, the weather calm and delightful, and the vegetation that of early spring. We were still upon the foot-hills of the mountains, where the soil is sheltered by woods and where rain falls much more frequently than in the open Sacramento Valley near the edge of which we then were. I have been in copious continuous rains of eighteen or twenty hours' duration, in the oak region of the mountain, when none fell in the valley below. Innumerable small streams have their rise through these foot-hills, which often fail to reach the river of the valley, but are absorbed in its light soil; the large streams coming from the upper part of the mountain make valleys of their own of fertile soil, covered with luxuriant grass and interspersed with groves.

The oak belt of the mountain is the favorite range of the Indians. I found many small villages scattered through it. They select places near the streams where there are large boulders of granite rock, that show everywhere holes which they had used for mortars in which to pound the acorns. These are always pretty spots. The clean, smooth granite rocks standing out from the green of the fresh grass over which the great oaks throw their shade, and the clear running water are pleasant to eye and ear.

After the rough passage and scanty food of the Basin these lovely spots with the delightful spring weather, fresh grass and flowers, and running water, together with the abundant game, tempted us to make early camps; so that we were about four days in coming down the valley.

Travelling in this way slowly along, taking the usual astronomical observations and notes of the country, we reached on the 9th of December the [Eliab] Grimes Rancho [del Paso] on what was then still known as *Rio de los Americanos*—the American Fork, near Sutter's Fort.

Captain Sutter received me with the same friendly hospitality which had been so delightful to us the year before.[22] I found that our previous visit had created some excitement among the Mexican authorities. But to their inquiries he had explained that I had been engaged in a geographical survey of the interior and had been driven to force my way through the snow of the mountains simply to obtain a refuge and food where I knew it could be had at his place, which was by common report known to me.

Being ourselves already recruited by the easy descent into the valley I did not need to delay long here. A few days sufficed to purchase some animals and a small drove of cattle, with other needed supplies.

Leaving the upper settlements of *New Helvetia,* as the Sutter settlement was called, on the 14th of December, I started to find my party which I had left in charge of Talbot when we had separated in the Basin on Walker Lake. Passing through the groves of oak which border the American Fork, we directed our route in a southeasterly course towards the Cosumné River.

The Cosumné Indians, who have left their name on this river, and which I had preserved on my map of the country, have been driven away from it within a few years and dispersed among other tribes; and several farms of some leagues in extent had already been commenced on the lower part of the stream. At one of these we encamped about eight miles above the junction of the Cosumné with the Mokelumné River, which a few miles below enters a deep slough in the tide-water of the San Joaquin delta.

Our way now lay over the well-remembered plains of the San Joaquin valley, the direction of our route inclining towards the mountains. We crossed wooded sloughs, with ponds of deep water, which nearer the foothills are running streams with large bottoms of fertile land; the greater part of our way being through evergreen, and other oaks. The rainy season, which commonly begins with November, had not yet commenced, and the streams were at the low stage usual to the dry season and easily forded. The Mokelumné where we crossed it is about sixty yards wide; the broad alluvial bottoms were here about five hundred yards wide. Leaving this river on the morning of the 16th, we travelled about twenty miles through open woods of white oak, crossing in the way several stream-beds, among them the Calaveras Creek. These have abundant water with good land nearer the hills; and the Calaveras makes some remarkably handsome bottoms.

Issuing from the woods we rode about sixteen miles over open prairie partly covered with bunch-grass, the timber reappearing on the rolling hills of the river Stanislaus in the usual belt of evergreen oaks. The level valley was about forty feet below the upland, and the stream seventy yards broad, with the usual fertile bottom-land which was covered with green grass among large oaks. We encamped in one of these bottoms, in a grove of the large white oaks previously mentioned.

The many varieties of deciduous and evergreen oaks which predominate throughout the valleys and lower hills of the mountains afford large quantities of acorns. Their great abundance in the midst of fine pasture-land must make them an important element in the farming economy of the country.

The day had been very warm. At sunset the temperature was 55° and the weather clear and calm.

At sunrise the next morning the thermometer was at 22° with a light wind from the Sierra N. 76° E. and a clear pure sky, against which the blue line of the mountains showed clearly marked. The way for about three miles was through woods of evergreen and other oaks with some shrubbery intermingled. Among this was a lupine of extraordinary size, not yet in bloom. Emerging from the woods we travelled in a southeasterly direction, over a prairie of rolling land, the group becoming more broken as we approached the Tuolumné River, one of the finest tributaries to the San Joaquin.

The hills were generally covered with a species of geranium (*erodium cicutarium*), in the language of the country *alfalferia,* a valuable plant for stock and considered very nutritious. With this was frequently interspersed good and green bunch-grass, and a plant commonly called *bur-clover*. This plant, which in some places is very abundant, bears a spirally twisted pod, filled with seeds that remain on the ground during the dry season, well preserved. This affords good food for the cattle until with the spring rains new grass comes up.

We started a band of wild horses on approaching the river and the Indians ran off from a village on the bank; the men lurking round to observe us.

The trail led sidling down the steep face of the hill to the river-bottom. The horse I was riding, one of those gotten at Sutter's, had been reclaimed from the wild herds, and seeing this wild herd scouring off he remembered his own free days and in mid-trail set

32

himself to bucking, in the way a California horse—wild or tame—knows how to do exceptionally. A wild horse broken to the saddle never forgets, and takes advantage of every chance he has to rid himself of his rider. If a girth breaks or a saddle turns he knows it. A rifle across the saddle and Indians to be watched and a bucking horse on a steep hill-side make a complicated situation, but we got to the bottom without parting company and my horse seemed only pleased by the excitement.

I give place to a recollection of another bucking horse which illustrates well the capacity in that way of the California horse of the civilized breed and the capacity of the Californian to sit him. After the capitulation of Couënga I was riding into Los Angeles at the head of the battalion and was met by Don Francisco de la Guerra[23] and other officers of the Californian force, who brought with them for me two fine horses, one gray, the other a *palomino* or tan-colored cream; both uncommonly large for Californian horses and just the size for a saddle-horse. Before changing my saddle I took a look at the two, and not liking the eyes of the gray I had Jacob put the saddle on the *palomino*. My friend Don Pedro Carillo,[24] a Californian, educated at Harvard—and who had taken sides with me and was one of my aides—took the gray. Of course, like all Californians, Don Pedro was a splendid horseman. He sprang lightly into the saddle, which was that of the country, with the usual *mochila* or large, stiff, leather covering to the saddle. But his right foot had not reached the stirrup when the gray commenced. He bucked from the start, going around in a circle about thirty yards across, bucking right along and with so much force that he jerked Don Pedro's sword from its scabbard, the pistols from the holsters and the *mochilas* from between him and the saddle. Everybody applauded his horsemanship. Francisco de la Guerra cried out *"Todavia es Californio!"* ("He is a Californian still.")

Californians generally were handsome, but even among them Don Pedro was a fine-looking man. He is yet living at Los Angeles, and we remain friends.

We encamped on the Tuolumné on bottom-land, open-wooded with large white oaks of the new species; and excellent grass furnished good food for the animals. The usual order of the camp was enlivened by the Indians, who were soon reconciled to our presence. About their huts were the usual *acorn cribs,* containing each some twenty or thirty bushels. The sunset temperature was pleasant, at 54°, and a clear atmosphere. Multitudes of geese and other wild fowl made the night noisy.

In the morning the sky was clear, with an air from the southeast and a hoar frost covering the ground like a light fall of snow. At sunrise the thermometer was at 24°, a difference from the preceding sunset of thirty degrees. Our course now inclined more towards the foot of the mountain and led over a broken country. In about seventeen miles we reached the Auxumné River—called by the Mexicans *Merced*—another large affluent of the San Joaquin, and continued about six miles up the stream, intending gradually to reach the heart of the mountains at the head of the Lake Fork of the Tularé.

We encamped on the southern side of the river, where broken hills made a steep bluff, with a narrow bottom. On the northern side was a low, undulating wood and prairie land, over which a band of about three hundred elk was slowly coming to water, feeding as they approached.

The next day was December the 19th; the weather continuing clear and pleasant, very unlike the winter days to which we were accustomed. We continued our journey in a southeasterly direction, over a broken and hilly country without timber, and showing only scattered clumps of trees from which we occasionally started deer.

In a few hours we reached a beautiful country of undulating upland, openly wooded with oaks, principally evergreen, and watered with small streams which together make the MARIPOSAS River. Continuing along we came upon broad and deeply-worn trails which had been freshly travelled by large bands of horses, apparently coming from the San Joaquin valley. But we had heard enough to know that they came from the settlements on the coast. These and indications from horse-bones dragged about by wild animals, wolves or bears, warned us that we were approaching villages of Horse-thief Indians, a party of whom had just returned from a successful raid. Immediately upon striking their trail I sent forward four of my best men, Dick Owens and Maxwell and two Delawares. I followed after with the rest of the party, but soon the Indian signs became so thick, trail after trail coming into that on which we were travelling, that I saw we were getting into a stronghold of the Horse-thieves, and we rode rapidly forward. After a few miles of sharp riding, a small stream running over a slaty bed, with clumps of oaks around, tempted me into making an early halt. Good grass was abundant, and this spot not long since had been the camping ground of a village, and was evidently one of their favorite places, as the ground was whitened with the bones of many horses. We had barely thrown off our saddles and not yet turned the horses loose, when the intermittent report of rifles, in the way one does not mistake, and the barking of many dogs and sounds of shouting faintly reached us, made us quickly saddle up again and ride to the sounds at speed.

Four men were left to guard the camp. In a short half mile we found ourselves suddenly in front of a large Indian village not two hundred yards away. More than a hundred Indians were advancing on each side of a small hill, on the top of which were our men where a clump of oaks and rocks amidst bushes made a good defence. My men had been discovered by the Indians and suddenly found themselves in the midst of them, but jumped from their horses and took to the rocks, which happened to be a strong place to fight them. The Indians were shouting at them in Spanish, and the women and children at the village howling at their best. Our men were only endeavoring to stand them off until we should get up, as they knew we would not be far behind. The Indians had nearly surrounded the knoll and were about getting possession of the horses when we came into view. Our shout as we charged up the hill was answered by the yell of the Delawares as they dashed down the hill to recover their animals, and the report of Owens' and Maxwell's rifles. Owens had singled out the foremost Indian, who did not go any farther up the hill, and the others drew a little back towards the village. Anxious for the safety of the men left behind, I profited by the surprise to withdraw towards our camp; checking the Indians by an occasional rifle shot, with the range of which they seemed to think they were acquainted. They followed us to the camp and scattered around among the rocks and trees, whence they harangued us, bestowing on us liberally all the epithets they could use, telling us what they would do with us. Many of them had been Mission Indians and spoke Spanish well. "Wait," they said. *"Esperate Carrajos*—wait until morning. There are two big villages up in the mountains close by; we have sent for the Chief; he'll be down before morning with all the people and you will all die. None of you shall go back; we will have all your horses."

I divided the camp into two watches, putting myself into the last one. As soon as it was fully dark each man of the guard crept to his post. We heard the women and children retreating towards the mountains. Before midnight the Indians had generally withdrawn, only now and then a shout to show us that they were on hand and attending to us. Otherwise nothing occurred to break the stillness of the night, but a shot from one of the Delawares fired at a wolf as it jumped over a log. In our experienced camp no one moved, but Delaware Charley crept up to me to let me know what had caused the shot of the Delaware who, with hostile Indians around, instinctively fired at a moving thing that might have been an Indian crawling towards our horses.

The Horse-thief tribes have been "Christian Indians" of the Missions, and when these were broken up by Mexico the Indians took to the mountains.[25] Knowing well the coast country, and the exact situation of the Missions where they had lived and the ranchos and the range which their horses were accustomed to, they found it easy to drive off the animals into the mountains, partly to use as saddle-horses, but principally to eat.

In time they became a scourge to the settlements. The great ranges which belonged with the ranchos not only supported many thousands of cattle, but also many hundreds of horses which were divided into bands, *"manadas."* The Indians were the vaqueros or herdsmen who attended to both; herding the cattle, and breaking in the colts. The Californians had great pleasure in their horses. On some ranchos there would be several hundred saddle-horses, in bands of eighty or a hundred of different colors; *Alazan* (sorrel) always the favorite color. Deprived of their regular food, the Indians took to the mountains and began to drive off horses. Cattle would not drive fast enough to avoid the first pursuit. In their early condition they had learned to eat wild horse-meat and liked it. Familiarity with the whites and the success of their predatory excursions made the Horse-thief Indians far more daring and braver than those who remained in fixed villages, whether in the mountains or on the valley streams which carried the name of the different tribes —the Cosumné, Mokelumné, Towalumné, and Auxumné Rivers. Probably all the streams if their Indian names could have been known, received their names from the small tribes who lived upon them.

The Indians of this country finding their food where they lived were not nomadic. They were not disposed to range, and seemed unaccustomed to intrude upon the grounds which usage probably made the possession of other tribes. Their huts were easily built and permanent; the climate was fine, they lived mostly in the open air, and when they died they were not put in the ground but up in the branches of the trees. The climate is such that a dead animal left on the ground simply dries up and only the eye gives knowledge of its presence.

The springs and streams hereabout were waters of the Chauchiles [Chowchilla] and Mariposas Rivers and the Indians of this village belonged to the Chauchiles tribe.

On some of the higher ridges were fields of a poppy which, fluttering and tremulous on its long thin stalk, suggests the idea of a butterfly settling on a flower, and gives to this flower its name of *Mariposas*—butterflies—and the flower extends its name to the stream.

We were only sixteen men. Keeping in the oak belt on the course I was pursuing would bring us farther among these villages, and I would surely have lost the cattle and perhaps some men and horses in attacks from these Indians. In the morning therefore I turned down one of the streams and quickly gained the open country of the lower hills. We had gained but a little distance on this course when an Indian was discovered riding at speed towards the plain, where the upper San Joaquin reaches the valley. Maxwell was ahead and not far from the Indian when he came into sight, and knowing at once that his object was to bring Indians from the river to intercept us, rode for him. The Indian was well mounted but Maxwell better. With Godey and two of the Delawares I followed. It was open ground over rolling hills and we were all in sight of each other, but before we could reach them a duel was taking place between Maxwell and the Indian—both on foot, Maxwell with pistols, the Indian with arrows. They were only ten or twelve paces apart. I saw the Indian fall as we rode up. I would have taken him prisoner and saved his life, but was too late. The Delawares captured his horse.

Riding along the open ground towards the valley after a mile or two we discovered ten Indians ahead going in the same direction. They saw us as well, but took no notice and did not quicken their gait. When we were about overtaking them they quietly turned into a close thicket which covered about eight acres. We gave the thicket a wide berth; for ten Indians in such a place were more dangerous than so many gray bear.

Turning now to the southward we continued on our way, keeping a few men towards the mountain to give early notice of the approach of any Indians. At evening we encamped in a spring hollow leading to the upper San Joaquin where it makes its way among the hills towards the open valley. We were at an elevation of 1000 feet above the sea; in latitude by observation 37° 07′ 47″. The day had been mild with a faint sun and cloudy weather; and at sunset there were some light clouds in the sky and a northeasterly wind, and a sunset temperature of 45°; probably rendered lower than usual by the air from the mountains, as the foot-hills have generally a warmer temperature than the lower valley.

During the day elk were numerous along our route, making at one time a broken band several miles in length. On the 21st the thermometer was at sunrise 33°; the sky slightly clouded, and in the course of the morning clouds gathered heavy in the southwest. Our route lay in a southeasterly direction, still toward the upper Joaquin, crossing among rolling hills, a large stream, and several sandy beds and affluents to the main river. On the trees along these streams as well as on the hills I noticed *mosses*. In the afternoon we reached the upper San Joaquin River, which was here about seventy yards wide and much too deep to be forded; a little way below we succeeded in crossing at a rapid made by a bed of rock below which, for several miles, the stream appeared deep and not fordable. We followed down it for six or eight miles and encamped on its banks on the verge of the valley plain.

At evening rain began to fall, and with this the spring properly commenced. In November there had been a little rain, but not sufficient to revive vegetation.

December 22d. Temperature at sunrise was 39°. During the night there had been heavy rain, with high wind, and there was a thick fog this morning, but it began to go off at 8 o'clock when the sun broke through. We crossed an open plain still in a southeasterly direction, reaching in about twenty miles the *Tularé Lake* River. This is the Lake Fork; one of the largest and handsomest streams in the valley, being about one hundred yards broad and having perhaps a larger body of fertile lands than any one of the others. It is called by the Mexicans the *Rio de los Reyes*. The broad alluvial bottoms were well wooded with several species of oaks. This is the principal affluent of the Tularé Lake, a strip of water which receives all the rivers in the upper or southern end of the valley. In time of high water it discharges into the San Joaquin River, making a continuous water-line through the whole extent of the valley. The lake itself is surrounded by lowlands and its immediate shores are rankly overgrown with bulrushes.

According to the appointment made when I left my party under Talbot, it was a valley upon the Lake Fork to which the guide Walker was to conduct him. Here I expected to find him.[26] The men, as well as the cattle and horses, needed rest; a strict guard had been necessary, as in the morning Indian sign was always found around our camp. The position was good in the open ground among the oaks, there being no brush for cover to the Indians, and grass and water were abundant. Accordingly we remained here a day and on the 24th entered the mountain, keeping as nearly as possible the valley ground of the river. While in the oak belt the travelling was easy and pleasant, but necessarily slow in the search for our people, especially here in this delightful part of the mountain where they should be found. Several days were spent here. At the elevation of 3500 feet the ridges were covered with oaks and pines intermixed, and the bottom-lands with oaks, cottonwoods, and sycamores. Continuing upward I found the general character of the mountain similar to what it was in the more northern part, but rougher, and the timber perhaps less heavy and more open, but some trees extremely large. I began to be surprised at not finding my party, but continued on, thinking that perhaps in some spread of the river branches I was to find a beautiful mountain valley. Small varieties of evergreen oaks were found at the observed height of 9840 feet above the sea, at which elevation *pinus Lambertiani* and other varieties of pine, fir, and cypress were large and lofty trees. The distinctive oak belt was left at about 5000 feet above the sea.

Indians were still around the camp at night and the necessity of keeping the animals closely guarded prevented them from getting food enough and, joined with the rough and difficult country, weakened them. For this, I usually made the day's journey short. I found the mountain extremely rocky in the upper parts, the streams breaking through cañons, but wooded up to the granite ridges which compose its rocky eminences. We forced our way up among the head springs of the river and finally stood upon the flat ridge of naked granite which made the division of the waters and was 11,000 feet above the sea. The day was sunny and the air warm enough to be not only very agreeable, but with exercise exhilarating, even at that height. Lying immediately below, perhaps 1000 feet, at the foot of a precipitous descent was a small lake, which I judged to be one of the sources of the main San Joaquin. I had grown, by occasional privation, to look upon water as a jewel beyond price, and this was rendered even more beautiful by its rough setting. The great value to us of the first necessaries of life made a reason why we so seldom found gold or silver or other minerals. Ores of iron and copper, and gold and silver, and other minerals we found, but did not look for. A clear cold spring of running water or a good camp, big game, or fossils imbedded in rock, were among the prized objects of our daily life. Owens, after the discovery of the gold in California, reminded me that he had once on the American Fork noticed some little shining grains which he could see from his horse and which afterward we decided was gold, but we were not interested enough at the time to give it attention; and Brecken-ridge too reminded me that he brought me in his hand some large grains which I carelessly told him were sulphurets of iron. These too were probably gold. As I said, this bed of summit granite was naked. Here and there a pine or two, stunted and twisted, and worried out of shape by the winds, and clamping itself to the rock. But immediately below we encamped in the sheltering pine woods which now were needed, for towards evening the weather threatened a change. The sky clouded over and by nightfall was a uniform dull gray, and early in the night the roar of the wind through the pines had at times the sound of a torrent. And the camp was gloomy. We had ridden hard, and toiled hard, and we were all disappointed and perplexed, wondering what had become of our people. During the night the Indians succeeded in killing one of our best mules. He had fed quietly into one of the little ravines, wooded with brush pines, just out of sight of the guard near by, and an Indian had driven an arrow nearly through his body. Apparently he died without sound or struggle, just as he was about to drink from the little stream.

The next day, December 31st, I made a short camp, the cattle being tender-footed and scarcely able to travel. To descend the mountain we chose a different way from that by which we had come up, but it was rocky and rough everywhere. The old year went out and the new year came in, rough as the country. Towards nightfall the snow began to come down thickly, and by morning all lay under a heavy fall. The chasms through which the rivers roared were dark against the snow, and the fir branches were all weighed down under their load. This was the end of the few remaining cattle. It was impossible to drive them over the treacherous ground. The snow continued falling, changing the appearance of the ground and hiding slippery breaks and little rocky hollows, where horse and man would get bad falls. Left to themselves cattle could easily work their way to the lower grounds of the mountain if not killed by Indians. We had great trouble in getting out from the snow region. The mountain winter had now set in, and we had some misgivings as we rode through the forest, silent now without a sound except where we came within hearing of water roaring among rocks or muffled under snow. There were three ridges to surmount, but we succeeded in crossing them, and by sunset when the storm ceased we made a safe camp between 9000 and 10,000 feet above the sea. The temperature at sunset when the sky had cleared was between eight and nine degrees.

The next day we reached the oak region, where spring weather, rain and sunshine, were found again. At an elevation of 4500 feet the temperature at the night encampment of the 3d of January was 38° at sunset and the same at sunrise; the grass green and growing freshly under the oaks. The snow line at this time reached down to about 6000 feet above the sea. On the 7th of January we encamped again on the Lake Fork in the San Joaquin valley. Our camp was in a grove of oaks at an Indian village, not far from the lake. These people recognized the horse of the Indian who had been killed among the hills the day after our encounter with the Horse-thief village, and which had been captured by the Delawares. It appeared that this Indian had belonged to their village and they showed unfriendly signs. But nothing took place during the day and at night I had a large oak at the camp felled. We were unencumbered and its spreading summit as it fell made a sufficient barricade in event of any sudden *alerte*.

We found the temperature much the same as in December. Fogs, which rose from the lake in the morning, were dense, cold, and penetrating; but after a few hours these gave place to a fine day. The face of the country had already much improved by the rains which had fallen while we were travelling in the mountains. Several humble plants, among them the golden-flowered violet (*viola chrysantha*) and *erodium cicutarium,* the first valley flowers of the spring, and which courted a sunny exposure and warm sandy soil, were already in bloom on the southwestern hill slopes. In the foot-hills of the mountains the bloom of the flowers was earlier. Descending the valley we travelled among multitudinous herds of elk, antelope, and wild horses. Several of the latter which we killed for food were found to be very fat. By the middle of January, when we had reached the lower San Joaquin, the new grass had covered the ground with green among the open timber upon the rich river bottoms, and the spring vegetation had taken a vigorous start.

We had now searched the San Joaquin valley, up to the headwaters of the Tularé Lake Fork, and failed to find my party. They were too strong to have met with any serious accident and my conclusion was that they had travelled slowly in order to give me time to make my round and procure supplies; the moderate travel serving meanwhile to keep their animals in good order, and from the moment they would have turned the point of the California Mountain the whole valley which they entered was alive with game—antelope and elk and bear and wild horses. Accounting in this way for their failure to meet me I continued on to Sutter's Fort, at which place I arrived on the 15th of the month, and remaining there four days I sailed on Sutter's launch for San Francisco, taking with me eight of my party. From Captain Sutter, who was a Mexican magistrate, I had obtained a passport to Monterey for myself and my men. At Yerba Buena,[27] as it was then called, I spent a few days, which Leidesdorff,[28] our vice-consul, and Captain Hinckley[29] made very agreeable to me. With Captain Hinckley I went to visit the quicksilver mine at New Almaden, going by water to please the captain. We were becalmed on the bay and made slow progress, failing in the night to find the entrance to the Alviso *embarcadero* and spending in consequence a chilled and dismal night in the open boat tied up to the rushes.[30] When the light came we found without difficulty the *embarcadero,* and the discomforts of the night were quickly forgotten in a fortifying breakfast. As may be supposed, the mineral being so rare, this visit to the quicksilver mine was very interesting. The owner, a Mexican of Mexico, who was also, I think, the discoverer, received us very agreeably and showed us over the mine and gave us all the specimens we were able to carry away from some heaps of the vermillion-colored ore which was being taken out.[31] At the time of our visit it could have been purchased for $30,000. While at Yerba Buena I wrote to Mrs. Frémont the following letter, which sums up briefly the incidents of our journey so far, and gives something of the plans I had in my mind for the future.

MEMOIRS, 427–52.

1. Richard L. Owings (1812–1902), more popularly known as Richard or Dick Owens, had been reared near Zanesville, Ohio. He went to the mountains in 1834 with Nathaniel Wyeth's second expedition and soon established a close friendship with Kit Carson. When the men of the third expedition became involved in the revolt in California, Owens became captain of Company A in JCF's battalion. He later went to Washington as a witness in the court-martial, but he was not called to testify. He returned to Taos, and in Jan. 1849 JCF wrote to JBF, "Owens goes to Missouri in April to get married, and thence by water to California" (letter in BIGELOW, 372). Owens did neither. He did leave Taos, but after a short stay in Colorado he settled in Delaware County, Ind. In 1854 he married, and in 1872 he moved to Circleville, Kans., where he spent the rest of his life (CARTER [1] and 19 April 1972 letter of Harvey L. Carter to the editors).

2. Pike's capture had been on the Rio Conejos, a western affluent of the Rio Grande, not far north of the present Colorado–New Mexico border; it occurred south of JCF's position.

In his diary, portions of which appeared in *Life* (6 April 1959), pp. 95–104, Edward M. Kern wrote that the party encamped at Hardscrabble on 25 Aug. where they met Bill Williams. Williams must have joined the expedition, for a voucher indicates that he was paid at Great Salt Lake (before the crossing of the desert) on 27 Oct. at the rate of $1 per day for services as a guide from 28 Aug.

3. In his entry of 2 Sept. Kern also mentions encountering several bands of buffalo.

4. JCF crossed the Grand [Colorado] River to the upper White, which led him down the Green River. Crossing the Green, he went up the Duchesne River, which he calls the Uinta on his map; today the name Uinta is applied to a northern affluent of the Duchesne. He then ascended the upper Duchesne, crossed a northeastern extension of the Wasatch Mountains, and followed the Provo River down to Utah Lake. From here the party moved to the present site of Salt Lake City.

5. Entitled "Carte générale du royaume de la Nouvelle Espagne . . . ," Baron Alexander von Humboldt's map of New Spain was first published in the *Atlas géographique et physique de royaume de la Nouvelle-Espagne* in Paris in 1811. For the northern portion of his map the German scientist relied heavily upon the cartography of Bernardo de Miera y Pacheco, who had mapped the 1776 expedition of Fray Francisco Atanasio Domínguez and Fray Silvestre Vélez de Escalante to the upper Colorado River basin and the Utah Valley. Lake Timpanogos on the Miera map, and consequently on the Humboldt map, resembles Salt Lake but is actually Utah Lake, which the missionary friars discovered. The Indian villages which they visited were on the Provo River east of Utah Lake and north of the city of Provo. A chapter on the Domínguez-Escalante expedition and a partial chapter on Humboldt and his use of the Miera data may be found in C. I. WHEAT, vol. 1; a translation of Escalante's journal and a colored copy of Miera's map may be found in BOLTON, along with a historical introduction.

6. Although JCF places this particular episode near Grantsville, it probably occurred in Skull Valley because of the character of the "run" (KORNS, 12n).

7. His 1848 map shows that he rounded the Oquirrh Mountains, camped at the springs of present-day Grantsville, then circled the Stansbury Mountains into Skull Valley before setting off across the Salt Desert.

8. Somewhere on the White River Joseph Reddeford Walker had joined the party as a guide (Talbot to Adelaide Talbot, 24 July 1846, DLC—Talbot Papers). In spite of JCF's statement that Walker knew nothing of the country confronting them, he must have been able to supply some information. In 1833 he had become lost in this region, and after much suffering he and his party had reached the head of the Humboldt and followed it to its sink. A bit later (p. 23) JCF admits that Walker was well acquainted with the country east of the Sierra.

9. Probably a reference to a preliminary movement across Skull Valley to Redlum Spring, where JCF camped before crossing the Cedar Mountains (KORNS, 14).

10. JCF must have reached a point beyond Grayback Mountain, or the fire would have been of no service in guiding Archambeault back across the desert (KORNS, 15).

11. It was in the next year—1846—that emigrant caravans took the desert route that came to be known as the Hastings Cutoff. Lansford W. Hastings, author of *The Emigrants' Guide to Oregon and California* (Cincinnati, 1845), probably met JCF at Sutter's Fort in Jan. 1846 and learned of the explorer's shortcut to California. In a few months he went east across the Sierra Nevada and, with the help of James M. Hudspeth and James Clyman, picked up the Walker-JCF trail where it intersected the emigrant road coming from Fort Hall on the Humboldt River. They followed it across the desert and eventually reached Fort Bridger on Blacks Fork. Clyman went on to St. Louis, but Hudspeth and Hastings waited for the westward-bound emigrants and were successful in persuading a number of emigrant groups to take the desert shortcut to California. Hudspeth conducted the mounted William H. Russell party as far as Skull Valley; Hastings took the Harlan-Young party down the steep canyons of the Weber and across the desert all the way to California. The Donner party, some days behind the Harlan-Young wagon train, attempted to follow, but Hastings sent back a message advising that they cut a road across the Wasatch. Their progress was so slow and their difficulties so great that they were caught by snow in the Sierra Nevada and reduced to starvation and cannibalism. Following the Donner tragedy, the Hastings Cutoff was discredited, but the gold rush fever of 1849 brought it into general use again. For some biographical details on Hastings, see ANDREWS [1] and [2].

12. JCF does not make much of his feat of crossing the desert. It was accomplished late in October, and his party was mounted. But emigrants, crossing in late summer and making fifteen miles a day with heavy-laden wagons and oxen, suffered incredibly.

13. From the east base of Pilot Butte, the expedition traveled in a southwesterly direction and probably camped at the spring on the north side of Morris Basin (CLYMAN, 330).

14. Whitton Spring, named after Jesse W. Whitton, is present Mound Springs or nearby Chase Springs in Independence Valley.

15. Before JCF put this name on his map, it was known as Mary's or Ogden's River.

16. According to Talbot's letter to his mother of 24 July 1846 (DLC—Talbot Papers) he was in charge of the main body, and according to Edward M. Kern the division of the party took place on 5 Nov. at Mound Springs—not after 8 Nov. on the waters of the Humboldt as is implied here (see Doc. No. 5).

17. JCF wrote Jessie from Yerba Buena, 24 Jan. 1846, that his volunteer party consisted of fifteen.

18. JCF's route from northeastern Nevada to Walker Lake had been roughly a diagonal one, and the table of latitudes and longitudes in the *Geographical Memoir* of 1848 permits a fairly easy tracing. After dividing his party, he led his own detachment south and west. Passing south of Franklin Lake, he went into Ruby Valley and across the Humboldt [Ruby] Mountains, probably by Harrison Pass. The camp of 8 Nov. was on Crane's branch, undoubtedly Twin Creek, an affluent of the south fork of the Humboldt. Proceeding south over tortuous ground, he went through Ruby Pass into Diamond Valley and camped on 11 Nov. at Conner Spring, named after one of his Delawares, James Connor. Continuing a southwest course, he skirted the Monitor Range and crossed the Toquima Range into Big Smoky Valley. Following along the east side of the Toiyabe Mountains, he rounded them at the southern end and proceeded to the east shore of Walker Lake, crossing two more low ranges on the way. FLETCHER, 435–38, MACK, 100–101, and NEVINS & MORGAN, xxvii–xxviii, also note in detail JCF's route across the Great Basin.

19. For the route of the main party, see Doc. No. 5, pp. 48–63.

20. This pass, which came to be known as Donner Pass, was first used by the California emigrants of 1844. See note 11 above for the Donner party in 1846.

21. Named for Aaron Hamilton, one of the few *voyageurs* who made the round trip to California with JCF. He was paid off in St. Louis in 1847.

22. NEW HELVETIA DIARY notes JCF's arrival on 10 Dec.

23. Francisco de la Guerra (1818–78), son of the wealthy, cultivated, and influential José de la Guerra y Noriega, would serve as mayor of Santa Barbara for several years after 1851.

24. After the American conquest of California, Pedro Carrillo, son-in-law of Juan Bandini, was made collector at San Pedro, San Diego, and finally at Santa Barbara, where he also became alcalde. He was elected a member of the California legislature in 1853, and in 1884 he unsuccessfully sought the position of register in the Los Angeles Land Office (RIEDER).

25. Between 1834 and 1836 the twenty-one California missions were secularized and their lands gradually divided among the private ranchos. By Governor Figueroa's proclamation of 9 Aug. 1834 half the property was supposed to go to the Indians, but even if a few of them did procure land, they retained it for only a few years. Some found employment on private ranchos or in the towns. Many sank into vice and drunkenness. Others left the coastal areas to live with Indian tribes in the interior. As for the Franciscan fathers, many remained at the mission churches to continue their religious duties (BEAN, 62–68; SERVÍN).

26. Walker mistook the Kern for the "Lake Fork" of the Tulares and halted there.

27. It was while at Yerba Buena in Jan. 1846 that JCF bestowed the name of

Chrysopylae or Golden Gate upon the strait uniting the Bay of San Francisco with the Pacific Ocean, "on the same principle that the harbor of Byzantium (Constantinople afterwards) was called Chrysoceras (golden horn)." See FRÉMONT [3], 32n.

28. William Alexander Leidesdorff (1810–48) had been appointed U.S. vice-consul in Oct. 1845 by Thomas Oliver Larkin. The son of a Danish father and a mulatto mother, he had grown up in the Danish West Indies and had come to California in 1841 as master of the *Julia Ann,* sometimes called simply the *Julia.* He obtained Mexican citizenship and a reputation as a prominent businessman and real estate owner (R. E. COWAN).

29. Massachusetts-born William Sturgis Hinckley was a Mexican official— captain of the port of San Francisco. He dated his permanent residence in California from 1840, although for many years before that time he had been trading in and out of California ports. Ironically, by dying in June 1846, Hinckley managed to escape arrest by JCF's men.

30. The Alviso embarcadero was at the head of the navigable slough that extends south from San Francisco Bay. In early mission days it was called the Embarcadero de Santa Clara de Asís and had played an important part in the life of the settlers at Mission Santa Clara and Pueblo de San Jose. The development of the quicksilver mines at New Almaden and the discovery of gold at Coloma were to stimulate anew Alviso's shipping industry (ABELOE, 428).

31. The owner, Don Andres Castillero, had discovered the New Almaden in 1845. JCF defied Gen. José Castro a few weeks after his visit to the mine, and Castillero was sent to Mexico to reiterate the danger of the American menace and to speed up military measures for California. For a history of the mine, see JOHNSON [2]; for Castillero's activities as a diplomat before 1845, see TAYS [1].

4. Frémont to Jessie B. Frémont

YERBA BUENA, January 24, 1846

I crossed the Rocky Mountains on the main Arkansas, passing out at its very head-water; explored the southern shore of the Great Salt Lake, and visited one of its islands. You know that on every extant map, manuscript or printed, the whole of the Great Basin is represented as a sandy plain, barren, without water, and without grass. Tell your father that, with a volunteer party of fifteen men, I crossed it between the parallels of 38° and 39°. Instead of a plain, I found it, throughout its whole extent, traversed by parallel ranges of lofty mountains, their summits white with snow (October) while below, the valleys had none. Instead of a barren country, the mountains were covered with grasses of the best quality, wooded with several varieties of trees, and containing more deer and mountain sheep than we had seen in any previous part of our voyage. So utterly at variance with every description, from authentic sources, or from rumor or report, it is fair to consider this country as hitherto wholly unexplored, and never before visited by a white man. I met my party at the rendezvous, a lake southeast of the Pyramid Lake; and again separated, sending them along the eastern side of the Great Sierra, three or four hundred miles in a southerly direction, where they were to cross into the valley of the San Joaquin, near its head. During all the time that I was not with them, Mr. Joseph Walker was their guide, Mr. Talbot in charge, and Mr. Kern the topographer. The eleventh day after leaving them I reached Captain Sutter's, crossing the Sierra on the 4th December, before the snow had fallen there. Now, the Sierra is absolutely impassable, and the place of our passage two years ago is luminous with snow. By the route I have explored I can ride in thirty-five days from the *Fontaine qui Bouit* River to Captain Sutter's; and, for wagons, the road is decidedly far better.

I shall make a short journey up the eastern branch of the Sacramento, and go from the Tlamath Lake into the Wahlahmath valley, through a pass alluded to in my report; in this way making the road into Oregon far shorter, and a *good* road in place of the present very bad one down the Columbia. When I shall have made this short exploration, I shall have explored from the beginning to end *this road to Oregon.*

I have just returned with my party of sixteen from an exploring journey in the *Sierra Nevada,* from the neighborhood of Sutter's to the heads of the Lake Fork. We got among heavy snows on the mountain summits; they were more rugged than I had elsewhere met them; suffered again as in our first passage; got among the 'Horse-thieves' (Indians who lay waste the California frontier), fought several, and fought our way down into the plain again and back to Sutter's. Tell your father that I have something handsome to tell him of some exploits of Carson and Dick Owens, and others.

I am now going on business to see some gentlemen on the coast, and will then join my people, and complete our survey in this part of the world as rapidly as possible. The season is now just arriving when vegetation is coming out in all the beauty I have often described to you; and in that part of my labors I shall gratify all my hopes. I find the theory of our Great Basin fully confirmed in having for its southern boundary ranges of lofty mountains. The Sierra, too, is broader where this chain leaves it than in any other part that I have seen. So soon as the proper season comes, and my animals are rested, we turn our faces homeward, and be sure that grass will not grow under our feet.

All our people are well, and we have had no sickness of any kind among us; so that I hope to be able to bring back with me all that I carried out. Many months of hardships, close trials, and anxieties have tried me severely, and my hair is turning gray before its time. But all this passes, *et le bon temps viendra* [and good times will soon be here].

Excerpt, first printed in *Niles' National Register,* 70 (16 May 1846):161, and later in the MEMOIRS, 452–53.

5. Journal of Edward M. Kern of an Exploration of the Mary's or Humboldt River, Carson Lake, and Owens River and Lake, in 1845

WASHINGTON, *September* 10, 1860.

SIR: In compliance with your request for information regarding a portion of the route pursued by the expedition to the Rocky Mountains and California under command of Capt. J. C. Frémont, in the year 1845, I inclose you a copy of my journal, which you are at liberty, if it will be in any way serviceable to you, to make such use of as you may think fit. Truly, your obedient servant,

EDW. M. KERN.

Capt. J. H. Simpson,
U.S. Corps Topographical Engineers.

[5 Nov. 1845–15 Feb. 1846]

November 5, 1845.—Whitten's Spring [Mound or Chase Springs]. To-day we parted company, the captain passing to the southward with a small party, to examine that portion of the Great Basin supposed to be a desert, lying between the Sierra Nevada and the Rocky

Mountains. The main body of the camp, under the guidance of Mr. Joseph Walker, are to move toward the head of Mary's or Ogden's [Humboldt] River, and down that stream to its sink or lake. From thence to Walker's Lake, where we are again to meet. I am to accompany the latter party in charge of the topography, &c. Crossing the [Pequop] mountains near our camp, we arrived about 1 o'clock p.m. at several springs of excellent water. These springs spread into a large marsh, furnishing an abundant supply of good grass for the animals. On the 6th, owing to a severe snow-storm, we were obliged to remain in camp. Having no timber but a few green cedars, fires were not very abundant.

On the 7th we commenced our ascent by a steep and rocky road. The snow was falling lightly when we started, but before we reached the summit, we were nearly blinded by the storm.[1] A short descent brought us into a pleasant valley, well watered by several small streams, and timbered with aspen and cottonwood. This is, really, a beautiful spot, surrounded by high mountains, those on the west covered with snow. Crossing a low range of hills, we entered another valley, that takes its waters from the snowy mountains on either side. The stream, after winding among the grass-covered hills, emerges into a plain, through which we could see Ogden's River flowing. Walker has give this creek the name of Walnut Creek, from one of his trappers having brought into his camp a twig of that tree found near its head; a tree scarcely known so far west as this. Camped on Walnut Creek, having made 14½ miles

November 8.—At about 6 miles from our camp of last night, we struck Ogden's River. It is about 25 feet wide here and about 2 feet deep, with a tolerable current. Crossing without difficulty, we struck the emigrant wagon-trail.[2] Continuing down it for a few miles, we encamped a little below where the river receives a tributary of considerable size, coming from the northwest. Made to-day about 14 miles.

November 9.—Still on the emigrant trail. This has proved of great assistance to our tired animals; they appear to have new life. Met to-day several Sho-sho-nee Indians, who report three separate parties of emigrants having passed this fall. About four miles above our camp of to-night are some hot springs [Elko], too hot to bear one's hand in. Walnut Creek empties into the river about 1½ miles below our camp. Made 19 miles.

November 10.—Crossed the river several times. At one point, the high, rocky ridges that bound the bottom came so close to the banks of the river, we were obliged to pass in the water. The timber is principally cottonwood.

November 11.—We left the river to avoid a bend it makes. Ascending some grassy hills, encamped at several springs. Bunch-grass plenty; 11 miles.

November 12.—Continued among the hills for about five miles, when we again struck the river. The country is becoming more open. The hills on the right make a wide sweep from the river, returning to it again at our camp of this evening, November 13. On the left bank the mountains are close and high and rugged in their character. Near our camp on this bank they make a bend forming a valley, through which one would suppose the river to flow. The character of the rocks is changing; more bold, basaltic.

The river presents but little variety, always the same winding, crooked stream. On the 23d November, we arrived at the [Humboldt] sink or lake. This lake is about 8 miles long by 2 in width; it is marshy, overgrown with bulrushes, at the upper end. On the eastern side is a range of low hills at the upper, and increasing in height at the lower end of the lake. On the western side is a level plain of clay mixed with sand. The country here becomes more desolate in its appearance. We have been fifteen days on this river, making a distance of nearly 200 miles. The grass has been generally good. The only timber is a few cottonwood trees and willows; the latter are in great abundance on its banks, though very small. The river-bottoms vary from 4 to 20 miles in width. Vegetation failing as we approach the sink, the soil becoming more sandy and sterile. The Indians we first met were better clad than one would suppose; having also a few horses among them. As we approached the sink, however, they appeared much more indigent and shy, hiding from us on our approach; raising smokes and other signs of warning to their friends of the approach of strangers. They belong to the Bannack tribe of Diggers, and are generally badly disposed toward the whites. Walker was attacked some two [twelve] years since by a party of them numbering, he thought, near 600; these he defeated without loss to his own party. The loss on the part of the Indians numbered 16.[3] Walker was engaged at that time exploring for a route into California, through the Sierra Nevada.

A curious feature of this river is the number of small streams near its banks and immediately in its bed. We tried the temperature of one on the 10th instant with a thermometer graduated to 160°, to which point the mercury rose in a few seconds. From its situation, forming as it does a long line of travel of the emigrant parties, this river will soon become an interesting and noted point in this now great wilderness. Portions of its immediate bottoms may be capable of cultivation; but the bare, sandy bluffs that surround or border it, produce little save bunch-grass, and no timber. Great numbers of ducks and geese are to be found in this region. A small gray duck is of excellent flavor. Provisions becoming scarce. Leaving our camp of the 24th November, on the outlet of the lake, we crossed a low, gravelly ridge, mixed with heavy sand, for 4 or 5 miles; we then struck a level plain resembling the dry bed of a lake, extending to a low range of hills on the western side 10 or 12 miles distant, and from 20 to 25 miles on the eastern side, running in a northeasterly direction, and continuing east of Ogden's or Mary's Lake, probably connecting with some of the high ranges visible from the river on the 18th and 19th. As on the plains on the western side of the Great Salt Lake, the incrustation yielded to the tread of our horses. Nothing can appear worse then the surrounding country; the glare of the white sand, relieved only by the rugged distant mountains, the absence of animal and vegetable life, make up a whole in the way of dreariness and desolation.

The outlet of Ogden's Lake, after running several miles toward the rim of this basin, forms a large marsh in the midst of the sand-hills. Our animals failing, we encamped among the sand-hills, without grass or water.

November 25.—A couple of hours' ride this morning brought us to the outlet of another lake [Carson Lake], where we encamped, having ridden twenty-five miles. The water in this stream is running, but is indifferently good. The banks are from 8 to 10 feet high; growth willow. Sand-hills on either side. On the east runs a low rocky range, beyond which are ridges and peaks of higher mountains. About eight miles below us this stream forms a large marsh, hidden from us by sand-hills. Walker tells me that its waters are extremely disagreeable. I found skulls of the natives killed here by Walker's party some ten [twelve] years since. The emigrants turn toward the California Mountains from the sink of Ogden's River. After a noon halt and rest to our animals, we crossed and continued down the river, camping near the lake.

November 26.—In a southeasterly direction nine miles along the

51

border of the lake. For 30 or 40 yards about its edge in width is a thick growth of bulrushes. It is a very pretty sheet of water; various kinds of fowl in abundance. The greatest length is about 11 miles. On the eastern side runs a low range of burnt rock hills. The lake is bounded on the west by a low range of mountains; about midway on the western side a stream [Carson River] enters it. Slightly timbered; probably cottonwood.

November 27.—In a southern course, over a level for about 3 miles, then crossing a low ridge of sand and burnt rock down an open ravine, leading into a larger plain, we made camp among the sand-hills, at some Indian wells of bad water, thoroughly impregnated with sulphur. These wells, with a little trouble, could be made a good watering-place; but, as they now are, it was with greatest difficulty that we could procure a sufficiency for our animals. There was plenty of good bunch-grass about camp; no fuel but greasewood. Continuing our route over low, heavy sand-hills, we rejoined Captain Frémont at our place of rendezvous, Walker's Lake. He had reached that point four days ahead of us, having traveled over a mountainous country, finding in his route plenty of grass, water, game, and Indians; the latter very shy, not being accustomed to the sight of white men in their desolate country. The river of Walker's Lake is a fine, bold stream, 30 to 40 feet wide, with considerable current, timbered with fine large cottonwoods, its bottoms covered with a luxuriant growth of grass, wild peas, and rushes. We had anticipated a glorious feast of fish on our arrival at this point, from the glowing descriptions Walker had given us of great quantities of fine salmon-trout which frequent the river and lake. In this, however, we were doomed to disappointment. The fishing season being over, "Carro hoggi" was the only reply we could obtain to our many signs and inquiries after the finny tribe from the few Indians that still lingered about the lake.

To-morrow (November 29) Captain Frémont leaves us again, this time to take his old trail of 1843, while the main body of camp will continue down the eastern slope of the Sierra Nevada, which Walker had discovered when exploring this section of the country some 10 years ago. We will remain here 9 or 10 days to recruit our animals, as many of them are exhausted.

December 8.—Once more took up our line of march. During our stay at our camp on Walker's River the weather has been clear and cold. Thermometer at sunset 23° above zero, and at sunrise 4°. The river frozen hard; it has been a strange mixture of winter and summer. The Indians are of much lower grade than any I have yet seen. They are, however, very friendly. I visited some of their huts near the mouth of the river. They had some very pretty decoy-ducks, made from the skin of those birds, neatly stretched over a bulrush float. There were four or five old women hovering over a fire of a few willow twigs of six or eight inches in length. I thought if the personification of witches ever existed, these were of them. Their withered bodies, almost entirely naked and emaciated, their faces smeared with dirt and tar, the dull, idiotic stare of their eyes, trembling from cold and dread of our intentions toward them, rendered them to me the most pitiable objects I had ever seen. A couple of children, nestling close to the fire, showed more the signs of wonder in their countenances than fear. Some of these children, notwithstanding the hardships of their lives, only dependent on grass-seeds and the few fish they can catch, any large game being unknown hereabouts, have really lively and interesting countenances; but the expression leaves them with youth; their future, being one of continued privation, soon dulls the light of the eye, and the face becomes heavy and stolid in expression. It was at this camp we have made our first essay on horse-meat. Throwing aside all antipathies I, with the others, enjoyed our meal. On this river, with but a couple of exceptions, is the only *large* timber we have met since leaving the Timpanogos. Traveling three miles on the river and about twelve on the shores of the lake, we made our camp among some low sand-hills. A range of burnt rock hills extends a few miles further back, while on the opposite side of the lake the dark mountains come bluff to the water's edge. No fuel but greasewood and grass. We longed heartily for the fires of our last ten-days' camp, the weather being excessively cold.

December 9.—Camped near the head of the lake. No grass; the water exceedingly bad and salty. Charley, (our cook) to improve(?) the already horrid taste given to our coffee by the bad water, added some greasewood or other noxious weed, giving it a flavor too unsavory even for appetites as keen-set as ours. This lake is about twenty-two miles in length, and eleven or twelve in the widest part. To the eastward of our camp runs a valley. About twelve miles down it Walker says he found springs of good water and an abundance of good grass, the springs forming a small lake. To-night the horses, driven to desperation by their bad fare, a large number of them eluding the vigilance of the guard escaped to the other side of the lake, where they were found in the morning, having discovered somewhat better grass than we had at our camp.

December 10.—Leaving camp we traveled up a valley leading from the southern end of Walker's Lake, a little east of south; at about eight miles we crossed a low ridge, heavy sand and scattering bunch-grass. Traveling up the general direction of a ravine, in a southeasterly course for about six miles, we made camp late at some springs near the foot of a basaltic rock ridge.

December 11.—Continued our route down the valley in a southerly direction. Walker's trail of two years ago passed to the left of our camp three or four miles. Passed several wells dug by the Indians, but they were dry. Also, a large corral or pen made of sage and cedars for the purpose of ensnaring deer. Continued about six miles into the mountains by a rough and broken road. Were unable to find water. In the evening we encamped among some of the largest sage I have ever seen. This gave us an abundance of fuel, and also served us in constructing pens about our different campfires as a protection from the cold. We soon forgot in slumber our lack of water. Here we killed our last beef, if what was left of the animal could be dignified by such a name.

December 12.—To-day we obtained a fine view of the great Sierra Nevada from the far north till it faded on the distant horizon far to the south of us. This bold and rocky barrier, with its rugged peaks, separates us from the valley of California. We are to travel along its base till by its lessening height it will offer but a slight obstacle to our passage across it. To the southeast and east of us mountain rises beyond mountain as far as the eye can see. Descending by a break-neck road we reached, toward evening, a small valley, where we made camp. We found a portion of the sand leveled very smooth and some willow hoops lying about, with fresh signs to convince us that the place had not long been vacated by a party of Indians.

December 13.—Still among the burnt rock hills, interspersed with grassy valleys. Descending into a large, open, grassy valley, we fed upon the dry bed of a stream that has both wood and water six or seven miles farther up. Camped at a large spring that spreads into a marsh.

December 14.—Traveled down the same valley. Water rises and sinks, breaking through a rocky ridge to the east; rising again in several cold springs at the entrance of the gap, runs a short distance and forms a stinking lake. Crossing the ridge by an Indian trail, we came into another valley watered by a fine warm stream, in which I took a delightful bath. Good grass and plenty—quite a treat for our tired animals. The boys brought in some roots they had found near a couple of Indian huts, the inmates having fled at their approach. The root was of some water-plant of good flavor. They were plaited together in ropes, something after the manner of doing up onions at home. Our old cook at fault again to-day, boiling a large piece of rosin soap in our coffee. Rather unlucky just now, when coffee is coffee.

December 15.—The same water of yesterday still finds its way into another valley more to the east. We crossed into this. Its greatest length is from north to south. On the eastern side is a high chain of mountains, about the height of those on eastern side of Utah Lake. The mountains throw out some small streams, which sink before they fairly reach the valley. The road in the forenoon of to-day broken and sandy. We have gained four days on Walker's route of 1843, from camp of December 10 to this place. A better route lies to the right of our road.

December 16.—To-day struck Owen's River. It is a fine, bold stream, larger than Walker's. The same chain of mountains bounds it on the east, while on the western side rises, like a wall, the main chain of the California Mountains. Our rations are becoming extremely scant. The men being all on foot, they feel their appetites much quickened by the additional exercise of walking. A few more days we hope will bring us to the land of plenty.

December 17 and 18.—Still on the river; obliged to keep some distance from it on account of a large marsh. Wild-fowl in abundance. Walker went in search of some salt, which he found, incrusted to the thickness of a quarter of an inch on the surface of the earth. The Indians are numerous here, though they keep out of sight. They are badly disposed. Colonel Childs [Joseph B. Chiles] had trouble with them here. They shot one of his men. Walker's party killed some twenty-five of them, while on his side some of his men were wounded and eight or nine horses killed.[4]

December 19.—Camped on [Owens] lake near the mouth of river. Grass poor. Ducks and geese plentiful.

December 20.—Traveling down the lake. Main California Mountains close on our right within half a mile of us. This lake is somewhat irregular in its shape, lying north and south; is about fifteen miles long, the widest part about seven miles. On the western side there are several capes. It is surrounded by high mountains. Water strong, disagreeable, salty, nauseous taste. There are Indian fires among the rocks within half a mile of us. None ventured nearer. They appear to be well supplied with horses, judging from the quantity of sign. Along the route of to-day we crossed several streams coming from the mountains, some of them dry; all slightly timbered with cottonwood.

December 21.—Leaving lower end of lake, we passed among some sandy hollows, falling into a larger ravine leading south. Passing a good camp for grass and water, the hollow narrowed, bounded by hills of minutely broken black rock, opening afterward into a large plain; camped at some springs on the slope of the main California Mountains; grass, fresh and green, owing to the late rains. To-day we met for the first time the yuca [Joshua] tree, nicknamed by the men "Jeremiah," in lieu of some better title. These trees have a grotesque appearance, a straight trunk, guarded about its base by long bayonet-shaped leaves; its irregular and fantastically shaped limbs give to it the appearance of an ancient candelabra. It bears a beautiful white flower. We passed to-day Child's [Walker's] cache, where, on account of his animals failing, he was obliged to bury the contents of his wagons, among which was a complete set of mill-irons.

December 22.—Passed to-day a salt-lake, half a mile long and about 200 yards wide; leaving this, we turned up a large hollow, for about four miles, to find a camp. At this point there may be a pass over the mountains, judging from the number of Indian trails joining together here. The ascent, however, is very steep, and it was judged advisable not to attempt it, our animals not being in a condition to undergo any such experiments. So we continued our route in a southerly direction, among the foot-hills of the mountains.

December 23 and 24.—Still among the hills. On the 23d, a mule was lost, with its pack. Archambeau[lt], Stradspeth [Benjamin M. Hudspeth], and [James T.] White were sent back in search of it; returned on the evening of the 24th, with the animal. The mule was loaded with, to us, a very valuable cargo, sugar and coffee, with some of the "possibles," of Stradspeth and White. The mule had wandered up one of the many ravines in the hillsides. When the Indians were discovered, they were sitting very coolly among the rocks, where they had driven the mule, dividing the spoils; there were three of them. Of the sugar they had made a just division, but the coffee was to them perfectly useless. They had already charred and pounded it, without coming to any satisfactory conclusion as to its use. The "possibles" shared the same fate as the eatables. Among the articles a blanket and an overcoat. Being three in their party, and being unable to divide these things equally in any other way, one had taken the blanket, and tearing the coat in two, gave a half of it to each of the others. On our men showing themselves, they fled precipitately, leaving the property behind. Collecting and rearranging the pack, the men started for camp, bringing with them, as proof of their victory, some bows and arrows, a large sack of sage-seed, about as digestible as sand, and a small sack of some compound, which we could not make out; it was very palatable with coffee, of a dark chocolate color.*

Our Christmas was spent in a most unchristmas-like manner. Our camp was made on the slope of the mountain, at some Indian wells of good water. The yuca tree is here in great abundance, furnishing us a plentiful supply of fuel. The camp-fires blazed and cracked joyously, the only merry things about us, and all that had any resemblance to that merry time at home. The animals, on account of grass, were guarded about a quarter of a mile from camp, higher up the mountain.

December 25.—Christmas day opened clear and warm. We made our camp to-day at some springs among the rocks; but little grass for our animals. Dined to-day, by way of a change, on one of our tired, worn mules, instead of a horse.

Turning from our camp of the 25th into the mountain by an easy ascent, and over a somewhat broken road, arriving on the 27th, on the head-waters of a river.† Continuing down this stream, on the 28th we made camp at its forks. This is the appointed place of rendezvous. There are no signs yet of the Captain. Our provisions have entirely failed; save the few remaining horses of our cavallada, there was not much prospect of obtaining fresh supplies. To have killed these would have been to deprive us of the means of transportation of our effects and the results of the expedition, in case we

---

* I have seen the same dish among the Indians of California; it is prepared from roasted grasshoppers and large crickets, pounded up, and mixed with, when procurable, some kind of animal grease.

† Now called Kern River.

are not joined by Captain Frémont in this place. A party of Indians visited our camp, from whom we traded a colt. The hunters brought in a few small deer, the meat extremely poor. A small piece of venison, with as much cold water as one could drink, furnished breakfast, dinner, and supper in one. We became reduced to acorns, and on this swinish food made our New-Year's feast. This forms the principal food of the natives, here and in the valley. Our camp is situated in a beautiful valley, about six miles in length, and well-timbered with pine, cedars, and cottonwood, while the mountains which surround it are of the usual growth of the Sierra, the majestic redwood, &c. The river is a bold stream, coming from the northeast. The Indians inhabiting this region are of the most degraded class, entirely naked, and with scarcely a sufficiency of food to sustain life. I was amused at coming suddenly on a half a dozen of these characters; being armed, they, probably having a dread of pistols, immediately commenced crossing themselves in the most devout manner, at the same time muttering "Christiano, Christiano," the probable extent of their Spanish, hoping to avert any evil intent we might have had toward them.

Since leaving Walker's Lake we have traveled through a country having a few pretty spots, but for the most part a sandy waste, broken by short chains and isolated mountains. Bunch-grass is found among most of the sand-hills. Water, save in the rivers, is not to be had in anything like a sufficiency. Piñon and willow are the principal timbers. From our camp of December 26, toward the south, as far as the eye could reach, lay a continued plain of sand, relieved only by an occasional hill of burnt rock rearing itself above the level, adding, if possible, to the desolation of the scene, with no game, save now and then a hare, and perchance a stray goat.[5] Lizards are here in abundance, and form the principal food of the hungry natives. At our camp the weather has been extremely fine, warm, and sunshine. On the 13th of January there was a severe storm of snow and sleet; a shower followed that soon removed all appearance of winter from the valley, but the mountains retained this, their first winter covering.

January 18, 1846.—Raised camp and traveled about five miles into the mountains, stopping for the night at the hunter's camp, in a pretty valley; snow about two feet deep. An abundance of the most beautiful timber, live-oak, pine, redwood, &c.

January 19.—To-day we reached the summit; snow $2\frac{1}{2}$ feet deep.

From here we had the first view of the much-wished-for Valley of California. It lay beneath us, bright in the sunshine, gay and green, while about us everything was clothed in the chilly garb of winter.

On the 21st January we reached the valley; our descent was rough and broken; the mountain well watered and densely timbered. Among the foot-hills are beautiful groves of live and other oaks, clear from growth of underwood; the fine grass gives the country the appearance of a well-kept park.[6] We passed two Indian villages; the huts were built of tulé or bulrush. The men entirely naked; the only covering the women possessed was a kind of petticoat made of tulé. The country is much cut up by gullies. The weather is warm like spring, the young grass and some few flowers just putting forth. Notice a small blue flower particularly very abundant.

Crossing several small streams that find their way into the great Tulare Lake, we encamped, on the evening of the 26th of January, on a fine bold stream.* The whole country is well watered, and capable of high cultivation. Oaks and willows in abundance. The river heads in the Sierra Nevada, running in a west, a little south, and then in a southerly direction. Walker thinking to make a cut-off at the bend, we were obliged to spend a most uncomfortable night at some holes of water, amid a storm of cold rain, with no fuel save a few willows.

January 28.—After searching in vain for the river, we camped, at 9 o'clock at night, among the foot-hills of the Coast range, without grass, water, or fire, having traveled through immense fields of old tulé, the horses sinking at almost every step as deep as their bellies; having to be hauled out only to sink again, owing to the loose rotten soil. This has been the most tedious day we have had since we entered the valley, and particularly trying to our animals in their present weak state. Cloudy and rainy all day.[7]

January 29.—Leaving our miserable camp of last night early this morning, we struck a northerly course, passing a large dry creek timbered with cottonwood, over a plain destitute of vegetation (the grass and shrubbery having been destroyed by the wild horses), we made camp on a large slough.‡ Manuel, to-day, killed a fat wild

---

* The Rio Reyes, or Lake Fork.

† Walker mistook this river for the South Fork of the San Joaquin.

‡ This slough, at high water, connects the waters of the San Joaquin with the great Tulare Lake.

horse—as acceptable a thing as could have happened, as we were out of meat, and had been so for two days.

January 30.—Continuing down the slough for four or five miles, we struck a bold stream—the San Joaquin. It is heavily timbered with oak and willow. Wild horses and elk begin to show themselves.

February 1.—Jim Connor and Wetowa (two Delawares) tracked a large grizzly bear to his thicket. The whole camp prepared themselves for the attack: after much difficulty, he was killed. This animal was one of the largest size; he must have weighted at least 900 pounds. This acquisition to our larder enlivened the spirits of the men, and mirth abounded at the various camp-fires that night; the song and joke, the accompaniments of plenty in the wilderness, could be heard everywhere.

Continuing up the valley toward Suter's fort, on the 6th we arrived and made camp on the Calaveras, a tributary of the San Joaquin. Messrs. Fabbol and Walker started on ahead to hear if they could obtain any tidings of Captain Frémont. They returned again in the evening in company with Big Fallen [Fallon], an old mountaineer, known more commonly by the sobriquet of "Le Gros."[8] From him we learned that the captain was at the pueblo of San José with the rest of his camp. The next morning Fallen and Walker started for the pueblo to give him intelligence of our whereabouts, while we would return to the crossing of the San Joaquin to await further orders. Yesterday Jim Secondi [Sagundai] (a Delaware) killed another bear, the counterpart of the one killed on the 1st instant.

February 11.—To-day we were joined by Carson and Owens, at the crossing. Crossing the river in boats or rafts, made of tulé.

February 15.—To-day we met a party of the boys with fresh horses, sent out to meet us. We passed through the pueblo of San José. The country between the pueblo and the Calaveras is beautiful, and well suited for cultivation; the streams are well timbered with different species of oaks. The flowering season is commencing, adding great beauty to the plains, by their variegated colors. The mission of San José is about twelve miles from the town, situated at the foot of a mountain, on the road from the crossing of the San Joaquin. It was formerly one of the richest missions in the upper country; it presents now but a poor appearance, and shows the evil resulting from the removal of the padres, whose posts were replaced by rapacious "administradors" of government. The building is very large and built of adobes; the roof is of tiles. Long rows of adobe buildings, one story high, used as the dwellings of the native converts, are now in a most dilapidated condition, scarcely affording shelter for the few miserable Indians who still cling to those hearths, where they had been raised, by the kindness of the founders, to something like civilization. The remains of the gardens and vineyards show the care and labor bestowed on the grounds by the fathers. Opposite to the mission, on an eminence, is the Campo Santro; the entrance to it is surmounted by a large cross. From here we can see an arm of the bay of San Francisco. The pueblo of San José is a small town of some 50 or 60 houses, most of them in a very crumbling condition, showing the slothful habits of the people. We arrived about noon at the "Laguna farm," where we rejoined Captain Frémont, who was anxiously awaiting our arrival.[9] Both parties were again united, without any serious accident having happened to either, and both had had their share of hard times.

Note.—When separating from Captain F. on Walker's Lake, Walker had given a description of the valley of California, where a river which he *supposed* to be the Rio Reyes (and on which we encamped from the 27th of December till the 18th of January, 1846, the same which is now called Kern's River), enters the valley, the description and the rude map which I made from it, answered to the markings of the country very well. Supposing we had entered the valley at the river Reyes, we crossed the several small streams that find their way into the Tulare Lake, and when reaching the Lake Fork or Rio Reyes, he (Walker) fancied himself on the South Fork of San Joaquin. I remember Walker's telling me that the river made a great bend to the southward, and to make a cut-off, we left its banks, and in expectation of again meeting it, traveled till we found ourselves climbing the Coast range. Walker had fallen into the error on a previous trip years ago, and had, in search of the river, crossed the Coast range toward Monterey. On his return trip he left the country by a more southern pass in the Sierra, which Captain Frémont calls Walker's pass. Walker's old pass was to the northward of this by what is now called Kern River. The mistake Walker made in the name of the river on which we had camped to wait for Captain Frémont was the cause of his failure to make a junction with us, as had been prearranged, at Walker's Lake; Captain Frémont, as will be found by his memoir of 1848, having ascended the Rio Reyes (proper) in search of our party.

E. M. K.

Printed as Appendix Q in SIMPSON, 477–86. This is apparently an abridgment of Kern's full journal of the trip to California, covering the period from 17 Aug. 1845 to 15 Feb. 1846, which in 1959 was in possession of Mr. and Mrs. Fred Cron of Dingman's Ferry, Pa. Some extracts of the original were published in *Life,* 6 April 1959. Capt. James Hervey Simpson was an old employer of Edward M. Kern and his brother, Richard H. After JCF's fourth expedition broke up in 1849, the Kern brothers had been left stranded in New Mexico, but they soon found employment with Simpson in drafting a report of his route from Fort Smith to Santa Fe. A few weeks later they accompanied him as artist-scientists on a military reconnaissance of the Navajo country. In 1860 Simpson was writing a report of his 1859 survey of a wagon route across part of the Great Basin and wished to have the benefit of Kern's knowledge gained from his travels with JCF.

1. The party crossed the Ruby Mountains by way of Secret Pass.

2. The emigrant wagon road to California came from Fort Hall to the Truckee River by way of the Humboldt.

3. Walker's battles with the Indians seem to have occurred in 1833 and 1834. WATSON, 53, 70, records that Walker's party killed some thirty-nine Paiutes in the Humboldt Sink country in Sept. 1833 on their route into California and some fourteen the next spring on their way out.

4. Kern has confused his facts and dates. The man shot was Milton Little, who received an arrow wound in the breast while on guard duty one night (William Baldridge narrative, pp. 3–4, CU-B). He was with the Walker detachment of the 1843 Chiles-Walker expedition to California. Walker used the pass which bears his name, but Chiles and his group kept to the Oregon Trail as far as Fort Boise, then struck off to the west, up the Malheur River, and on to the waters of the Sacramento (GIFFEN [2], 39–43). As noted above, the bloody battles with the Indians occurred in 1833 and 1834.

5. Kern was looking across the Mojave Desert.

6. They probably reached the valley of California in the vicinity of White River (FARQUHAR, 93).

7. On this day and perhaps again on 30 Jan., Kern—who was collecting western birds—obtained specimens of *Buteo regalis* (Gray), the ferruginous hawk (A.O.U. 348). In notes he made later for ornithologist John Cassin, he wrote that some of his party shot it for the mess kettle whenever opportunity offered, finding it "very good eating." Cassin already knew the bird as *Falco ferrugineus* Licht., *Abh. K. Acad. Berlin* (1838) and as *Archibuteo regalis* Gray, *Genera of Birds,* vol. 1, pt. 1 (May 1844). He gave Kern credit, however, for first bringing it to the attention of American naturalists— perhaps an inadvertence—and indicated that its range was rather restricted. Actually the bird ranged as far east as Minnesota, but too little collecting had been done by 1846 to establish the full range. See Kern to Cassin, 11 May 1852 (PPAN), and CASSIN, 159–62 and plate 26. Biologist and author Paul R. Cutright has kindly contributed his own knowledge to this note and has done some further checking at the Academy of Natural Sciences of Philadelphia. A few additional bird specimens collected by Kern are on deposit at the academy.

8. We have no information on Fabbol beyond the fact that he was a member of JCF's 1845 expedition. He seems not to have been a member of the California Battalion. A native of St. Louis, William O. Fallon had spent many years in the Rocky Mountain fur trade, would participate in the Bear Flag Revolt, and would recruit for JCF's California Battalion, in which he himself served. He would also head the Donner Fourth Relief and serve as guide for General Kearny when he went east in 1847 (ANDERSON, 296–300; BRYANT, 261–65).

9. "Laguna farm" was Rancho la Laguna Seca, which belonged to William

Fisher (d. 1850), a sea captain from Boston who had been living in California for a number of years and who had purchased the rancho of four square miles in 1845. Fisher settled his family there after JCF's February visit.

6. Excerpt from the *Memoirs*

[24 Jan.–20 Feb. 1846]

After finishing my letter[1] I set out towards evening for Monterey with Mr. Leidesdorff, who was kind enough to give me the advantage of his company. His house was one of the best among the few in Yerba Buena—a low bungalow sort of adobe house with a long piazza facing the bay for the sunny mornings, and a cheerful fire within against the fog and chill of the afternoons. His wife, a handsome, girl-like woman, Russian from Sitka, gave the element of home which had been long missing to my experience.[2] He was a cheerful-natured man, and his garden and his wife spoke pleasantly for him.

We had started rather late and on the plain beyond the Mission Dolores in the darkness and the fog we lost our way, but wandering around we were at last rejoiced by hearing the barking of dogs. This soon brought us to the rancho of Don Francisco Sanchez,[3] for which we were looking, and where we were received with the cordial hospitality which in those days assured a good bed and a savory supper to every traveller, and if his horse happened to be tired or hurt by any accident a good one to replace it for the journey.

The next day we rode along the bay shore, the wooded and fertile character of which needs no describing, and stopped for the night with Don Antonio Sunol.[4] This was my first ride down the valley of San José, and I enjoyed even the passing under the oak groves with the branches cut off to a uniform height by the browsing herds of cattle, listening the while to Leidesdorff's account of the fertility of the country's vegetation. His descriptions of this part of the country were especially interesting to me. He was a lover of nature and his garden at San Francisco was, at that time, considered a triumph.

After a half day's riding from the Gomez rancho,[5] across the Salinas plains, we reached Monterey and went directly to the house of our consul, Mr. Larkin.[6] I had come to Monterey with the object of obtaining leave to bring my party into the settlements in order to refit and obtain the supplies that had now become necessary. All the camp equipment, the clothes of the men and their saddles and horse gear, were either used up or badly in want of repair.

The next morning I made my official visits. I found the governor, Don Pio Pico,[7] absent at Los Angeles. With Mr. Larkin I called upon the commanding general, Don José Castro,[8] the prefect,[9] alcalde,[10] and ex-Governor Alvarado.[11] I informed the general and the other officers that I was engaged in surveying the nearest route from the United States to the Pacific Ocean. I informed them farther that the object of the survey was geographical, being under the direction of the Bureau of Topographical Engineers, to which corps I belonged; and that it was made in the interests of science and of commerce, and that the men composing the party were citizens and not soldiers.

The permission asked for was readily granted, and during the two days I stayed I was treated with every courtesy by the general and other officers.[12]

This permission obtained I immediately set about arranging for supplies of various kinds[13] and for sending fresh horses to meet our people; with such supplies of lesser luxuries as I knew would be grateful to them; and by the middle of February we were all reunited in the valley of San José, about thirteen miles south of the village of that name on the main road leading to Monterey, which was about sixty miles distant.[14]

.   .   .   .

The place which I had selected for rest and refitting was a vacant rancho called the *Laguna*, belonging to Mr. Fisher. I remained here until February, in the delightful spring season of a most delightful climate. The time was occupied in purchasing horses, obtaining supplies, and thoroughly refitting the party.

I established the rate of the chronometer and made this encampment a new point of departure. Observations put it in longitude 121° 39′ 08″, latitude 37° 13′ 32″. This point is but a few miles distant from what is now the Lick Observatory.

Many Californians visited the camp, and very friendly relations grew up with us.[15] One day amusements were going on as usual, the Californians showing our men their admirable horsemanship. One of the largest vultures which are often seen floating about overhead had been brought down with a broken wing by one of our rifles. This was the point on which we excelled, as the others in perfect horsemanship. The vulture was sitting on the frame of a cart to which he had been tied; he had gotten over his hurt and would have been treated as a pet, but his savage nature would not permit of any approach. By accident a Californian had gotten a fall and the whole camp was shouting and laughing, and Owens, his mouth wide open, was backing towards the cart to rest his arm on the wheel, forgetful of the vulture. The vulture with his long, red neck stretched out was seizing the opportunity—we all saw it and Owens saw our amusement, but not quite in time to escape the grip of the vulture.

It was quite a picture. The vulture lying in wait, and Owens' unconsciousness, and the hearty laugh which cheered the bird's exploit. Owens got off with a sharp pinch and a torn sleeve.

.   .   .   .

MEMOIRS, 453–56.

1. To Jessie B. Frémont, 24 Jan. 1846, Doc. No. 4.

2. Leidesdorff was unmarried. After his premature death Army officer Joseph Libbey Folsom purchased all right and title to his estate from Leidesdorff's mother and surviving brothers and sisters, who were living on the island of St. Croix (R. E. COWAN). The steamer which the vice-consul purchased from the Russian American Company in the fall of 1847 for use in his hide and tallow trade became known as the *Sitka*—at least after she sank—having been constructed in the Russian port of that name (J. H. KEMBLE).

3. Owner of Rancho San Pedro in San Mateo County, Francisco Sanchez later organized a Californian force which captured Lieut. Washington Allon Bartlett and five men on 8 Dec. 1846. The Americans were engaged in a foray to carry off cattle. It is Wiltsee's opinion that Sanchez hoped to organize a revolt of all Upper Californians to cooperate with José María Flores's revolt south of the Tehachapi (see WILTSEE [1], 123–28).

4. Antonio María Suñol (ca. 1800–1865), a native of Spain, had deserted from the French naval service and settled in San Jose, where he became subprefect in 1841. By that time, too, he had acquired the Rancho San Jose del Valle.

5. Rancho Verjeles, owned by José Joaquín Gómez, who had the reputation of being friendly to the United States. Thomas Oliver Larkin was captured by the Californians at the Gómez rancho in Nov. 1846.

6. Born in Massachusetts, Thomas Oliver Larkin (1802–58) had come to California in 1832 and gradually built up a prosperous trade. He served as U.S. consul at Monterey, and in 1846 Archibald Gillespie brought a secret dispatch appointing him "Confidential Agent in California," under the authority of which he launched a propaganda campaign to separate California from Mexico peacefully, in furtherance of President Polk's expansionist policy. He was actually not very sympathetic to the Bears, as will become

José Castro. From a portrait in the Bancroft Library.

evident later. Larkin was appointed U.S. naval agent by Commodore Stockton in Aug. 1846—an appointment confirmed by President Polk in March 1847, and one which JCF tried unsuccessfully to obtain in 1848.

7. Pío Pico (1801–94), sympathetic to English rather than American interests in California, was actually the provisional governor, though his claim to the office was confirmed in Mexico, and on 18 April 1846 he took the oath as constitutional governor.

8. Gen. José Castro (ca. 1810–60) had a long career of public service. Although he often switched sides in California politics and conflicts, he was consistent in his patriotism and genuinely concerned about the American threat in California.

9. Manuel de Jesús Castro (b. 1821), a cousin but not a supporter of Gen. José Castro in his political rivalry with Pío Pico. After the Angeleños revolted against Gillespie, Manuel de Jesús Castro was put in command of the northern division. When Flores was defeated, Castro fled to Mexico with him but later returned to San Francisco, although he never became a U.S. citizen (PIONEER REGISTER).

10. The alcalde of Monterey in Jan. 1846 was Manuel Díaz, owner of a Sacramento rancho and somewhat friendly to the United States (PIONEER REGISTER).

11. Juan Bautista Alvarado (1809–82) had been governor, first revolutionary and then constitutional, of California from 1836 to 1842. He was the grantee of several ranchos, including the famous Las Mariposas, which Larkin was to purchase for JCF on 10 Feb. 1847.

12. Historians have usually considered JCF's request to winter and provision his men in California a verbal one, and JCF himself in an interview in Dec. 1884 with the historian Josiah Royce remembered the request as being verbal (Royce's memorandum of an interview with JCF and JBF, CU-B). Certainly no letter of JCF to Castro has been found. However, to a copy of his own letter to the prefect of the Second District, Larkin has added this interesting note, implying that the request had been a written one: "The General was at his own request officially informed by Captain Fremont of his motives in coming here, which motives were accepted by Gen. Castro in not answering the letter" (LARKIN, 4:186–87). In the same 1884 interview with Royce, JCF recalled obtaining permission not only to rest and resupply the party on the frontiers—i.e., in the San Joaquin Valley—but to travel through the country and examine the passes to the coast. Talbot wrote his mother that the captain had permission "to pass through the country & buy stores and recruit generally" (letter of 24 July 1846, DLC—Talbot Papers), but it must be remembered that Talbot had been in the San Joaquin Valley at the time of JCF's visit to Monterey and could know only what the explorer might have told him. In his court-martial defense, probably written by Benton, the implication is that JCF had permission to winter in the valley of the San Joaquin. Certainly Larkin gave the impression that JCF's men were to be left on the frontiers of the Second Department and that as soon as JCF obtained the necessary supplies in Monterey, he would continue on to Oregon (Larkin to Manuel de Jesús Castro, 29 Jan. 1846, LARKIN, 4:186–87). In Doc. No. 15 Larkin implies that JCF's later difficulty with the Mexican authorities arose from his camping too near towns, but another document, later by one day, indicates that General Castro may have changed his policy after granting permission. "Since then the General states, that he has received by the Hannah, positive orders from Mexico, to drive Captain Fremont

from the Country" (Larkin to "The Commander of any American Ship of War, in San Blas, or Mazatlan," 9 March 1846, LARKIN, 4:243–44). General Castro wrote to the Minister of War from Monterey on 6 March, "But two days ago I was much surprised at being informed that this person [JCF] was only two days' journey from this place" (CAL. HIS. SOC. DOCS., 4:375).

13. On 1 March 1846 Larkin wrote the U.S. consul at Vera Cruz that he had purchased for JCF's party "common shirts at over three dollars each, common heavy jackets twelve to fourteen dollars." On 6 March he forwarded to Joel Giles two drafts, one for $1,000 and one for $800, both drawn by JCF on the chief of the Topographical Bureau. JCF received cash for his drafts. Both letters are in LARKIN, 4:215–17, 235–36.

14. The brief account which JCF gives of the activities of the Talbot-Walker-Kern detachment is omitted here, as Kern's journal (Doc. No. 5) gives a fuller account.

15. But apparently there were also some irritations, as the next document will indicate.

7. Frémont to José Dolores Pacheco

Camp Near Road to Santa Cruz
February 21, 1846

SIR:

I received your communication of the 20th,[1] informing me that a complaint had been lodged against me in your office for refusing to deliver up certain animals of my band, which are claimed as having been stolen from this vicinity about *two months* since; and that the plaintiff further complains of having been insulted in my camp.

It can be proven on oath by thirty men here present, that the animal pointed out by the plaintiff has been brought in my band from the United States of North America. The insult of which he complains, and which was authorized by myself, consisted in his being ordered immediately to leave the camp. After having been detected in endeavoring to obtain animals under false pretences, he should have been well satisfied to escape without a severe horse-whipping.

There are four animals in my band which were bartered from the Tulare Indians by a division of my party which descended the San Joaquin Valley. I was not there present, and if any more legal owners present themselves, these shall be immediately delivered upon proving property. It may save some trouble to inform you that, with this exception, all the animals in my band have been

68

Thomas Oliver Larkin. From a print in Walter Colton, *Three Years in California* (New York, 1850). Courtesy of the University of Illinois Library.

purchased and paid for. Any further communications on this subject will not, therefore, receive attention. You will readily understand that my duties will not permit me to appear before the magistrates of your towns on the complaint of every straggling vagabond who may chance to visit my camp. You inform me that unless satisfaction be immediately made by the delivery of the animals in question, the complaint will be forwarded to the Governor. I would beg you at the same time to give to his Excellency a copy of this note. I am, very respectfully, Your obedient servant,[2]

J. C. FRÉMONT
U.S. Army

Printed in CAL. HIS. SOC. DOCS., 4:374. José Dolores Pacheco (d. 1852) was alcalde and justice of the peace at San Jose in 1846.

1. Not found.

2. Besides the theft of a mule or a horse, three of JCF's men were accused of, when under the influence of liquor, offering insults to the family of Angel Castro, uncle of Gen. José Castro (Larkin to Secretary of State, duplicate copy, 27 March 1846, DNA-59, Consular Despatches, Monterey, Calif.). While JCF made amends immediately, the event undoubtedly focused attention on him and his men. Patriotic Californians, who had heard rumors that 1846 was to bring "great changes over the face of California" and who saw John Marsh and other native-born Americans visiting the camp of the explorer, became suspicious of JCF's real motives in traveling and camping within the vicinity of Monterey, sometimes within eight miles of the town.

8. Excerpt from the *Memoirs*

[22 Feb.–3 March 1846]

Resuming the work of the expedition, on the 22d March [Feb.] we encamped on the Wild-Cat Ridge on the road to Santa Cruz, and again on the 23d near the summit. The varied character of the woods and shrubbery on this mountain, which lay between my camp and the Santa Cruz shore, was very interesting to me, and I wished to spend some days there, as now the spring season was renewing vegetation, and the accounts of the great trees in the forest on the west slope of the mountains had roused my curiosity. Always, too, I had before my mind the home I wished to make in the country, and first one place and then another charmed me. But none seemed perfect where the sea was wanting, and so far I had not stood by the open waves of the Pacific. The soft climate of the San José valley was very enticing, and in the interior I had seen lovely spots in the midst of the great pines where the mountains looked down, but the sea was lacking. The piny fragrance was grateful, but it was not the invigorating salt breeze which brings with it renewed strength. This I wanted for my mother. For me, the shore of "the sounding sea" was a pleasure of which I never wearied, and I knew that along this coast the sea broke deep against bold rocks or shining sands. All this I had reason to believe I would find somewhere on the Santa Cruz shore. We remained on the upper portion of the mountain several days. The place of our encampment was two thousand feet above the sea, and was covered with a luxuriant growth of grass a foot high in many places.

At sunrise the temperature was 40°; at noon, 60°; at four in the afternoon, 65°, and 63° at sunset, with very pleasant weather. The mountains were wooded with many varieties of trees, and in some parts with heavy forests. These forests are characterized by a cypress (*taxodium*) of extraordinary dimensions, which I have already mentioned among the trees in the Sierra Nevada as distinguished among the forest trees of America by its superior size and height. Among many we measured in this part of the mountain a diameter of nine or ten feet was frequent, sometimes eleven; but going beyond eleven only in a single tree, which reached fourteen feet in diameter. Above two hundred feet was a frequent height. In this locality the bark was very deeply furrowed and unusually thick, being fully sixteen inches on some of the trees. It was now in bloom, flowering near the summit, and the flowers consequently difficult to procure.

This is the staple timber-tree of the country, being cut into both boards and shingles, and is the principal timber sawed at the mills. It is soft and easily worked, wearing away too quickly to be used for floor; but it seems to have all the durability which anciently gave the cypress so much celebrity. Posts which had been exposed to the weather three-quarters of a century, since the foundation of the Missions, showed no marks of decay in the wood and are now converted into beams and posts for private dwellings. In California this tree is called the *Palo Colorado, Redwood*.

Among the oaks in this mountain is a handsome, lofty evergreen tree, specifically different from those of the lower grounds, and in its general appearance much resembling hickory. The bark is smooth, of a white color, and the wood hard and close-grained. It seems to prefer the north hillsides, where some were nearly four feet in diameter and a hundred feet high.

Another remarkable tree of these woods is called in the language of the country *Madrona*. It is a beautiful evergreen with large, thick, and glossy digitated leaves; the trunk and branches reddish colored and having a smooth and singularly naked appearance, as if the bark had been stripped off. In its green state the wood is brittle, very heavy, hard, and close grained; it is said to assume a red color when dry, sometimes variegated, and susceptible of a high polish. This tree was found by us only in the mountains. Some measured nearly four feet in diameter and were about sixty feet high.

A few scattered flowers were now showing throughout the forests, and on the open ridges shrubs were flowering; but the bloom was not yet general. On the 25th of February we descended to the coast near the northwestern point of Monterey Bay, losing our fine weather, which in the evening changed to a cold southeasterly storm that continued with heavy and constant rains for several days.

The rain-storms closed with February, and the weather becoming fine, on the 1st of March we resumed our progress along the coast. Over the face of the country between Santa Cruz and Monterey, and around the plains of San Juan, the grass, which had been eaten down by the large herds of cattle, was now everywhere springing up and flowers began to show their bloom. In the valleys of the mountains bordering the Salinas plains wild oats were three feet high and well headed. The Salinas River runs through these plains, which are some fifty miles in length.

Pursuing our course to the southward I encamped on the afternoon of March 3d at the Hartnell rancho,[1] which is on a small creek-bed well out on the plain. We were now passing Monterey, which was about twenty-five miles distant.

The Salinas valley lay outside of the more occupied parts of the country; and I was on my way to a pass, opening into the San Joaquin valley, at the head of a western branch of the Salinas River.

MEMOIRS, 456–58.

1. William E. P. Hartnell (1798–1854), an Englishman who had been engaged in trade in California as early as 1822, was the owner of the Rancho Alisal or Patrocinio. He was administrator of the Mexican customs house at Monterey, and he was to render valuable service to both Mexicans and Americans as an interpreter and translator. For an appreciation of Hartnell's varied career, see DAKIN.

9. Frémont to Thomas Oliver Larkin

In Camp, March 5th 1846

My dear Sir

It would have afforded me pleasure to thank you personally for the kindness of your late letters,[1] but I am unwilling to leave my party and the presence of my little force might be disagreeable to the authorities in Monterey.

I therefore practise the selfdenial which is a constant virtue here and forego the pleasure I should have found in seeing some little of society in your capital. Having seen nothing, what shall I say now to those who ask me of Hastings' accounts?[2]

The bearer is one of my trustworthy men[3] and I send him to you for any intelligence you may have received from the States, and beg you to give him the newspapers you spoke of in your last. As you may judge, your letter woke up some strong memories and since then my occupations here have lost something of their usual interest. But I shall soon be laboriously employed; the spring promises to be a glorious one, and a month or two will pass quickly and usefully among the flowers while we are waiting on the season for our operations in the north.

This evening I encamp on the Monterey river, where I will expect the return of my messenger tomorrow afternoon. If Mr. Hartnall [Hartnell] could conveniently find the astronomical positions of Mr. Douglas[4] which he mentioned, they would be of use to me now in my journey southward.

I need hardly say that it will afford me pleasure to be of any service to you at home and I shall always be glad to hear from you. Can you tell me at about what time the letters I left with you will reach Washington? In May perhaps? Please offer my regards to Mrs. Larkin; I must certainly endeavor to see you again before leaving the country, and in the mean time am, Yours truly,

J. C. Frémont

Thomas O. Larkin Esqre
Consul for the United States at Monterey

Printed in LARKIN, 4:227–28.
1. Larkin's letters have not been found.
2. A reference to Lansford W. Hastings's promotional lectures and literature

on California, particularly to *The Emigrants' Guide to Oregon and California* (Cincinnati, 1845). See Doc. No. 3, n. 11.

3. Alexander Godey, according to William D. Phelps, master of the bark *Moscow,* who claimed to be present when the messenger arrived at the consulate (PHELPS, 279).

4. David Douglas (1799–1834), Scottish botanical explorer, had collected in the Pacific Northwest and California before he met a tragic death in the Hawaiian Islands.

10. Thomas Oliver Larkin to Frémont

MONTEREY, March 5th, 1846

SIR

I have just received two letters from the Commandant General of California, and the Prefecto of this District, who inform me they have sent you official letters,[1] enclosing me the copies. The following is a translation, which with my answer I will send to you in English.[2] I remain, Dear Sir, Yours sincerely,

(Signed) THOMAS O. LARKIN

To Captain J. C. Fremont, U.S. Army

Printed in LARKIN, 4:228.

1. The original letters of Gen. José Castro and prefect Manuel de Jesús Castro have not been found, but Larkin sent translations of his copies to the Secretary of State, James Buchanan (see our Doc. Nos. 11 and 12).

2. See Larkin to José Castro and Manuel de Jesús Castro, 6 March 1846, Doc. No. 13.

11. José Castro to Frémont

Commandant General of Upper California
[5 March 1846]

With this date I say to Captain J. C. Fremont the following:

At seven o'clock this morning the Commandant General was given to understand that you and the party under your command have entered the towns of this Department, and such being prohibited by our laws I find myself obligated to advertise you that on the receipt of this you will immediately retire beyond the limits of this same Department such being the orders of the supreme Government and the subscriber is obligated to see them complied with.

And the undersigned has the honor of transcribing the same to the Consul of the United States of America for its knowledge of the same. God & Liberty. Monterey March 5th 1846.

(Signed) José Castro

Mr. Thomas Larkin
Consul of the U.S. America In this Port

Translated copy enclosed in Larkin to Secretary of State, 5 March 1846, no. 36 (DNA-59, Consular Despatches, Monterey, Calif.).

12. Manuel de Jesús Castro to Frémont

Prefect of the Second District
Monterey March 6th [5th] 1846

Captain J C Fremont
Sir

"I have learnt with surprise that you against the laws of the authorities of Mexico have introduced yourself into the towns of this Departmental district under my charge with an armed force under a commission which must have been given you by your government only to survey its own proper lands.

In consequence this Prefectura now orders that you will immediately on receipt of this without any pretext return with your people out of the limits of this territory. If not this office will take the necessary measures to cause respect to this determination."

I have the honor to transcribe this to you for your intelligence that you may act in the case as belongs to your office and that he may comply with the expressed order. God & Liberty. Monterey March 5th 1846.

(Signed) Manuel Castro

Mr. Thomas O Larkin
Consul of the U.S. of America

Translated copy enclosed in Larkin to Secretary of State, 5 March 1846, no. 36 (DNA-59, Consular Despatches, Monterey, Calif.).

13. Thomas Oliver Larkin to José Castro and Manuel de Jesús Castro

Consulate of the United States
MONTEREY March 6th 1846

SIR

The undersigned Consul of the United States has the honour to acknowledge the receipt of your official note of yesterday containing a copy of your letter and orders to Capt J C Fremont, U. S. Army (now encamped near the Salinas River) with his men, to leave this country immediately.

The undersigned understood that your letter was yesterday carried to Captain Fremont, by an officer having some eight or ten men under his charge and that at this moment there is a large number of armed men collecting in this town for the purpose of going to the camp of that American officer. He would therefore take the Liberty of saying that although he is well aware that you, as a Mexican officer and a patriot, are bound to take every step that may redound to the integrity and interest of your country, he would further observe that his countrymen must not be unjustly or unnesesarily harrased from causes that may arise from false reports, or false appearances, and would recommend, that if any party are going to the Camp of Captain Fremont that it may be commanded by a trustworthy & experienced officer, which may prevent affairs on the meeting of the two parties from being brought to some unhappy conclusion. The undersigned has the honor to subscribe himself as your most obedt. [servant],

(Signed) THOMAS O. LARKIN

To Don Jose Castro, Commandant General of Upper California & Sr. Don Manuel Castro, Prefecto of the 2d District

Copy enclosed in Larkin to Secretary of State, 9 March 1846, no. 37 (DNA-59, Consular Despatches, Monterey, Calif.).

14. Manuel de Jesús Castro to Thomas Oliver Larkin

Prefecture of the Second District
[8 March 1846]

The undersigned Prefect of this District has received the note of the consul of the U.S. Mr. Thomas O Larkin dated 6 Inst. and in answer thereto has the honour to say that far from replying in it that he will order the captain of the U.S. army Mr J C Fremont to leave immediately with his force of Armed Troops (according to the acceptation of the word camp which he uses in his communication) the limits of this Department transgressing the principles established amongst civilized nations he defends his unjust introduction. The undersigned when he ordered Capt Fremont to march back founded himself on repeted orders & decrees from the Supreme Government of the Mexican Republic which prohibits the introduction not only of troops belonging to any power but even that of Foreigners who do not come provided with legal Passports and not on False Reports and False appearances as the Consul of the U.S. says in his said note. The undersigned promises the Consul of the United States that as far as lays in his power Those persons who are subject to the laws of the country and may harrass the subjects of his nation who are under the protection of said laws shall be punished according to the same, after the necessary prooffs shall be given, and the customary formalities gone through. The undersigned makes known to the Consul of the U.S. that if he desires to avoid that the force of Capt. Fremont may come to an unfortunate end meeting with the force of the Department, he ought to inform said Captain Fremont that since he entred this Department with an armed force wether through malice [or] error, he must now either blindly obey the authorities or on the contrary experience the misfortunes which he has sought by his crime. The Undersigned subscribes &c &c God & Liberty, Monterey March 8th 1846.

(Signed) Manuel Castro

Consul of the U. S. of North America Mr. Thomas O Larkin

Translated copy enclosed in Larkin to Secretary of State, 9 March 1846, no. 37 (DNA-59, Consular Despatches, Monterey, Calif.).

15. Thomas Oliver Larkin to Frémont

Consulate of the United States
MONTEREY, CALIFORNIA, March 8th, 1846

SIR

With this you have my Consular answer[1] to the General & Prefecto's letter to you of last week, of which I had the honour to receive copies from them. I also add the Señor Prefecto's second letter[2] to me of this day. By your Messenger of last week, I forwarded some U. S. Newspapers, a Spanish Grammar, some Magazines, and English copies of the General and Prefecto's letters to you on the 5th Inst. I then informed you that there was an American Brig (Brig Hannah, of Salem) at anchor in this port, bound to Mazatlan, whose Supercargo[3] I had requested to remain here untill the third day to enable you to send letters to the United States if you were so inclined. I cannot tell whether my letter[4] reached you, but heard of your man being almost at your Camp day before yesterday. I have now to inform you (and my information is derived from the current reports of the day) that General Castro was on the plain last night with about sixty people. Many more from the Ranchos joined him today. At this moment some forty men are preparing to leave Monterey to join the party. I should think tomorrow he might have two hundred men or perhaps more. Many of the common people will join through choice, others by being so ordered by the General. Among the other class, there are some looking on the affair with indifference, some perhaps with favor to either side as their friendship to the present authorities or their own interest may govern them. Respecting the result there are various opinions.

It is not for me to point out to you your line of conduct. You have your Government Instructions. My knowledge of your character obliges me to believe you will follow them. Nor can I offer any advice not knowing those instructions. Should you have no orders to enter this country the authorities are by their own laws correct in saying you can not remain with a company of armed men. You of course are taking every care and safe guard to protect your men, but not knowing your situation, and the people who surround you, your care may prove insufficient. You are officially ordered to leave the Country; I am shure you will use your own discretion on the subject. Your danger may remain in supposing that no uncommon means will be taken for your expulsion. Although the expressions of the common people under the passions of the moment, breathe vengeance in every form against you, I cannot conclude that so much will be put in force, should they succeed in overpowering you. I therefore only wish you to suppose yourself in a situation where you must take every measure to prevent a supprise, from those you may consider partially friends. Should my ideas be correct, the act perhaps will originate, not from the heads, or the respectability of the Country, but from those of a more head-strong class, who having fought so many (called) battles, may considered themselves invencible.

Your encamping so near Town has caused much excitement. The Natives are firm in the belief that they will break you up, and that you can be entirely destroyed by their power; in all probility they will attack you. The result either way may cause trouble hereafter to Resident Americans. I myself have no fear on the subject, yet believe the present state of affairs may cause an interruption in business. Should it be impossible or inconvenient for you to leave California at present, I think on a proper representation to the General and Prefecto, an arraingment could be made for your Camp to be continued, but at some greater distance; which arraingment I would advise, if you can offer it. I never make to this Government an unreasonable request, therefore never expect denial, and have for many years found them well disposed towards me. You cannot well leave your people. Should you wish to see me, I will immediately visit your Camp. Please answer directly by the Bearer. I am Yours Truly, in haste,

(Signed) Thomas O. Larkin

Captain J. C. Fremont
U. S. Army. Alisal
24 miles from Monterey

Copy enclosed in Larkin to Secretary of State, 9 March 1846, no. 37 (DNA-59, Consular Despatches, Monterey, Calif.).
1. See Larkin to José Castro and Manuel de Jesús Castro, 6 March 1846, Doc. No. 13.
2. See Manuel de Jesús Castro to Larkin [8 March 1846], Doc. No. 14.
3. Gregorio Ajuria was supercargo of the *Hannah*.
4. This letter not found.

16. Memorandum of Directions to Courier

Consulate of the U.S. of N. America
MONTEREY 8th March [1846]

You will proceed as quick as possible, by all means to Capt Fremont tomorrow. You will show your passport and the letter to any person who as an officer may demand to see them. Should you by force have to deliver up my letter, do so but endeavour to know the person who takes it. Should the letter be taken from you, endeavour to see Capt. Fremont and tell him I sent you with the letter and who took it from you. You will tell him to guard himself against acts of treachery at night, and not to place any faith in having a regular warfare, should there be any regular fighting, and by no means depend on the natives.

Note. One copy given to a native and another to a foreigner,[1] the latter being two days on the road, fell into the hands of the General and gave him the letters on the latter promising to forward as directed. On the second day Capt. Fremont had left. General Castro, twenty days afterward informed me that he had forwarded the letters the man gave him to Capt Fremont, when he had actualy sent them to Mexico, where they were published. He at the same time informed his Government that Capt. Fremont was driven away and that in May all other Americans would be.

(Signed) THOMAS O. LARKIN

Copy 8 in Larkin to Secretary of State, 20 July 1846, no. 54 (DNA-59, Consular Despatches, Monterey, Calif.).

1. The "foreigner" to whom Larkin entrusted a copy of the letter of 8 March was one of JCF's own men, Joseph Stepp of Quincy, Ill., who had been with him since the start of the expedition in May 1845 as a hunter and gunsmith (Larkin to Frémont, 31 May 1846, Doc. No. 30). BRANDON, 79, and HAFEN & HAFEN, 24, believe Stepp's correct name to be Stepperfeldt, but the voucher carries the shorter version, which was at least his preference. The "native" returned to the American Consulate in nine or ten hours, bringing a letter from JCF (our Doc. No. 18). The total distance traveled was about sixty miles (Larkin to Secretary of State, 27 March 1846, LARKIN, 4:270–73).

17. José Castro's Proclamation

[8 March 1846]

The Citizen José Castro Lieut Col. of the Mexican army and commander in chief of the Department of Cal.

———

Fellow citizens: A band of robbers commanded by a Capt. of the U.S. Army, J. C. Fremont, have, without respect to the laws & authorities of the Department daringly introduced themselves into the country and disobeyed the orders both of your Commander in Chief & of the Prefect of the district, by which he was required to march, forthwith, out of the limits of our Territory: & without answering their letters he remains encamped at the farm "Natividad" from which he sallies forth, committing depredations, and making scandalous skirmishes.

In the name of our native country I invite you to place yourselves under my immediate orders at headquarters, where we will prepare to lance the ulcer which (should it not be done) would destroy our liberties & independence for which you ought always to sacrifice yourselves, as will your friend & fellow citizen.

Head quarters at "San Juan"
(Signed) José Castro

8 March 1846

Edward M. Kern's copy (CSmH).

18. Frémont to Thomas Oliver Larkin

[9 March 1846]

My Dear Sir

I this moment received your letters and without waiting to read them acknowledge the receipt which the Courier requires instantly. I am making myself as strong as possible in the intention that if we are unjustly attacked we will fight to extremity and refuse quarter, trusting to our country to avenge our death. No one has reached my camp and from the heights we are able to see troops (with the glass) mustering at St. Johns and preparing cannon. I thank you for your kindness and good wishes and would write more at length as to my intentions, did I not fear that my letter will be intercepted; we have in no wise done wrong to the people or the authorities of the country, and if we are hemmed in and assaulted, we will die every man of us, under the Flag of our country. Very truly yours,

(Signed) J. C. FREMONT

P.S. I am encamped on the top of the Sierra at the head water of stream which strikes the road to Monterey, at the house of D. Joaquin Gomez.

J. C. F.

Consulate of the United States
MONTEREY, March 10, 1846

This letter wrote in haste by Captain Fremont with his pencil, I received last night at 8 o'clock. I permit the translation at the request of D. Manuel Diaz, Alcalde of Monterey (he having given yesterday a passport to my Courier to go to the Camp and return to me) with the hopes of its allaying the present sensation, bringing affairs to a better understanding, and that the authorities may not suppose I have any improper correspondence with Captain Fremont.

(Signed) THOMAS O. LARKIN

Copy (DNA-45, Area 9 File, Pacific). Also copy 10 in Larkin to Secretary of State, 20 July 1846 (DNA-59, Consular Despatches, Monterey, Calif.). Larkin's note was added to the letter when he permitted a Spanish translation to be taken by William Hartnell for Manuel Díaz. He later became upset because Hartnell had translated "refuse quarter" into "I will not give quarter," thus making JCF's statement the very reverse of what he intended. So Larkin wrote Abel Stearns in Los Angeles, asking him to see if the governor's copy (forwarded by Díaz) was actually in Hartnell's writing and also to try to exchange it for the true copy. He added a curious note: "From Captain Fremont's visit, I am under the idea that great plans are meditated to be carried out by certain persons" (Larkin to Stearns, 19 March 1846, no. 17, in Larkin to Secretary of State, 20 July 1846, no. 54, DNA-59, Consular Despatches, Monterey, Calif.).

19. Thomas Oliver Larkin to Frémont

Consulate of the United States
MONTEREY, CALIFA., March 10th 1846

SIR

Your letter of yesterday I received last night at eight o'clock. Thank you for the same. It took from me a weight of uneasiness respecting your situation. The Alcalde of Monterey has requested from me a copy in Spanish of your letter. Not knowing what you might approve of in the case, I had some objection. On second thoughts I considered that the Alcalde having given the Courier a passport (without which he would not go) carrying of the letters both ways were made public, and people might put a wrong construction on our correspondence. I gave it to him with the following addition.[1]

I also considered the letter contained nothing of importance to keep secret, and now annex my letter of this morning to the Alcalde.[2] As you may not have a copy of your letter, I send one. My Native Courier said he was well treated by you, that two thousand men could not drive you. In all cases of Couriers, order your men to have no hints or words with them, as it is magnified. This one said a man pointed to a tree, and said there's your life. He expected to be led to you, blindfolded, says you have sixty two men well armed, &c. &c.

You will without thought of expence or trouble, call on me, or send to me, in every case or need, not only as your Consul, but your friend and Countryman. I am Yours truly,

(Signed) THOMAS O. LARKIN

To Capt. J. C. Fremont at his camp
U.S. Army

Copy 13 in Larkin to Secretary of State, 20 July 1846, no. 54 (DNA-59, Consular Despatches, Monterey, Calif.).
1. See Frémont to Larkin, [9 March 1846], Doc. No. 18.
2. See Larkin to Díaz, 10 March 1846, Doc. No. 20.

20. Thomas Oliver Larkin to Manuel Díaz

Consulate of the U. S.
MONTEREY, March 10th, 1846

SIR,

I am not confident that Capt. Fremont may approve of my giving you a translation of his hasty wrote letter. As you allow the Courier to travel to the camp and return, and hoping this letter may on being known, bring affairs to some better understanding, I send you the translation you request.[1]

It may be that the authorities of this Department expect something from me as U. S. Consul under the present state of affairs; yet I know nothing that I can do. I have verbally offered my services whenever required, and now do the same in writing. Capt. Fremont has his own instructions, and has not to be ordered by this Consulate, yet I would with pleasure allay the present sensation if in my power.

I can only add that I would respectfully advise that you would in your letter to the General today, say that I would take the liberty to propose that he should send a letter to Capt. Fremont requesting one hour's conversation before any extreme measures are taken, as I am of the firm opinion, should that officer be attacked, much bloodshed would ensue, that may cause not only loss of life to many of the present parties, but cause hereafter much expence, trouble, and perhaps farther loss of life to many of our respective nations, and I am satisfied that no present or future advantage will be obtained by the country from the circumstances as they now appear. I have reason to believe that Capt. Fremont only waits a few days to rest his horses (having purchased his provisions) and intends to remove immediately from California, yet it may be impossible for him to do so, while surrounded by people with hostile intentions towards him. Will you please send a copy of this letter to the Commandant General D. José Castro. I have the honour to remain Yours respectfully,

(Signed) THOMAS O. LARKIN

To Don Manuel Diaz   Monterey
1st Alcalde

Copy 15 in Larkin to Secretary of State, 20 July 1846, no. 54 (DNA-59, Consular Despatches, Monterey, Calif.).

1. Larkin sent a Spanish translation of the 9 March 1846 letter of JCF, our Doc. No. 18.

21. José Castro's Proclamation

[13 March 1846]

Fellow-citizens—a party of highwaymen who, without respecting the laws or authorities of the department, boldly entered the country under the leadership of Don J. C. Frémont, captain in the U.S. army, having disobeyed the orders of this comandancia general and of the prefecture of the 2d district, by which said leader was notified immediately to march beyond the bounds of our territory; and without replying to the said notes in writing, the said captain merely sent a verbal message that on the Sierra del Gavilan he was prepared to resist the forces which the authorities might send to attack him. The following measures of this command and of the prefecture, putting in action all possible elements, produced as a result that he at the sight of 200 patriots abandoned the camp which he occupied, leaving in it some clothing and other war material, and according to the scouts took the route to the Tulares. Compatriots, the act of unfurling the American flag on the hills, the insults and threats offered to the authorities, are worthy of execration and hatred from Mexicans; prepare, then, to defend our independence in order that united we may repel with a strong hand the audacity of men who, receiving every mark of true hospitality in our country, repay with such ingratitude the favors obtained from our cordiality and benevolence.

Headquarters at San Juan Bautista, March 13, 1846.

Printed translation in BANCROFT, 5:19. Castro's claim to have driven out JCF and the American cowards posted in the Billiard Room in Monterey (Larkin to Secretary of State, 27 March 1846, no. 38, DNA-59, Consular Despatches, Monterey, Calif.).

22. Excerpt from the *Memoirs*

[9 March–24 May 1846]

Descending the southeastern side of the ridge we halted for the night [9–10 March] on a stream about three miles from the camp of

85

General Castro, a few miles from our fort.[1] The next day we resumed our route, and emerging into the valley of the San Joaquin on the 11th we found almost a summer temperature and the country clothed in the floral beauty of spring. Travelling by short stages we reached the Towalumne River on the evening of the 14th. By observation, in latitude 37° 25′ 53″, and longitude 120° 35′ 55″.

On the 21st we entered the Sacramento valley, and on the 22d encamped at a favorite spot opposite the house of Mr. Grimes.[2] As already mentioned, his house was not far from Sutter's Fort. We remained several days here on the American River, to recruit our animals on the abundant range between the Sacramento and the hills.

On the 24th we broke up camp with the intention of making an examination of the lower Sacramento valley, of which I had seen but little above Sutter's Fort.[3] I left the American River ten miles above its mouth; travelling a little east of north in the direction of the Bear River settlements. The road led among oak timber, over ground slightly undulating, covered with grass intermingled with flowers.

At sunrise on the 25th the temperature was a few degrees above the freezing point with an easterly wind and a clear sky.

In about thirty miles' travel to the north, we reached the Keyser rancho,[4] on Bear River; an affluent to *Feather* River, the largest tributary of the Sacramento. The route lay over an undulating country—more so as our course brought us nearer the mountains—wooded with oaks and shrubbery in blossom, with small prairies intervening. Many plants were in flower and among them the California poppy unusually magnificent. It is the characteristic bloom of *California* at this season, and the Bear River bottoms, near the hills, were covered with it. The blue fields of the nemophyla and this golden poppy represent fairly the skies and gold of California.

I was riding quietly along with Godey through the oak groves, the party being several miles off nigher to the hills, when we discovered two Indian women busily occupied among the trees on the top of a hill, gathering plants or clover-grass into their conical baskets. Taking advantage of the trees we had nearly reached the top of the hill, thinking to surprise these quick-eyed beings. Reaching the top we found nothing there except the baskets—apparently suddenly dropped and the grass spilled out. There were several bushes of a long-stemmed, grass-like shrub, and searching around to see

86

what had become of them, we discovered two pairs of naked feet sticking out just above the top of the bushes.

At the shout we raised two girls to whom the feet belonged rolled out of the bushes into which they had only time to dive as we neared the top of the hills, thinking perhaps that we had not seen them. They were but little alarmed and joined in the laugh we had at their ostrich-like idea of hiding. It appeared that they belonged to a village not far away towards the hills. Ranging around in that beautiful climate, gathering where they had not the trouble to sow, these people had at that time their life of thorough enjoyment. The oaks and pines and grasses gave them abundant vegetable food, and game was not shy.

We crossed several small streams, and found the ground miry from the recent rains. The temperature at four in the afternoon was 70°, and at sunset 58°, with an easterly wind, and the night bright and clear.

The morning of the 26th was clear, and warmer than usual; the wind southeasterly, and the temperature 40°. We travelled across the valley plain, and in about sixteen miles reached Feather River at twenty miles from its junction with the Sacramento, near the mouth of the *Yuba,* so called from a village of Indians who live on it. The river has high banks—twenty or thirty feet—and was here one hundred and fifty yards wide, a deep, navigable stream. The Indians aided us across the river with canoes and small rafts. Extending along the bank in front of the village was a range of wicker cribs, about twelve feet high, partly filled with what is there the Indians' staff of life—acorns. A collection of huts, shaped like beehives, with naked Indians sunning themselves on the tops, and these acorn cribs, are the prominent objects in an Indian village.

There is a fine farm, or rancho, on the Yuba, stocked with about three thousand head of cattle, and cultivated principally in wheat, with some other grains and vegetables, which are carried by means of the river to a market at San Francisco. Mr. [Theodor] Cordua, a native of Germany, who is proprietor of the place, informed me that his average harvest of wheat was twenty-five bushels to the acre, which he supposed would be about the produce of the wheat lands in the Sacramento valley. The labor on this and other farms in the valley is performed by Indians.

The temperature here was 74° at two in the afternoon, 71° at four, and 69° at sunset, with a northeasterly wind and a clear sky.

At sunrise of the 27th the temperature was 42°, clear, with a northeasterly wind. We travelled northwardly, up the right bank of the river, which was wooded with large white and evergreen oaks, interspersed with thickets of shrubbery in full bloom. This was a pleasant journey of twenty-seven miles, and we encamped at the bend of the river, where it turns from the course across the valley to run southerly to its junction with the Sacramento. The thermometer at sunset was 67°, sky partially clouded, with southerly wind.

The thermometer at sunrise on the 28th was at 45° 5', with a northeasterly wind. The road was over an open plain, with a few small sloughs or creeks that do not reach the river. After travelling about fifteen miles, we encamped on *Butte* Creek, a beautiful stream of clear water about fifty yards wide, with a bold current running all the year. It has large, fertile bottoms, wooded with open groves, and having a luxuriant growth of pea vine among the grass. The oaks here were getting into general bloom. Fine ranchos have been selected on both sides of the stream, and stocked with cattle, some of which were now very fat. A rancho [Esquon] here is owned by [Samuel] Neal, who formerly belonged to my exploring party. It may be remembered that in my last expedition I had acceded to his request to be left at Sutter's where he was offered high wages, with a certain prospect of betterment, where good mechanics were in great request. He was a skilful blacksmith, and had been and was very useful to me, as our horses' feet were one of the first cares. But his uniform good conduct rendered him worthy of any favor I could grant, and he was accordingly left at Sutter's when we resumed our march homeward. In the brief time which had elapsed he had succeeded in becoming a prospering stockman, with a good rancho. There is a *rancheria* (Indian village) near by, and some of the Indians gladly ran races for the head and offals of a fat cow which had been presented to us. They were *entirely* naked. The thermometer at two in the afternoon was at 70°, two hours later at 74°, and 65° at sunset; the wind east, and the sky clear only in the west.

The temperature at sunrise the next day was 50°, with cumuli in the south and west, which left a clear sky at nine, with a northwest wind, and temperature of 64°. We travelled twenty miles, and encamped on Pine Creek, another fine stream, with bottoms of fertile land, wooded with groves of large and handsome oaks, some attaining to six feet in diameter, and forty to seventy feet in height.

At four in the afternoon, the thermometer showed 74° and 64° at sunset; and the sky clear, except in the horizon.

March 30.—The sun rose in masses of clouds over the eastern mountains. A pleasant morning, with a sunrise temperature of 46° 5', and some *mosquitoes*—never seen, it is said, in the coast country; but at seasons of high water abundant and venomous in the bottoms of the Joaquin and Sacramento. On the tributaries nearer the mountains but few are seen, and those go with the sun. Continuing up the valley, we crossed in a short distance a large wooded creek, having now about thirty-five feet breadth of water. Our road was over an upland prairie of the Sacramento, having a yellowish, gravelly soil, generally two or three miles from the river, and twelve or fifteen from the foot of the eastern mountains. On the west it was twenty-five or thirty miles to the foot of the mountains, which here make a bed of high and broken ranges. In the afternoon, about half a mile above its mouth, we encamped on Deer Creek, another of these beautiful tributaries of the Sacramento. It has the usual broad and fertile bottom-lands common to these streams, wooded with groves of oak and a large sycamore (*platanus occidentalis*), distinguished by bearing its balls in strings of three to five, and peculiar to California. Mr. Lassen, a native of Germany, has established a rancho here, which he has stocked, and is gradually bringing into cultivation.[5] Wheat, as generally throughout the north country, gives large returns; cotton, planted in the way of experiment, was not injured by frost, and succeeded well; and he has lately planted a vineyard, for which the Sacramento valley is considered to be singularly well adapted. The seasons are not yet sufficiently understood, and too little has been done in agriculture, to afford certain knowledge of the capacities of the country. This farm is in the 40th degree of latitude; our position on the river being in 39° 57' 00", and longitude 121° 56' 44" west from Greenwich, and elevation above the sea five hundred and sixty feet. About three miles above the mouth of this stream are the first rapids—the present head of navigation—in the Sacramento River, which, from the rapids to its mouth in the bay, is more than two hundred miles long, and increasing in breadth from one hundred and fifty yards to six hundred yards in the lower part of its course.

During six days that we remained here, from the 30th March to the 5th April, the mean temperature was 40° at sunrise, 52°.5 at nine in the morning, 57°.2 at noon, 59°.4 at two in the afternoon, 58°.8 at four, and 52° at sunset; and at the corresponding times the dew point was at 37°.0, 41°.0, 38°.1, 39°.6, 44°.9, 40°.5; and the moisture in a cubic foot of air 2.838 grs., 3.179 grs. 2.935 grs., 3.034 grs., 3.766 grs., 3.150 grs. respectively. Much cloudy weather and some showers of rain, during this interval, considerably reduced the temperature, which rose with fine weather on the 5th. Salmon was now abundant in the Sacramento. Those which we obtained were generally between three and four feet in length, and appeared to be of two distinct kinds. It is said that as many as four different kinds ascend the river at different periods. The great abundance in which this fish is found gives it an important place among the resources of the country. The salmon crowd in immense numbers up the Umpqua, Tlamath [Klamath], and Trinity Rivers, and into every little river and creek on the coast north of the Bay of San Francisco; and up the San Joaquin River, into the Stanislaus, beyond which the Indians say they do not go. Entering all the rivers of the coast far to the north, and finding their way up into the smaller branches which penetrate the forests of the interior country, climbing up cataracts and lesser falls, this fish had a large share in supporting the Indians—who raised nothing, but lived on what Nature gave. "A Salmon-Water," as they named it, was a valuable possession to a tribe or village, and jealously preserved as an inheritance. I found the "Salmon-waters" in the forests along the eastern flank of the Cascade range below the Columbia River.

In the evening of the 5th we resumed our journey northward,[6] and encamped on a little creek near the Sacramento, where an emigrant from "the States" was establishing himself, and had already built a house. It is a handsome place, wooded with groves of oak, and along the creek are sycamore, ash, cottonwood, and willow. The day was fine, with a northwest wind.

The temperature at sunrise the next day (April 6th) was 42°, with a northeasterly wind. We continued up the Sacramento, which we crossed in canoes at a farm on the right bank of the river. The Sacramento was here about one hundred and forty yards wide, and with the actual stage of water, which I was informed continued several months, navigable for a steamboat. We encamped a few miles above, on a creek wooded principally with large oaks. Grass was good and abundant, with wild oats and pea vine in the bottoms. The day was fine, with a cool northwesterly breeze, which had in it the air of the high mountains. The wild oats here were not yet headed.

The snowy peak of Shastl [Shasta] bore directly north, showing out high above the other mountains. Temperature at sunset 57°, with a west wind and sky partly clouded.

April 7.—The temperature at sunrise was 37°, with a moist air; and a faintly clouded sky indicated that the wind was southerly along the coast. We travelled toward the Shastl peak, the mountain ranges on both sides of the valleys being high and rugged, and snow-covered. Some remarkable peaks in the Sierra, to the eastward, are called *the Sisters,* and, nearly opposite, the Coast Range shows a prominent peak, to which in remembrance of my friend Senator Linn, I gave the name MOUNT LINN,[7] as an enduring monument to recall the prolonged services rendered by him in securing to the country our Oregon coast. I trust this reason will protect it from change. These giant monuments, rising above the country and seen from afar, keep alive and present with the people the memory of patriotic men, and so continue their good services after death. Mount Linn and Mount Shastl keep open to the passing glance each an interesting page of the country's history—the one recording a successful struggle for the ocean boundary which it overlooks, the other the story of a strange people passed away. And so, too, these natural towers call attention from the detail of daily occupation to the larger duties which should influence the lives of men.

Leaving the Sacramento, at a stream called Red Bank Creek, we entered on a high and somewhat broken upland, timbered with at least four varieties of oaks, with *mansanita (arbutus Menziesii)* [*Arctostaphylos* sp.] and other shrubbery interspersed. The *mansanita* is the strange shrub which I met in March of '44 in coming down from the Sierra Nevada to Sutter's Fort, and which in my journal of that time I described as follows: "A new and singular shrub, which had made its appearance since crossing the mountain, was very frequent to-day. It branched out near the ground, forming a clump eight to ten feet high, with pale green leaves of an oval form, and the body and branches had a naked appearance as if stripped of the bark, which is very smooth and thin, of a chocolate color, contrasting well with the pale green of the leaves." Out of its red berries the Indians made a cider which, put to cool in the running streams, makes a pleasant, refreshing drink. A remarkable species of pine, having leaves in threes (sometimes six to nine inches long), with bluish foliage, and a spreading, oak-shaped top, was scattered through the timber. I have remarked that this tree grows lower down the mountains than the other pines, being found familiarly associated with oaks, the first met after leaving the open valleys, and seeming to like a warm climate. It seems that even among inanimate things association levels differences. This tree, growing among oaks, forgets its narrow piny form and color, and takes the spreaded shape of the oaks, their broad summits, and lesser heights. Flowers were as usual abundant. The splendid California poppy characterized all the route along the valley. A species of clover was in bloom, and the berries of the *mansanita* were beginning to redden on some trees, while others were still in bloom. We encamped, at an elevation of about one thousand feet above the sea, on a large stream called Cottonwood Creek, wooded on the bottoms with oaks, and with cotton-woods along the bed, which is sandy and gravelly. The water was at this time about twenty yards wide, but is frequently fifty. The face of the country traversed during the day was gravelly, and the bottoms of the creek where we encamped have a sandy soil.

There are six or seven rancherias of Indians on the Sacramento River between the farm where we had crossed the Sacramento and the mouth of this creek, and many others in the mountains about the heads of these streams.

The next morning was cloudy, threatening rain, but the sky grew brighter as the sun rose, and a southerly wind changed to northwest, which brought, as it never fails to bring, clear weather.

We continued sixteen miles up the valley, and encamped on the Sacramento River. In the afternoon (April 8th) the weather again grew thick and in the evening rain began to fall in the valley and snow on the mountains. We were now near the head of the lower valley, and the face of the country and the weather began sensibly to show the influence of the rugged mountains which surround and terminate it.

The valley of the Sacramento is divided into upper and lower— the lower two hundred miles long, the upper known to the trappers as Pitt [Pit] river, about one hundred and fifty; and the latter not merely entitled to the distinction of upper, as being higher up the river, but also as having a superior elevation of some thousands of feet above it. The division is strongly and geographically marked. The Shastl peak stands at the head of the lower valley, rising from a base of about one thousand feet out of a forest of heavy timber. It ascends like an immense column upwards of fourteen thousand feet (nearly the height of Mont Blanc),[8] the summit glistening with snow, and visible, from favorable points of view, at a distance of one hundred and forty miles down the valley. The river here, in descending from the upper valley, plunges down through a cañon, falling two thousand feet in twenty miles. This upper valley is one hundred and fifty miles long, heavily timbered, the climate and production modified by its altitude, its more northern position, and the proximity and elevation of the neighboring mountains covered with snow. It contains valleys of arable land, and is deemed capable of settlement. Added to the lower valley, it makes the whole valley of the Sacramento three hundred and fifty miles long.

April 9.—At ten o'clock the rain which commenced the previous evening had ceased, and the clouds clearing away, we boated the river, and continued our journey eastward toward the foot of the Sierra. The Sacramento bottoms here are broad and prettily wooded, with soil of a sandy character. Our way led through very handsome, open woods, principally of oaks, mingled with a considerable quantity of the oak-shaped pine. Interspersed among these were bosquets or thickets of *mansanita,* and an abundant white-flowering shrub, now entirely covered with small blossoms. The head of the valley here (lower valley) is watered by many small streams, having fertile bottom lands, with a good range of grass and acorns. In about six miles we crossed a creek twenty or twenty-five feet wide, and several miles farther descended into the broad bottoms of a swift stream about twenty yards wide, called Cow Creek, so named as being the range of a small band of cattle, which ran off here from a party on their way to Oregon. They are entirely wild, and are hunted like other game. A large band of antelope was seen in the timber, and five or six deer came darting through the woods. An antelope and several deer were killed. There appear to be two species of these deer—both of the kind generally called black-tailed; one, a larger species frequenting the prairies and lower grounds; the other, much smaller, and found in the mountains only. The mountains in the northeast were black with clouds when we reached the creek, and very soon a fierce hailstorm burst down on us, scattering our animals and covering the ground an inch in depth with hailstones about the size of wild cherries. The face of the country appeared as whitened by a fall of snow, and the weather became unpleasantly cold. The evening closed in with rain, and thunder rolling around the hills. Our elevation here was between one thousand and eleven hundred feet. At sunrise the next morning the thermometer was at 33°. The surrounding mountains showed a continuous line of snow, and the high peaks looked wintry. Turning to the southward, we retraced our steps down the valley, and reached Lassen's, on Deer River, on the evening of the 11th. The Sacramento bottoms between Antelope and Deer River were covered with oats, which had attained their full height, growing as in sown fields. The country here exhibited the maturity of spring. The California poppy was everywhere forming seed-pods, and many plants were in flower and seed together. Some varieties of clover were just beginning to bloom. By the middle of the month the seed-vessels of the California poppy which, from its characteristic abundance, is a prominent feature in the vegetation, had attained their full size; but the seeds of this and many other plants, although fully formed, were still green-colored, and not entirely ripe. At this time I obtained from the San Joaquin valley seeds of the poppy, and other plants, black and fully ripe, while they still remained green in this part of the Sacramento—the effect of a warmer climate in the valley of the San Joaquin. The mean temperature for fourteen days, from the 10th to the 24th of April, was 43° at sunrise, 58° at nine in the morning, 64° at noon, 66° at two in the afternoon, 69° at four, and 58° at sunset (latitude 40°). The thermometer ranged at sunrise from 38° to 51°, at four (which is the hottest of those hours of the day when the temperature was noted) from 53° to 88°, and at sunset from 49° to 65°. The dew point was 40°.3 at sunrise, 47°.3 at 9 in the morning, 46°.1 at noon, 49°.2 at 2 in the afternoon, 49°.2 at 4, and 46°.6 at sunset; and the quantity of moisture in a cubic foot of air at corresponding times was 3.104 grs., 3.882 grs., 3.807 grs., 4.213 grs., 4.217 grs., 3.884 grs., respectively. The winds fluctuated between northwest and southeast, the temperature depending more upon the state of the sky than the direction of the winds—a clouded sky always lowering the thermometer fifteen or twenty degrees in a short time. For the greater number of the days above given the sky was covered and the atmosphere frequently thick with rain at intervals from the 19th to the 23d.

Here at Lassen's I set up the transit and during the nights of the 14th and 16th (April) obtained good observations of moon culminations which established the longitude of the place in 120° 56′ 44″, latitude obtained 39° 57′ 04″. This was the third of my main stations and the place of observation was upon Deer River half a mile above its mouth in the Sacramento and opposite Lassen's house.

On the 24th I left Lassen's, intending to penetrate the country, along the Cascade ranges north into Oregon, and connect there with the line of my journey of '43, which lay up the Fall [Deschutes] River of the Columbia and south to the great savannah, or grassy meadow-lake through which flows from among the ridges of the Cascade Mountains the principal tributary or rather the main stream of the waters which make the Tlamath Lake and River. It is a timbered country, clothed with heavy pine forests that nourish many streams.

Travelling up the Sacramento over ground already described, we reached the head of the lower valley in the evening of the second day and in the morning of the 26th left the Sacramento, going up one of the many pretty little streams that flow into the main river around the head of the lower valley.[9] On either side low, steep ridges were covered along their summits with pines, and oaks occupied the somewhat broad bottom of the creek. Snowy peaks which made the horizon on the right gave a cool tone to the landscape, and the thermometer showed a temperature of 71°, but there was no breeze and the air was still and hot. There were many runs and small streams, with much bottom-land, and the abundant grass and acorns, both of excellent quality, made it a favorite resort for game. The frequent appearance of game furnished excitement, and together with the fine weather, which made mere breathing an enjoyment, kept the party in exhilarated spirits. At our encampment among oak groves in the evening, we found ourselves apparently in a bear garden, where the rough denizens resented our intrusion and made a lively time for the hunters, who succeeded in killing four of them after we had encamped. During our skirmishing among the bear this afternoon we had overtaken and slightly wounded one, just enough to irritate him. At this moment Delaware Charley's horse fell near by the bear. To save Charley we had all to close in on the bear, who was fortunately killed before he could get the Delaware. In his fall the hammer of his gun struck Charley on the bridge of his nose and broke it in the middle. We had no surgeon, but I managed to get it into good shape and it healed without trace of injury. I was always proud of this surgical operation, and the Delaware was especially pleased. He was a fine-

Buttes in the Sacramento Valley. From an engraving in Frémont's *Memoirs.*

looking young man, and naively vain of his handsome face, which now had a nose unusual among his people; the aquiline arch had been broken to knit into a clear straight line, of which he became very vain.

At sunset the weather was pleasant, with a temperature of 56°. I had only an observation for latitude, which put the camp in 40° 38' 58", and the elevation above the sea was one thousand and eighty feet. The day following we found a good way along a flat ridge; there was a pretty stream in a mountain valley on the right, and the face of the country was already beginning to assume a mountainous character, wooded with mingled oak and long-leaved pine, and having a surface of scattered rocks, with grass or flowers, among them the three-leaved poppy, its parti-colored blossoms waving on the long stem above the grass, and gaining for itself the name *mariposas,* already mentioned because of its resembling living butterflies. I speak often of the grass and the flowers, but I have learned to value the one and the other lends a beauty to the scenery which I do not like to omit, and the reader can always imagine for himself the brightness they give when once he has had described the glorious flowers of this country, where the most lovely hues are spread in fields over both hill and plain. At noon, when we were crossing a high ridge, the temperature was down to 61°, and where we encamped at an elevation of two thousand four hundred and sixty feet, on a creek that went roaring into the valley, the sunset temperature was 52°.

The next day I continued up the stream on which we had slept, and with it the mountain slope rose rapidly, clothed with heavy timber. On crossing one of the high ridges, snow and the great [sugar] pine [*Pinus*] *Lambertiani* appeared together, and an hour before noon we reached a pass in the main ridge of the Sierra Nevada, in an open pine forest at an elevation of only four thousand six hundred feet, where the snow was in patches and the deciduous oaks were mingled with the pines. The thermometer was at 50°, and we were not above the upper limit of the oak region. This pass is in about the fortieth degree of latitude, and is in the terminating point of the northern link of the Sierra Nevada chain, which the Cascade range takes up with the link of the Shastl peak. Between the points of these links the upper Sacramento River breaks down on its way to the Bay of San Francisco and the Tlamath River to the sea.

97

Going through this pass and descending the mountain, we entered into what may be called a basin or mountain valley, lying north and south along the ranges of the Cascade Mountains. Here we found a region very different from the valley of California. We had left behind the soft, delightful climate of the coast, from which we were cut off by the high, snowy mountains, and had ascended into one resembling that of the Great Basin, and under the influence of the same elevation above the sea; but more fertile and having much forest land, and well watered. The face of the country was different from that of the valley which we had just left, being open and more spread into plain, in which there were frequent lakes as well as rivers. The soil itself is different; sometimes bare. At times we travelled over stretches in the forest where the soil was a gray or yellowish-white pumice-stone, like that which I have seen along the Cascade range in travelling south from the Columbia River, where the soil was covered with splendid pine forests, but where there was hardly a blade of grass to be found. Very different from this the compact growth of grass and flowers which belong to the California valley, where the rich soil had accumulated the wash of ages from the mountains, and where the well-watered land and moisture of the air combine to cover the country with its uncommon and profuse vegetation. The country where we now were was not known to any of the men with me, and I was not able to communicate with any of the Indians, who in this region were unfriendly—from these I might have learned the names by which the natural features were known to them. Except in some of its leading features I regarded this district as not within the limits of fixed geography, and therefore I thought it well to give names to these; to some at the time, and to others afterward, when I came to making up a map of the country. And this was also necessary, as otherwise I could not conveniently refer to them.

On the 29th of April I encamped on the upper Sacramento [Pit River], above Fall River, which is tributary to it. I obtained observations here, which gave for longitude 121° 07′ 59″, and for latitude 40° 58′ 43″; and the next day again encamped on it at the upper end of a valley, to which, from its marked form, I gave the name *Round Valley* [Big Valley]. By observation the longitude here is 121° 01′ 23″, latitude 41° 17′ 17″. On the first of May I encamped on the southeastern end of a lake, which afterwards I named Lake Rhett [Tule Lake, which has been reclaimed] in friendly remembrance of Mr. Barnwell Rhett, of South Carolina, who is connected with one of the events of my life which brought with it an abiding satisfaction.[10] I obtained observations here which placed this end of the lake in longitude 121° 15′ 24″, and latitude 41° 48′ 49″.

This camp was some twenty-five or thirty miles from the lava beds, near which Major-General [E. R. S.] Canby was killed by the Modocs, twenty-seven years later; and when there was some of the hardest fighting known in Indian history between them and our troops.[11]

This Indian fighting is always close, incurring more certain risk of life and far more sanguinary, than in the ordinary contests between civilized troops. Every Indian fights with intention, and for all that is in him; he waits for no orders, but has every effort concentrated on his intention to kill. And, singularly, this Indian fighting, which calls for the utmost skill and courage on the part of men, is not appreciated by the Government, or held worthy of the notice given to the milder civilized warfare.

When we left Round Valley in the morning Archambeau[lt], who was an inveterate hunter, had gone off among the hills and towards the mountain in search of game.

We had now entered more into the open country, though still a valley or high upland along the foot of the main ridge, and were travelling north; but the route of the day is often diverted from its general course by accidents of country and for convenient camping grounds. Archambeau did not come in at night, and when the morning came and did not bring him I did not move camp, but sent out men to look for him. Since leaving the California Mountains we had seen no Indians, though frequently we came upon their tracks and other sign. All through this country there were traces of them. Doubtless our camp-fires had discovered us to them, but they hovered around out of our way and out of sight. The second day passed and still no trace of Archambeau had been found, and the greater part of the third was passed in scouring the country. There would have been little difficulty in a prairie region, but in a broken or hilly country much ground cannot be covered and the search is restricted to a small area. We had now been in camp three days and I began to be seriously disturbed by his absence. Game had been found scarce in the immediate neighborhood. He had nothing with him but a little dried meat when he turned off from the party, expecting to rejoin us before night, and the Indians in the region through which we were travelling were known to be hostile and treacherous, with a fixed character for daring. Parties from as far north as the Hudson Bay Company's post who had penetrated here had met with some rough experiences, and the story of trapper adventure hereabout was full of disaster.[12] On one occasion a large party of trappers from the north were encamped on one of the streams of the Cascade range, and having been led into carelessness by the apparent friendly conduct of the Indians, were every man killed.[13] It was easy to waylay a single man, especially if he were intent on game. I had always been careful of my men, and in all my journeyings lost but few, and with rare exceptions those were by accident or imprudence. Naturally disposed that way, I had always endeavored to provide for their safety so far as the nature of our exposed life permitted, for in case of accident, as we had no surgeon, I was myself the only resource. A man lost from camp was likely also to lose his life. In such circumstances every hour increases the danger of his situation. And so about sunset we were greatly relieved when a shout from the men on guard roused the camp and we saw Archambeau creeping slowly in, man and horse equally worn out. Searching for game, he had been led off and entangled among the hills until the coming night roused him and the darkness cut off all chance of reaching camp. His search was as fruitless on the following days. He did not meet game, and his horse being kept close at hand at night had no chance to feed, and was nearly as tired as himself. And he had probably owed his life to his good eyes. These were unusually fine, with an instant quickness to catch a moving object or any slight difference in color or form of what lay before him. I was riding with him on the prairie one day, off from the party, when he suddenly halted. "Stop," he said, "I see an antelope's horns." About fifty steps away an antelope was lying in the tall grass, and the top of its horn was barely visible above it, but he not only saw it but shot and killed it. And this time his eyes had served him well again. They were ranging around taking in all before him when he caught sight of a party of Indians. They were travelling directly across his line of way, making towards the coast mountains, probably going to some river in which there were salmon. If they had been coming towards him they would have seen him, or if they had crossed his trail behind him his life would have been lost. He saw them as they were coming up out of a broad ravine and in the instant got his horse out of sight down the

100

Moving Camp. From an engraving in Frémont's *Memoirs*.

slope of a hill. "My heart was in my mouth for a moment," he said. The danger of his situation had already brought on the hurry and excitement which often deprives a man of all prudence. In such mishaps a man quickly loses his head, but at this stage, happily, he struck our trail.

The arrival of Archambeau relieved and spread pleasure through the camp, where he was a general favorite. He was Canadian, tall, fine looking, very cheerful, and with all the gayety of the *voyageur* before hard work and a rough life had driven it out. He had that light, elastic French temperament that makes a cheerful companion in travelling; which in my experience brings out all there is of good or bad in a man. I loved to have my camp cheerful and took care always for the health and comfort which carry good temper with them. Usually, on leaving the frontier, I provided the men with tents or lodges, but by the time we had been a month or two on the road, they would come to me to say that it was hard on them to have to put up their lodge at night when they were tired, and that they made a delay in the morning when starting. So usually their shelters were gladly left behind and they took the weather as it came.

Meantime the days while we had been waiting here were not lost. Our animals had been resting on good grass, and when in the morning the welcome order was given to move camp, they made the lively scene which Mr. Kern gives in the picture [p. 101]. This was an order which the animals were always prone to resist promptly, and their three days' rest made them do it now with unusual vigor. But the men, too, refreshed by rest and cheered by the recovery of their companion, entered with equal spirit into the fray, and soon we were again on the trail, the animals settled down to their orderly work.

Archambeau was himself again in the morning after a night's rest, and good meals among companions, but his horse was let to run loose for some days, in order to recover its useful strength. With the animals refreshed we made a long stretch and encamped on a stream flowing into Lake Rhett, which I called McCrady [Lost River]. This was the name of one of my boyhood's friends [Edward McCrady], living in Charleston, who came this evening into my mind, and I left his memory on the stream. In such work as I was engaged in there is always much time for thinking, or ruminating, as it may better be called; not upon the road, but often at night, waiting for the hour when the work belonging to it may begin.

In the forenoon of the sixth we reached the Tlamath Lake [Upper Klamath Lake] at its outlet, which is by a fine, broad stream, not fordable. This is a great fishing station for the Indians, and we met here the first we had seen since leaving the lower valley. They have fixed habitations around the shores of the lake, particularly at the outlet and inlet, and along the inlet up to the swamp meadow, where I met the Tlamaths in the winter of '43–44, and where we narrowly escaped disaster.

Our arrival took them by surprise, and though they received us with apparent friendship, there was no warmth in it, but a shyness which came naturally from their habit of hostility.

At the outlet here were some of their permanent huts. From the lake to the sea I judged the river to be about two hundred miles long; it breaks its way south of the huge bulk of Shastl Peak between the points of the Cascade and Nevada ranges to the sea. Up this river the salmon crowd in great numbers to the lake, which is more than four thousand feet above the sea. It was a bright spring morning, and the lake and its surrounding scenery looked charming. It was inviting, and I would have been glad to range over it in one of the Indian canoes. The silent shores and unknown mountains had the attraction which mystery gives always. It was all wild and unexplored, and the uninvaded silence roused curiosity and invited research. Indigenous, the Indians like the rocks and trees seemed part of the soil, growing in a state of rude nature like the vegetation, and like it nourished and fed by nature. And so it had been back to a time of which nothing was known. All here was in the true aboriginal condition, but I had no time now for idling days, and I had to lose the pleasure to which the view before me invited. Mr. Kern made the picture of it [p. 104] while we were trading with the Indians for dried fish and salmon, and ferrying the camp equipage across the outlet in their canoes.

The Indians made me understand that there was another large river [Williamson] which came from the north and flowed into the lake at the northern end, and that the principal village was at its mouth, where also they caught many fish.

Resuming our journey, we worked our way along between the lake and the mountain, and late in the day made camp at a run, near

where it issued from the woods into the lake and where our animals had good feed. For something which happened afterward, I gave this run the name of Denny's Branch. Animals and men all fared well here.

May 7.—The weather continued refreshingly cool. Our way led always between the lake and the foot of the mountains, frequently rough and blocked by decaying logs and fallen trees, where patches of snow still remained in the shade, over ground rarely trodden even by an Indian foot. In the timber the snow was heavy and naturally much heavier towards the summits and in the passes of the mountains, where the winter still held sway. This year it had continued late and rough. In the late afternoon we reached a piece of open ground through which a stream ran towards the lake. Here the mountain receded a little, leaving a flat where the woods, which still occupied the ground, left us a convenient open space by the water, and where there was grass abundant. On the way along from the outlet no Indians had been seen and no other sign of life, but now and then when the lake was visible a canoe might be seen glancing along. But in the morning, as we were about to leave camp, a number of them came in. I could not clearly find where they had come from, though they pointed up the lake. Perhaps from some valley in the mountain on this stream, or perhaps they had followed our trail. This was most likely, but if so they were not willing to tell. They would not have done so with any good intent, and they knew well enough that we were aware of it. They said that they were hungry, and I had some mules unpacked and gave them part of our remaining scanty supply of dried meat and the usual present which an Indian, wild or tame, always instinctively expects.

We continued our route over the same kind of ground, rendered difficult by the obstructions which the wash of the rain and snow, and the fallen timber, the undisturbed accumulations of the many years, had placed in these forests. Crossing spurs of mountains and working around the bays or coves between the ridges or winding among the hills, it is surprising how a long day's march dwindles away to a few miles when it comes to be laid down between the rigorous astronomical stations. We had travelled in this direction many such days when we encamped in the afternoon of the 8th of May. A glance at the mountains, which are shown in the view of the lake, gives some idea of the character of this unexplored region. By unexplored, I wish to be understood to say that it had never been explored or mapped, or in any way brought to common knowledge, or rarely visited except by strong parties of trappers, and by those at remote intervals, doubtless never by trappers singly. It was a true wilderness. There was the great range of mountains behind the coast, and behind it the lakes and rivers known to the trappers, and that was all, and the interest attached to it was chiefly from the disaster which had befallen them. And from their reports, rude and exaggerated outlines, and Turtle Lakes and Buenaventura Rivers, had been marked down at the stations of the Fur Company.[14] All this gave the country a charm for me. It would have been dull work if it had been to plod over a safe country and here and there to correct some old error.

And I had my work all planned. The friendly reader—and I hope that no unfriendly eyes will travel along with me over these lines; the friends may be few and the many are the neutral minds who read without reference to the writer, solely for the interest they find. To these I write freely, letting the hues of my mind color the paper, feeling myself on pleasant terms with them, giving to them in a manner a life confession in which I hope they find interest, and expecting to find them considerate and weighing fairly, and sometimes condoning the events as we pass them in review. My reading friend, then, who has travelled with me thus far will remember that some seventeen months before this time, in the December of '43, in coming south from the Columbia, I encamped on a large savannah, or meadow-lake [Klamath Marsh], which made the southern limit of my journey. I met there a Tlamath chief and his wife, who had come out to meet me and share his fate, whether good or bad, and the chief had afterward accompanied me and piloted me on my way through the forest and the snow. Where I had encamped this night I was only some twenty miles in an air-line from their village and I was promising myself some pleasure in seeing them again. According to what the Indians at the south end of the lake had told me, I had only to travel eastward a short march and I would find a large village at the inlet of the river, which I knew must be that on which my friendly chief lived, some twenty miles above. And his Indians, too, like all the others along these mountains, had the character of normal hostility to the whites.

My plans when I started on my journey into this region were to connect my present survey of the intervening country with my camp on the savannah, where I had met the Tlamaths in that December;

and I wished to penetrate among the mountains of the Cascade ranges. As I have said, except for the few trappers who had searched the streams leading to the ocean, for beaver, I felt sure that these mountains were absolutely unknown. No one had penetrated their recesses to know what they contained, and no one had climbed to their summits; and there remained the great attraction of mystery in going into unknown places—the unknown lands of which I had dreamed when I began this life of frontier travel. And possibly, I thought, when I should descend their western flanks some safe harbor might yet be found by careful search along that coast, where harbors were so few; and perhaps good passages from the interior through these mountains to the sea. I thought that until the snow should go off the lower part of the mountains I might occupy what remained of the spring by a survey of the Tlamath River to its heads, and make a good map of the country along the base of the mountains. And if we should not find game enough to live upon, we could employ the Indians to get supplies of salmon and other fish. But I felt sure that there was game in the woods of these mountains as well as those more to the south. Travelling along the northern part of this range in December of '43, I had seen elk tracks in the snow, and at an old Cayuse village in the pine forest at the foot of the mountains, only about sixty miles farther north, there were many deer horns lying around. This showed that we should probably find both elk and deer, and bear, in the mountains, and certainly on the slope towards the sea, where every variety of climate would be found, and every variety of mast-bearing trees, as in the oak region of the Sierra Nevada. And I had not forgotten how fascinated I had been with the winter beauty of the snowy range farther north, when at sunrise and at sunset their rose-colored peaks stood up out of the dark pine forests into the clear light of the sky. And my thoughts took the same color when I remembered that Mr. Kern, who had his colors with him, could hold these lovely views in all their delicate coloring.

How fate pursues a man! Thinking and ruminating over these things, I was standing alone by my camp-fire, enjoying its warmth, for the night air of early spring is chill under the shadows of the high mountains. Suddenly my ear caught the faint sound of horses' feet, and while I was watching and listening as the sounds, so strange hereabout, came nearer, there emerged from the darkness— into the circle of the firelight—two horsemen, riding slowly as though horse and man were fatigued by long travelling. In the foremost I recognized the familiar face of Neal, with a companion whom I also knew. They had ridden nearly a hundred miles in the last two days, having been sent forward by a United States officer who was on my trail with despatches for me; but Neal doubted if he would get through. After their horses had been turned into the band and they were seated by my fire, refreshing themselves with good coffee while more solid food was being prepared, Neal told me his story. The officer who was trying to overtake me was named Gillespie.[15] He had been sent to California by the Government and had letters for delivery to me.[16] Neal knew the great danger from Indians in this country, and his party becoming alarmed and my trail being fresh, Mr. Gillespie had sent forward Neal and [Levi] Sigler upon their best horses to overtake me and inform me of his situation. They had left him on the morning of the day before, and in the two days had ridden nearly a hundred miles, and this last day had severely tried the strength of their horses. When they parted from him they had not reached the lake, and for greater safety had not kept my trail quite to the outlet, but crossed to the right bank of the river, striking my trail again on the lake shore. They had discovered Indians on my trail after they had left Gillespie, and on the upper part of the lake the Indians had tried to cut them off, and they had escaped only by the speed and strength of their horses, which Neal had brought from his own rancho. He said that in his opinion I could not reach Gillespie in time to save him, as he had with him only three men and was travelling slow.

A quick eye and a good horse mean life to a man in an Indian country. Neal had both. He was a lover of horses and knew a good one; and those he had with him were the best on his rancho. He had been sent forward by the messenger to let me know that he was in danger of being cut off by the Indians.

The trail back along the shore at the foot of the mountains was so nearly impassable at night that nothing could be gained by attempting it, but everything was made ready for an early start in the morning. For the relief party, in view of contingencies, I selected ten of the best men, including Carson, Stepp, Dick Owens, Godey, Basil, and Lajeunesse, with four of the Delawares.[17]

When the excitement of the evening was over I lay down, speculating far into the night on what could be the urgency of the message which had brought an officer of the Government to search so far after me into these mountains. At early dawn [9 May] we took the backward trail. Snow and fallen timber made the ride hard and long to where I thought to meet the messenger. On the way no Indians were seen and no tracks later than those where they had struck Neal's trail. In the afternoon, having made about forty-five miles, we reached the spot where the forest made an opening to the lake, and where I intended to wait. This was a glade or natural meadow, shut in by the forest, with a small stream and good grass, where I had already encamped. I knew that this was the first water to which my trail would bring the messenger, and that I was sure to meet him here if no harm befell him on the way. The sun was about going down when he was seen issuing from the wood, accompanied by three men.

He proved to be an officer of the navy, Lieutenant Archibald Gillespie of the Marine Corps. We greeted him warmly. All were glad to see him, whites and Indians. It was long since any news had reached us, and every one was as pleased to see him as if he had come freighted with letters from home, for all. It was now eleven months since any tidings had reached me.

Mr. Gillespie informed me that he had left Washington under orders from the President and the Secretary of the Navy, and was directed to reach California by the shortest route through Mexico to Mazatlan.

He was directed to find me wherever I might be, and was informed that I would probably be found on the Sacramento River. In pursuance of his instructions he had accordingly started from Monterey to look for me on the Sacramento. Learning upon his arrival at Sutter's Fort that I had gone up the valley, he made up a small party at Neal's rancho, and guided by him, followed my trail and had travelled six hundred miles to overtake me; the latter part of the way through great dangers.[18]

The mission on which I had been originally sent to the West was a peaceful one, and Mr. Bancroft had sent Mr. Gillespie to give me warning of the new state of affairs and the designs of the President. Mr. Gillespie had been given charge of despatches from the Secretary of the Navy to Commodore Sloat, and had been purposely made acquainted with their import.[19] Known to Mr. Bancroft as an able and thoroughly trustworthy officer, he had been well instructed in the designs of the Department and with the purposes of the Administration, so far as they related to California.

Through him I now became acquainted with the actual state of affairs and the purposes of the Government. The information through Gillespie had absolved me from my duty as an explorer, and I was left to my duty as an officer of the American Army with the further authoritative knowledge that the Government intended to take California. I was warned by my Government of the new danger against which I was bound to defend myself; and it had been made known to me now on the authority of the Secretary of the Navy that to obtain possession of California was the chief object of the President.

He brought me also a letter of introduction from the Secretary of State, Mr. Buchanan, and letters and papers from Senator Benton and family. The letter from the Secretary was directed to me in my private or citizen capacity, and though importing nothing beyond the introduction, it accredited the bearer to me as coming from the Secretary of State, and in connection with the circumstances and place of delivery it indicated a purpose in sending it. From the letter itself I learned nothing, but it was intelligibly explained to me by the accompanying letter from Senator Benton and by communications from Lieutenant Gillespie.

This officer informed me that he had been directed by the Secretary of State to acquaint me with his instructions, which had for their principal objects to ascertain the disposition of the California people, to conciliate their feelings in favor of the United States; and to find out, with a view to counteracting, the designs of the British Government upon that country.

The letter from Senator Benton, while apparently of friendship and family details, contained passages and suggestions which, read by the light of many conversations and discussions with himself and others at Washington, clearly indicated to me that I was required by the Government to find out any foreign schemes in relation to California and, so far as might be in my power, to counteract them.[20]

Neal had much to talk over with his old companions and pleasurable excitement kept us up late; but before eleven o'clock all were wrapped in their blankets and soundly asleep except myself. I sat by the fire in fancied security, going over again the home letters. These threw their own light upon the communication from Mr. Gillespie, and made the expected signal. In substance, their effect was: The time has come. England must not get a foothold. We must be first. Act; discreetly, but positively.

Looking back over the contingencies which had been foreseen in the discussions at Washington, I saw that the important one which carried with it the hopes of Senator Benton and the wishes of the Government was in the act of occurring, and it was with thorough satisfaction I now found myself required to do what I could to promote this object of the President. Viewed by the light of these deliberations in Washington, I was prepared to comprehend fully the communications brought to me by Mr. Gillespie.[21]

Now it was officially made known to me that my country was at war,[22] and it was so made known expressly to guide my conduct. I had learned with certainty from the Secretary of the Navy that the President's plan of war included the taking possession of California, and under his confidential instructions I had my warrant. Mr. Gillespie was directed to act in concert with me. Great vigilance and activity were expected of us both, for it was desired that possession should be had of California before the presence in her ports of any foreign vessel of war might make it inconvenient.

I had about thought out the situation when I was startled by a sudden movement among the animals. Lieutenant Gillespie had told me that there were no Indians on his trail, and I knew there were none on mine. This night was one of two when I failed to put men on guard in an Indian country—this night and one spent on an island in the Great Salt Lake. The animals were near the shore of the lake, barely a hundred yards away. Drawing a revolver I went down among them. A mule is a good sentinel, and when he quits eating and stands with his ears struck straight out taking notice, it is best to see what is the matter. The mules knew that Indians were around, but nothing seemed stirring, and my presence quicting the animals I returned to the fire and my letters.

I saw the way opening clear before me. War with Mexico was inevitable; and a grand opportunity now presented itself to realize in their fullest extent the far-sighted views of Senator Benton, and make the Pacific Ocean the western boundary of the United States. I resolved to move forward on the opportunity and return forthwith to the Sacramento valley in order to bring to bear all the influences I could command.

Except myself, then and for nine months afterward, there was no other officer of the army in California. The citizen party under my command was made up of picked men, and although small in number, constituted a formidable nucleus for frontier warfare, and many of its members commanded the confidence of the emigration.

This decision was the first step in the conquest of California.

My mind having settled into this conclusion, I went to my blankets under a cedar. The camp was divided into three fires, and near each one, but well out of the light, were sleeping the men belonging to it. Close by along the margin of the wood which shut us in on three sides were some low cedars, the ends of their boughs reaching nearly to the ground. Under these we made our beds.

One always likes to have his head sheltered, and a rifle with a ramrod or a branch or bush with a blanket thrown over it answers very well where there is nothing better. I had barely fallen to sleep when I was awakened by the sound of Carson's voice, calling to Basil to know "what the matter was over there?" No reply came, and immediately the camp was roused by the cry from Kit and Owens, who were lying together—"Indians." Basil and the half-breed, Denny, had been killed. It was the sound of the axe being driven into Basil's head that had awakened Carson. The half-breed had been killed with arrows, and his groans had replied to Carson's call, and told him what the matter was. No man, with an Indian experience, jumps squarely to his feet in a night attack, but in an instant every man was at himself. The Delawares who lay near their fire on that side sprung to cover, rifle in hand, at the sound of the axe. We ran to their aid, Carson and I, Godey, Stepp, and Owens, just as the Tlamaths charged into the open ground. The fires were smouldering, but gave light enough to show Delaware Crane jumping like a brave as he was from side to side in Indian fashion, and defending himself with the butt of his gun. By some mischance his rifle was not loaded when he lay down. All this was quick work. The moment's silence which followed Carson's shout was broken by our rifles. The Tlamath chief, who was at the head of his men, fell in front of Crane, who was just down with five arrows in his body —three in his breast. The Tlamaths, checked in their onset and disconcerted by the fall of their chief, jumped back into the shadow of the wood. We threw a blanket over Crane and hung blankets to the cedar boughs and bushes near by, behind my camp-fire, for a defence against the arrows. The Indians did not dare to put themselves again in the open, but continued to pour in their arrows. They made no attempt on our animals, which had been driven up by Owens to be under fire of the camp, but made frequent attempts to get the body of their chief. We were determined they should not have it, and every movement on their part brought a rifle-shot; a dozen rifles in such hands at short range made the undertaking too hazardous for them to persist in it. While both sides were watching each other from under cover, and every movement was followed by a rifle-shot or arrow, I heard Carson cry out: *"Look at the fool. Look at him, will you?"* This was to Godey, who had stepped out to the light of my fire to look at some little thing which had gone wrong with his gun; it was still bright enough to show him distinctly, standing there—a fair mark to the arrows—turning resentfully to Carson for the epithet bestowed on him, but in no wise hurrying himself. He was the most thoroughly insensible to danger of all the brave men I have known.

All night we lay behind our blanket defences, with our rifles cocked in our hands, expecting momentarily another attack, until the morning light enabled us to see that the Indians had disappeared. By their tracks we found that fifteen or twenty Tlamaths had attacked us. It was a sorrowful sight that met our eyes in the gray of the morning. Three of our men had been killed: Basil, Crane, and the half-breed Denny, and another Delaware had been wounded; one-fourth of our number. The chief who had been killed was recognized to be the same Indian who had given Lieutenant Gillespie a salmon at the outlet of the lake.[23] Hung to his wrist was an English half-axe. Carson seized this and knocked his head to pieces with it, and one of the Delawares, Sagundai, scalped him. He was left where he fell. In his quiver were forty arrows; as Carson said, "the most beautiful and warlike arrows he had ever seen." We saw more of them afterward. These arrows were all headed with a lancet-like piece of iron or steel—probably obtained from the Hudson Bay Company's traders on the Umpqua—and were poisoned for about six inches. They could be driven that depth into a pine tree.

This event cast an angry gloom over the little camp. For the moment I threw all other considerations aside and determined to square accounts with these people before I left them. It was only a few days back that some of these same Indians had come into our camp, and I divided with them what meat I had, and unpacked a mule to give them tobacco and knives.

On leaving the main party I had directed it to gear up as soon as the men had breakfasted and follow my trail to a place where we had encamped some days back. This would put them now about twenty-five miles from us. Packing our dead men on the mules, we started to rejoin the main camp, following the trail by which we had come. Before we had been two hours on the way many canoes appeared on the lake, coming from different directions and apparently making for a point where the trail came down to the shore. As we approached this point the prolonged cry of a loon told us that their scout was giving the Indians warning of our approach. Knowing that if we came to a fight the care of our dead men would prove a great hindrance and probably cost more lives, I turned sharply off into the mountain, and buried, or *cached* them in a close laurel thicket.

With our knives we dug a shallow grave, and wrapping their blankets round them, left them among the laurels. There are men above whom the laurels bloom who did not better deserve them than my brave Delaware and Basil. I left Denny's name on the creek where he died.

The Indians, thrown out by our sudden movement, failed in their intended ambush, and in the afternoon we found our people on the stream where we had encamped three days before. All were deeply grieved by the loss of our companions. The Delawares were filled with grief and rage by the death of Crane and went into mourning, blackening their faces. They were soothed somewhat when I told them that they should have an opportunity to get rid of their mourning and carry home scalps enough to satisfy the friends of Crane and the Delaware nation. With blackened faces, set and angry, they sat around brooding and waiting for revenge.

The camp was very quiet this evening, the men looking to their arms, rubbing and coaxing them. Towards evening I went over to the Delaware fire and sat down among them. They were sitting around their fire, smoking and silent. It did not need to speak; our faces told what we were all thinking about. After a pause I said, "Swonok bad luck come this time. Crane was a brave. Good man, too. I am very sorry." "Very sick here," he said, striking his hand against his breast; "these Delaware all sick." "There are Indians around the camp, Swonok," I replied. "Yes, I see him. Me and Sagundai and Charley gone out and see him in woods." "How many?" "Maybe ten, maybe twenty, maybe more." "Where did they go?" "Up mountain. He not long way." "Listen, Swonok, we kill some. These same men kill Crane. How best kill him?" The chief's eyes glittered and his face relaxed, and all the Delawares raised their heads. "You go in morning? Which way?" "Only three, four mile, to creek which you know over there," said I pointing up the lake; "next day, big Indian village." Swonok turned to Sagundai

James Sagundai. From a portrait in Frémont's *Memoirs*.

and the two chiefs spoke earnestly together for a few moments, the others deeply interested, but gravely listening without speaking. "Captain," said Sagundai, "in the morning you go little way, stop. These Delaware stay here. Indian come in camp, Delaware kill him."

In the morning, when we were ready to start, the Delawares rode out some moments ahead, halting after a few hundred yards until we came up; then, leaving their horses with us, they returned on foot and got into a thicket among some young pines near the camp ground. We continued our way and halted, no one dismounting, at a little run about a quarter of a mile distant. It was not long before the stillness was broken by a scattered volley, and after that, nothing. Shortly Swonok came up. "Better now," he said; "very sick before, better now." They had taken two scalps. The Tlamaths, as expected, had rushed into the camp ground, so soon as they thought it safe, and met the rifles of the Delawares. Two were killed and others wounded, but these were able to get away. Fortunately for them, the cracking of a dry branch startled the Tlamaths and the Delawares were too eager to shoot as well as usual. I moved on about three miles to a stream where the grass was good and encamped. Choosing an open spot among the pines we built a solid corral of pine logs and branches. It was six feet high and large enough to contain all our animals. At nightfall they were driven into it, and we took up our quarters outside, against the corral; the fires being at a little distance farther out and lighting up, while they lasted, the woods beyond. I obtained observations which put this camp in longitude 121° 58′ 45″ and latitude 42° 36′ 45″.

Continuing our route along the lake we passed around the extreme northwestern bay and after a hard day's march encamped in the midst of woods, where we built again a corral for the night. In the morning there were many canoes on the lake, and Indians had been about during the night, but the lesson they had learned served to keep them warily aloof in daylight. We were not very far from the principal village at the inlet which the Indians whom I had met when I first reached the lake had described to me; and the arms being all carefully examined and packs made secure, we started for it. When within a few miles I sent Carson and Owens ahead with ten men, directing them to reconnoitre the position of the Indians, but if possible to avoid engaging them until we could come up. But, as we neared the mouth of the river, the firing began. The party was dis-

Battle with Indians in Oregon in 1846. From an engraving in Frémont's *Memoirs*.

covered and had no choice but to open the fight, driving the Indians who were on this side to the other side of the river. As I rode up I saw a dead Indian sitting in the stern of a canoe, which the current had driven against the bank. His hand was still grasping the paddle. On his feet were shoes which I thought Basil wore when he was killed.[24] The stream was about sixty yards wide and a rapid just above the mouth made it fordable. Without drawing rein we plunged in and crossed to the farther side and joined our men who were pressed by a large body of Indians. They had abandoned their village and were scattered through a field of sage-brush, in front of the woods. But this time the night was not on their side and the attack was with us. Their arrows were good at close quarters, but the range of the rifle was better. The firing was too severe for them to stand it in open ground and they were driven back into the pine woods with a loss of fourteen killed. They had intended to make a hard fight. Behind the sage-bushes where they had taken their stand every Indian had spread his arrows on the ground in fan-like shape, so that they would be ready to his hand. But when our close fire drove them from the brush they were compelled to move so quickly that many did not have time to gather up their arrows and they lay on the ground, the bright, menacing points turned toward us. Quantities of fish were drying, spread on scaffolds, or hung up on frames. The huts, which were made of tall rushes and willow, like those on the savannah above, were set on fire, and the fish and scaffolds were all destroyed.

About a mile from the village I made my camp on a *clairière* in the midst of woods, and where were oaks intermingled with pines, and built a strong corral. Meantime I kept out scouts on every side and horses were kept ready saddled. In the afternoon Indians were reported advancing through the timber; and taking with me Carson, Sagundai, Swonok, Stepp, and Archambeau, I rode out to see what they were intending. Sacramento knew how to jump and liked it. Going through the wood at hand-gallop we came upon an oak tree which had been blown down; its summit covered quite a space, and being crowded by the others so that I was brought squarely in front of it, I let Sacramento go and he cleared the whole green mass in a beautiful leap. Looking back, Carson called out, "Captain, that horse will break your neck some day." It never happened to Sacramento to hurt his rider, but afterward, on the Salinas plain, he brought out from fight and back to his camp his rider who had been shot dead in the saddle.

In the heart of the wood we came suddenly upon an Indian scout. He was drawing his arrow to the head as we came upon him, and Carson attempted to fire, but his rifle snapped, and as he swerved away the Indian was about to let his arrow go into him; I fired, and in my haste to save Carson, failed to kill the Indian, but Sacramento, as I have said, was not afraid of anything, and I jumped him directly upon the Indian and threw him to the ground. His arrow went wild. Sagundai was right behind me, and as I passed over the Indian he threw himself from his horse and killed him with a blow on the head from his war-club. It was the work of a moment, but it was a narrow chance for Carson. The poisoned arrow would have gone through his body.

Giving Sacramento into the care of Jacob, I went into the lodge and laid down on my blankets to rest from the excitement of which the day had been so full. I had now kept the promise I made to myself and had punished these people well for their treachery; and now I turned my thoughts to the work which they had delayed. I was lost in conjectures over this new field when Gillespie came in, all roused into emotion. "By heaven, this is rough work," he exclaimed. "I'll take care to let them know in Washington about it." "Heaven don't come in for much about here, just now," I said; "and as for Washington, it will be long enough before we see it again; time enough to forget about this."

He had been introduced into an unfamiliar life in joining me and had been surprised into continued excitements by the strange scenes which were going on around him. My surroundings were very much unlike the narrow space and placid uniformity of a man-of-war's deck, and to him the country seemed alive with unexpected occurrences. Though himself was not, his ideas were, very much at sea. He was full of admiration for my men and their singular fitness for the life they were leading. He shared my lodge, but this night his excitement would not let him sleep, and we remained long awake; talking over the incidents of the day and speculating over what was to come in the events that seemed near at hand. Nor was there much sleeping in the camp that night, but nothing disturbed its quiet. No attack was made.

The night was clear and I obtained observations here which gave what may be assumed for the longitude of the outlet 121° 52′ 08″, and for its latitude 42° 41′ 30″. To this river [Williamson] I gave the name of my friend, Professor Torrey, who, with all the enthusiasm that goes with a true love of science, had aided me in determining the botany of the country.

The next day we moved late out of camp and travelled to the southward along the lake. I kept the ground well covered with scouts, knowing the daring character of the Tlamaths. We made a short day's march and encamped in woods and built a corral. On the following day we continued the march, still in the neighborhood of the lake, and in the evening made camp at its southeastern end, on a creek to which I gave the name of one of the Delawares, We-to-wah. Indians were seen frequently during the day. Observations placed the mouth of this creek in longitude 121° 41′ 23″, latitude 42° 21′ 23″. As had become usual we made a corral to secure the safety of the animals. This was our last camp on the lake. Here I turned away from our comrades whom I had left among the pines. But they were not neglected. When the Tlamaths tell the story of the night attack where they were killed, there will be no boasting. They will have to tell also of the death of their chief and of our swift retaliation; and how the people at the fishery had to mourn for the loss of their men and the destruction of their village. It will be a story for them to hand down while there are any Tlamaths on their lake.[25]

The pines in these forests were mostly full-grown trees, and for many a year our log forts around the lake will endure, and other travellers may find refuge in them, or wonder, in the present quiet, what had once broken the silence of the forest. Making open spots in the woods where the sunshine can rest longest, the trees that encircle them will be fuller-headed and grass and flowers will be more luxuriant in the protection of their enclosure, so that they may long remain marked places.

The next day brought no unusual incident. On the day following I was travelling along a well-worn trail when I came upon a fresh scalp on an arrow which had been stuck up in the path. Maxwell and Archambeau were ahead, and in the evening they reported that riding along the trail they met an Indian who, on seeing them, laid down a bunch of young crows which he had in his hand, and forthwith and without parley let fly an arrow at Maxwell, who was foremost. He threw himself from his horse just in time to escape the arrow, which passed over the seat of his saddle, and, after a brief interchange of rifle-balls and arrows, the Indian was killed and his scalp put up in the trail to tell the story. We were getting roughened into Indian customs.

Our route was now among the hills over ground where we had already just travelled in going north and bordering the valley of the upper Sacramento, which, as I have said, was known to trappers under the name of Pitt River. The spring now gave its attraction and freshness to the whole region. The rolling surface of the hills was green up to the timbered ridges of the Cascade range which we were skirting along; but, above, the unconquerable peaks still were clothed with snow, and glittered cool in their solitary heights.

Chapter XIV.

. . . .

On one of these days, being hurried forward by rifle-shots ahead, we found Owens, with Stepp and Jacob, engaged with a party of Indians who had attacked them with as little ceremony as the Indian who had taken Maxwell for a mark. One of them was left behind when the others took to the thicker timber. These Indians deserve their reputation for daring, but their bravery is imprudent and un-calculating. Like tigers, their first spring is the dangerous one.

We were skirting still the wooded foot-hills of the great mountains, and, journeying along, had reached the head of a rocky, wooded ravine, down which a trail that we had been following led into a cañon. I was passing along its edge when a strong party of Indians suddenly issued from among the rocks and timber, and commenced an attack. They were promptly driven into cover of the wood and down the ravine into the brush, with a number wounded. One brave refused to be dislodged from behind a rock in the brush on the side of the ravine, from which he kept up a dangerous flight of arrows. He had spread his arrows on the ground and held some in his mouth, and drove back the men out of range for some moments, until Carson crept around to where he could get a good view of him and shot him through the heart. Carson gave the bow and arrows to Mr. Gillespie. The Indians had seemed bent on speeding their parting guest, but this was the last encounter we had with them.

Their ambush had been well laid. They had thought we would certainly follow the trail into the cañon, where, between their arrows and the rocks which they would have hurled down upon us, we would have had a *mauvais quart d'heure* [bad time of it] and lost men as well as animals. But in a bad country I usually kept clear of such places, and in all this journey, except on the night at Denny's Creek, committed but one imprudence, which was in passing along the shore of the lake where a high, naked ridge, its face so literally strewed over with jagged fragments of rock as to be absolutely inaccessible from below, skirted the water for a number of miles. The Indians could have rained arrows and rock down upon us, and we could neither have got at them without great loss, nor got our animals out of the way. I breathed more freely when I was at the end of this pass, and felt mortified that I needed a lesson.

We were now approaching the rougher country into which breaks the point of the last link of the Sierra Nevada, and at nightfall encamped on its waters. We crossed the mountain upon a different line, nearer to the head of the lower Sacramento valley, and, descending, entered into a truly magnificent forest. It was composed mainly of a cypress and a lofty white cedar (*Thuya gigantea*) one hundred and twenty to one hundred and forty feet high, common in the mountains of California. All were massive trees, but the cypress was distinguished by its uniformly great bulk.[26] None were seen so large as are to be found in the coast mountains near Santa Cruz, but there was a greater number of large trees—seven feet being a common diameter—carrying the bulk eighty or a hundred feet without a limb.

At an elevation of four thousand six hundred feet the temperature at sunset was 48° and at sunrise 37°. Oaks already appeared among the pines, but did not show a leaf. In the meadow-marshes of the forest grass was green, but not yet abundant, and the deer were poor. Descending the flanks of the mountain, which fell gradually toward the plain, the way was through the same deep forest. At the elevation of about three thousand feet the timber had become more open, the hills rolling, and many streams made pretty bottoms of rich grass; the black oaks in full and beautiful leaf were thickly studded among the open pines, which had become much smaller and fewer in variety, and when we halted near midday, at an elevation of two thousand two hundred feet, we were in one of the most pleasant days of early spring, cool and sunny, with a pleasant breeze, amidst a profusion of flowers; many trees in dark summer foliage, and some still in bloom. Among these the white spikes of the horse-chestnut, common through all the oak regions, were conspicuous. We had again reached summer weather, and the temperature at noon was 70°. The plants we had left in bloom were now generally in seed, and many, including the characteristic plants, perfectly ripe.

In the afternoon we descended to the open valley of the Sacramento, one thousand feet lower, where the thermometer was 68° at sunset and 54° at sunrise. This was the best timbered region that I had seen, and was the more valuable from its position near the head of the valley of the lower Sacramento, and accessible from its waters.

On the 24th of May we reached again Lassen's, and in the evening I wrote to Senator Benton; a guarded letter,[27] chiefly to call the attention of Mr. Buchanan to the Indians among whom I had been travelling, especially to the fact that they were unfriendly to us but friendly to the English, by whom they were supplied with arms from a Hudson Bay's post[28] on the Umpqua conveniently near to the coast. In the vague condition of affairs until the arrival of Commodore Sloat, my own movements depended upon circumstances and of them I could say but little.

MEMOIRS, 470–99.

1. JCF's log fort atop one of the peaks in the Gabilan Range was probably not on the one now called Fremont Peak but on one two miles distant, known as Hill 2146. It is at the head of Steinbach Canyon and outside of Frémont State Park, which was created in 1934 (GUDDE, 114, citing Fred B. Rogers). After remaining on the peak three days, the pole bearing the American flag fell to the ground, and using this as an indication to his men that it was time for them to take up their scientific duties again and be on their way, JCF proceeded inland to the valley of the San Joaquin. He rationalized that he had given Castro sufficient time to execute his threat of driving them out. "Besides," he wrote, "I kept always in mind the object of the Government to obtain possession of California and would not let a proceeding which was mostly personal put obstacles in the way" (MEMOIRS, 460). Gen. José Castro claimed a victory (Doc. No. 21), but he made no effort to attack or follow JCF. In fact, Archibald Gillespie reported to the Secretary of the Navy that Castro had boasted to Henry Mellus that he had not intended to attack JCF but had used the circumstances to suit his purposes and to insure his position in Mexico City (18 April 1846, AMES [1], 135–40). Talbot expressed a similar view of the Mexican general's personal motives when he wrote his mother that Castro really wanted to use the incident to oust Pío Pico as governor (24 July 1846, DLC—Talbot Papers). For some time Larkin was unaware of JCF's movements and wrote the Secretary of State that it was generally supposed he had gone to Santa Barbara, where an American vessel had been sent in February by the consul with funds and provisions for the explorer (2 April 1846, LARKIN, 4:275–77).

2. Eliab Grimes (d. 1848), a native of Massachusetts, was a well-known

Honolulu merchant when he selected this rancho in the Sacramento Valley in 1842. The grant was confirmed in 1844, but Grimes preferred to spend most of his time in San Francisco.

3. While JCF was examining the lower Sacramento Valley, Talbot was sent to San Francisco to buy supplies (Talbot to Adelaide Talbot, 24 July 1846, DLC—Talbot Papers; NEW HELVETIA DIARY, 24 March and 9 April 1846).

4. An old friend of John Sutter and a native of the Austrian Tyrol, Sebastian Keyser was half-owner of the William Johnson rancho on Bear River.

5. Peter Lassen (1800–1859) was a Dane—not a German—who had learned blacksmithing before he arrived in Boston in 1831. He soon moved to St. Louis, went overland to Oregon in 1839, and later to California on the *Lausanne*. By the end of 1844 he was a naturalized Mexican and the grantee of this rather isolated northern rancho near Deer Creek. After JCF's visit he laid out the village of Benton City and tried unsuccessfully to attract immigrants to the area (SWARTZLOW).

6. JCF had stayed at Lassen's six days, 30 March to 5 April 1846. As he will note later, he returned to Lassen's again on 11 April and remained until 24 April. It was during these stays at Lassen's that he reputedly purchased stolen horses from the Indians, angering Sutter (Sutter to José Castro, 13? May 1846, CAL. HIS. SOC. DOCS., 6:82–83). Kit Carson notes that during their stay at Lassen's (he fails to note that there were two visits) "some Americans that were settled in the neighborhood came in stating that there were about 1000 Indians in the vicinity making preparations to attack the settlements; requested assistance of Frémont to drive them back. He and party and some few Americans that lived near started for the Indian encampment. Found them to be in great force, as was stated. They were attacked. The number killed I cannot say. It was a perfect butchery. Those not killed fled in all directions, and we returned to Lawson's" (CARSON, 101). Another of JCF's men affirms that an attack was made on the Indians in April (Thomas S. Martin's dictated narrative, 1878, pp. 13–14, CU-B), and Henry L. Ford said that he organized one of the companies (ROGERS [1], 29:135).

The *Memoirs* do not mention this Indian slaughter *before* the trip to Oregon, and Thomas E. Breckenridge remembers it as having occurred *after* the return from Oregon and as having been done by the settlers with the assistance of about half of JCF's men. They had to slip "away from camp quietly one by one" because JCF refused to go on a raid against the Indians, but he did promise aid if the settlers were attacked. Although Breckenridge did not participate, he learned of some of the details and much later wrote, "By noon the settlers were ready to march against an Indian village twelve miles away and consisting of about 150 bucks and about 250 squaws and children. They arrived at the village late in the afternoon and found the Indians engaged in a war dance. I think that the fact of finding the village engaged in a war dance made the settlers worse for the order was to ask no quarter and to give none. The settlers charged into the village taking the warriors by surprise and then commenced a scene of slaughter which is unequalled in the West. . . . There was from 120 to 150 Indians killed that day" ("Recollections of Thomas E. Breckenridge," p. 56, MoU). That the Indians of northern California were restless in the spring of 1846 is exemplified by their burning a house on Pierson B. Reading's Rancho Buenaventura (ABELOE, 485). And, curiously, an 1856 biography of JCF contains a picture of the charge upon the Indians at "Redding's" rancho (UPHAM, facing p. 232).

124

Both in the MEMOIRS, 502–3, 516–17, and in his description of his California expedition, JCF takes responsibility for chastising the Indians *after* the return from Oregon but notes extreme provocation—in fact, he alleges protection of the settlers against impending attack. "I then descended into the Sacramento valley where I found the American settlers in excitement & alarm. I learned that General Castro had caused a general rising of the Indians, with the avowed object of destroying the crops & farms of the Americans & extirpating them from the country. The settlers came to me & requested my protection & assistance which I undertook to give them. Being joined by about 20 of them I proceeded to the head of the lower Sacramento valley, where four or five hundred Indians had gathered together and anticipating them in the very act of their descent on the settlements I attacked & defeated & entirely dispersed them" (JCF's description of his California expedition, 27 June [1855], KyLoF—James Guthrie Papers).

If there was a full-scale attack by JCF's men upon the Indians of California in the spring of 1846, which is not too clear, it was made before the trip to Oregon. There is little corroborating evidence that JCF participated in a June war against the Indians. It is possible that some of his men went along on Sutter's and Pierson B. Reading's not too successful expedition against the Indians of the Mokelumne between 3 and 7 June 1846 (NEW HELVETIA DIARY, 41; DILLON, 240).

7. Not the present Mount Linn in Tehama County but another high peak to the west.

8. Mount Shasta towers 14,162 feet above sea level in northern California; at 15,781 feet, Mont Blanc in France is the highest mountain in the Alps.

9. The JCF-Preuss map of 1848 shows that JCF ascended the Sacramento as far as a stream which he called the Nozah River, presently known as Battle Creek. It is south of Redding.

10. Robert Barnwell Rhett (1800–1876), formerly Robert Barnwell Smith, began a legal career in his home town of Beaufort. In 1832 he was elected attorney general of South Carolina and in 1837 was sent to Congress, where he served for more than a decade. It was he who in Aug. 1848 made the presentation to JCF of an ornamented sword and belt—gifts from the citizens of Charleston to a son who had done honor to South Carolina and the nation.

11. E. R. S. Canby was shot down on 11 April 1873 while attempting to arrange a truce with the Modocs, whom he had been sent to subdue. In 1925 the Lava Beds National Monument was established in northeastern Siskiyou County on the boundary of Modoc County. See HEYMAN for a biography of Canby and MURRAY for an account of the war.

12. The first official Hudson's Bay Company trapping party to enter Alta California was led by Peter Skene Ogden, who trekked through the northeastern corner during his 1826–27 Snake country expedition. In 1829 Alexander R. McLeod had taken a brigade as far south as present-day Stockton, and in 1829–30 Ogden, who had journeyed down the east face of the Sierra Nevada, came back through the central valley of California, taking a thousand pelts in the San Joaquin basin and exploring the Sacramento from San Francisco Bay to its headwaters. The year 1832 saw yet two more penetrations by the Hudson's Bay Company. Michel Laframboise took a route up the Rogue River to its confluence with the Applegate. Proceeding to Upper Klamath Lake, he then turned southward to the Pit River and from there into the Sacramento Valley. Near the Marysville or Sutter Buttes he was joined by the second expedition, under the command of John Work. The

parties combined to forage for furs in and around San Francisco Bay, but in May 1833, near Fort Ross on Bodega Bay, they again separated and took different routes home to Fort Vancouver. In his journal Work frequently comments on the troublesomeness of the Indians and their theft of expedition horses and traps. The Indian menace did not deter the Hudson's Bay Company from sending out an occasional land expedition to hunt furs in California. For journals of the early expeditions, see OGDEN and WORK; for a biographical sketch of Laframboise, see NUNIS [1].

13. JCF may be referring to the attack on Jedediah S. Smith and his party of trappers in 1828 by Indians of the Umpqua River region. Fifteen men were killed, but Smith and three others escaped.

14. It was noted on p. 125, n. 12, that for some time the Hudson's Bay Company had been sending its fur brigades into southern Oregon and northern California. The 1834 Arrowsmith map of British North America might be called an Ogden map, since it represented Peter Skene Ogden's knowledge of the West. Chief factor John McLoughlin at Fort Vancouver had relayed Ogden's sketches to company offices in England, which in turn had sent them to the heirs of Aaron Arrowsmith. The 1838 map of Capt. Washington Hood was drawn to illustrate the report of Senator Lewis F. Linn on a bill to authorize the U.S. president to occupy the Oregon territory. The map was said to have been prepared "with much care and labor" under the direction of J. J. Abert, the chief of the Bureau of Topographical Engineers. In reality it was almost an exact copy of the 1834 Arrowsmith map. JCF undoubtedly had access to the Hood map as well as to information on Oregon and California which the Charles Wilkes expedition had acquired in 1841. In fact, JCF's 1843–44 survey had made several contributions to the Wilkes maps of Oregon and California, which were not published until 1844 and 1845. On JCF's own 1845 map the Willamette and upper Sacramento valleys and the coastal regions of Oregon and California are blank. The Wilkes map of Oregon Territory was good for the main Oregon region and indicates that Wilkes had access to Jedediah Smith's 1831 map of the West, and perhaps even to one that Smith may have drawn while wintering at Fort Vancouver between Dec. 1828 and March 1829. JCF is correct in maintaining, however, that the region had never been thoroughly explored or mapped. For a discussion of the various maps mentioned here, see C. I. WHEAT, 2:119–39, 146–48, 177–78.

15. According to his wife, Archibald H. Gillespie (1813–73), a Marine and former officer on the *Brandywine,* was selected as confidential agent because he had an excellent command of Spanish. After interviews with President Polk and Secretaries of the Navy and State, Gillespie left New York in November, crossed Mexico in civilian garb, and journeyed from Mazatlán to Monterey via Honolulu in the sloop of war *Cyane.* On 17 April he was in Monterey harbor and in contact with the American consul, Thomas Oliver Larkin, and on the next day delivered to him the Secretary of State's 17 Oct. 1845 dispatch. He had committed it to memory and destroyed it before reaching Vera Cruz, but he now wrote it out again. By this dispatch Larkin was appointed a "Confidential Agent in California" and was instructed to "exert the greatest vigilance in discovering and defeating any attempts which may be made by Foreign Government to acquire a control" over California (James Buchanan to Larkin, 17 Oct. 1845, LARKIN, 4:44–47). Buchanan wrote that if the Californians wished to unite "their destiny" with the United States, "they would be received as brethren." "Their true policy, for the

present, in regard to this question, is to let events take their course," unless an attempt should be made to transfer them to Great Britain or France. Receipt in Washington of disturbing news of British activities in the Northwest and Mexico was allegedly responsible for Gillespie's mission and the new duties for Larkin. From Monterey, Gillespie went on to Yerba Buena (24 April) and was at Sutter's Fort on 28 April seeking JCF. For a biography of Gillespie, see MARTI.

16. The letters which Gillespie had for JCF were family letters. Although Benton's letter (see JCF's reference to it in Doc. No. 28) seems to have led him to expect an important communique from Buchanan, there was only a message from the Secretary of State introducing Gillespie, which read:

WASHINGTON, November 3, 1845

My Dear Sir: The bearer hereof, Mr. Archibald H. Gillespie, is about to visit the northwest coast of America on business, and has requested me to give him a letter of introduction to you. This I do with pleasure, because he is a gentleman of worth and respectability, and is worthy of your regard. I do not deem it probable that he will fall in with you; but, if he should, allow me to bespeak for him your friendly attention. He will be able to communicate to you information on the health of Mrs. Fremont and Col. Benton and his family. From your friend, very respectfully,

JAMES BUCHANAN

The letter was printed in the *National Intelligencer,* 12 April 1848, as a part of Benton's speech on the California Claims, delivered in the Senate on 10 April 1848.

17. There is a misplaced comma separating Basil and Lajeunesse. The name was Basil Lajeunesse. Stepp was not with JCF but with Gillespie's small party of six, which was trying to overtake JCF.

18. Gillespie arrived at Lassen's on 1 May to find that JCF had left eight days earlier. The five men who accompanied him in search of the explorer were Lassen, Stepp, Neal, Sigler, and Gillespie's Negro servant Ben Harrison (Gillespie to Larkin, 24 May 1846, LARKIN, 4:393–94).

19. Navy Department dispatches dated 24 June and 17 Oct. 1845 had instructed Sloat to seize California in the event of actual hostilities between the United States and Mexico (DNA-45, Confidential LS). In letters of 19 Nov. 1845 and 17 March 1846 Sloat acknowledged receipt of the 24 June instructions and a copy of the 17 Oct. dispatch to Larkin, the original of which Stockton was carrying out on the *Congress.* Since Gillespie felt it necessary to memorize and destroy his copy of the Larkin dispatch before journeying across Mexico, it is doubtful that he retained any written message when he reached Sloat at Mazatlán in February, but he may have written it out from memory for Sloat as he did later for Larkin. Sloat wrote Bancroft, "Lieut. Gillespie reached here some days since and was immediately sent forward to his destination [Monterey via Oahu] agreeable to the verbal orders delivered me from his Excellency the President of the U. States and the Honl. Secretary of the Navy." He also added, "The Squadron is in fine order and ready for any service" (25 Feb. 1846, DNA-45, LR, Commanding Officers of Squadrons, Pacific, 1846–47).

20. For a discussion of Benton's enigmatic letter and JCF's instructions or lack of instructions from the government, see the introduction, pp. xxviii–xxxii.

21. Thirty years earlier in the description of his California expedition,

JCF stated even more succinctly his comprehension of the communications brought by Gillespie. See the introduction, p. xxxi. But see also his 25 July 1846 letter to Benton (Doc. No. 52), in which he implies that his return to the Sacramento Valley was a voluntary one, i.e., that he was not being recalled by Gillespie, and that his participation in the Bear Flag movement was of his own responsibility.

22. Not true. Hostilities had actually begun on the Texas-Mexico border, but Gillespie brought only the news that war seemed imminent.

23. Stern believes the attack on the JCF party was made by the Klamath Indians of the Iuhlalonkini division rather than the Hot Creek Modocs, to whom Lindsay Applegate, the first agent on the Klamath Reservation, had assigned responsibility for the deed (STERN, 235–37).

24. These were perhaps not Basil Lajeunesse's shoes, if STERN, 236–37, is correct in believing that JCF's reprisal fell not upon his attackers but upon Klamaths of the Eukskni division.

25. The swiftness of JCF's reprisal did not break the spirit of the Klamaths. Rather, it left a legacy of bitterness and was undoubtedly a factor in drawing them into the hostile camp in the Molalla War, soon to follow.

26. Present-day botanists are unable to identify this cypress.

27. See Doc. No. 28.

28. Fort Umpqua, a Hudson's Bay Company post in Douglas County, Ore.

23. Charles William Flügge to Frémont

MONTEREY March 26th 1846

J C Fremont Esqre
U S Army
SIR

Returned on this coast from the Sandwich Islands, I have been informed of your visit to California which gives me an opportunity of writing to you, and of reminding you of your business transaction with me when last we saw each other on the Sacremento. I at that time had no idea that I in vain should have to wait two years, without seeing fulfilled a promise given, and made by you to me, that is: to remit the amount of $1291.93 cts in specie, immediately to this coast, as amount of your draft, for that amount on Colonel J. J. Albert [Abert] Cheif of the Topografical at Washington City D.C. The offer was made by you spontaniously at the time when you thought it to be derogatory to the Credit of the U.S. and when you felt much offended at my chargeing a discount on Bills drawn by you on the Government. Even to my letters adressed to you, and Colonel J. J. Albert which I sent by way of Mazatlan and Mexico, I have not received the shortest answer. Under these circumstances I have seen proper to consult T. O. Larkin Esqr U.S. Consul at this place, and have requested the favour of his acting for me in this affair. According to this Gentlemans views on the subject I am entitled to add interest of 1 per cent a month from the time the money might have been received here and add to the discount usual on this Coast, in case I should be obliged to wait longer for the money. In such case I should request the favour of your delivering into the hands of the said T. O. Larkin Esq, a regular set of Bills of exchange in my favour lawfully drawn, and for such sum as would be produced by adding to the princapal a/c $1291.93 cts. The interest at 1 per cent per month, and the discount on your draft for $237.25 I have been obliged to loose $30. A long serious illness which brought me near the grave, and later compelled me to seek medical aid in another part of the world, has made me feel the want of this money greatly, but now live in hopes you will bring the matter to a final close. It would be very difficult to dispose of your drafts, if not drawn in the above mentioned manner, and I therefore request the favour of your according to my wish. I Remain Sir With much respect Your Obedient Servent,

(Signed) C. W. FLUGGE

[*Cover bears note:*] The original sent this day to Capt. Fremont. June 1st 1846.

Printed in LARKIN, 4:265–66. A German emigrant to California in 1841, Charles William Flügge (d. 1852) had a rancho on the Feather River and a store in Los Angeles. He had furnished supplies to JCF on his visit to California in the spring of 1844. JCF had given him a voucher for $237.25 (see Vol. 1, Doc. No. 95, item 109), but the voucher for the "business transaction" involving $1,291.93 has not been found, although it was drawn on the chief of the Topographical Bureau and therefore must have been a legitimate expedition expenditure.

24. Frémont to Jessie B. Frémont

SACRAMENTO RIVER, (lat. 40°)
April 1, 1846

It is hard to say when I shall see you, but about the middle of the next month, at latest, I will start for home. The Spaniards were somewhat rude and inhospitable below, and ordered us out of the country, after having given me permission to winter there. My sense of duty did not permit me to fight them, but we retired slowly and growlingly before a force of three or four hundred men, and three pieces of artillery. Without a shadow of a cause, the governor suddenly raised the whole country against me, issuing a false and scandalous proclamation. Of course I did not dare to compromise the United States, against which appearances would have been strong; but, though it was in my power to increase my party by many Americans,[1] I refrained from committing a solitary act of hostility or impropriety. For my own part, I have become disgusted with everything belonging to the Mexicans. Our government will not require me to return by the southern route against the will of this government; I shall therefore return by the heads of the Missouri, going through a pass of which your father knows, and be at Westport about 1st September. I go in about two weeks through from the Tlamath lake to the Walamath valley, to make a reconnaissance of the pass which I mentioned to you before. Say many kind things for me to all the family. Glad will I be when finally we turn our faces homeward.

Printed in *Niles' National Register*, 71 (21 Nov. 1846):190. It is obviously an extract. An even shorter extract was given to President Polk in Benton's letter of 9 Nov. 1846, which was printed in the *National Intelligencer*, 11 Nov. 1846. The letter was written from Lassen's, sixty miles above New Helvetia. On the previous day, 31 March, JCF had written Larkin applying for funds; Larkin forwarded them in gold by a courier who seems to have been Samuel Neal (NEW HELVETIA DIARY, 4 and 14 April 1846). While the letter has not been found, it apparently gave no news about the explorer's journey from the Monterey vicinity. However, Larkin understood from the courier that JCF had not seen a single Californian during his journey from the Gabilan (Larkin to Buchanan, 17 April 1846, LARKIN, 4:288–90).

1. Larkin wrote the Secretary of State that JCF "received verbal applications from English and Americans to join his party and could have mustered as many men as the natives. He was careful not to do so, and although he discharged five or six of his men, he took no others in their place" (2 April 1846, LARKIN, 4:275–77).

25. Frémont to James Clyman

[April? 1846]

To James Clyman, Esq.
at Yount's Mills, California
DEAR SIR:

Your favor of the 21st ultimo[1] has been received through the kindness of Mr. Flint, some time since, but as the subject matter is one of the gravest importance I have taken time to consider before venturing upon a definite reply. I am placed in a peculiar position. Having carried out to the best of my ability, my instructions to explore the far west, I see myself on the eve of my departure for home, confronted by the most perplexing complications. I have received information to the effect that a declaration of war between our Government and Mexico is probable,[2] but so far this news has not been confirmed. The California authorities object to my presence here and threaten to overwhelm me. If peace is preserved I have no right or business here; if war ensues I shall be out numbered ten to one and be compelled to make good my retreat pressed by a pursuing enemy. It seems that the only way open to me is to make my way back eastward, and as a military man you must perceive at once that an increase of my command would only encumber and not assist my retreat through a region where wild game is the only thing procurable in the way of food. Under these circumstances I must make my way back alone and gratefully decline your offer of a company of hardy warriors And remain Yours Respectfully,

JOHN C. FREMONT

Camp on Feather River [?]
December 19th 1845. [!][3]

Printed in CLYMAN, 193, from Ivan Petroff's "Abstract of Clyman's Note-Book," p. 26 (CU-B). James Clyman (1792–1881), born in the foothills of the Blue Ridge Mountains of Virginia, had a varied and adventurous career as surveyor, Rocky Mountain trapper, and pioneer in Illinois and Wisconsin. He emigrated to Oregon in 1844 and the next year from Oregon to California as a leader of the McMahon-Clyman party. At the time of the writing of this letter, Clyman was preparing to return east again. He would come back to California in 1848 as guide to a company of emigrants, marry in 1849, and settle down to farm life. In 1846 Clyman's camp was eighteen miles from the flour and saw mills which George C. Yount had built on his princely grant in the heart of the Napa Valley near present-day Yountsville.

1. Charles Camp, the editor of Clyman's reminiscences and diaries, thinks Clyman wrote his letter to JCF on 21 Jan. 1846. He had seen Isaac Flint on that day, and JCF mentions that Flint had brought the letter to him. It is most likely that JCF wrote in April, his "21st ultimo" meaning 21 March, the date on which Clyman wrote in his diary of JCF's troubles at the Mission San Juan, although JCF could not have sent a letter from Lassen's to Yount's Mills by 31 March—the date on which Clyman was there—unless Clyman had been expected to linger longer at his camp in the Napa Valley. Clyman's offer seems to have been a genuine one to return to the States with JCF and not a scheme for a movement against the Californians (CLYMAN, 192–94, 198–203). Isaac F. Flint, from Wisconsin, had come to California in 1845. In the PIONEER REGISTER Bancroft speculates that he returned east with Clyman in the spring of 1846, but Camp does not identify him as a member of the eastbound party (CLYMAN, 235).

2. It is difficult to explain this statement of JCF's, for Gillespie did not reach him in Oregon until 9 May. It may be that rumors of war had been gleaned from newspapers sent by Larkin (see Doc. Nos. 15 and 30, 8 March and 31 May 1846). If these newspapers did not reach him at San Juan before 10 March, perhaps he saw them a few days later at New Helvetia.

3. The date appearing on Ivan Petroff's copy of JCF's letter to Clyman is obviously wrong; possibly even the place is incorrect, although probably not. JCF probably wrote the letter from his camp at Lassen's either between 30 March and 5 April or between 11 and 24 April, the dates of his two visits to Lassen's. Although addressed to Clyman at Yount's Mills, the letter may actually have been carried to Clyman's camp on Bear River, a small stream running into Feather River. Clyman was there from 16 to 23 April, completing his preparations for the homeward journey and waiting for additions to his party. He may also have waited for JCF's answer there. On 23 April he began ascending the mountains on his way east; on 24 April JCF left Lassen's for Oregon.

26. Frémont to William A. Leidesdorff

LASSEN'S FARM, SACRAMENTO RIVER;
April 23. 1846

DEAR SIR,

Enclosed you find a draft for the amount of your bill and expenditures made in my favor. I shall start for the States in a few days and therefore will not have the satisfaction of a reply to my late letters to you,[1] as I am informed that you have left for Monterey.

I trust that on your return, or thereabouts, you will write me a line at Washington, and give me the current news. Repeating my thanks for your kindness, which I hope for an occasion to reciprocate, I am, Very truly yours,

J. C. Frémont

ALS, RC (CU-B).

1. JCF left for Oregon the next day; his letters to Leidesdorff have not been found.

The Bear Flag Revolt
and the Conquest of California

27. Frémont to Thomas Oliver Larkin

MY DEAR SIR

Not being able to detain a present opportunity to write to you, I will beg you only to forward the enclosed through some of our friends in Mazatlan, so that it may *not be interrupted*. Please see to this for me. I will write you soon more at length and acknowledge all favors. Yours truly,

J. C. FREMONT

Thom. O Larkin Esq
Consul for the United States at Monterey

Printed in LARKIN, 4:390. The enclosure was JCF's letter to Benton, 24 May 1846, Doc. No. 28.

28. Frémont to Thomas H. Benton

SACRAMENTO RIVER, (Lat. 40°)
May 24, 1846

MY DEAR SIR:

Most unexpectedly, and in a remote region of the northern mountains, I had the great pleasure to receive your letters. An express from Mr. Gillespie overtook me, the man being Neal, whom you will remember as having been left by me here in the last expedition. No other man here would have had the courage and resolution to follow us. I had the good fortune to save the lives of Mr. Gillespie and party from the Indians. In a charge at night by the Tlamath Indians I lost three men killed and had one dangerously wounded, being then with a detached party of fourteen men. You will regret to hear that among the killed was my old companion, Basil Lajeunesse. We afterwards fought the nation from one extremity to the other, and have ever since been fighting, until our entrance into the Lower Sacramento valley. I have but a faint hope that this note will reach you before I do; but the object for which I write is a pressing one and therefore I make the experiment.

The Tlamath lake on our last map I find to be only an expansion of the river above, which passes by an outlet through a small range of mountains into a large body of water to the southward. This is the true Tlamath lake, and the heart of the Tlamath nation. It is on the east side of a range of mountains, (the Cascade.) Directly west, and comparatively near at hand, is the Umpqua river. *Here the British have a post.* Why do they keep it there? The trade in fur will not justify it. If there is to be any war with England, it is of great importance that they should instantly be driven from this and similar posts before they furnish the Indians with fire arms, and engage them in their service. These Indians are considered by the Willamette missionaries (who have been able to have only a slight knowledge of those in the north) as the most savage and warlike Indians on the continent. So said Mr. Lee. This post maintains an intercourse with the Tlamaths and other mountain Indians, and furnishes them with the tomahawks and iron arrow-heads, with which they fought us. They are the bravest Indians we have ever seen; our people (my camp, Carson, &c.) consider them far beyond the Blackfeet, who are by no means so daring. You know that the Indians along the line of the Columbia are well supplied with fire arms, ammunition, and horses—hardly a man having less than forty or fifty of the latter; that they are brave, friendly to the British, and unfriendly to us. These things may be worthy of Mr. Buchanan's attention. Your letter led me to expect some communication from him, but I *received nothing.* I shall now proceed directly homewards, by the Colorado, but cannot arrive at the frontier until late in September.[1] I saw a notice of your illness in the papers, and your letter relieved me of much anxiety. I trust that I will be able to force my way through this rough voyage, and find all well on the frontier. We certainly commenced our voyage when some malicious and inauspicious star was in the ascendant, for we find enemies and difficulty everywhere. I detain Mr. Gillespie's courier to write only to yourself; believing, too, that when this reaches you I shall be near at hand. The letters from home have taken off half the length of the journey, and I have courage now for the rest. Very truly and repectfully,

J. C. FREMONT

Printed in *National Intelligencer*, 11 Nov. 1846. This letter also appeared in *Niles' National Register*, 71 (21 Nov. 1846):190–91, and MEMOIRS, 499. Undoubtedly portions were deleted before its contents were made public.
1. JCF's actions indicate that he had no intention of proceeding "directly homewards." Perhaps the statement was included to mislead the Californians should the letter fall into their hands.

29. Frémont to Archibald H. Gillespie

LASSEN'S RANCH, RIO DEL SACRAMENTO
May 25th 1846

SIR,

There is required for the Support of the Exploring party under my command, at present almost entirely destitute, the following amount of Supplies with which I respectfully request that I may be furnished from the public Stores.

The unfriendly disposition of this Government in the present doubtful position of affairs has made it very difficult for me to obtain provisions, in any case only to be had at very exorbitant prices; and to obtain them from our Squadron would materially aid the surveys with which I am charged and very much expedite my return to the States.

Lead (American rifle)	300 lbs.
Powder	1 Keg
Purcussion Caps	8000
Russia Duck	250 yds.
Flour	5 bbls.
Sugar	600 lbs.

Coffee—Tea

Pork   1 bbl.

Medicines (common cases, emetics, purges, fever &
    ague &c)

Soap   1 Box

Salt   1 Sack

Tobacco   300 lbs.

$\frac{1}{2}$ Inch Rope for tent   30 fathoms

Iron for horse shoes

Very Respectfully Sir Your Obdt. Servant,

J. C. Frémont
Bt. Capt. U. S. Topl. Engineers

Lt. Archibald Gillespie
U. S. Marine Corps, Sacramento River

LS, RC (DNA-45, Area 9 File, Pacific). Endorsed in John B. Montgomery's hand with the note "Transfered to me with letter of Lieut. Gillespie of June 9, 46." Earlier Gillespie had written Larkin that he was to go to Yerba Buena to obtain the supplies for JCF's camp "& by so doing prevent any further trouble," but he cautioned the consul not to say anything about his mission (Gillespie to Larkin, "At Peter Lassen's," 24 May 1846, LARKIN, 4:393–94). On 1 June Commander Montgomery had received through Larkin a communication from Lieutenant Gillespie detailing the attack upon the JCF party by the Indians, and the *Portsmouth* had thereupon moved to the Bay of San Francisco (DUVALL, 11–13). By 7 June Gillespie was at Yerba Buena, his late arrival having been occasioned by a call at Dr. John Marsh's, where he landed some thirteen Indians who had been on a visit to Sutter's Fort.

30. Thomas Oliver Larkin to Frémont

Consulate of the United States of America
Monterey California, May 31st, 1846

Captain J. C. Fremont
Sir

Your letter of a few lines I have just received, also one for Col. Benton.[1] I was very happy to hear from you. I did expect to have a long letter from you a month back and supposed it must have miscarried. I have never been able to tell whether you received any Newspapers while you were at Sn. John's, or package of letters by

Mr. Neale. Did you receive a duplicate of the letter the Californian gave you when entrenched near the Sn John's Mission, also a copy of my letter to this Alcalde. Mr. Step gave them to Castro, who told me he forwarded them to you. "Quien sabe." By two conveyances I forwarded to Hon. James Buchanan all my correspondence respecting your affairs near Sn. John's. Your letter to me was badly translated by saying, you would give no quarter, in place of asking none. The same day I had a new one made and sent to the Governor and General. For fear the latter should by *mistake,* send the wrong one, I sent one with Mr. Hartnells certificate of the mistake, to our Minister in Mexico. As he is not there, Consul [John] Black should have it.[2] With it went my request to publish it in Mexico, if the wrong one was made public. Your Californian business shall not suffer if I can prevent it.

I have been keeping some N. O. & N. York papers for Come. Stockton, but cannot resist the opportunity of sending them to you. In one you will find a pretty Bee story for your published Books of Travels. In another paper you will read of a visit paid by some Indians with a long name to Col. Benton. Had a talk with Mrs. Fremont, and tried to make acquaintance with your child, but the little one declined an introduction to his [her] Father's Mountain Friends. One of the papers contained a long story of a Governor, who it appeared married a Miss Frances, one of Col Benton's Kinsfolks, which caused some trial, where Mrs. Freemont and two sisters attended Court as witnesses.[3] All the Herald's and other papers have something to say about California, half of them relative to the gallant Capt. Fremont and Lady. I really think *when* I see Washington, I shall become acquainted with one I hear so much of.

I thank you for your former kind offer of services when you may arrive at Washington, yet know not how I can claim them at present. I have neither demands nor favour to ask of our Government, nor odds, to use a Western expression. What time may require, time must bring to light. You are aware that great changes are about to take place in a country we both are acquainted with. To aid this, I am giving up business, holding myself in readiness for the times to come and the results, therefore drawing myself into the political vortex. This in time may bring my name too prominent forward, that I may be assailed by others at home for their own purposes. Should this ever happen, you may render me service. I have a relation in Washington, Mr. E. L. Childs, P. O. Department, who writes me in January, that he ordered one of your Books from Boston to be sent to me, but could not obtain it. I presume you have it. If so, please let me have it, sending it to W. A. Leidesdorff. Your Messenger arrived late tonight. I have many letters to write, and am tired. By my letter to Mr. Gillespie wrote this morning, you have the news of the day.[4] If I had time I would enclose you a letter of introduction to my Friend and Correspondent, Mr. Childs, and should like to have you call and see him. Although you did not mention it, I suppose you, Mr. Talbot and others of your company, received the letters, and yourself the public documents I forwarded by Mr. Gillespie. I received Mr. Talbot's receipt for the 500$ I sent by Mr. Neale.

With this I send to you a letter I have had some time in my hands from Charles W. Flugge.[5] He went to Captain Sutter's to meet you, says you ought to have sent him out his money, Etc. He has vexed me twice on the subject. I always told him you can make your part of the affair correct, and I only have one side of it from him. If the story is as Mr. Flugge makes it and the money is still due him, and should you approve of it, you can send to me by carefull conveyance, a sett of drafts in his name for the amount due him, and he shall receive them from me. Respecting the interest due him from the time it could have reached here via Cape Horn, and the discount on a draft, you will decide for yourself. Of this I know nothing. Respecting his small draft he sold, he lost nothing, as the owners of drafts in California, know they are not in Cash, worth their face. Should the discount suit me and you send Mr. Flugge a draft, perhaps I may send him, to the Pueblo de los Angeles, the cash for it.

Wishing you a speedy, safe, and pleasant journey to our Capital, and that from there, I may here from you, I am Sir, your most obedient,

(Signed) THOMAS O. LARKIN

Printed in LARKIN, 4:409–11.

1. See Frémont to Larkin, 24 May 1846, and Frémont to Benton, 24 May 1846, Doc. Nos. 27 and 28. JCF had sent the letters by Samuel Neal, who was serving as Gillespie's courier. Neal made excellent time from Lassen's rancho to Monterey. The NEW HELVETIA DIARY recorded his arrival at Sutter's Fort on 25 May and his immediate departure. High water forced him to return to the fort, but on 27 May he started again for Monterey by way of Sonoma and reached Larkin on 31 May.

2. Wilson Shannon, the last American minister to Mexico before the

break in relations which preceded the Mexican War, had asked for his passport on 8 May 1845.

3. Larkin is referring to the marital problems of Sally McDowell, a niece of Thomas H. Benton, who in June 1841 had married Francis Thomas (1799–1876), a man twenty years her senior. At the time he was a U.S. congressman from Maryland, but within a few months he was elected governor of that state. In 1845 Thomas publicly charged his wife with infidelities, and as a result a libel suit was filed in Washington (*U.S.* v. *Thomas*) in which Benton acted as the family's manager and arranged for counsel to assist the public prosecutor. A public meeting was held in Lexington, Va., to testify to the purity of Mrs. Thomas. Thomas filed for divorce in Maryland, and Sally filed a counter suit in Richmond. Early in 1846 the divorce was granted, and later Sally married a Presbyterian minister and Thomas rehabilitated himself from his "paranoia" (CHAMBERS, 216, 254, 301–3).

4. This letter to Gillespie, 1 June 1846 (really 31 May 1846), must have been written several hours before the arrival of Neal (LARKIN, 4:407–8).

5. See Flügge to Frémont, 26 March 1846, Doc. No. 23.

31. John B. Montgomery to Frémont

U. S. Ship Portsmouth
BAY OF ST. FRANCISCO June 3d 1846

SIR,

On the 31st. ulto. the day previous to my sailing from Monterey, a courier from Lieut. Gillespie to the U. States Consul arrived, bringing the only definite inteligence of your movement & position since my arrival at that port on the 22d. of April last. The instructions under which I am now serving, and which may detain me until late in the fall, or longer upon this coast, having relation specifically to the object of affording protection to the Persons & Property of Citizens of the U. States and of maintaining a watchful care over the general interests of our country, without reference in any manner to the enterprise in which you are so actively engaged; the nature and subject of which I am ignorant, except so far as I may have been rightly informed by paragraphs casually met with in public prints. I beg leave however (availing myself of the return Messenger) to assure you Sir, of the interest I feel in the successful prosecution and issue of the Public interests committed to your direction, And without desiring information further than you may deem necessary, to enable me to aid & facilitate your operations, to express my sincere

John Berrien Montgomery. From a portrait in the possession of
Montgomery's great-grandson, John M. Mahon.

desire & readiness to serve you in any manner consistent with other duties.[1]

Permit me to say Sir, that if you should find it convenient to visit the U. S. Ship Portsmouth during her stay in this port, that I with the officers of the Ship will be most happy to see you.

I shall remain here probably three weeks unless unforseen circumstances requiring an earlier movement and my present intention is to return to Monterey. I am Sir, Very Respectfully Your obt. Servt.,[2]

> JNO. B. MONTGOMERY
> Commander
> U. S. N.

To
Capt. J. C. Fremont
Upper California

Lbk (DNA-45, no. 22, Officers' Letters, Letterbooks of J. B. Montgomery). John Berrien Montgomery (1794–1873), scion of a naval family, was in command of the *Portsmouth* from 10 Nov. 1844 to 6 May 1848. He retired as a captain in 1861, but he served throughout the Civil War as commodore on shore duty and was promoted to rear admiral in 1866. The best biography of this dedicated naval officer, who evidenced much diplomatic ability, is ROGERS [2]. In the letter which Neal had carried to Larkin from Lassen's ranch, Gillespie had written, "I send this messenger to get such news as you have & to give us some information in relation to the vessels of war—where they are & whether the Congress has arrived. I enclose a note from [for] the Commodore, which please lock up, if he should have sailed" (Gillespie to Larkin, 24 May 1846, LARKIN, 4:393–94). The editors are unable to determine which "Commodore" Gillespie was referring to—Stockton of the *Congress,* the vessel mentioned in the letter; John D. Sloat; or John B. Montgomery (actually a commander) of the *Portsmouth?* Already noted is the fact that before leaving San Francisco for Sutter's Fort in April, Gillespie received word from Larkin by a fast rider that the *Portsmouth* had arrived at Monterey on 22 April and that "Captain Montgomery is of the opinion that Commodore Sloat may by the next Mail (six or eight days) have a declaration on the part of the United States against Mexico in which case we shall see him in a few days to take the Country" (Larkin to Gillespie, 23 April 1846, and Gillespie to Larkin, Yerba Buena, 25 April 1846, LARKIN, 4:340–41, 346–47). If the JCF-Gillespie note had been intended for Stockton or Sloat, Larkin gave it to Montgomery, and it accounts for his sailing to San Francisco harbor on 1 June and anchoring at Sausalito, where the *Portsmouth* would have land communications with Sonoma.

1. Two phrases in this letter of Montgomery to JCF are striking and immediately bring questions to mind. In what *enterprise* is JCF now engaged? What *public interests* are committed to his direction? Why is Montgomery so ready to serve—and to serve apparently on instructions from

JCF? In spite of his declarations to Benton (Doc. No. 28), JCF seems not to be planning to go home immediately.

2. The courier Samuel Neal, who had been on board during the passage of the *Portsmouth* from Monterey to Sausalito, left the ship on 3 June to carry Montgomery's letter to JCF (DUVALL, 12).

32. John B. Montgomery to Frémont

U. S. Ship Portsmouth
BAY OF ST. FRANCISCO June 10th 1846

SIR,

Since writing you by "Neil" on the 3rd. Inst. I have been informed by Lieut. Gillespie of your present position and circumstances; and made acquainted with your design, soon to proceed South with your party as far as Santa Barbara; before striking across the country for the U. States. I am also informed by Lt. Gillespie of your having expressed to him a desire for the presence of a vessel of war at St. Barbara, during the period of your sojourn in the vicinity of that port. Now Sir, I am happy to say, that I feel myself at liberty to visit any or all the Ports upon this coast, should the Public interests require it, and and if on receipt of this you shall still think the presence of a Ship of War at Santa Barbara may prove serviceable to you in carrying out the views of our Government, and will do me the favor by the return boat to communicate your wishes, with information as to the time you will probably reach that part of the coast; I will not fail (Providence permitting) to meet you there with the Portsmouth.

I feel gratified Sir, in having it in my power to forward you by Lt. Hunter, the amount of funds asked for in your name by Lieut. Gillespie; with most of the articles of stores &c. required to meet the demand of your urgent necessities; regretting only, my inability to furnish the whole.[1] You will oblige me by signing the requisitions & receipts annexed to the several invoices transmitted by Lt. Hunter & with a view to the settlement of Purser J. H. Watmough's Accounts at the Navy Department.[2] Be pleased to give an order, or bill (in duplicate) on the proper Department of Government, payable to Purser Watmough's order, to the 4th. Auditor of the Treasury for

146

the aggregate amount of money & Pursers Stores Supplied. Articles having no prices affixed need only to be receipted for.

Lieut. Gillespie informs me that you may find it convenient to visit the Portsmouth at Santa Barbara should we have occasion to go there. With this prospect in view I beg leave again to assure you, that we shall all on board be most happy to see you. Very Respectfully I am Sir, Your Obt. Servt.

JNO. B. MONTGOMERY
Commander

To
Capt. J. C. Fremont
Bt. Capt. U.S. Topl. Engineers
Upper California

Lbk (DNA-45, no. 22, Officers' Letters, Letterbooks of J. B. Montgomery).
1. Lieut. Benjamin F. Hunter of the *Portsmouth* later became acting captain of Company C in Stockton's battalion. In addition to the supplies listed in Doc. No. 29, JCF had asked for $1,500.
2. Two months later purser James H. Watmough was put in command of the Santa Clara garrison, in which capacity he made a successful campaign against the Indians on the Stanislaus.

33. Jessie B. Frémont to Frémont

WASHINGTON
June 16, 1846

MY DEAREST HUSBAND,

A Mr. Magoffin[1] says he will be at Bent's Fort a month from to-morrow, and that he will leave a letter for you, so I write, dearest husband, to tell you how happy I have been made by hearing of you up to the 31st of March, through Mr. Larkin. Only the day before, I had received the Mexican account of your being besieged by Gen. Castro, and I was much relieved by what Mr. Larkin says—that you could present yourself at Monterey, alone, if you wished, and not be harmed. But I hope that as I write you are rapidly nearing home, and that early in September there will be an end to our anxieties. In your dear letter[2] you tell me that *le bon temps viendra,* and my faith in you is such that I believe it will come: and it will come to all you love, for during your long absence God has been good to us and kept in health your mother and all you love best. This opportunity of writing only presented itself last night, so that there is not time for a letter from your mother herself, but I had one from her two days ago in which she tells me that during the warm weather she will remain at a place about ten miles from Mount Pleasant. Her stay in the country did her health much good last fall and indeed it has been good generally throughout the winter. Her heart has been made glad by your brilliant success, and your late promotion, although it distressed her to anticipate more separations, could not but be most gratifying in many respects. You must let me make you my heartiest congratulations. I am sorry that I could not be the first to call you Colonel. It will please you the more as it was entirely a free will offering of the President's, neither father nor I nor anyone for us having asked or said we would like it.

So your merit has advanced you in eight years from an unknown second lieutenant, to the most talked of and admired lieutenant-colonel in the army. Almost all of the old officers called to congratulate me upon it, the Aberts among them, and I have heard of no envy except from some of the lower order of Whig papers who only see you as Colonel Benton's son-in-law. As for your Report, its popularity astonished even me, your most confirmed and oldest worshipper. Lilly has it read to her (the stories, of course) as a reward for good behavior. She asked Preuss the other day if it was true that he caught ants on his hands and eat them—he was so amazed that he could not answer her, and she said, "I read it in papa's lepote; it was when you were lost in California." Father absolutely idolizes Lilly; she is so good and intelligent that I do not wonder at it. And then you should see his pride in you!

Mother's health has been worse than ever during the winter, but the force of the disease seems now to have expended itself, and she is quite well again. That gave me a reason for staying at home quietly as I wished, and I have read so much that is improving that you will be very pleased with me. Your mother was kind enough to send me your daguerreotype, and it hangs over the head of my bed and is my guardian angel, for I could not waste time or do anything you did not like with that beloved face looking so kindly and earnestly at me. I opened a new history of Louisiana, a week or two ago, and it commenced with the Spanish discoveries on the southern part of the continent. I was by myself, Lilly asleep, and reading by our lamp. When I came to De Soto's search for the fountain of youth, I stopped, for it seemed as if pleasant old days had returned; and then I remembered so well what you once wrote to me that I could not help bursting into tears. Do you remember, darling?

It was soon after we were married, and you wrote me, "Fear not for our happiness; if the hope for it is not something wilder than the Spaniards' search for the fountain in Florida, we will find it yet." I remembered it word for word, although it was so long since I read it. Dear, dear husband, you do not know how proud and grateful I am that you love me. We have found the fountain of perpetual youth for love, and I believe there are few others who can say so. I try very hard to be worthy of your love.

I had meant to tell you of many things which might interest, but it would take a day to choose out from the year's accumulation. The road you have discovered is spoken of as giving you more distinction than anything you have yet done. I had to publish almost all your letter, and like everything you write it has been reprinted all over the country. I have some beautiful poetry to show you on our motto *le bon temps viendra*. Editors have written to me for your biography and likeness, but I had no orders from you and then you know it would look odd to leave out your age, and you never told me how old you were yet.

How old are you? You might tell me now I am a colonel's wife— won't you, old papa? Poor papa, it made tears come to find you had begun to turn gray. You must have suffered much and been very anxious, "but all that must pass." I am very sorry you did not get our letters. Yours gave so much happiness that I grieved you could not have had as much from ours. You will of course come on here as soon as you get back. I wanted to go to St. Louis to meet you, but father says I had better not, as it will be very uncomfortable and even dangerous to go out in the worst of the season, and I don't want to be sick, for I am not going to let you write anything but your name when you get home. And then we will probably have to be at Jefferson Barracks during the winter and until the new regiment is ready for the field. Father says you are to accept the appointment as it was given, with the understanding that you were to be kept on scientific duty under the direction of the Senate. Mr. [Daniel] Webster says it would be too great a loss to the science of the country if you were stopped in your onward course. If I begin telling you the sincere compliments from people whose names are known in Europe as well as America I would need a day.

You must have a few to think of, however. Edward Everett, Mr. Gallatin, Stevens (Central America), Davis, the author of "Jack Downing," a Dr. Barrett of Connecticut, a botanist who sent me his herbarium of American grasses (for which he wants the buffalo and bunch grasses) are among the Northern men.[3] The South Carolinians claim you bodily, and Dr. Grayson[4] of Charleston wrote one of the most beautiful of all the notices I saw. Your early and steady friends, Mr. McCrady and Mr. Poinsett, were the first to whom I sent well-bound copies of your book. You are ranked with DeFoe [Daniel Defoe]. They say that as *Robinson Crusoe* is the most natural and interesting fiction of travel, so Frémont's report is the most romantically truthful. I have a letter from the President of the Royal Geographical Society, Lord Chichester [Colchester],[5] who says he could not help preparing a paper on your travels to be read at their meeting—and more and more and many more of the same.

Mr. Magoffin has come for the letter and I must stop. I have not had so much pleasure in a very great while as today. The thought that you may hear from me and know that all are well and that I can tell you again how dearly I love you makes me as happy as I can be while you are away.

All Jacob's relations are well. I see Mrs. Talbot and her daughter constantly. They are so grateful to you for your mention of Theodore.

Farewell, dear, dear husband. In a few months we shall not know what sorrow means. At least, I humbly hope and pray so.

Your own affectionate and devoted wife,

JESSIE B. FRÉMONT

Printed in NEVINS, 301–4. Nevins cites the location of the letter as the Bancroft, but that library has no record of it (William M. Roberts to Mary Lee Spence, 26 May 1971).

1. James Wiley Magoffin (1799–1868), a native of Kentucky, had long been interested in trade with Santa Fe and Chihuahua. He had resided within Mexican territory for some nineteen years, spoke Spanish fluently, and knew many influential Mexicans. Benton introduced him to President Polk, and when Magoffin sped west to Bent's Fort with JBF's letter, he also carried important ones to Kearny from Polk and the Secretary of War. As a result of these messages and a conference with Magoffin, Kearny gave the trader a letter to Governor Manuel Armijo and ordered a military escort, commanded by Capt. Philip St. George Cooke, to accompany him to Santa Fe under a flag of truce. By clever diplomacy and perhaps bribery, Magoffin made pos-

sible a bloodless occupation of New Mexico by Kearny. Magoffin intended to repeat the process in Chihuahua for Gen. John E. Wool, but his previous success imperiled his venture. He was captured, and only his resolution, wealth, and resourcefulness enabled him to stay alive until finally freed by U.S. troops (BENTON [1], 2:682–84; CLARKE, 126–38).

2. JCF's letter of 24 Jan. 1846 from Yerba Buena.

3. Most of the "Northern men" mentioned by JBF had national reputations. Edward Everett (1794–1865), Unitarian clergyman and statesman, had been the U.S. minister to Great Britain, and at the time of JBF's letter he was president of Harvard University. Albert Gallatin (1781–1849), former Secretary of the Treasury in both Jefferson's and Madison's administrations, would seek information from JCF when the latter returned from his third expedition (Doc. No. 213). Noted for the study of Mayan civilization and for volumes on his travels in Central America and Yucatán, John Lloyd Stephens (1805–52) would initiate the building of the Panama Railroad. Various letter writers used the pseudonym "Major Jack Downing," which had been originated by Seba Smith, but New York businessman Charles Augustus Davis (1795–1867) was the most popular to do so. At least eight printings of his *Letters of J. Downing, Major, Downingville Militia, Second Brigade, to His Old Friend, Mr. Dwight, of the New-York Daily Advertiser* were issued in 1834. Although both JBF and an obituary notice in the New York *Times* (27 Jan. 1882) give Barrett as the name of the Connecticut physician, botanist, and mineralogist, this was actually the English-born Joseph Barratt.

4. Not a doctor but a lawyer, William John Grayson (1788–1863) was a member of an old South Carolina family. He had been in Congress in the 1830s, but at the time of JBF's letter he was collector of the port of Charleston. In the fifties he turned poet, both for self-expression and as an apologist for the South, with *The Hireling and the Slave* his best-known poem.

5. Charles Abbot (1798–1867), Lord Colchester, an officer in the Royal Navy, was president of the society from 1845 to 1847.

34. Frémont to John B. Montgomery

NEW HELVETIA, CALIFORNIA; June 16 1846.

SIR,

I had the gratification to receive on the 6th. your letter of the 3d. Inst; and the farther gratification to receive yesterday by the hands of Lieut. Hunter your favor of the 10th. conveying to me assurances of your disposition to do any thing within the scope of your instructions to facilitate the public service in which I am engaged.[1] In acknowledging the receipt of the stores with which you have supplied us, I beg you to receive the earnest thanks of myself and party for the prompt & active kindness, which we are all in a condition fully to appreciate. My time today has been so constantly engrossed that I could make no opportunity to write, and as it is now nearly midnight you will permit me to refer you to Lieut. Hunter for an account of the condition of the country, which will doubtless have much interest for you. The people here have made some movements with the view of establishing a settled & stable Government, which may give security to their persons & property.[2] This evening I was interrupted in a note to yourself by the arrival of Genl. Vallejo and other officers, who had been taken prisoners & insisted on surrendering to me.[3] The people and authorities of the country persist in connecting me with every movement of the foreigners, & I am in hourly expectation of the approach of Genl. Castro.[4]

My position has consequently become a difficult one. The unexpected hostility which has been exercised towards us on the part of the military authorities of California has entirely deranged the plan of our survey & frustrated my intention of examining the Colorado of the gulf of California, which was one of the principal objects of this expedition. The suffering to which my party would be unavoidably exposed at this advanced period of the year by deprivation of water during intervals of three and four days, renders any movement in that direction impracticable.

It is therefore my present intention to abandon the farther prosecution of our exploration and proceed immediately across the mountainous country to the eastward in the direction of the head waters of the Arkansaw river, and thence to the frontier of Missouri, where I expect to arrive early in September. In order to recruit my animals and arrange my equipage for a long journey, I shall necessarily be compelled to remain here untill about the first of July. In the mean time should any thing be attempted against me, I cannot, consistently with my own feelings and respect for the national character of the duty in which I am engaged, permit a repetition of the recent insults we have received from Genl. Castro. If therefore, any hostile movements are made in this direction, I will most assuredly meet or anticipate them; and with such intention I am regulating my conduct to the people here. The nature of my instructions & the peaceful nature of our operations, do not contemplate any active hostility on my part even in the event of war between the two countries; and therefore although I am resolved to take such *active* and precautionary measures as I shall judge necessary for our safety, I am not authorized to ask from you any other than such assistance, as without incurring yourself unusual responsibility, you would feel at

liberty to afford me. Such an emergency could not have been anticipated in any instructions; but between indians on the one hand and
a hostile people on the other, I trust that our Government will not
severely censure any efforts to which we may be driven in defence of
our lives and character. In this condition of things I can only then
urgently request that you will remain with the Portsmouth in the
Bay of San Francisco, where your presence will operate strongly to
check proceedings against us; and I would feel much more security
in my position should you judge it advisable to keep open a communication with me by means of your boats. In this way you would
receive the earliest information, and you might possibly spare us the
aid of one of your surgeons in case of accident here. Repeating my
thanks for the assistance you have rendered us and regretting my inability to visit you on board the Portsmouth, I am Sir, very respectfully Your Obedt. Servt.

J. C. FRÉMONT
Bt. Capt. Topl. Engineers
U.S. Army

Capt Jno. B. Montgomery
U. S. Ship Portsmouth
Bay of San Francisco
California

ALS, RC (DNA-45, Area 9 File, Pacific).
1. Interesting accounts of the delivery of the stores to JCF are to be found
in DOWNEY, 28–33, and DUVALL, 13–22. In addition to Lieutenant Hunter and
the boat's crew and pilot, the launch carried Gillespie and his servant; purser
Watmough; the assistant naval surgeon on the *Portsmouth*, Marius Duvall;
R. Eugene Russell, one of JCF's *voyageurs;* and a "lawless Frenchman,"
probably David Beauchamp, who had been discharged by JCF in February.
2. The "movements" to which JCF referred were two. On 10 June a party
of twelve or fourteen American settlers, led by Ezekiel Merritt, seized a
caballada of horses as they were being driven from Sonoma to Santa Clara,
where José Castro was organizing his forces. The rumor had spread that
they were to be used by him to drive the American settlers from the Sacramento Valley. Commanding the small horse guard of nearly a dozen Californians were Lieut. Francisco Arce and Lieut. José María Alviso. The
Californians were permitted to continue their journey armed and mounted,
but the captured horses were delivered to JCF's camp, which he was moving
from the Sutter Buttes to the more strategic location of his old camp on the
American River. Four days later (14 June) a group of thirty-odd Americans,
initially led again by Ezekiel Merritt, captured undefended Sonoma, the
stronghold of Mexican power in the north. The next day the independent
Bear Flag Republic was established, with William B. Ide in command. For
Larkin's account of these events, see his letter to Foxen D. Atherton, 20 July

1846, NUNIS [2]. See also Jacob P. Leese, "Bear Flag Statement" (CU-B), and IDE [2].

3. Gen. Mariano G. Vallejo, Capt. Salvador Vallejo, and Lieut. Col. Victor Prudon were taken prisoner at Sonoma and incarcerated at Sutter's Fort. The Vallejos' brother-in-law, Jacob P. Leese, who had accompanied the three as interpreter, was also ordered imprisoned. Mariano Guadalupe Vallejo (1807–90), secularizer of the Mission San Francisco Solano, founder of the town of Sonoma, and owner of large tracts of land north of the Bay of San Francisco, including Rancho Petaluma, was the dominant native Californian in provincial affairs north of Monterey. Although he often warned the central government of the danger inherent in such establishments as Sutter's New Helvetia, he was more receptive to U.S. influence than European. Generous and able, he was elected to the constitutional convention in 1849 and to the first state senate. His brother, Salvador Vallejo (1814–76), whom he had established at Sonoma and who was often in command of the post or fighting Indians, was of a rougher nature. Victor Prudon, a Frenchman who had come from Mexico to California in 1834 to teach, had become Mariano G. Vallejo's secretary in 1842 and was living in Sonoma when the Bear Flaggers appeared. Jacob Primer Leese (1809–92), Ohioan by birth and former employee of Bent, St. Vrain and Company, had come to California in 1833. For a time he was in partnership with Nathan Spear and William S. Hinckley, but a quarrel disrupted the alliance. A few years after Leese married Rosalia Vallejo, he transferred his business and residence to Sonoma, becoming alcalde in 1844–45, often quarreling with Prudon, in turn never being completely trusted by Mariano G. Vallejo, and eventually leaving his family. See MC KITTRICK and TAYS [3] for the influence and interrelationships of the Vallejo family.

4. James H. Gleason wrote his uncle, William Paty, in Oahu, "It is generally believed here [Monterey] that Captain Frémont is the mover in the revolution" (3 July 1846 letter in GLEASON). Little wonder that Gleason and others persisted in connecting JCF with the movements of the Americans. The circumstances of his return to the Sacramento Valley convinced many Californians that he had been called back by Gillespie and was merely biding his time. Sutter wrote Mariano G. Vallejo, "I think Senor Fremont has to wait until the arrival of the frigate *Congress,* which has Commodore Stockton aboard, to receive orders, in case war is declared" (1 June 1846, CAL. HIS. SOC. DOCS., 6:185). JCF sent messengers advising American settlers to organize for their mutual safety. William B. Ide tells of having received by the hand of an Indian "agent" on 8 June at his cabin on Josiah Belden's Rancho Barranca Colorada the following unsigned message: " 'Notice is hereby given, that a large body of armed Spaniards on horseback, amounting to 250 men, have been seen on their way to the Sacramento Valley, destroying the crops, burning the houses, and driving off the cattle. Capt. Frémont invites every freeman in the valley to come to his camp at the Butes, immediately; and he hopes to stay the enemy, and put a stop to his'—(Here the sheet was folded and worn in-two, and no more is found)" (IDE [2], 30). Both of Merritt's "capturing parties" had set out from JCF's camp, and by the explorer's own account, Merritt was his "Field Lieutenant" among the settlers (MEMOIRS, 509), of which there was a constant flow to his camp. It was not until 20 June that he decided "to govern events" rather than "to be governed by them" and openly began participating in the Bear Flag movement (MEMOIRS, 520). Here, in justice to William B. Ide, should be mentioned his claim to be the real conqueror of California. He maintained that when the

Americans moved in on Sonoma, the majority understood, because of the "advice" of JCF, that their only business was to take certain principal men prisoner in order to provoke Castro *"to strike the first blow"* in a war with the United States. It was he who rallied them to independence and conquest. In fact, he contended, his plans were so far carried out, before JCF undertook the direction of affairs, that the subsequent military acts were needless (IDE [2], 28–46).

35. John B. Montgomery to Frémont

U. S. Ship Portsmouth
Sau Solito, June 23, 1846

Sir,

By Lieut. Hunter who reached the ship on Saturday Evening [20 June] from your camp, I had the pleasure to receive your letter of the 16th inst. announcing the seasonable reception of the stores forwarded by him. The last few days have teemed with important events; pointing in my view, to results momentous to the interests of California and our own Country. I have determined to remain where I am at present, looking after the interests of our country and countrymen, requiring to be watched at this crisis, and readily comply with your suggestion to keep open the communication with your camp, by means of my boats; in pursuance of which it is intended to send a boat in the morning (tomorrow) in charge of Lieut. Revere[1] (who will hand you this) and another on Saturday next, by return of which you will be pleased to inform me, whether a third boat will be likely to reach you at your present camp or not. The Surgeon of the *Portsmouth* (Doctor Henderson) goes in the boat, with orders to remain with you until the return of the next boat, or longer should you desire it.[2] Altho aware that the public mind in California was prepared for a change of Government, I little expected the movement to take place at this time or in the manner it has. The capture of the horses and the surprise at Sonoma were master strokes, but should have been followed up by a rush upon Santa Clara, where Castro, with the residue of ordnance & munitions in the country, might have been taken by thirty men at any time previous to Saturday Evening. Castro must feel sensibly the loss of the two Vallejos & Prudon as well as that of the arms & munitions taken at Sonoma.[3]

Mariano Guadalupe Vallejo. From a print in the Bancroft Library.
Courtesy of George P. Hammond.

I have exchanged communications with the commanders on both sides, and others; preserving a strict neutrality and avowing my purpose of scrupulously adhering to this principal; while I confess my sympathies are wholly with the gallant little band in arms for mutual defence.[4] Individuals and small parties from this section have been joining the insurgents at Sonoma daily I am informed, and Lt. Hunter brings intelligence of Sutter's union with them.[5] An irregular force of one hundred and fifty are said to have joined Castro at Santa Clara on Saturday brought from the vicinity of Monterey by Emanuel Castro the Sub-Prefect of that place, and I am just informed that they are expected to cross the *Straits,* and take horses at point St. Pedro where a number have been collected for their use this evening, and move directly upon Sonoma. If this is the case we shall soon know the result.

I yesterday heard of the arrival of the United States ship *Cyane* at Monterey, where the *Congress* is also daily looked for from the Islands, where she arrived on the 13th of May. Not a word of news has yet been received by the *Cyane,* but I think she must bring from Mazatlan something respecting our Mexican concerns.

I received a letter from Castro a few days since a copy of which, as it relates solely to your imagined operations, I have thought it well to send you with my reply.[6] Also two proclamations this moment received.[7]

Should anything of consequence reach me from the *Cyane* before sending the next boat, I will not fail to communicate it to you. In the meantime permit me to subscribe myself Very Respectfully Your Obt. Servt.,

JNO. B. MONTGOMERY
Commander

To Capt. J. C. Fremont
U. S. Topl. Engineers,
Sacramento, Upper California

N.B.—Since writing the above, I have heard there is no probability of Castro's movement upon Sonoma for several days; they are using great efforts to purchase arms, etc.

Lbk (DNA-45, no. 22, Officers' Letters, Letterbooks of J. B. Montgomery).
1. Lieut. Joseph Warren Revere (1812–80) would publish an account of his part in the conquest of California in 1849 under the title *A Tour of Duty in California*. Resigning from the Navy in 1850, he became a rancher and

trader. When the Civil War broke out, he became colonel of the 7th New Jersey Volunteers and ultimately a brigadier general.

2. Andrew A. Henderson was assistant surgeon on the *Portsmouth* and in 1847 was surgeon in Stockton's battalion.

3. In his 15 June 1846 letter addressed to Commodore Stockton, but delivered to Commander Montgomery by special messenger William L. Todd, William B. Ide had written that "8 Field Pieces, 200 stand of arms, a great quantity of cannon, canister and Grape shot, and little less than 100 lbs. of powder had been captured" (CAL. HIS. SOC. DOCS., 1:82–83). Mariano G. Vallejo's biographer, Tays, maintains that the brass cannon were "small and mostly unserviceable" and the muskets "shop worn and out of repair" (TAYS [3], 17:164).

4. Mariano G. Vallejo had immediately (14 June) sent Don José de la Rosa to Montgomery to inform him of what had happened at Sonoma and to request that he use his authority or exert his influence to prevent the commission of acts of violence by the insurgents, since they denied acting under the authority of the United States and seemed to be without an effective leader. Vallejo petitioned Montgomery to send an officer or a letter that would save the helpless Sonoma inhabitants from violence and anarchy (statement of the interview between El Senor Don José de la Rosa and Commander Montgomery, by Lieut. W. A. Bartlett, CAL. HIS. SOC. DOCS., 1:79–80). On the other side, William B. Ide sent William L. Todd with a letter addressed to Commodore Stockton, but delivered to Montgomery, which recounted the events of 10 and 14 June, justified the establishment of the Bear Flag Republic, assured that private property would be protected, and expressed an earnest desire "to embrace the first opportunity to unite our adopted and rescued country, to the country of our early home" (copy of William B. Ide's letter, 15 June 1846, CAL. HIS. SOC. DOCS., 1:82–83).

5. Sutter's union with the Bear Flaggers was not an enthusiastic one, but he did agree to man and prepare his fort for the coming events. However, his hospitable treatment of his distinguished California prisoners irritated JCF, and soon the command of the fort was entrusted to Edward M. Kern, the artist and topographer of the expedition.

6. In his letter of 17 June 1846 Gen. José Castro had asked Montgomery for an explanation of JCF's conduct in invading California, taking possession of the military post of Sonoma, and imprisoning the commander and some residents of the post. He termed these "scandalous and unwarrantable offences." In his reply of the next day Montgomery assured Castro of his "entire conviction" that JCF's visit had reference only to "scientific researches" and was in no manner whatever, "either by authority of the United States Government or otherwise," connected with the movement against Sonoma. He referred to the unjustifiable and "gratuitous" demonstration against JCF in March and regretted that Castro had fallen into error a *"second time."* Furthermore, he pointed out that to charge JCF with cooperating in the Sonoma affair was to impugn the integrity of the U.S. government (both letters in CAL. HIS. SOC. DOCS., 2:69–71).

7. The proclamations which Montgomery forwarded to JCF were probably the two issued by José Castro from Santa Clara on 17 June 1846 and ordered "published, circulated, and fixed in the customary conspicuous places" by the alcalde. One called upon Castro's countrymen to sacrifice themselves in the defense of liberty, independence, and "the true religion possessed by our fathers," and the second assured protection to foreigners, provided "they mix

in no revolutionary movements." Larkin forwarded copies to the Secretary of State in his 24 June 1846 letter, no. 50b. They are also nos. 29 and 30 in the report which he sent with his letter of 20 July 1846.

36. Frémont's Commission as Lieutenant Colonel

[26 June 1846]

The President of the United States of America, To All Who Shall See These Presents, Greeting:

Know Ye, that reposing special trust and confidence in the patriotism, valor, fidelity and abilities of John C. Fremont, I have nominated, and by and with the advice and consent of the Senate, Do Appoint him Lieutenant Colonel in the Regiment of Mounted Riflemen, in the service of the United States: to rank as such from the twenty seventh day of May, eighteen hundred and forty six. He is therefore carefully and diligently to discharge the duty of Lieutenant Colonel, by doing and performing all manner of things thereunto belonging. And I do strictly charge, and require all Officers and Soldiers under his command to be obedient to his orders as Lieutenant Colonel. And he is to observe and follow such orders and directions, from time to time, as he shall receive from me, or the future President of the United States of America, or the General or other superior Officers set over him, according to the rules and discipline of War. This Commission to continue in force during the pleasure of the President of the United States, for the time being.

Given under my hand, at the City of Washington, this twenty sixth day of June, in the year of our Lord one thousand eight hundred and forty six, and in the seventieth year of the Independence of the United States.

By the President.   James K. Polk
                        Wm. L. Marcy, Secretary of War

Basic printed form (DNA-94, Register of Army Commissions, Issued and Distributed, vol. 11, 1846–47). The original was sent to Benton; on 3 Nov. 1846 the Adjutant General's Office notified JCF that it was sending a certified copy to California by Col. Richard B. Mason of the 1st Dragoons (Lbk, DNA-94, LS, 23:109). JCF received the news of his promotion (but probably not a copy of the commission) when he returned to Monterey in the ship *Sterling* on 27 or 28 Oct. 1846. The records do not show any formal acceptance of his lieutenant colonelcy, and the first communication received by the Adjutant General's Office after his appointment was the letter dated 17 Sept. 1847 reporting himself in arrest pursuant to the orders of Brigadier General Kearny (S. Cooper to R. Burgess, Lbk, DNA-94, LS, 28:371).

37. John B. Montgomery to Frémont

U. S. Ship Portsmouth
Yerba Buena June 26, 1846

Sir   ,

Since writing to you by Lieutenant Revere, a force of Seventy Californians moving from Santa Clara towards Sonoma after passing the narrows of the Bay, twelve miles to the Nd. of my anchorage, were met by a party of fifteen of revolutionists, and checked, or as reported, compelled to fall back with the loss of two killed & two wounded, two of the fifteen also falling by the fire of their opponents.[1] This first success, tho seemingly a small affair, cannot fail I think to give a favorable impulse to the operations of the insurgents, and attract at once, numbers of the Foreign residents to their aid. Although neutral in my position, I cannot be so in feeling, and am anxiously looking for farther intelligence, believing that inactivity in the circumstances can form no part of the policy of the Sonoma party.

Castro has written to me saying that "He had received advice from various sources, that the boats of the American ship *Portsmouth* go about the Bay of San Francisco armed, for the purpose of examining its trade, &c." This of course I have very honestly denied, but informed him that I had sent two Boats since the 10th inst. to your camp, and deemed it proper in the circumstances to notify him of my intention to despatch another for the purpose of communicating with you at the close of the week, since which I have heard nothing from him. He is at Santa Clara with about seventy men it is said.

I have directed Lt. Bartlett[2] to bring Surgeon Henderson with him when he returns, unless your detention beyond the period named for your final departure for the U. States should render his further continuance important, of which you will please be the judge. Lieut. Bartlett will hand you Sir a package for the Honorable Secretary of the Navy, which if perfectly convenient (not otherwise), I will thank you to take charge of and forward from any point of communication most convenient to yourself.

[*Commander Montgomery's letterbook then indicates that the following extracts from Thomas Oliver Larkin's letter of 20 June 1846 (which he had received on 25 June) were included for JCF's information:*]

"From a *confidential* letter dated May 18, 1846 Mazatlan, I learn from Com. Sloat that he expected to be here as soon as the "Cyane" and will have all his vessels on this coast. He is informed from our Government that I shall be prepared to give him the necessary information, consult and advise with him relative to future measures. From this I must suppose there are dispatches sent to me that I have not rec'd. The misfortune is that our Mazatlan consul was not aware of the sailing of the "Cyane" for this port. Therefore I am deprived of my mail, yet the information desired could hardly come via Mexico. I must believe they are on the road over the mountains.

"Com. Sloat adds that supposing I shall understand him he does not write more particulars. I presume he only calls off this port and then proceeds to San Francisco. The officers are not aware of the squadrons coming to California the Commodore wishing it to remain a secret. He was in expectation of reaching here before Captain Melvine [Mervine]. I therefore look for him daily. I believe he expects me to go on board for San Francisco.

"You will see into the affair as you can, as I can not explain it."

[*Montgomery indicates that he made some remarks on the above extract but did not record them. He then concluded his letter:*]

Wishing you Sir, a safe and pleasant journey to your country & home I have the honor to subscribe myself Very Respectfully Your obt. Servt.,[3]

JNO. B. MONTGOMERY
Commander

To
Capt. J. C. Fremont
U. S. Topgl. Engineers
Upper California

Lbk (DNA-45, no. 22, Officers' Letters, Letterbooks of J. B. Montgomery). See also Larkin to Montgomery, Monterey, 20 June 1846 (DNA-45, Area 9 File, Pacific).

At the suggestion of Vice-Consul Leidesdorff, the *Portsmouth* had moved on 23 June from Sausalito to Yerba Buena, to protect the vice-consul's property and that of other American citizens from "the probable outrages of the Californians" (DUVALL, 24–25). From Monterey, James H. Gleason wrote to his uncle, "The U. S. Ship 'Portsmouth' . . . supplies in a secret manner Ide's party with provisions and ammunition" (3 July 1846 letter in GLEASON).

1. Montgomery is referring to the encounter of the small force under Bear Flagger Henry L. Ford with the much larger force of Joaquín de la Torre on 24 June. Actually only one Californian seems to have been killed at this engagement at Olompali. Since the Americans maintained they had no casualties as a result of the engagement, Montgomery must refer to the murder of Thomas Cowie and George Fowler, who had been taken prisoner a few days earlier by a small band of Californians. Before the engagement of 24 June Ford asserted he had sent to the Sacramento a report that Castro was crossing with troops at Carquinez Strait with the intention of attacking Sonoma (ROGERS [1], 29:266–69).

2. Lieut. Washington Allon Bartlett of the *Portsmouth*, who has been identified by HUSSEY [1] as author of "The Farthest West" letters from California in 1846, arrived at Sutter's Fort on 28 June to find that JCF had left with reinforcements for Sonoma on 23 June. On 29 June Bartlett, in company with John Bidwell, set out overland for Sonoma.

3. It may have been a surprise when Gillespie came on board the *Portsmouth* the next day, 27 June, to inform Montgomery that JCF was at San Rafael, some twelve miles distant (DUVALL, 26).

38. Frémont to John B. Montgomery

SONOMA: July 5th. 1846

SIR,

I have the pleasure to acknowledge the receipt at this place of your two communications, dated June 23d & 26th, the latter highly interesting, in connection with the present crisis. I trust that by the time you receive this note, the arrival of Com. Sloat will have put an end to your neutral position.

Besides owing you my acknowledgments for the professional aid of Dr. Henderson, I am much indebted to you for the pleasure of his acquaintance, as our pursuits appear to have been somewhat similar. I found him with Lt. Bartlett here on my arrival, 2 days since.[1]

A military organization of the force under arms was yesterday made at this place, and farther than this, I have nothing of present interest to communicate to you.[2] I shall today continue my road towards Sutter's Fort, on the Sacramento.[3] Foreigners from below are daily arriving at this post, and we have information that upwards of 100 good men are now in the upper part of the Sacramento valley, on their road from Oregon. The intelligence was brought by a party of 7 men who were in advance. Of these, 5 were wounded, one very dangerously, in an attack by the Indians. This man was shot through the body and is lying at one of the upper settlements.

I forward this by Lt. Bartlett, who is about starting, and to my great regret, Dr. Henderson accompanies him.

I trust that, in case anything of moment should occur, you will not find it inconsistent with your convenience and the strict neutrality of your position to give me some information. Thanking you in the meantime for your recent kindness, I am Sir, very respectfully Your obedient servt.,

J. C. FRÉMONT
Bt. Capt. U. S. Topl. Engineers

Captain Jno. B. Montgomery
U. S. Ship *Portsmouth,* Bay of San Francisco

ALS, RC (DNA-45, Area 9 File, Pacific).
1. Note that JCF spends no time recounting his activities since his first arrival at Sonoma on 25 June. He left the next day for Mission San Rafael with a force augmented to about 125 to search for Joaquín de la Torre and to intercept additional forces which Castro might send across San Francisco Bay. During the course of this search Ramón and Francisco de Haro, twin brothers who were carrying a message to Torre and were accompanied by their uncle, José de los Reyes Berreyesa, fell into the hands of JCF's party near San Rafael, and all three were shot to death (for details, see Doc. No. 52, n. 6). Another intercepted letter, written expressly to fall into JCF's hands, led him to believe that Torre planned to attack Sonoma the next morning and caused him to make a night march (28–29 June) back to Sonoma. This left the Californians a clear path of retreat to Sausalito, where they commandeered a launch from Capt. William A. Richardson, crossed the bay to San Pablo, and rejoined Castro. The next day Castro's reunited force marched south. JCF then busied himself by making two small raids south of the bay. On 1 July, with about twelve men, perhaps as many as twenty, he crossed the Golden Gate from Sausalito in a launch borrowed from the American ship *Moscow.* Its captain, William D. Phelps, acted as pilot. JCF spiked the cannons of the old ungarrisoned Spanish fort, Castillo de San Joaquin, at present Fort Point beneath the southern end of the modern Golden Gate Bridge. On 2 July he sent ten men, commanded by Robert Semple, to Yerba Buena to capture the alcalde, William S. Hinckley. But Hinckley had died a few days before, so Robert Ridley, the harbor master, was taken instead and sent as a prisoner to Sutter's Fort. The capture of Ridley must have delighted Leidesdorff, who had long predicted that the cockney would get his "just due." When JCF returned to Sonoma, he found Dr. Henderson and Lieutenant Bartlett there and celebrated a victorious Fourth of July (MEMOIRS, 525–26; PHELPS, 290; RADCLIFFE). Later Robert B. Semple certified that his party went to Yerba Buena on 1 July (CSmH), but Montgomery definitely dates it "mid day" 2 July (LARKIN, 5:94–96). For his

services on that July day, Phelps later attempted to collect $10,000, but Archibald Gillespie certified that "there was no enemy present, and the sole object Captain Frémont had in view was to prevent the Californians from using the guns at any future time. There was no risk or personal danger incurred, and the service would be well paid for at fifty dollars" (*Presidential Message on the Accounts of John C. Fremont*, Senate Exec. Doc. 109, p. 71, 34th Cong., 1st sess., Serial 825).

2. A four-company battalion was organized to conquer Castro. JCF was in command, Gillespie was adjutant, and Henry L. Ford, Granville P. Swift, and John Grigsby were elected captains of three companies. But since the fourth company was made up largely of men from the exploring expedition, JCF appointed its commander, Richard Owens. JCF later noted that if he had withdrawn, the independence movement "would have collapsed with absolute ruin to the settlers." In accepting the position of command, he addressed the settlers and "dwelt on the responsibility which I had assumed as an officer of the United States Army, trusting to them to do nothing which would discredit themselves or our country" (MEMOIRS, 526; ROGERS [4], 54–56; MARTI, 61).

3. Grigsby and his company of about fifty men were left to garrison Sonoma; the remainder proceeded to the Sacramento. En route, parties were sent out to procure horses and cattle to mount and feed the battalion.

39. John D. Sloat to John B. Montgomery

Flag Ship Savannah
MONTEREY, July 6th. 1846

SIR,

Since I wrote you last evening I have determined to hoist the Flag of the U. States at this place tomorrow as I would prefer being sacrificed for doing too much than too little.

If you consider you have sufficient force or if Fremont will join you, you will hoist the Flag of the United States at Yerba Buena or any other proper place and take possession in the name of the United States, of the Fort, and that portion of the Country. I send you a copy of my summons to the Military Commandant of Monterey to surrender the place and also my Proclamation to the People of California which you will have translated into Spanish and promulgate many copies in both languages.[1] I have sent a similar letter to Genl. Castro with an addition of an invitation for him to meet me at this place to enter into a capitulation.

I will send you a duplicate copy of these documents tomorrow by land which I hope will reach you before the boat can get up. You will secure the Bay of San Francisco as soon as possible at all events. It is my intention to go up to San Francisco as soon as I can leave this [place] which I hope will not be many days.

Mr. Larkin advises that you should not send by Courier anything that would do harm to make public and should you have anything that you consider important for me to know you can send the Launch down again.

I am very anxious to know if Capt. Fremont will cooperate with us. Mr. Larkin is writing to him by the Launch and you will please put him in possession of his letter as soon as possible.

I have not time to write more at present. Very Respectfully Your Obdt. Servt. &c.

JOHN D. SLOAT
Commde. in Chief &c.

Copy of enclosure 1 in Sloat to George Bancroft, 31 July 1846 (DNA-45, Pacific Squadron, Commodore Sloat's Cruise, 1844–46). The letter was sent to Montgomery at San Francisco. Commodore John D. Sloat (1781–1867), commander of the Pacific Squadron since 1844, had finally arrived at Monterey on 2 July and had been briefed on the California situation by Larkin. But it was not until after the arrival of the *Portsmouth*'s launch with letters from Montgomery detailing JCF's cooperation with the Bear Flaggers that he decided to make California a part of the United States (MC LANE, 83). Although Sloat was greatly concerned about his own health and turned over his command to Stockton before the month was out, he was not put on the reserve list until 1855.

1. The "Summons" and the "Proclamation" are not printed here but may be found in CAL. HIS. SOC. DOCS., 2:352–54. In the latter, which Larkin helped compose, Sloat exhibited tact and conciliation. He declared that although he came "in arms with a powerfull force," he came not as an enemy to California but as a friend. He assured the "peaceable" inhabitants that they would enjoy "the same rights and privileges as the Citizens of any other portion" of the nation; pointed out the benefits of a permanent, secure government; and guaranteed freedom of religion, security of property, and, to those not disposed to accept the privileges of U.S. citizenship, the right to move out of the country. He also invited the local officials to retain their offices.

40. Thomas Oliver Larkin to Frémont

Consulate of the United States of America
MONTEREY, CALIFORNIA, July 7th, 1846

DEAR SIR

From the circumstances of the Country of which you will soon be informed, you may be induced to send to the States a few men to carry despatches, in which case you will please give the Commodore [Sloat] and myself timely notice. I by all means recommend it. No vessel will, I presume, leave here for Mazatlan under thirty days, making 90 to 100 to reach Washington. Even under present circumstances, she may not sail, and if she does, the letters are not safe going through Mexico. It is of every importance that letters go to our different Departments immediately. You are better aware than myself of the time of year, and whether a few men can travel or not. Should you not feel justified in detaching the men from your company, if it is of service, I will make the demand on you for them. The Commodore wishes you at once to cooperate with him under the new state of affairs, and inform him immediately, calling on Capt. Montgomery for a Launch if you need it, to bring him information of your willingness to do so. By land you can immediately send me a Courier with a letter in your handwriting without either of our signatures, merely saying you will fall into the plan offered. You [will] please shew this to Mr. Gillespie. I am Sir your most obdt. servt.,

(Signed) THOMAS O. LARKIN

Captain J. C. Fremont

Copy 38 in Larkin to Secretary of State, 20 July 1846, no. 54 (DNA-59, Consular Despatches, Monterey, Calif.). The letter was sent "open" to Commander John B. Montgomery, who was asked to read, seal, and forward it immediately.

41. John B. Montgomery to Frémont

U. S. Ship Portsmouth
YERBA BUENA, July 9th 1846

SIR,

Last evening I was officially notified of the existence of war between the United States & the Central Government of Mexico, and have this morning taken formal possession of this place, and hoisted our Flag in the Town. Commodore Sloat who took possession of Monterey on the 7th Inst. has directed me to notify you of this change in the political condition of California and to request your

Sutter's Fort about 1846. From a lithograph in Joseph Warren Revere, *A Tour of Duty in California* (New York, 1849). Courtesy of the Library of Congress.

presence at Monterey with a view to future arrangements [and] co-operation at as early a period as possible.

I forwarded at two o'clock this morning a despatch from Commodore Sloat to the Commandant of Sonoma with an American Flag for their use should they stand in need of one.

Mr. Watmough who will hand you this will give you all news. Very Respectfully I am Sir, Your Obt. Servt.,

JNO. B. MONTGOMERY

To Capt. J. C. Fremont
U. S. Top. Engineers
Santa Clara.

Lbk (DNA-45, no. 22, Officers' Letters, Letterbooks of J. B. Montgomery). By an order of the same date, purser James H. Watmough of the *Portsmouth* was instructed to proceed to Santa Clara and to San Jose, if necessary, to intercept JCF. JCF was at Sutter's Fort when he received the news on the evening of 10 July that the American flag was flying over Monterey and Yerba Buena. The next morning the Stars and Stripes were raised over the fort.

42. John D. Sloat to Frémont

Flag-Ship Savannah, BAY OF MONTEREY
July 9, 1846

SIR:

You will, no doubt, have received the information before this that I have hoisted the flag of the United States at this place, on the 7th instant; as yet all is quiet and no resistance of any kind has been made.

I immediately sent to General Castro a copy of my proclamation to the inhabitants of California, and a summons to surrender forthwith to the American arms the forts, military posts, and stations, under his command, together with all troops, arms, munitions of war, and public property of every description under his control and jurisdiction, with an invitation for him to meet me immediately at this place to enter into articles of capitulation, that himself, officers, soldiers, and the inhabitants of California, may receive assurances of perfect safety to themselves and property.

I have this moment learned, by an Englishman just arrived from General Castro, at the Pueblo, that General Castro was probably at St. John's last evening, and that you would probably be at the Pueblo at the same time.

I have not as yet received any communication from General Castro.[1]

It is thought he will be in to-morrow, or send some communication. The Englishman says that when the general read my proclamation to his troops, he expressed his approbation of it: if he is wise, he will make no resistance.

I have here the frigate *Savannah,* of fifty-four guns, the sloops of war *Cyane* and *Levant,* of twenty-four guns each, armed with 32-pounder long guns, 68-pounder shell guns, and 42-pounder carronades, with a large complement of men, and am every moment in expectation of the arrival of the frigate *Congress,* with sixty 32-pounder long guns, at this place, and the sloop *Erie* with long 18's at San Francisco.[2] I am extremely anxious to see you at your earliest convenience; and should General Castro consent to enter into a capitulation, it is of the utmost importance that you should be present. I hope, therefore, that you will push on with all possible despatch, or, at any rate, let me hear from you immediately.

Captain Montgomery sent his launch down, which I despatched on the 6th, informing him that I should take possession of this place on the next day in the name of the United States, and sent him a copy of my summons and proclamation, and also orders to take possession of Yerba Buena and the Bay of San Francisco immediately, requesting him to inform you of these facts without delay. I have also sent him three couriers with the same orders (in cipher), which I have no doubt have reached him, and am confident that the flag of the United States is now flying there.

Although I am in expectation of seeing General Castro, to enter into satisfactory terms with him, there may be a necessity of one hundred men, well mounted, who are accustomed to riding, to form a force to prevent any further robbing of the farmers' houses, &c. by the Indians. I request you to bring in as many men up to that number with you, or send them on under charge of a trusty person, in case you may be delayed for a day or two. Should you find any

Government horses on the road, please bring them in. Very respectfully, your obedient servant,

JOHN D. SLOAT
Commander-in-Chief of the U. S.
Naval Forces in the Pacific Ocean, etc.

Captain J. D. Frémont.

Printed in *National Intelligencer,* 6 Dec. 1847, and MEMOIRS, 530–31.

1. On the very day Sloat wrote JCF, Castro answered the naval officer's
summons. "I say to your excellency that for the resolution of affairs of such
great gravity it is necessary for me to put myself in accord with his excellency
the Governor and Honorable Assembly of the Department as the legitimate
authorities which represent the towns which compose it, in the understanding
that I will defer with pleasure to the opinion of those officials." In addition
to saying that he must go south to consult with Governor Pico and the Assembly, he wrote that he was resolved "to omit no sacrifice" to preserve the
integrity and independence of his country as long as he could count on a
single man "in this cause which is as just as it is national" (José Castro to
Sloat, San Juan Bautista, 9 July 1846, both original and translation in CAL.
HIS. SOC. DOCS., 2:354–55).

2. As noted earlier, Sloat had arrived at Monterey from Mazatlán in his
flagship *Savannah* on 2 July, almost two weeks after the arrival of the *Cyane*
(19 June), captained by William Mervine, from the same Mexican port, and
two days after the *Levant* (30 June), apparently from Mexico. The *Congress,*
sailing from Hawaii with Commodore Stockton aboard, did not anchor in
Monterey Bay until 15 July, and the storeship *Erie* put in on 4 Sept. and was
fitted out as a cruiser. The *Portsmouth,* under the command of John B.
Montgomery, had arrived at Monterey about 22 April but in June, at the
request of Larkin, shifted her anchorage to San Francisco. When Commodore
Sloat transferred the command of the Pacific Squadron to Stockton on 29
July, he sailed for home on the *Levant.* A good account of the U.S. Navy's
role in the conquest of California is BAUER.

43. Mariano G. Vallejo to Frémont

[NEW HELVETIA]
[11 July 1846]

MY RESPECTED SIR:

Yesterday I had the pleasure of having received word from one of
your officers that today we would have a meeting for which I have
been eagerly waiting for the whole day, but the day being almost
over, I fear that you will not have time, and both to calm the restlessness of the gentlemen who share my jail and for my own satisfaction,

Monterey about 1846. From a lithograph in Joseph Warren Revere, *A Tour of Duty in California* (New York, 1849). Courtesy of the Library of Congress.

I wish that you would let us know if our imprisonment, which has been aggravated by a complete incommunicado since last June 16, has ended. I do not have to tell you about the way in which we have been deprived of our freedom because you know about it, but the national flag of North America that today is waving over this fortress suggests to me that the change has already taken place and a prosperous future is in store for this country to whose destiny I cannot be indifferent. Therefore today I was delighted that you have issued the proclamation which was probably published when the flag that changes the destiny of California was raised high, and that it is bound to have a direct influence over those of us, whose deep-down conviction is that the state of the nation cannot be worse than the state in which it was before the change.

[*No signature*]

Copy in Spanish (CU-B). The editors wish to thank Mrs. Sara de Mundo Lo, University of Illinois Library, for translating this document and Doc. Nos. 142 and 163.
Vallejo was being detained at Sutter's Fort by order of JCF.

44. Thomas Oliver Larkin to Frémont

Consulate of the United States of America
MONTEREY, CALIFORNIA, July 12th, 1846

SIR

From the route you have taken I presume you did not receive my last letter (of this past week).[1] Commodore Sloat is very anxious to see you, waiting for your cooperation. I have given him to understand that jointly with you, his business will become light in comparison to what he now has on hand. I presume you to have entered the Pueblo [San Jose] today. The Como. wishes you to reach Monterey with all the men you can bring, or with a few come in, and have the others follow directly. He wants to form a Company under pay to cut off the horse stealing, crimes in general throughout the Country that requires a force or bear arms against any body of soldiers who may be met to fight him. General Castro has wrote to the Como. that he must go South to see the Governor & Assembly.[2] I hope they settle the business peaceably. You can promise men to

172

take up arms in the name of the United States at fifteen or twenty dollars per month. They can in a great measure choose their own officers. Should you be able to purchase any horses or saddles before you come in, funds are here for payment.

I strongly recommend a few of your former men to carry home despatches. Of this more when we meet. Hoping to see you tomorrow I am your most obedient servant,

(Signed) THOMAS O. LARKIN

Captain J. C. Fremont

Printed in LARKIN, 5:129–30.
1. Our Doc. No. 40.
2. See p. 170, n. 1.

45. Frémont to Edward M. Kern

AMERICAN FORK, July 12. 46

DEAR SIR,

Without regard to any order that you may receive in my absence, you will retain Messrs. Vallejo, Preuxdon [Prudon], Leese, and Carillo[1] at the fort, of which you are hereby placed in full command. I will probably see you again in 10 days, when we will make preparations for our homeward voyage. Iron and confine any person who shall disobey your orders—shoot any person who shall endanger the safety of the place. Respectfully, Yrs.

J. C. FRÉMONT

I leave Jean Droil [François Gendreau][2] in charge of my cavallada [caballada] and of the cattle. He will be at or near Perry's house.[3] Send vaqueros to him when you want a beef.   J.C.F.

ALS, RC (CSmH). Addressed, "Mr. Kearne, Commandr. Fort Sacramento."
1. Seeking information about the imprisonment of his brother-in-law, Mariano G. Vallejo, Julio Carrillo had arrived at Sutter's Fort in the latter part of June. And although Lieut. John S. Missroon at Sonoma had given him a passport to and from the fort, Edward Kern refused to allow him to leave. He had been forced to join the ranks of the prisoners, who now included not only Robert Ridley and those taken at Sonoma but also José Noriega and Vicente Peralta, who had stopped at the fort on 20 June. It was

173

not until 3 Aug. that Carrillo and Mariano G. Vallejo were released and not until 8 Aug. that Salvador Vallejo, Prudon, Leese, Ridley, Noriega, and Peralta were paroled. This was largely due to the solicitation of Larkin and to naval orders—not to any order of JCF's (TAYS [3], 17:224–29). Later the Spanish vice-consul at Santa Barbara sought reparation from the U.S. government for the unjust imprisonment suffered by Noriega through the orders of JCF (see correspondence between R. B. Mason and Cesareo Lataillade, House Exec. Doc. 17, pp. 427, 430, 31st Cong., 1st sess., Serial 573). A document in CSmH, dated Fort Sacramento, 11 July 1846, and appearing to be a parole of Vicente Peralta, José Noriega, and others, seems merely to express the wishful thinking on the part of the prisoners that they be released.

2. François Gendreau's name appears in JCF's financial vouchers as François Jeandreau and in other California records as Gendran, Gendron, Geandreau, and even Jondro. He was a Canadian with a Walla Walla Indian wife. Gendreau was an employee of Sutter's, and he later commanded the company of Walla Wallas organized by Sutter for JCF's southern campaign in the winter of 1846 (see Frémont to Kern, 20 Nov. 1846 [Doc. No. 90], and DILLON, 254).

3. Probably Perry McCoon (d. 1851), a former sailor in the British Navy who had worked at Sutter's Fort. In 1845 he moved to a farm of his own nearby (NEW HELVETIA DIARY, 38, 43; PIONEER REGISTER).

46. Robert F. Stockton to Frémont

Memoranda

[22 July 1846]

1st. Capt. Fremont and Lieut. Gillespie will, in a letter addressed to me, volunteer, for themselves and the men with them, to serve under my command as long as I may be in possession of California and desire their services.

2d. They may increase the number of their forces to 300 men.

3d. Their men must all be enlisted, and put under the military laws of the United States in every respect.

4th. The men may receive ten dollars a month, besides their rations.

5th. All their supplies, such as tobacco, &c., will be charged to them.[1]

R. F. STOCKTON
Commander

Printed in *National Intelligencer,* 6 Dec. 1847. This was one of the documents presented to the court on 3 Dec. 1847 in the trial of JCF for mutiny, disobedience, and conduct prejudicial to good order and discipline, but it was not printed in the official proceedings.

Robert Field Stockton. From a daguerreotype of the Chicago
Historical Society.

Robert Field Stockton (1795–1866) had arrived on the *Congress* at Monterey on 15 July and had been appointed commander-in-chief of all forces and operations on land in California by Commodore Sloat. He had superintended the construction of the first propeller-driven warship—the *Princeton*—and commanded it for two years. More than a naval officer, Stockton was an influential businessman and wealthy landowner from New Jersey with a reputation for flamboyant, unconventional, and adventurous action—in a sense the prototype of the aggressive American nationalist of the 1830s and 1840s.

Larkin suspected that Stockton was sent to California for a special reason. To Abel Stearns in Los Angeles on 24 May he had written, "I look daily for Com. Robert Stockton in the Congress, who left Norfolk, October 30. . . . He is a man worth from 25 to 30,000 dollars, per year, with yet larger expectations. In the Clay and Polk canvass of 1844, I understand he spent 20,000 dollars in the New Jersey election. . . . Com. Stockton was called to Washington a day or two before he sailed. He is a man I believe much in the confidence of Mr. Polk. I believe that Emigration will exceed one thousand this year, perhaps two. . . . Now when you understand all this, and see the signs of the times, knowing what we do of this and affairs here, what object can you suppose a Commodore of Capt. Stockton's wealth rank and prospects had in leaving all, and coming to the North Pacific. Hardly to take charge of a squadron to see to Whalers and some merchants ships" (LARKIN, 4:391–92). A few days later, over the signature "Paisano," Larkin wrote Moses Yale Beach & Sons of the New York *Sun* about the ball which the *Portsmouth* had given for the native inhabitants and added, "The Portsmouth now gentle lays at here a[n]chorage waiti[n]g for the Commodore [i.e., Stockton] who will on his arrival give a Ball of some discription or other according to the finale of Mr. Slidel & mission last Feb & March in the 'gran Capital.' Be his Ball and party as it may, it will end pleasantly and to the satisfaction of many as they can not long endure the present state of self government" (LARKIN, 4:404–6).

On 31 May Larkin informed Gillespie that Stockton could hardly be in Monterey harbor before 15 or 20 June—as though to warn him and JCF not to move too quickly (LARKIN, 4:407–9).

Soon after the Mexican War, Stockton resigned from the Navy and as New Jersey's Democratic senator entered Congress, where he urged various naval reforms, including the abolition of flogging. For more details on his life, see STOCKTON and PRICE.

1. As ten days had elapsed since JCF penned Doc. No. 45 to Kern, a résumé of his activities may be helpful in putting the present document into perspective.

On 12 July JCF had left the American River for Monterey, going by way of the San Joaquin Valley and crossing the mountains to the Mission San Juan Bautista. Arriving there on 17 July, he was joined by Archibald Gillespie, who brought the happy news that Commodore Stockton had arrived. But he also brought the less felicitous tidings that Sloat was disturbed over the lack of knowledge of the authority under which the Marine lieutenant and JCF were operating. JCF left a small detachment to garrison San Juan and proceeded with 160 or 170 men to Monterey, which he reached on 19 July. Accompanied by Gillespie, JCF went on board the *Savannah* for an interview with Sloat. Regarding this meeting, Gillespie reported to the Secretary of the Navy, "Commodore Sloat . . . did not express himself as satisfied with either of us, and appeared extremely distressed at the thought of responsibility in any way connected with ourselves. Commodore Sloat up to this moment has not recognized the operations or the command of Cap't Fremont, and at our late interview, required that a letter should be addressed to him by Cap't Fremont, showing by what authority we were in the country, and under what orders we had been acting. This letter has not been written, and very fortunately and to save all difficulty, Commodore Sloat gave the command of all operations on shore to Commodore Stockton, which circumstances has inspired confidence in the volunteers, and already given a new aspect to the position of affairs in this quarter" (Gillespie to Secretary of the Navy, 25 July 1846, AMES [1], 277–78). In testimony in 1848 before the subcommittee of the Senate Military Affairs Committee considering the California Claims, JCF stated that he had told Sloat that he was acting on his own responsibility and without written authority from the government to justify hostilities—a view which was reiterated in the *Memoirs* and in a *Century* magazine article (*California Claims,* Senate Report 75, p. 113, 30th Cong., 1st sess., Serial 512; MEMOIRS, 534; "The Conquest of California," *Century,* n.s., vol. 19 [1890–91]).

As soon as Sloat had appointed Stockton commander-in-chief of all forces and operations on land, Stockton took JCF and his troops into the service of the United States as the "Battalion of California Volunteers." However, the official muster rolls of the California Battalion, made later, show 7 July 1846 as the date of entry into service for those who had been in JCF's battalion on that date. This was the date on which Sloat occupied Monterey (ROGERS [3], 18).

Gillespie and JCF must have breathed further sighs of relief when Sloat, in poor health, sailed on 29 July in the *Levant* for the United States, leaving the vigorous and aggressive Stockton in command of the Pacific Squadron.

47. Robert F. Stockton to Frémont

U. S. Frigate Congress
BAY OF MONTEREY, July 23, 1846

SIR:

You are hereby appointed to the command of the California battalion of United States troops, with the rank of major. Respectfully, your obedient servant,

R. F. STOCKTON
Commander-in-chief, &c.

To Major Fremont,
Commanding California battalion

Printed in *Message of the President of the United States, Communicating the Proceedings of the Court Martial in the Trial of Lieutenant Colonel Frémont,* Senate Exec. Doc. 33, p. 175, 30th Cong., 1st sess., Serial 507.

Hereafter, this document will be cited as CT. MARTIAL. And since the supplement to the present volume of *The Expeditions of John Charles Frémont* is a facsimile edition of the government document, all references to CT. MARTIAL are also references to it.

48. Robert F. Stockton to Frémont

United States Frigate Congress,
MONTEREY BAY, July 23, 1846.

SIR:

You will please to embark on board the United States ship Cyane,[1] with the detachment of troops under my command, on Saturday afternoon.

The ship, at daylight on Sunday morning, will sail for San Diego, where you will disembark your troops and procure horses for them, and will make every necessary preparation to march through the country at a moment's notice for me.[2]

You will endeavor to encamp so near San Diego as to have a daily communication with the Cyane, which will remain at anchor there, until you receive orders to march.

The object of this movement is to take, or to get between, the Colorado and General Castro.

I will leave Monterey in this ship for San Pedro, so as to arrive there about the time that you may be expected to have arrived at San Diego.[3]

I will despatch a courier to you from San Pedro, to inform you of my movements. Faithfully, your obedient servant,

R. F. STOCKTON
Commodore, &c.

Captain Fremont,
United States army.

Copy of enclosure 11 in Stockton to George Bancroft, 22 Aug. 1846 (DNA-45, Pacific Squadron, Commodore Stockton, 1846–47). Also in "The Report of the Secretary of the Navy," 5 Dec. 1846, which formed a part of the *Message of the President of the United States to the Two Houses of Congress,* 8 Dec. 1846, House Exec. Doc. 4, p. 674, 29th Cong., 2nd sess., Serial 497.

1. On this same day Samuel F. DuPont had been ordered by Stockton to relieve Capt. William Mervine as commander of the twenty-gun sloop *Cyane.* Mervine was assigned to the frigate *Savannah* (DU PONT, 34–35).

2. When the ship sailed on 26 July, she had, in addition to her own crew of 120, about 165 battalion men with saddles and packs but no horses.

3. Larkin wrote Buchanan on 29 July that he was to go south with Stockton "for the purpose of seeking a personal interview with the Governour and Legislature of California with the view of entering into some arrangement with them as the constitutional authorities of the country to settle the present state of affairs around us. This once done the people will become calm and submit to the existing state of things lately brought about" (LARKIN, 5:180–82). Through Abel Stearns, one of the more influential Americans in Los Angeles, Larkin urged the local civil and military officers to form a government under Stockton's authority. When his efforts failed, perhaps because Stockton desired them to fail, Larkin wrote Stearns from the *Congress*, 7 Aug., "You will bear in mind that I have done all I could to prevent the visit of 800 soldiers to your city and to avert the evils that must necessully attend a Campagn by such men thorg [through?] the country from St D. to the Sacramento. The Commo intends to proceed at once to hostilities and deal with this department as a part of R. Mexico" (LARKIN, 5:187).

49. Thomas Oliver Larkin to Frémont

Consulate of the United States of America
MONTEREY CALIFORNIA July 24th 1846

SIR

By verbal orders of Commodore John D Sloat, I wrote you on the 7th and 12th instant on certain affairs. Since your arrival in Monterey you have verbally informed me that you did not receive the letter of the 12th and you have not sent me any Official answer to either. Commodore Sloat has since informed me verbally that he has concluded not to keep up the cavalry, nor any other force for the interiour of the Country, and therefore will not act on the subject of my letters.

Therefore as I have acted only on verbal orders, you will please consider all requests or instructions of mine in any former letters I have written to you as countermanded and not to be further acted on from this date. I am Sir with great respect, Yours very Truly,

(Signed) THOMAS O. LARKIN

Captain J. C. Fremont
United States Army, Monterey

Printed in LARKIN, 5:158.

50. Frémont to William A. Leidesdorff

CARMEL, July 24. 1846

DEAR SIR,

I have shipped to your address by ship Sterling, Capt. [George W.] Vincent, a box marked with my name and containing property be-- longing to Mr. Knight.[1] You will much oblige me by paying charges and forwarding the same by an early opportunity to New Helvetia, consigned to Mr. Edd. Kerne, commdg. at Fort Sacramento. Very Respectfully Your Obedt. Servt.

J. C. FRÉMONT

Capt. Leidesdorff
U.S. Consul at Yerba Buena

ALS, RC (CU-B). Addressed; endorsed.
1. William Knight (d. 1849), a settler on the Sacramento, had taken an active part in the Bear Flag Revolt. He had come to California in 1841 in the Workman-Rowland party from New Mexico (PIONEER REGISTER).

51. Frémont to Archibald H. Gillespie

CARMEL, July 25 [1846]

DR. SIR,

The new arrangement is of course *corriente* [in operation], and the camp will be held in readiness to move at 3 in the morning. Very respectfully,

J. C. FRÉMONT
U. S. Army

Capt. Archibald Gillespie
Adjt., Cal. Battn.

ALS, RC (Eleutherian Mills Historical Society Library, Greenville, Del.). Addressed to Gillespie at Monterey. Endorsed: "All right! Countermand the Boats 'til Sunrise tomorrow. A. H. G."

52. Frémont to Thomas H. Benton

Mission of Carmel, July 25, 1846

My Dear Sir:

When Mr. Gillespie overtook me in the middle of May, we were encamped on the northern shore of the greater Tlamath Lake. Snow was falling steadily and heavily in the mountains, which entirely surround and dominate the elevated valley region into which we had penetrated; in the east, and north, and west, barriers absolutely impassable barred our road; we had no provisions; our animals were already feeble, and while any other way was open, I could not bring myself to attempt such a doubtful enterprise as a passage of these unknown mountains in the dead of winter.[1] Every day the snow was falling; and in the face of the depressing influence exercised on the people by the loss of our men, and the unpromising appearance of things, I judged it inexpedient to pursue our journey further in this direction, and determined to retrace my steps, and carry out the views of the Government by reaching the frontier on the line of the Colorado river. I had scarcely reached the lower Sacramento, when General Castro, then in the north (at Sonoma, in the Department of Sonoma, north of the bay of San Francisco, commanded by General Vallejo), declared his determination immediately to proceed against me, and after defeating me to proceed against the foreigners settled in the country, for whose expulsion an order had just been issued by the Governor of the Californias.[2] For these purposes Castro immediately assembled a force at the Mission of Santa Clara, a strong place, on the northern shore of the Francisco Bay. You will remember how grossly outraged and insulted we had already been by this officer; many in my own camp, and throughout the country, thought that I should not have retreated in March last. I felt humiliated and humbled; one of the main objects proposed by this expedition had been entirely defeated, and it was the opinion of the officers of the squadron (so I was informed by Mr. Gillespie) that I could not again retreat consistently with any military reputation. Unable to procure supplies elsewhere, I had sent by Mr. Gillespie to Captain Montgomery, commanding the United States ship of war Portsmouth, then lying at Monterey, a small requisition for such supplies as were indispensably necessary to leave the valley; and my animals were now in such a state that I could not get out of the valley, without reaching the country which lies on the east side of them in an entirely destitute condition. Having carefully examined my position, and foreseeing, I think, clearly, all the consequences which may eventuate to me from such a step, I determined to take such active and anticipatory measures as should seem to me most expedient to protect my party and justify my own character. I was well aware of the grave responsibility which I assumed, but I also determined that, having once decided to do so, I would assume it and its consequences fully and entirely, and go through with the business completely to the end. I regret that, by a sudden emergency, I have only an hour for writing to all friends, and that therefore from the absence of detail, what I say to you will not be clearly understood.

Castro's first measure was an attempt to incite the Indian population of the Joaquin and Sacramento valleys, and the neighboring mountains, to burn the crops of the foreigners and otherwise proceed immediately against them. These Indians are extremely numerous, and the success of his measure would have been very destructive; but he failed entirely. On the 6th of June I decided on the course which I would pursue, and immediately concerted my operations with the foreigners inhabiting the Sacramento valley. A few days afterwards, one of Castro's officers, with a party of 14 men, attempted to pass a drove of two hundred horses from Sonoma to Santa Clara, via New Helvetia, with the avowed purpose of bringing troops into the country. On the 11th they were surprised at daylight on the Consumné River by a party of 12 from my camp. The horses were taken, but they were (the men) dismissed without injury. At daybreak on the 15th, the military fort of Sonoma was taken by surprise, with 9 brass pieces of artillery, 250 stands of muskets, some other arms, and a quantity of ammunition. General Vallejo, his brother (Captain Vallejo), Colonel Greuxdon [Prudon], and some others were taken prisoners, and placed at New Helvetia, a fortified post under my command. In the meantime a launch had reached New Helvetia with stores from the ship Portsmouth, now lying at Yerba Buena, on Francisco Bay. News of General Castro's proceedings against me in *March* had reached Commodore Sloat at Mazatlan at the end of that month, and he had immediately despatched the ship Portsmouth to Monterey, with general instructions to protect American interests in California.

These enterprises accomplished I proceeded to the American settlements on the Sacramento, and the Rio de los Americanos, to obtain reinforcements of men and rifles.

The information brought by Mr. Gillespie to Captain Montgomery, in relation to my position, induced that officer immediately to proceed to Yerba Buena, whence he despatched his launch to me. I immediately wrote to him, by return of the boat, describing to him fully my position and intentions,[3] in order that he might not, by supposing me to be acting under orders from our Government, unwittingly commit himself in affording me other than such assistance as his instructions would authorize him naturally to offer an officer charged with an important public duty; or, in fine, to any citizen of the United States.

Information having reached me from the commanding officer at Sonoma, that his post was threatened with an attack by a force under General Castro, I raised camp on the American Fork on the afternoon of the 23rd, and, accompanied by Mr. Gillespie, at two in the morning of the 25th reached Sonoma, with ninety mounted riflemen, having marched eighty miles. Our people still held the place, only one division of Castro's force, a squadron of cavalry, numbering seventy men, and commanded by Joaquin de la Torre (one of his best officers), having succeeded in crossing the straits (Francisco Bay). This force had attacked an advance party of twenty Americans, and (was) defeated with the loss of two killed and two or three wounded. The Americans lost none. This was an unexpected check to the Californians, who had announced their intentions to defeat our people without firing a gun; to beat out their brains with their *"tapaderos,"* and destroy them *"con cuchillos puros."*[4] They were led to use this expression from the circumstances that a few days previously they had captured two of our men (an express), and after wounding, had bound them to trees, and cut them to pieces while alive, with an exaggeration of cruelty which only Indians would be capable of.[5] In a few days *de la Torre* was driven from the country, having barely succeeded in effecting his escape across the straits, the guns (six large and handsome pieces) spiked at the fort on the *south* side of the entrance to Francisco bay, and the communication with the opposite side entirely broken off, the boats and launches being either destroyed or in our possession. Three of Castro's party having landed on the Sonoma side in advance, were killed on the beach;[6] and beyond this there was no loss on either side. In all these proceedings, Mr. Gillespie has acted with me. We reached Sonoma again on the evening of July 4th, and in the morning I called the people together, and spoke to them in relation to the position of the country, advising a course of operations which was unanimously adopted. California was declared independent, the country put under martial law, the force organized and officers elected. A pledge, binding themselves to support these measures, and to obey their officers, was signed by those present. The whole was placed under my direction. Several officers from the Portsmouth were present at this meeting. Leaving Captain Griggsby [Grigsby][7] with fifty men in command of Sonoma, I left that place on the 6th, and reached my encampment on the American Fork in three days. Before we arrived at that place, General Castro had evacuated Santa Clara, which he had been engaged in fortifying, and with a force of about four hundred men, and two pieces of artillery, commenced his retreat upon St. John's, a fortified post, having eight pieces of artillery, principally brass. On the evening of the 10th we were electrified by the arrival of an express from Captain Montgomery, with the information that Commodore Sloat had hoisted the flag of the United States at Monterey, and taken possession of the country. Captain Montgomery had hoisted the flag at Yerba Buena, and sent one to Sonoma, to be hoisted at that place. One also was sent to the officer commanding at New Helvetia, requesting that it might be hoisted at his post.

Independence and the flag of the United States are synonymous terms to the foreigners here (the northern, which is the stronger part, particularly), and accordingly I directed the flag to be hoisted with a salute the next morning. The event produced great rejoicing among our people. The next day I received an express from Commodore Sloat, transmitting to me his proclamation, and directing me to proceed with the force under my orders to Monterey. The registered force actually in arms, and under my orders, numbered two hundred and twenty riflemen, with one piece of field artillery, and ten men, in addition to the artillery of the garrison. We were on the eve of marching on Castro when this intelligence arrived; accordingly, I directed my march upon Monterey, where I arrived on the evening of the 19th, with a command of one hundred and sixty mounted riflemen and one piece of artillery. I found also there Commodore Stockton in command of the frigate Congress, and Admiral Seymour, in command of her Britannic Majesty's ship Collingwood, of 80 guns.[8] I have been badly interrupted, and shall scarcely be able to put you in full possession of occurrences.

To come briefly to a conclusion, Commodore Sloat has transferred the squadron, with California and its apurtenances, into the hands of Commodore Stockton, who has resolved to make good the possession of California. This officer approves entirely of the course pursued by myself and Mr. Gillespie, who, I repeat, has been hand-in-hand with me in this business. I received this morning from Commodore Stockton a commission of major in the United States army, retaining command of my battalion, to which a force of eight marines will be attached. We are under orders to embark to-morrow morning on board the Cyane sloop of war, and will disembark at *San Diego,* immediately in the rear of Castro. He is now at the *Pueblo de los Angeles,* an interior city, with a force of about 500 men, supposed to be increasing. The design is to attack him with my force at that place. He has there seven or eight pieces of artillery.

Commodore Sloat, who goes home by way of Panama, promises to hand or send you this immediately on his arrival at Washington, to which he goes direct. It is my intention to leave this country, if it is within the bounds of possibility, at the end of August. I could then succeed in crossing the Rocky Mountains; later it would not be possible, on account of the snow; and by that time a territorial Government will be in operation here. Yours, very truly,

J. C. FREMONT

Hon. Thomas H. Benton
United States Senate, Washington

Printed in *National Intelligencer,* 11 Nov. 1846; also in Washington *Daily Union,* 9 Nov. 1846, and MEMOIRS, 545–47. Benton actually laid the private letter before the president "in the absence of official information on the subject of Lieutenant Colonel (then Captain) Fremont's operations in Upper California" to show the "unwilling manner in which he became involved in hostilities with the Mexican authorities of that province, before he had heard of the war with Mexico . . . and especially to disprove the accusation made officially against him by Governor Castro, of having come into California with a body of United States troops, under the pretext of a scientific expedition, but in reality to excite the Americans settled in that province to an insurrection against the Mexican Government."

1. For a man who had crossed the Sierra in Feb. 1844, JCF seems to be overemphasizing the problems of snow in the Oregon mountains in mid-May. He had not mentioned snow in his letter of 24 May to Benton.

2. On 30 April 1846 the subprefect of San Francisco had given the American vice-consul there a copy of an order which he had received from the prefect of Monterey. Noting that many strangers had purchased land, Manuel

Castro wrote that he had "concluded to order all Justices of towns under their charge, that they cannot under the most strong responsability, permit nor authorize sale or cession whatever of land or of said class of property, without regulation by right, and in favour of Mexican citizens, advising those foreigners that are not naturalized and legally introduced, that whatever purchase or acquisition they make will be null and void, and will be subject (if they do not retire voluntarily from the country) to be expelled from it whenever the government finds it convenient" (Francisco Guerrero y Palormares to William Leidesdorff, 30 April 1846, LARKIN, 4:354). While this order does not seem to be retroactive, but merely sets a policy for the immediate future, there were various rumors of possible expulsion. In a circular Larkin noted, "From April to June the foreigners in the Sacramento Valley, were continually harassed by verbal reports & written proclamations, that they must leave California" (Larkin to "Several Americans," 8 July 1846, LARKIN, 5:119–21). Several months earlier he had reported to the Secretary of State that "General Castro is now thinking of taking up to the Sacramento in July, some two or three hundred men, with the ostensible purpose of opposing the Emigrants expected. Yet it can hardly be supposed he is in earnest in his intention. Should he be, he only hastens the crisis" (17 April 1846, DNA-59, no. 42, Consular Despatches, Monterey, Calif.). The expulsion of American settlers would probably have been impossible, even if it had been genuinely contemplated. However, the Mexican authorities did consider the idea of acquiring Sutter's Fort as a barrier against American immigration (DILLON, 236).

3. See Frémont to Montgomery, 16 June 1846, Doc. No. 34.

4. I.e., to beat out their brains with the leather stirrup covers of the Mexican saddles and destroy them simply with knives.

5. The slain men were George Fowler and Thomas Cowie.

6. JCF is referring to the shooting of Francisco and Ramón de Haro, twin brothers from San Francisco, and their uncle, José de los Reyes Berreyesa, an old ranchman from Santa Clara, by Kit Carson, Granville P. Swift, and Neal (probably John Neal) after they were captured at the embarcadero in San Rafael. Talbot gave no details when he wrote his mother, "We killed 3 spies here [San Rafael] from the main force across an arm of the bay of San Pablo" (Talbot to Adelaide Talbot, 24 July 1846, DLC—Talbot Papers). After talking with John Sears in Sonoma in Sept. 1846, Marius Duvall, the assistant surgeon on board the *Portsmouth,* rejected the Carson-Swift-Neal allegation that the three Californian victims carried orders from Castro directing Joaquín de la Torre to slaughter foreigners without distinction of sex or age. He was convinced that the blood of these men was on the conscience of JCF, who, he was persuaded, had given covert orders not to take prisoners (DUVALL, 53–54). Richard B. Mason, military governor of California, wrote Col. Jonathan D. Stevenson, "I have been told that Carson was of or commanded the party that went to meet them, and upon starting, asked what orders he had to give, to which F. replied, 'You know the orders, we want no prisoners, or we cannot take care of prisoners' or words to that effect. The party darted off and soon met and shot down an old man & two boys, they being unarmed. This is as I hear the story, and I should like to know Carson's version of it" (Mason to Stevenson, Monterey, 28 Feb. 1848, CLU—J. D. Stevenson Papers).

JCF's degree of responsibility for the atrocity was to become an issue in the presidential campaign of 1856. Alexander Godey wrote a letter to John

O. Wheeler defending JCF and claiming that Carson had shot the Californians when they resisted arrest (12 Sept. 1856, HAFEN & HAFEN, 263–75). Gillespie, however, charged that the men were deliberately shot in cold blood. He did not say that JCF gave the orders, but that after the deed was done, JCF commented "It is well!!!" and let the bodies lie on the ground all night ([1856] memorandum, CLU—Gillespie Papers).

In his MEMOIRS, 525, JCF justified the execution on the grounds that it was in retaliation for the brutal killing of Cowie and Fowler, and he attributed the deed to his scouts, "mainly Delawares." Kern wrote home to his brother that the butchering of Cowie and Fowler had "produced an order from our side to take no more prisoners" (Edward M. Kern to Richard H. Kern, Fort Sacramento, 27 July 1846, CSmH).

7. Tennessean John Grigsby (ca. 1806–76), who had been one of the most active in fomenting the Bear Flag Revolt, had come to California in 1845 with William B. Ide. After the California Battalion was reorganized in Nov. 1846 for the southern campaign, Grigsby commanded Company E.

8. Commander of the British Pacific Squadron, Rear Adm. Sir George F. Seymour had been on his flagship at Mazatlán while Sloat was there. The *Collingwood* arrived in Monterey the day after Stockton and stayed a week, fitting new spars. JCF and his supporters were wont to say that their prompt cooperation with the Bear Flaggers spurred Sloat into action and thus averted any scheme the British might have had for establishing a protectorate over California.

53. Frémont to Samuel F. DuPont

S. DIEGO, Aug. 3d. 1846

MY DEAR SIR,

One of Mr. Bandini's[1] servants, Pedro, I am told, goes in your launch.[2] Will you do me the favor to direct him to use much precaution with the accompanying letter and give it into the hands only of D. Alejandro[?][3] himself? Very respectfully,

J. C. FREMONT

Capt. Dupont
Ship Cyane

ALS, RC (Eleutherian Mills Historical Society Library, Greenville, Del.). Addressed to DuPont at San Diego. On 26 July JCF and his men sailed south from Monterey on the *Cyane,* captained by Samuel F. DuPont, to cut off the escape of General Castro. They reached San Diego on 29 July, where they took possession and raised the American flag without a shot being fired against them. For a description of the occupation, see DU PONT, 34–35.

1. Juan Bandini (1800–1859), born and educated in Lima, Peru, came to California as a young man and soon became engaged, sometimes unwisely, in politics, holding various offices. At the time of Stockton's move on Los Angeles in Aug. 1846, Bandini was Governor Pico's secretary and a member

of the Assembly, but he soon espoused the American cause and with Don Santiago E. Argüello aided JCF in procuring horses and supplies, deeds which caused him to be viewed as a traitor by Pico (MEMOIRS, 563–65).

2. The *Cyane's* launch was sent to San Pedro to report the capture of San Diego to Commodore Stockton.

3. The "accompanying letter" for D. Alejandro has not been found. D. Alejandro could possibly be David W. Alexander, whom Captain DuPont made collector of the port of San Pedro on 17 Aug. 1846. He was likewise appointed to that position by JCF in 1847.

54. Robert F. Stockton to Frémont

U. S. Frigate Congress
BAY OF SAN PEDRO
August 6th. 1846
Thursday night

SIR:

I have to inform you that on my arrival here this morning I learned that Alvarado left the Pueblo [Los Angeles] on Sunday morning with 50 men, and that Castro marched on Wednesday with the remainder of their forces, amounting in all to about 250 men.

They say that they have gone to a place called Allamitos [Alamitos],[1] eight leagues south east of Pueblo. If this be true, they must be about half way between us. I will get as near to him as I can without horses. I can not of course chase him. I must try to intercept him, on his retreat before you.

I will probably be encamped at Temple's Farm,[2] which is about midway between this and Pueblo on the main road on Wednesday night, where I will await your arrival that we may march into Pueblo together.

If therefore you are prepared in every respect to march against Castro, you will join me with your forces at Temple's Farm, as soon as you can.

If you are not so prepared you had better embark on board the Cyane and join me by the way of San Pedro.

If you should have good reason to believe that Castro has gone in a different direction, and especially if he attempts to get to the southward of you, you are at liberty to exercise your own judgment, whether it will be better for you to pursue him, or to join me. Faithfully, Yr. obdt. servt.,

R. F. STOCKTON
Commander in chief &c. &c.

To Major Fremont
Commanding California Battalion
St. Diego

P. S. Since writing the above, I have intercepted a letter signed by Pico and Castro, brothers of the General and Governor, I believe, brought this evening by a courier from Pueblo, written it would seem in answer to one written by a Californian officer on shore here announcing my arrival, in which this officer is desired to keep a lookout on the *movements of the enemy*.

"Allamitos" I understand is a Ranch. The last news is that Castro's men are daily leaving him, and that they are very badly equipped.[3]

Lbk (DNA-45, Entry 395 [E-20-A], Letterbook of Robert F. Stockton, 1846–47). The letter was brought to San Diego by the *Cyane*'s launch.
On 1 Aug., three days after JCF had landed at San Diego, Stockton sailed from Monterey with 360 Marines and seamen aboard the *Congress*. Going south with Stockton was Larkin, who hoped to work through influential Americans in Los Angeles to get the Mexican civil and military officers to raise the American flag and form a government under Stockton's authority. Stockton touched at Santa Barbara on 4 Aug., ran up the U.S. flag, and left a small garrison in charge. As this letter indicates, he was in San Pedro two days later.
1. Los Alamitos was owned by Abel Stearns. It had been a part of the large grant made to Manuel Nieto in 1784, originally including all the land lying between the Santa Ana and San Gabriel rivers from the mountains to the sea (R. G. COWAN; ABELOE, 151).
2. Stockton is probably referring to John Temple's land and adobe mansion, built in 1844, in the vicinity of present Long Beach. It, too, had been a part of the old Nieto grant. John Temple (1798–1866), an energetic Massachusetts Yankee who had come to California in 1827, acquired Los Cerritos through marriage and purchase. Success attended most of his ventures in Los Angeles. He opened the first general store, had the first market, and with his brother, Francis Pliny F., was the builder of the first office structure— Temple Block (ABELOE, 151–52).
3. BANCROFT, 5:261–66, notes that Castro and Pico had scarcely been able to raise 200 men and that the citizenry was reluctant to fight against the Americans. Furthermore, the local authorities were apathetic and quarreling among themselves. But after its occupation Larkin wrote an exaggerated account of the power of the Californians in Los Angeles. "The soldiers & farmers collected together in this place by the General, Governor & Prefect of Monterey, amounted to about five hundred men. They had sufficient powder, many very handsome pieces of brass artillery, in good order & an incredible number of

carbines & muskets all over the country, with as many horses & bullocks as they chose to take from the farms; the Officers & principal friends of the Genl. & Govr., were well provided with pistols and swords, and most of these people had a full knowledge of roads, mountains & country." But between 9 and 11 Aug. parties of between twenty and sixty men left the city, "and on the arrival of the United States forces in the town on the 13 inst., not an armed soldier was to be found." He added that the people were completely subdued (23 Aug. 1846, LARKIN, 5:214–16).

55. Robert F. Stockton to Frémont

U. S. Frigate Congress
BAY OF SAN PEDRO
August 9th. 1846

SIR:

Castro has returned to a place within two miles of the Pueblo.

I send to you a young man who will show you the way to "Temple's Rancho." Faithfully, Yr. obdt. servt.,

R. F. STOCKTON
Commander in chief &c. &c.

To
Major Fremont
California Battalion. &c. &c.

Lbk (DNA-45, Entry 395 [E-20-A], Letterbook of Robert F. Stockton, 1846–47). The day after landing at San Pedro, Stockton had received two commissioners—Pablo de la Guerra and José María Flores—who presented a note from Castro demanding an explanation of Stockton's purposes and pointing out that negotiations could not take place until all hostilities were suspended. BANCROFT, 5:268–76, believes that at this point Castro was disposed to accede to the U.S. wishes of voluntarily raising the American flag, and writes that Stockton was also aware that Castro might submit if negotiations were entered into. But Stockton did not want voluntary submission: he wished to avoid continuing the Californians in power on any basis. So he not only rejected the Mexican overtures for negotiations but also insisted on their raising the American flag in such a manner that Castro could not submit without great humiliation. The Californian refused to yield and informed Governor Pico that the country could not be defended and that he was leaving to report to the supreme government in Mexico. Pico submitted Castro's communication to the Assembly on 10 Aug., admitting in a speech that he saw no possibility of a successful defense. He also stated that he was leaving with the general to report to the national authorities and recommended that the Assembly dissolve—which it did. Castro disbanded his military force, and on the night of 10 Aug. he and Pico left the capital and went their separate ways. Castro slipped through the San Gorgonio Pass to the Colorado River and took the Sonora route into Mexico, never to return to California. Pico went to his Santa Margarita rancho, where he found his flight to Mexico temporarily cut off by the advancing Americans. His stay in Mexico was short, however, and in the middle of 1848 he was again in California.

Stockton's march to Los Angeles began on 11 Aug., but when Castro's flight was known, 150 sailors were sent back to San Pedro. Captain Phelps of the *Moscow*, who had arrived at that port on 12 Aug., started overland to overtake Stockton's forces, and he described them as they moved out from Temple's rancho: "The invading army, as it now moved over the plains, presented quite an imposing appearance. First came the full band of music, followed by Captain Zeilin and his marines; then Lieut. Schenck and the web-feet; Lieut. Tighlman, and a battery of four quarter-deck guns, mounted on as many bullock carts' the carriages of the guns were secured by the breechings, and ready for instant service; each cart was drawn by four oxen, —the baggage ammunition followed in similar teams; the Purser, Doctor, and some other officers,—part of them mounted on rather sorry looking horses, and others on foot. The total force was about three hundred and fifty" (PHELPS, 300). In a dispatch to Buchanan, Larkin says the force was 250 men (23 Aug. 1846, LARKIN, 5:214–16).

On 12 Aug., perhaps at the invitation of some of the Angeleños, Larkin, Passed Midshipman Charles H. Baldwin, and a servant pushed on ahead to the Government House in the city. Stockton arrived the next day, and a bit later—about 4 P.M.—JCF's forces, now mounted, joined those under Lieut. James F. Schenck in the gardens outside the town. The combined forces entered the capital. The brass band played "Hail Columbia," and the Stars and Stripes were hoisted in the plaza. The ship's crew took quarters within the walls of the Government House, and JCF's forces camped near the river (PHELPS, 302–5; LARKIN, 5:214–16).

Before joining Stockton's forces, JCF had learned of Castro's retreat and had hoped to cut him off before he could reach the Colorado, but finding that Castro's horses were superior, he soon gave up the chase. The commander of the *Cyane* recorded that Castro "buried his guns in the most ingenious way in the sands, carrying on the carriages much further and leaving thus the wheel tracks to mislead; but the unerring eye of one of the Delaware Indians in Frémont's party detected the trail" (DU PONT, 50). On 17 Aug. JCF started in pursuit of Governor Pico, a chase which he carried on half-heartedly and which ended by his writing to Pico "assuring him of protection to his person and property, and inviting him to return to the city [Los Angeles]" (MEMOIRS, 566; PHELPS, 302–5). Although Pico did not then decide to return, JCF heard afterward that "he thoroughly appreciated my sincere desire to save himself from annoyance and his affairs from derangement, and to publicly show my respect for him and his official position" (MEMOIRS, 655).

In his Senate speech opposing the nomination of Kearny for the brevet rank of major general, Benton said he had the letter from Pico, in the original Spanish, addressed from his retirement in Sonora to JCF, offering to come in person, if necessary, in the interests of preserving peace and order and disclaiming all use of his name to the contrary. "Fremont," Benton said, "should keep it forever, as the high testimony of his exalted conduct in California" (Washington *Daily Union*, 1 Sept. 1848), but unfortunately the letter has been lost to history.

JCF was at San Diego when he received word of the official declaration of war with Mexico. He left Gillespie there and hastened back to Los Angeles to communicate with Stockton (PHELPS, 303–5).

56. Robert F. Stockton to Frémont

CIUDAD DE LOS ANGELES
August 24th. 1846

SIR,

By the Mexican newspapers I see that war has been declared both by the United States and Mexico,[1] and the most vigorous measures have been adopted by Congress to carry it to a speedy conclusion.

Privateers will no doubt be fitted out to prey upon our commerce, and the immense value of that commerce in the Pacific Ocean, and the number of valuable men engaged in it, requires immediately all the protection that can be given to them, by the Ships under my command.

I must therefore withdraw my forces from California as soon as it can be safely done, and as soon as you can enlist men enough to garrison this City, Monterey, San Francisco, Santa Barbara and San Diego; and to have a sufficient force besides to watch the Indians and other enemies.

For these purposes you are authorized and required to increase your present force to three hundred men.

Fifty for San Francisco, Fifty for Monterey, Twenty five for Santa Barbara, Fifty for this City, and Twenty five for San Diego; and one hundred to be kept together, with whom those in the several garrisons can at short notice be called upon at anytime in case of necessity to act.

I propose before I leave the Territory to appoint you to be the Governor, and Captain Gillespie the Secretary thereof; and to appoint also the Council of State, and all the other necessary officers.

You will therefore proceed without delay to do all you can to further my views and intentions thus frankly manifested. Supposing that by the 25th of October, you will have accomplished your part of these preparations, I will meet you at San Francisco on that day to complete the whole arrangement, and to place you as Governor over California.

You will dispose of your present force in the following manner, which may be hereafter altered as occasion may require.

Captain Gillespie to be stationed at this City, with Fifty men and officers in the neighbourhood—Twenty five men with an officer at Santa Barbara—Fifty men and officers at Monterey, and Fifty at San Francisco.

If this be done at once I can at any time safely withdraw my forces, as I proceed up the coast to San Francisco; and be ready after our meeting on the 25th of October to leave the desk and the camp, and take to the ship and to the Sea. Faithfully Yr. Obdt. Servt.

R. F. STOCKTON
Commander in Chief and Governor of the Territory of California

To Major Fremont
California Battalion
Ciudad de los Angeles

LS (DNA-45, Pacific Squadron, Commodore Stockton, 1846–47). An unsigned copy is in DLC—Polk Papers, where the endorsement notes "Recd. Nov 30. 1846." The letter was printed in "Report of the Secretary of the Navy" in *Message of the President of the United States to the Two Houses of Congress,* 8 Dec. 1846, House Exec. Doc. 4, 29th Cong., 2nd sess., Serial 497. At the time of Stockton's writing, the U.S. flag was flying at every commanding position in California, and ostensibly the conquest of California was complete. Stockton proclaimed martial law but indicated that the people might choose their local civil officers.

1. President Polk signed the declaration of war on 13 May 1846, four days after the receipt of the news that a small squadron of dragoons, constituting part of the command of Gen. Zachary Taylor, had been fired upon by Mexican forces in the area north of the Rio Grande, not far from Point Isabel, Tex. The news of the declaration was received in California on 17 Aug., when the *Warren* came into San Pedro.

57. Robert F. Stockton to James K. Polk

Private

CIUDAD DE LOS ANGELES
August 26th. 1846

DEAR SIR:

You will no doubt be informed by the Secretary of State and the Navy Department of the doings of the Frigate Congress under my command at Honolulu and in California, and you will be enabled to judge of my conduct, without a word from me on the subject—how far I have fulfilled my own promises, and to what degree I have come up to your expectations.

By the month of October, I think I will have the whole civil government of the Territory, in peaceful and successful operation—the foreign population is now so small in comparison with the native population, that I am of opinion that a mixed government of old and new forms will be at present most beneficial and wise.

I will therefore make the Organic Laws of the Territory very few and strong, and leave as much of the old municipal regulations in force, as will be consistent with the entire change of Government.

The most important and serious subject connected at present with the Government of California, and on which account this letter is principally written, is the arrival at San Francisco of some of the Mormons,[1] and the expected arrival of a great many more, who are likely to give me more trouble than our "decided enemies."

You will see by my Proclamation of the 17th that I have had my eye upon them.[2] I write *this* private letter and sent it overland by Express, that you may if you see fit send me by the return messenger some instructions on the subject, or let me work it out on my own responsibility.

We have taken most of the Military leaders, and will no doubt take the others who have not fled to Mexico. I have Expresses going constantly from one end of the Territory to the other, and all is now peaceful and quiet.

My word is at present the law of the land. My person is more than regal. The haughty Mexican Cavalier shakes hands with me with pleasure, and the beautiful women look to me with joy and gladness as their friend and benefactor. In short all of power and luxury is spread before me, through the mysterious workings of a beneficient Providence.

No man could or ought to desire more of power and respect, but my work is almost done here, and my duty calls me again upon the ocean, to protect as well as I may, the lives and property of our fellow citizens engaged in commerce. I will go without the least hesitation, and will transfer my power to other hands without repining.

As soon as I can safely do so I will appoint Major Fremont Governor and Captain Gillespie Secretary of the Territory. They both understand the people and their language and I think are eminently qualified to perform the duties, which I shall assign to them, until your pleasure is made known to me.

The ardent zeal shown by them throughout deserves this compliment; besides they are fully possessed of my views, which if they are worth anything, may be some advantage to them.

The Battalion increased to three hundred picked men, will be kept in the service, and will be quite sufficient to defend the Territory.

I enclose my last order to Major Fremont, that you may see how the force will be disposed of. I earnestly request you to confirm them in their places, as the most salutary arrangement that can be made for the good of the Territory.

One word for my officers and crew—more devoted men never walked a ship's deck. They are quite willing to stay with me as long as I stay, and go with me wherever I may go, and I should be sorry to leave them behind.

Will you not compliment them *under your own hand in a general order?* giving me permission to bring the ship and them home with me, *as soon as the war is over.*

They deserve it, they did the work; and have secured by their toil and daring this beautiful Empire. I have made this request of the Secretary, but your name would be better.

Major Fremont will send this letter with my despatches to the Secretary of the Navy, by Express[3] over the mountains, and in four months I will if nothing happens to prevent, be at San Francisco to get your reply, which I hope you will return immediately, that no unnecessary delay may take place in my operations here. Your faithful friend and obdt. servt.,

R. F. STOCKTON

To His Excellency
James K. Polk
President of the United States
Washington, D. C.

Lbk (DNA-45, Entry 395 [E-20-A], Letterbook of Robert F. Stockton, 1846–47).

1. About 240 Mormons had arrived at San Francisco on the *Brooklyn* on 31 July 1846.

2. The proclamation excluded from the territory those who would not agree to support the existing government, promised religious liberty to those who

did pledge allegiance, and forbade on penalty of deportation the carrying of arms without special permission. The provision, "Nor will any persons, come from where they may, be permitted to settle in the Territory, who do not pledge themselves to be, in all respects, obedient to the laws which may be from time to time enacted by the proper authorities of the Territory," was particularly aimed at the Mormons. Stockton's proclamation to the people of California, 17 Aug. 1846, is printed in House Exec. Doc. 4, pp. 669–70, 29th Cong., 2nd sess., Serial 497.

3. The express was Kit Carson, who was ordered to go to Washington in sixty days (CARSON, 111). With fifteen men and fifty mules, each mule carrying one bushel of dried corn, he left Los Angeles on 5 Sept. When he met General Kearny 175 miles from Santa Fe at present-day Socorro on the Rio Grande, thirty-one days later, only eighteen mules had survived (*Missouri Republican,* 16 Nov. 1846). According to JCF, Carson was selected "to insure the safety and speedy delivery of these important papers, and as a reward for brave and valuable service on many occasions. . . . He was to go direct to Senator Benton at Washington, who would personally introduce him to the President and Secretary of the Navy, and to whom he could give in fulness the incidental detail always so much more interesting than the restricted official report. . . . On his way he would see his family at Taos, New Mexico, through which lay his shortest road to the frontier. It was a service of high trust and honor, but of great danger also. . . . He went off, charged with personal messages and personal feelings, and I looked to his arrival at home and the deep interest and pleasure he would bring to them there, almost with the pleasure I should feel in getting there myself—it was touching home. Going off at the head of his own party with carte blanche for expenses and the prospect of novel pleasure and honor at the end was a culminating point in Carson's life" (MEMOIRS, 567). JCF never forgave Kearny for turning Carson back and using him as his guide to California, sending the dispatches on to Washington by Fitzpatrick, who incidentally was also highly regarded by JCF and who had been with him on the 1843–44 expedition. Philip St. George Cooke grumbled that with Kearny's order, the express for JCF's mail was able to requisition twenty-one of the best mules in Santa Fe (COOKE, 93).

58. Robert F. Stockton to Frémont

CIUDAD DE LOS ANGELES
August 27th. 1846

SIR:

On my arrival in this City I found that the Furniture had all been removed from the Government House, and that the Archives of the Government had also been carried off.

Some of the Furniture has been restored since my Proclamation

Christopher Carson. From a print at the University of Illinois. Collection of Donald Jackson.

on that subject by an individual; and I have reason to believe there is more of it in the City—and that there are some important Public Documents in the House of a citizen.

You are therefore authorized and required to seize the Archives, and all other Public Property that you may be enabled to find in this City, or elsewhere in the Territory; and to keep them securely until a future Governor and the Legislative Council shall otherwise direct. Faithfully, Yr. obdt. servt.,

R. F. Stockton
Governor and Commander in Chief of the Territory of California

To
Major Fremont
California Battalion
Ciudad de los Angeles

Lbk (DNA-45, Entry 395 [E-20-A], Letterbook of Robert F. Stockton, 1846–47).

59. Robert F. Stockton to Frémont

Ciudad de los Angeles
August 31st. 1846

Sir:

You will proceed as soon as your other duties will permit, to St. Johns near Monterey, and ascertain the views of Captain Fauntleroy and Mr. McLane in relation to remaining in the service of the Territory, and the number of men under their command, and how many of them will enter for the Battalion.[1]

You will then go on to San Francisco, where you will see Commander Montgomery, who will inform you how many men he has enlisted into the service of the United States, who will answer for the Battalion.

After which you may adopt the best measures to get rid of any surplus, or to supply any deficiency. The Battalion may consist of Three hundred, exclusive of officers.

If you should fall in with Lieutenant Maddox[2] you will also ascertain his views and wishes as to remaining in the service of the Territory. Faithfully, Yr. obdt. servt.,

R. F. STOCKTON
Commander in Chief of the Territory of California

To
Major Fremont
California Battalion

Lbk (DNA-45, Entry 395 [E-20-A], Letterbook of Robert F. Stockton, 1846–47).
1. Daingerfield Fauntleroy (d. 1853) had been temporarily relieved of his duties as purser on the *Savannah* on 8 July 1846 by Commodore Sloat in order to organize a company of dragoons. The company, made up of sailors from the warships in Monterey Bay and civilian volunteers, would garrison San Juan Bautista, an outpost to the defenses of Monterey. Naval Acting Lieut. Louis McLane (1819–1905) of the *Levant* was the first lieutenant in Fauntleroy's troop. For the activities of these horse marines in July and August in guarding the lines of communication to the north and south and in quelling marauding Indians, see MC LANE, 84–86, and AMES [2]. Fauntleroy was ordered back to his duties as purser on 18 Sept. 1846, and McLane turned his attention to recruiting for the California Battalion. When its reorganization was complete, he was captain of artillery (later major) and was subsequently one of JCF's commissioners who signed the Treaty of Cahuenga.
2. Lieut. William A. T. Maddox (1814–89) had commanded the Marine squad raising the U.S. flag in San Diego a few weeks earlier, and after the reoccupation of Los Angeles he had gone to Monterey with the companies of Henry L. Ford and Granville P. Swift. Near San Luis Obispo they captured and paroled some Californian officers, including José de Jesús Pico, who was later to break his parole. Commodore Stockton arrived at Monterey with the *Congress* on 15 Sept., and on the 18th Maddox was made commandant of the Central District with the rank of captain in the California Battalion (BANCROFT, 5:282, 289–90). In 1857 he helped suppress the Plug-Ugly riot in Washington, D.C., and from that year to 1878 was stationed in Philadelphia in charge of the Marine Battalion's assistant quartermaster's office. Three naval destroyers have been named for him (DNA-45, Entry 464, Subject File ZB; NAVAL SHIPS, 4:188–90).

60. Robert F. Stockton to Frémont

CIUDAD DE LOS ANGELES, September 1, 1846

SIR:

The amount of money for which you have made a requisition cannot be furnished you at this time. Mr. [William] Speiden, the purser of the Congress, says he can only spare twenty thousand dollars; which I hope will answer your purposes until we hear from home, and receive information from the government how and where (if hostilities continue) we can be furnished with funds.[1]

It is quite probable that we may not be able to get any money at Mazatlan. Respectfully, your obedient servant,

R. F. STOCKTON,
Commander-in-chief, &c.

Major Fremont, California battalion

Printed in CT. MARTIAL, 290.
1. JCF had already obtained $1,000 in gold, "equal to sixteen dollars to the ounce or doubloon," on 16 Aug. from purser Speiden, $500 on 25 Aug., and $1,000 on 27 Aug. 1846 (see *Presidential Message on the Accounts of John C. Fremont*, Senate Exec. Doc. 109, pp. 14–17, 34th Cong., 1st sess., Serial 825).

61. Frémont's Appointment as Military Commandant

[LOS ANGELES]
[2 Sept. 1846]

KNOW ALL MEN BY THESE PRESENTS:

That I, Robert F. Stockton, governor and commander-in-chief of the territory of California, reposing special confidence in the ability and patriotism of Major J. C. Fremont, of the United States army, do hereby appoint him to be the military commandant of the territory of California.

To have and to exercise all the powers and privileges of that office until the governor of the said territory shall otherwise direct.

Therefore, by these presents, I do hereby command all civil and military officers and citizens to obey him accordingly.

Given under my hand on this second day of September, Anno Domini one thousand eight hundred and forty-six.

R. F. STOCKTON

Ciudad de los Angeles, Sept. 2, 1848 [1846]

Printed in CT. MARTIAL, 110.

62. Robert F. Stockton to Frémont

U. S. Frigate Congress
BAY OF SAN PEDRO
September 4th. 1846

SIR:

When you send orders to Captain Ford[1] to proceed to San Francisco, you will please to write to Lieutenant Maddox, that it is my wish that he should go to that place and await my arrival, or the arrival of this Ship; when he will report himself to the Commanding officer for further orders.

You will also leave with Captain Gillespie for Lieutenant Maddox, a note to the same effect, in case he should return to the Pueblo. Faithfully, Yr. obdt. servt.,

R. F. STOCKTON

Governor and Commander in Chief of the Territory of California

To

Major Fremont

Military Commandant of the Territory of California, Ciudad de los Angeles.

Lbk (DNA-45, Entry 395 [E-20-A], Letterbook of Robert F. Stockton, 1846–47).

1. Born Noah Eastman Ford in New Hampshire in 1822, this officer had taken the name of his brother, Henry L. Ford, after deserting from the dragoons at Carlisle Barracks, Pa. He stowed away for California, worked for Sutter as a hunter, took a prominent part in the Bear Flag Revolt, and commanded in the fight at Olompali. As noted in Doc. No. 59, n. 2, he had gone south with JCF and returned north by land with Maddox. Ford later commanded Company B of the reorganized California Battalion and was killed in 1860 by the accidental discharge of his pistol (ROGERS [1]).

63. Frémont to Pierson B. Reading

CIUDAD DE LOS ANGELES; Sepr. 4. 1846

SIR,

You will immediately embark in the U. S. ship Congress, about to sail for the Bay of San Francisco, *via* Monterey.

On your arrival at Monterey you will please obtain information in regard to a *cavallada* [*caballada*] of horses (350), which were left in charge of the commanding officer at St. Johns on our departure for San Diego;[1] and have it in readiness for delivery to an officer who will be despatched with a party of men for that purpose. The officer sent will be directed to report to you at Monterey.

You will please be particularly careful to let no animals be taken from the band by any of the men who go up with you on board the ship. As the *cavallada* will be immediately sent to the Sacramento, any private horses in it can be there returned to their owners. Very respectfully Your Obedt. Servt.,

J. C. Frémont,
Military Commandant of California

ALS, RC (C). Addressed, "Reading, Paymaster California Battalion of U. S. Forces, Angeles, California." Pierson B. Reading (1816–68), a native of New Jersey, had come to California in 1843 in the Chiles-Walker party. Business failures in the cotton market in Vicksburg and New Orleans had prompted his emigration (STEGER). He worked for Sutter, was an active Bear Flagger, and some of the volunteers would have preferred Reading to JCF as commander of the battalion (HARLAN, 84–85). After the war Reading devoted his attention primarily to business—mining and the development of his Rancho Buenaventura in Shasta County—although in 1851 he was an unsuccessful candidate for governor.

1. The commanding officer was Daingerfield Fauntleroy.

64. Frémont to Archibald H. Gillespie

Ciudad de los Angeles; Sepr. 7. 1846

Sir,

Lieut. G. B. Wilson,[1] with a detachment of twenty men from company E., has been placed in occupation of the *Caxon Pass* [Cajon Pass], through which leads the *"Spanish trail"* from New Mexico. He has been directed to guard, so far as his small force will admit, the neighboring approaches from Sonora; reporting all occurrences worthy [of] notice immediately to yourself, and keeping you at all times well informed of the general condition of the Frontier.

He is farther directed to pursue, bring back, and deliver to you at this post, all persons attempting to pass the Frontier committed to his *surveillance*. Very Respectfully Your Obedt. Servt.,

J. C. Frémont
Military Commandant of California

Capt. Archibald Gillespie
Military Commandant of the Southern Department of California

ALS, RC (CLU—Gillespie Papers). Endorsed.
1. JCF has made an error in the initials of Benjamin Davis Wilson (1811–78), who was known in California as Benito. A native of Tennessee, he had immigrated to California in the Workman party from New Mexico, where he had resided for years as a trapper and trader. Within a few weeks after occupying Cajon Pass, he was captured with nineteen other Americans at the Chino rancho, the home of Isaac Williams, some twenty-five miles east of Los Angeles. Wilson later became the second mayor of Los Angeles, the city's foremost railroad booster, and state senator for two terms.
In his "Observations" Wilson implies that Williams betrayed the U.S. force to gain favor with the Californians (WILSON, 106–10).

65. Frémont to Thomas Oliver Larkin

Mission of San José
[Sept.? 1846]

DEAR SIR

I have examined carefully the business of which we were speaking, approve your intentions, and enter into the agreement with you accordingly.[1]

This is a pretty place, this mission.[2] The gardens or orchards might be made handsome places but, to render them valuable, whoever possesses them in the new state of things should *possess also the water* which no[w] supplies these vineyards and which comes from a ravine or arroyo in the hills behind. A handsome plain of good land extends from the hills towards the bay and could be well watered and highly cultivated.

There are some valuable bodies of land from this around the bay towards the Mountain Diavolo [Diablo] and lying under it. Two of these are between Pinole[3] and Marsh's, one, next and adjoining Pinole belongs to the Welch family (a brother in law of Forbes)[4] and the other to the mother in law of Tom Bowen,[5] a drunken vagabond about the Pueblo San José. These lands lie upon the bay. I shall be glad to hear from you at any opportunity and should like to see you at an early day. *Call upon me when necessary.* Yours truly,

J. C. FREMONT

I understand that *one* of the orchards here belongs to Alvarado.

Thomas O. Larkin Esqre
Naval Agent for the U. States in California

Printed in LARKIN, 5:255–56.
1. JCF's business agreement with Larkin is not known.
2. The Mission San Jose in Alameda County is some distance from the Pueblo de San Jose. With a party of thirty-five or forty men, JCF had left Los Angeles on 11 Sept. At Santa Barbara he detached Talbot and nine men to garrison that town and, guided by William Knight, proceeded north toward the Sacramento Valley (MEMOIRS, 570–72). He stopped at the Mission San Jose and other settled places to recruit for his battalion of 300 and to sound out the American settlers on their attitude toward enlisting in a battalion which Stockton desired to organize for a movement on Mexico (see Doc. No. 66). This letter indicates that while he was caring for public business, JCF was not adverse to promoting his private interest—that of acquiring valuable land. It may have been at this time or earlier that he acquired several fifty-vara lots in San Francisco (as did Stockton and Sloat), which Leidesdorff later hired Jacob W. Harlan to fence (HARLAN, 110).
3. The Pinole rancho, Contra Costa County, owned by Ignacio Martínez.
4. The family of William Welsh, who had come to California as a sailor, probably from Scotland, was a large one—there being eight sons and daughters. The brother-in-law was James Alexander Forbes (d. 1881), also a Scot and the British vice-consul in California.
5. Tom Bowen's distillery business failed in 1844. A trapper from New Mexico, Bowen had been living in San Jose since 1836 (PIONEER REGISTER: GIFFEN [2], 25).

66. Robert F. Stockton to Frémont

(Private)

United States Frigate Congress
HARBOUR OF SAN FRANCISCO, September 28, 1846

SIR:

I am here anxious to know what prospect there is of your being able to recruit my thousand men, for a visit to Mexico.

Let me know as soon as possible, many serious arrangements will have to be made, all requiring more or less time, which, you know in war, is more precious than "rubies." Your faithful and obedient servant,

R. F. STOCKTON
Governor, &c.

To Major Fremont, Military Commandant of the Territory of California.

Copy of enclosure 4 in Stockton to George Bancroft, 23 Nov. 1846 (DNA-45, Pacific Squadron, Commodore Stockton, 1846–47). On 19 Sept. Stockton had written confidentially to Capt. William Mervine, now in command of the *Savannah,* that he had sent JCF north to see how many men he could recruit, "with a view to embark[ing] them for Mazatlan or Acapulco, where, if possible, I intend to land and fight our way as far on to the city of Mexico as I can." He wanted Mervine to have the ships of the squadron located where he might get them together as soon as possible. And on 1 Oct. he wrote the Secretary of the Navy that he would send the *Savannah* "on her cruise tomorrow, and the Portsmouth in a few days, and will follow myself in the Congress as soon as I can (if not sooner superseded by Commodore Biddle), to carry out my views in regard to Mexico, with which I have not thought it necessary or expedient yet to acquaint the Department." Both letters are printed in *Report of the Secretary of the Navy, Communicating Copies of Commodore Stockton's Despatches Relating to the Military and Naval Operations in California,* Senate Doc. 31, pp. 13–15, 30th Cong., 2nd sess., Serial 531.

But Stockton's vision of shaking hands with General Taylor at the gates of Mexico City was shattered the very day he penned the note to the Secretary of the Navy. John Brown, better known as Juan Flaco, arrived with Gillespie's pleas for immediate aid, for the Angeleños had risen in revolt and his garrison was under siege. In fact, before Stockton could send relief, Gillespie was forced to move out of Los Angeles (28 or 29 Sept.) to San Pedro, where his force was to surrender its artillery to the Californians and embark on the *Vandalia* for Monterey. The *Vandalia* was able to remain at San Pedro, but for a time the men were confined to the ship (MARTI, 75–83).

Stockton canceled his plans to go to Mexico, sent William Mervine in the *Savannah* to aid Gillespie, and hastily summoned JCF to San Francisco from the Sacramento Valley, instructing him to bring as many men and saddles as he could procure.

Larkin, who in time became a prisoner of the rebels, attributed the disturbances to Gillespie's "harshness" and Stockton's "cheap way of conducting." From the Government House in Los Angeles he wrote to his wife on 14 Dec., "I hear from many of the People of the Country that had Dr. Gilcrist, Lt. A. Grey, or any proper and prudent person been left here by the Como all this disturbance would not have happened. It appears even from the Americans that Captain AHG punished fined and imprisoned who and when he pleased without any hearing. I always told the Como he should have granted the Mexican officers their request to be sent to Mexico. He would not that, and his cheap way of conducting—with Capt Gillespie's harshness has brot the country to its present pass. Its done, I am a Prisoner" (LARKIN, 5:310–15).

67. Robert F. Stockton to Frémont

U. S. Frigate Congress
HARBOUR OF SAN FRANCISCO
October 1st. 1846

SIR:

I send a Boat to Sonoma for you, in the hopes that the news from the South has brought you on in this direction; and that you will be ready with your men to embark with me. I will wait until the 4th for you, or the return of the boat.

Bring with you as many men as you can. If I hear that you are on the road this way, I'll wait for you. Hurry! Faithfully, Yr. obdt. servt.,

R. F. STOCKTON
Commodore &c.

To
Major Fremont
Military Commandant of the Territory of California

[*On the back of the envelope:*] The Boats will wait an answer from Major Fremont.

Lbk (DNA-45, Entry 395 [E-20-A], Letterbook of Robert F. Stockton, 1846–47).

68. Frémont to Edward M. Kern

Camp Cosùmné river, Oct. 4 [1846]

DEAR SIR,

Please send me our brand (letter F) should Cosgrave[1] not have left. Yrs. truly,

J. C. FRÉMONT

Do not detain your mail [?] for me as Commodore Stockton leaves today, but send him immediately with information [to] the neighboring people that we want men.

Lieut. Kerne,
Comdg. Fort Sacramento

The greater part of the Sonoma people will [?] have embarked in the Congress, but there may be some remaining who could overtake us. We leave tomorrow.

DS, RC (CSmH).
1. "F" was branded on all the horses belonging to JCF's exploring party. Anthony Cosgrave, a blacksmith, had been a member of JCF's exploring party. He would later use his talents in working on a gun carriage at Santa Barbara (DNA-217, T-135, voucher 191; DNA-92, California Claims Board, receipt dated 5 Feb. 1847).

69. Frémont to Edward M. Kern

[FORT SACRAMENTO]
[7 Oct. 1846]

Received of Lieut. E. M. Kern Commanding Military Post Fort Sacramento, Four Horses & the following articles for the use of the California Battalion.
77 lbs Tobacco
1 Keg 25 lbs Powder

J. C. FRÉMONT
Military Commandant of U. S. Forces in California
Oct 7 1846

DS, RC (CSmH).

70. Robert F. Stockton to Frémont

Congress
October 13th. 1846

DEAR SIR:

Captain Vincent will remain at Santa Barbara until you will be able to decide on your course of action.

I will thank you to write to me by him, to inform me of your probable approach towards the Angeles.

Wishing you great success and honor, I am most truly Yours faithfully,

R. F. STOCKTON

To
Major Fremont
Military Commandant of the Territory of California

Lbk (DNA-45, Entry 395 [E-20-A], Letterbook of Robert F. Stockton, 1846–47).

71. Frémont to William A. Leidesdorff

Ship Sterling, Oct 14th 46

DEAR SIR,

I would be indebted to you to forward immediately the enclosed. Should Dr. Marsh need any assistance in his arrangements[1] for me please supply him with the necessary funds until my return. Yours truly,

J. C. FRÉMONT

Capt. W. Leidesdorff

ALS, RC (CU-B). Endorsed. The enclosure has not been identified. JCF had embarked on the merchant ship *Sterling* with about 160 men the previous day, under orders to proceed to Santa Barbara, where he was to procure horses to march to Los Angeles. He and his force had arrived in San Francisco from the Sacramento region on 12 Oct., having traveled the last stage of their journey in a fleet of boats commanded by Midshipman Edward Beale, whom Stockton had sent to look for him (MEMOIRS, 574–75).

1. Dr. John Marsh (d. 1856), a native of Massachusetts with a medical

diploma from Harvard, came to California in 1836 via Wisconsin, Missouri, New Mexico, and Sonora. He acquired a rancho at the foot of Mount Diablo, which he named Brentwood and where he became wealthy in livestock (LYMAN). His "arrangements" are not known. While Marsh was much interested in politics and wanted California to become a part of the United States, he actually took little part in the political troubles of 1846–47.

72. Frémont to Edward M. Kern

Excerpt

Ship Sterling off Monterey Oct 22/46

DEAR SIR:

. . . .

Many of the emigrants who will come to us, will necessarily leave their families unprovided for & without supplies. I know that you have but little in the way of shelter to offer them, but please do for them in that respect all that you can; for any supplies that they may need, please send to Capt. Leidesdorff (at Yerba Buena) who will forward them to you. I have already written to him to that effect.

. . . .

Tell Jean Dreau [Gendreau] that I have directed the Walla Wallas who shall come to me to leave their families in his charge, & let him know that you will send to Yerba Buena for any supplies that the families may want.

. . . .

Truly yours,

J. C. FRÉMONT

Lt. E. M. Kern
Commg. Sac. Dist.

Copy of excerpt in the draft of a letter of Edward M. Kern to Archibald Gillespie, 11 March 1853 (CSmH). Kern was trying to answer Gillespie's queries regarding events in the conquest of California. He noted that there were from fifty to sixty women and children at Sutter's Fort to whom he supplied rations. He extracted the above letter from JCF, and one from John B. Montgomery, 2 Nov. 1846 (not printed here), as his authority for doing so. He also noted that he had had horses under his charge, sometimes as many as 800. "I kept them at a grazing camp & used them for the transportation of recruits from my post to different parts of the lower country.

. . . A good number of them taken from the Sonoma side from the Rancho of Genl. Vallejo were national Horses and branded with the Govt. Iron of the Mission of San Rappael. . . . Genl. Kearny took possession of the whole band when he came to the Fort without receipting for them to me. There were then there as well as my memory serves me (my papers having been lost in the Mts. in 48 & 49 with Fremont) about Five hundred head. What became of the balance after he had selected sufficient for his homeward journey I do not know."

73. Frémont to John B. Montgomery

Ship Sterling, Off San Antonio; 22d. Oct. 46

SIR,

This note will be handed you by Mr. D. Burruss,[1] who will be able to give you some interesting information, should the recent occurrences below be not already known to you. I have despatched Mr. Burruss to the Sacramento Valley, via Sonoma; on very urgent business for the government, and I will be greatly indebted for any facility it may suit your convenience to afford him forwarding him on his way. For four or five days past we have been becalmed within a few miles of our present position, vainly endeavoring to make Monterey. A boat will be despatched in the morning which will probably anticipate our arrival several days, should the calm continue. With much respect, Your Obedt. Servt.,

J. C. FRÉMONT
Military Commandant of California

Captain J. B. Montgomery
U. S. Ship Portsmouth,
Commanding Northern Department of California, San Francisco Bay

ALS, RC (DNA-45, Area 9 File, Pacific). Endorsed: "Recd. at San Francisco." JCF and Stockton had sailed on separate vessels for the south, but on the first evening out of San Francisco the *Sterling* became separated from the *Congress* in the fog. When two days later she fell in with the *Vandalia*, JCF learned that the insurrection against Gillespie had spread over all of the southern half of California and that the Californians had driven stock into the interior. As mounts were not to be had, JCF decided to sail to Monterey, collect horses, men, provisions, and ammunition, and march overland. As this letter indicates, the lack of wind slowed his voyage to Monterey, but he finally entered the harbor on 27 Oct. Welcoming him at Monterey was the news of his appointment as lieutenant colonel in the Army (CT. MARTIAL, 378).

1. JCF was sending the popular Charles D. Burrass, sometimes referred to as Burroughs or Burruss, to recruit and equip members for the California Battalion. He was from St. Louis and was in command at the battle of Natividad on the Salinas Plains, 16 Nov. 1846—a battle in which he lost his life (Doc. No. 90; 26 June 1847 letter of William R. Russell, *Missouri Republican*, 17 May 1847; *California Star*, 21 Aug. 1847).

74. Charles D. Burrass to Frémont

YERBA BUENA Oct 26th 1846

SIR,

You will pay to W. A. Leidesdorff Thirty Dollars in payment of one Rifle Gun Bullet Moulds & shot pouch. For the use of California Battalion. Yrs. Respectfully,

C. D. BURRASS

Major J. C. Fremont
Military Commandant of California

ALS, RC (CU-B). Endorsed.

75. Frémont to Robert F. Stockton

[MONTEREY]
[27 Oct. 1846]

.   .   .   .   .

We met the *Vandalia* with information of the occurrences below. Mr. Howard[1] represented that the enemy had driven off all the horses and cattle, so that it would be impossible to obtain either for transportation or supplies. Under the circumstances, and using the discretionary authority you have given me, I judged it of paramount necessity to haul up immediately for this port, with the intention to send for all the men who could be raised in the north, and for the band of horses which I had left on the Consumné. In the meantime we should be able to check the insurrection here, and procure horses and supplies, so as to be in readiness to march to the southward immediately on the arrival of our reinforcements.

.   .   .   .

[J. C. Frémont]

Excerpt, printed in MEMOIRS, 579–80. The complete letter has not been found, but its contents are substantiated by Stockton in a letter to the Secretary of the Navy, 23 Nov. 1846, from San Diego (STOCKTON, Appendix A, pp. 4–6).

For our determination of date, see Mervine to Frémont, 14 Nov. 1846, Doc. No. 84. The letter was received from the *Malek Adhel* by Stockton, who was off the coast of San Diego about 1 Nov.

1. Bostonian William Davis Merry Howard (1819–56), who had been supercargo of the *Vandalia* from 1843 to 1845, was now associated with Henry Mellus in the mercantile business in San Francisco. The two men had purchased the property of the Hudson's Bay Company. For biographical details and some of Howard's letters to his second wife, see WHITWELL.

76. John B. Montgomery to Frémont

U. S. Ship Portsmouth
SAN FRANCISCO, Oct. 29th. 1846

SIR,

Your letter by Mr. Burrass reached me on the evening of the 27th & in two hours after he was on his way in one of my boats to Sonoma, with orders to Lieut. Revere at that post to speed him on his way to Fort Sacramento.

On the 11th inst. receiving intelligence from Lieut. Maddox of the agitated state of affairs about Monterey & the probability of an attack upon that place I despatched boats to Sonoma & the Fort Sacramento, with direction to the officers in command to go on with enlistments for the general Service & forward couriers from the Fort to intercept & hasten the arrival of approaching Emigrants which was promptly done by Mr. Kern who has sent down in my launch twenty-four men with an intimation that others will be ready to come down on the return of the boat which I shall not now send since Mr. Burrass informed me that all will be required to attend the caballada which he expects to obtain at the Fort.

Several days since I directed Mr. [Lansford W.] Hastings to proceed to the Pueblo of San Jose & to engage such of the emigrants as may have reached that place & despatched at the same time a party of men with orders to collect all good horses between this & the Pueblo for the Public Service to be forwarded in a few days with the troops collecting here, probably in charge of Capt. Grigsby should he return to this place.

Having had much difficulty heretofore in procuring rifle caps I have deemed it proper to purchase a lot of 10,000 which I hope to forward you by Capt. Grigsby whose receipt in your behalf will be required. I have also purchased & supplied each recruit with a horn of rifle powder to be included in the receipt.

All the troops forwarded from here will be supplied with Blankets, necessary clothing & tobacco from the Stores of the Portsmouth, an account of which I will cause to be forwarded to be charged to their respective accts. of pay.

I sincerely hope Sir that you may be enabled to effect all necessary arrangements for a speedy movement upon the enemy in the South before the advance of the rainy season shall present new difficulties to be overcome.

The natives I suppose will take great encouragement from their late Success in driving back the main force of the Savannah, the news of their victory, as it is termed having been already extensively circulated through the country with the view of enticing all to their Standard. It was an unfortunate mistake under the circumstances to attempt an advance from the coast without cannon.

Permit me Sir to express to you my sincere congratulations on your recent promotion of which I am informed by my son in a letter received a few days since from Mazatlan. I am Sir Very Respy. Your Obt. Servant,

JNO. B. MONTGOMERY
Military Commandant of the Northn. Dept. of
Calif. & Commander of U. S. Ship Portsmouth

To
Lieut. Col.
J. C. Fremont
Military Commandant of California

Lbk (DNA-45, no. 22, Officers' Letters, Letterbooks of J. B. Montgomery).

77. Frémont to Edward M. Kern

MONTEREY, Octr. 30. 1846

DEAR SIR,

I send Mr. Foster[1] to aid in enlisting men for us. Please give your aid. Colonel Wm. H. Russell[2] will be with you soon after you receive this.

Congress has given swords to the officers engaged in the battle at Rio Grande, and promoted [Zachary] Taylor to be Brigadier General, with the Brevet of Major General. Col. Kearney is in New Mexico with 5000 men. I trust that you have fully recovered your health. Yours truly,

J. C. FREMONT
Lt. Colonel U. S. Army

Lieutenant Kerne
Fort Sacramento

ALS, RC (Morristown National Historical Park, Morristown, N.J.).
1. Joseph E. Foster, who was killed a few weeks later at the battle of Natividad with Charles D. Burrass and Hiram Ames.
2. William H. Russell (1802–73), sometimes known as "Owl" Russell, was a new arrival in California, having come in August from Missouri with a party of emigrants. A lawyer, he had served as representative for Nicholas County in the Kentucky legislature and as U.S. marshal for the District of Missouri. He was to become a major in the California Battalion, help frame the Treaty of Cahuenga, and serve JCF as secretary of state. Upon the demise of the JCF administration, Russell went back to the States by the southern route and became a principal witness for the explorer in his court-martial. He returned to California in 1849 and practiced law in San Jose and elsewhere. For additional biographical details, see MORGAN, 2:460–61.

78. John B. Montgomery to Frémont

U. S. Ship Portsmouth
SAN FRANCISCO, Nov. 3rd. 1846

SIR,

By Captain Libby of Tasso[1] I forward you 8,000 rifle percussion caps, two thousand having been served to troops who are soon to join you. More can not be obtained at this place. The whole stock of lead in the market and our ships supply has been exhausted in furnishing balls to recruits. A small quantity of Rifle powder, in canisters, remains in the hands of Mr. Mellus² which can be had if wanted.

We are today transporting horses from Sausalito to this place, and I hope in a few days that a strong Party and Caballada will proceed to Monterey.

In haste, I am Sir Respy. Your Obt. Servt.,

JNO. B. MONTGOMERY
Commanding Northn. Dept. & U. S. Ship Portsmouth

Please sign & return me the enclosed receipt.

To
Lt. Col. J. C. Fremont
Military Commandant of California, Monterey

Lbk (DNA-45, no. 22, Officers' Letters, Letterbooks of J. B. Montgomery).
1. Capt. Elliot Libbey, master of the *Tasso* in 1845–48 and of the *Commodore Shubrick* in 1847. A note in JCF's name, but written and signed by William H. Russell (to Capt. John B. Montgomery), 4 Nov. 1846, from Yerba Buena, asks Montgomery to pay William H. Davis the value of 15,000 percussion caps bought for the U.S. troops "under my command and sent to my headquarters in the bark Tasso" (CtY). William Heath Davis (1822–1909) had just established himself as a merchant in San Francisco, but he had been in and out of California for many years, acting as clerk and agent for various commercial firms. For a biography of this Honolulu-born son of a Boston shipmaster, see ROLLE [1]. Davis's own history of events and life in California may be found in his *Seventy-five Years in California* (San Francisco, 1929).
2. Henry Mellus (1815–60) made his first voyage to California in 1835 on the *Pilgrim* with Richard Henry Dana. He settled permanently in California in 1839 as the agent or supercargo of the vessels of William Appleton and Co. In 1845 he formed a partnership with W. D. M. Howard and amassed a considerable fortune through the firm of Mellus & Howard in the San Francisco region.

79. John B. Montgomery to Frémont

U. S. Ship Portsmouth
YERBA BUENA, Nov. 4th. 1846.

SIR,

The following arms have been purchased by this ship & have been issued to the men whose names are specified.

One Rifle for $20 to Robt. Neil

One Rifle for $25 to Peter (an Indian)

One Rifle for $25 to George Smith

Eight Rifles delivered to Capt. Grigsby for which he has given his receipt (bill not rendered). The men, Neil, Peter, & Smith, have signed receipts for their rifles.

Besides the above arms purchased there have been delivered of arms brought from Sonoma, the following for which receipts are taken.

To Amasa Heit [Hoyt?]	one musket
To C. F. Caldwell	one musket
To J. C. Furgason [Ferguson]	one musket
To Jno. Frederick	one musket
To Andrew Farley	one shot rifle
To George Coats	one carbine
To Thomas Frith [Firth?]	one carbine
To Frank Wilcox	one carbine

Each Recruit who has passed through the ship has been furnished with caps to make up 115 [15?] (Percussion) & from one to two lbs. of lead, with a horn of rifle powder beside such clothing as the store room of the ship could furnish; of the latter, I send you herewith a statement of amounts, issued to the Volunteers, as set opposite their respective names to be deducted from their accounts in final settlement. I am Respy. Yr. Obt. Servt.

JNO. B. MONTGOMERY
Comdg. Northn. Dept. of Calia.
& of the U. S. Ship Portsmouth

To
Lt. Col. J. C. Fremont
Military Comdt. of California

Lbk (DNA-45, no. 22, Officers' Letters, Letterbooks of J. B. Montgomery).

80. Frémont to Jacob Antoine Moerenhout

MONTEREY, November 7th. 1846

SIR:

Two communications addressed by yourself to Captain William A. Maddox, Commandant of Monterey, have been referred by him for my consideration.[1]

From the representation made to me by Captain Maddox, I am satisfied that the claim for damages which has been brought forward, is highly exaggerated, and altogether unfounded in fact. I have accordingly directed him to furnish this office with a certified statement of the case, which appears clearly sufficient to invalidate the claim.[2]

In the present disorganized condition of the country, when the civil officers have been suspended in the exercise of their usual functions, the French Consul could not have reasonably expected that subjects of his nation should continue in the enjoyments of their customary political and commercial privileges, or that any exception in their favor should be made from such restrictions and regulations as to the military authorities of the Territory might appear expedient and salutary.

As the French Consul appears to entertain very different views, his farther residence at Monterey would evidently create embarrassment and lead to a frequent correspondence, for which, at this time, there can be neither the necessary leisure nor disposition.

Reminding Mr. Moerenhout that he is accredited to the Mexican Department of California, and that the present exercise of his functions is due only from the courtesy of the officer representing the United States, I have judged it advisable and proper to enclose a passport to San Francisco, in the hope that, as it would be very satisfactory to the authorities now in this Department, it would not be disagreeable to the French Consul to transport his office to that place.

Availing myself of this occasion to offer to Mr. Moerenhout the assurance of my great personal consideration, I am, very respectfully,

(Signé) J. C. FREMONT,
Lieut. Colonel U. States Army, and
Military Commandant of the
Territory of California

Mr. J. A. Moerenhout,
Consul for His Majesty the King of the French

Copy enclosed in R. B. Mason to R. Jones, 28 March 1849, transmitting procedures of board of officers investigating complaint by the French minister (DNA-94, LR, M-376 1849). A copy is also in DNA-45, Area 9 File, Pacific. Author of the celebrated *Voyages aux îles du grand océan* (Paris, 1837), Jacob Antoine Moerenhout (ca. 1797–1879) had arrived in California in Oct. 1846 to take up his duties as French consul. He came from Tahiti, where he had been engaged in trade and where he had represented as consular agent not only France but also the United States for a short time. For a biographical sketch, see NASATIR, 12:155–58.

1. The first letter of Moerenhout to Maddox, commander at Monterey, 4 Nov. 1846, complained of the revocation of a permit previously given to Clement Panaud to take care of business interests in San Jose. The French consul charged that the revocation was made on the "frivolous" pretext that Panaud had two pistols in his house in Monterey. The second letter, dated 7 Nov., noted JCF's discourtesy in failing to reply (Maddox had told Moerenhout that the matter had been referred to JCF) and informed Maddox that he maintained "all the rights of the Frenchman, Panaud, who is exposed to total ruin, in consequence of the severe measures adopted towards him by the American authorities." Copies of Moerenhout's letter to Maddox are in R. B. Mason to R. Jones, 28 March 1849 (DNA-94, LR, M-376 1849).

2. The American version was that Panaud had been arrested because he was carrying pistols, contrary to the order of the military commandant that only those in the service of the United States could bear arms.

81. Jacob Antoine Moerenhout to Frémont

To Lieut. Colonel Frémont
Military Commandant of the Territory of California

Consulate of France at Monterey
MONTEREY, November 8th. 1846

The Undersigned, Consul of France at Monterey, has received the letter which Lieut. Col. Frémont, Military Commandant of the Territory of California did him the honor to address to him, under date of yesterday. The Undersigned considers it his duty to observe to the Colonel, in reply—

(1) That the invoice which he had the honor to present to Capt. Maddox is an exact copy of the original, which M. Panaud gave him, and which he declares to be true.[1]

(2) That he has required nothing of an exceptional nature in favor of the people of his nation; that he limited himself to soliciting verbally, from Capt. Maddox some slight favors for Frenchmen, such as receipts for horses which had been taken from them, or permits for those who, having come to Monterey on business, wished to return to their residences at Santa Cruz.

(3) That so far from having wished to render himself troublesome, or importunate, as Colonel Frémont seems to intend to insinu-

ate, the Undersigned, notwithstanding the injuries suffered by his countrymen, has made but one request officially, and in writing in favor of Panaud, because in withdrawing from the said Panaud the permit given him by Capt. Maddox to go to the interior, he has been gratuitously wronged, and has been exposed by this severe measure to the loss of the goods which he had despatched, as also of others which he had on the way, and at San José and at Santa Cruz.

It will doubtless appear very strange, that, for such acts, and in a case in which the Undersigned has remained strictly within the duties and attributes of his office, he should receive notice that it would be proper for him to change his residence and his Consulate. The Undersigned has therefore the honor to send back to Col. Frémont the permit of Captain Maddox, as, being the Consul of His Majesty the King of the French, in this country, it is only the King of the French or his Government which can order him to change his residence. The Undersigned will nevertheless make known to his Government the invitation to this effect, which he has received from Col. Frémont, in his character of Military Commandant of the Territory of California.

With regard to the paragraph of Col. Frémont's letter in which he says that the Undersigned is only accredited to California, a Department of Mexico, the Undersigned acknowledges that he does not comprehend it entirely, but although he does not consider himself required to give any explanation on this subject here, he will add, that, having been appointed Consul for His Majesty the King of the French for this country since the month of April, 1845, he has naturally received, at the request of his Government, his exequâtur from the President of the Republic of Mexico. With regard to the favorable reception given to him by Commodore Stockton, the Undersigned made it his duty, as it was his pleasure, to announce the fact himself to his Government.

The Undersigned will conclude this letter, by protesting against the official measure which Col. Frémont has adopted, and, as he cannot regard it as otherwise than as shewing a formal intention to intimidate him, & to suspend the free exercise of the principal and almost the only attributes of his office, those of protecting and defending the interests of his countrymen, the Undersigned conceives it to be his duty to inform Col. Frémont, that he will take the first occasion to make known to the French Government the manner in which his complaints and his official acts have been treated, supporting his statement by the correspondence and other documents relating thereto.

The Undersigned prays Colonel Frémont to accept the assurance of his high consideration.

J. A. Moerenhout,
Consul of France

Copy of a translated version enclosed in R. B. Mason to R. Jones, 28 March 1849, transmitting procedures of board of officers investigating complaint by the French minister (DNA-94, LR, M-376 1849). See also copy in French in DNA-45, Area 9 File, Pacific.

1. JCF's view was that Panaud's claim was "grossly false" (see Frémont to Marcy, 28 Sept. 1847, Doc. No. 223) and that referring it "had been a conspiracy to defraud." If Panaud did have a valid—though greatly exaggerated —claim, as Larkin seemed to think, he renounced it on 10 Nov. "voluntarily and without any compulsion" (see enclosure in Frémont to Secretary of War, 4 Oct. 1847, Doc. No. 225; testimony of Larkin, 21 July 1848, in report of board of officers, enclosed in R. B. Mason to R. Jones, 28 March 1849, DNA-94, LR, M-376 1849). Moerenhout, however, wrote a different story to the French Minister of Foreign Affairs: "He [Frémont] called M. Panaud before the judge and several officers, and after having greatly intimidated him, especially on account of a slight error in the [his] account, he made him sign a written agreement by [which] he renounced all demands for indemnity. On this condition they gave him a permit to take himself and his servants to San José and Santa Cruz to transact his business, and a receipt for the horses that they had taken from him." Panaud, who had only yielded on account of fear in signing these agreements, believed it wise not to go himself to Santa Cruz (Moerenhout to Minister of Foreign Affairs, 22 Nov. 1846, NASATIR, 12:170–71).

82. Frémont to John B. Montgomery

Monterey, November 10th. 1846

Sir,

I acknowledge the receipt of your letters of the 29th and 30th ultimo, and at the same time express to you my great gratification and thanks for your assistance which I assure you contrasts remarkably with the apparent inactivity of our officers in the north. None of the men you forwarded to the Pueblo have yet come in and I have recd. no communication whatever from Mr. [Lansford W.] Hastings or Capt. Weaver.[1] I experience much embarrassment in the apparent irresponsibility of officers who make no reports of their position or proceedings. In the meantime the rainy season is setting in rapidly and we shall certainly suffer by our delay.

We are much in want of several articles which I am informed the Euphemia[2] has just brought to San Francisco and I will beg of you the favor to purchase for me by the enclosed list. On it I have placed some articles which possibly you can spare me from the stores of the Portsmouth. I will arrange with Mr. Larkin to pay to your order the amount of purchase from the Euphemia.

I have been informed that you are about to cause to be sold the Julia Ann, a prize brought in by the Warren,[3] and one of my principal reasons in sending to you this courier is to know if some arrangement cannot be made by which she may be put at my disposition. Such a vessel would be of great importance to operate in communication with us along the coast, and for many things and in many cases would be invaluable.

I make this enquiry and these suggestions with some reserve, not knowing how far my proposition may be consistent with other arrangements, or proprieties of service. At all events I hope you may be induced to delay the sale.

An apology will be necessary for troubling you with so many requests, but I hope you will find it in the fact, that these things are really of great importance to me, and I cannot elsewhere apply with the confidence that they will be attended to properly. Out of various rumors, the most reliable intelligence here is that Com. Stockton has entered the Pueblo without opposition. One of our horseguards was fired upon and wounded by the Californians a few days since—an inexperienced man who was off his post.

I thank you for your congratulations on my promotion. To me, it was the more agreeable because entirely unexpected.

I hope the courier will arrive in time to enable you to forward the articles I have asked for by Mr. Brennan;[4] if not I will send to the Pueblo of San José for them. Would it not be advisable to put an embargo on the munitions of war brought by the Euphemia and on all others? Very truly & Respectfully,

J. C. FRÉMONT,
Lt. Colonel U. S. Army, & Commandant of California

Captain J. B. Montgomery
Military Commandant Northern Department &
Commanding U. S. Ship Portsmouth

Two Hundred thousand percussion caps—I am informed that the Euphemia brings three or four hundred thousand.

One thousand lbs. American lead.

Any holster pistols or sabres

One Hundred prs. blankets.

10 or 15 cases of canister (if of lead) and *small Grape shot.*

30 yds stout cotton canvass.

ALS, RC (DNA-45, Area 9 File, Pacific). Endorsed.

1. JCF undoubtedly means Capt. Charles M. Weber (1814–81), successful San Jose businessman and owner of Rancho Campo de los Franceses. He was engaged in the work of collecting horses and supplies for the California Battalion. Because of his hostility to JCF, he declined to serve in the battalion, but was made captain of the San Jose Volunteers. DUVALL, 72, is of the opinion that Weber's means of commandeering mounts and equipment were sometimes obnoxious and unjustifiable. For an excellent sketch of Weber's life, see HAMMOND & MORGAN.

2. The *Euphemia* was a Hawaiian brig of 150 tons with Thomas Russum, an Englishman, as master and William Heath Davis as supercargo and part owner.

3. The 133-ton schooner *Julia Ann* may have been brought into port by the *Warren,* but she had been captured off La Paz in Sept. 1846 by the *Cyane* (E. L. Stetson to Larkin, 28 Sept. 1846, LARKIN, 5:253–54). COLTON, 125, describes her as "a beautiful vessel," riding "the water like a duck" and sailing "with the speed of the wind," her masts raking "to an angle that might startle a Baltimore clipper."

4. Probably Samuel Brannan (1819–89), Mormon elder who had arrived at Yerba Buena on the *Brooklyn,* 31 July 1846, with a colony of approximately 240 Saints. For a biography, see BAILEY.

5. At the bottom of the enclosure is a note on the action taken with regard to JCF's request: "Forwarded of the within 407 lbs. of lead purchased on shore, a quantity of loose grape shot (268 lbs.) (copper) from the Port and a number of rifles furnished by Mr. Leidesdorff. Sent to Santa Clara by boat Novr., 13th."

83. John B. Montgomery to Frémont

U. S. Ship Portsmouth
SAN FRANCISCO, Nov. 13th. 1846

SIR,

Your letter by courier of the 10th inst. reached me yesterday & after the most diligent search & enquiring on Shore & among the Shipping I find it impossible to obtain the articles named in your memorandum as needed for the public Service except 407 lbs. of lead purchased from the Euphemia. None of the articles required (owing to the extensive requisitions recently made upon the Portsmouth) being included in our present list of Stores on board. Loose copper Grape shot can be supplied from the post a moderate quantity of which I have directed to be put up in bags or barrels to be forwarded to the Pueblo of San Jose in one of my boats with the lead & a number of rifles sent by Mr. Leidesdorff where I think you had best send for them if you can as I am not apprised of there being any other means by which they can be safely forwarded to Monterey.

I regret exceedingly Sir that the circumstances attending the position of the prize Schooner Julia at present filled with captured merchandise leaves me no power to comply with your requisition for her service in the manner proposed except in a case of extreme necessity. She cannot be sold until after condemnation & no adjudication in her case can be effected until ordered by the Commander in Chief who is not yet apprised of her capture.

I hope that all the volunteers & caballada from the Pueblo & fort Sacramento will have reached Monterey swelling your force to more than five hundred before you receive this.

From the Pueblo I have heard they were to move yesterday morning.

I am now about to transfer the charge of this Department to Capt. Joseph B. Hull of the Warren & shall only await the arrival of bread to leave this port for more active tho' perhaps not more important & stirring service than has fallen to our lot during the war.[1]

I will now close Sir with a matter of intelligence brought by the Warren which I have no doubt may be relied upon, viz. That Col. Kearny who entered San Fe with five thousand men some months since has despatched from there one thousand mounted riflemen for service in Calia. I cherish the hope that you may fall in with them before you return from the south. With sentiments of respect I am your Ob't. Serv't.

JNO. B. MONTGOMERY
Military Comdt. of Calia. &
Comdr. of the U. S. Portsmouth

Lt. Col. J. C. Fremont
Military Commandant of California, Monterey

Lbk (DNA-45, no. 22, Officers' Letters, Letterbooks of J. B. Montgomery).
1. Montgomery and the *Portsmouth* did not sail for San Diego until 5 Dec.

The further delay in turning over the command and governorship of the "Northern District" to Hull was due to the loss of a launch from the *Warren* with Montgomery's sons, William H. and John E., aboard. Bound for the Sacramento on 13 Nov., the launch carried a crew and money to pay the garrison at Sutter's Fort. Neither boat nor crew was ever heard from again, and the presumption was that the craft was upset and the men drowned. But many believed that the crew mutinied, murdered the Montgomerys, and made off with the payroll (DOWNEY, 73–78; ROGERS [2], 87–91).

84. William Mervine to Frémont

U. S. Frigate Savannah
BAY OF MONTEREY, November 14th. 1846

SIR,

I am directed by Commodore R. F. Stockton, in the event of finding you here, to offer you any assistance that I can possibly give, to prepare you for the campaign; and to say that, "having failed after every exertion to reach Monterey to join you at the time specified in your letter of the 27th October," he, "concluded to return to San Diego as the most certain and speediest means of rejoining you."[1]

I have an Iron 4 Pounder—Ship Gun—mounted upon a good pair of cart wheels; also two new pairs of cart wheels and axles which are at your service. Respectfully &c. &c.

WILLIAM MERVINE

Lbk (DNA-45, Letterbooks of Officers at Sea, E-14 (A), William Mervine, vol. 1, 1846). Capt. William Mervine (1791–1868), in command of the *Savannah*, was still smarting from a defeat by the Californians. After the Angeleños revolted and drove out Archibald Gillespie and his forces, Stockton ordered Mervine to sail south and give the Americans aid. Landing at San Pedro on 7 Oct., Mervine and a portion of his crew joined Gillespie's men and advanced on Los Angeles, only to be outmaneuvered and pounded by a small cannon. He was forced to retreat to his ship and await the arrival of Stockton, and all of southern California slipped back into the hands of the local citizens. Although he had been sent north to give whatever aid JCF might need in preparing for his march to Los Angeles, he took no further active part in the war. He did remain in the Navy—an enemy of Gillespie's—and retired as a rear admiral in 1866 (MARTI, 87–91, 122–23; AMES [1]).

1. Stockton was eventually able to "buoy the bar" and get the *Congress* into the harbor of San Diego. He was there when Edward Stokes arrived on 3 Dec. with a letter from Gen. Stephen Watts Kearny at Warner's rancho. The letter advised him of the general's approach and expressed the wish that Stockton send a party to open communications with him (Kearny to Stockton, 2 Dec. 1846, CT. MARTIAL, 186).

85. Frémont to William Mervine

Sir,

I have the honor to acknowledge your communications of yesterday and this morning, in which you desire to be informed if the present strength of the garrison is adequate to the protection of the place, and farther offer me any aid in your power from the Savannah.

In my opinion the force under command of Capt. Wm. A. Maddox is insufficient to the successful defence of the fort and the protection of the town: a reinforcement of thirty men and an officer, would enable him to maintain both, and render the presence of a Ship of War unnecessary.[1]

I am informed that a prize Brig called the Julia Ann has been brought by the Warren to San Francisco, and farther informed that she would probably be sold at that place. Such a vessel would be of great importance to operate in communication along the coast, and would otherwise be extremely serviceable: if therefore, no other disposition of her has been already made, I would suggest to you that she be fitted out in such capacity, and that the Commanding Officer be accordingly directed to cooperate with and report to me for duty.

The circumstances of the country will render it advisable to detail a force from the Squadron for the occupation of the Pueblo of San José, which will operate effectually to check the inhabitants between Monterey and San Francisco: Our movement to the Southward will necessarily leave the interior exposed.

I feel pleasure in expressing my thanks for the aid you have afforded me, and am With much respect &c. &c. &c.

J. C. Fremont
Col. U. S. Army & Military Commdt. of California

Capt. William Mervine
Comdg. U. S. Frigate Savannah

Postscripture

I am unable to account for the delay which the men sent to me by Capt. Montgomery are making at the Pueblo of San José. I would be under much obligation to you, if you would send to Captain Charles Webber [Weber], who is now at San José, a positive and absolute order to march immediately, with all the Volunteers who may have entered the service of the United States, and join me at Monterey, or wherever else I may designate.

Those men who have not procured saddles can procure them on joining me. Ut. Supra.

J. C. Fremont

Lbk (DNA-45, Letterbooks of Officers at Sea, E-14 (D), Correspondence of William Mervine, vol. 8, 1846).

1. The next day Mervine ordered Midshipman Alexander B. Abercrombie "with a detachment of thirty Seaman & ordinary Seamen" from the *Savannah* to report to Lieut. William A. T. Maddox at Monterey (Mervine to Abercrombie, 15 Nov. 1846, DNA-45, Letterbooks of Officers at Sea, E-14 (A), William Mervine, vol. 1, 1846).

86. William Mervine to Frémont

U. S. Frigate Savannah
Bay of Monterey, Nov. 15th. 1846

Sir,

Agreeably to your request, I send you William Miller,[1] 1st class Musician, with his account[2] enclosed herewith. He is desirous of being permanently transferred to your command, but that must receive the sanction of the Commander in Chief. Very Respectfully &c. &c. &c.

William Mervine
Captain

Lieut. Col. J. C. Fremont
Military Comdt. of California

Lbk (DNA-45, Letterbooks of Officers at Sea, E-14 (A), William Mervine, vol. 1, 1846).

1. William D. Miller became a bugler for JCF (downey, 128–31).
2. Not found.

87. Frémont to William Mervine

MONTEREY, November 16th. 1846

DEAR SIR, .

I understand that, under the opinion that we had already commenced our march to the Southard, some persons in the Sacramento are engaged in *forming a battalion* to act as a reserve. Such a course will naturally weaken our forces, be of no manner of service to us, and create a large additional expenditure, for which we shall not be prepared.

The Warren has not brought a Dollar, but for reasons you will immediately perceive, this should not be made public here.

I therefore, suggest that, all additional enlistments should by an express order from yourself, be immediately discontinued throughout the Territory,—making an exception of the recruiting officers appointed by me, and who will soon be in—and that all men now enlisted immediately report to me at St. Johns, it being intended that the different Posts should be garrisoned by troops from the Squadrons. It cannot be expected that we should ration the families of Emigrants who do not aid me in the field.

I respectfully urge upon you the propriety and necessity of having it clearly understood that no persons will be received or paid who do not engage in the service of and report to the Military Commandant of the Country.

By giving me your aid in this way the public service will receive material benefit.

At present I am much harrassed by numerous appointments of irresponsible men, who obey nobody, and are more often drunk than sober.

I find that Webber [Weber] desires to remain at the Pueblo, and with your permission I will arrange the business between him and Hastings.[1]

I am glad that the day signals recurred to you, we will act accordingly.

I am indebted to you for the painting on our Flag—it is handsome, and if you will permit it, I should like to compensate the artist. Very Respectfully &c. &c. &c.

J. C. FREMONT
Lt. Col. U. S. Army

Captain Wm. Mervine
Senior Officer Northn. California.
U. S. Ship Congress [*Savannah*] &c.

Lbk (DNA-45, Letterbooks of Officers at Sea, E-14 (D), Correspondence of William Mervine, vol. 8, 1846).
1. Mervine had already directed John B. Montgomery to send a "positive order" to Captain Weber to join JCF with every volunteer in Monterey, and to have Lansford W. Hastings remain at San Jose for the time being (Mervine to Montgomery, 15 Nov. 1846, DNA-45, Area 9 File, Pacific). And this Montgomery did, although he indicated that if it were still "impracticable" for Weber to do so, he might remain in command at San Jose (Montgomery to Charles M. Weber, 18 Nov. 1846, CSmH). Weber remained at San Jose; Hastings went south to join JCF at Monterey.

88. William Mervine to Frémont

U. S. Frigate Savannah
Bay of Monterey, Nov. 16th. 1846

Sir,

Your letter of this date is received, and as I am much engaged just now in preparing to get underweigh, you will excuse my saying more than, that, all the suggestions contained therein shall be attended to.

You can make the arrangements you speak of with respect to Hastings.

Your Requisitions have be[en] complied with, with the exception of substituting "catridges" for "tube Boxes." Very Respectfully &c. &c. &c.

Wm. Mervine
Capt. U. S. Navy

Lieut. Col. J. C. Fremont
U. S. A. & Military Comdt. of California

Lbk (DNA-45, Letterbooks of Officers at Sea, E-14 (A), William Mervine, vol. 1, 1846).

89. Frémont to Charles M. Weber

Mission of San Juan
Nov 19th 1846

SIR

As we are exceedingly in want of horses and mules, You will please deliver to Lieut Wm. Blackburn[1] all that have been collected by yourself or other officers under your command. I am anxiously awaiting the arrival of those men, from the neighborhood of the Pueblo, that Capt. Mervine informed me would be ordered to join my command. I am, Very Respectfully Your Obt. Servt.

(Signed) J. C. FREMONT
Lt Col Comdg. Calif. Battalion & Mil. Comdt. California

Capt. Chas. Weber
Pueblo San José

Copy (CSmH). JCF had come from Monterey, where he had been organizing, equipping, and provisioning his California Battalion, to the Mission San Juan Bautista. Tom Hill, a Delaware Indian scout, and Charley McIntosh, a half-breed, had slipped through the enemy lines to bring information on the plight of two small American forces which had met a large group of Californians on 16 Nov. The encounter became known as the battle of Natividad, as it was fought principally on the Rancho Natividad, which adjoined the Gómez rancho where Thomas Oliver Larkin had been captured by a Castro detachment on the night of 15–16 Nov. JCF gives some details of the battle in his 20 Nov. letter to Kern (Doc. No. 90). See also ROGERS [1], 29:336–41.

1. Second Lieut. William Blackburn (1814–67), of Company A artillery, was a Virginia cabinetmaker who immigrated to California in 1845. Before joining the battalion, he served in the Fauntleroy dragoons. When peace came, he settled in Santa Cruz and served as alcalde and later as county judge before turning his attention to agriculture (PIONEER REGISTER).

90. Frémont to Edward M. Kern

Mission St. John's, Nov. 20. 1846

MY DEAR SIR,

I received your note by Mr. Burrus [Burrass], taken from his person after he was killed.[1] The party which he commanded in con-

229

junction with one of 25 under Lieut. Thompson[2] encountered a Californian force 150 strong, at the mouth of the Gomez Canada, on the Salinas plain. The Californians were defeated, losing 10–20 killed and a considerable number wounded. They carried their wounded and some of their dead. Ten of the latter were counted on the field. We have lost in killed four; viz, Capt. Burruss, Joseph [E.] Foster, Hiram Ames and ——— Cooper; two severely wounded and others slightly—all now doing well.[3] The Californians were ran about 2 miles and night stopped the fight. Our men acted nobly but very imprudently; only forty of them were in the fight when they charged. We have lost good men.[4] Tell the Wallawalah chief[5] that his men fought bravely and none of them were hurt. Tom Hill killed three Californians and received two slight wounds.[6] I wish you [to indicate to him] (I have promised this to the Walawalahs) that his men cannot get back in a moon & a half [*sketch of a moon and a half-moon*]. It will require 2 moons. I desire you to supply the families of those Walawalahs who are with me, with beef and flour regularly; and to give regular rations to Jeandrois' [Gendreau's] family.

I regret exceedingly that you cannot be with me, and sympathize with your bad health, but hope the cool weather will relieve you.[7] I shall leave this in a few days. We expect close skirmishing and one hard fight. At this time we are over 300 men and shall have four pieces of artillery. I hope yet that Capt. Sutter will arrive with his Indians—if they do not join us here they can be of no service.[8] Yours truly,

J. C. FREMONT

Lieut Kerne
Commanding Sacramento District

P. S. Talbot and his party are with us.
                    ut Supra.
We heard cannon last evening at Monterey—I left that place 3 days since—Captain Maddox is in command there with 125 men, and 6 pieces artillery. Merrit recaptured San Diego without loss—25 men against 80–120 Californians.[9]
                    ut Supra

ALS, RC (CSmH).
1. Charles D. Burrass was bringing twenty-two men, a cannon, and a large drove of horses and mules from the Sacramento district to augment

JCF's battalion and supplies at Monterey. Nineteen-year-old Edward Kemble, a participant in the battle of Natividad, in an article appearing in the *California Star*, 21 Aug. 1847 (reprinted in E. C. KEMBLE, 59–64), reported that ten Walla Wallas "under the command of one Brennard" and two Delawares were attached to the Sacramento company. Brennard has not been identified, and it is possible that Kemble, who soon became editor of the *Star*, made an error. According to Sutter (DILLON, 254), François Gendreau was captain of the Walla Walla detachment, and Gendreau's name appears on the roster of the California Battalion. The letter above implies that Gendreau was in command of the Walla Wallas.

2. Bluford K. Thompson, who was actually captain—not lieutenant—of Company G, California Battalion, had recruited a motley party of rancheros, runaway sailors, Negroes, Englishmen, and Germans at San Jose for JCF's battalion. A gambler by profession, Thompson was later acquitted of a murder charge but was obliged to leave California in 1848. He was himself killed in a new quarrel on the Sweetwater.

3. Like Burrass and Thompson, Joseph E. Foster, sometimes called "Captain," and St. Louisan Hiram Ames were also 1846 immigrants to California. William Thorne, not Cooper, was killed at Natividad, although he may have been called Billy the Cooper (ROGERS [1], 29:338; ROGERS [3]). Wounded were James Cash, William McGlone, Henry Marshall, and James Hays.

4. JCF's battalion sustained its greatest losses of the war here at Natividad.

5. Piopiomoxmox or Yellow Serpent was the chief of a band of forty warriors and their families who came back to New Helvetia in Sept. 1846 to hunt, trade for cattle, and visit the grave of Elijah, the chief's son, slain more than a year before by an American residing in California. Rumors that the warriors numbered 250 and were coming in vengeance brought terror to the American community, and many preparations were made to meet the invasion (see REVERE, 148–63; HEIZER; AMES & HUSSEY). On 11 Aug. 1847 Joseph Libbey Folsom, chief of the Quartermaster Department station at San Francisco, reported to William T. Sherman that JCF, on his way out of California with General Kearny in June 1847, had given the Walla Walla Indians about a hundred of the public horses in payment for their services in the war.

6. Tom Hill (ca. 1811–ca. 1860), a Delaware scout, had been one of Kit Carson's men in 1834. In 1839 he joined a band of Nez Perce Indians living in the buffalo country of Montana and in 1846 was part of the so-called Walla Walla invasion of California. Following his adventure as a scout for Burrass, he became a scout with JCF's forces on the winter march through rain and mud to Los Angeles (HAINES).

7. In a letter of 2 Nov. 1846 George McKinstry, Jr., wrote Pierson B. Reading that Edward M. Kern was in bed at Fort Sutter "shaking finely with the chills" (MORGAN, 1:217).

8. Sutter was recruiting Indians on the Stanislaus and Mokelumne rivers—"old horse thieves who had reformed," as he termed them (DILLON, 254). He also helped enlist a company of native California Indians to serve at New Helvetia and thus release the old garrison for service in the south.

9. San Diego had been recaptured sometime between 8 and 11 Oct. by a small force variously reported as twenty-five or forty men, including John Bidwell and sailors from the whaler *Stonington*. The assault was commanded by Ezekiel Merritt. On appeal by Merritt for reinforcements, Mervine at San

Pedro chartered the whaler *Magnolia* out of New Bedford and sent it with Lieut. George Minor, two midshipmen, thirty-five sailors, and fifteen volunteers dashing to the rescue. This group landed near the mouth of the San Diego River and built fortifications, but for some time San Diego was a no-man's-land. The Americans were unable to dislodge the Mexicans from the hilltops or to procure cattle and horses. For an account of the siege of San Diego, see POURADE, 3:87–94. Ezekiel Merritt had commanded the party that seized Arce's horses in June and organized the Bear Flaggers' descent on Sonoma.

91. William Mervine to Frémont

U. S. Frigate Savannah
BAY OF SAN FRANCISCO, Nov. 21st. 1846

SIR,

The state of the country on my arrival here was represented to be such as to render the landing of the Brass Gun at the Embarcadero of Santa Clara extremely hazardous, without a sufficient force to escort it down to you, which could not be spared.[1] I have, therefore, sent it down in the "Julia", and hope it will arrive in time; if not, it will remain on board the Schooner, and follow you down the coast.

Manuel Castro is at the head of a party of about sixty men, maurading about the country. Some of his gang made prisoner of T. O. Larkin, during the night of the day after his leaving Monterey.[2] Very Respectfully &c. &c. &c.

WILLIAM MERVINE
Captain

Lieut. Col. J. C. Fremont
Military Commdt. of Calia.

Lbk (DNA-45, Letterbooks of Officers at Sea, E-14 (A), William Mervine, vol. 1, 1846).

1. Mervine had requested that the brass gun which Capt. Joseph B. Hull had taken out of the prize brig *Malek Adhel* be sent to the embarcadero at Santa Clara (Mervine to John B. Montgomery, 1 Nov. 1846, DNA-45, Area 9 File, Pacific).

2. Larkin had left Monterey on 15 Nov. for San Francisco to be with his wife and children after learning that his youngest daughter, Adeline, was seriously ill. He stopped for the night at the rancho of José Joaquín Gómez, and about midnight was captured and escorted on horseback to Manuel Castro's camp on the Salinas River. Held as a hostage for several weeks, he was taken to Santa Barbara and then to Los Angeles as the Californians retreated (LARKIN, 5:xiv–xv).

92. Frémont to William Mervine

St. Johns Mission
Nov. 27th. 1846

Sir,

I have directed all officers, civil and military, who come properly within my jurisdiction, to abstain from any farther offensive proceedings against the Californians, residing and being in the Northern Department; and that they permit them to pursue their usual lawful business without molestation.

Believing this to be the best as well as most humane course, and satisfied of the present peaceable disposition of the greater part of the inhabitants here, I have to request that you will sustain it by your influence and authority.

I have given to numbers of residents in this vicinity general passports and safeguards, any violation of which will be punished according to the usages of war by a summary Court Martial.

Some of the proceedings instituted by Captain Charles Weber against the people here are very little honorable to the United States, and I have publicly and fully disclaimed them as disgraceful. I feel certainly assured that nothing of this nature will be countenanced by yourself and therefore call your attention to them.

I am in hopes that Captain Weber will not now have any farther power to destroy the people and force out against us those who otherwise would have been willing to remain quiet.[1]

I beg to insist strongly upon this subject with you, as I believe that any farther hostile measures in the Northern Department are totally unnecessary. They will cause unnecessary expense and bloodshed. No persons are in arms beyond a few straggling robbers whom a small force is sufficient to check and chastise.

I should feel it unnecessary to make these representations to you were the commission of Military Commandant of California received by me from Commodore Stockton, of any authority among his Officers: but under the actual circumstances I should feel myself humiliated by attaching it to my name.

I have only therefore to beg of you that you will do me the favor to sustain the conciliatory measures which I have judged it advisable to adopt here, and that you will cause my passports and safeguards to be respected by the officers of this department. Any violation of them will certainly be punished to the full extent of the ability that law and circumstances may leave in my power.

We are just about raising camp and I hope in a few weeks to be able to send some satisfactory news.[2] Begging you to receive the assurances of personal regard I am, Very Respectfully your Obdt. Servt.,

J. C. FRÉMONT
Lt. Col. U. S. Army Commdg. California Battalion U. S. Troops

Captain Wm. Mervine
Senior Captain in North California.
Commanding U. S. Frigate Savannah, San Francisco

LS (DNA-45, LR by Secretary of the Navy from Commanding Officers of Squadrons, Pacific Squadron, Commodore Stockton, 1846–47). Endorsed. The body of the letter was written by Talbot, who, suffering "starvation, cold, nakedness and every sort of privation" after being driven from Santa Barbara by the Californians under the command of Manuel Garfias, had managed to rejoin JCF at Monterey a day or two before the battle of Natividad (Talbot to Adelaide Talbot, 15 Jan. 1847, DLC—Talbot Papers).

1. Weber's methods of requisitioning horses and equipment for JCF met resistance, and Henry Mellus and W. D. M. Howard in particular protested the crippling of their business (John B. Montgomery to Charles M. Weber, 2 Nov. 1846, CSmH). The commandant of the Northern District actually appointed a commission to investigate complaints against Weber, but the order was later annulled, and the alcalde of San Jose was directed to take the affidavits of the aggrieved.

2. Shortly after sending off this letter, JCF and his motley battalion started from San Juan on their march to Los Angeles to cooperate with Stockton against the army of José María Flores, commanding insurgent forces in the south. Flores's design was to confine American naval officers to the seaports by the practical technique of driving all stock into the interior, making it impossible for the American Navy to mount and provision a land force. "Against the naval force only," JCF wrote, "his plan would have been easily successful, but it became impossible when in addition he had against him the active force of my command, which cut his plan at the root and turned it against himself. I had at my back the constantly increasing emigrant force, and the mountains, which I knew better than himself" (MEMOIRS, 593).

93. Excerpt from the *Memoirs*

[28 Nov. 1846–13 Jan. 1847]

Working and waiting for the reinforcements from the valley, the weeks passed on until the end of November, when we moved from San Juan, and, halting a few days for our supply of beef cattle, took up the line of march for Los Angeles. Our route lay up the San Benito River, and thence over the hills into the Salinas valley.[1] The march was made under difficult circumstances. Winter weather and cold rain-storms for days together; the roads and trails muddy; the animals weak for want of food; the strength of the old grass washed out by the rains, and the watery new grass without sustenance. Many of the horses, too weak for use, fell out by the way and were left behind, and part of the battalion was soon on foot.

Attached to the battalion was a company of Indians; some Walla-wallahs and a few Delawares from the Columbia River, the rest Indians from the Sacramento. These were to act as scouts under the command of Captain Richard Jacob,* of Louisville, Kentucky. Regularly during the march a part of this company encamped, without fires, one to three miles in advance of the battalion; the other part about the same distance in the rear; so that no traveller on the road escaped falling into our hands.

The battalion numbered about four hundred and thirty men.[2] Their only provision was the beef which was driven along,[3] but this was good, and the men were in fine health. Cold weather and the exposed marches gave wholesome appetites. Perfect order was maintained on the march and in the camp, and private property was respected absolutely. No man left the camp without a pass, and the column passed over the country without giving reasonable cause for complaint to any Californian.[4]

In such a march, it may be supposed, there was no superfluity of baggage, and the men rode or walked in the rain and slept wet at night, but there was surprisingly little complaint and no disorder. As always, there were in the command some men who were useless and some who were worse, but these were kept under watchful eyes, and gave little trouble. In the forepart of the day of the 14th December I encamped on the mountain near San Luis Obispo. In the afternoon I went with William Knight to a point on the hills which overlooked the mission, and watched for awhile, but in the distance we could discover nothing to indicate whether or not there was a force at the place. The night was rainy. Saddling up after nightfall, about nine o'clock we surrounded the mission buildings and captured the few people found there. Some took to the roofs of the mis-

* Afterwards Lieutenant-Governor of Kentucky and son-in-law of Senator Benton.

235

sion, but none got away. To avoid turning the people out of their houses in the stormy weather, I quartered the battalion in the mission church, putting a regular guard over the altar and church property. We found in the town some *frijoles* and other vegetables, and crushed wheat, which were bought and distributed among the men by way of luxuries.

Upon information, I sent men around the neighborhood, and in all some thirty men fell into our hands, among them an officer who had been wounded at the Encinal, and Don [José de] Jesús Pico,[5] who was at the head of the insurrection in that quarter. Don Jesús had broken his parole, and was put before a court-martial and sentenced to be shot.

Among the papers seized here was an original despatch from General Flores, by which we learned of the action at San Pasqual, but it made no mention of the officer commanding on the American side.

The hour for the execution of Don Jesús Pico had arrived and the battalion was drawn up in the plaza in front of my windows. The rough travelling had put the men in bad humor and they wanted to vent it upon something. They looked upon Pico as in part cause of their hardships and wanted to see him die. Don Jesús was about to be led out. The door of my room was abruptly opened by Captain Owens, who showed in a lady in black, followed by a group of children. They were the wife and children of Pico. She had prevailed upon Owens, who was kind as well as brave, to bring her to me. On entering the lady threw herself on her knees, she imploring the life of her husband, the children crying and frightened. "He did not know," she said, "that he was committing such a crime. He went with the *hijos del pais* to defend the country because he was ashamed to stay behind when the others went to fight. He did not know it was so wrong." I raised her from her knees and told her to go home and remain quiet, and I would presently let her know.[6]

I sent Owens to bring me Don Jesús. He came in with the gray face of a man expecting death, but calm and brave, while feeling it is near. He was a handsome man, within a few years of forty, with black eyes and black hair. I pointed through the window to the troops paraded in the square. He knew why they were there. "You were about to die," I said, "but your wife has saved you. Go thank her."

He fell on his knees, made on his fingers the sign of the cross, and said: "I was to die—I had lost the life God gave me—you have given

236

me another life. I devote the new life to you." And he did it, faithfully.

Don Jesús was a cousin of Don Andres Pico who commanded at San Pasqual, and who was married to a lady of the Carrillo family. When the march was resumed he accompanied me and remained with me until I left California, always an agreeable companion and often rendering me valuable service—perhaps sometimes quite unknown to myself.[7]

Contracting space requires me here to pass lightly over incidents of the march, beyond the Mission.[8] On Christmas eve we encamped on the ridge of Santa Ines [Ynez] behind Santa Barbara.[9] The morning of Christmas broke in the darkness of a southeasterly storm with torrents of cold rain, which swept the rocky face of the precipitous mountain down which we descended to the plain. All traces of trails were washed away by the deluge of water, and pack-animals slid over the rocks and fell down the precipices, blinded by the driving rain. In the descent over a hundred horses were lost. At night we halted in the timber at the foot of the mountain, the artillery and baggage strewed along our track, as on the trail of a defeated army. The stormy day was followed by a bright morning, with a welcome sun, and gathering ourselves into an appearance of order we made our way into the town. There was nothing to oppose us, and nothing to indicate hostility; the Californian troops having been drawn together in a main body near Los Angeles. I remained here some days to refresh the battalion and repair damages. The gun crews wanted sights to their guns, and to please them I had the guns tried and sighted.[10]

Pending this delay Don Jesus brought me word that a lady wished to confer with me. He informed me that she was a woman of some age, highly respected and having a strong connection, over which she had the influence sometimes accorded to women of high character and strong individuality.*

---

* I had retained only the Christian name of this lady, but in reply to a letter I have received the following telegram:

San Luis Obispo, California, November 10, 1886.

To General J. C. Frémont, 1310 Nineteenth Street, Washington, D. C.

Received your letter. The lady who urged you for peace with the Californians at Santa Barbara is Bernarda Ruiz. She died eight years ago.

J. de Jesus Pico

In the interview I found that her object was to use her influence to put an end to the war, and to do so upon such just and friendly terms of compromise as would make the peace acceptable and enduring. And she wished me to take into my mind this plan of settlement, to which she would influence her people; meantime, she urged me, to hold my hand, so far as possible. Naturally, her character and sound reasoning had its influence with me, and I had no reserves when I assured her that I would bear her wishes in mind to act when the occasion came, and that she might with all confidence speak on this basis with her friends. Here began the Capitulation of Couenga [Cahuenga].

With damage from hard marching and stormy weather repaired, and the men restored by their rest in comfortable quarters to good condition and good humor, the march was resumed on the 17th [3 Jan.]. On our way across the plain below Santa Barbara a corps of observation of the enemy's cavalry, some fifty to one hundred men, hovered about us, without doing or receiving any harm. It did not come within my policy to have any of them killed, and a few shots from our guns that went uncomfortably near dispersed them.

There is a maritime defile called the *Rincon,* about fifteen miles south of Santa Barbara and fifteen miles long. A mountain ridge here skirts the sea, leaving a narrow beach floored with a hard, particolored bitumen. The defile was passed without opposition. Herealong we were flanked by a gunboat, under the command of Lieutenant Selden, of the navy, which Commodore Stockton had sent, to be of aid to me in some possible emergency.[11] He was watchful over the whole situation and prompt to aid wherever he saw an opening. On the morning of the 9th Captain [George W.] Hamlyn [Hamley], master of the *Stonington,* which had so useful a part at San Diego, came into my camp at "The Willows," below the Rincon.[12]

Captain Hamlyn was the bearer of a despatch to me from Commodore Stockton, whom he had left at San Luis Rey, and passing through San Diego had embarked on the brig *Malek Adhel* and landed at San Buenaventura, which is at the southern entrance of the Rincon Pass. He was accompanied by my friend Don Pedro Car[r]illo, by whose aid he had found an Indian who guided them past the camp of the horsemen who had been observing us, and brought them to me at "The Willows."

This is the letter which he brought me from the commodore:

[Not reprinted here, but included as Stockton to Frémont, 3 Jan. 1847, Doc. No. 101.]

We entered the Pass of San Bernardo [San Fernando] on the evening of the 12th,[13] expecting to find the enemy there in force, but the Californians had fallen back before our advance and the Pass was undisputed. In the afternoon we encamped at the mission of San Fernando,[14] the residence of Don Andres Pico, who was at present in chief command of the Californian troops. Their encampment was within two miles of the mission, and in the evening, Don Jesús, with a message from me, made a visit to Don Andres. The next morning, accompanied only by Don Jesús, I rode over to the camp of the Californians, and, in a conference with Don Andres, the important features of a treaty of capitulation were agreed upon.

A truce was ordered;[15] commissioners on each side appointed; and the same day a capitulation agreed upon. This was approved by myself as Military Commandant representing the United States, and Don Andres Pico, Commander-in-Chief of the Californians. With this treaty of Counega [Cahuenga][16] hostilities ended, and California left peaceably in our possession; to be finally secured to us by the treaty of Guadalupe Hidalgo in 1848.

MEMOIRS, 597–601. Talbot wrote his mother that the battalion left San Juan on 26 Nov., but in view of the fact that he dated a letter for JCF to William Mervine (Doc. No. 92) from San Juan on 27 Nov., the date of 30 Nov. as given by McLane is more likely the accurate one (Talbot to Adelaide Talbot, 15 Jan. 1847, DLC—Talbot Papers; MC LANE, 91). Lieut. Edwin Bryant in Company H of the battalion implies that the start was made on 28 Nov. (BRYANT, 365–68). Bryant (1805–69), former editor of the Lexington, Ky., *Reporter,* was chiefly responsible for raising Company H from the newly arrived emigrants to California, of which he was one, but the command was given to Richard T. Jacob, a JCF favorite (Sacramento *Daily Union,* 9 Dec. 1871; E. C. KEMBLE, 90–97). Bryant's *What I Saw in California,* published shortly after the author's return east with General Kearny, went through several editions and, along with McLane's journal, is useful in supplementing JCF's much later account of his march from San Juan Bautista to Cahuenga. In the struggle between Kearny and JCF in California, Bryant sided with Kearny and was appointed by him to serve as alcalde of San Francisco.

1. GIFFEN [1] has a fine secondary account, accompanied by a map, of the battalion's march from San Juan Bautista to Los Angeles. She notes the distance covered and the campsite for each day. OUTLAND differs on a few of the bivouacs, particularly after the battalion left Mission San Buenaventura on 6 Jan. 1847.

2. In addition to the Indians, the battalion was made up of many members of JCF's exploring party, volunteers from the American settlements, and newly arrived emigrants. For the most part, they furnished their own ammunition and equipment and were capable of bearing the fatigue and

privations endured by veteran troops. Attached to the battalion were three pieces of artillery and an ammunition wagon under the command of Lieut. Louis McLane of the Navy (MC LANE, 91). "In the appearance of our small army," Bryant wrote, "there is presented but little of 'the pomp and circumstance of glorious war.' There are no plumes nodding over brazen helmets, nor coats of broadcloth spangled with lace and buttons. A broad-brimmed, low-crowned hat, a shirt of blue flannel, or buckskin, with pantaloons and moccasins of the same, all generally the worse for wear, and smeared with mud and dust, make up the costume of the party, officers as well as men. A leathern girdle surrounds the waist, from which are suspended a bowie and a hunter's knife, and sometimes a brace of pistols. These, with rifle and holster-pistols, are the arms carried by officers and privates. A single bugle (and a sorry one it is) composes the band" (BRYANT, 366).

3. In addition to the 1,900 horses and mules on the quartermaster's roll, the battalion was driving 300 head of cattle (MC LANE, 91). Ordinarily thirteen beeves were slaughtered each day, and in the early stages of the march, replacements were secured from missions and ranchos along the way. This was also true for horses that gave out. At the Mission San Miguel on 10 Dec. the battalion feasted on mutton, *frijoles,* and *tortillas,* and wheat became more readily available as they proceeded south (BRYANT, 372, 383, 390).

4. BRYANT, 374, also observed that "the deportment of the battalion might be cited as a model for imitation." But there were others who did not share his opinion. A resident of Santa Barbara, William A. Streeter, remembered JCF saying that he had destroyed all the property he could find of those who were out in arms against him, and reported that the battalion commander's original intention had been to enter Santa Barbara "with fire and sword" (STREETER, 164). While the battalion was in the vicinity of Mission San Miguel, a scouting party burned the ranch house of Mariano Soberanes and took him and his sons prisoner (MC LANE, 112; GIFFEN [1], 221).

5. As captain of defense and justice of the peace at San Luis Obispo, José de Jesús Pico (b. 1807) had been paroled earlier, but he had broken that parole, participated in the battle of Natividad, and supported José María Flores in the general uprising in the south.

6. DOWNEY, 126, wrote, "We all knew the Colonel was a little tender on sex, and along before the conference was ended it was the generally received opinion in camp that there would be no hanging done." Javaela Villavicencio's pleading had saved her husband, but an Indian who had been spying on the battalion on the orders of Pico had been summarily executed on 13 Dec. in full view of Indians from a neighboring ranchería (BRYANT, 373). CUTTS, 161, contains what is reputedly Talbot's description of Pico's pardon, probably written by JBF.

7. Pico, owner of Piedra Blanca, which later became a part of George Hearst's estate of San Simeon, not only aided JCF in bringing about the Treaty of Cahuenga but also accompanied him on his famous ride from Los Angeles to Monterey in March 1847 when the worried governor sought an interview with Kearny (see Doc. No. 166, n. 1). Later he would serve for a time as assessor of San Luis Obispo County and in 1852–53 as a member of the state legislature.

8. After the Mission San Luis Obispo camps were made near Rancho Nipomo, owned by William Goodwin Dana, a native of Massachusetts who had become quite influential in California, and at Rancho Tinaquaic, owned by Benjamin Foxen, a former English sailor who over the years was to build

a large California estate in spite of spending four years in jail for killing Agustín Dávila in 1848 (BRYANT, 377–78; PIONEER REGISTER).

9. Guided by Foxen, the battalion crossed the Santa Ynez ridge by way of San Marcos Pass. The artillery had to be unlimbered and carried by the men over the pass and down the precipitous mountain. During the descent "the wind blew almost with the force of a tornado" (BRYANT, 380). JCF has been unjustly accused of poor judgment in taking the San Marcos Pass instead of the road through Gaviota. The latter pass is a narrow one, and rumors were afloat that the Californians intended to make a stand there. Furthermore, to take the route through Gaviota would have limited his mobility—he would have had the ocean on one side and the steeply rising hills on the other.

10. For an account of the reoccupation of the almost deserted town of Santa Barbara, see ELLISON, 256–69.

11. Lieut. Edward A. Selden, who had been a midshipman on board the U.S.S. *Columbus*, commanded the prize schooner *Julia*, in earlier days called the *Julia Ann*. He had arrived in the Santa Barbara roadstead on 30 Dec. and landed a cannon for the use of the battalion (BRYANT, 386). See Doc. No. 99 for JCF's instructions to Selden.

12. "The Willows" was about two miles east of present-day Fillmore (OUT-LAND, 412–13).

13. On the morning of 11 Jan. "the artillery, horses and baggage, with an advance-guard and escort," went through the narrow pass, while the main body took a circuitous route over a ridge of hills to the right of the main road (BRYANT, 390).

14. Before arriving at the Mission San Fernando at about 1 P.M. on 11 Jan., the battalion had been met by two Californians, who informed them of Kearny's and Stockton's victories at San Gabriel and the Mesa and of the American reoccupation of Los Angeles on 10 Jan. A Frenchman also brought a letter (probably Doc. No. 102) to JCF from Kearny (BRYANT, 390–91).

15. See Doc. No. 103, and note that it bears the date 12 Jan. 1847.

16. See Doc. No. 106, and note that the Articles of Capitulation bear the date 13 Jan. 1847.

94. Stephen Watts Kearny to Robert F. Stockton

SAN DIEGO
December 22d 1846

DEAR COMMODORE

If you can take from here sufficient force to oppose the Californians now supposed to be near the Pueblos, & waiting for the approach of Lieut. Col. Fremont I advise that you do so, & that you march with the force as early as possible in the direction of the Pueblos by which you will either be able to form a junction with Lieut. Col. Fremont or make a division very much in his favor.

Four Unidentified Members of the California Battalion. From a photograph taken 29 Aug. 1848, Washington, D.C., in the Los Angeles County Museum of Natural History.

I do not think that Lieut. Col. Fremont should be left unsupported to fight a battle upon which the fate of California may for a long time depend if there are troops here to act in concert with him. Your force as it advances might surprise the enemy at the San Louis [San Luis Rey] Mission & make prisoners of them. I shall be happy in such an expedition to accompany you, & to give you any aid, either of head or hand of which I may be capable. Yours Truly,

(Signed) S. W. KEARNY
Brig. Genl.

Copy of enclosure C-1 in Kearny to R. Jones, 30 Jan. 1847 (DNA-94, LR, K-120 1847, f/w K-209 1846). Kearny and the remnants of his Army of the West had limped into San Diego on 12 Dec. The American force had been badly mauled by the Californians on 6 Dec. in the battle of San Pasqual, suffering casualties of twenty-one or twenty-two dead and almost as many injured, the general himself being wounded. However, Kearny wrote to the adjutant about the "victory" gained over "more than double our force," despite the fact that his force was not able to move from "Mule Hill" until the arrival of a relief party under Lieut. Andrew V. F. Gray—sent by Stockton after urgent pleas for aid came to the commodore's headquarters. The Historical Division of the Army War College declared in 1928, "General Kearny did not sustain a defeat at San Pasqual" (quoted in CLARKE, 230), and Kearny's biographer rates San Pasqual an American victory, since the force was able to march ultimately to its goal: San Diego (CLARKE, 229–32). Stockton, Benton, and JCF stigmatized it as a defeat, and so have many historians. Except for John S. Griffin, the assistant surgeon, and Maj. Thomas B. Swords, the quartermaster, every line officer who fought in the battle of San Pasqual received awards for gallant and meritorious service. "A grand affair for the Brevet of Major Gen'l to be conferred," Swords wrote bitterly to Griffin (GRIFFIN [2], 33:266–67). Many details of the battle were revealed during JCF's court-martial (CT. MARTIAL, 63–66). For a historical discussion, see WOODWARD, CLARKE, 195–232, and MARTI, 92–101.

95. Robert F. Stockton to Stephen Watts Kearny

Head Quarters
SAN DIEGO
December 23d. 1846

DEAR GENERAL

Your note of yesterday was handed to me last night by Capt. Turner[1] of the Dragoons. In reply to that note, permit me to refer

Stephen Watts Kearny. From a mezzotint engraving in the Library of Congress.

you to the conversation held with you yesterday morning at your Quarters. I stated to you distinctly that I intended to march upon St. Louis Rey as soon as possible, with a part of the forces under my command—that I was very desirous to march on to the Pueblo to cooperate with Col. Fremont, but my movements after taking St. Louis Rey would depend entirely upon the information that I might receive as to the movements of Col. Fremont, and the enemy. It might be necessary for me to stop the pass at San Felipe, or march back to San Diego.

Now my dear General, if the object of your note is to advise me to do any thing which would enable a large force of enemy to get into my Rear & cut off my communication with San Diego, and harass the safety of the garrison, and the Ships in the harbour, you will excuse me for saying, I cannot follow such advice.

My purpose still is to march for St. Louis Rey as soon as I can get the Dragoons & Riflemen mounted which I hope to do in two days. Faithfully Your Obdt. Servt.

(Signed) R. F. STOCKTON
Commander in chief & Governor of the Territory of California

To Brig. Genl. W. S. Kearny
U.S. Army

Copy of enclosure C-2 in Kearny to R. Jones, 30 Jan. 1847 (DNA-94, LR, K-120 1847, f/w K-209 1846).
1. Henry Smith Turner (1811–81), Kearny's aide and adjutant and a kinsman of Robert E. Lee, kept a journal of his march from Fort Leavenworth to Warner's rancho with the Army of the West and another of his return east with Kearny in the summer of 1847. Both have been edited recently by Dwight L. Clarke (see TURNER). Turner would resign from the Army in July 1848 and embark on a financial career in St. Louis with his wife's wealthy uncle, James H. Lucas. A fellow officer and friend in California, William T. Sherman, became manager of the firm's San Francisco branch bank in the 1850s.

96. Stephen Watts Kearny to Robert F. Stockton

SAN DIEGO
Dec 23d 1846

DEAR COMMODORE

I have received yours of this date, repeating, as you say, what you stated to me yesterday, & in reply I have only to remark, that if I had so understood you, I could not have written my letter to you of last evening—you certainly could not for a moment suppose that I would advise or suggest to you any movement, which might endanger the safety of the Garrison and the ships in the harbor. My letter of yesterday's date stated that "if you can take from here &c &c." of which you were the Judge & of which I knew nothing. Truly yours,

(Signed) S. W. KEARNY
Brig. Genl.

Comd. R. F. Stockton
Comd U.S. Navy &c &c
San Diego

Copy of enclosure C-3 in Kearny to R. Jones, 30 Jan. 1847 (DNA-94, LR, K-120 1847, f/w K-209 1846).

97. Robert F. Stockton to Stephen Watts Kearny

Head Quarters
SAN DIEGO
December 24th. 1846

DEAR GENERAL

The animals for our march are being selected today, & although not in very good condition, I propose to move on the Road to [Pueblo] de los Angeles on Monday at 10 A.M. & open if possible a communication with Col. Frémont's force, now supposed to be approaching the Pueblo.

I expect to be joined by one hundred Indians, who with the Mounted Men will be ready at any time to make a forced march back to San Diego, in the event of the insurgents attempting to get in our rear to attack the garrison.

You were kind enough to say that you would accompany me on this march—nothing could be more serviceable, & nothing more gratifying to me personally than your presence and I sincerely hope that your health will permit you to do so. Faithfully Your Obdt. Servt.

(Signed) R. F. STOCKTON
Commodore &c.

Brig Genl. W. S. Kearny
U.S. Army

Copy of enclosure C-5 in Kearny to R. Jones, 30 Jan. 1847 (DNA-94, LR, K-120 1847, f/w K-209 1846).

98. Robert F. Stockton to Frémont

Head Quarters
SAN DIEGO
December 24th. 1846
6 o'clock P. M.

MY DEAR COLONEL:

I hope to leave on Monday with five hundred men and six pieces of artillery, able I think to conquer the whole Country. I send this to you to urge you to take great care how you charge the insurgents, or how you chase them. They will run until they get you in disorder and separated, and suddenly turn and charge—do not let them get behind you; they are so expert in horsemanship that you cannot hope to compete with them in that art, or that of dodging or running: therefore keep your men quiet and steady—let the enemy do the charging and your Rifles will do the rest.

I hope to be at St. Luis Rey on Wednesday. If you have *even one chance* against you, join me before fight and we can do as we see fit afterwards. The bearer[s] will tell you all the news and our route. Send them back as soon as possible.

God bless you and prosper our Country. Very Truly Yours,

R. F. STOCKTON

Lieut. Col. Fremont
Military Commandant of California

Lbk (DNA-45, Entry 395 [E-20-A], Letterbook of Robert F. Stockton, 1846–47).

99. Frémont to Edward A. Selden

ANTA BARBARA, Jan 2d 1847

SIR,

You will please proceed with your vessel to the western extremity of the Rincon[1] and awaiting there the appearance of my force, endeavor to cooperate with me, should it become necessary to force a passage.

I am informed that the Eastern extremity of the passage which is called Punta Gorda, is occupied by the Enemy with at present, but one piece of artillery. On the morning of the 4th instant my advance will enter the passage which in the meantime you will keep under strict surveillance, and give me immediate information of any movement or increase of force; using for that purpose the subjoined signals. Your slight force and want of boats make it difficult for you to render efficient assistance. You will however do the best you can, and after the passage of the Rincon make your way to Commodore Stockton, whom you will acquaint with our Situation and intended movements. Having procured the necessary supplies for your vessel you will immediately return to San Pedro and await there farther communication from me. One gun, followed after an interval of five minutes by a rocket, and succeeded by a blue light on the beach will be understood by you as a signal for a boat. You will reply by a rocket and blue light. I am with Respect Your Obdt. Servt.

(Signed) J. C. FRÉMONT
Lt. Col. U.S. Army

Captain George [Edward A.] Selden
Schooner Julia
Bay of Santa Barbara

Copy 19 (1) enclosed in Kearny to R. Jones, 11 Sept. 1847 (DNA-94, LR, K-217 1847, f/w K-209 1846). For details on the taking of the schooner *Julia Ann*, see Doc. No. 82, n. 3.
1. For JCF's description of the pass, see p. 238.

8

100. Frémont to Robert F. Stockton

Santa Barbara
Jany. 2d. 1847

Sir

I reached this place on the 28th ultimo, with an effective force of about three hundred and fifty men and three pieces of artillery.

Bad weather and poor horses have harassed and impeded our movements, making our advance extremely slow.

I shall leave our present position in the afternoon and on the 4th pass the Rincon, the eastern extremity of which is occupied by a force of the Californians, with the strength of which I am not informed. Lieut. Selden, in the Julia, will cooperate with me at that point.

I shall thence march directly to the Pueblo de los Angeles, and if not met by the enemy, on the road, will attack him at the town. I am very Respectfully Your Obedient Servant,

(Signed) J. C. Frémont
Lt. Col. U.S. Army
Commdg. Cal. Battalion

Commodore R. F. Stockton
Governor & Commander in Chief of Territory of California

Copy 19 (2) enclosed in Kearny to R. Jones, 11 Sept. 1847 (DNA-94, LR, K-217 1847, f/w K-209 1846).

101. Robert F. Stockton to Frémont

Camp at San Louis Rey,
January 3, 1847

My Dear Colonel:

We arrived here last night from San Diego, and leave to-day on our march for the City of the Angels, where I hope to be in five or six days. I learn this morning that you are at Santa Barbara, and send this despatch by the way of San Diego, in the hope that it may reach you in time. If there is one single chance against you, you had better not fight the rebels until I get up to aid you, or you can join me on the road to the Pueblo.

These fellows are well prepared, and Mervine's and Kearny's defeat have given them a deal more confidence and courage. If you do fight before I see you, keep your forces in close order. Do not allow them to be separated, or even unnecessarily extended. They will probably try to deceive you by a sudden retreat, or pretended runaway, and then unexpectedly return to the charge after your men get in disorder in the chase. My advice is to allow them to do all the charging and running and let your rifles do the rest.

In the art of horsemanship, of dodging, and running, it is in vain to attempt to compete with them.

In haste, very truly, your friend and obedt. servt.

R. F. STOCKTON

To Lieut. Col. Fremont.

P. S. I understand that it is probable they will try to avoid me & fight you separately.

Lbk (DNA-45, Entry 395 [E-20-A], Letterbook of Robert F. Stockton, 1846–47). Also in CT. MARTIAL, 272–73, with the second clause of the first sentence in the second paragraph italicized. See p. 238 for JCF's description of Hamley's arrival with this letter from Stockton.

102. Stephen Watts Kearny to Frémont

PUEBLO DE LOS ANGELES
Sunday, January 10, 1846 [1847], 4 p. m.

DEAR FREMONT:

We are in possession of this place, with a force of marines and sailors, having marched into it this morning. Join us as soon as you can, or let me know, if you want us to march to your assistance; avoid charging the enemy; their force does not exceed 400, perhaps not more than 300. Please acknowledge the receipt of this, and despatch the bearer at once. Yours,

S. W. KEARNY,
Brigadier General, U. S. Army

Lieutenant Colonel J. C. Fremont
Mounted riflemen, commanding, &c. &c.

Printed in CT. MARTIAL, 73. This is undoubtedly the letter which the Frenchmen had brought JCF on 11 Jan. 1847 near the Mission San Fernando (BRYANT, 391) and is evidence that JCF knew of the route of the Californians before he ordered a truce on 12 Jan. (Doc. No. 103).

Kearny testified at the court-martial that he considered this letter and his letters of 12 and 13 Jan. 1847 to JCF to be "semi-official," and that he kept no copies (CT. MARTIAL, 72). He does not mention that Stockton was in Los Angeles, but JCF undoubtedly learned that he was from various messengers and Californians. "[We] camped in the Mission of San Fernando . . . and received authentic information that Commodore Stockton had defeated˙ Flores . . ." (MC LANE, 102).

103. Frémont's Proclamation

[12 Jan. 1847]

To ALL TO WHOM THESE PRESENTS SHALL COME GREETING:

Know ye that in consequence of propositions of peace or cessation of hostilities, being submitted to me as commandant of the Californian Battalion of United States Forces, which has so far been acceded to by me, as to cause me to appoint a board of commissioners to confer with a similar board appointed by the Californians, and it requiring a little time to close the negotiations, it is agreed upon and ordered by me, that an entire cessation of hostilities shall take place until tomorrow afternoon (Jan. 13th) and that the said Californians be permitted to bring in their wounded to the mission of San Fernandez [Fernando], where also if they choose, they can remove their camp, to facilitate said negotiations.

Given under my hand and seal this twelfth day of January 1847.

J. C. FRÉMONT,
Lieut. Colonel U. S. Army & Military Commandant of California

DS, enclosure in Stockton to George Bancroft, 15 Jan. 1847 (DNA-45, Pacific Squadron, Commodore Stockton, 1846–47). The body of this document and the Articles of Capitulation, 13 Jan. 1847, are in the hand of Theodore Talbot.

104. Stephen Watts Kearny to Frémont

PUEBLO DE LOS ANGELES,
Tuesday, January 12, 1847, 6 p.m.

DEAR FREMONT:

I am here in possession of this place, with sailors and marines. We met and defeated the whole force of the Californians on the 8th and 9th; they have not now to exceed 300 men concentrated; avoid charging them, and come to me at this place. Acknowledge the hour of receipt of this, and when I may expect you. Regard to Russell. Yours,

S. W. KEARNY,
Brigadier General

Lieutenant Colonel Fremont

Printed in CT. MARTIAL, 73.

105. Stephen Watts Kearny to Robert F. Stockton

Hd Qrs. Army of the West
CIUDAD DE LOS ANGELOS, Jany. 13 '47

SIR

I fear from the armistice which I this morning saw, signed by Lieut Col Fremont & sent to me by you, that our countrymen under Col. *F.* are entirely ignorant of our being here, that they are embarassed in their movements & I further fear, that unless something is done at once to inform them of the true State of affairs here, that they may capitulate and retire to the upper country to avoid so serious an evil. I advise & offer to take one half of this command, from 250 to 300 men & march at once to form a junction with Lieut Col. Fremont. Very Respectfully Yr. Obt. Servt.

S. W. KEARNY
Brig. Genl.

Comdr. R. F. Stockton, U.S. Navy
Gov of California, Comdg. U. S. forces

Copy of enclosure D in Kearny to R. Jones, 30 Jan. 1847 (DNA-94, LR, K-120 1847, f/w K-209 1846). On the copy to Jones, Kearny observed in a note dated 27 Jan., "No answer recd. to this but a verbal reply that Com. S. did not think Lieut. Col. F. was in any danger."

106. Articles of Capitulation

[13 Jan. 1847]

Articles of Capitulation made and entered into, at the Ranch of Cowenga this Thirteenth day of January, Anno Domini Eighteen Hundred and forty seven between P. B. Reading, Major Louis Mc-Lane Jr. Commdg. Artillery, Wm. H. Russell Ordnance Officer, Commissioners appointed by J. C. Frémont, Lieut. Colonel, United States Army, and Military Commandant of the Territory of California, and Jose Antonio Carrillo, Commdt. Escuadron, Augustin Olvera, Diputado, Commissioners appointed by Don Andres Pico, Commander-in-Chief of the Californian Forces under the Mexican Flag.

Article 1st

The Commissioners on the part of the Californians agree, that their entire force shall on presentation of themselves to Lieut. Col. Frémont deliver up their artillery and Public Arms, and that they shall return peaceably to their homes conforming to the Laws and Regulations of the United States and not again take up arms during the war between the United States and Mexico, but will assist and aid in placing the country in a state of peace and Tranquillity.

Article 2nd

The Commissioners on the part of Lieut. Col. Frémont agree and bind themselves on the fulfillment of the 1st Article by the Californians, that they shall be guaranteed protection of Life and property whether on parole or otherwise.

Article 3d

That until a Treaty of Peace be made and signed between the United States of North America and the Republic of Mexico, no Californian or other Mexican citizen shall be bound to take the oath of allegiance.

Article 4th

That any Californian or other citizen of Mexico, desiring is permitted by this Capitulation to leave the country without let or hindrance.

Article 5th

That in virtue of the aforesaid articles, equal rights and privileges are vouchsafed to every citizen of California as are enjoyed by the citizens of the United States of North America.

Article 6th

All officers, citizens, Foreigners, or others shall receive the protection guaranteed by the 2nd Article.

Article 7th

This Capitulation is intended to be no bar in effecting such arrangements as may in future be in justice required by both parties.

P. B. READING, Major California Battalion
WM. H. RUSSELL, Ord. Officer of Calif. Batt.
LOUIS McLANE JR., Comdg. Artillery California Battalion

JOSÉ ANTO. CARRILLO[1]   AGUSTÍN OLVERA[2]
Comandte. de Escuadrón   Diputado

Approved,

J. C. FRÉMONT,

Lt. Col. U. S. Army and Military Commandant of California
Aprobado

ANDRÉS PICO

Comandte. de Escuadron y Jefe de los fuerzas nacionales en California

---

DS, enclosure in Stockton to George Bancroft, 15 Jan. 1847 (DNA-45, Pacific Squadron, Commodore Stockton, 1846–47). The body of the Articles of Capitulation and the JCF proclamation of 12 Jan. 1847 are in the hand of Theodore Talbot; the signatures to the Articles of Capitulation are those of Reading, Russell, McLane, Carrillo, Olvera, JCF, and Pico. The original Spanish text of the articles, with the signatures of the commissioners, JCF, and Pico, is in CU-B. The *Annual Publications* of the Historical Society of Southern California, 15 (1932):303–10, reproduces it in facsimile and also gives an English translation which varies considerably from the Talbot document.

The signing took place at the home of Don Tomás Feliz, at the north end of Cahuenga Pass and within a few hundred feet of the Rio de Porciuncula (Los Angeles River). A stretch of El Camino Real wound its way nearby, linking Mission San Fernando with El Pueblo de los Angeles. The site is now within the limits of Universal City. The agreement was reached in the morning, and William H. Russell was dispatched to Los Angeles to report the capitulation. The treaty is known as the Treaty of Cahuenga, the name being derived from that of a former Gabrielea Indian rancheria located nearby.

Stockton's earlier unwillingness to treat with the Californians, and his irritation at their surrender to JCF, come through in the letter to Bancroft by which he forwarded the armistice and the Articles of Capitulation. "It seems that not being able to negotiate with me, and having lost the battles of the 8th [on the banks of the San Gabriel River] and 9th [the Mesa], they met Colonel Fremont on the 12th instant, on his way here, who not knowing what had occurred, he entered into the capitulation with them, which I now send to you; and although I refused to do it myself, still, I have thought it best to approve it." It already has been noted that when JCF made peace with the Californians, he knew of the American occupation of Los Angeles.

A naval surgeon wrote in his journal that Lieut. George Minor, who had commanded the garrison at San Diego, said that Stockton called JCF "a coward, traitor, and other such harsh names" after he learned of the treaty with the Californians (DUVALL, 95).

1. José Antonio Carrillo (1796–1862) had been in and out of public life for twenty-five years when he signed the Treaty of Cahuenga. In 1846 he joined Castro at Santa Clara as major general of the Californian forces, but he did not flee with his commander to Mexico in August. In fact, he was second in command when Flores drove Gillespie out of Los Angeles.

2. Agustín Olvera had served as secretary and member of the Assembly under both Pío Pico and José María Flores. After the American conquest he became a lawyer and a judge, and in 1856 he was appointed receiver of the U.S. Land Office at Los Angeles (PIONEER REGISTER).

107. Stephen Watts Kearny to Frémont

CIUDAD DE LOS ANGELES
January 13th, 1847—12 (noon)

DEAR FREMONT:

We are in force in this place—sailors and marines—join us as *soon as possible.* We are ignorant of your movements, and know nothing of you further than your armistice of yesterday. Yours,

S. W. KEARNEY,
Brigadier General

Lieut. Col. Fremont

Printed in CT. MARTIAL, 73–74.

Andrés Pico. From a photograph in the Henry E. Huntington Library and Art Gallery.

108. Stephen Watts Kearny to Frémont

CIUDAD DE LOS ANGELES
January 13th, 1847—2 p.m.

DEAR FREMONT:

We have been here since the 10th—have plenty of marines and sailors—we know nothing of you except your armistice of yesterday, signed by yourself. I have sent several letters to you, and fear they have been intercepted, as I have received no answer. Come here *at once* with your whole force and join us, or, if you cannot, let me know it, and I will go to you. The enemy cannot *possibly* have near you more than 300, most *probably* not more than 150 men. Acknowledge the *hour* of receiving this, and send back the bearer *at once,* and write but little, as it may get into the hands of the enemy instead of mine.

We defeated the enemy on the 8th and on the 9th, during our march. Since then, they have been much scattered, and several, no doubt, gone home.

I repeat we are ignorant of every thing relating to your command, except what we conjecture from your armistice, signed by yourself. Yours,

S. W. KEARNY,
Brigadier General

Do not charge the enemy.

Lt. Col. J. C. Fremont
Mounted Riflemen, &C., &c.

Printed in CT. MARTIAL, 74. Under questioning at the court-martial Kearny said he did not recall underscoring "Do not" of "*Do not* charge the enemy," and was of the opinion that if JCF had charged the enemy without sabres, he would have been defeated.

109. Frémont to Stephen Watts Kearny

On the march, Jany. 13th 1846 [1847]

DEAR SIR,

I have the honor to report to you my arrival at this place with 400 mounted riflemen and six pieces of artillery, including among the latter two pieces lately in the possession of the Californians.[1] Their entire force, under the command of D. Andro Pico, have this day laid down their arms and surrendered to my command. Very respectfully Yr. Obdt. Servt.

J. C. Frémont
Lt Col. U.S. Army, and Military Commandant of the Territory of California

Brig. General S. W. Kearny
Commanding U. S. Forces,
Pueblo de los Angeles

ALS, RC, enclosure 3 in Kearny to R. Jones, 11 Sept. 1847 (DNA-94, LR, K-217 1847, f/w K-209 1846). Endorsed. Russell carried not only the Articles of Capitulation to Los Angeles on the evening of 13 Jan. but also this letter to Kearny, who claimed that it constituted an official report of the California Battalion to him and a recognition that he was JCF's commander. JCF maintained at his court-martial that this was a private letter, written in reply to Kearny's four urgent, familiar, informative letters of 10, 12, and 13 Jan., and not a reporting of the battalion. Furthermore, JCF pointed out that Kearny's letters had not revealed that Stockton was with him at Los Angeles, and he intimated that such information had been deliberately withheld (CT. MARTIAL, 6–7, 72–74, 400–405).

Russell testified that he had, indeed, first called upon Kearny and delivered the letter, but on being told that Stockton was in command, went to him to report the capitulation; JCF had given him instructions "carefully to inquire as to who was in chief command, and to make my report accordingly." He added, "No such contingency was contemplated, I think, by Lieutenant Colonel Fremont, when he dispatched me on that mission, as the command being claimed by them both [Kearny and Stockton]" (CT. MARTIAL, 243–45, 257, 263).

After reporting to Stockton, Russell returned to dine with Kearny and Capt. Henry S. Turner and spent the night in Kearny's quarters. The next morning, 14 Jan., he rode out of Los Angeles to meet JCF, who was marching toward the city at the head of the battalion, and conducted him to the quarters assigned by Stockton. He reported that conversations with Kearny and Stockton indicated that both were anxious to confer upon JCF the office of governor. "I told him [JCF] . . . that I was satisfied, from what had occurred, that General Kearny was a better friend of his than Stockton; but, from Kearny's own admission, I regretted to have to give it as my opinion that we should have to look to Commodore Stockton still as commander-in-chief, and submitted to implicitly, as I thought, by Kearny" (Russell's testimony, CT. MARTIAL, 263). Benjamin D. Wilson remembered the streets being full of rumors that JCF did not intend to recognize the superiority of either Stockton or Kearny (WILSON, 123).

1. Later JCF charged that Kearny never reported to the government the recovery of a cannon which he had lost at the battle of San Pasqual, and this fact, he said, evidenced "his temper towards me" (CT. MARTIAL, 45).

110. Articles of Capitulation, Additional Article

[16 Jan. 1847]

That the paroles of all officers, citizens and others of the United States and of naturalized citizens of Mexico are by this foregoing capitulation cancelled and every condition of said paroles from and after this date are of no farther force and effect and all prisoners of both parties are hereby released.

Ciudad de los Angeles, Jany. 16th. 1847

Approved   Signed
J. C. FRÉMONT   P. B. READING
Lieut. Col. U. S. Army   Major Calfa. Battalion
Mility. Comdt. of California

                                                      LOUIS MCLANE, JR.
                                                      Commdt. Artillery
                                                      Califora. Battalion

                                                      WM. H. RUSSELL
                                                      Ordnance Officer
                                                      California Battalion

ANDRES PICO   JOSÉ ANTONIO CARRILLO
Commdt. of Squadron and   Commdt. of Squadron
Chief of the National forces of California   AGUSTÍN OLVERA
                                                      Deputado

I do hereby certify that the within is a correct copy of the Capitulation effected between the U. States and California. El Pueblo de Los Angeles. January 17th. 1847.

(Signed) P. B. READING
Major Cala. Battalion

Copy (DNA-45, Area 9 File, Pacific). English copies of the Articles of Capitulation, 13 Jan. 1847, and the Additional Article, 16 Jan. 1847, were forwarded by W. Branford Shubrick to the Secretary of the Navy on 28 Jan. 1847. The Navy Department acknowledged their receipt on 10 May.

The Quarrel
with Stephen Watts Kearny

111. Stephen Watts Kearny to Robert F. Stockton

Hd. Qrs. Army of the West
CIUDAD LOS ANGELES
January 16. 1847

SIR

I am informed that you are now engaged in organizing a civil government & appointing officers for it in this Territory. As this duty has been especially assigned to myself by orders of the Presdt. of the U. S. conveyed in letters to me from the Secy. of War of June 3 & 18. 1846[1] the original of which I gave to you on the 13th & which you returned to me on the 14th & copies of which I furnished you with on the 26 Decr.

I have to ask if you have any authority from the Presdt., from the Secty. of Navy, or from any other channel of the Presdt. to form such government & make such appts.? If you have such authority & will shew it to me, or furnish me with certified copies of it, I will cheerfully aquiesce in what you are doing. If you have not such authority I then demand that you cease all further proceedings relating to the formation of a civil government for this territory, as I cannot recognize in you any right in assuming to perform duties confided to me by the President. Very Respectfully Yr. Obt. Servt.

(Signed) S. W. KEARNY
Brig. Genl. U.S.A.

Com. R. F. Stockton
U. S. Navy
Actg. Govnr.

Copy of enclosure E-2 in Kearny to R. Jones, 30 Jan. 1847 (DNA-94, LR, K-120 1847, f/w K-209 1846). Endorsed.
1. For an extract of the 18 June 1846 letter, see the enclosure in Doc. No. 113.

112. Robert F. Stockton to Stephen Watts Kearny

Head Quarters
Ciudad de los Angeles
January 16th. 1847.

Sir

In answer to your note received this afternoon I need say but little more than that which I communicated to you in a conversation at San Diego—That California was conquered & a civil government put into successful operation—That a copy of the laws made by me for the government of the Territory, & the names of the officers selected to see them faithfully executed were transmitted to the President of the United States before your arrival in the Territory.[1]

I will only add, that I cannot do anything, nor desist from doing anything or alter anything on your demand; which I will submit to the President & ask for your recall. In the meantime you will consider yourself suspended from the command of the U. S. Forces in this place.[2] Faithfully Yr. Obdt. Servt.

R. F. Stockton
Commander in chief

To
Brvt. Brig Genl.
S. W. Kearny

LS, enclosure in Kearny to W. L. Marcy, 21 Sept. 1847 (DNA-94, LR, K-275 1847). Endorsed. A copy may also be found as enclosure E-3 in Kearny to R. Jones, 30 Jan. 1847 (DNA-94, LR, K-120 1847, f/w K-209 1846).
1. Stockton and Kearny had talked on 28 Dec. at San Diego about the War Department's order to Kearny in regard to the civil government of California (CT. MARTIAL, 79).
2. On cross-examination at the court-martial Kearny testified that he considered the word "suspend" applicable to the sailors and Marines, and he accordingly gave up command over them but continued in command of the dragoons (CT. MARTIAL, 117, 121).

113. William H. Emory to Frémont

Head qrs. Army of the West
C<small>IUDAD</small> <small>DE</small> <small>LOS</small> A<small>NGELES</small>
January 16th. 1847

By direction of Brig. Genl. Kearny I send you a Copy of a Communication to him from the Secty. of War, dated June 18th. 1846 in which is the following "These Troops and such as may be organized in California will be under your Command,"—The General directs that no change will be made in the organization of your Battalion of Volunteers or Officers appointed in it without his Sanction or approval being first obtained. Very Respectfully,

(Signed) W. H. E<small>MORY</small>
Lt. & Act Asst. Adj. General

To
Lt. Col. J. C. Frémont
Mounted Riflemen Commdg. Battn. California Vol.

[Enclosure]

William L. Marcy to Stephen Watts Kearny

War Department
W<small>ASHINGTON</small> June 18th. 1846

S<small>IR</small>

. . . . .

I have nothing of importance to add to the despatches which have been already forwarded to you. Since my last letter it has been determined to send a small force round Cape Horn to California. The Arms, cannon & Provisions to be sent to the Pacific will be accompanied by one Compy. of Artillery of the Regular Army; arrangements are now on foot to send a Regt. of Volunteers by sea. These troops & such as may be organized in California, will be under your command. More than common solicitude will be felt here in regard to the expedition committed to you & it is desired that you should avail yourself of all occasions to inform the Government of your progress & prospects. The President desires your opinion as early as you are in a situation to give it, of the practicability of your reaching California in the course of this Autumn or in the early part of next winter. I need not repeat the expression of his wishes, that you should take military possession of that Country as soon as it can be safely done. I am with great respect Your Obt. Servt.

(Signed) W. L. MARCY
Sec of War

To Col. S. W. Kearny

Copy of enclosure 1 in Kearny to R. Jones, 11 Sept. 1847 (DNA-94, LR, K-217 1847, f/w K-209 1846). A copy without the enclosure is in Kearny to R. Jones, 17 Jan. 1847 (DNA-94, LR, K-97 1847, f/w K-209 1846). Kearny's January letter to Jones bears the endorsement "Recd. Monday night—by Majr. Emory, May 3d. 1847. R. Jones." A duplicate had already been received by the Adjutant General on 20 April 1847.

Kearny's order through Emory was another play in the power struggle between Stockton and Kearny. The general is here trying to get JCF not to recognize Stockton's appointment of Gillespie as major of the California Battalion—an appointment made necessary by the fact that JCF was to become governor.

Kearny later maintained that he wrote this order to JCF before receiving Stockton's letter of 16 Jan., but in any case, by Emory's testimony it was not delivered until after dusk on 16 Jan. (CT. MARTIAL, 78, 118, 163) and apparently after the receipt of Stockton's letter suspending him from the command of the troops at Los Angeles (except the dragoons of the regular army).

Gillespie's commission is dated 18 Jan., but he recalled having learned that he was to become major of the battalion on either 16 or 17 Jan. (CT. MARTIAL, 203).

William Hemsley Emory (1811–87) of Maryland, a West Point graduate and lieutenant in the Corps of Topographical Engineers, had been assigned to the Army of the West as its senior engineering officer. Undoubtedly he was responsible for saving Kearny's life in the battle of San Pasqual. The general soon sent him east with dispatches, and en route Emory probably wrote a number of letters which appeared in various journals. Since they were highly critical of Stockton's and JCF's roles in California, they aroused the ire of Benton, who, however, was unable to block a double brevet to Emory for his services in California. His *Notes of a Military Reconnaissance from Fort Leavenworth to San Diego,* published in 1848 by order of Congress in an edition of 10,000 copies, is really the official report of the march of the Army of the West. Soon after the Mexican War, Emory became the astronomer of the U.S.-Mexican Boundary Commission, and during the Civil War was breveted a major general. He retired in 1876 as a brigadier general.

114. Frémont's Appointment as Governor

[16 Jan. 1847]

To all whom it may concern, greeting:

Having, by authority of the President and Congress of the United States of North America, and by right of conquest, taken possession of that portion of territory heretofore known as upper and lower California; and having declared the same to be a territory of the United States, under the name of the territory of California; and having established laws for the government of the said territory, *I, Robert F. Stockton,* governor and commander-in-chief of the same, do, in virtue of the authority in me vested, and in obedience to the aforementioned laws, appoint *J. C. Fremont,* esq. governor and commander-in-chief of the territory of California, until the President of the United States shall otherwise direct.

Given under my hand and seal, on this sixteenth day of January, Anno Domini, one thousand eight hundred and forty-seven, at the Ciudad de los Angeles.

R. F. Stockton
Governor, &c.

Printed in CT. MARTIAL, 175–76. Months later William H. Russell, who had been appointed secretary of state, was confident that he and JCF had gone "not later than the middle of the afternoon" to Stockton's quarters to receive their commissions. Stockton, on the other hand, believed the commissions had been delivered at an evening interview (CT. MARTIAL, 196–97, 263). At this time, too, he thought he had shown Kearny's letter of 16 Jan. and read his own reply (see Doc. Nos. 111 and 112), and recalled JCF stating during this visit that he had received a letter from Kearny which he intended to answer the next day.

JCF did not actually take up his duties as governor until three days later, when Stockton left Los Angeles for San Diego.

115. Stephen Watts Kearny to Frémont

January 17 [1847]

Dear Colonel:

I wish to see you on business. Yours,

S. W. Kearny
Brigadier General

Lieut. Col. Fremont

Printed in ct. martial, 76.

116. Frémont to Stephen Watts Kearny

Ciudad de los Angeles
Jany. 17. 1847

Sir

I have the honor to be in receipt of your favor of last night,[1] in which I am directed to suspend the execution of Orders which in my capacity of Military Commandant of this Territory I had received from Commodore Stockton, Governor & Commander in Chief of California.[2]

I avail myself of an early hour this morning to make such a reply as the brief time allowed for reflection will enable me.

I found Commodore Stockton in possession of the Country exercising the functions of Military Commandant and Civil Governor, as early as July of last year; and shortly thereafter I received from him the Commission of Military Commandant, the duties of which I immediately entered upon, and have continued to exercise to the present moment.

I found also on my arrival at this place some three or four days since, Commodore Stockton still exercising the functions of Civil and Military Governor with the same apparent deference to his rank on the part of all officers, (including yourself) as he maintained and required when he assumed in July last.

I learned also in conversation with you, that on the march from San Diego recently to this place you entered upon & discharged

268

duties implying an acknowledgement on your part of supremacy, to Commodore Stockton.[3]

I feel myself therefore with great deference to your professional & personal character constrained to say, that, until you & Commodore Stockton adjust between yourselves the question of rank, where I respectfully think the difficulty belongs, I shall have to report and receive orders as heretofore from the Commodore. With consideration of high regard I am Your Obedt. Servt.,

J. C. FRÉMONT
Lt. Col U. S. Army and Military Commandant of the Territory of California[4]

To
Brig. Genl. S. W. Kearny
U.S. Army

LS, enclosure 2 in Kearny to R. Jones, 11 Sept. 1847 (DNA-94, LR, K-217 1847, f/w K-209 1846). Endorsed: "Refuses to comply with orders of the War Department." This is one of many documents submitted by Kearny to support the charges and specifications against JCF, which had accompanied his 11 Sept. letter. From California the general had already sent to Washington three copies of JCF's "insubordinate" letter.

JCF personally delivered the letter. He had gone to Kearny's quarters at the general's request, and while there Kit Carson brought the letter, it having been left with Talbot to copy (CT. MARTIAL, 38, 76, 228). JCF signed it and gave it to Kearny. According to his testimony later, Kearny advised JCF to take the letter back and destroy it and he would forget it. JCF refused and noted that Stockton would support him. "I told him," Kearny testified, "that Commodore Stockton could not support him in disobeying the orders of his senior officer and that, if he persisted in it, he would unquestionably ruin himself. He told me that Commodore Stockton was about organizing a civil government and intended to appoint him as governor of the territory. I told him Commodore Stockton had no such authority, that authority having been conferred on me by the President of the United States. He asked me if I would appoint him governor. I told him I expected shortly to leave California for Missouri; that I had, previous to leaving Santa Fe, asked for permission to do so, and was in hopes of receiving it; that as soon as the country was quieted I should, most probably organize a civil government in California, and that I, at that time, knew of no objections to my appointing him as the governor. He then stated to me that he would see Commodore Stockton, and that, unless he appointed him governor at once, he would not obey his orders, and left me" (CT. MARTIAL, 39).

This attempt to depict JCF as bargaining for the governorship is not very convincing. If the testimonies of Stockton and Russell are to be credited, all the forms bestowing the governorship on JCF had been completed the day before and the commission bears the date 16 Jan., while the appointment itself had been promised by Stockton six months earlier (see Doc. No. 56). Furthermore, if there was still a possibility of JCF obeying his orders and becoming Kearny's appointee, why did Kearny leave Los Angeles for San

Diego the next morning (18 Jan.) without informing JCF that he was going or where he was going (CT. MARTIAL, 87)? However, it must be noted that JCF makes no mention in his letter to Kearny of having received his commission as governor from Stockton. But perhaps that is only natural, since Kearny's order to him of 16 Jan. had dealt only with the question of military superiority.

There seems to have been a real question in Kearny's mind about his supreme authority in California. In writing to his wife about the "blow-out" between Commodore Stockton and Kearny, Turner noted, "Kearny is nothing but will remain in the country until the action of the President is received, with respect to the extraordinary behavior of Stockton and Fremont" (Turner to Julia Turner, 30 Jan. 1847, TURNER, 149–50).

On being cross-examined by the defense at the court-martial, Kearny admitted that about a week after receiving this 17 Jan. letter of JCF's, he decided he would arrest JCF, but he did not communicate this fact to him (or to Benton, to whom he wrote in March and May) until the time of the actual arrest on 22 Aug. at Fort Leavenworth (R. Jones to Benton, 24 Aug. 1847, Doc. No. 209; CT. MARTIAL, 41).

1. See Doc. No. 113.

2. See Doc. No. 61.

3. These duties, which implied Kearny's acceptance of Stockton as the supreme official in California, were enumerated by JCF in a letter to Benton, 3 Feb. 1847, and again at his court-martial (see Doc. No. 131 and CT. MARTIAL, 438–39).

4. In a biography of Kearny, Clarke implies that since JCF had elected to continue service under Stockton, a more appropriate title following the signature would have been "Major in the Naval battalion" (CLARKE, 258).

117. Stephen Watts Kearny to Robert F. Stockton

Hd Qrs. Army of the West
Ciudad de los Angeles
January 17. 1847

Sir

In my communication to you of yesterday's date, I stated that I had learned that you were engaged in organizing a civil government for California. I referred you to the Presdts. instructions to me (the original of which you had seen and copies of which I furnished you) to perform that duty and I added that if you had any authority from the Presdt. or any of his organs for what you were doing, I would cheerfully acquiesce & if you have not such authority, I demanded that you cease further proceedings in the matter! Your reply of the same date refers me to a conversation held at San Diego

& adds that you "cannot do anything, nor desist from anything nor alter anything on your (my) demand."

As, (in consequence of the defeat of the army on the 8th & 9th Inst. by the troops under my command, & the capitulation entered into on the 13th inst. by Lieut. Col. Fremont with the leaders of the Californians, in which the people under arms & in the field agreed to disperse & remain quiet and peaceable,) the country may now for the first time be considered as conquered & taken possession of by us, and as I am prepared to carry out the President's instructions to me which you oppose, I must for the purpose of preventing collision between us & possibly a civil war in consequence of it, remain silent for the present, leaving with you the great responsibility of doing that for which you have no authority & preventing me from complying with the Presdt's orders. Very Respectfully Yr. Obt. Servt.

(Signed) S. W. KEARNY, Brig Genl.

Com. R. F. Stockton
U.S. Navy
Actg. Gov. of Califa.

Copy of enclosure E-4 in Kearny to R. Jones, 30 Jan. 1847 (DNA-94, LR, K-120 1847, f/w K-209 1846). Endorsed. On the same day Kearny sent a short note to Stockton, whom he addressed as "acting Governor of California," informing him of his intention to leave Los Angeles the next day with the small party which had escorted him to California (CT. MARTIAL, 195). He went to San Diego and on 31 Jan. sailed for Monterey.

Naval officer McLane's opinion of the three senior officers at Los Angeles was not very high. Stockton, "unscrupulous & energetic," had played a "grab" game; JCF was an "ambitious Ass, and entirely wanting in Military Knowledge & feeling, though persevering & cunning"; and Kearny, who he felt was "repressed" by his defeat at San Pasqual, had shown "great want of moral courage & unfitness for command" (MC LANE, 104–5).

118. Frémont to William A. T. Maddox

EL PUEBLO DE LOS ANGELES
January 17, 1847

SIR:

You will comply on the part of the United States with the article in the capitulation made with the Californians on the 13th instant, also with the additional articles of the 16th.

For the benefit of all the military commanders north of this place, I send by the bearer, Don Joaquin de la Tore,[1] a correct copy of the above mentioned capitulation.

You will please transmit this information to all United States officers in command of posts and forces to the north. Very respectfully, your obedient servant,

J. C. FREMONT
Lieutenant Colonel U. S. Army

Capt. W. Maddox
Military Com'dt. of Middle Dep't of California

Printed in appendix to Senator Benton's speech opposing the nomination of Brigadier General Kearny for major general, Washington *Daily Union,* 10 Oct. 1848.

1. Joaquín de la Torre (ca. 1812–55) had commanded the Californians in the skirmish at Olompali and had fought in the Natividad campaign (PIONEER REGISTER).

119. Robert F. Stockton to Frémont

Head Quarters
CIUDAD DE LOS ANGELES
January 19th. 1847

SIR:

In answer to your enquiries in regard to the Salaries of the different officers of the Government of California, I enclose to you a letter from Mr. Larkin,[1] whose experience in the Country had better be your guide in relation to that matter until you hear from the President of the United States.[2] Faithfully, Yr. obdt. servt.,

R. F. STOCKTON

To His Excellency
J. C. Fremont
Governor of the Territory of California

Lbk (DNA-45, Entry 395 [E-20-A], Letterbook of Robert F. Stockton, 1846–47).
1. Larkin's letter not found.
2. On this day Stockton left for San Diego with a small escort. Soon after

his departure the California Battalion was paraded, and Russell read publicly JCF's appointment as governor of California and his own as secretary of state (BRYANT, 414).

120. Frémont to Abel Stearns *et al.*

To Messrs.
  D. Abel Stearns
  E. Celis[1]
  C. W. Flügge
Gentlemen:

You are hereby commissioned and authorized by me, as Governor of California, to institute and enquire at your earliest convenience into the losses of property, whether effected by thefts on the part of the soldiers or breakages by the improper violence of the men, or by any other means sustained, on the part of the citizens, of the port of San Pedro, and of the Ciudad de los Angeles, and its vicinity, whilst the same were in possession of the troops of the United States whether under command of Commodore Stockton, Genl. Kearny or myself, and make report of the same with every particular to me.[2]

Your acceptance of this commission will be so considered by me unless notified to the contrary. Very respectfully Your Obt. Servant,

J. C. Frémont,
Governor & Commander in Chief of California

LS, RC (CSmH). It has already been noted that at the time of the American conquest, Abel Stearns (1798–1871) was a confidant of Larkin's and a most influential citizen of Los Angeles. He was probably also the wealthiest man in all of California. Born in Massachusetts, he had emigrated to Mexico about 1826 and settled in Los Angeles in 1833 as a trader in hides, tallow, and liquor. In 1840 he married Arcadia Bandini, daughter of Juan Bandini, and over the next few years gradually expanded his land and cattle holdings and built an imposing residence named El Palacio. For an excellent sketch of Stearns's activities to 1848, see WRIGHT.

1. Eulogio de Célis (d. 1868) had come to California in 1836 as an employee of the Acapulco merchant Henry Virmond, a transplanted German. He made Los Angeles his home until 1853, becoming a businessman and landowner. See Doc. No. 231 for the cattle contract he made with JCF.

2. Many of the claims submitted to the commission are in the Stearns Papers at the CSmH, but others are scattered in various collections, including the T. W. Norris Collection at the CU-B. The approved claims were signed by JCF as well as the three commission members. WRIGHT, 230, notes that at least two summaries of the claims were compiled. One, dated 12 April 1847, contained the names of forty-two individuals and totaled more than $5,295; the other, dated 29 April, bore twelve names and a total of more than $22,077. Stearns was on the second list with a claim of $4,605.50.

121. Frémont to Felipe Lugo *et al.*

CIUDAD DE LOS ANGELES
21st Jany. 1847

To
   Don Felipe Lugo
   Don Macedonio Aguilar
   Don Thomas Sanchez
GENTLEMEN,

You are hereby appointed by me as Governor of California a board of survey to ascertain the number of cattle killed, and to whom they belonged, by the U. S. Forces under the command of Commodore Stockton & Genl. Kearney, and report the same with all needful particulars to me at your earliest convenience.

Your acceptance of this commission will be considered a matter of course unless you instruct me to the contrary. Very Respectfully,

J. C. FRÉMONT
Governor & Commander-in-Chief of California

Attest:
WM. H. RUSSELL
Secy. of State

LS, RC (Los Angeles County Museum of Natural History). In Los Angeles at one time or another, Felipe Lugo (b. ca. 1808) had been *juez,* Macedonio Aguilar (b. ca. 1809) *juez de campo,* and Tomás Sanchez (1802–82) collector of taxes. After the American occupation Lugo became a justice of the peace and a supervisor, residing at La Mesa. Aguilar acquired that portion of Rancho La Ballona, or Wagon Pass, out of which present-day Palms was carved. Sanchez was sheriff of Los Angeles County from 1859 to 1867 (PIONEER REGISTER; ROLLE [2], 155).

122. Frémont's Circular

[LOS ANGELES]
[22 Jan. 1847]

The peace of the country being restored, and future tranquillity vouchsafed by a treaty made and entered into by Commissioners respectively appointed by the properly authorized California Officers on the one hand, and by myself, as Military Commandant of the United States Forces in the District of California, on the other, by which a civil government is to take place of the Military, an exchange of all prisoners, &c. &c. forthwith ensure to the end that order and a wholesome civil police should obtain throughout the land. A copy of which said treaty will be immediately published in the Californian newspaper, published at Monterey.

Therefore, in virtue of the aforesaid treaty, as well as the functions that in me rest as Civil Governor of California, I do hereby proclaim order and peace restored to the country, and require the immediate release of all prisoners, the return of the civil officers to their appropriate duties, and as strict an obedience of the Military to the civil authority as is consistent with the security of peace, and the maintenance of good order when troops are garrisoned.

Done at the Capitol of the Territory of California, temporarily seated at the Ciudad de los Angeles, this 22d day of January, A. D. 1847.

J. C. FREMONT
Governor and Commander-in-Chief of California

Witness: W. H. RUSSELL, Secretary of State.

Printed in the Monterey *Californian,* 6 Feb. 1847. The same issue carries a Spanish translation. The *California Star* (San Francisco), 6 Feb. 1847, gives a slightly different version in English and Spanish.

123. Frémont to Mariano G. Vallejo

Sir,

I have the honor to transmit you the Commission of a Member of a council of State, intended to exercise the functions of a legislative body, in the Territorial Government of California.

Your great influence in the country with the high respect and regard entertained for your person by the Californians will render your services of great value in tranquillizing the people and effecting the restoration of order and civil Government.

I shall feel great pleasure in being associated with you in the accomplishment of these objects and trust that it will not be incompatible with your private engagements to accept the post offered you.

The bearer, Mr. Knight has always shown attachment to your family and a disposition to avert from the Californians the bad consequences of the Movement in which they were recently engaged. I can therefore with some propriety recommend him to your friendly regard.

With Sentiments of respect and consideration, I am Sir, Your Obt. Servt.

J. C. Frémont,
Governor & Commander in Chief of California

Genl. Guadaloupe Vallejo
Sonoma

LS, RC (CU-B). Addressed. In addition to Vallejo, the new councillors were Thomas Oliver Larkin, Juan Bandini, Santiago Argüello, Jr. ("the 2nd," as Larkin expresses it), Juan B. Alvarado, David Spence, and Eliab Grimes (Larkin to Mariano G. Vallejo, 22 Jan. 1847, larkin, 6:16–17). Vallejo's appointment was made by Stockton, and JCF merely forwarded the commission. For Vallejo's acceptance, see Doc. No. 142.

The council was to convene at Los Angeles on 1 March, but no meeting was ever held. Gillespie placed the blame to some extent on Larkin, writing that if he had shown a willingness, all the councillors would have come. But Larkin wrote Stockton that even though the commodore had sent the *Cyane* to transport the commissioners from the northern part of California, Commodore Shubrick had prevented her return. "The members could not go by land and reach in time. . . . They also objected moving in the business until your despatches by Mr. Norris should reach you as they said there were naval and military officers on the coast, who could annul anything you or Colonel

Fremont might do. . . . Had we endeavoured to open the cession I think we should have been prevented" (Gillespie to Larkin, 1 April 1847, and Larkin to Stockton, 13 April 1847, LARKIN, 6:82–83, 100–101).

124. John Grigsby to Frémont

CITY OF ANGELS Jan. 22nd 47

SIR

A period having arrived in my opinion my services may be dispensed with I have thought proper to, and do hereby tender to your Excellency my resignation of the office of Captain of Company E. of the California Regiment, which office I have had the honor to hold during the last three months, and which resignation I hope your excellency will have the goodness to accept.

I have the honor to remain Sir, your obt. & humble servt.

JOHN GRIGSBY
Commanding Company E. of the Cal. Regiment

To
J. C. Fremont
Governor & Commander in Chief of the Military Force in California

ALS, RC (CSmH).

125. Frémont to Pierson B. Reading

EL PUEBLO DE LOS ANGELES
January 23rd. 1847

SIR,

In the *absence* of funds in your department, you are authorized to issue due bills, in making settlements with such Troops as shall be discharged from the service. Respectfully, etc.

J. C. FRÉMONT
Lt. Col. Commdg. Battn. and Govr. of California

LS, RC (C).

126. Frémont to Pierson B. Reading

Head Qrs. California Battn.
CIUDAD DE LOS ANGELES
Jany. 23d. 1847

To Major P. B. Reading
Paymaster of California Battalion
SIR,

In consequence of there being no defined arrangements in the Army Regulations for the rank or pay of an Ordnance Officer in a command corresponding to my own, I hereby direct you to settle with W. H. Russell who discharged the duties of Ordnance Officer, as Captain, entitled to full pay as Commandant of a Company, which commission he holds under me and to compute his pay from the 8th of Oct. 1846 to 21st Jany. 1847 the date of his resignation.

J. C. FRÉMONT,
Lt. Col. U S A & Commandr. in Chief of California

LS, RC (CSmH).

127. Frémont to Juan Bandini

CIUDAD DE LOS ANGELES
Executive Department
23d Jany. 1847

To
Juan Bandini
SIR,

The civil department of the government of California being now in full operation, and cherishing an anxious desire that the vacant offices of Alcalde and other municipal Stations be filled by proper and suitable incumbents, and in a manner most acceptable to the citizens of the Territory; and reposing entire confidence in your capacity and friendly disposition to aid me by suggestion and useful advice,

I respectfully invite you to meet me in the Executive Council room on Tuesday the 26th instant to confer on those various subjects. Very Respectfully Your Obt. Servt.

J. C. Frémont
Governor & Commdr. in Chief of the Territory of California

LS, RC (CSmH). A few days before JCF wrote this invitation, Stockton had named Bandini to the legislative council.

128. Frémont to John Temple

[Los Angeles]
[25 Jan. 1847]

$1500

Received of Mr. John Temple the sum of fifteen hundred dollars in cash for the use of the United States, for which sum I promise (in the name of the United States as Governor of California) to pay two per cent. per month until paid, said percentage being customary in this Territory.

Angeles Capital of California Jany. 25th 1847

(Signed) J. C. Frémont
Govr. of California

I certify the above to be a true copy of the original which I this day saw in the possession of Mr. Temple.

Los Angeles California
May 13th 1847

A. J. Smith[1]
1st Drag.

Copy of enclosure 18 in Kearny to R. Jones, 11 Sept. 1847 (DNA-94, LR, K-217 1847, f/w K-209 1846).
1. Capt. Andrew Jackson Smith (1815–97) of the 1st Dragoons had come to California with the Mormon Battalion.

129. Frémont to John K. Wilson

ANGELES, Jany. 25th 1847

To
Capt. J. K. Wilson
Light Artillery
SIR

You are hereby authorized and directed to raise a company of men to constitute the second company of Artillery in the California Service, and for that purpose are detached from your present command.

You will please report the number you may be able to enlist, with as little delay as possible.

You are authorized to enlist the men for 3 months and to promise them as compensation twenty five dollars per month. Respectfully,

J. C. FREMONT
Lt. Col Commanding California Forces in the United States Service

Copy of enclosure 4 in Kearny to R. Jones, 11 Sept. 1847 (DNA-94, LR, K-217 1847, f/w K-209 1846). John K. Wilson was a midshipman on the *Savannah*.

130. John B. Montgomery to Frémont

U. S. Ship Portsmouth, SAN DIEGO, Jan. 26. 1847

SIR,

Under the pressure of your many and important engagements at this moment, I should not now call your attention to the subject of this communication, but for the possibilities that another opportunity may not be presented.

Will you therefore do me the favor to acknowledge the receipt of two rolls which I forwarded to you by water from San Francisco to Monterey in Octo. or Novr. last ex[h]ibiting a statement of clothing &c. issued from the Purser's stores of the U. S. Ship Portsmouth under my command, to a number of volunteers while on their way to join your command at the latter place, stating if you please the ag[g]re-gate amt. of said issues as set forth in the rolls—to be deducted from the pay accts. of the Volunteers, respectively, on final settlement with them.

Purser Watmough will forward your account for the same made in the required form—with a receipt annexed—which I will thank you to sign which [will] be used as a voucher in settlement with Navy Department. I have the Honor to be Sir, Your Obt. Servt.,

Jno. B. Montgomery
Commander U. S. S. P.

To his Excely. J. C. Fremont
Governor of California at the Pueblo de los Angeles

Lbk (DNA-45, no. 22, Officers' Letters, Letterbooks of J. B. Montgomery).

131. Frémont to Thomas H. Benton

[Los Angeles]
[3 Feb. 1847]

.   .   .   .

Knowing well the views of the cabinet, and satisfied that it was a great national measure to unite California to us as a sister State, by a voluntary expression of the popular will, I had in all my marches through the country, and in all my intercourse with the people acted invariably in strict accordance with this impression, to which I was naturally farther led by my own feelings. I had kept my troops under steady restraint and discipline, and never permitted to them a wanton outrage, or any avoidable destruction of property or life. The result has clearly shown the wisdom of the course I have pursued. . . .[1]

When I entered Los Angeles I was ignorant of the relations subsisting between these gentlemen [Stockton and Kearny], having received from neither any order or information which might serve as a guide in the circumstances. I therefore, immediately on my arrival, waited upon the governor and commander-in-chief, Commodore Stockton; and, a few minutes afterwards, called upon General Kearney. I soon found them occupying a hostile attitude, and each denying the right of the other to assume the direction of affairs in this country.

The ground assumed by General Kearney was, that he held in his hand plenary instructions from the President directing him to conquer California, and organize a civil government, and that consequently he would not recognize the acts of Commodore Stockton.

The latter maintained that his own instructions were to the same effect as Kearney's; that this officer's commission was obsolete, and never would have been given could the government have anticipated that the entire country, seaboard and interior, would have been conquered and held by himself. The country had been conquered and a civil government instituted since September last, the constitution of the territory, and appointments under the constitution, had been sent to the government for its approval, and decisive action undoubtedly long since had upon them. General Kearney was instructed to conquer the country, and upon its threshold his command had been nearly cut to pieces, and, but for the relief from him (Commodore Stockton) would have been destroyed. More men were lost than in General Taylor's battle of the 8th. In regard to the remaining part of his instructions, how could he organize a government without first proceeding to disorganize the present one? His work had been anticipated; his commission was absolutely void, null, and of no effect.

But if General Kearney believed that his instructions gave him paramount authority in the country, he made a fatal error on his arrival. He was received with kindness and distinction by the commodore, and offered by him the command of his land forces. General Kearney rejected the offer, and declined interfering with Commodore Stockton. This officer was then preparing for a march to Ciudad de los Angeles, his force being principally sailors and marines, who were all on foot (fortunately for them), and who were to be provided with supplies on their march through an enemy's country where all the people are cavalry. His force was paraded, and ready to start, 700 in number, supported by six pieces of artillery. The command, under General Stockton, had been conferred upon his first lieutenant, Mr. Rowan.[2] At this juncture General Kearney expressed to Commodore Stockton his expectation that the command would have been given to him. The commodore informed the general that Lieutenant Rowan was in his usual line of duty, as on board ship, relieving him of the detail and drudgery of the camp, while he himself remained the commander-in-chief; that if General Kearney was willing to accept Mr. Rowan's place, under these circumstances, he could have it. The general assented. Commodore Stockton called up his officers and explained the case. Mr. Rowan gave up his post generously and without hesitation; and Commodore Stockton desired them clearly to understand that he remained the commander-in-chief; under this arrangement the whole force entered Angeles; and on the day of my arrival at that place General Kearney told me that he did then, at that moment, recognize Commodore Stockton as governor of the territory.

You are aware that I had contracted relations with Commodore Stockton, and I thought it neither right nor politically honorable to withdraw my support. No reason of interest shall ever compel me to act towards any man in such a way that I should afterwards be ashamed to meet him. . . .[3]

Both offered me the commission and post of governor; Commodore Stockton to redeem his pledge to that effect, immediately, and General Kearny offering to give the commission in four or six weeks. . . .[4]

I was named Governor, and immediately proclaimed peace and order restored to the country; and, like the waters of some small lake over which a sudden storm had passed, it subsided instantly into perfect tranquility, from one extremity to the other. A Californian gentleman, Don Pedro Carillo, arrived yesterday evening from Santa Barbara, and told me that he heard a group of boys in the street singing to their guitar

> "Vivan los Estados Unidos
> Y viva el Coronel Frémont,
> Quien nos ha aseguardo las vidas."

> "Long live the United States
> And long live Colonel Frémont,
> Who has secured to us our lives."[5]

.   .   .   .

Throughout the Californian population, there is only one feeling of satisfaction and gratitude to myself. The men of the country, most forward and able in the revolution against us, now put themselves at my disposition, and say to me, *'Viva usted seguro, duerme usted seguro,'* (live safe, sleep safe,) 'we ourselves will watch over the tranquility of the country, and nothing can happen which shall not be known to you."[6] The unavailing dissatisfaction on the part of (———) own people, was easily repressed, the treaty was ratified.[7]

.   .   .   .

The incomplete letter printed here has been pieced together by the editors from various sources, and there is no assurance that the proper sequence has been divined. Before the military court JCF said he would have been willing to read his 3 Feb. 1847 letter to Benton to the court as his sole defense had it not been for the treatment he had received, "the secret purpose to arrest," and the various publications against him. He said that the letter was received by Benton in May at St. Louis and was sent to President Polk, "whose endorsement is on the back, in his own hand writing, stating it to have been received from Mr. Christopher Carson on the 8th of June" (CT. MARTIAL, 379–80). The sources from which the letter was extracted are given in the notes below.

1. Extract printed in CT. MARTIAL, 380.

2. Lieut. Stephen Clegg Rowan (1808–90), formerly of the *Cyane,* served as major in the march of Stockton's battalion from San Diego to Los Angeles, and was slightly wounded in the battle of the Mesa. He remained in the naval service, becoming commodore in 1862; he was on the retired list as vice-admiral in 1889.

3. Printed in BIGELOW, 197–98.

4. Extract printed in CT. MARTIAL, 393.

5. Extract from Benton's speech opposing the nomination of Brigadier General Kearny for the brevet of major general, Washington *Daily Union,* 1 Sept. 1847.

6. In his Senate speech opposing the nomination of Kearny for the brevet of major general, Benton included the Spanish phrase "Estan preparados los hijos del pais para sostener á usted," which he translated as "The children of the country are prepared to sustain you."

7. Extract printed in CT. MARTIAL, 380.

132. William Speiden to Frémont

United States Ship Congress,
SAN DIEGO, February 4, 1847

SIR:

I have been directed by Commodore Stockton to furnish you with any amount of funds that could be disposed of after paying the bills of the Government at this place, and I regret to inform you that there is not a sufficient sum on hand to liquidate said account.

The barque Guypuzcouno [*Jóven Guipuzcoana*] is daily expected here from the [Hawaiian] Islands with money,[1] and we also are in expectation of the arrival of the Erie from Callao with funds, and shall be pleased to attend to your demands so soon as the above expectations are realized.[2]

I have the honor to be, most respectfully, your obedient servant,

WM. SPEIDEN
Purser United States Navy

His Excellency J. C. Fremont,
Governor of the Territory of California

Printed in *National Intelligencer,* 6 Dec. 1847. One of the documents presented to the military court on Friday, 3 Dec. 1847, but not published in the official report.

1. When the *Jóven Guipuzcoana* did arrive from the Hawaiian Islands, she had but half the funds expected (Archibald H. Gillespie to Thomas Oliver Larkin, 15 March 1847, LARKIN, 6:37). However, on 24 Feb. 1847 JCF did receive $6,500 at San Diego from purser Speiden (see voucher, *Presidential Message on the Accounts of John C. Fremont,* Senate Exec. Doc. 109, p. 15, 34th Cong., 1st sess., Serial 825).

2. In addition to the $9,000 obtained from Speiden—$2,500 in Aug. 1846 and $6,500 in Feb. 1847—JCF had received other money from Navy funds. Through Gillespie, he had been paid $10,850 in 1846 as military commandant of California; $4,000 as major commanding U.S. forces; and $4,195.40 plus $1,338.13 for provisions and clothing as lieutenant colonel, U.S. Army. In all, he received $29,383.53 through Gillespie and Speiden from the Navy Department (see A. O. Dayton, Fourth Auditor's Office, 15 Aug. 1856, to Secretary of Treasury, *Presidential Message on the Accounts of John C. Fremont,* pp. 13–14).

133. Frémont to Antonio José Cot

[LOS ANGELES]
[4 Feb. 1847]

I the undersigned Governor of California, for the United States of North America, acknowledge that I have received from Don Antonio José Cot, merchant of this city, Two thousand dollars in hard cash, which he has furnished this Government for the public service. And I bind myself in the name of the United States Government to return the said sum within the term of two months from this date, paying for interest three per cent per month, or one hundred & twenty dollars. But if at the expiration of this term the Government should see fit still to make use of these two thousand dollars, Mr. Cot agrees that the interest shall run for four months longer at 2 per cent per month, or one hundred and sixty dollars for the 4 months. And for the fulfillment of what has been stipulated I bind myself as Governor of California.

$2000   Angeles   4th February 1847   J. C. FREMONT

I have furthermore received from the said Mr. Cot the sum of one thousand dollars in the terms expressed above.

$1000   Angeles   20th February 1847   J. C. FREMONT

I have received from Mr. Fremont the sum of one hundred and eighty dollars for the interest of two months on the three thousand dollars mentioned in this obligation. Angeles 12th April 1847

ANTONIO JOSÉ COT
A copy of the original
(Signed) ANTONIO JOSÉ COT

Translated copy enclosed in R. B. Mason to R. Jones, 21 June 1847 (DNA-94, LR, M-1113 1847, f/w K-209 1846). Antonio José Cot (d. ca. 1860), a Spanish trader from Lima, had been the resident manager in Los Angeles of Mancisidor and Company. Because he was a Spaniard and supposedly unfriendly to Mexican interests, he was ordered out of California in the late 1820s, but he returned to Los Angeles in the mid-1830s to engage in commerce. About the time that JCF was borrowing money from him, Cot was purchasing San Luis Rey.

Because of his feud with Kearny, JCF had a most difficult time financing his "government" and supplying the California Battalion, but all U.S. officials in California lacked money. Lieut. Col. Philip St. George Cooke, under the date of 12 March, expressed the situation accurately and humorously: "Gen. Kearny is supreme—somewhere up the coast; Col. Frémont supreme at Pueblo de los Angeles, Commodore Stockton is 'commander-in-chief' at S. Diego;—Commodore Shubrick, the same at Monterey; and I, at San Luis Rey; and we are all supremely poor; the government having no money and no credit; and we hold the territory because Mexico is poorest of all" (COOKE, 283).

134. Theodore Talbot *et al.* to Frémont

CIUDAD DE LOS ANGELES
4th Feby. 1847

To
His Excellency,
J. C. Frémont
Govr. of California
SIR,

We constituting the command of Adjt. J. T. Talbot, placed by your order at Santa Barbara, were forced by an attack of a much superior Californian force, to abandon the town with all the little property we then had with us, of which the subjoined account is a true & faithful schedule which under the circumstances we think ought to be made good to us by the Govt., and respectfully petition your Excellency, to approve and order the same to be paid.

J. T. TALBOT	CHARLES SCHEIBER [SCHREIBER]
F[RANCIS] BRIGGS	ELIJAH MOULTON
R. E. RUSSELL	JOHN STEVENS
THOMAS E. BRECKENRIDGE	WILLIAM CHENOOK [CHINOOK]

United States Dr.
Qmr. Dept.
To J. Theodore Talbot

Oct. 3d. To 1 saddle complete (2 pair mochisns)	$40.00
1 pair Spurs—6.00; 1 Bridle—5.00	11.00
9 Shirts @ $3.	27.00
1 Suit of Fine Blue Cloth	36.50
2 pr. pants @ 5.00	10.00
1 pair Bottas	12.00
2 Blankets @ 8.00	16.00
	152.50

Received of Jacob R. Snyder[1] Qr. Master California Battalion, U. States Troops the sum of one hundred fifty dollars amount of above bill.
Angeles, Feb. 6, 1846 [1847]   J. THEODORE TALBOT

287

United States Dr.
QMr. Dept.
To Robert E. Russell

Oct. 3d. To 1 Bridle	10.50
1 pr. of spurs	5.00
1 Blanket	7.50
5 Calico shirts @ 3.00	15.00
1 pair of pants	10.00
1 silk handkf.	2.50
	50.50

Received of Jacob R. Snyder Quartermaster, California Battalion the sum of fifty-50/100 dollars in full.

R. E. RUSSELL

United States Dr.
Qmr. Dept.
To Thos. E. Breckenridge

Oct. 3d. To 3¾ yds of Blue Cloth	$22.50
1 pr. pants	4.75
1 Blanket	5.00
3 shirts 3.00	9.00
2 Cotton Hdkfs.	2.50
1 Saddle complete	35.00
1 Bridle	4.00
1 Spur	7.00
	89.25 [89.75]

Recd. of Jacob R. Snyder Quartermaster, California Battalion, the sum of $89.25/100 in full.

THOMAS E. BRECKENRIDGE

United States Dr.
Qmr. Dept.
To Francis Briggs

Oct. 3d. To 1 saddle complete	16.00
1 Bridle	7.00
1 pr. Spurs	6.00
1 pr. pants	4.00
2 Shirts	4.00

1 Blanket	3.00
	40.00

Received of Jacob R. Snyder, Quartermaster of California Battalion the sum of Forty dollars in full of above account.

F. Briggs

Angeles, March 9[?] 1847

United States Dr.
Qmr. Dept.
To Charles Screiber [Schreiber]

Oct. 3d. To Two good Blankets	$10.00
2 Hickory Shirts	6.00
Shaving apparatus	3.00
	19.00

Received of J. R. Snyder, Quartermaster of California Battalion U. States Forces the sum of nineteen dollars amount of above bill, Angeles Feb. 17th. 1847   Charles Schreiber

United States Dr.
Qmr. Dept.
To John Stephens [Stevens]

Oct. 3d. To 1 saddle complete	$45.00
1 Bridle & 1 pr. Spurs	

Received of Jacob R. Snyder Quartermaster of California Battalion U. States Forces the sum of 45 dollars amt. of above bill. Angeles, March 9th. 1847   John Stevens

United States Dr.
Qmr. Dept.
To E. Moulton

Oct. 3d. To 1 Saddle & Bridle	$ 8.00
1 pr. pants	3.00
1 pr. Drawers	2.00
1 shirt	3.00
	$16.00

Received of Jacob R. Snyder Quartermaster of California Battalion U. States Forces, the sum of sixteen dollars amt. of above bill

Angeles, March 9, 1847

his
E. X Moulton
mark

United States Dr.
Qmr. Dept.
To William Chenook
1846

Oct. 3d. To 1 Saddle with rigging	$20.00
2 Blankets	8.00
1 coat	10.00
3 yds. of Blue Cloth	18.00
1 spurs	3.00
1 pr. drawers.	2.00
	61.00

Received of Jacob R. Snyder Quartermaster of California Battalion U. S. Troops the sum of Sixty one dollars amount of above bill.

Angeles, Apr. 18, 1847

his
William X Chenook
mark

Witness: P. B. Reading

The above accounts are accordingly hereby approved.

February 5th. 1847

J. C. Frémont,
Govr. of California

DS (DNA-92, enclosed in J. R. Snyder to Col. C. F. Smith, 25 Oct. 1853, Vouchers, Receipts, and Other Papers Relating to the Settlement of Claims, 1847–48 [unarranged], Microfilm Roll 8). The letter and the claims are in the hand of Theodore Talbot and are typical of the smaller claims. JCF had also placed two other men at Santa Barbara with Talbot—a French creole, St. Vrain Durand, and a "New Mexican Spaniard" named Manuel. Except for Schreiber, Durand, Moulton, and Manuel, the young men were all about twenty years of age (MEMOIRS, 596; *California Claims,* Senate Report 75, pp. 52–54, 30th Cong., 1st sess., Serial 512). R. Eugene Russell was a son of William H. Russell, JCF's secretary of state. William Chinook was the Oregon Indian boy whom JCF had taken east when he returned from his 1843–44 expedition. Under the name of William Perkins he was discharged on 16 June 1847 at Johnson's farm, Upper California. Schreiber, whose second given name seems to have been Frederix, was an 1833 German emigré and a friend of George Engelmann and Gustave Koerner. After his service with JCF, he became a farmer in St. Clair County, Ill. In addition to

Schreiber, Talbot, Russell, Breckenridge, and Chinook had all been members of JCF's third expedition.

1. Born in Philadelphia, Jacob Rink Snyder (1812–78) had come from Missouri to California in 1845 and with several others, including William Blackburn, commenced the business of whip-sawing lumber and making shingles from the redwoods near Santa Cruz—a business which they continued until the outbreak of hostilities between the Californians and Americans. Snyder then joined JCF's battalion as quartermaster. After the war he was successively and sometimes simultaneously: surveyor general of the Middle Department of California, a member of the banking firm of James King of William, a state senator, assistant treasurer of the U.S. mint at San Francisco, president of the Society of California Pioneers, and a Sonoma rancher. For additional biographical details, see "Excerpts from the Memorial . . . to Major Jacob Rink Snyder," *Quarterly* of the Society of California Pioneers, 8 (1931):203–5.

135. Frémont to Louis McLane

CIUDAD DE LOS ANGELES
5th Feby 1847

SIR

I feel it my duty as the representative of the United States government in California to instruct you to proceed forthwith North as far as in your discretion may seem necessary, and exercise your best efforts in enlisting troops for the term of six months, compensation to be $—— per month, to be employed in the service of the United States, and at such points in the territory of California as in my judgment they are most required.

You are furthermore instructed to proceed as far as the town of Yerba Buena on the San Francisco bay, and examine diligently into the state of the naval or military defence of that town, and particularly to enquire into the best means of fortifying the mouth of the bay against the ingress of all enemies, and I particularly recommend to you to cause to be commenced the erection of a fort or battery on White island, calculated, when completed to prevent the entrance of any ship or vessel that may be forbidden to do so by said United States.

To enable you to carry into effect the foregoing instructions you are hereby authorized, and required to call on all officers under my command to extend to you any assistance of money, men, or property that in your judgment may be necessary to accomplish the same.

In witness whereof, I have hereunto set my hand and affixed my seal, at the capital of California, this date before written.[1]

J. C. Frémont
Governor of California

Attest:
Wm. H. Russell
Sec of State

To
Major Louis McLane
U. States Army
California Regt.

LS, RC (DNA-94, LR, K-217 1847, f/w K-209 1846). Endorsed: "Recd. by Genl K. from Mr. McLane March 3d. '47." This was enclosure 15 in Kearny to R. Jones, 11 Sept. 1847, and is in support of Kearny's charges against JCF.
1. McLane "reluctantly" went north to raise men and money. When he reached Monterey, Commodore Shubrick terminated his mission (MC LANE, 110, 112).

136. Frémont to James Buchanan

Pueblo de los Angeles
Feby. 6th. 1846 [1847]

To
Hon. James Buchanan
Sec. of State
Sir,

The civil government which in various parts of California had been temporarily suspended by a dangerous insurrection being happily again in full and vigorous operation, throughout the territory, and having myself recently, and in fulfillment of the arrangements transmitted for your consideration in September last, been appointed to the office of chief magistrate of the country, I have thought it important and necessary in the discharge of my official relations to draw immediately your attention to our actual necessities, and to present for your approval such measures as the security of the territory and the public interest have rendered it urgently expedient to adopt. The great embarrassment that I at present experience as the principal representative of the United States government is the want of money to enable me to pay off the troops under my command; and to cancel such other obligations, as I have been compelled to come under in prosecuting a war in a country where no supplies whatever were furnished me by my own government, and where most articles are scarce and extravagantly high.

I consider the temper of the Californians decidedly favorable to annexation with the United States, and I see no obstacle to the entire accomplishment of the views of my government regarding this country, but an adequate and regular supply of money.

The credit system is but little understood in this country where the manner of the people are primitive and simple and finance but little known. For example I could buy easily a horse or mule for fifteen dollars cash, when I could not get him for less than thirty dollars credit, if indeed I could get him at all.

I have also been compelled to raise money at the most usurious rates of interest to avoid the falsification of pledges that I have made as an officer of the United States, and which threatened if not redeemed, to be likely to produce mutiny and dissatisfaction among the troops and generally to be productive of the worst consequences. I have made the foregoing representation which really falls short of my distress for the want of money, to prove the necessity of my being furnished forthwith with an adequate supply, and regularly hereafter be kept in funds so as to avoid a recurrence of the difficulties that I have had to contend with for the want of it.

In the absence of instructions from the United States predicated on a certainty of what has occurred in this remote region, where a regular and uniform correspondence cannot exist, I have considered an early meeting of the representatives of the people essentially prudent, as well to furnish undoubted proof that our designs in this favoured land are to make it an integral part of our republican government, as to adopt some wholesome municipal regulations absolutely required by the late unsettled condition of affairs. A proclamation has accordingly been already issued that the first assembly or convocation of the legislative council shall take place on the 1st of March proximo. With a view to conciliate the feelings of the people and secure at as early a day as possible the adjustment of many vexed and harrassing claims, I have established several boards of Commissioners with full and plenary power to institute enquiries, and audit all claims occasioned [?] by spoilations committed by the American troops during the progress of the recent insurrection. The commissioners have been selected with a due regard to their integrity and capacity, and I respectfully recommend that by your ratification the results of their investigations be made definitive and binding upon the government. The large majority of the claimants are poor people and payment cannot be long delayed to them without creating great dissatisfaction.

This letter will be handed to you by Mr. Theodore Talbot, a young gentleman of your city who accompanied me on the recent Exploring Expedition, and whose continued presence in this country during the progress of the events which induced the present change, together with his general ability and habits of observation, will make him useful in conveying to you a clear and accurate knowledge of California. This made a principal reason in selecting him as the bearer of these despatches to you; my own situation being one of so much difficulty, and so much embarrassed by uncertainty, that I feel it impossible in the midst of many causes for anxiety and through incessant interruptions and calls on my attention, to furnish you with a connected history of events here. It may be due myself as an officer of the U. States government, cherishing the fullest regard to discipline and submission to the properly constituted civil authorities at home, and at all times anxiously inclined to support the dignity of our Government, to add; that I hold my office as do all others under me by no stronger tenure than the will of the President, and am ready at any moment to lay it down, or observe a contrary course touching the municipal regulations of the country, when the pleasure of the President is made known to me.

In conclusion I respectfully offer for your consideration my remote position and want of information as a justification of any informalities of official conduct. My principal objects have always been the interest and the approbation of my government, and in the pursuit of these great ends my measures have been such as I regard incidental to the extraordinary powers I am called upon to exercise, and to the large discretion which must always be permitted to the governor of a province so remote as California.

With sentiment of great consideration and personal regard, I have the honor to be Your Obedt. Servt.

J. C. FRÉMONT,
Governor of California

ALS, RC (DNA-107, LR, S-215 [65]). On the first page of the letter appears this notation: "June 4th. 1847. Recd. from Mr. Talbot personally & referred to the Secretary of War." Endorsed: "Department of State 4 June 1847. The within communication from Colonel Fremont is respectfully referred to the Secretary of War; because the Government of California being derived from the War making power & resting upon military authority, that officer ought to receive his instructions from the War Department. James Buchanan."

In a letter to Stephen Watts Kearny, 11 June 1847, Secretary of War William L. Marcy mentioned that a letter to the Secretary of State from JCF, dated 3 Feb. 1847, had been referred to him. Since it likewise dwelt on the need for money, Marcy has probably made a mistake on the date, and the so-called 3 Feb. letter is really the 6 Feb. letter (*New Mexico and California,* House Exec. Doc. 70, pp. 28–31, 30th Cong., 1st sess., Serial 521).

137. Frémont to W. Branford Shubrick

CIUDAD DE LOS ANGELES,
7 Feby. 1847

SIR,

I had the honor at a late hour of last night, to receive your favor of the 25th ultimo,[1] and fully coinciding with the opinion that you express, that a cooperation of our respective commands, as a precautionary measure at least, is of primary importance, I hasten to acknowledge its receipt, and signify to you my earnest desire to see you and consult on the measures calculated in our judgments to be the most certain of making our labors conduce to the interest of our Government.

Not having had as you remarked any communication since your arrival on this coast with Commodore Stockton, you seem not to have been made acquainted with the fact that by a commission from the Commodore I had been placed in command of the territory, as civil Governor, which I beg leave herewith to communicate to you.

It is also proper to advise you that Genl. Kearney, who comes to California with instruction from the Sec of War, dated as early as June last, (designed for a state of affairs which he by no means found, to wit, the country still unconquered, and which of course being intended for that very different circumstances, cannot have application here) claims himself to have supreme command in California, which position I felt it my duty to deny him, and in language respectful but decisive of my purpose communicated to him.

The subjoined reasons led me to the conclusion I adopted; = The conquest of California was undertaken and completed by the joint efforts of Commodore Stockton & myself in obedience to what we regarded paramount duties from us to our Governt; = that done, the next necessary step in order, was the organization of a civil government designed to maintain the conquest by the exercise of mild and wholesome civil restraints over the people rather than by the iron rule of a military force.

The result of our labors, which were precisely what were contemplated by the instructions of Genl. Kearney, were promptly communicated to the Executive of the Union by an express which has not yet brought back the approval or disapproval of the Govt.

Genl. Kearney's instructions being therefore to the letter fully anticipated by others; = I did not feel myself at liberty to yield a position so important to the interests of my country until, after a full understanding of all the grounds, it should be the pleasure of my government that I should do so.

I trust the foregoing explanation will fully satisfy you that the position I take is an incident to the extraordinary circumstances surrounding me, and is borne out by a rigid adherence to the line of duty.

The insurrection which broke out here in September last, and which it required a considerable force and a large expenditure of money to put down, has left me in rather an embarrassed condition for funds to redeem my engagements to my men, and to cancel the necessary obligations created by the Quartermaster and Commissariat departments of the Command; = If, therefore, you can at an early day advance me a considerable sum of money it will tend greatly to subserve the interests of the country and relieve an embarrassment which as an officer of the Govt. heavily presses me.

I start off simultaneous with this a courier to the United States with important despatches, but thinking perhaps that you might wish to avail yourself of so good an opportunity of forwarding despatches, I have ordered him to remain on the border of the settlements until the return of my courier from you. The precise point where my courier will remain recruiting his animals being at this time unknown to me, you will please send your despatches by the return courier to me and I will forward them to the party homeward bound.

With considerations of high respect, I am sir, your obedt. servt.

J. C. FRÉMONT
Governor of California

To
Commodore W. Branford Shubrick
Commanding U. S. Naval Forces in the Pacific Ocean
Bay of Monterey

ALS, RC (DNA-94, LR, K-217 1847, f/w K-209 1846). Endorsed: "Received 13 Feby. 1847, W. B. S." "Recd. from Com. S. March 1, S. W. K." Enclosure 5 in Kearny to R. Jones, 11 Sept. 1847, and used in support of the military charges against JCF. Copy in DNA-45, Area 9 File, Pacific. William Branford Shubrick (1790–1874), who had arrived at Monterey on the *Independence* on 22 Jan., replaced Stockton as commander of the Pacific Squadron by reason of seniority. After his superior officer, Commodore James Biddle, arrived on the *Columbus* in early March, Shubrick took command of the squadron blockading Mexican ports. However, he is best remembered for his command of the expedition sent to settle difficulties with Paraguay in 1858–59.
1. Shubrick's letter to JCF of 25 Jan. has not been found.

138. Juan B. Alvarado to Frémont

[10 Feb. 1847]

In the port of Monterey of Upper California on the tenth day of the month of February in the year of One Thousand eight hundred and forty-seven, before me Walter Colton, Justice of the Peace of this demarcation, and before the subscribing witnesses, appeared Don Juan Bta. Alvarado and says: That for himself and in the name of his wife Da. Martina Castro de Alvarado and other heirs and successors, and whoever of them shall have title, voice and repute in whatever manner, he sells and conveys in public sale and perpetual alienation by right of inheritance forever and ever to John C. Fremont, a tract which belongs to him in ownership, by concession made to him by the Most Excellt. Señor Commandant General and Governor of the Department Don Manuel Micheltorena, with date 29th Feby 1844. Said tract is called "Las Mariposas" it has an extent of ten sitios de ganado mayor,[1] and is situated between the limits of the Sierra Nevada and the Rivers known by the name of

Chauchilas [Chowchilla], de la Merced and San Joaquin. The vendor declares that he has not alienated nor burdened it, and that it is free from every public burden, and as such he sells it to the purchaser in the price of three thousand dollars ($3000) which he has received to his entire satisfaction; that henceforth he may use it and dispose of the dominion, ownership and other whatever right may aid him in the said tract, renouncing it and transferring it to the purchaser, that he may dispose of it, as of his own thing: the vendor obligating himself that this sale shall be certain, secure and effective to him, (the vendor) and that he will not disturb him, or institute a law suit against him, and that in all cases if there shall be any claim set up, he will be bound to indemnify the purchaser for all the damages and prejudices which may have been occasioned to him. To which effect, he transfers on this date to the purchaser, the said title of concession, and to the observance of all the foregoing he obligates all his property present and future, and with them he submits himself to the Laws and to Jurisdiction of the Judge who may have cognizance of his causes, in order to compel him to its fulfilment, and oblige him, as if by final judgement, admitted and passed in authority of a thing adjudged, renouncing the laws which might favor him in the promises.

(Signed) Juan B. Alvarado.
[*Seal*]

(Signed)   Walter Colton[2]
            Chief Magistrate
Witness   Wm. Ed. Hartnell
Witness   Wm. R. Garner[3]

On said day, month, and year, appeared also before me and the said Witnesses, Da. Martina Castro de Alvarado, wife of Don Juan Bta. Alvarado and said: That in her name and those of her heirs and successors, and of whoever of them shall have title, voice and repute, in whatever manner, she gives for well sold the before mentioned place, and that she spontaneously and voluntarily renounces all right which she and her said heirs may have to it.

(Signed)   Martina Castro de Alvarado
"Witness"
Wm. R. Garner
"Witness"
Wm. Ed. Hartnell

WALTER COLTON
Chief Magistrate of Monterey

Office of California Land Commission
Los Angeles, Septr. 27th. 1852

I certify the foregoing to be a true and correct Translation of the
original on file in this office in Case No. 1.

(Signed) Geo. Fisher
Sect'y

Filed in Office Septr. 18th. 1852

(Signed) Geo. Fisher
Sect'y

Translated copy (DNA-49, California Private Land Claims Dockets,
Docket 1, pp. 88–89). The original documents by which Las Mariposas was
conveyed to Alvarado and then to JCF were first located in the archives at
Monterey, but with the conclusion of the American conquest, those pertaining to land titles were placed in the Office of the U.S. Surveyor for California
in San Francisco. Here they remained until 1906, when they were destroyed
by fire following the earthquake. Fortunately, copies may be found in Docket
1, which is the transcript of the proceedings in the case before the Board of
U.S. Land Commissioners, the District Court of the United States for the
Northern District of California, and the Supreme Court.

Larkin purchased Las Mariposas for JCF and charged him a commission
of $7\frac{1}{2}$ percent, or $225 (CRAMPTON, 27). Located not far from Yosemite Valley,
the vast grant was to cause JCF endless trouble, and it was not until 19 Feb.
1856 that he received a U.S. patent. It was a "floating grant," with no set
boundaries, and the vendor's title was by no means absolute. Because of the
Indian menace, Alvarado had been unable to comply with the provisions for
survey and settlement; in addition, one of terms of the grant had forbidden
the sale or alienation of the property. The legal problems were further complicated by the discovery of gold in 1849.

Before he left California in June 1847, JCF sought the aid of a friend in
establishing a settlement on the grant. He gave a power of attorney to
Pierson B. Reading, who sent Joseph W. Buzzell with men, money, and
equipment to build a house and corral, but Indian hostility forced the aban-
donment of Buzzell's four attempts to occupy Las Mariposas (CRAMPTON,
28–30).

En route to California in 1849, JCF encountered a party of Sonorans on
their way to the goldfields. He made arrangements with them to proceed to
Las Mariposas and work the gold that he believed could be found there, on a
fifty-fifty basis (Jessie B. Frémont, "Great Events during the Life of Major
General John C. Frémont," pp. 98, 109, CU-B). Apparently Alexander Godey
went along to supervise them and to prospect for gold. In the summer of
1849 JCF visited the grant and had Charles Preuss survey and draft a map of
the tract (William C. Jones's testimony to the Board of California Land
Commissioners, DNA-49, California Private Land Claims Dockets, Docket 1,
p. 99). This map seems not to have been preserved, but in a letter to a friend
JBF indicates that her husband had paid Preuss $500 for some 1849 services

in California (JBF to Elizabeth Blair Lee, 4 May [1857?], NjP—Blair-Lee Papers).

1. Ranges for a lot of cattle, or ten leagues.

2. A Congregationalist minister and former journalist, Walter Colton (1797–1851) had served as naval chaplain aboard the *Congress* before being appointed alcalde at Monterey by Commodore Stockton. At the time of the Mariposa transaction he was publishing the *Californian* with Robert Semple and gathering material for his famous *Three Years in California,* which was published in 1850 after he left California (DRURY).

3. An English sailor who had been forcibly put ashore in California in 1824 by the captain of a whaler, William Robert Garner (1803–49) was secretary, translator, and guide to Walter Colton. At Colton's urging, Garner began writing a series of letters on California which were to appear in 1847 and 1848 in the Philadelphia *North American and United States Gazette* and in the New York *Journal of Commerce.* In 1970 the letters were collected and edited and may be found in GARNER, along with a biographical sketch of their writer.

139. Frémont to Willard P. Hall

Government House
ANGELES, 11th Feby. 1847

To
Hon. Willard P. Hall
SIR

The position I occupy as the chief representative of the U. S. Government in California, renders it an imperative duty on me, that I should prudently but with energy exert all the power with which I am clothed to retain the conquest we have made, and strengthen it by all means possible.

The Executive Office of California, which I understand centers supreme civil and military command in the territory was actually assigned me as early as September last, and my entering on the duties of the same was postponed only in consequence of an insurrection that broke out in this portion of the territory, which it took some months to quell; that done I assumed the office of Govr., as had been previously arranged.

I learn with surprise and mortification that Genl. Kearney, in obedience to what I cannot but regard as obsolete instructions from the Sec. of War, means to question my right, and viewing my position and claim clear and indisputable I cannot without considering myself derelict to my trust and unworthy the station of an American officer, yield or to permit myself to be interfered with by any other, until directed to do so, by the proper authorities at home predicated on full and ample despatches that I forwarded to Washington as early as August of last year.

I require the cooperation, with a view to the important object of preserving the peace and tranquility of California, of every American citizen and soldier in the territory and must expressly inhibit from all quarters all arguments and intimations that may tend to weaken my authority by inducing the belief that my present position is an act of usurpation, unjust, and will not be sanctioned by my government.

Intimations, not perhaps susceptible of positive proof, have reached me that you were using your talents, and high character as a member of the American Congress, in your intercourse with the citizens of this place and the troops under my immediate command to raise doubts, if not questioning altogether the legitimacy or validity of my tenure of office.

I feel myself constrained therefore in obedience to the behests, and high interests of my government, as well as the respect I cherish for the position you occupy to enquire of you in frankness whether the intimations alluded to have any foundation in fact or truth.

Cherishing a confident belief that you must on reflection concur with me, in thinking, that at this juncture, any move calculated to weaken me, or embarrass, must be inexpedient and improper, I trust a frank negative answer from you will dissipate my doubts, and admonish me that the enquiry I have made was altogether unnecessary. With considerations of high respect I am your obt. servt.

J. C. FRÉMONT
Governor of California

LS, RC (DNA-94, LR, K-217 1847, f/w K-209 1846). Addressed and endorsed. Enclosure 6 in Kearny to R. Jones, 11 Sept. 1847, and presented against JCF at the court-martial as evidence that he was endeavoring to persuade Hall, a man of influence, to aid and abet him in resisting and making mutiny against Kearny.

Willard P. Hall (1820–82) was a young lawyer who had enlisted as a private in the 1st Missouri Cavalry under Col. Alexander W. Doniphan soon after the beginning of the Mexican War. On the Santa Fe Trail, word reached him that he had been elected to Congress from his home district, but he continued on with the troops and helped to construct the code of civil laws known as the "Kearny code" for New Mexico. He went on to California with the Mormon Battalion and returned east with General Kearny to take his seat in the House of Representatives—belatedly, for the term had begun on 4 March. During the Civil War Hall served first as provisional lieutenant governor and later as governor of Missouri. In his testimony at JCF's court-martial Hall indicated that his position in California was that of a private in Company C of the first regiment of Missouri Mounted Volunteers (CT. MARTIAL, 209).

140. Jacob R. Snyder to Edward M. Kern

ANGELES Feb. 11th. 1847

DR. SIR

Thirty Saddles and thirty two horses, you will please to receive from the Tularie Indians, who have been in the employ of the U. States Government; Should the Indians not bring in the horses and saddles Please send for them.

By order of Lieut. Col. J. C. Fremont

JACOB R. SNYDER
Quartermaster

N.B.
Jose Jesus[1] is the Chief of the tribe.

ALS, RC (CSmH).
1. Siyakum chief José Jesus and his people occupied the area between French Camp Slough and the Stanislaus River. The chief had long been unfriendly to the Californians, and he and some of his warriors were enlisted by Sutter for Company H of the California Battalion (ROGERS [3]; BANCROFT, 5:360n).

141. W. Branford Shubrick to Frémont

U. S. Ship Independence
MONTEREY, February 13th. 1847

SIR,

I have the honor to acknowledge the receipt of your letter of the 7th instant, and shall detain your courier as short a time as possible, for my answer, and will also avail myself of your kind offer to forward despatches to the United States.

When I wrote to you on the 25th ultimo, I was not informed of the arrival of Brigadier General Kearny in California, and addressed you as the Senior Officer of the Army in the Territory. On the 28th, however, having understood that the General was at "Los Angeles," I addressed a similar letter to him.

On the 8th instant, General Kearny arrived in this harbor, in the sloop of war "Cyane", and left by the same conveyance, on the 11th for San Francisco. While the General was here we consulted freely, as enjoined on me by my instructions, and on him by his, on the measures necessary to be taken by us for the security of the Territory of California.[1]

I am looking daily for the arrival of Commodore Stockton in this harbor, when I shall of course receive from him a full account of the measures taken by him while in command of the Squadron.

It is to be hoped that the pleasure of the President of the United States on this subject of the organization of a civil government, and of the measures taken by Commodore Stockton and yourself, may be soon known; and it will give me pleasure at all times, to cooperate with the Civil Government as well as with the Military Commander in Chief for the peace and security of the Territory.

I regret to say that not anticipating any unusual draft on them, the funds brought with me are barely sufficient with the most economical expenditure to meet the wants of the Squadron. I am, Very Respectfully, Sir, Your Obedt. Servt.[2]

W. BRANFORD SHUBRICK
Commander in Chief
United States Naval Forces.

Lieut. Colonel Frémont &c. &c. &c.
"Los Angeles."

Copy (DNA-45, Area 9 File, Pacific).
1. More than a month later, and after the receipt of new instructions from Washington, Kearny wrote an account of his visit with Shubrick which indicates that on 8 Feb. he was indeed in doubt about the supremacy of his civil authority in California (see CT. MARTIAL, 96–99).
2. On the same day Shubrick wrote the Secretary of the Navy that he felt the appointment of JCF was "prematurely taken by Commodore Stockton." But since the appointment had been communicated to the president in August, he soon expected more information and would therefore await such information, "and confine myself for the present to arrangements for the quiet possession of the territory, and for the blockade of the coast of Mexico" (Shubrick to George Bancroft, 13 Feb. 1847, CT. MARTIAL, 296). Later Stockton questioned Shubrick's ethics in expressing himself so frankly to the

Secretary of the Navy. In the unpleasant correspondence that resulted between the two naval officers, Shubrick sought the advice of his friend James Fenimore Cooper in answering Stockton (Cooper to Shubrick, 5 Aug. 1849, J. F. COOPER, 6:58–62).

142. Mariano G. Vallejo to Frémont

SONOMA, 15 Feb. 1847

Governor J. C. Fremont
RESPECTED SIR:

I received with gratitude your favorable [letter] of the past 22 of January enclosing the honorable commission Your Excellency R. F. Stockton had conferred upon me. The desire burns in me incessantly that in this, the country of my birth, the peace, order and prosperity of which it is capable will reign and that it will be the consequence of a wise and just government and it has been very flattering that without meriting it, you have found me capable of contributing 300 pesos to the big enterprise of regenerating this Dept. assigning me a place in the council that must be organized and if I have accepted the delicate task it is only because I have confidence and depend more in the cleverness and patriotism of my dignified colleagues than in my poor ability, which is very insufficient, for performing such an arduous assignment of whose requirements I am still ignorant.

With no less pleasure than that which you show in your aforesaid [letter] I forsee positive advantages for the country as a result of your cooperation and I hope to see realized the wishes that you express in the same [letter] concerning the restoration of the order and tranquility that are so needed.

You have always seen me, when the circumstances required it, to subordinate my own interest to that of the public well-being and to abandon the repose and domestic comfort to work hard for the well-being of my fellow citizens; I find myself now still in the same patriotic mood and to prove it, I have not been stopped by reason of conscience or by my deteriorated health or by the class of prisoner in which I still find myself and I shall be ready to start my march as soon as the H. Sr. D. T. O. Larkin, who wrote to me that he was coming to Yerba Buena to lead the members of the Council, arrives, and even without waiting for him I would have left today if my failing health, which would be now worsened by the navigation had not prevented it.

We have favorably viewed your recommendation in favor of M. Knight as we shall always do with respect to any order that you wish to give us.

Yours truly, with the most high esteem, kisses your hand.

[*Unsigned*]

AL, translation of a draft in CU-B. The letter actually sent has apparently been lost. Before surrendering the governorship of the conquered territory of California to JCF in Jan. 1847, Stockton had appointed Vallejo to the legislative council (see Doc. No. 123).

143. Robert F. Stockton to Frémont

U. S. Frigate Congress
HARBOUR OF SAN DIEGO
February 16th. 1847

MY DEAR SIR,

Will you do me the favour to appoint Don Santiago Arguello,[1] Collector for this port in the place of Don Pedro C. Carrillo, who has removed to Santa Barbara.

We have but three days bread on board and no money; I shall therefore remain here until I get money, Bread and Despatches.

On Monday next is the 22nd of February. Suppose you come down to San Diego on Sunday with your Suite, and visit the Ship on Monday; when I will give a fete in honor of the day and the Governor. Faithfully, Yr. obdt. servt.,

R. F. STOCKTON

To His Excellency
Governor J. C. Fremont
Ciudad de los Angeles

P. S.

Bring Russell along to write an account of it for the Californian, for the edification of General Kearny.

Lbk (DNA-45, Entry 395 [E-20-A], Letterbook of Robert F. Stockton, 1846–47). Philip St. George Cooke records that the "Secretary of State"

(Russell) stopped at the Mission San Luis Rey on the evening of 21 Feb. He was on his way to San Diego to represent the government at the ball (COOKE, 280).

1. Santiago E. Argüello (ca. 1813–57), acting as captain, had enrolled a company in San Diego in Dec. 1846 to serve three months in the California Battalion. JCF granted Stockton the favor requested in this letter, and Argüello served as collector of the port of San Diego until June 1847.

144. Frémont to Pierson B. Reading

ANGELES February 16th 1847

SIR

In effecting settlements with the officers connected with the Battalion, you are authorized to allow in their accounts Forage and servant hire as specified in the Pay Table without requiring of them certificates of having constantly kept or employed the horses and servants as allowed agreeably to their respective ranks. Respectfully,

J. C. FRÉMONT,
Lieut. Col. Comm'd'g. Battn. and Governor of California

LS, RC (C).

145. Frémont to Archibald H. Gillespie

CIUDAD DE LOS ANGELES
17 Feby. 1847

SIR

I avail myself of a momentary freedom, or respite from a vexatious headache to reply to your communication of yesterday's date.

Recognizing Commodore Stockton as civil and military Governor of California, and thereby invested with full power to represent & bind the U. S. government in all his official acts, and of course, the rate of pay promised to the Vols [Volunteers];—I feel as his successor as if I had no other election than to ratify all the promises and engagements entered into by him whilst acting as Govr.

I therefore, authorize and require all his contracts with the Vols. to be redeemed to the letter, without expressing any opinion as to the propriety of the measures adopted by him. Very Respectfully Your Obt. servt.,

J. C. FRÉMONT
Govr. of California

To Arch. H. Gillespie
Major Califa. Battln.

LS, RC (CLU—Gillespie Papers). Addressed. Endorsed: "Col. Frémont in reply to inquiry in relation to an increase of pay from $10 to $25. Los Angeles, Feby. 17th 1847. Russell's writing; Frémont's signature."

146. Frémont to Jacob R. Snyder

[LOS ANGELES]
[22 Feb. 1847]

TO ALL TO WHOM THESE PRESENTS SHALL COME
GREETING:

Know ye, that I, J. C. Fremont, Governor of California, in virtue and by the authority of powers vested in me as such, and in the consideration of the entire and perfect confidence that I repose in the capacity, integrity and favorable disposition cherished by Jacob R. Snyder towards the public service, do hereby constitute, ordain, and appoint him, superintendent of the Mission of San Gabriel with authority and power to take full and entire control of said Mission of San Gabriel, to employ labour to make all needfull repairs and to do aught else with said Mission, as in his judgement and discretion may conduce, by such expenditure and labour to the public interest.

In testimony whereof I have hereunto set my name, and have caused the seal of the Territory of California to be affixed at the Ciudad de Los Angeles the Capitol of California this Twenty second day of February A. D. Eighteen hundred and forty seven.

Attest
WM. H. RUSSELL
Sec'y of State

J. C. FRÉMONT
Governor of California
[Seal]

Facsimile, printed in the *Quarterly* of the Society of California Pioneers, 8 (1931):210.

147. W. Branford Shubrick to Frémont

U. S. Ship Independence
Monterey, February 23rd 1847

Sir,

Since my letter to you of the 22nd[1] Passed Midshipman McLane of the Navy has arrived at this place under some instructions from you,[2] and as I understand your courier has not yet left, I avail myself of him to send this.

Mr. McLane informs me that there are several officers of the Navy doing duty with the volunteers under your command. I desire that all such be immediately returned to the Squadron, unless General Kearny who, I am instructed, is the Commanding Military Officer in California, and invested by the President with the administrative functions of Government over the people and Territory, should wish their services on land. I am, Sir, Very Respectfully Your Obdt. Servt.[3]

(Signed) W. Branford Shubrick
Commander in Chief of the Naval Force

Lieutenant Colonel J. C. Frémont
U. S. Army
Pueblo de Los Angeles.

Copy of enclosure 10 in Kearny to R. Jones, 11 Sept. 1847 (DNA-94, LR, K-217 1847, f/w K-209 1846).

1. Not found, although a special search was made of the pertinent series of naval records. Perhaps Shubrick refers to his letter of 25 Jan. 1847, not found.

2. Not only Louis McLane but, more important, Lieut. J. M. Watson had arrived in Monterey on or before 20 Feb. with significant dispatches from Washington, including one from the Secretary of the Navy dated 5 Nov. 1846 and addressed to Stockton, but given in his absence to Shubrick. It reads: "The president has deemed it best for the public interests to invest the military officer commanding with the direction of the operations on land, and with the administrative functions of government over the people and territory occupied by us. You will relinquish to Colonel Mason or to General Kearney, if the latter shall arrive before you have done so, the entire control over these matters and turn over to him all papers necessary to the performance of his duties" (CT. MARTIAL, 51–53). It would be interesting to know if this is JCF's *first* information that Kearny was to have supreme command in the territory, or if Shubrick's letter of 22 Feb. had stated clearly the nature of these instructions from Washington. If not, this is a very cursory and obscure way of informing JCF that a bearer of new instructions

308

had arrived in California and that JCF would be foolish to persist in his defiance of Kearny. True, these instructions were sent by the Navy Department before the receipt of Stockton's letters of the previous August and September with news of the conquest of California and his plans for the establishment of a civil government.

Before the naval courier reached Shubrick in Monterey, Kearny had received from Col. Richard B. Mason on 13 Feb. in San Francisco a copy of the Navy Department's dispatch plus one from Winfield Scott, general-in-chief of the Army. Dated 3 Nov. 1846, Scott's dispatch instructed Kearny to muster the California Volunteers, organized by Stockton, into the Army and reiterated that the senior officer of the land forces was to be the governor of the province (CT. MARTIAL, 48–50). But Kearny did not inform JCF of the new orders. Later, when he was cross-examined in Washington about his failure to do so, he stated that he was not in the habit of communicating to his juniors the instructions he received unless required to do so (CT. MARTIAL, 102). Sometime in March Stockton received from Commodore Biddle the instructions of 5 Nov. 1846 from the Navy Department, but he did not furnish JCF with a copy of these instructions (CT. MARTIAL, 200).

Although Kearny and Stockton never officially communicated the new instructions to JCF, he must have known their nature after receiving this 23 Feb. 1847 letter from Shubrick, as well as newspaper reports of new instructions, sometime in early March. On 5 March Gillespie wrote Larkin, "Fremont received some [newspapers] by the courier who came down lately but he has not favored our eyes with a sight of them" (LARKIN, 6:37–38). The *California Star* of Yerba Buena, 20 Feb., reported that Kearny had received new instructions and additional powers from Washington. Perhaps this issue of the *Star* had not reached JCF in Los Angeles when Gillespie wrote— or perhaps it had, and this was why JCF was keeping the papers from his colleagues. Gillespie noted that "everything is very quiet & has the appearance of remaining so; indeed, the policy adopted by Fremont, should secure it. . . ." He also chided Larkin: "You people in Monterey, I fear, think too much of the rising sun [i.e., Kearny]. Take care it may be eclipsed, and you will be all lost in the fog!"

It seems almost certain, then, that JCF did know by early March of the new instructions to the Navy and Army, but he also believed that even later instructions were on the way to California. He doubted very much that President Polk, once he was informed of the conquest of California by Stockton and JCF, would refuse to approve Stockton's appointing him as governor. On 1 March Larkin wrote W. D. M. Howard, "He [JCF] yet expects by Secretary Norris the approval of appointment as Governor by Mr. Polk" (LARKIN, 6:32–33). And Gillespie, piqued over Shubrick's and Kearny's refusal to honor the financial commitments of officers of the California Battalion, wrote Larkin, "The movements at your place [Monterey] certainly looked very much like the desertion of those in the country, whom you know have done the work. . . . Shubrick had nothing to do with the acts of Commo. Stockton previous to his arrival, and Gen'l. Kearney had less, until he received the last instructions; and then courtesy would have dictated a different procedure, had he not been actuated by personal motives, and a feeling of importance. However, let it all go for what it is worth. The sequel will show whether the Government will sustain such a course as has been pursued against the officers, sent to this country before those last comers were thought of. The Army Gents may think they have caught the hare, but I doubt much if they will hold it" (Gillespie to Larkin, "Angeles," 1 April 1847, LARKIN, 6:82–83).

3. Richard B. Mason wrote Henry S. Turner that JCF had said he paid no attention to this communication of Shubrick's in regard to the naval officers on duty with the California Battalion, "and did not communicate it to the officers concerned, because it did not reach him through Com. Stockton, by whose orders the officers were put on duty with the Battalion and on account of the manner and want of courtesy on the part of Commodore Shubrick in communications with him on the subject" (Mason to Turner, 10 April 1847, enclosure D in Kearny to R. Jones, 3 May 1847, DNA-94, LR, K-202 1847, f/w K-209 1846).

148. Stephen Watts Kearny to Frémont

Head Qrs. 10th Military Department
MONTEREY (U.C.) March 1st. 1847

SIR:

By Dept. Orders No. 2 of this date, (which will be handed to you by Capt. Turner 1st Dragoons A.A.A. Genl for my Command) you will see that certain duties are there required of you as Commander of the Battalion of California Volunteers.[1]

In addition to the duties above referred to, I have now to direct that you will bring with you, & with as little delay as possible all the Archives & Public Documents & Papers which may be subject to your Control & which appertain to the Government of California, that I may receive them from your hands at this Place, the Capitol of the Territory.

I have directions from the Genl. in chief, not to detain you in this Country against your wishes, a moment longer than the necessities of the service may require & you will be at liberty to leave here, after you have complied with these instructions & those in the "Orders" referred to. Very Respectfully Your Obdt. Servt.

(Signed) S. W. KEARNY
Brig. Genl. & Governor of California

To
Lt. Col. J. C. Frémont
Regt. of Mounted Riflemen
Commdg. Battn. of Califa. Vols.
Ciudad de los Angeles

Copy enclosed in Kearny to R. Jones, 15 March 1847 (DNA-94, LR, K-166 1847, f/w K-209 1846). Endorsed. Also in BIGELOW, 200–201. This letter to JCF and departmental orders no. 2 were carried to Los Angeles by Capt. Henry S. Turner after Kearny's return to Monterey from a reconnaissance of the Bay of San Francisco. There, as noted in Doc. No. 147, n. 2, Kearny had received instructions from Washington dated 3 and 5 Nov. 1846 which, without question, gave him supreme authority in California. Turner left Monterey on 2 March and delivered orders no. 2 to JCF in Los Angeles on 11 March (CT. MARTIAL, 148). The following day he had an interview with JCF, who, he said, informed him that he would proceed the next day to the Mission San Gabriel to execute the order (CT. MARTIAL, 148). JCF apparently did not go personally but sent the adjutant of the battalion, William N. Loker, who was unsuccessful in mustering members of the California Battalion into service (CT. MARTIAL, 134).

To his wife, Julia, Turner had already written that Kearny had not displayed "his usual firmness and decision of character in dealing with Frémont" and attributed this temporizing course to fear of offending Benton. "Were I to behave as Frémont has done he would cause me to be put in irons, and would pursue me with a bitterness that would drive me to desperation. Yet this man is permitted to escape without a murmur. He says that he will prefer charges against Frémont and cause him to be tried, but I do not believe it. I think he will do nothing calculated to give displeasure to Col. Benton" (Turner to Julia Turner, 22 Feb. 1847, TURNER, 154–59).

1. See Doc. No. 149.

149. 10th Military Department Orders No. 2

Hd. Qrs. 10th Military Dept.
MONTEREY, March 1, 1847

Orders No. 2

I With a view to regular payment, it is necessary that the Battalion of California Volunteers, now, under the command of Lt. Col. Frémont, of the Army and Stationed at the Ciudad de los Angeles, if not originally mustered under the law of May 13 and the supplemental law of June 18, 1846, should now be mustered into service under those laws. This muster will be made at once by Lt. Col. Fremont. Should any men of that Battalion be unwilling to continue in service under the above named laws, they will be conducted by Lt.

Col. Frémont to Yerba Buena via Monterey, and be there discharged.

II Lt. Gillespie of the Marines now serving with the Battalion of California Volunteers is relieved from that duty, he will repair to Washington City, and will report himself to the Commanding officer of his Corps.

III Lieut. Col. P. S. Cooke[1] now in Command of the Mormon Battalion, is entrusted with the supervision of the Southern Mil. District, for the protection and defence of which he will make the necessary provision, posting his command (to consist of Company C. 1st Dragoons, the Mormon Battalion, and the California Volunteers) at such places, as he may deem most eligible.

IV Lieutenant Colonel Cooke will designate an officer to receive all public property which the senior naval officer, at San Diego, may be caused to be turned over.

V Major Swords,[2] quartermaster, and Paymaster Cloud,[3] will repair to head-quarters, at Monterey, and report themselves to the general commanding.

By order of Brig. Genl. S. W. Kearny.

H. S. Turner
Capt. A.A.A. Genl.

Copied for Adj. Genl., Lt. Col. Fremont & Cooke [and] of Par. 2 for Com. of Marine Corps at Washington.

DS (DNA-393, Order Book, 10th Military District, vol. 8, Feb.–Dec. 1847).

1. Virginian Philip St. George Cooke (1809–95), one of the youngest men ever to graduate from West Point, would devote forty-six years of his life to the Army. He held a captaincy in the 1st U.S. Dragoons (as well as a commission, dating from 16 Feb. 1847, as a major in the 2nd Dragoons), but he had really come to California as a lieutenant colonel in command of the Mormon Battalion. The battalion arrived in San Diego on 29 Jan. 1847, and Kearny sent it to the Mission San Luis Rey, fifty-three miles from San Diego, on the road to Los Angeles. Cooke's journal of his epic and arduous overland march was published by the government in 1849 (Senate Doc. 2, 31st Cong., spec. sess., Serial 547) and was republished by the author in 1878 (with additions) under the title *The Conquest of New Mexico and California*. But Cooke's greatest contribution to military history was a manual, the first written on cavalry field tactics. For a biography of Cooke, see YOUNG. For Kearny's letter to Cooke, which Turner carried south, see CT. MARTIAL, 140–41.

2. Maj. Thomas B. Swords (ca. 1807–86) was chief quartermaster of the Army of the West, and returned east with Kearny in the summer of 1847. He was breveted brigadier general and major general for his services in the Quartermaster Department during the Civil War.

3. Paymaster Jeremiah H. Cloud had come to California with the Mormon Battalion. He died at Sutter's Fort on 4 Aug. 1847 after a fall from a horse.

150. Shubrick-Kearny Circular

To all whom it may concern, be it known,

That the President of the United States, desirous to give and secure to the People of California a share of the good government and happy civil organization enjoyed by the People of the United States, and to protect them at the same time, from the attacks of foreign foes, and from internal commotions,—has invested the undersigned with separate and distinct powers, civil and military; a cordial co-operation in the exercise of which, it is hoped and believed will have the happy results desired.

To the Commander-in-Chief of the Naval Forces, the President has assigned the regulation of the import trade,—the conditions on which vessels of all nations, our own as well as foreign, may be admitted into the ports of the Territory, and the establishment of all Port Regulations.

To the Commanding Military Officer, the President has assigned the direction of the operations on land, and has invested him with administrative functions of government over the People and Territory occupied by the forces of the United States.

Done at MONTEREY, Capital of California, this first day of March, A. D. 1847.

W. BRANFORD SHUBRICK,
Commander-in-Chief of the Naval Forces
S. W. KEARNY, Brig. Gen'l. U. S. A. and Governor of California

Printed copy found in Kearny to R. Jones, 15 March 1847 (DNA-94, LR, K-166 1847, f/w K-209 1846). A copy was sent south with Turner to JCF (CT. MARTIAL, 102). The circular appeared in the *California Star* on 6 March 1847 and for several successive weeks. Kearny and Shubrick selected Monterey as the temporary capital.

151. Stephen Watts Kearny's Proclamation

[MONTEREY]
[1 March 1847]

TO THE PEOPLE OF CALIFORNIA

The President of the United States having instructed the undersigned to take charge of the civil government of California, he enters upon his duties with an ardent desire to promote as far as he is able, the interests of the country and the welfare of its inhabitants.

The undersigned has instructions from the President to respect and protect the religious institutions of California, and to see that the religious rights of the People are in the amplest manner preserved to them, the constitution of the United States allowing every man to worship his Creator in such a manner as his own conscience may dictate to him.

The undersigned is also instructed to protect the persons and property of the quiet and peaceable inhabitants of the country against all or any of their enemies, whether from abroad or at home; and when he now assures the Californians that it will be his duty and his pleasure to comply with those instructions, he calls upon them all to exert themselves in preserving order and tranquility, in promoting harmony and concord, and in maintaining the authority and the efficiency of the laws.

It is the wish and design of the United States to provide for California with the least possible delay, a free Government similar to those in her other Territories, and the people will soon be called upon to exercise their rights as freemen in electing their own Representatives, to make such laws as may be deemed best for their interest and welfare. But until this can be done, the laws now in existence and not in conflict with the constitution of the U. States, will be continued until changed by competent authority; and those persons who hold office, will continue in the same for the present, provided they swear to support the constitution and to faithfully perform their duty.[1]

The undersigned hereby absolves all the inhabitants of California from any further allegiance to the Republic of Mexico, and will consider them as citizens of the United States; those who remain quiet and peaceable will be respected in their rights and protected in them; should any take up arms against, or oppose the Government of the Territory, or instigate others to do so, they will be considered as enemies and treated accordingly.

When Mexico forced a war upon the United States, time did not permit the latter to invite the Californians as friends to join her standard, but compelled her to take possession of the country to prevent any European Powers from seizing upon it, and in doing so, some excesses and unauthorized acts were no doubt committed by persons employed in the service of the United States, by which a few of the inhabitants have met with a loss of property; such losses will be duly investigated, and those entitled to remuneration will receive it.

California has for many years suffered greatly from domestic troubles; civil wars have been the poisoned fountains which have sent forth trouble and pestilence over her beautiful land. Now these fountains are dried up; the Star Spangled Banner floats over California, and as long as the sun continues to shine upon her, so long will it float there, over the natives of the land, as well as others who have found a home in her bosom; and under it, agriculture must improve and the arts and sciences flourish, as seed in a rich and fertile soil.

The Americans and Californians are now but one People; let us cherish one wish, one hope, and let that be for the peace and quiet of our country. Let us as a Band of Brothers unite and emulate each other in our exertions to benefit and improve this our beautiful, and which soon must be our happy and prosperous home.

Done at Monterey, Capital of California, this first day of March, A. D. 1847, and in the 71st year of Independence of the United States.

S. W. KEARNY, Brig. Gen.
U. S. A. and Governor of California

Printed copy, in English and Spanish, enclosed in Kearny to R. Jones, 15 March 1847 (DNA-94, LR, K-166 1847, f/w K-209 1846). The proclamation was actually issued on 4 March, after the departure of Turner for the south, but was back-dated to 1 March. The *California Star,* 20 March 1847 (and for many weeks thereafter), printed it in English and Spanish.
1. Article 3 of the Articles of Capitulation had guaranteed that no Californian or Mexican citizen should be compelled to take the oath of allegiance, but this provision made an oath mandatory for officeholders.

152. Frémont to Pierson B. Reading

[2 March 1847]

Know all men by these Presents, that I, J. C. Fremont, Governor of the Territory of California, and in virtue thereof legal representative of the United States of North America, clothed with general and extensive powers, in consideration of the necessity of having an agent to represent this integral part of the United States of North America in foreign parts as well as the entire confidence that I feel and repose in the favorable disposition, integrity, capacity and business habits of Major Pearson [Pierson] B. Reading, United States Paymaster for the United States troops in California, do surely constitute, ordain and appoint him my true and special agent and attorney to proceed with blank bonds signed by myself in my fiduciary character and countersigned by William H. Russell, Secretary of State, to Mazatlan, Lima, or any other place that he may elect to negotiate certain loans for the use and benefit of the United States. It is the intention of this instrument or letter of attorney to invest my said agent Major Pearson B. Reading with power fully to regulate the rates of interest, fill up the dates which are left blank in the bonds and do everything necessary to be done towards accomplishing the loans for the amounts respectively set forth in the bonds. I further more authorize my said agent to charter or instruct the charter of the barque Guipuzcoana and to employ the services of such agent or agents as my aforesaid agent may deem necessary to enable him to effect the loans or object of his mission, hereby pledging and binding myself in my fiduciary character and as such the faith and honor of the Government of the United States of North America to sanction, ratify and confirm each and every one of his said acts. In faith whereof I have hereunto set my hand and caused the seal of the Territory of California to be affixed this second day of March A. D. 1847, at the Ciudad de los Angeles, Capital of California.

J. C. FREMONT,
Governor of California
[*Seal*]

Attest
WM. H. RUSSELL
Secretary of State

LS, RC (C).

153. Contract for Purchase of Alcatraz Island

In consideration of Francis Temple having conveyed to the United States of North America a certain Island commonly called White or Bird [Alcatraz] Island situated near the mouth of San Francisco Bay, I, J. C. Fremont Governor of California, and in virtue of my office as aforesaid hereby oblige and bind myself as the legal representative of the United States and my successor in office to pay the said Francis Temple, his heirs or assigns the sum of five thousand dollars (5000) to be paid at as early a day as possible after the receipt of funds from the United States.[1]

In witness whereof I have hereunto set my hand and have caused the seal of the territory of California to be affixed at the Ciudad de Los Angeles the capital of California this 2 day of March A.D. 1847.

(Signed) J. C. Fremont
Gov. of California

Attest
Wm. H. Russell
Secty of State

I hereby certify the above to be a true copy of the original document now in the hands of Mr. Temple a resident of this place.

J. D. Stevenson
Col. 7 Regt.

Pueblo de los Angeles
13 May 1847

I certify that on the 2d day of March 1847 I delivered to Gov. J. C. Fremont the Title to the above mentioned Island.

Ciudad de los Angeles May 13th 1847
Francis Temple

Enclosure 16 in Kearny to R. Jones, 11 Sept. 1847 (DNA-94, LR, K-217 1847, f/w K-209 1846).
1. Many years later JBF wrote an account of the circumstances surrounding the purchase, probably in an attempt to justify her husband's actions. His attention had first been called to the military importance of the island by reading in Vancouver's *Voyages* that "a true course for a vessel entering the harbor from seaward, was to bring Fort Point into a line with Alcatraz

Island." On hearing that the French consul wished to acquire it, JCF made overtures on behalf of the United States to the owner, Temple, who had apparently acquired it from William Workman. Workman in turn had received it "in the regular and usual form, under a special decree of the Mexican Government by Don Pio Pico." Temple, fearful that the United States might not pay, refused to sign the contract until JCF executed his personal bond. The United States did, indeed, decline to recognize the purchase, and eventually JCF paid through Simon Stevens of New York the $5,000 plus interest to the holder of the bond, and thus claimed to be the owner of the island. However, in 1858 the U.S. government forcibly took possession, and JCF's 1859 legal action to eject the officer in charge of fortifying the island could not be prosecuted without the consent of Congress, which was refused ("Great Events during the Life of Major General John C. Frémont," pp. 29–31, CU-B; *California Claims,* Senate Report 75, p. 16, 30th Cong., 1st sess., Serial 512).

154. Frémont to Eulogio de Célis, 3 March 1847

[See Mason to Jones, 9 Oct. 1847, Doc. No. 231.]

155. Frémont to Archibald H. Gillespie

Government House
5th March 1847

SIR

Circumstances having caused me to postpone my intention of leaving the Capital at present you will therefore consider all the orders predicated on that idea recalled by reason of their inapplicability, and you will proceed in the exercise of your usual and ordinary duties, as if no such special orders had been issued. Very respectfully Your obt. servt.

J. C. FRÉMONT
Governor of California

To
Majr. A. H. Gillespie
California Battn.
U. S. Forces

LS, RC (CLU—Gillespie Papers). Addressed. Endorsed: "Countermand of order March 3, 1847." The body of the letter is in Russell's hand, the signature is JCF's. The 3 March 1847 order has not been found.

156. Frémont's Circular

[Los Angeles]
[9 March 1847]

To all to whom these presents shall come
Greeting

Know ye that I J. C. Fremont Governor of California, and in virtue thereof the legal representative of all the various interests of the United States on the coast of said Territory of California, and in pursuance of a custom of precedent established by my predecessor in office Governor R. F. Stockton, do by these presents give full authority and permission to the Brig Primavera, William Stenner[1] Master to trade on any portion of the coast of California on terms, and with the same immunities as merchant vessels of the United States.

Said Brig Primavera[2] is sailing under Mexican colours, but is owned by worthy, and good citizens residents of California. In testimony whereof I have hereunto set my hand, and have caused the seal of California to be affixed at the Ciudad de los Angeles the Capitol of California this 9th day of March A. D. 1847.

J. C. Frémont
Governor of California

attest
Wm. H. Russell
Sec. of State

Copy (DNA-393, 10th Military Department, Frémont Circular). Endorsed.
1. This may have been the same William Stenner, a native of Massachusetts, who had come to California in 1831 as a mate aboard the *Ayacucho*. For two years he had been in charge of the hide houses at San Diego (pioneer register).
2. The *Primavera* was a Mexican brig captured the previous August by the *Cyane* while sailing from San Diego to San Pedro.

157. Philip St. George Cooke to Frémont

Hd. Qrs. South. Mil. Dist.
SAN LUIS REY, 14 March 1847

SIR,

I request you to send me information of the number of men of the Battalion of California Volunteers that have been mustered into service agreeably to 10th Mil. Dept. Order No. 2; and what protection will be afforded to the Artillery and Ordnance stores at San Gabriel.

If possibly, none of the Battalion have consented to be regularly mustered and continued in service, I suggest the necessity of delaying for a few days, until they shall be relieved, the commencement of their march for Yerba Buena. The importance of speedy information on these points will be evident. Very respectfully Yr. obt. servant,

(Signed) P. ST. GEO. COOKE
Lt. Col. Comdg.

To Lt. Col. J. C. Fremont
or Officer comdg. the Battn. California Volunteers,
Ciudad de los Angeles.

Copy of enclosure H in Kearny to R. Jones, 3 May 1847 (DNA-94, LR, K-202 1847, f/w K-209 1846). After conferring with JCF in Los Angeles, Turner went on to the Mission San Luis Rey with the order placing Cooke in command of the southern half of California (COOKE, 284). Cooke then sent this letter of inquiry by a courier who reached JCF's headquarters in Los Angeles on 16 March (see Doc. No. 160).

158. Frémont to Richard Owens

CIUDAD DE LOS ANGELES
15th March 1847

SIR:

In the performance of a portion of my official duties, it become necessary that I should visit in person on the Northern District of the Territory, where I shall probably be detained some 15 or 20 days, and the better to possess you of my views in my absence, and to render your authority in the meantime undoubted, I have considered it proper to issue the following orders.

1st. You will continue with the entire Battalion at San Gabriel, observing order, vigilance, and exercising as much discipline as in your discretion can be prudently enforced.

2d. You will make no war whatever from San Gabriel in my absence unless to repel an actual invasion, or obey the order of any officer that does not emanate from me.

3d. You will take the best possible care of the public arms, and munitions belonging to the Command, and turn them over to no Corps without my special order.

4th. The general police of the garrison and strict regard to the public interest will of course as Comdt. ad. interim, constantly engage your best efforts. Very Respectfully Your Obdt. Servt.

(Signed) J. C. Frémont
Lieut. Col. U. S. Army
Comdt. of California Battalion

To
Capt. Richard Owens
Actg Comdt. of Cal. Battalion.

Copy of enclosure F, no. 1, in Kearny to R. Jones, 3 May 1847 (DNA-94, LR, K-202 1847, f/w K-209 1846). Acting on these orders, Owens refused to deliver up the ordnance to Cooke, who rode to the Mission San Gabriel on 24 March in an effort to persuade him to do so or to permit Midshipman John K. Wilson, acting as captain of artillery and ordnance in the California Battalion, to comply with Cooke's pointed order to turn over the ordnance and ordnance stores to a subordinate. These refusals caused Cooke to write on 25 March to Capt. Henry S. Turner in Monterey, "My God! to think of a howitzer brought over the deserts with so much faithful labour by the Dragoons: the howitzer with which they have four times fought the enemy, & brought here to the rescue of Lt. Col. Fremont & his volunteers to be refused to them by this Lt. Col. Fremont, and in defiance of the orders of his General:—I denounce this treason, or this mutiny which jeopardizes the safety of the Country, and defies me in my legal command and duties! by men, too, who report and say they believe that the enemy approaches from without & are about to rise in arms around us" (see copy F in Kearny to Jones, 3 May 1847, same file).

159. Israel Brockman to Frémont

CITY OF ANGELS
March 15th. 1847

To your excellency Col. J. C. Fremont
Sir:

I am under the necessity of applying to you for my immediate discharge from the service. It is the first time I have asked it and I trust you will grant it for the reason Mr. Stanley, deceased,[1] and myself have or own a waggon and team in co-partnership beside other property which Mr. Craig, Stanley's Administrator, cannot dispose of without my consent. As Mr. Craig is going to the States the ensuing season and has Stanley's debts to collect and take them home to his family I think it very necessary that I should immediately repair to the upper country to see to the disposal of Mr. Stanley's property which cannot be done otherwise.[2] I hope my anxiety will be my excuse. Your most obent.,

ISRAEL BROCKMAN

ALS, RC (Society of California Pioneers—Jacob Rink Snyder Collection). Addressed, "To his excellency Lieut. Col. J. C. Fremont present Guipuscuana [*Jóven Guipuzcoana*]." The outside of the letter bears the names of Israel Brockman, G. S. Carter, and D. Manuel Requena.

Israel Brockman and the two men mentioned in the body of the letter, John Craig and Larkin Stanley, were three of an eight-man party which traveled to California in 1846. All joined Company D of the California Battalion, with Brockman becoming a sergeant. G. S. Carter was also a sergeant in Company D. Requena (ca. 1804–76) was a native of Yucatán. He had come to California in 1835 to trade and remained in Los Angeles until his death, except for a brief time when he retired across the Mexican frontier for political reasons. He was a citizen of excellent standing and much local influence (PIONEER REGISTER).

1. Larkin Stanley died on 12 Dec. 1846 when the California Battalion was nearing Mission San Luis Obispo. His death is described by BRYANT, 13 Dec. 1846, and by Craig in a 4 Oct. 1847 letter to a friend in MORGAN, 1:133–43.

2. Craig and his party left Sutter's on 22 May 1847 (NEW HELVETIA DIARY).

160. William H. Russell to Philip St. George Cooke

CIUDAD DE LOS ANGELES
16th March 1847

SIR

I am instructed by Govr. Fremont to acknowledge a few moments since the receipt of your communication of the 14th Inst. and to say in reply that the Vols. constituting the California Battn. decline without an individual exception to be mustered into the U. S. service conformable to order No. 2 of the 10th Mil. Dept. referred to by you.[1]

The Govr. considers it unsafe at this time, when rumor is rife with a threatened insurrection to discharge the Battn. and will decline doing so, and whilst they remain in service, he regards this force quite sufficient for the protection of the artillery and ordnance stores at the mission of San Gabriel. I am with considerations of respect Your obt. servt.

WM. H. RUSSELL
Sec of State

To
P. St. Geo. Cooke
Lieut Col. Comdg.
Mission San Luis Rey

ALS, RC, enclosure 8 in Kearny to R. Jones, 11 Sept. 1847 (DNA-94, LR, K-217 1847, f/w K-209 1846). Endorsed: "Recd. at 2 P.M. 17 March 1847." This 16 March letter of Russell's arrived at the Mission San Luis Rey while Turner was still there. After Cooke showed him the letter, Turner concluded that JCF did not really intend to execute Kearny's orders and set out immediately for Monterey to inform the general of that fact. Although he stopped at Los Angeles, he did not call upon JCF, and, much to his surprise, the explorer made his appearance in Monterey on 25 March, the day after Turner arrived (enclosure 7, same file; Henry S. Turner to Julia Turner, 31 March 1847, TURNER, 161–62).

1. William N. Loker, who had become JCF's adjutant after Talbot's departure for Washington on 25 Feb. with dispatches, had been assigned the task of going to Mission San Gabriel to determine if any members of the California Battalion wished to be mustered into U.S. service—as outlined by orders no. 2 of the 10th Military Department. None desired to make the change, but Cooke doubted "that steps were taken to allow the men of that battalion to decide knowingly." He looked upon them generally as "good Citizens; but cruelly and studiously misguided and deceived" (Cooke to Turner, 25 March 1847, enclosure F in Kearny to R. Jones, 3 May 1847, DNA-94, LR, K-202 1847, f/w K-209 1846).

323

161. Thomas Oliver Larkin to Frémont

MONTEREY March 16, 1847

Lieut. Col. J. C. Fremont
SIR

I wrote to you by Juan Flaco[1] and by Mr. Knight, to which I have no answer to this date.

I have taken the deed from Alvarado for the ten or eleven leagues of land.[2] The drafts sent to Oahu allowing the discount will cover the sale.

Mr. Green[3] is obliged to go South to see Commodore Stockton, and yourself to settle his account. He has borrowed at two per cent, per month over six thousand dollars in cash. He can go no farther in his business until he can recover some part of his claims. You will oblige us both by assisting him. Hoping to see you soon I do not write much at present. I regret exceedingly that former Government arrangements cannot be carried out.[4] I hear very favourable reports of your gaining popularity among the Californians.[5] You have acted as Governor of California, and you will so be known by the United States at large, and although the time was short, it will be of future service to you in the public opinion. More of these affairs when we meet. I am Your Obdt. Servant.

(Signed) THOMAS O. LARKIN

Printed in LARKIN, 6:59.

1. Popularly known as Juan Flaco, John Brown (ca. 1800–1859), a Swedish emigrant to California in 1828, often served as a courier to Los Angeles, Monterey, and San Diego. He made a fast and dramatic ride from Los Angeles to San Francisco in Sept. 1846 with Gillespie's urgent appeal for aid, and he probably carried one of Kearny's letters to JCF before the latter's arrival in Los Angeles. From 1853 until his death he was employed as a vaquero and caretaker on the ranch of Edward W. Howison, sixty miles northeast of Stockton (DOFFLEMYER).

2. A reference to Larkin's purchase of Las Mariposas for JCF from Alvarado for $3,000, 10 Feb. 1847.

3. Paul Geddes (1810–89), a defaulting bank clerk in Pennsylvania, built a new career in California under the name Talbot H. Green. In the 1851 campaign for the mayoralty of San Francisco, he was recognized and denounced. In 1846 and 1847, acting as Larkin's agent, he furnished a large portion of the supplies purchased by the California Battalion and the naval forces at Monterey. From 17 Sept. 1846 to Oct. 1847 he served, by appointment from Capt. William Mervine, as collector of the port of Monterey. For an article on Green, see HUSSEY [2].

4. A reference to the failure of the council to meet on 1 March, and an implication that all the arrangements made by Stockton for the governance of the territory had ceased, including JCF's term as governor.

5. JCF had indeed ingratiated himself with the native Californians. He wore a sombrero and gave gala balls. Marius Duvall, an assistant naval surgeon, reported a rumor that some Californians had offered to join JCF and fight General Kearny (DUVALL, 93).

162. Thomas Oliver Larkin to Frémont

MONTEREY March 16, 1847

Col. J. C. Fremont
SIR

I think it would save you and the paymaster some trouble, by giving to Mr. Green a draft of large amount, and he undertake to pay off the Riflemen, and others, when in funds. Mr. Green, should he meet you, will offer some plan of arrangement to this effect. I remain, Yours Sincerely,

(Signed) THOMAS O. LARKIN

Printed in LARKIN, 6:59.

163. Citizens of Los Angeles to Frémont

[LOS ANGELES]
[18 March 1847]

MR. JUAN C. FREMONT, GENERAL COMMANDER AND
GOVERNOR OF CALIFORNIA

The undersigned, with the knowledge that you are ready to depart for Monterrey and convinced that this step is not only not advisable but also highly jeopardizes the security of the populations in the southern part of the country, we therefore can do no less than to beg of you to desist for now from your departure for the following reasons.

The country has just emerged from a dangerous crisis and resents the events, therefore it is no wonder that although secret, the resentments that caused the previous subversions still last.

The most important aspect to which you must direct your political effort is toward these populations; they have suffered infinite troubles and they were [in] the original theater [of events] and the evils of war still are alive and if to so grave a circumstance he turns his back, the one who with tact has known how to calm the worries and find the ways toward a national peace, things may arrive at a pitiful situation for which you are responsible.

It is not our purpose to question the reasons found by the "jefes" who are in Monterrey for issuing with such latitude the decree signed the first of the current March, which right we reserve for ourselves; but we want to point out that the effect of your departure from this city might have as a result consequences that are not easy to see from the beaches of Monterrey.

You have managed to gain the confidence of all this neighborhood, they are happy with your vigilance and enthusiasm to keep good order, and for all these reasons it is important in our circumstances to make use of the occasion to amalgamate the good will in order to avoid public calamity.

With sincerity we express our opinions to you and we do not doubt that pursuing the happy ending of events, you will take into consideration our just observations.

Therefore we ask that you remain in this city and that you consult with the appropriate people about the best ways of achieving security.

Thus we beg of you and we hope to be obliged swearing as to the sincerity of the stated matter.

City of Los Angeles, Capital of California, the 18 of March 1847. Signed[1] B. D. Wilson, Abel Stearns, Alejandro Bell, Eulogio Celis, John Temple, Plenio F. Temple, Luis [Buchet?], John Keys, John Atkinson, Franco. [Francisco] Figueroa, Gaspar [Osante?], [Prudon?], William Wolfskill, Lemuel Carpenter, Dobson, Jordan Pacheco, L. Rubideau [Robidoux], Thomas A. Sanchez, Jacildo Aguilar, Julian Chavez, Jn. Luis Vignes, Juan Bandini, Miguel Pryor.

AL, translation of a draft in CSmH.
1. The names listed are not holograph signatures. A clean copy of this draft, but with no names attached, is also in CSmH.

164. Frémont to William Workman

Angeles, March 20th '47

My dear Sir,

I had the pleasure to receive a few minutes since a letter from Mr. Wilson,[1] acquainting me with the regret felt by the people at my departure,—and the farther gratification to learn from him that you had been kind enough to express your entire approbation of my official conduct and your confidence in the success of the measures which I had adopted for the promotion of the public interest. Being much pressed today by many engagements I can only delay to thank you for your friendly disposition to me and to acquaint you briefly with my object in visiting the northern part of the Territory.

You are aware that in the performance of our official duties, and in the exercise of our discretion as the legal representatives of the United States in this remote country, Commodore Stockton and myself have contracted extensive liabilities and become responsible for many interests which it will be difficult for new authorities to support, without some understanding with us. You will also readily understand that for our official conduct we are responsible only to our government, and that therefore in assuming the control of affairs here General Kearny should likewise have assumed all our liabilities. I have therefore decided to go directly to Monterey with the view of requiring as an act of common justice and propriety, due alike to my own character and that of the government I have represented, that this assumption of our responsibilities be made by my successor. Without this assumption it is impossible that I should [make] a formal delivery or transfer of the government, and in such an event I shall immediately return to this place in order to concert with our friends on such measures as may appear advisable in such an emergency. I trust that I shall then receive your aid and countenance in my efforts to support the integrity of my administration. I am with much respect your obedt. servt.

J. C. Frémont

Mr. William Workman
at the Puente

ALS, RC (CU-B). Addressed; endorsed. A native of England, William Workman (1800–1876) had come to California in 1841 from New Mexico, where he had long been a trader at Taos. With a fellow emigrant, John Rowland, he was granted Rancho La Puente, embracing some 48,000 acres in the San Gabriel Valley. Together with Juan Avila and Eulogio de Célis, he appeared under a flag of truce at Stockton's camp on 10 Jan., indicating that the Angeleños would not resist American reoccupation if promised protection and kind treatment. Much later Workman entered the banking business in Los Angeles with his son-in-law, Francis Pliny F. Temple; the failure of the enterprise in 1876 ruined the fortunes of both.

1. See Citizens of Los Angeles to Frémont, 18 March 1847, Doc. No. 163.

165. William H. Russell to David W. Alexander

CIUDAD DE LOS ANGELES
21st March 1847

SIR

You are hereby ordered and permitted in the case of F. Huttman [Hüttmann][1] to receive government payment in payment of his custom house duties.[2] Very respectfully,

J. C. Fremont
Governor of California
By
WM. H. RUSSELL
Sec of State

To
David W. Alexander
Collector of the Port of San Pedro

N.B. Mr. Huttman will be entitled to the usual discount by prompt payment.

W. H. R.
For
J. C. Fremont
Govr.

ALS, RC, enclosure 11 in Kearny to R. Jones, 11 Sept. 1847 (DNA-94, LR, K-217 1847, f/w K-209 1846). Addressed; endorsed. Before becoming collector at the port of San Pedro, Irishman David W. Alexander had been in trade in New Mexico and Los Angeles. He acquired the ranchos of Tujunga and Providencia and later became Los Angeles County sheriff.

1. Francis Hüttmann was master and supercargo of the English bark *Callao*.

2. "Government payment" referred to the use of "due bills" from the paymaster and quartermaster of the California Battalion as negotiable. According to Kearny, these were bought up by Hüttmann at 25 or 30 percent discount. As collector, Alexander had accepted more than $1,700 in this form of paper before receiving Kearny's order to honor nothing but "Specie, Treasury Notes or Drafts" in payment of customs house duties (Kearny to David W. Alexander, 26 April 1847, copy enclosed in Kearny to R. Jones, 1 May 1847, DNA-94, LR, K-245 1847, f/w K-209 1846). Kearny promised Alexander that since he was led into the mistake by the error of others, the amount he had received from Hüttmann would be passed to his credit. After Kearny left for Washington, Richard B. Mason wrote the Adjutant General requesting that JCF be required to refund immediately the $1,700 that the Treasury of California had thus lost by his "illegal order" (Mason to R. Jones, 21 June 1847, DNA-94, LR, M-1113 1847, f/w K-209 1846).

The "due bills" which David W. Alexander had received were invoiced in Los Angeles on 13 May 1847 by acting assistant quartermaster Lieut. John W. Davidson as follows, a copy of which may be found as enclosure 13 in Kearny to R. Jones, 11 Sept. 1847 (DNA-94, LR, K-217 1847):

One due bill, signed Arch. H. Gillespie, endorsed J. C. Fremont, in favor of N. M. Pryor, dated March 27/47 for	$ 500.00
One due bill, signed P. B. Reading, payr. Cal. Bat. in favor of Michael Foley, dated March 26/47 for	114.00
One due bill, signed P. B. Reading, payr. Cal. Bat. in favor of John W. [ ] dated Feb. 23/47 for	182.00
One due bill, signed P. B. Reading, Payr. Cal. Bat. in favor of William D. Miller, dated Feby. 23/47 for	256.54
One due bill signed P. B. Reading, Payr. Cal. Bat. in favor of J. R. Snyder, dated March 14/47 for	100.00
One due bill, signed P. B. Reading, Payr. Cal. Bat. in favor of J. P. Long, dated March 8th/47 for	16.37½
One due bill, signed P. B. Reading, Payr. Cal. Bat. in favor of John Hoit, dated Feby 24/47 for	52.27
One due bill, signed J. R. Snyder QMr. in favor of Henry King, dated March 5/47 for	30.00
One due bill, signed J. R. Snyder Q Mr. in favor of John Dobenbliss, dated Feby. 12/47 for	105.00
One due bill signed J. R. Snyder Q Mr. in favor of Maj. Henry King, Comm. Cal. Bat. dated Mar. 26/47 for	248.07
One due bill, signed J. R. Snyder Q Mr. in favor of Henry King, dated March 15/47 for	40.00
One due bill, signed J. R. Snyder Qr. Mr. in favor of John Dobenbliss dated Feby. 22/47 for	55.00
One due bill, signed J. R. Snyder Qr. Mr. in favor of Edwin Bryant, dated Jany. 28/47 for	15.00
One due bill, signed J. R. Snyder Q Mr. in favor of Lieut. Hiram Rheusaw, dated March 9/47 for	16.50
Am't.	$1731.41½

166. Stephen Watts Kearny to Richard B. Mason

Head Qrs. 10th Mil. Dist.
MONTEREY, March 27th 1847

SIR,

You will proceed to the Southern Military District of this Territory, and inspect the troops in that quarter. You are hereby clothed with full authority to give such orders and instructions in that country, upon all matters whatever, both civil and military, as in your judgement, you may think conducive to the public interest. You will then return to this place. I am Sir very respectfully &c.[1]

(Signed) S. W. KEARNY
Brig Genl. &c
Gov. of Califa.

Col. R. B. Mason
1st Dragoons

Copy of enclosure A in Kearny to R. Jones, 3 May 1847 (DNA-94, LR, K-202 1847, f/w K-209 1846). Endorsed. On 13 Feb. Richard B. Mason (1797–1850), a colonel in the 1st Dragoons, had arrived ill in San Francisco on the *Erie,* a naval storeship commanded by the brother of Henry S. Turner. A descendant of a prominent Virginia family, he had brought out the dispatches from Washington which clearly made Kearny military and civil governor of California, a position to which Mason was to succeed in June.

1. Kearny's order to Mason came after an interview with JCF on the previous day at the general's headquarters in Monterey. Accompanied by his Negro servant, Jacob Dodson, and José de Jesús Pico, JCF had ridden from Los Angeles to Monterey in three days, ten hours. As the distance was then estimated at 400 miles, much of it through mountainous country, the trip was regarded as quite a feat. Reputedly, JCF covered 125 miles on each of two days, exchanging nine tired mounts for eight fresh ones at Pico's San Luis Obispo home. He made the journey, JCF said, to warn Kearny of a possible new insurrection in the south and to determine whether the general would honor the fiscal commitments he had made as governor under Stockton's appointment (CT. MARTIAL, 422). Kearny testified that he had no recollection of JCF's asking that he assume the government's responsibilities. JCF was not pleased with the interview nor with the presence of Mason as a witness but, upon reflection, finally indicated that he would obey Kearny as his superior officer because, as he later stated in his own defense, he believed there was on foot a design to depose him "by force and violence" from the governorship of California (CT. MARTIAL, 106–7, 422–23). During the interview JCF also offered to resign his commission, which Kearny refused, and on that afternoon—20 March—the explorer began the ride back to Los Angeles. The

Californian, 27 March 1847, printed some of the details of the epic ride; after JCF's court-martial began, the *National Intelligencer,* 22 Nov. 1847, gave an account to its readers, acknowledging that the details provided by Dodson had been revised by JCF.

167. Stephen Watts Kearny to Frémont

Head Qrs. 10th Mil. Dept.
Monterey, Califa. March 28. 1847.

Sir

This will be handed to you by Col. Mason, 1st Dragoons, who goes to the Southern Military District, clothed by me with full authority to give such orders and instructions upon all matters both civil and military in that section of country, as he may deem proper and necessary.[1] Any instructions he may give to you, will be considered as coming from myself.

I deem it proper to suggest to you, that should there be at the Pueblo any unsettled accounts or demands against the Government, incurred by your orders or approval, which you may not have already authenticated and completed for the action of the Disbursing Officers, that you at once do so, as it may be necessary for you to proceed from here to Washington—and should there be any of the Party which accompanied you from Missouri still with you and under pay from the Topographical Department, you will cause them to come to this place, that they may be returned home and discharged and be of no further expense to the U. States, unless they prefer being discharged at once in this country.

In 12 days after you have embarked the Volunteers at San Pedro, I desire to see you in this place. Very respectfully Your Ob. Servt.

(Signed) S. W. Kearny
Brig. Genl. & Gov. of Califa.

Lieut. Col. J. C. Frémont
Regt. of Mounted Riflemen
Commdg. Battn. Califa. Vols.

Copy of enclosure B in Kearny to R. Jones, 3 May 1847 (DNA-94, LR, K-202 1847, f/w K-209 1846). Endorsed.

1. Mason sailed on 28 March and reached Los Angeles early in April (see Doc. No. 168).

168. Richard B. Mason to Frémont

PUEBLO DE LOS ANGELES
April 5th. 1847

SIR:

I have just arrived at this place and am at the house of Mr. Pryor,[1] where I request the pleasure of seeing you this evening.[2] Very Respectfully Yr. Obt. Servt.

(Signed) R. B. MASON
Col. 1st Dragoons

Copy of enclosure in R. B. Mason to H. S. Turner, 10 April 1847, which is in turn enclosure D in Kearny to R. Jones, 3 May 1847 (DNA-94, LR, K-202 1847, f/w K-209 1846). Endorsed: "Recd. April 22d. 1847."

1. The home of Nathaniel M. Pryor, a Kentucky silversmith and clock-maker, was south of the Plaza between First and Commercial streets. Pryor had come to California in 1828 and operated a vineyard.

2. The interviews between Mason and JCF were conducted in the presence of Cooke. On 6 April Mason and JCF rode out to the Mission San Gabriel to see the California Battalion. The troops were paraded, and Mason reported to Kearny that none were willing to continue in the service under the laws of May and June 1846; furthermore, the soldiers claimed a right to be discharged at Los Angeles (Mason to Turner, 10 April 1847, DNA-94, K-202 1847, enclosure D in Kearny to R. Jones, 3 May 1847, f/w K-209 1846).

169. Frémont to Richard B. Mason

ANGELES April 7th 1847

SIR:

Agreeably to your directions[1] I enclose the names of those men belonging to the Cal. Battalion, whose term of service is unexpired. You will find appended a note from the Adjutant relative to the terms on which they enlisted. The refusal of the Volunteers to reenlist or to be mustered into service, rendering it impossible to comply with the orders of General Kearny, it would perhaps be advisable that I rcccive from yourself an order relative to my further proceedings.

I enclose a memorandum of what I supposed yesterday to be your desire in the circumstances, and which according to the terms of the contract with me will be the readiest method of closing their connections with the U. States. Very Respectfully Your Obt. Servt.

(Signed) J. C. FREMONT
Lt. Col. U. S. Army

To
Col. R. B. Mason
1st Dragoons, U.S. Army

[*Enclosure*][2]

Benjamin Wrighter	Co. A.	Feby. 1st		. . . Compy. A. Artillery	
Luther Perkins	" "	" 15		. . . V. Weaver	Jan 27th
William Belly [Belty]	" B	Jany. 28		. . . H. Sanders [Saunders]	" "
C. H. Smith	" E	Feb. 1st		. . . D. H. [S.] Carriger	" "
L. D. Vincenhaler [Lorenzo D. Vinsonhaler]	" "	"	"	. . . B. E. Kellog	" "
D. L. Lytton [D. S. Litten]	" "	"	"	. . . F. Giggsby [Grigsby]	" "
John Gard	" "	"	"	P. Raymond	" "
Charles Gard	" "	"	"	. . . W. McDonnel	" "
B. A. Reed[3]	" "	"	"	. . . J. Greenwood	" "
Jacob Bonsell	" "	"	"	. . . A. J. Loper	" "
Hiram Brock	" "	"	"	. . . D. Harsh	" "
James Reese [Rees]	" "	"	"	. . . S. Carriger	" "
J. W. Johnson	" "	"	"	. . . W. Bennett	" "
Jos. O. Donne [Joseph O'Donnel]	" "	"	"	. . . G. Carr	" "
J. D. Spitler	" "	"	"	. . . I. Davis	" "
J. M. Roberts	" "	"	"	. . . B. [T.?] Painter	" "
				Wm. Wood	" "
				J. H. Kellogg[3]	" "

Agreeably to your Order I enclose a list of names of men belonging to the Cal. Battalion whose terms are unexpired. These men were reenlisted with the understanding that when their services were no longer thought necessary by your self they should be discharged and permitted to return to their homes. Very Respectfully Your Obt. Servt.

(Signed) WM. N. LOKER
Adj. Cal. Battl.

Lt. Col. Frémont
Comdg. Cal. Battn.
Angeles, April 7th 1847

Will Col. Mason give an order to Lt. Col. Frémont to discharge the California Battalion on such terms as his contract with the men calls for—that of $25 per month—and also to provide transportation for such as may require it, from the place of discharge to the place of Enlistment.

Copy of enclosure in R. B. Mason to H. S. Turner, 10 April 1847, which is a part of enclosure D in Kearny to R. Jones, 3 May 1847 (DNA-94, LR, K-202 1847, f/w K-209 1846).

1. Probably an allusion to Mason's letter of 6 April 1847, not found, referred to again in Mason to Frémont, 9 April 1847, Doc. No. 179; it is possible that Mason's directions were given orally.

2. As transcription of the document was difficult, what appear to be the correct names or initials are given in brackets. Unless specifically noted, all names are listed in one of three sources: ROGERS [3]; PIONEER REGISTER; "Receipt Roll" of Companies A, B, C, D, E, and F, California Battalion, item 137, and Appendix D of the SNYDER CALENDAR.

3. B. A. Reed and J. H. Kellogg are not listed in any of the above sources.

170. Richard B. Mason to Frémont

PUEBLO DE LOS ANGELES
April 7. 1847

SIR,

The term of service of the Battalion of California Volunteers (with a few individual exceptions) having already expired, and as they now claim to be discharged from the service at their present position, on the ground, as well as on the pledge which, you yesterday informed me, was made to them by yourself, at the time of raising the Corps, to induce them to enter the service: Viz "that they should be discharged when the country was quiet at any time & place they should demand it, even though the term of service for which they were engaged might not have expired." That this promise was made to them under the circumstances it was, may be kept in good faith, you are relieved from so much of the execution of Department Orders No. 2 of the 1st March 1847, as requires you to march them to Yerba Buena. You will therefore be pleased to "muster them out of service" *at once* at their present Cantonement.

The Naval Officers now serving with your Battalion, you will immediately relieve from duty, and order them to repair to Monterey and report to Commodore Biddle.

I had just written the foregoing when I received your letter of today & its enclosures. The Volunteers having claimed to be discharged at their present post, I cannot order any transportation to be furnished in kind to them from the place of discharge to the place of Enlistment, further than to say that the Sloop of war, Warren, Capt. Hull, now at San Pedro, will take to Yerba Buena as many as one hundred—the ship cannot accommodate a greater number. I have no instructions to give touching your contract with the men so far as it relates to their pay. That the Warren may not be unnecessarily detained at her present anchorage which is an exposed one, those who go in her must be embarked on Friday next, & I desire that you conduct them to the ship yourself, taking care to have properly noted on the rolls those who take passage in her. Horses & Horse Equipage will be furnished the Topographical party, that the General requires you to take to Monterey, from those now in possession of your Battalion. All other Public property in the possession of your Corps or any individual thereof, beyond what may be necessary to mount the Topographical party, you will cause to be turned over to Lt. Davidson,[1] 1st Dragoons for which he will give the proper receipts. Any further answer to your communication has been anticipated in that part of this letter written before its reception. Very Respectfully Your Obt. Servt.

(Signed) R. B. Mason
Col. 1st Dragoons

Lt. Col. J. C. Frémont
U. S. Army Comdg. Cal. Volunteers

Copy of enclosure in R. B. Mason to H. S. Turner, 10 April 1847, which is a part of enclosure D in Kearny to R. Jones, 3 May 1847 (DNA-94, LR, K-202 1847, f/w K-209 1846).

1. Lieut. John Wynn Davidson (d. 1881), later brevet brigadier general, had been in charge of the two howitzers which Kearny had brought over mountain and desert from Santa Fe to California. Soon after Mason wrote this letter, Davidson became acting assistant quartermaster at Los Angeles.

171. Frémont to Richard B. Mason

ANGELES, April 8th 1847

SIR:

Immediately on the receipt of your letter of yesterday, I sent the Adjutant to San Gabriel with your permission for passage of the Troops on board the Warren, but up to this time have received no reply. I will send an officer to you with the first intelligence received from the Garrison. Very Respectfully, Your Obt. Servt.

(Signed) J. C. FRÉMONT
Lt Col Rifm.

Col. R. B. Mason
1st Dragoons, Angeles

Copy of enclosure in R. B. Mason to H. S. Turner, 10 April 1847, which is a part of enclosure D in Kearny to R. Jones, 3 May 1847 (DNA-94, LR, K-202 1847, f/w K-209 1846).

172. Frémont to Richard B. Mason

ANGELES, April 8th. 1847

SIR:

The insecurity will render it very dangerous for the men now being discharged here to travel unarmed. I therefore respectfully request that they may be allowed to retain their Arms, myself becoming responsible for the safe delivery of these at Monterey or Yerba

Buena. I am informed by the Paymaster that the accounts of the men will not be ready in time for any considerable number of them to embark in the Warren. Very Respectfully Your Obdt. Servt.

(Signed) J. C. Frémont
Lt. Col Rifl. Regt.

Col. R. B. Mason
U.S. Dragoons
Angeles

Copy of enclosure in R. B. Mason to H. S. Turner, 10 April 1847, which is a part of enclosure D in Kearny to R. Jones, 3 May 1847 (DNA-94, LR, K-202 1847, f/w K-209 1846).

173. Richard B. Mason to Frémont

ANGELES, April 8th 1847

SIR:

The Company of Volunteers that have lately been discharged at San Diego had some horses, and perhaps some other public property in their charge. Those horses, I learn, are now in the possession of Ex Lt. Aguillo[1] who refuses to give them up to Capt. Hunter[2] of the Mormon Battalion Commanding that post. Be pleased to inform me whether you have at any time, given any instructions touching, the detention of this public property. I am very Respectfully Your Obdt. Servt.

(Signed) R. B. MASON
Col. 1st Drags.

Lt. Col. J. C. Frémont
U. S. Army, Comdg. Cal. Volunteers

Copy of enclosure in R. B. Mason to H. S. Turner, 10 April 1847, which is a part of enclosure D in Kearny to R. Jones, 3 May 1847 (DNA-94, LR, K-202 1847, f/w K-209 1846).
1. A reference to former captain Santiago E. Argüello (see Doc. No. 143).
2. A native of Kentucky, Jesse D. Hunter (1804–77), commanding Company B of the Mormon Battalion, had been placed in charge of the San Diego garrison by Cooke. After the Mormons were discharged, Hunter remained in California and on two occasions acted as U.S. Indian agent (TYLER, 120, 271, 281; PIONEER REGISTER).

174. Richard B. Mason to Frémont

PUEBLO DE LOS ANGELES
April 8th 1847

SIR:

I am this moment in the receipt of your letter of this date. Your battalion was ordered to Yerba Buena in their *armed* and organized capacity, there to be discharged, & transportation both by land and water was at hand for their accommodation. *The order has not been obeyed,* but their discharge claimed at their present post, it has been accorded to them, and I am not at liberty to leave in their hands any of the public property, nor am I authorized to detain the Warren, her presence being elsewhere required, for their accommodation now that they have ceased to be soldiers.

Had orders been obeyed no "insecurity" would have been felt or "danger" apprehended, for the want of arms. Your Battalion have made their election and must abide their choice. It has been nearly *one* month since you received orders relative to the discharge of your battalion, and surely, the accounts of the men ought to have been prepared in that time. Very Respectfully Your Obdt. Servt.

(Signed) R. B. MASON
Col. 1st Dragoons

Lt. Col. J. C. Frémont
Mtd. Riflemen, Comadg. Cal.
Volunteers

Copy of enclosure in R. B. Mason to H. S. Turner, 10 April 1847, which is a part of enclosure D in Kearny to R. Jones, 3 May 1847 (DNA-94, LR, K-202 1847, f/w K-209 1846).

175. Frémont to Richard B. Mason

ANGELES, April 8. 1847

SIR:

I have the honor to be in the receipt of your communication requiring me to put you in possession of Orders which I have previously given to Capt. Arguillo [Argüello], lately of the Californian Battalion.

It will in my judgement be a sufficient explanation of the course pursued by Captain Arguillo to state, that in view of his own accountability he is entirely justified in refusing to deliver to any other order than my own, any property which may have been placed by me in his custody and safe keeping. I am very Respectfully Your Obt. Servt.

(Signed) J. C. FRÉMONT
Lt. Col. Rifle Regt.

Col. R. B. Mason
U. S. Dragoons, Angeles

Copy of enclosure in R. B. Mason to H. S. Turner, 10 April 1847, which is a part of enclosure D in Kearny to R. Jones, 3 May 1847 (DNA-94, LR, K-202 1847, f/w K-209 1846).

176. Richard B. Mason to Frémont

PUEBLO DE LOS ANGELES
April 8th 1847

SIR,

Your third note of this date is received, in reply to mine of this morning which you have misconstrued. I merely required to know whether you had given any instructions touching the detention of certain public property; and did not as you suppose call on you to to put me in possession of the Orders, if indeed any had been given: but I now direct that you furnish me with a full copy of any order that you have given for the detention and refusal to be turned over to any one, of the property alluded to in my first letter of today. I am Respectfully Yr. Obdt. Servt.

(Signed) R. B. MASON
Col. 1st Dragoons

Lt. Col. J. C. Frémont
Mounted Riflemen
Comdg. Cal. Vols.

Copy of enclosure in R. B. Mason to H. S. Turner, 10 April 1847, which is a part of enclosure D in Kearny to R. Jones, 3 May 1847 (DNA-94, LR, K-202 1847, f/w K-209 1846).

177. Frémont to Richard B. Mason

CIUDAD DE LOS ANGELES
April 9th. 1847

SIR:

I am in receipt of your order of the 9th [8th] inst. requiring me to furnish to you a full copy of any order relative to the detention of public property, addressed by me to Capt. Arguillo [Argüello] of the California Battalion.

In reply I have the honor to inform you that as the commandant of the California Battalion, no such order has been addressed by me to Capt. Arguillo. Very Respectfully Yr. Obdt. Servt.

(Signed) J. C. FRÉMONT
Lt. Col. Rifle Regt.

Col. R. B. Mason
1st Dragoons

Copy of enclosure in R. B. Mason to H. S. Turner, 10 April 1847, which is a part of enclosure D in Kearny to R. Jones, 3 May 1847 (DNA-94, LR, K-202 1847, f/w K-209 1846).

178. Richard B. Mason to Frémont

ANGELES, April 9th. 1847

SIR:

If you desire it you can retain any of the public Arms for the use of the Topographical party whilst on their march to Monterey. Be pleased to let me know the number of the *original party* that still remain, as such, under pay, and that will accompany you to Monterey, what number of Animals will be required for their march.

I have not yet received the list of horses & horse equipage that I asked you for on the 6th inst.;[1] be pleased to let me have it at your earliest convenience. I am Respectfully Your Obdt. Servt.

(Signed) R. B. MASON
Col. 1st Dragoons

Lt. Col. J. C. Frémont
Mounted Riflemen

Copy of enclosure in R. B. Mason to H. S. Turner, 10 April 1847, which is a part of enclosure D in Kearny to R. Jones, 3 May 1847 (DNA-94, LR, K-202 1847, f/w K-209 1846).
1. This 6 April 1847 letter has not been found, and, as noted earlier, Mason's request of 6 April may have been a verbal one. He certainly did not include it among the copies of his correspondence with JCF which he forwarded to Henry S. Turner.

179. Frémont to Richard B. Mason

CIUDAD DE LOS ANGELES
April 9th 1847

SIR,

I am in receipt of your letter of this date making of me several interrogations relative to a party of men under my command during a Geographical Exploration, under the direction of the War Department. I have the honor to reply to your interrogations in order as follows, viz: The number of the party properly belonging to that expedition, and now under my Command, is twenty four, so nearly as I can recollect, the list not being here at hand.

The number of Animals required for the march of that party, including transportation of the instruments and property belonging to the expedition, will be about one hundred and twenty.

Agreeably to the orders of General S. W. Kearny requiring me to march my Exploring party to Monterey, I had already properly equipped them for the journey.

In regard to the Statement which is referred to as having been required on the 6th inst. I have to reply that I did not myself know the number of horses or quantity of equipage at this place in the possession of the Quartermaster, the number & quantity frequently varying according to the necessities of the service here.

Immediately on the receipt of your instructions I directed this officer to transfer the property to Lt. Davidson as early as could be done without confusion, or neglect to his accountability, & to furnish you with a list of the same. He informs me that he has appointed this afternoon for the transfer.[1] I am very Respectfully Your Obdt. Servt.

(Signed) J. C. Frémont
Lt. Col. Rifle Regt.
Commanding Exploring Expedition to Oregon & California

Col. R. B. Mason
1st Dragoons

Copy of enclosure in R. B. Mason to H. S. Turner, 10 April 1847, which is a part of enclosure D in Kearny to R. Jones, 3 May 1847 (DNA-94, LR, K-202 1847, f/w K-209 1846).

1. The actual transfer of property took place on 11 April. The following list, which may be found as enclosure E-4 in Kearny to R. Jones, 3 May 1847, indicates how meager and poor it was:

Invoice of public property this day turned over by Mr. J. R. Snyder Qr. M. Califa Battalion to Lieut. J. W. Davidson, 1 Drgs., a. a. Qr. M., U.S. A. viz:

30 Thirty horses—in bad condition
2 Two mules—in bad condition
50 Fifty Saddle trees—Serviceable
22 Twenty-two Saddle trees—unserviceable
70 Seventy wooden Stirrups
8 right Iron stirrups
2 Two Pack Saddle trees—Serviceable
1 One " " " Unserviceable
3 Three Spurs
3 Three Bridle-bits—unserviceable
3 Three tents—serviceable
5 Five " unserviceable
20 Twenty bars of iron, weighing each 14 lbs.
14 Fourteen tent poles
15 Fifteen Singletrees
12 Twelve Shovels
3 Three Pick Axes
13 Thirteen pieces of Canvass—whole 90 yds.

(Signed) J. R. Snyder
Q. M. Califa. Bat.

Angeles
April 11. 1847
(Copy)
(Sd.) J. W. Davidson
Lieut. Drags. a. a. q. m.

180. Robert F. Stockton to Archibald H. Gillespie

Private

U. S. Frigate Congress
Harbor of San Diego
April 10th 1847

Dear Sir:

In your letter of the 5th by Mr. Bandini, you say that you desire to see me and that if I remain here beyond the 10th, you will come on for that purpose.

I send this by Flacco (who has just arrived, 2 o'clock P.M.) to say that I will remain here until the morning of the 17th that you may have the opportunity to see me before I go North. I expect to go home soon myself and therefore you had better not fail to be here by the 16th and as much sooner as you can.

Ask Colonel Fremont for a copy of the Commission as Governor which I gave him and to endorse on it the date he received it.

Commodore Biddle[1] has treated me with great respect and kindness. He has sent to me the last orders from the Secretary, which were addressed to me, but which Commodore Shubrick did not see fit to send. They are very gratifying to me, besides which I have a private letter from the Secretary which is all that I could desire it to be.

It would have been better for you perhaps if you had seen me before, and you cannot now see me too soon. You may rely upon it that I will bring this matter out triumphantly if I am not baulked by my own friends.

I have taken my gloves off and they will find Commodore Stockton the same man he was twenty years ago, and a hard customer at any thing they may drive him to. I mean to make clean work of it. I have begun by sending an article to the Californian in answer to an Editorial,[2] which no doubt you saw.[3]

But you may rely upon it that sudden fits and starts wont answer. Our course must be well considered, firm and determined. I say therefore you *had better see me as soon as possible*.

You will consider this letter *strictly confidential,* and do not *intimate to any one* my views and intentions. I do not want *any one else* to know my purposes. From my letters, I judge that Commodore

Sloat has done no good at home for you or Fremont, but you shall know all when you see me. Very Sincerely & Truly Yours,

R. F. STOCKTON

Major A. H. Gillespie

LS (CLU—Gillespie Papers). Endorsed.

1. Commodore James Biddle (1783–1848) arrived at Monterey from Callao just as Henry S. Turner started south early in March with Kearny's department orders no. 2. He replaced Shubrick as naval commander of the Pacific Squadron.

2. Referring to American preparations for the move on Los Angeles, an editorial in the *Californian*, 13 Feb. 1847, had stated, "Commodore Stockton announced to the officers that the *whole expedition* was placed under the command of General Kearny, himself holding his station as commander-in-chief of California, and Gen. Kearny did command the *whole expedition."*

3. Stockton's long article dealing with the question of supremacy in California between him and Kearny was not printed in the *Californian* until 17 July 1847. The delay was due not only to the belief of one of the editors that the controversy was a "personal difficulty" between the two men and might be much better settled in the United States, but also to his fruitless attempts, by letter and personal interview, to learn from Kearny "the facts" which occurred at San Diego before the march of the American forces on Los Angeles. Kearny intimated that if Robert B. Semple published Stockton's letter and its accompanying vouchers, he would hold him accountable. The editor judiciously waited until Kearny left California and then published the article. It began with a letter from Stockton dated 10 March 1847 from aboard the *Congress* in San Diego harbor. It branded as untrue the editorial statement of 13 Feb. 1847 that the *whole expedition* had been under the command of Kearny. Stockton wrote, "On the request of General Kearny, and with the consent of Lieut. Rowan (to whom, with the consent of Lieut. Minor, who had previously held it, I had given the command only the night before), I appointed General Kearny to command the troops, and so announced it; at the same time stated distinctly that I still retained my own position as commander-in-chief; the word California did not pass my lips upon that occasion." Stockton's letter was followed by one from purser William Speiden, 16 March 1847, likewise contradicting the editorial and avowing himself to be the author of a letter which had appeared in the *Californian* on 28 Jan. 1847. The first Speiden letter had given an account of the march to Los Angeles and treated Stockton as commander-in-chief. Next followed the statements of Speiden and three other naval officers— Stephen C. Rowan, George Minor, and J. Zeilin—attesting that Kearny had been second in command to Stockton. The article ended with a statement by fourteen naval officers, some commissioned, some not, attesting to the truth of Speiden's January account of the march to Los Angeles and the chain of command. Stephen C. Rowan, who was later to hedge, probably because of the influence of Lieut. William Radford, Kearny's brother-in-law, specifically stated, "I believe the written account [Speiden's] of our march to be circumstantially correct" (*Californian*, 28 Jan., 13 Feb., 26 June, 17 July 1847; *National Intelligencer*, 4 Feb. 1848).

181. Richard B. Mason to Frémont

Sir,

Be pleased to furnish me with a list of such civil appointments as you have made in this territory, setting forth the names of the individuals appointed, to what office & when.

I would prefer seeing myself as I told you in conversation today such of the official records as you have, civil & military, that I may judge whether they contain any information that may be useful to me, or influence me in the discharge of any of those duties with which Genl. Kearny, the Govnr. of the Territory, has charged me. I therefore desire that you submit the whole of them, civil & military, to me early in the day tomorrow as I am making efforts to leave here the next day for Monterey. I am very Respectfully Your Obdt. &c.

(Signed) R. B. Mason
Col. 1 Dragns.

Lt. Col. J. C. Fremont
Mtd. Riflemen

Copy of enclosure in R. B. Mason to Kearny, 26 April 1847, which is enclosure E-2 in Kearny to R. Jones, 3 May 1847 (DNA-94, LR, K-202 1847, f/w K-209 1846).

182. Frémont to Richard B. Mason

Ciudad de los Angeles
April 13th. 1847

Sir

I have the honor to be in receipt of your communication of last Evening requiring from me a list of civil appointments made by me in this territory and farther demanding to be put in possession of such official records as I may have, civil or military.

In compliance with your order I send by the hands of the former or late adjutant of the Cala. Battalion, Mr. W. N. Loker the few papers pertaining to that Battalion which I can at present find. These I request to be returned to me.

Such brief record of my official acts as Govnr. of the territory that were preserved by me has been *forwarded to the United States.*[1]

My position here having been denounced as usurpation by General Kearny I could not anticipate from him any call for these papers and in requiring [?] myself from the general government means & authority to comply with my engagement, it became necessary that these and their objects should be thoroughly made known.

The permanent civil appointments made by me are two, viz: Don Santiago Argüello to be collector of the customs for the port of San Diego.

Don Pedro Carrillo to be collector for the customs for the Port of Santa Barbara. I am very respectfully Your obdt. Servt.

(Signed) J. C. FRÉMONT
Lt. Col. Rifle Regt.

Col. R. B. Mason
1st Dragoons

Copy of enclosure in R. B. Mason to Kearny, 26 April 1847, which is enclosure E-3 in Kearny to R. Jones, 3 May 1847 (DNA-94, LR, K-202 1847, f/w K-209 1846).

1. Presumably these papers were carried east by William H. Russell, JCF's former secretary of state, who left California about 23 March (CT. MARTIAL, 260).

183. Frémont to Richard B. Mason

CIUDAD DE LOS ANGELES, April 14, 1847

SIR:

I have the honor to request through my friend, Major P. B. Reading, who will hand you this note, that you apologize for the injurious language applied to me this day. Very Respectfully, your obedient servant,

J. C. FREMONT
Lieut. Col. Mounted Riflemen

Col. R. B. Mason
Col. Dragoons, Ciudad de los Angeles

Printed in BIGELOW, 205–6. Also in Washington *Daily Union,* 3 Sept. 1848, in Benton's speech opposing the nomination of Kearny for the brevet of major general, as were the other letters dealing with the altercation between JCF and Mason. Benton states that Mason's determination to have JCF produce the horses, which had been sent to graze in the country in preparation for his contemplated expedition to General Scott in Mexico, was responsible for the challenge to a duel. Mason sent twice for the former governor to come to "the tavern" to answer questions about the horses. JCF resented Mason's manner of questioning and used language which in turn caused Mason to reply, "None of your insolence, or I will put you in irons."

184. Richard B. Mason to Frémont

ANGELES, April 14, 1847

SIR:

I have just received your note of this evening, and can only repeat in writing, what I stated to you verbally, when we parted, viz: "I thought you intended to be so. You best knew whether you did or did not." Your not disavowing it, left me to infer that I was not mistaken; with that impression upon my mind, I can say nothing more until it be removed. I am, respectfully, your obedient servant.

R. B. MASON

Lieut. Col. J. C. Fremont
Mounted Riflemen

Printed in BIGELOW, 206.

185. Frémont to Richard B. Mason

CIUDAD DE LOS ANGELES, April 14, 1847

SIR:

An apology having been declined, Major Reading will arrange the preliminaries for a meeting, requiring personal satisfaction.[1] Very respectfully, your obedient servant,

J. C. FREMONT
Lieut. Col. Mounted Riflemen

Col. R. B. Mason
First Dragoons, Ciudad de los Angeles

Printed in BIGELOW, 206.

1. Jacob W. Harlan recorded many years later that he had "heard persons tell queer yarns about the ceremonies, and scrapings, and bowings" which passed between Mason and Pierson B. Reading when the latter carried the challenge to a duel. Mason verbally accepted and selected double-barreled shotguns, a firearm for the use of which he was famous. After the weapons had been chosen, Reading learned that JCF could not have hit "the side of a hay-stack" (HARLAN, 85–86).

One naval officer opined that Mason had "played bluff" and would suffer. "He provoked the quarrel by giving way to his temper & should have fought like a Gentleman & not like a Western bully or Texas cutthroat" (MC LANE, 113).

186. Richard B. Mason to Frémont

ANGELES, April 15, 1847

SIR:

With a view of the adjustment of my *private affairs*, it is necessary that I return to Monterey, before I afford you the meeting you desire. We shall probably reach there within a few days of each other, I will then, as soon as circumstances permit, arrange the necessary preliminaries for the meeting. I am respectfully your obedient servant,

R. B. MASON

Lieut. Col. Fremont
Mounted Riflemen

Printed in BIGELOW, 207.

187. Frémont to Richard B. Mason

CIUDAD DE LOS ANGELES, April 15, 1847

SIR:

I am in receipt of your letter of this date, and in reply have the honor to state that I will hold myself in readiness for a meeting at Monterey, at such time as you may designate. I am, very respectfully, your obedient servant,

J. C. FREMONT
Lieut. Col. Mounted Riflemen

Col. R. B. Mason
First Dragoons, Ciudad de los Angeles

Printed in BIGELOW, 207.

188. Robert F. Stockton to Archibald H. Gillespie

Confidential

[SAN DIEGO]
[April 1847]

MY DEAR SIR:

I have called Flacco back to say to you that if you are on sufficiently good terms and *other circumstances justify it* you had better try to make up the quarrel between Fremont & Mason and suggest to Mason at all events to wait at the Angeles until he can see me. It may be too late when they get to Monterey. Yours,

R. F. STOCKTON

ALS, RC (CLU—Gillespie Papers). Addressed. Endorsed: "Commod. Stockton San Diego Mar 1847. To make up the quarrel between Mason & Fremont." Gillespie has obviously made a dating error in the endorsement. Stockton must have written the letter sometime between 17 and 21 April.

189. Robert F. Stockton to Archibald H. Gillespie

Confidential

U. S. Frigate Congress
Harbor of San Diego
April 23rd. 1847

My Dear Sir:

I have your letter by Flacco, 9 A. M. Nothing has occurred here since my last. I hope you sent on my Despatches without delay. I have written to Fremont to say that I hope to leave San Pedro for Monterey on 1st May, immediately after the arrival of my "Courier" from Monterey. When you come down to San Pedro, get Johnson & Alexander to sign that letter.[1] I have not of course said to Fremont anything about your letter, as he did not allude to the matter in his letter[2] to me.

We must stand by him, let what may come—whether Bondage or Stripes. Very truly yours,

R. F. Stockton

P. S. Flacco says he can go to Monterey and *back to San Pedro* by *tomorrow week,* which will be 1st May. If you have not sent my despatches on before he arrives, please to send him with them without delay. I give him Fifty Dollars.

Major A. H. Gillespie

ALS (CLU—Gillespie Papers). Endorsed: "Commo. Stockton, San Diego, April 23d. 1847 asking more favors!"
1. Johnson and Alexander have not been identified, and the contents of the letter are unknown.
2. Not found.

190. Stephen Watts Kearny to Frémont

Head Qrs., 10th Mil. Dept.
Monterey, Califa. May 4, 1847

Sir:

It has been reported here, by some of the Discharged Men of the Battalion of California volunteers, just arrived from the Pueblo de los Angeles, that a challenge has passed between Col. Mason, of the 1st Dragoons, and yourself, the meeting to take place at or near Monterey.

As I am about leaving here for the South,[1] in consequence of rumors of an excitement among the People in that District of country, it becomes my duty to inform you that the good of the Public Service, the necessity of preserving tranquillity in California, imperiously require, that the meeting above referred to should not take place at this time, and in this country, and you are hereby officially directed by me to proceed no further in this matter.

A similar communication has been addressed to Colonel Mason. Very respectfully, Your Ob. Servt.

(Signed) S. W. KEARNY
Brigadier General

Lieutenant Colonel Fremont,
Regiment Mounted Rifles, Monterey.

N.B.   A letter to same purport, and of same date, addressed to Col. Mason.

Copy of enclosure in Kearny to R. Jones, 21 Jan. 1848 (DNA-94, LR, K-12 1848); also in BIGELOW, 208–9. The attention of the War Department was brought to this order in Jan. 1848 by Benton, JCF's counsel, who requested that Kearny be required to communicate it to that department (Benton to Adjutant General, 8 Jan. 1848, DNA-94, LR, F-8 1848; Benton to Adjutant General, 15 Jan. 1848, enclosed in Kearny to Adjutant General, 21 Jan. 1848, DNA-94, LR, K-12 1848). Benton alleged that this order of Kearny's and James Biddle's letter to Mason (enclosure in Mason to Frémont, 19 May 1847, Doc. No. 191) were attempts to extricate Mason from the affair. Kearny's act of postponing the duel by this order was a strange proceeding, since his duty by military regulations was to arrest both parties.

1. Kearny arrived in Los Angeles on 9 May. He was accompanied by Col. Jonathan D. Stevenson, who commanded the New York Volunteers, which was replacing the Mormon Battalion as the garrison for the city.

191. Richard B. Mason to Frémont

MONTEREY, May 19, 1847

SIR:

The affair between us has been made public here by the arrival, about the 4th instant, of some of the discharged men of the late battalion of California volunteers from Los Angeles.

I did not expect that this affair would have gained publicity until it had finally been terminated, but it has turned out otherwise. The result is, it has come to the knowledge of the general, and you doubtless have received, as well as myself, a communication from him upon the subject.[1] This unforeseen and unexpected circumstance, together with reasons which you will find in the copy of a letter on the next page, dated on the 4th of the present month, renders it proper that the meeting should be postponed to some future time and place.

I am inclined to believe that, under the existing state of things, you will at once see the propriety of this course. I am, respectfully, Your obedient servant,

R. B. MASON

Lieut. Col. Fremont

[*Enclosure*]

James Biddle to Richard B. Mason

U. S. Ship Columbus
MONTEREY, May 4th, 1847

MY DEAR COLONEL:

A party of Californian volunteers, recently under Lieut. Col. Fremont, have just arrived on their way to the north. They state publicly that at Puebla a challenge had passed between yourself and Lieut. Col. Fremont, and that on the arrival of the latter here, a hostile meeting would take place. I learn that this statement is generally credited on shore. As your personal friend, and the friend of your public character, this statement has given me great pain. You cannot but be sensible that, in the present condition of things in California, personal collisions between the officers must be highly injurious to the public interest. You cannot but know that it is the duty of all of us to suppress for the moment every angry feeling of a personal nature, and to give ourselves zealously, cordially, and exclusively to the public service. Permit me to appeal to your patriotism, and to your sense of public duty, and upon these grounds to entreat that any contemplated hostile meeting may be postponed. Elsewhere, and at another time, it may not be improper, but here, in the present distracted state of affairs, it could have no other result than to injure the public, and to injure your military reputation. I remain, very truly Your friend, &c.,

JAMES BIDDLE[2]

Col. Mason, U. S. Army, Monterey

Printed in BIGELOW, 209.

1. JCF had left Los Angeles on 13 May (Kearny to R. Jones, 13 May 1847, no. 11, DNA-94, LR, K-238 1847) and was now in Monterey. BIGELOW, 208, maintains that JCF called at Mason's quarters to let the future governor of California know of his presence and availability for the duel, and that Kearny's order of 4 May (Doc. No. 190) was delivered to him afterward. But apparently JCF already knew that Kearny had forbidden the duel from a previous conversation with him in Los Angeles.

2. JCF's father-in-law resented Biddle's interference in the controversy. In his speech opposing the nomination of Kearny for the brevet of major general, Benton said, "As for Commodore Biddle, there were reasons why he should not have interfered at all, where a member of my family was concerned, except by taking a position on the highest pinnacle of honor, impartiality, and humanity. I had struck the house of Biddle in striking the Bank of the United States; but never after it was down. I do not kick the dead lion. I made war upon him in his high and palmy state: since his fall, no one has ever heard me name him. I say nothing of him, his family, or the bank. The same reserve should have prevented Commodore Biddle from interfering to the prejudice of my son-in-law on the far distant coast of the Pacific" (Washington *Daily Union*, 3 Sept. 1848).

192. Frémont to Abel Stearns

Camp on the Salinas river near Monterey
May 19, 1847

MY DEAR SIR,

I send you this note by Jacob, whom business requires me to send to your city. I regret that I have not my affairs sufficiently arranged to write you on matters of business by so certain a conveyance, but I will endeavor to find another equally so before I leave. I was disappointed not to see you before but hope that no unpleasant accident detained you at the rancho. On some subjects of general importance to the country I should have been [glad] to have had your views and did wrong to postpone informing myself to so late an hour. I[t] might have been useful at home. When you reply to this which I trust you will not fail to do by Jacob I will thank you to mention any one particular thing or measure which may occur to you as useful here at this time.

Nothing of interest is going on here, so far as is known to me. Every thing and every body appear quiet, the only busy people are the horse thieves. I am told that one of the rancheros sent in word that they had heard of a new governor and would like to see some of his men. Even the newspaper formerly published here has been removed to Yerba Buena.[1] Mr. Larkin is there at present and I suppose will soon locate himself there.[2]

I have commenced my preparations for the homeward march and in about a week shall be ready to start.

Commodore Biddle goes home in the Columbus immediately after the departure of our party. Commodore Shubrick will remain in command. He had been sent to capture Guaymas, Mazatlan and Acapulco, and the Preble has been sent to bring him back. Please present my remembrances to the family. I am with much respect & regard Your Obedt. Servt.,

J. C. FRÉMONT

ALS, RC (CSmH).
1. A reference to the *Californian*.
2. In 1848 Larkin went to San Francisco permanently.

193. Frémont to Richard B. Mason

MONTEREY, May 22d. 1847

SIR:

I have the honor to acknowledge the receipt, on yesterday, of your note of the 19th instant, accompanied by a copy of a letter from Commodore Biddle to yourself.

The object of your note appears to be to induce me to consent to a further, and indefinite postponement of a meeting. If such be your desire I am willing to comply with it, trusting that you will apprise me of the earliest moment at which the meeting can take place

San Francisco in 1846. From a lithograph in Walter Cotton, *Deck and Port* (New York, 1850). Courtesy of the University of Arizona Library.

consistently with your convenience and sense of propriety. I am most respectfully, Your obedient servant,

John C. Fremont

Col. R. B. Mason, Monterey

Printed in bigelow, 210–11.

194. Abel Stearns to Frémont

Angs. May 23d. 1847

Charles J. Fremont Esqr.
Dear Sir:

By your servant Jacob I rec'd this morning yours of the 19th inst. I regret not to have seen you the morning before you left as I had intended; my delay was caused by some difficulties which took place between the servants and which I had to settle. I arrived in the morning a short time after you left. Have the Publishers of the "Californian" taken fright that they have moved from Monterey to San Franco. or do they wish to pass the warm season in the fog of the latter place?

As you are about to leave this "Western Star" for the more brilliant ones of the east, it is to be supposed you will communicate immediately with the Govt. or heads of department and from your acquired knowledge of the affairs and people of this *not little* important Territory you will use your influence to secure to California what is *most desired* by all good Citizens both native and foreign residents. 1st that this may never be returned to Mexico, 2d. that the Government of the U. S. will as soon as possible establish a permanent territorial govt. with a wise and select council named by the government itself, 3d. as the judiciary department of Califa. is in a bad state or I may say we have none at all, that the govt. of the territory be empowered to appoint all the necessary officers to this most impor[tant] branch of all governments, 4th. and not least, procure to send a number of Catholick Clergymen who understand the Castillian Language, men of liberal principles and good moral Character. Such men would be of much importance both to the govt. and welfare of the people. 5th. Should Califa. ultimately compose a part of the U. S. a govt. armed Steamer would be of importance to play [ply] between this and Panama as probably at present the most prompt means of facilitating the interests and communications of the govt. and people its master. 6th. Should war continue with Mexico some additional force of regular troops should be sent here.

I have thought proper to note the above observations which perhaps might Serve you as a memorandum to remind you a little of the place you are to leave, and its necessities.

You will undoubtedly inform some of your friends (Merchants in the States) that there is a scarcity of goods in Califa. of every description, some well assorted cargoes would return the merchant a sure profit. Dry goods, groceries, hard crockery & Glass ware, furniture, Boots Shoes, Hats &c. all are wanted.

[Unsigned]

Draft, SC (CSmH). Also in HAW.GOOD [1], 90–91. This is a reply to JCF's letter of 19 May 1847.

195. Richard B. Mason to Frémont

MONTEREY, CAL., May 24, 1847

SIR:

I have the honor to acknowledge the receipt of your letter of the 22d instant. I shall certainly promptly inform you when the peculiar official obligations, under which I find myself placed in this country, are so far removed as to enable me to meet you.[1] I am, respectfully, Your obedient servant,

R. B. MASON

Lieutenant-Colonel J. C. Fremont, U.S.A.

Printed in BIGELOW, 211.
1. According to the Frémonts, Mason sent a note in 1850 which informed JCF that if he would come out to St. Louis, he should have the satisfaction which Mason promised him in 1847. The session of Congress in which JCF was a senator was closing, and he was about to depart to California with his family. He ignored the note, and Mason died before the year was over (BIGELOW, 213).

196. Pierson B. Reading to Frémont

MONTEREY, CALIF., May 27, 1847

DEAR SIR:

In reply to your favor of yesterday, I will state that immediately after having delivered your challenge to Colonel Mason, he informed me that he would give you the desired meeting, *and said to me,* in order that there might be as little delay as possible, he would inform me (though informally) that he would select double-barrelled shot-guns as the weapons to be used on the occasion. I replied to him at once that I should lose no time in obtaining such a weapon for Colonel Fremont—that in the morning I should have him provided with a good gun. When I delivered the challenge to Colonel Mason, it was about eight o'clock in the evening, though you received this written acceptance, through his friend Captain [Andrew Jackson] Smith, near noon the following day, in which he proposed that the meeting should take place at Monterey, distant from the Puebla de los Angeles about four [hundred] miles. This gave us considerable surprise, as we expected and were fully prepared to have taken the field that day—forming our opinions from the character of his conversation to me the preceding evening.

Since that period, your correspondence with Colonel Mason contains the history of this affair.

I am, most respectfully, your very obedient servant,

P. B. READING

Lieutenant-Colonel J. C. Fremont, U.S.A.

Printed in BIGELOW, 211–12.

197. 10th Military Department Orders No. 19

Head Qrs. 10th Mil. Dept.
MONTEREY, CALIFORNIA, May 29, 1847

I. General Kearny being under orders to proceed to the U. States, will leave here on the 31st inst. for Washington.

The Command of the 10th Mil. Dept. and consequently the office of Governor of California, will devolve upon Col. R. B. Mason of the 1st Dragoons.

II.   The General will be accompanied to the U. States by Lieut. Col. Fremont, Regt. of Mounted Riflemen, Major Swords Qr. Mr., Capts Cook & Turner 1st Dragoons & Asst. Surgeon Sanderson,[1] Mormon Battalion.

III.   Lieut. Col. Fremont will discharge such men of his Topogl. Party as may desire to continue in California, the remainder with those men who came to this country under Lieut. Emory, Topl. Engineers, will accompany Genl. Kearny to the U. States to be there discharged.

IV.   Lieut. Col. Fremont will turn over to Lieut. Halleck, Engineers, for Lieut Warner Topl. Engineers, the Instruments in his charge belonging to the Topl. Dept. taking receipts for the same.[2]

By order of Brig. Genl. S. W. Kearny

H. S. Turner
Capt. A.A.A. Genl.

DS (DNA-393, 10th Military Department, LR, General Orders 19, May 29, 1847). Endorsed. JCF and some of the men of his old topographical party had appeared at Monterey at an hour fixed by Kearny, to be reviewed and given orders by the general. The explorer asked if he might go to Yerba Buena to get the botanical and geological specimens he had been collecting, but Kearny refused permission (CT. MARTIAL, 113–14).

1. George B. Sanderson would resign from the Army when Kearny reached Fort Leavenworth. The Mormon volunteers had intensely disliked the "fiendish doctor" but were unsuccessful in resisting "his calomel and arsenic," which he administered with an old iron spoon (TYLER, 146–47).

2. Lieut. Henry Wager Halleck (1815–72) resigned from the Army in 1854 and became a member of the influential San Francisco law firm of Halleck, Peachy, & Billings. During the Civil War he was commissioned a major general and succeeded JCF in command of the Department of Missouri. From 23 July 1862 to 9 March 1864 he was military adviser to President Lincoln, with the anomalous title of general-in-chief. His fellow officer William Horace Warner, who had come to California with Kearny, was killed by Indians in Sept. 1849 while surveying in the Sierra Nevada.

198. Frémont to J. J. Abert

Monterey, California
May 29. 1847

Sir:

I have drawn on you, under this date for $924.63/100 in favor of Talbot H. Green on account of advances made by him for supplies to the Exploring Company, under my command, which' please honor and charge to Your most Obedient Servant,

J. C. Frémont
Lt. Col. U. S. A.

To
Col. J. J. Abert
Chief of the Topographical Bureau
City of Washington
District of Columbia

ALS, RC (DNA-77, LR). Endorsed: "Recd. Sep. 27th. 1847."

199. J. J. Abert to Frémont

Bureau of Topogl. Engs.
Washington June 11. 1847.

Sir,

Your letter of the 5th February '47[1] by Mr. Talbott[2] has been duly received.

Eight drafts drawn by you upon this Bureau, each for 500 dollars, have been accepted and paid, and a ninth draft for 1500 dollars has been accepted, and will also be paid on maturity, making a total of 5500 dollars (of drafts from California).

It is to be regretted that you have not had an opportunity of transmitting any vouchers of your expenditures, as you are thereby placed in the attitude of delayed settlements.[3] The enclosed copy of the law on this subject, and of a late regulation, will apprise you of the necessity of exertions in these respects. We are obliged to report delinquents under this law, but your situation, and the extreme difficulty if not impossibility that you could transmit accounts and vouchers, have always been received by the President as an adequate explanation. I have advised Mr. Talbott to hand in whatever vouchers he may have, on your account, as this could be considered a rendering of accounts under the law, and would prevent the necessity of future explanations for some time to come.

Although no official information has been received of your acceptance of the appointment of Lt. Colonel of the Rifles, yet as well from your letter of the 5th February as from other sources it is not doubted that you have accepted. It would probably under such circumstances be agreeable to you to be relieved as far as practicable from the responsibilities of your former position. You are therefore authorized to deliver to Lieut Warner of the Corps of Topographical Engineers any instruments or other public property belonging to this Bureau, and under your care, taking his duplicate receipts for the same, one of which on being transmitted to this office will acquit you of existing responsibility on this account.

The Bureau will be glad to receive the results of the observations of your late tour, promised in your letter of the 5th February. Respectfully Sir Your Obt. Servt.

(Signed) J. J. ABERT
Col. Corps T. E.

Lbk (DNA-77, LS, 10:125–26).

1. JCF's letter of 5 Feb. 1847 is registered as having been received but is no longer present. A summary of the letter accompanying the register entry, and the copy of a letter of J. J. Abert to Robert Campbell, indicate that JCF had informed Abert that he had closed his connection with the Topographical Bureau as of 30 Sept. 1846, "when in consequence of my position being transferred to the military the men enlisted by me for Topographical Service were either discharged or enlisted in the U. S. Military Service." He had empowered Theodore Talbot to settle his accounts. He also promised to furnish the results of his expedition as soon as possible. The eight drafts of $500 to which Abert refers seem to have been drawn in favor of Thomas Oliver Larkin (Register of Letters Received by the Topographical Bureau; Abert to Robert Campbell, 4 June 1847, DNA-77, LS, 10:121–22).

2. Traveling with Christopher Carson, Edward F. Beale of the Navy, and R. Eugene Russell (son of JCF's secretary of state), Talbot had left California on 25 Feb. with dispatches for Washington. Their route was by way of Santa Fe and St. Louis (*Missouri Republican,* 17 May 1847). For the first twenty days out of California, Beale, who was very ill, had to be lifted on and off his horse by Carson (CARSON, 116–17). Beale delivered his communiques at the Navy Department on 31 May, and Talbot his at the Topographical Bureau on 3 June. On 7 June JBF, accompanied by Carson, called on President Polk and delivered JCF's long 3 Feb. letter addressed to Benton.

In his diary Polk wrote, "Mrs. Fremont seemed anxious to elicit from me some expression of approbation of her husband's conduct, but I evaded [making any]." He confided to his journal that he considered JCF "greatly in the wrong" for refusing to obey the orders issued by Kearny, who the president thought was also right in his controversy with Stockton, but he hoped the matter would pass over quickly without the necessity of an investigation by a court-martial. In the evening the president saw Carson a second time and had a "full conversation" with him on the state of affairs in California, "especially in relation to the collision between the land and naval commanders." On 14 June Carson called on the president again with JBF, who expressed a desire that her husband be retained in California (POLK, 3:52, 54, 61). The next day Carson left for California with dispatches for Kearny and the commander of the Pacific Squadron. On the day of his departure, 15 June 1847, a long article appeared in the Washington *Daily Union,* based not upon a personal interview but on a "description of this singular man" provided by "a gentleman, who had seen much of Carson. . . ."

3. On 3 July 1847 Abert wrote the Third Auditor that Talbot had deposited in the Bureau of Topographical Engineers vouchers for payments in the amount of $9,923.48 made by JCF on his third expedition. The chief of the bureau likewise noted that Robert Campbell of St. Louis was acting as JCF's agent in paying claims (Abert to Peter Hagner, DNA-77, LS, 10:151).

200. James Buchanan to Frémont

Private

WASHINGTON 11 June 1847

MY DEAR SIR,

I have received your despatch of the 6th February last & referred it to the Secretary of War.

It may be proper to explain to you the reason why this was done. The civil government of California is at present but a mere emanation from the war making power. It rests upon military authority alone & as such is justified from necessity under the law of nations. It is temporary in its character & has never yet been recognized by Congress. Under these circumstances the Secretary of War is the appropriate channel through which the military Governor should address the President. This, you have doubtless long since learned from the President's message of December last.

I regret exceedingly the controversy which has arisen between General Kearney & Commodore Stockton. We are all very sorry that you have been involved in it. We doubt not, however, that all difficulties were terminated on the receipt in California of the orders issued by the Secretary of the Navy to Commodore Stockton of the 5th November last & those of General Scott to General Kearney of the 3d of the same month. From their date, you will at once perceive that these instructions were founded upon general principles, & could not possibly have had a personal application to yourself as Governor. General Scott directs General Kearney to consult your wishes in regard to your return home & not to detain you "a moment longer than the necessities of the service may require." I need not say that this was intended in kindness to yourself.

Your military career in California has increased your high reputation & the President had evinced his sense of your previous services by your appointment as Lieutenant Colonel. Your course must be onward & you have a bright future before you.

I was much pleased with Carson. He will return to you a second lieutenant in the Rifle Regiment.[1] I suggested the propriety of his appointment to the President & Secretary of War & they acceded to it without a moment's hesitation.

It is scarcely possible to form any opinion in regard to the conduct of Mexico. I should not be astonished to hear any day that a Treaty of peace has been concluded, & I shall not be much disappointed should the war continue for years to come. Chaos reigns supreme in that ill fated country. Its government is that of a military despotism without its stability. It is perpetually changing according to the interest or caprice of the army but never grows better. Until this corrupt army shall be destroyed, there can be no hope of deliverance for the people. On a small scale, it enacts the part of the Pretorian Guards.

I shall not give you any family news, because I know Carson will take this to you in abundance from the fountain head.

With the most sincere wishes for your health and prosperity, I remain very respectfully your friend,

J. B.

Colonel Fremont.

AL, SC (PHi—Buchanan Papers). The endorsement conveys the information that the letter was being carried to JCF by Lieutenant Carson.

1. The Senate refused to confirm the appointment, and although Carson heard of its rejection in Santa Fe, he continued on to California to deliver the dispatches (CARSON, 121).

201. Jessie B. Frémont to Frémont

[WASHINGTON]
[ca. 14 June 1847]

MY DEAR HUSBAND:

Kit Carson is waiting to take a letter to you. Nothing I can say will express in the littlest degree the love and yearning in my heart —the grief that I cannot be with you. It hurts too much even to write. Besides, I would not make you unhappy by my repining. Kit will tell you everything. I am sending you myself—in miniature. I lay with it over my heart last night. I pray you wear it over yours until *le bon temps viendra.* Your devoted wife,

JESSIE

Printed in PHILLIPS, 116. Catherine Coffin Phillips cites the letter as being in the Frémont Papers, location undesignated. The Bancroft Library, the logical depository, has no record of it (William M. Roberts to Mary Lee Spence, 26 May 1971). Apparently the miniature Jessie sent JCF was the one painted by John Wood Dodge in the winter of 1845.

202. Thomas H. Benton to Roger Jones

ST. LOUIS, June 14, 1847

To the Adjutant General:
SIR:

I enclose you a printed article cut from the Missouri Republican of this day's date, (marked A,)[1] containing accusations against Lieut. Col. Fremont, which, if true, will require him to be cashiered. I do not believe they are true; but justification is not to rest upon *belief;* and as he cannot remain in the army with such accusations against him, and is not here to attend to his own justification, it becomes my duty to attend to it for him, and to ask his immediate *recall,* and a general court martial upon him.

The writer of the article enclosed (marked A) is —— ——, and I give his name as a witness to justify the arrest of Lieut. Col. Fremont, and to be examined on his trial.

I also enclose you printed articles (marked B and C) to the same effect, the former from the Louisville Journal[2] and the latter from the New Orleans Picayune,[3] founded upon reports given out by *Major W. H. Emory,* late Lieutenant of Topographical Engineers; upon which also I ask the immediate arrest and trial of Lieut. Col. Fremont, and give the name of the said Major Emory as a witness to prove the charges in the papers B and C, and to justify his immediate recall, arrest, and trial.

It is not necessary to acknowledge the receipt of the communication to me at *this* place, as I shall soon be in Washington to give the subject a personal attention.

Requesting that you will lay this communication immediately before the President and Secretary at War for their decision, I have the honor to be, sir, yours, most respectfully,

Thomas H. Benton

P. S. When the foregoing was written I expected the editor of the paper (Missouri Republican) to insert the name of the writer of the article (A) in the blank left for that purpose. After taking time for *reflection,* he *declines* to do so.* I have therefore to say that the last paragraph of the communication, seeming to exclude all the officers at San Diego but the two arriving with the Mormon battalion after the events, the question of authorship is narrowed down to those two; and as one of them, to wit, Capt. Smith, of the dragoons, has connexions and correspondents in this city, I feel authorized to name *him* as the writer, and as the witness to be summoned. But, anxious to do Capt. Smith no wrong, I shall have this statement submitted to the editor for his contradiction, if the truth permits it to be contradicted.

T. H. B.

*I showed this postscript, as well as the letter to which it is appended, to Mr. A. B. Chambers, the editor of the Missouri Republican, and he replied that he neither affirmed nor denied that Capt. Smith was the author.

Robert Campbell

*Republican Office,
St. Louis, June 15, 1847

Sir:

On reflection, I must decline giving the name of the author of the communication which appeared in the Republican of yesterday in relation to the events in California. Yours, respectfully,

A. B. CHAMBERS

Col. R. Campbell

Printed in *National Intelligencer*, 25 Nov. 1847. Not found in DNA. However, on 24 Aug. 1847 (Doc. No. 209) Roger Jones acknowledged that his office had received Benton's 14 June letter and referred it to the Secretary of War. Benton and William C. Jones gave a copy of the letter to the editors of the *National Intelligencer* following the court-martial session on 24 Nov. Benton noted for the benefit of the public that he had revoked at the War Office the name of Captain Smith as the author of the article in the *Missouri Republican*, substituting that of Maj. Philip St. George Cooke.

1. The article from the *Missouri Republican*, 14 June 1847, is in CT. MARTIAL, 129–33. In court JCF wanted to ask Cooke if he were its author, but the court ruled that the question could not be put (CT. MARTIAL, 133).

2. For the article from the Louisville *Journal*, see enclosure in Frémont to Jones, 27 Sept. 1847, Doc. No. 221.

3. The newspaper article from the New Orleans *Picayune*, 22 April 1847, is in CT. MARTIAL, 169–71.

203. Frémont to Stephen Watts Kearny

NEW HELVETIA, UPPER CALIFORNIA
June 14, 1847

SIR:

In a communication which I received from yourself, in March of the present year, I am informed that you had been directed by the commander-in-chief not to detain me in this country against my wishes, longer than the absolute necessities of the service might require.

Private letters, in which I have entire confidence, further inform me that the President has been pleased to direct that I should be permitted the choice of joining my regiment in Mexico, or returning directly to the United States. An application which I had the honor to make to you at the Ciudad de los Angeles, for permission to proceed immediately to Mexico, having been rejected,[1] and the duties of the exploring expedition, which had been confided to my direction, having been terminated by yourself, I respectfully request that

Thomas Hart Benton. Courtesy of the Library of Congress.

I may now be relieved of all connexion with the topographical party, which you have taken under your charge, and be permitted to return to the United States. Travelling with a small party by a direct route, my knowledge of the country and freedom from professional business, will enable me to reach the States some forty or fifty days earlier than yourself, which the present condition of affairs and a long absence from my family make an object of great importance to me.

It may not be improper to say to you that my journey will be made with private means, and will not therefore, occasion any expenditure to the government. I have the honor to be, with much respect, your obedient servant,

J. C. FRÉMONT,
Lieut. Colonel, mounted rifles

Brigadier-General S. W. Kearney,
Commanding western army,
Nueva Helvetia, Upper California

Printed in CT. MARTIAL, 280–81.
1. JCF had applied to Kearny for permission to join General Taylor's army in Mexico about 10 or 11 May, and the defense in the court-martial implied that he had 120 picked horses and 60 men ready to go, with *pinoli* and dried beef for their support (CT. MARTIAL, 103).

204. Stephen Watts Kearny to Frémont

Camp Near New Helvetia, (CALIFORNIA,)
June 14, 1847

SIR:

The request contained in your communication to me of this date, to be relieved from all connection with the topographical party (nineteen men) and be permitted to return to the United States with a small party made up by your private means, cannot be granted.

I shall leave here on Wednesday, the 16th instant, and I require of you to be with your topographical party in my camp (which will probably be fifteen miles from here) on the evening of that day, and to continue with me to Missouri.[1] Very respectfully, your obedient servant,

S. W. KEARNEY.
Brigadier-General

Lieut. Col. Frémont,
Regiment mounted riflemen, New Helvetia

Printed in CT. MARTIAL, 281.
1. JCF made two later requests to leave Kearny's command. After crossing the Sierra Nevada in 1847, he applied for permission to go directly through the Great Basin to the States in order to complete and correct his 1845 route to California, which had passed south of the Great Salt Lake. He sent Kearny a sketch showing that such a route would cut approximately 400 miles from the one Kearny was traveling, and that mapping it would be advantageous to future travelers and emigrants. Again, at Fort Laramie, JCF asked to return with his topographical party to the Missouri frontier by a shorter route than the one by Fort Leavenworth. This request was also denied (CT. MARTIAL, 282).

205. Richard B. Mason to Roger Jones

Head Quarters, 10th Mily. Dept.
MONTEREY, CALA. June 21, 1847

SIR

An opportunity offering to San Francisco, I send off this letter in the hopes that it will overtake my despatch to you of the 18th inst. at that place, and that both will reach you at the same time.

A claim has today been presented to me against the United States of so extraordinary a nature, that I deem it proper to send it to you for the information of the Department.[1]

You will perceive it is for money borrowed at an enormous rate of interest by Lt. Col. Fremont from one Antonio José Cot, and that too in the official character of Governor of California, when he knew that General Kearny his superior and commanding officer was here in the country.

In the same manner the Lt. Col. gave orders and caused the collector of customs at San Pedro, to receive in payment of custom house dues, a large amount, say about $1700.00 of depreciated paper signed by individuals in no way responsible to the government.

Genl. Kearny has gone home prepared to lay all the facts attending that transaction before the War Department.

The object that I now have in view is to request that Lt. Col. Fremont may be required to refund immediately the seventeen hundred dollars that the Treasury of California has thus lost by his illegal order. The money is wanted to defray the expense of the civil department in this country. I am Respectfully Your Obt. Servt.

RICHARD B. MASON
Com'dg.

Brig. Genl. R. Jones
Adjt. Genl. U. S. A.
Washington, D. C.

LS, RC (DNA-94, M-1113 1847, f/w K-209 1846). Endorsed: "Respectfully submitted. R. Jones, A. G. Nov. 16th."
1. The enclosure—Frémont to Antonio José Cot, 4 Feb. 1847, Doc. No. 133—is not reproduced here.

206. Thomas H. Benton to Frémont

ST. LOUIS, June 22. 1847

MY DEAR SIR,

I have written you fully on the points which concern your public conduct,[1] and add this note in relation to Jessie Ann & little Lilly. Be under no uneasiness about either of them; they are both my children, & will share all my cares and affections equally with the rest. They are both exceedingly well, and have no want but that of your return. Lilly is one of the finest children in the world, every way, in mind, temper, and behaviour. No child could be a more universal favorite. Mrs. Benton's health has been greatly impaired by a paralytic attack, but it leaves her without any sign of paralysis except weakness & some defect of memory and of speech. The rest are all well, Ran[2] pursuing his studies under a clergyman in Kentucky.

I added steam power to the Saw [?], which works regularly & successfully. Yours truly & sincerely,

THOMAS H. BENTON

ALS, RC (CLSM).

1. Benton's letter has not been found.

2. A reference to John Randolph Benton, JBF's seventeen-year-old brother. He had accompanied JCF on his 1842 expedition as far as Fort Laramie. "Ran" did not pursue his studies long; by 25 Oct. he was in President Polk's office requesting a lieutenancy in the Army. When refused, he left in an outburst of passion and profanity (POLK, 3:201–3). Not only was the young man a family problem, but he also suffered from ill health and died in 1852, having been received into the Catholic church by Father Pierre-Jean de Smet (CHAMBERS, 388–89).

The Arrest and
Court-Martial of Frémont

207. Stephen Watts Kearny's Order for the Arrest of Frémont

Fort Leavenworth
August 22d. 1847

Orders

1st. Lieut Col. Fremont of the Regt. of Mounted Riflemen will turn over to the officers of the different Departments at this Post the Horses, mules & other Public property in the use of the Topo. Party now under his charge, for which receipts will be given. He will arrange the accounts of those men (19 in number) so that they can be paid at the earliest possible date. Lieut Col. Fremont having performed the above duty, will consider himself under arrest & will then repair to Washington City & report himself to the Adjutant General of the Army.

· · · · ·

DS (DNA-94, LR, K-205 1847, f/w K-209 1846). Endorsed: "Respectfully laid before the Sec. of War. No charges accompany this order of arrest. R. Jones, AG, Sepr. 7th. Returned Sept. 25." JCF was handed a copy of the arrest order in the presence of Lieut. Col. Clifton Wharton, commanding at Fort Leavenworth (CT. MARTIAL, 114–15).

208. Thomas H. Benton to Roger Jones

WASHINGTON CITY, Aug. 22d. 1847

To the Adjt. Genl.

SIR,

I reduce to writing for the purpose of being filed with the papers of the case what I said to you in person a few days ago, that believing it to be probable, as reported, that Genl. Kearny has arrested Lt. Col. Fremont in California and ordered him home for trial, I do not now ask for a decision on my application to have him ordered home for arrest and trial; but if it should be found that he is not so arrested & ordered home, then my application remains in full force. Yours respectfully,

THOMAS H. BENTON.

ALS, RC (DNA-94, LR, B-766 1847). First endorsement: *"Remarks:* [The papers in this case (whatever they may be) must have been addressed to the Sec. of War, as they have not been seen by the Adjut. General, &c. The wishes of Col. Benton shall be attended to whenever the occasion offers.] Recd. August 23d. R. Jones, AG." Second endorsement: "Col. Benton sent for my perusal today, a letter he has just recd. from Genl. Kearny, dated Monterey, March 17th from the tone of which he now believes that the report of the arrest of Lieut. Col. Fremont, is incorrect. I am very confident myself that there is no truth in the Report, as I informed Col. Benton a few days ago. R. Jones, AG, August 24th. Respectfully laid before the Sec. of War. R. Jones, Aug. 24." Third endorsement: "Note: I find that I am mistaken: 'The papers in the case' (Col. Benton's letter to the Adt. Genl. of June 14) were recd. June 25 when I was in New York & were immediately delivered to the Sec. of War, of which I knew nothing until within the last half hour. R. Jones. 2 o'clock. August 24th." Fourth endorsement: "Retd. 27 Aug. 1847 with 543—Respectfully laid before the Sec. of War, with Col. Benton's previous letter of June 14th. R. Jones, Sept. 14th. 1847." Fifth endorsement: "Copy of the letter furnished to Lt. Col. Fremont, Mounted Riflemen, Sept. 28, 1847. See letter to him, dated Sept. 27th."

209. Roger Jones to Thomas H. Benton

A. G. O. WASHINGTON, August 24. 1847

SIR:

I acknowledge the receipt of your note of the 22d. last evening, referring to the case of Lieut Col. *Fremont,* and will with pleasure give the desired attention to the subject.

Your letter of June 14th was received the 25th of that month, in my absence on duty in the City of New York, and was on the same day laid before the Secretary of War by Major Freeman.[1]

General Kearny's unofficial note to you from Monterey of March 17, which you did me the honor to send to-day for my perusal, confirms, I am glad to think the previous opinion entertained, that Lieutenant Colonel Fremont has not been arrested by the General, &c. I am Sir, &c. &c.

R. JONES
Adjt. Genl.

Lbk (DNA-94, LS, 24:152).
1. Bvt. Maj. William Grigsby Freeman (d. 1866) was Assistant Adjutant General (HEITMAN).

210. Frémont to the Citizens of St. Louis

St. Louis, August 30th, 1847

GENTLEMEN:

I had the pleasure this morning to receive your letter of this date, in which, with many kind assurances of welcome and congratulations on my return,[1] you honor with the strong expression of your approbation, my geographical labors during the recent explorations in Oregon and North California, and the military operations in which sudden emergencies involved me in California.

I beg you to receive my earnest acknowledgments for the very favorable notice you have bestowed upon the published results of those expeditions, and I regret that events which interrupted and more recent circumstances which abruptly terminated the last exploration, will permit me to give only a brief and imperfect account of California and of the intervening basin, which it had been the great object of the expedition to explore and determine.

The labor of many years in the interest of science, undertaken and sustained with only a distant hope of gaining your good opinion, has received, in the rapid progress of events, an earlier reward than I could possibly have hoped for or anticipated; but I am free to say that the highest pleasure I received from the perusal of your letter

377

was derived from your decided approval of my political course in North California. Circumstances there made us, in connection with the emigrants to that country, involuntary witnesses and unwilling actors at the birth of a great nation; but to which we now consider it our great good fortune to have aided in securing the blessings of peace with civil and religious liberty.

Placed in a critical and delicate position, where imminent danger urged immediate action, and where the principal difficulty lay in knowing full well what must be done; where, in a struggle barely for the right to live, every effort to secure our safety involved unusual and grave responsibilities, I could only hope from your forbearance a suspension of judgment, until, with full possession of facts, you would be able to determine understandingly.

I had the gratification on my arrival to find that neither remoteness of situation nor the more immediately important and interesting events at home had diverted your attention from our conduct, but that from a knowledge only of the leading occurrences in California, it had been fully and completely justified and sustained.

I regret that, under present circumstances, I cannot have the pleasure of meeting you at the dinner which you have done me the honor to offer me, but I beg you to accept the assurances of the high and grateful sense which I entertain of your kindness and regard, and of the very flattering manner in which you have expressed it.

With sentiments of respect and consideration, I am, gentlemen, your very obedient servant,

J. C. FREMONT

Printed in *National Intelligencer,* 23 Sept. 1847. Although JCF declined the public dinner, he did receive his friends at the residence of Col. Joshua B. Brant the next day between 10 A.M. and 2 P.M. (*Missouri Republican,* 31 Aug. 1847).

1. JCF, who had been absent two and a half years, had been greeted by his wife, made anxious by the rumors that he was being brought east under arrest. Twenty-four-year-old Jessie had gone up the Missouri River to the town of Kansas (Kansas City), Mo., to spend "some weary days of suspense" in a log cabin, stifling in the late summer heat. With a flair for the dramatic, she later recorded that meeting and the changes in her husband.

"The years and the experiences of those years of great events had made their telling mark on Mr. Fremont and he was still further changed by his dress, the unfamiliar Spanish riding dress of Californians. But the great change was in the stern set look of endurance and self control which the past few months had forced upon him; and with it a silent repressed storm of feeling which entirely dominated his old, light-hearted courtesy and thought for others. He had not thought to meet me up there and could not recover himself instantly from the long indignation of the return journey and the crowning insult that morning at Fort Leavenworth where, after leaving him waiting outside while Kearny and his officers were being welcomed by the resident officers, he was summoned within to be put under arrest.

"I only knew of this from his faithful men. Himself he could not put it into speech. I saw the need for silence, but when under pretext of looking after the men and horses, Mr. Fremont escaped from notice into the coming night, Godey told me of the astounding conduct of General Kearny. 'But now,' he said, 'we have seen the Colonel safe home—we would not trust him with Kearny. *We* were not under Kearny's orders—the prairies were free and we came along to watch over the Colonel—he's safe now!' " ("Great Events during the Life of Major General John C. Frémont," pp. 51–52, CU-B).

211. Thomas H. Benton to F. R. Conway

BLUE LICK (KY.) Sept. 3d, 1847

DEAR SIR:

I thank you for your note of the 19th ult. and the paper enclosed. If the article to which you called my attention merely concerned myself, I should leave it to do its office, without saying a word to lessen or impair its force; but as the design is to injure Col. Frémont, by representing me as preferring charges against him, and becoming his prosecutor, merely to obtain sham acquittal, I think proper to say, (and to give you leave to publish it) that I have preferred no charges against Col. Frémont, and have not become his prosecutor, but that I did send to the war office the charges made against him by others, and gave the name of the supposed writers as witnesses to prove what they wrote, at the same time expressing my disbelief of their truth, and asking a court martial. An article from the Missouri *Republican* was one of those so sent. Nothing was added to them, or taken from them. The charges were sent exactly as published, and were the charges of the *publishers* and *writers,* not mine; and it is *they* who are to be summoned to prove them. They (the writers and publishers) will be summoned, and all other witnesses that they want summoned, and all the charges tried which they have preferred, or shall prefer, or which any other person shall prefer. The trial which I have asked for is intended to be a real one, and not a *"farce,"* or a *"whitewashing,"* as the editor of the Republican supposes. It shall cover everything imputed, or to be imputed against Col. Fremont; and his accusers shall all be witnesses. If, under these circumstances, it becomes a *"farce, and a whitewashing affair,"* the fault will be their own.

I am here with Mrs. Benton, for the benefit of her health, which is such as not to admit of my leaving her to go on to Missouri this fall. This must be my apology to my southern friends, whom I expected to visit this month. Yours, very truly and respectfully,

THOMAS H. BENTON

Printed in Washington *Daily Union*, 17 Sept. 1847, from the St. Louis *Reveille*. Frederick Rector Conway, a long-time resident of St. Louis, was a nephew of Gen. William Rector.

212. Thomas H. Benton to James K. Polk

Private

WOODFORD CO., KEN.
Sep. 10. 1847

DEAR SIR:

I have had full conversations with Col. Fremont, and am certain that the public interest & the future welfare of California requires that the government should have a full knowledge of everything that has been done there, and that such knowledge is necessary to enable it to do justly between individuals, and, what is more, act safely for the future welfare of the province. Without going into particulars I can say that you ought to know things which have happened, & that you can only know them authentically through the court martial on Col. F., or at least, a court of inquiry.

Col. F. cannot give you information, while charges hang over him; and besides, he wants every thing judicially brought out. He is a party concerned, and wishes proof alone to decide everything. Military etiquette will not even allow him to call to pay his respects to you while he is in a state of arrest, and I know of no means except his trial which can give you the information which you ought to possess, and that with as little delay as possible. I would not write thus if I was not convinced that the public interest and the future welfare of California require you to know all that has happened.

Col. F. will be urgent for a court martial, or at all events for a court of inquiry, and that not merely on his own account, but for the higher & nobler object of giving information to the government which it ought to possess. Respectfully, Sir, your friend and fellow citizen,

THOMAS H. BENTON

ALS, RC (DLC—Polk Papers).

213. Albert Gallatin to Frémont

NEW YORK 15 Sept. 1847

SIR

I am now preparing a recapitulation of the extent of our knowledge of the languages of the Indians within the United States, and of the geographical features of the country they occupy, including also Oregon, California the great interior basin or California desert and the territory drained by the Rio Colorado of California.[1]

In the explanatory map annexed to that essay, you have of course been my guide for all that fell within your personal knowledge. You circumnavigated, if I may use the expression, the western, southern and eastern boundaries of the great interior basin, or California desert; but you are silent respecting its northern limit, which I presume to about lat. 41°. You would confer a great obligation on me by communicating correct information respecting the route, or routes, from Fort Hall on Snake river, through the desert, to the settlements in California. Permit me to state the various points, concerning which I am most desirous of being enlightened.

Is there but one place at which, on leaving California, the Sierra Nevada can be crossed? and is the point of departure from the river Joaquin, or from the Sacramento?

There is much discrepancy in the manuscript or printed maps within my reach, respecting the water courses, having no issue to the sea, which are occasionally found in or near the route of the emigrants, through the Desert.

In Farnhams map, on which I place but little reliance, a water course, called Marys river, is laid down more than one hundred miles long, running from northeast to southwest, terminating in a lake, the southern extremity of which is placed a few minutes north of lat. 38° and in long. 118°.

Newspaper accounts state, that, on your last journey you returned by the way of the Trucky or Salmon trout river.

In a manuscript map prepared in the year 1831 under the direction of General Ashley, a water course, called Budger's [Bridger's] Fork, is laid down running from east to west in lat. 41°, from a point nearly due south of Fort Hall to long. 118°. From this point the Fork is made to run due north and to unite with the Owyhee river. This was an erroneous conjecture; and it appears to have been since ascertained, that Budger's Fork has no issue to the sea and terminates in a lake or is lost in the sands. A short account of your return journey will throw a new light on the subject and settle those questions.[2]

I have not the honor of a personal acquaintance with you and do not wish to be indiscreet, or to encroach on your time and avocations. I will be grateful for any information which, without trespassing on these, you may be pleased to communicate.

I pray you to accept the assurance of my distinguished consideration and have the honour to be Your most obedient servant,

[*Unsigned*]

Col J C Fremont
Washington

AL, SC (NHi).
1. For years Gallatin had exhibited an intense interest in ethnology and western U.S. geography. He had advised Jefferson in the planning of the Lewis and Clark expedition in 1803. A generation later he had planned a significant essay and map, "A Synopsis of the Indian Tribes within the United States East of the Rocky Mountains," *Transactions* of the American Antiquarian Society (1836), vol. 2.
2. Gallatin referred to this map, produced from the data of Jedediah S. Smith, in a later publication in *Transactions* of the American Ethnological Society, 2 (1848):xxxvii: "J. S. Smith was no writer. We have nothing from him but the track of his routes, and a few scattered notes, incorporated in a manuscript Map prepared under the direction of the late General Ashley, Charles de Ward draughtsman, 1831." We have not located the map or identified the draftsman. It is not clear what river he is here calling Bridger's Fork. C. I. WHEAT, 2:136, assumed it was the Bruneau River, rising in southwest Idaho and meeting the Snake eighteen miles southwest of Mountain Home.

214. Frémont to Roger Jones

C. Street, WASHINGTON CITY, Sep. 17th. 1847

To the Adjutant General,

SIR,

According to the orders of Brigadier General Kearny, I have the honor to report myself to you in person, in a state of arrest, and to make the following requests:

1. A copy of the charges filed against me by the said General.
2. A copy of the orders under which the said General brought back from California to the United States myself and the topographical party of which I formerly had the command.
3. A copy of the communications from Senator Benton asking for my arrest and trial on the charges made in the newspapers against me, and which application from him I adopt and make my own.
4. That charges and specifications, in addition to those filed by General Kearny be made out in form against me on all the newspaper publications which have come, or shall come to the knowledge of the office, and on all other information oral or written.
5. That I may have a trial as soon as the witnesses now in the United States can be got to Washington, for although the testimony of the voice of California, through some of its most respectable inhabitants is essential to me, and also that of Commodore Stockton, who has not yet arrived from that province, yet I will not wish the delay of waiting for these far distant witnesses, and will go into trial on the testimony now in the United States, part of which is in the State of Missouri, and may require thirty days to get it to Washington. I therefore ask for a trial at the end of that time.

These requests I have the honor to make, and hope they will be found to be just, and will be granted. I wish a full trial, and a speedy one. The charges against me by Brigadier General Kearny, and the subsidiary accusations made against me in newspapers, when I was not in this country, impeach me in all the departments of my conduct, (military, civil, political, and moral,) while I was in California, and if true would subject me to be cashiered and shot under the rules and articles of war, and to infamy in the public opinion. It is my intention to meet these charges and accusations in all their extent; and for that purpose to ask a trial upon every point of allegation or insinuation against me, waiving all objections to forms and technicalities, and allowing the widest range to all possible testimony. These charges and accusations are so general and extensive as to cover the whole field of my operations in California, both civil and military, from the beginning to the end of hostilities, and as my operations, and those of which I was the subject or object extend to almost every act and event which occurred in the country during the eventful period of these hostilities the testimony on my trial will be the history of the conquest of California, and the exposition of the policy which has been heretofore pursued there, and the elucidation of that which should be followed hereafter. It will be the means of giving valuable information to the Government, which it might not otherwise be able to obtain, and thus enlighten it, both with respect to the past and the future. Being a military subordinate, I can make no reports, not even of my own operations; but my trial may become a report, and bring to the knowledge of what it ought to know, not only with respect to the conduct of its officers, but also in regard to the policy observed, or necessary to be observed with regard to the three fold population (Spanish Americans, Anglo Americans, and aboriginal Americans) which that remote province contains. Viewed under these aspects of public interest, my own personal concern in the trial, already sufficiently grave acquires an additional and public importance, and for these high objects as well as to vindicate my own character from accusations both capital, and infamous, it is my intention to require and to promote the most searching examination into every thing that has been done in that quarter.

The public mind has become impressed with the belief that great misconduct has prevailed in California, and, in fact, it would be something rare in the history of remote conquests and governments, where every petty commander might feel himself invested with proconsular authority, and protected by distance from the supervision of his government, if nothing wrong or culpable has been done by the public agents of the United States in that remote province. The public believes it; and the charges filed against me by Brigadier General Kearny—the subsidiary publications made against me whilst I was not in this country—my arrest on the frontier, and the premonitory rumors of that event—the manner of my being brought home for trial, not in irons as some newspapers suppose, but in chains stronger than iron, and with circumstances of ostentatious and galling degradation—have all combined to present me as the great malefactor, and the sole one.

Heretofore I have said nothing, and could have said nothing, in my own defence. I was ignorant of all that was going on against me —ignorant of the charges sent from California,—ignorant of the intended arrest, and of the subsidiary publications to prejudice the public mind. What was published in the United States in my favor, by my friends, was done upon their own view of things here, and of which I knew nothing. It was only on my arrival on the frontier of the United States that I became acquainted with these things, which concerned me so nearly. Brought home by General Kearny, and marched in his rear, I did not know of his design to arrest me until the moment of its execution at Fort Leavenworth. He then informed me, that among the charges which he had preferred were mutiny, disobedience of orders, assumption of powers, &c. and referred me to your office for particulars. Accordingly I now apply for them; and ask for a full and speedy trial, not only on the charges filed by the said General, but on all accusations contained in the publications against me.

The private calamity[1] which has this evening obtained for me permission from the Department to visit South Carolina, does not create any reason for postponement or delay of the trial, or in any way interfere with the necessary preliminaries.

Hoping then, Sir, that you will obtain and communicate to me an early decision of the proper authorities on these requests, I remain your most obedient servant.

J. C. FRÉMONT,
Lieut. Col. Mounted Rifles

ALS, RC (DNA-94, LR, F-212 1847). Also printed in the Washington *Daily Union,* 18 Sept. 1847, and the *National Intelligencer,* 20 Sept. 1847. Endorsed: "Respectfully submitted to the Sec. of War. The charges preferred by Genl. Kearny were submitted the 13th inst. R. Jones, AG, Sept. 18th. See letter of Septr. 27th. R. Jones."
1. JCF had learned of the serious illness of his mother, Ann B. Hale.

215. Jessie B. Frémont to Albert Gallatin

WASHINGTON CITY 20th Sep. 1847

SIR,

At Mr. Frémonts request I opened his letters & finding one from you I hasten to answer it so far as to assure you that he will take pride in the pleasure of contributing in any way to your materials for your intended work.

When he returns from the South, which will probably be in a week, he will answer you at length; in the meantime I am very respectfully Sir Your &c.

JESSIE BENTON FRÉMONT

The Hon. Albert Gallatin

ALS, RC (NHi). Endorsed.

216. Frémont to Roger Jones

CHARLESTON 20th September 1847

SIR

On the eve of my departure from Washington where I remained but one day, (in consequence of the receipt of a letter informing me of the illness of my mother)[1] I requested a friend to have my report to you published in the Union, as the best and as it seemed to me, the most respectful mode of answering the accusations which had been publicly made against me. On reflection, I fear I have been led to a violation of official Etiquette in such a publication without your permission, by my anxiety to offer some public vindication of my conduct.[2]

If my Report has not yet been published, I have written to prevent it, unless with your consent, which I now request. If it has appeared I must beg your acceptance of this apology for its publication & ask your sanction.

I have availed myself of the first cessation of travel on my way to Aiken, to address you, & am very respectfully Your obedient servt.

J. C. FREMONT
Lt. Col. U. S. A.

Adjutant Genl. Roger Jones
Washington City,
D.C.

LS, RC (DNA-94, LR, F-217 1847). Endorsed: "Respectfully laid before the Sec. of War. R. Jones, AG. See letter of Sepr. 27th. R. J."
1. His mother died before JCF could reach Aiken, and he took the body to Charleston for interment (see Vol. 1, p. 11n).
2. The editors suspect that this is a sham repentance on JCF's part, and that his sending the 17 Sept. letter to the Washington *Daily Union* (Doc. No. 214) was a deliberate and considered act, perhaps prompted by advice from Benton.

217. Jessie B. Frémont to Edward F. Beale

WASHINGTON CITY, Sepr. 20th 1847

MY DEAR SIR,

I heard this evening that you asked for orders for the Pacific, which is I hope a mistake—for a selfish reason I wish your stay a little longer in the country. Mr. Frémonts trial will take place in a month & I think he wishes you as a witness to some facts. More positively I cannot speak for he is in Charleston & not until I hear from him in answer to a letter I shall write tonight, can I give you a decided reason for postponing your departure. I hear with great pleasure of your improved health & if you can render Mr. Frémont the service of remaining a month longer on land I hope to judge of your improvement myself. Very truly yours,

JESSIE BENTON FRÉMONT

ALS, RC (DLC—Decatur House Papers). Edward Fitzgerald Beale (1822–93), a young officer aboard the *Congress* and the son of distinguished naval forebears, had been a part of Gillespie's command which joined Kearny before the battle of San Pasqual. He had subsequently crawled through enemy lines to seek aid for Kearny's battered forces. When JBF penned her plea, Beale had been in Washington more than three months, having been ordered east with dispatches by Stockton. Within the next few years Beale was to make several journeys from ocean to ocean, on one of them carrying the first official news of California gold to Washington. After his resignation from the Navy in 1851, he superintended briefly some of Stockton's investments in the Sacramento area, was superintendent of Indian affairs in California, experimented with camels as beasts of burden in the Southwest, and commanded the wagon survey along the thirty-fifth parallel from Fort Smith, Ark., to California. In the 1860s he became surveyor general of California and Nevada and in the 1870s minister to Austria-Hungary. For additional biographical details, see RINGLER and BONSAL; the latter contains many inaccuracies.

218. Jessie B. Frémont to James K. Polk

[21 Sept. 1847]

To the President,
SIR,

I enclose you this notice from the St. Louis Whig paper, the Republican,[1] and after reading it you will see the manifest injustice to Mr. Frémont of letting his accusers escape from the investigation of the charges they have made against him. There is an impression prevalent that Genl. Kearny also is to obtain orders for Mexico, at once.

You have the power to do justice & I ask it of you that Mr. Frémont be permitted to make his accusers stand the trial as well as himself. Do not suppose Sir, that I lightly interfere in a matter properly belonging to men, but in the absence of Mr. Frémont I attend to his affairs at his request. I trust he will be returned in a week, when agreeably to your request he will have the honor of calling on you. The precarious situation of his mother & my own want of health are I hope a sufficient apology for not having presented myself to Mrs. Polk. Very respectfully yours,

JESSIE BENTON FRÉMONT

Tuesday evening
Sepr. 21st 1847.

ALS, RC (DLC—Polk Papers).
1. The notice which JBF enclosed must have been from the *Missouri Republican* of 13 Sept. 1847, whose editors understood that orders had been received from Washington directing Capt. Henry S. Turner to proceed to Santa Fe and Maj. Philip St. George Cooke to Mexico. The journal noted, "These gentlemen have just returned from California, and the sudden order

Edward Fitzgerald Beale. From an engraving in Frémont's *Memoirs*.

to proceed upon such distant service, looks as if the President did not intend to be in a hurry about ordering a Court Martial to investigate the charges against Col. Fremont." On 30 Sept. Emory was ordered to join his regiment in Mexico, but that was superseded by an order of 7 Oct. to be present at JCF's court-martial as a witness for the defense (R. Jones to Emory, 7 Oct. 1847, DNA-94, LS, 24:228). The Adjutant General's Office informed Turner on 27 Sept. 1847 that he would be required as a witness for the prosecution (R. Jones to Kearny *et al.*, 27 Sept. 1847, DNA-94, LS, 24:214).

219. An Unidentified Correspondent to Frémont

MEMPHIS   SCOTLAND Co., Mo. Sept. 21st 1847

DEAR FRIEND:

I take this opportunity to inform you I am well at present and hope these few lines may find you enjoying the same blessing. I wrote to you at St. Louis, but I suppose you had left there before the letter got there. I see you went to Washington under arrest. It grieves me to the heart to hear of such taking place. Yes and after suffering as we did and after doing what you did to take the Country and that without money or provisions in a great measure and worse than all with only or about one hundred and sixty or seventy men. You marched from one end of California to the other only—see how after we had nothing but mule or horse meat to eat and without water— all this to carry out the object for which you was sent—seeing this and knowing that you was doing every thing in your power to take the Country and save the life of every men you had and with as little Expence as possible. When I was sick and the Spaniards took up arms the second time, I was determined to not be taken as we had marched through the Country without loosing a man and seeing you had done every thing in your power to save all your men and also was doing my duty as a soldier to not let them catch me but make my way to you if possible after seeing the interest you took in the welfare of your men and the good management in saving us. I felt that I could not be taken by consent. The Spaniards wanted me to give up and they would put me on parole and let me go as other Americans was but as a soldier this I could never submit to. I know I would not [have] suffered as much as I did if I had given myself up to them, that is, in the way of provision, and in mind, I knew it would trouble you to hear of one of your men falling in their hands.

I was determined on my part from what I had seen of your love and management for your hands not to have it said that the Spaniards had taken one of your men prisoner.

When I first herd the Spaniards had taken up arms I went with Mr. Branch[1] to see the owners of the Schooner you once had taken at Sandiago and showed them a letter Mr. Branch had and wanted them to set sail that evening for Monterey. I soon found out I was on a bad lead and how to get away from the Spaniards that was on the Beach was my next undertaking. I stayed on the Schooner two days and nights and then I left the vessel and went ashore just at dark. I lay on the sand about two hours thinking if the Spaniards was watching for me they would in this time give me out and leave, so I started then to go on to Mr. Branches fifteen miles. I followed the road about three quarters mile where I had to pass a cave where the farmers deposited their potatoes to keep them dry untill the ships would carry them off when I got nearly opposite the cave I saw fire which was struck with a flint and steel. I then stoped one moment and the person spoke. The instant he spoke I started up the road as hard as my legs would carry me. I ran about one hundred yards and came to the forks of the Road—one leading to the beach and the other leading to a house not far off. I took the road leading to the house. I thought they would least suspect me of going that way. I ran about one hundred yds. [on] the road leading to the house and then lay down about 25 steps off the side the road. I lay there about 10 minutes and there came along three Spaniards. I was lying in the forks of the Road but nearest the road leading to the house. One Spaniard came that Road and Two went the other road that led to the beach. The reason they did not catch me there I think was this: the farmers that had potatoes there had some Indians to watch that none was stolen and the Spaniards put the Indians to watch for me, and as they was in the cave they did not discover the signal until it was to late. After they passed me I got up and traveled to the Mountain. I there rested a little while and traveled all night. Made about 15 miles that night. I lay close to the Road and slept what I could that day. Went that night close to Mr. Branches and watched all night to see if the Spaniards was there watching for me. I could discover none. I lay round about there two days and two nights and about 4 hours. During this time I never eat one mouthful of victuals. I then went to the Mountains and stay there about one week. I then came in the Spanish settlement where there was a Dutchman lived

that I was acquainted with. I saw one of the Indians that was working for him. I told the indian in Spanish to tell the Dutchman to
come and see me. We there agreed that I would stay in the willows
close to the house and he would send me something to eat by the
indians which he did for eight days. I was still expecting you every
day. The Eighth day I left and went to the Mountains. I stay there
some several weeks. At length harmer[2] concluded he would go with
me to Monterey if we could get a pilot. I went to Mr. Branches and
got him to send me an Indian that was acquainted with the Country
and we would go through the mountains and try to get to Monterey
or some place where we could hear of you. While I lay in the Mountains I often heard the sound of Com. Stocktons cannon as he was
passing up and down the coast. I killed several Beeves to live on
while I was in the Mountains that belonged to the Spaniards. When
I concluded to leave the Mountain I was in and go in search of you,
Harmer another man and two indians [were] then in [my] company. I started these two Indians out to hunt for some of the Spaniards horses so as we could ride; in a little time we had 14 or 15
horses. Some belonging to Spaniards and some of your horses that
had given out near Mr. Denny [William G. Dana]. All was ready
and we left the mountain. We traveled day and night as long as we
had a horse that could go—all the horses gave out about 30 miles
before we reached Monterey. I then took it a foot leaving the other
men with the broke down horses. It was about two hours before
day. I walked hard till day light. This was on the Salenus [Salinas]
River. After light I had to take to the mountains and travel through
them until I arrived at Monterey. I then got on board the Schooner
that sailed for St. Barbara and there I overtook you. . . .

AL incomplete, RC (CU-B). Despite the many details this man relates of
his service with JCF, we have been unable to identify him. He seems not to
have been a member of Talbot's party, which had been driven out of Santa
Barbara into the mountains by a Californian force under Manuel Garfias
and had similar experiences. Talbot's party was able to join JCF in Monterey
in time to march south with the battalion. Furthermore, it did not include
Harmer, who is mentioned by the letter writer.
    1. Francis Z. Branch, who was living on his Rancho Santa Manuela in
Arroyo Grande Valley, thirteen miles south of Mission San Luis Obispo.
His aid would indicate that the letter writer's troubles began north of Santa
Barbara.
    2. ROGERS [3] lists Richard M. Harmer as being a member of Capt. William
A. T. Maddox's company, which saw most of its service in the vicinity of
Monterey in the fall of 1846.

220. Roger Jones to Frémont

W. D. A. G. O. WASHINGTON, Sept. 27. 1847.

SIR:

Herewith I enclose "General Orders" No. 32 of this date,[1] detailing the court martial by order of the President for your trial on charges and specifications recently filed against you by Brigadier General Kearney of the Army; and such other charges, (if any) as may seem to require investigation.[2]

It is contrary to the usage and practice of the service, to arraign an officer of the army on charges based upon anonymous newspaper publications, unvouched for by any one to sustain them.

The Judge Advocate will in due time furnish you with a copy of the charges upon which you are to be tried.

You will please to report in person to the presiding officer of the court at the time and place specified in the order. The time appointed for the meetings of the Court, (November 2d.) is at as early a date as will enable the distant members and witnesses to attend.

With respect to the orders under which you were brought back from California to the United States by General Kearney, I believe there was no special order for that purpose; the authority under which the General acted was derived, it may be supposed, from his general instructions from the War Department and as the officer commanding in chief the land forces in California.

Agreeably to your request, I enclose herewith copies of the communications from the Hon. Mr. Benton, respectively dated June 14th and August 22d.[3] requesting your arrest and trial.

With respect to the publication in the "Union" on the 18th instant, of your official note to the Department dated the 17th (the subject of your letter of the 20th,) it is proper to remark that you are correct in apprehending (as you state to be the case on further reflection) that such publication would be contrary to the proprieties of the military service. But, under the circumstances as explained by you, no exception will be taken to it.

Please to consider this communication as the answer to your letters of the 17th and 20th of September which have been duly submitted to the Secretary of War. I am, Sir, &c.

R. JONES, Adjt. Genl.

Lbk (DNA-94, LS, 24:210-11).

1. See CT. MARTIAL, 2. The word "President" was inadvertently omitted from the order, but when that omission was ascertained, the Adjutant General sent a substitute order on 26 Oct. (see Doc. Nos. 243 and 244).

2. Kearny had filed against JCF a single charge of mutiny, with eight specifications and nineteen supporting documents (Kearny to R. Jones, 11 Sept. 1847, DNA-94, LR, K-217 1847). As finally drawn by the judge advocate, however, there were three charges: (1) mutiny, (2) disobedience of the lawful command of his superior officer, and (3) conduct to the prejudice of good order and military discipline. For the numerous specifications, see CT. MARTIAL, 4-27.

3. See Doc. Nos. 202 and 208.

221. Frémont to Roger Jones

WASHINGTON CITY Sep. 27. 1847

SIR,

I have the honor to request that the enclosed paper may be filed in the War Office in addition to the Charges made against me by Genl. Kearny. Very respectfully Your Obedient Servant,

J. C. FRÉMONT
Lt. Col. Mounted Riflemen

To Genl. Roger Jones
Adjt. Genl., Washington City

[*Enclosure from the Louisville* Journal]
Friday, April 30, 1847.

THE DIFFICULTIES IN CALIFORNIA.—We mentioned, on Wednesday, that the New York Courier and Enquirer spoke of a serious difficulty as having occurred in California between Gen. Kearney and Com. Stockton. Yesterday we learned something further upon the subject.

Com. Stockton's despatches have been published in the Washington Union. Yesterday, a bearer of despatches passed through this city on his way to Washington. We learn by a gentleman direct from California that Com. Stockton's despatches are full of false representations. Our informant, whom we consider worthy of the fullest reliance, makes a statement very discreditable to Com. Stockton and Lieut. Col. Fremont. We will give the outlines of this statement.

Com. Stockton, it is well known, had been acting for some

months as Governor of California. Gen. Kearney, at the head of a body of troops, went out to California, with authority from the President of the United States to supersede Stockton in the Governorship of the territory. When he arrived at the village of San Pasqual with a force short of one hundred men, all worn out by a march of two thousand five hundred miles across the desert, he ecountered two hundred Mexicans. At the head of seventy of his men he charged the Mexicans, and, after a desperate fight, in which he lost thirty-five killed and wounded, he put the enemy to flight. One of his principal officers was killed, and all the rest, as well as himself, were wounded. After the battle, he found himself without horses or mules and consequently without the means of moving forward with his emaciated, worn-out, and wounded men. In his condition he sent seventy-five miles to Com. Stockton with a representation of his situation and a requisition for horses and a reinforcement of men. Stockton rudely refused to grant his requisition, remarking—"Let him stay where he is, he has no business to come out here to supersede me!"

With the greatest difficulty, Gen. Kearney succeeded in reaching San Diego where Stockton was stationed, and, finding there more men than were necessary to garrison the town, he requested Stockton to let him have a portion of them for the purpose of marching on the Puebla de los Angelos, the centre of Mexican power in California. Stockton peremptorily refused to let him have the men. The refusal created great dissatisfaction among Stockton's own officers, who were consequently on the point of rebelling against his authority and joining Kearney, but the latter exerted his influence in suppressing the movement. Subsequently Stockton, finding that the opinions of all were against him, granted a portion of his force to Gen. Kearney, who then moved upon Los Angelos and captured it after a sharp conflict. Kearney was the commanding officer in this battle although Stockton, in his despatches, represents himself as the leader.

After the taking of Los Angelos, Lieut. Col. Fremont arrived there with his troops and reported himself and them to Gen. Kearney as his superior officer. Learning that Gen. Kearney had authority from the U. S. Government to act as Governor of California, he requested the General to appoint *him* Governor. Gen. K. declined doing so at that time, but said that he would take the matter into consideration and let Col. Fremont know his decision in a few days. Fremont, angry that his request was not at once complied with, withdrew his troops from Gen. Kearney's command without author-ity, went to Com. Stockton, and solicited from *him* the appointment of Governor; and, strange to say, Stockton actually assumed the power to appoint Fremont Governor, although Kearney was upon the ground with a Governor's commission from the President of the United States!

These facts, and a great many others of the same character, we are informed, are set forth in Gen. Kearney's despatches, which will be published in Washington city in a few days.

LS, RC (DNA-94, LR, F-233 1847, f/w F-255 1847). Endorsed: "Re-ferred to the Judge Advocate. R. Jones, Sept. 27. 1847." The body of the letter was written by JBF, the signature is JCF's. On the reverse side are two notes: the first is in Benton's hand, the second signed by JCF.

"I was in Louisville the day of this publication. Capt. Emory arrived there the day before, from California, and was understood to be the informant. In consequence I addressed him a note immediately through Major T. L. Smith at Washington, and have never understood that he denied being Prentice's informant."

"I affirm that this publication is entirely untrue both as it concerns Com. Stockton and myself. J. C. Frémont, Lt. Col. Mtd. Riflemen."

222. William L. Marcy to Frémont

War Department
WASHINGTON, September 27, 1847

SIR,

The enclosed papers were sent sometime since, by the Secretary of State to this Department for the purpose of having measures adopted to investigate the charges therein preferred by the French Govern-ment, and to ascertain the true character of the transactions referred to, so that the Secretary of State might be able to make a proper reply to the application of the French Minister.[1]

These papers now transmitted to you for such explanations as you are enabled, and may deem proper, to give. Should it be necessary or required to take further steps in the case, and to obtain the testimony or explanations of other persons than yourself in California or the United States, I shall be obliged to you for the names and residences of such persons and for any statements as to the facts which may be established by them relative to the matter referred to in the enclosed papers. Such suggestions from you as will enable this Government to ascertain the facts of the case and to present it in its true character to that of France is respectfully desired. I am, with great respect, Your Obt. Serv.,

W. L. MARCY
Secretary of War

P. S. The papers herewith sent are the copies from the State Department, and you are requested to return them, but should you desire copies of them they will be furnished.

Lbk (DNA-107, LS, 28:47).
1. The French minister to the United States, Alphonse Pageot, had called Buchanan's attention to the proceedings of JCF and other American officers against Clement Panaud and his clerk, Théophile Dague. He expressed the hope that once the U.S. government was assured of the validity of the complaints, it would "call to a severe account the officers who had been guilty of these outrages, and will amply indemnify those individuals for the losses and injuries which they have sustained" (Pageot to Buchanan, 28 June 1847, with seven enclosures, DNA-94, LR, M-376 1849). The enclosures were: (1) J. A. Moerenhout to W. A. T. Maddox, 4 Nov. 1846, complaining of the revocation of a travel permit for Panaud; (2) Maddox to Moerenhout, 4 Nov. 1846, stating that the complaint had been referred to JCF for an answer; (3) Moerenhout to Maddox, 7 Nov. 1846, protesting against JCF's failure to respond by letter or action; (4) JCF to Moerenhout, 7 Nov. 1846, our Doc. No. 80; (5) Moerenhout to JCF, 8 Nov. 1846, our Doc. No. 81; (6) Maddox to Moerenhout, 8 Nov. 1846, stating that future communications about Panaud should be addressed directly to JCF; and (7) the deposition of Théophile Dague, 23 Nov. 1846, detailing his cruel treatment at the hands of the Americans, with the implication that they had stolen $420 in gold from him.

223. Frémont to William L. Marcy

WASHINGTON CITY Sep. 28th. 1847

SIR,

I have the honor to acknowledge the receipt of your communication of the 27th. inst. accompanied by the documents referred by the Secretary of State to the Department of War, and requiring from me some explanation in regard to charges preferred by the French government for outrages & injuries said to be inflicted upon certain French subjects, by the American authorities in that territory.

In reply I respectfully make the following statements, which are necessarily brief in the absence of books & other papers to which I might refer for certain information.

1. That portion of the territory where the events under consideration occurred was at that time in a state of insurrection and had been declared to be under the government of strict martial law.

2. Certain regulations deemed by the commandant of Monterey necessary to the safety of the place, had been violated by the complainant M. Pannaud who was in consequence, arrested by Capt. Maddox. Out of this arrest grew the correspondence between the French consul and the American authorities and the claim for damages made by said Pannaud.

3. The case was referred by me to the civil authorities (Walter Colton being the Judge or Alcalde) and Pannaud being required to make oath to the claim, which he, & the consul of France in his name, had preferred, did entirely refuse to do so preferring rather to make a formal renunciation of his claims, which was accordingly done.[1] Thomas O. Larkin Esq. and Captain Maddox were present on this occasion, conducting the case, which was as a matter of course considered to be terminated. It was considered by me that the preferring of the claim had been a conspiracy to defraud and it could have been incontestibly proved that said claim was grossly false. With this knowledge claimant had been required to certify on oath to its correctness.

4. It may not be improper to state for the information of the Department and in justification of my letter to the Consul of France that I had understood from Mr. Larkin and other respectable merchants of California that the said consul was known during his residence in the Sandwich Islands to be a man of troublesome character, much disposed [to] create & foment difficulties; for these reasons I considered his absence from the seat of operations at that time highly expedient.[2]

In the case of T. Dague I have to state that this man was brought to my encampment at the mission of Saint Johns by one of the Captains of the California Battalion U. S. troops, charged with being a spy. A court martial was accordingly called, consisting of officers of the Battalion and after a full hearing said Dague was condemned & sentenced to receive twenty-six lashes. The sentence was as a necessary measure approved by me and partially executed, the criminal receiving eighteen lashes. My presence with him & attention to him after the infliction of the punishment, was due simply to humanity & not from any belief in the innocence of the prisoner. Of the loss of money alledged by him I heard nothing at the time, nor at any subsequent time during my residence at California.[3] When I shall be in possession of my papers I may be able to communicate if desired farther information from the proceedings of the court martial & other notes; although at the time neither of these cases much occupied my attention.

I also respectfully refer the Department to Thomas O. Larkin late American Consul at Monterey & Capt. Wm. A. Maddox, for more detailed information.[4] I am very respectfully Sir, Your obedient Servant,

J. C. FRÉMONT,
Lieut. Col. Mounted Riflemen

Hon. Wm. Marcy
Sec. at War.

LS, RC (DNA-107, F-98 [66]). Endorsed: "Entd. Oct. 9 '47."

1. The French consul believed Panaud renounced his claims out of fear (see Doc. No. 81, n. 1).

2. Moerenhout had been a resident of the Society Islands, not the Sandwich Islands. His enemies there may have considered him a "troublesome character," because he proved their equal in intrigue, but—as Moerenhout pointed out to the board of officers convened to inquire into the affair—his conduct in the Society Islands had nothing to do with his service as French consul at Monterey (see J. A. Moerenhout's testimony, 19 June 1848, in report of the board of officers summoned to hear complaints of certain Frenchmen, DNA-94, LR, M-376 1849).

3. A twenty-two-year-old Frenchman in the employ of Panaud, Théophile Dague had been seized at the ranch of José Joaquín Gómez after the battle of Natividad because, he said, he had chastised some of JCF's men, whom he accused of stealing articles from the Gómez house. Testimony of others indicated that he may have used language abusive of the American officers and flag. Dague fainted during the flogging, and when he revived, he charged that his money belt containing $420 in gold was missing from his body (see Dague's testimony, 28 Sept. 1848, same file).

4. Because of incomplete evidence, the board of officers felt unable to report all the facts. It did conclude that there had been no reason for JCF to suggest that Moerenhout remove his office to San Francisco, and that Clement Panaud had indeed suffered losses, not only when he was prevented personally from attending to the sale of his goods but also by the detention and flogging of Dague, who had been sent to San Jose to take care of Panaud's business (report of the board of officers, 29 Jan. 1849, same file).

224. Thomas H. Benton to Frémont

Dear Sir,

Letters from Jessie of the 28th arrived this morning, containing the order for your trial at Fortress Monroe. The place will not prevent me from attending, tho inconvenient to both of us; I shall therefore hasten the conclusion of my business to this State, and propose to start back in a week.

With respect to the trial upon Kearneys charges, they are absurd, as he did not assume the command until after the 1st of March, and did not go to California by *virtue* of his orders, and acted under Stockton when he got there, and gave you mere orders of contradiction over the California Battalion raised under Stockton, of which he did not assume the command until he settled the question of authority with Stockton's superior (Com. Shubrick).

With respect to the newspaper publications, they cannot be considered as anonymous, Capt. Emory being mentioned by me as the imputed author (which he has not denied) and besides the editors of the Picayune, Louisville Journal, St. Louis Republican & Pittsburg Gazette, all vouch the respectability of the informant, and they are not anonymous.

The court is a very respectable one. The acquittal upon the charges is easy enough, but you are entitled to credit for your conduct in California, and the misconduct of others deserves to be exposed. These gentry shall all have their conduct brought out. The drawing up of the written defense will afford a proper occasion for an ample view of your conduct, and will become a great historical document. The authentic & formal demand which you have made for a trial on all the publications against you, and no one appearing to sustain them, is received by the public as a vindication, and the publication of the letter in [the] Union, and thence into other papers, covers all the authors of these publications, Emory especially, with the opprobrium of calumniators. That publication has given the course to public opinion on the whole subject.

I conceive that you have a *right* to a court of inquiry on the newspaper publications, and I look upon it as the duty of congress to enquire into the conduct of all the officers in the California conquest. This I will attend to myself: as to the court of Inquiry, it has not yet been refused and, it would be easy for some members of the court martial to constitute it. I will write frequently.

THOMAS H. BENTON

ALS, RC (CLSM). Also in F. M. WHEAT, 153.

225. Frémont to William L. Marcy

WASHINGTON CITY, Oct. 4th 1847

To the Hon. Mr. Marcy,
SIR,

In looking through my papers I find the within renunciation of claim by Clement Pannaud one of the plaintiffs in the case recently submitted by the French minister to the Secretary of State & referred to yourself.[1]

I respectfully enclose it for your information & request that itself or a copy may be returned to me. Very respectfully Sir your Obdt. Servt.,

J. C. FRÉMONT,
Lt. Col. U. S. A.

[*Enclosure*]

Copy
Magistrate's Office, MONTEREY
November 10' 1846

I hereby voluntarily and without any compulsion do declare that I renounced all claims, of whatever nature may have been made in my behalf by Mr. Morenhout, Consul of France against the Government of the United States of America in his official letter of the 7th instant to William A. T. Maddox Esq. Military Commandant of the Middle Department of California.

(Signed) CLEMENT PANAUD
(Signed) Witness and Interpreter
W. E. P. HARTNELL

(Signed)
Witness
WM. R. GARNER

401

The above document was drawn, signed and delivered in my presence and in my office this 10th day of November 1846.

WALTER COLTON
Chief Magistrate

The above is a true copy of the original document as drawn by the Secretary of the Magistrate's Office.

WILLIAM R. GARNER
Secretary of the Magistrate's Office

ALS-JBF, RC (DNA-107, LR, F-96 [66]). Endorsed: "Ansd. 6 Oct. 1847."
  1. See Marcy to Frémont, 27 Sept. 1847 and Frémont to Marcy, 28 Sept. 1847, Doc. Nos. 222 and 223. For background documents, see Frémont to Moerenhout, 7 Nov. 1846, and Moerenhout to Frémont, 8 Nov. 1846, Doc. Nos. 80 and 81.

226. William L. Marcy to Frémont

War Department
WASHINGTON, Oct. 6, 1847

SIR,

I have the honor to return, herewith, as requested by you, the paper accompanying your letter of the 4th. instant purporting to be a copy of an act executed by C. Panaud in California, renouncing claims made in his behalf against the United States: a copy of the paper now returned has been made and filed with your letter. Very respectfully Your Obt. Servt.,

W. L. MARCY
Secretary of War

Lt. Col. J. C. Fremont, U.S.A.
Washington City

Lbk (DNA-107, LS, 28:65).

227. Thomas H. Benton to Frémont

WOODFORD CO. KEN. Oct. 7, 1847

DEAR SIR,

The copy of the Judge Advocates letter of the 1st ins. to you, came to hand today, and in looking over the ten specifications, I find all of them to be anterior to the settlement of the question of rank with Shubrick, and consequently all amounting to the same thing. I do not know when the settlement of the question was militarily, or regularly, communicated to you, but *if so communicated at all,* it must have been late in March; consequently all the specifications refer to acts done before Kearny had [been] relieved of the land command, and made that change known to you. We shall demolish him with all ease, & overwhelm him with disgrace.

The newspaper article from the Louisville Journal being put into the hands of the Judge Advocate, without instructions what to do with it, seems to leave it to your option to require charges upon it, and will be so considered if you do not. I, therefore, recommend you to require charges and specifications to be made out on all the points they contain, and even take the charge without specifications: Emory, of course, to be a witness. To make sure I recommend you to specify the points, by no means omitting one which you will find in some of the publications, that you and Stockton had mismanaged &c. until Kearney arrived to set all right.

The fellow Bryant is in Lexington, and to meet him summon —— Brown [?][1] of the same neighborhood who is well spoken of by our friends for his faithful conduct towards you.

I wanted Hall to be summoned: we will finish his career in Mri. [Missouri]. He has been making speeches against you. I will write to my friends in the Platte country for a statement of what he has said.

Kearny brought all his witnesses from California with him, and all of them your enemies, & most of them engaged with him against you. He little knows how this will be turned against him. A military superior, perfidiously concealing his design, collects charges and witnesses to be used against a person ignorant of his design, conducted by him as a prisoner 3000 miles without giving him a chance to defend himself by bringing testimony to the scene of operations.

It is not only base, but shows a design to convict by unfair & foul means.

You will have to employ counsel: it will be more nominal than otherwise as I shall do the work. I would suggest Fendall,[2] who has been employed for the family in Sally McDowell's case.[3] It will be hard for you to get counsel to go to Fortress Monroe to be gone, one, two [or] three months. This may be a reason for a change of place. It will be a new case if, after Kearny has brought you [from] California without witnesses, the government shall send you to a fort in the sea, to be tried without counsel! It will be a case for the interference of your friends, & for accepting the *aid* from Charleston which will pay counsel fees. I shall be with you to the end, if it takes up the whole session of Congress.

If the place of trial is not changed before I get there, I will make a point of it.

I repeat: I wish you to require the judge advocate to make out charges on all the points of accusation, or insinuation against you, in the publications even dispensing with specifications where the charge was only in general terms, and for that purpose to name each point yourself in the words of the publications. The pardon of Jesus Pico—the capitulation granted Andres Pico—the duel affair with Mason must all be in.

Use your privilege of summoning witnesses without stint.

You will want copies of all orders to the Naval commanders in Cal. & to Kearny also. Yours,

B.

ALS, RC (CLSM). Addressed to JCF at C Street in Washington. Also in F. M. WHEAT, 151–53.

1. F. M. WHEAT transcribes the almost illegible surname as Brennan, whose identity the editors have been unable to determine. He may have had in mind Samuel Brannan, the chief of the Mormon colony, who reached San Francisco on 31 July 1846 and whose name was sometimes written as Brennan. Although Brannan had learned the printer's trade in Ohio and traveled through many parts of the country, he seems never to have been in Kentucky. Soon after reaching San Francisco, Brannan began publishing the *Star*. He was not summoned from California to testify, and more likely Benton is referring to William Brown, who was summoned as a witness (CT. MARTIAL, 298). Brown himself is an elusive figure. A Mr. Brown of Lexington, Ky., traveled part of the way to California with Edwin Bryant and William H. Russell in 1846 (BRYANT, 49), and a Lieutenant Brown commanded Russell's escort from California in the spring of 1847 (GARRARD, 328). Garrard indicates that only two years earlier the young lieutenant had emigrated to California and from there had visited the Hawaiian Islands. He returned to California

in the closing days of the war and received an appointment as an officer in the California Battalion. Brown's name, however, does not appear on the battalion's rosters (ROGERS [3]).

2. Philip Ricard Fendall (1794–1868), a highly respected Washington lawyer, had attended Princeton University, practiced law in Alexandria, and under the pseudonym "Patrick Henry" authored the pamphlet *An Argument on the Powers, Duties, and Conduct, of the Hon. John C. Calhoun, a Vice President of the United States, and President of the Senate* (Washington, D.C., 1827). He was consulted by Benton when the latter, acting under a power of attorney from JCF, sold Las Mariposas to Thomas Denny Sargent in 1852 (see Fendall to Frémont, 28 Feb. 1852, to be published in Vol. 3).

3. For details of Sally McDowell's case, see Doc. No. 30.

228. Thomas H. Benton to Frémont

WOODFORD CO. KEN.
[8 Oct. 1847]

DEAR SIR,

This Friday, and setting out on our return on Monday, this is the last letter I shall write you on the subject of the trial. I have a full view of the whole case—Kearney's as well as yours—and am perfectly at ease. You will be justified, and exalted: your persecutors will be covered with shame & confusion. The process through which you have gone is bitter; but it will have its Sweet. You will realize what Lord Palmerston said to Mr. Van Buren when he was rejected by the Senate, "that it was an advantage to a public man to be, in the course of his life, the subject of an outrage."

I mentioned yesterday the subject of the counsel, nominal only, for I should do the main work. You had as well let this rest until I arrive. I shall make advantage out of it. It would probably be impossible to get suitable counsel to go to Old Point Comfort for an indefinite period, & to study a new subject, and if you could find one the fee would be such as you could not pay. I should not propose less than $2000. If, therefore, the War Dept. perseveres in sending you to a fortress in the Atlantic ocean to be tried, for acts done on the Pacific, it will be sending you to be tried without counsel after bringing you across the continent to be tried without knowing it, & without a chance of getting testimony from California. I shall know how to make advantage out of all this, and it will force me, if it was not my previous attention [intention], to act as your counsel.

You may be at ease. The enemy is now in our hands, and may the Lord have mercy upon them; for I feel as if I could not. Love to all, & yours truly,

THOMAS H. BENTON

You will want Commodore Sloat to shew the commencement of your service under the Naval officers, and McLane who was a naval officer & one of your commissioners. Your Service under Naval officers commenced under Sloat & finished under Shubrick, when Kearney relieved him, & made known the change regularly to you.

ALS, RC (CLSM). Also in F. M. WHEAT, 153.

229. J. J. Abert to Frémont

Bureau of Topogl. Engs.
WASHINGTON October 8. 1847

SIR,

The enclosed is a notice of one of your drafts,[1] for which the means to meet were lately put in your hands. Please attend to it in time. Respectfully Sir Your Obt. Servt.

J. J. ABERT
Col. Corps T. E.

Lbk (DNA-77, LS, 10:237).
1. Not identified.

230. J. J. Abert to Frémont

Bureau of Topogl. Engs.
WASHINGTON October 9. 1847

SIR,

Your letter has been received.[1] The draft was not accepted there is therefore no accountability in the Bureau for it. It is one of your own. The sole right of drawing on this Bureau was on account of the appropriation for Surveys & if the draft had been paid by this Bureau it would have been paid & could have been paid only out of the funds which were lately put in your hands for the very purpose of enabling you to meet these drafts yourself. Future settlements, may show that many of your expenses are not chargeable upon the Survey fund, but I doubt the propriety of permitting such an apprehension to induce you to allow this draft to go unpaid & be protested which will be the case if you continue of the opinion expressed in your letter of this morning. Respectfully Sir Your Obt. Servt.

(Signed) J. J. ABERT
Col. Corps T. E.

Lbk (DNA-77, LS, 10:237).
1. JCF's letter to Abert, 8 Oct. 1847, giving his reasons for not feeling at liberty to pay a draft drawn on Abert for $767.32 out of the funds in his hands on account of military and geographical surveys, was listed in the register when received but is no longer on file.

231. Richard B. Mason to Roger Jones

Head Quarters, 10th Mily. Dept.
MONTEREY, CALIFORNIA
October 9th 1847

SIR,

I have the honor herewith to enclose to you the papers relating to a certain contract entered into on the 3rd day of March 1847, by Lieut. Colonel Frémont, Mounted Rifleman, with a Don Eulogio de Célis a resident of Ciudad de los Angeles California, but professing to be a Subject of the Queen of Spain. The paper marked A is a copy of this contract, with Lt. Col. Frémonts certificate bearing date April 26, 1847, that the contract had been complied with on the part of Don Eulogio de Célis, and that he Frémont had executed to him in payment, a note for the sum of Six thousand, nine hundred and Seventy-five dollars.

Lt. Col. Frémont left California in the month of June 1847, giving no notice to General Kearny or myself of the existence of such a contract, or that he had pledged the faith of his Government for the redemption of it by the payment of the sum of $6975, nor had I the least Idea of this obligation until applied to by Col. Stevenson in his letter marked 1, whether I would recognize the Contract and redeem the Bond at maturity. This letter was accompanied by those marked A. B. C. D. E. and F, which show that in fact, notwithstanding the certificate of Lt. Col. Frémont, Mr. Célis never delivered to the commissary of the California Battalion one single head of beef cattle under this contract, and that not one of these six hundred cattle were slaughtered for the use of that Battalion, but on the contrary that they have been delivered to a Mr. Stearns of Los Angeles, in two parcels, one of four hundred and eighty one, on the 1st day of May, and another of one hundred and nineteen, on the 6th day of July 1847, both of which dates are subsequent to the discharge of the California Battalion commanded by Lt. Col. J. C. Frémont. There is no doubt that these cattle are the same Six hundred, contracted for by Lt. Col. F. on the 3d. of March 1847. Mr. Celis stated it positively in his letter marked D, and the receipts for them by Stearns marked B and F specially state, that he Stearns receipts for them in the name and behalf of Lieut. Col. Frémont. These deliveries occurred at the time when a Garrison was stationed in Los Angeles, with a commissioned agent of the Commissary Department of the army Lieut. Davidson, to take charge of any subsistence stores intended for public use, yet these cattle furnished by a formal contract, are delivered to a private individual, upon a Special agreement (as he Stearns says) to breed on shares for the term of three years. I have endeavoured to procure from Mr. Stearns, a copy of the agreement he has made with Lt. Colonel Frémont for taking care of these cattle, but his letters marked 7 and 10 positively assert that he regards these cattle as the private property of Lieut. Frémont: but that the agreement by which he holds them, is a verbal one, witnessed by a Mr. Hensley,[1] Midshipman Wilson and Lt. Gillespie U. S. Navy. Midshipman Wilson has endorsed on the paper 10, that he knows nothing of it, and the other two Gentlemen have gone to the United States in Company with Commodore Stockton, and cannot be referred to by me. Thus stand the facts, and I am applied to, to know whether payment will be made upon the paper marked 2, which is a certificate that the sum of 6975 dollars is due to Mr. Célis for supplies furnished the California Battalion, which supplies are clearly and plainly the lot of Six Hundred breeding cows now in the hands of a private individual, not one of which has been used for public purposes. This note becomes due on the 18 day of December 1847, and bears an interest of 24 per centum per annum after that date.

In connection with this subject I call your attention to the paper marked 3 wherein Lt. Col. Frémont has bound himself and future Governors of California to pay the sum of Two thousand five hundred dollars, at the expiration of Eight months from the date of March 3, 1847, or in default thereof, that the note shall bear an interest of 24 per cent per annum—this too, when the A A Qr. Master at Monterey, had been more than a month in the Country, with a supply of money applicable to the proper expenses of the Army in California. Mr. Célis states that it was partly to secure this loan of money, that Lt. Col. Fremont made with him the liberal bargain for cattle, for which the price is about 40 per cent higher than the market price at the time. Both of these notes are soon due and Mr. Célis is going to make application for payment; as he claims to have fulfilled his part of a Contract, for the redemption of which the good faith of the Government of the United States is pledged, by an officer thereof: but as the whole transaction, as shown by the accompanying papers, appears to me of such a character, that I shall not order payment of the money to Mr. Célis, but refer all the papers to the Department, for such action as they may consider proper in the case. I have the honor to be Your most Ob. Servt.

R. B. MASON
Col. 1 Drag.
Com'dg.

Genl. R. Jones
Adjt. Genl.
Washington

[*Enclosures*]

A. Contract between Eulogio de Célis and Frémont and Frémont's Certificate of Compliance

[LOS ANGELES]
[3 March 1847]

This article of agreement made and entered into this third day of March in the year eighteen hundred and forty seven, by and between

Eulogio de Célis a resident of the City de Los Angeles Capital of Upper California of the first part and J. C. Fremont Governor of California and legal representative of the Government of the United States of North America of the second part. Witnesseth That the said Eulogio de Célis has sold to J. C. Fremont Governor of California aforesaid a lot of six hundred head of cattle of good merchantable kind and Suitable for beef to be delivered to the Commissary of the troops under the immediate command of Governor Fremont in number, corresponding with the requisitions of the Commissary and the said Governor Fremont binds himself and his Successors in office to pay to said Eulogio de Célis his heirs, executors, administrators or assigns at the expiration of eight months the sum of Six thousand dollars without defalcation. It is expressly understood between the above contracting parties that if said Eulogio de Célis fails to deliver good merchantable cattle when required to do so by the Commissary that the Contract is to be considered null and void by the said Governor Fremont, he paying to Eulogio de Célis, ten dollars per head for the number delivered and it is farther understood that the hides of the above cattle are to be delivered on application to the said Eulogio de Célis to whom they belong according to agreement. In testimony of the above the said parties have hereunto set their hand and affixed their Seals at the City de Los Angeles the Capital of California, the day and year before within.

Signed in presence of   (Signed) EULOGIO DE CÉLIS
Wm. H. Russell, Secy. of State   [*Seal*]
        (Signed) J. C. FRÉMONT
        Gov. of California
        [*Seal*]

I do hereby certify that Don Eulogio de Célis has complyed to within obligation and contract on his part by delivering the number of cattle as specified Angeles April 26th 1847 and in payment of I have this day executed to said Célis my note for the sum of Six thousand nine hundred, and seventy five dollars, including the hides of the full number of cattle.

        (Signed) J. C. FRÉMONT
        Lt. Col. U.S.A.

I hereby certify the above to be a true and faithful copy of the contract between J. C. Fremont Gov. of California & Eulogio de Célis,

and of the certificate of Lt. Col. Fremont, U. S. A. of said Célis's completion or fulfillment of the aforesaid contract.
"date of copy"

Los Angeles, California
June 17th. 1847

A. J. SMITH
Lt. 1st Dragoons
U. S. Army

B. Translation of Abel Stearns to Eulogio de Célis

[LOS ANGELES]
[1 May 1847]

I have received from Don Eulogio de Celis, four hundred and eighty-one head of cattle on account of Mr. J. C. Fremont, Lieut. Colonel of the Army of the United States, which cattle exists in my possession.

Angeles May 1st. 1847
(Signed) ABEL STEARNS

481 head of cattle

C. Jonathan D. Stevenson to John W. Davidson

Head Qrs. Southn. Mil. Dist. California
CIUDAD DE LOS ANGELES
7 June 1847

SIR,

It having been reported to me that some time in the month of March last, 600 Head of Beef cattle, were accounted for on account of U. S. Government, by Lt. Col. Frémont and delivered by his authority to Abel Stearns Esqr. of this place, I have to request that you will at the earliest moment possess yourself of all the facts, and circumstances of the case with a view to recover the property if it legally belongs to the Government of the U States. Very Respectfully Your Obdt. St.

J. D. STEVENSON
Col. Comdg.

J. W. Davidson
A. A. Qt. Master

D. Translation of Eulogio de Célis's Certificate of Facts

[LOS ANGELES]
[8 July 1847]

The undersigned certifies: that the Government & *Commandant* of this territory Mr. J. C. Fremont, finding himself short of resources for the support of the armed force which under his command co-operated towards the pacification of the country, solicited from various individuals a loan for the object indicated, and the under-signed having been requested through the medium of Mr. Charles Flügge to furnish provisions and cash, the accompanying Contract took place, the cash having been delivered immediately, without interest for the term of eight months, and the cattle was to be de-livered when it might be wanted, it being understood that the terms of payment should run on from the day of the contract on account of the cattle being moveable property which could not be consumed in two nor three months, and besides was augmenting daily it con-sisting chiefly of cows. It is likewise added that the contract was complied with on the part of the declarant, to the satisfaction of the Governour, who not having time to consume said cattle on account of having received a superiour order to deliver up the command, and disband the force, he ordered said cattle to be delivered to Mr. Abel Stearns, as I understand in the quality of a deposit until the Govern-ment should dispose of it.

Angeles 8th July 1847
(Signed) EULOGIO DE CELIS

E. Frémont to Eulogio de Célis

[LOS ANGELES]
[3 March 1847]

Eight months after date, I, J. C. Fremont Governor of California and thereby the legal agent of the Government of the United States of North America, in consideration of the sum of Two Thousand five Hundred Dollars being loaned or advanced to me, for the bene-fit of the said Government of the United States by Eulogio de Celis, do hereby promise and oblige myself in my fiduciary character as Governor aforesaid and my successors in office to pay to said Eulogio de Celis, his heirs, executors, administrators or assigns, the aforesaid sum of Two Thousand five Hundred Dollars ($2500) without defalcation.

It is agreed and understood that if the aforesaid sum of Two Thousand five hundred Dollars is not paid on or before maturity it is to draw interest at the rate of two per cent. per month from the time it falls due.

In testimony whereof, I have hereunto set my hand and have caused the seal of the territory to be affixed at the City de Los Angeles the Capital of California this third day of March in the year Eighteen Hundred and forty seven.

J. C. Fremont
Governor of California

True copy of Original
S. C. Foster[2]

F. Translation of Abel Stearns to Eulogio de Célis

[Los Angeles]
[7 July 1847]

I have received from Don Eulogio de Célis one hundred and nineteen head of cattle on account of Mr. J. C. Fremont, Lieut. Colonel of the Army of the United States, and said cattle remains in my possession according to agreement.

Angeles 7th July 1847

119 head of cattle   (Signed) Abel Stearns

1. Jonathan D. Stevenson to Richard B. Mason

Head Qts. Southn. Mily. Dist. (Califa.)
Ciudad de los Angeles
July 12, 1847

Colonel,

On the 17th of June A. A. Qt. Mastr. Davidson called on me with a resident of this place, named Celis, who had exhibited to him a contract made with Lt. Col. Fremont for the delivery of 600 head of Beef cattle, and enquired whether the Government would recognize the contract, and pay the bond at maturity. The A. A. Qt. Mastr. deeming it proper to consult me, called with Mr. Celis. After exhibiting such papers on the subject as he had in his possession I requested that he would furnish the Qt. Mastr. with copies, and give him all the information in his power, as to the disposition that was made of the cattle, and in short every species of information as well in relation to the cattle as to the cause that lead to the original contract; and that the A. A. Qt. Mastr. might act officially I addressed him an official letter requiring him to make all necessary enquiries and report the result to me; on the 6th I received from him the papers (marked "A" and "B") together with a copy of my communication to him "C". I have since obtained and forward with the others the statement of Celis (marked "D") of all particulars connected with the contract together with a copy of the note given by Lt. Col. Frémont (marked "E") for $2500 loaned him by Celis to obtain which the contract for the cattle was undoubtedly made. This matter in my judgement clearly shows the whole transaction to have been unjustifiable and calculated to defraud the Government although such may not have been the intention of the Government officer who made the contract.

The whole is respectfully submitted for your adjudication. I have the honor to be Very Respectfully Your Obdt. Servt.,

J. D. STEVENSON
Col. Comd. Southn. Mil. Dist Califa.

Col. R. B. Mason
Govr. of California

N. B.   Since writing the above I have received from Célis an additional receipt given him by Stearns (Marked "F") for 119 head of cattle making the delivery of the 600 complete on the 7th July whereas the certificate of Col. Fremont that the contract is complied with bears date 26 April 1847.

J. D. STEVENSON
Col.

14 July 1847

2. Frémont's Certificate of Indebtedness to Eulogio de Célis

[26 April 1847]

This is to certify that there is due from the United States to Don Eulogio de Celis, the sum of six Thousand, nine hundred and Seventy-five Dollars on account of Supplies furnished by him for sub-sisting United States Troops in Service in this Territory and under my command.

The above sum for which this obligation is given shall be subject to an interest of two per centum per month, after the expiration of the term of eight months from the 18th day of April 1847 until paid.

Angeles California, April 26th. 1847

(Signed) J. C. FREMONT
Lt. Col. U. S. A.

I certify that the above is a true copy of the Certificate held by Don Eulogio de Célis at Monterey, Cal. August 26, 1847

W. T. SHERMAN[3]
1st Lieut. 3rd Art.

3

[Another copy of Frémont's note to Eulogio de Célis, 3 March 1847 (see pp. 412–13)]

4. Jonathan D. Stevenson to Richard B. Mason

Head Qts. S. M. District (Califa.)
CIUDAD DE LOS ANGELES
August 11. 1847

COLONEL,

Enclosed you will receive the translation of Celis's communication in relation to the contract with Lt. Col. Fremont for Beef Cattle. I learn from Doctor Foster the interpreter here that in conversation with Celis the day before he left here for Monterey, Celis stated that he should place the notes in the hands of some person at Monterey to be presented at maturity to the successor of Govr. Fremont and if they were not paid have them protested and forwarded to the Spanish Minister at Washington to be presented by him either at the War or Treasury Offices for payment. Mr. Stearns is still at his rancho some 25 miles from here. I shall write him immediately and if there is no probability of his returning here in time to forward his answer to you by next mail I will send some person down to deliver the letter and get his answer. I also enclose you the receipts for Two Ensigns forwarded by the U. S. Ship Lexington. I have the honor to be Very Respectfully Your Obdt. St.,

J. D. Stevenson
Col. Comdg. S. M. Dist. (Califa.)

Colonel R. B. Mason
U. S. Dragoons
Govr. of California

5. Jonathan D. Stevenson to Richard B. Mason

Head Qts. S. M. District (Califa.)
Ciudad de los Angeles
August 12th. 1847

Colonel,

I have the honor to enclose you a copy of my note to Mr. Stearns making the enquiry relative to the cattle he holds, as p[er] receipts in your possession. I also enclose his answer which you will perceive I have certified to as being the original. Very Respectfully Your Obdt. St.,

J. D. Stevenson
Col Com'dg. S. M. Dist.

Col. R. B. Mason
1st U. S. Dragoons
Govr. of California

6. Jonathan D. Stevenson to Abel Stearns

Head Qts. S. M. District (Califa.)
Ciudad de los Angeles
August 11. 1847

Sir,

Don Eulogio de Celis of this Ciudad presented to me in the month of June last a contract made between himself and Lt. Col. Fremont for Six hundred head of Beef Cattle together with certain evidences of the fulfillment of his part of the contract, at the same time enquiring whether payment for said cattle would be made by the Qt. Mastr. of this Post or any other person at the time stipulated in the contract. I immediately forwarded a certified copy of the contract

416

and all the accompanying papers to Col. Mason, Military Commander and Governor of California, the only person in my judgement who could properly answer the enquiry of Mr. Celis. Among the vouchers presented by Celis and forwarded to Col. Mason were two receipts of yours for 600 head of Cattle; the last mail brought me a reply from Col. Mason to my communication accompanying said documents directing me to make the following enquiry of you to which I will thank you for an answer at your earliest convenience.

Extract

H. Qts. 10th Mily. Dept.
Santa Barbara Aug. 1st, 1847

You will enquire of Mr. Stearns what Cattle these are he holds, by what tenure he holds them, whether he considers them his own property, that of Lt. Col. Fremont or that of the United States. I have the honor to be Very Respectfully Your Obdt. St.

(Signed) J. D. Stevenson
Col. Comd. S. M. District

Abel Stearns, Esqr.

7. Abel Stearns to Jonathan D. Stevenson

Angeles Agt. 12th. 1847

Dear Sir,

In reply to your official letter of yesterday, I would observe that I hold in my possession six hundred head of cattle (the major part breeding cows) received from Don Eulogio de Celis on account of Lt. Col. J. C. Fremont.

I hold these cattle by agreement and for the term of three years to return the same number and class at the end of the term with one half of increase, excepting such as may be lost in any way whatever and not for want of care on my part.

I consider the cattle as the private property of Lt. Col. J. C. Fremont, not being instructed by him to the contrary. I have the honor Sir to be your very Obt. Servt.,

Abel Stearns

To Col. J. D. Stevenson
Comd. South. Mil. Dist. Califa.

I certify this be an original document handed me by Mr. Stearns in person within the last hour.

J. D. STEVENSON
Col. Comdg. Los Angeles

Head Qts. S. M. Dist. Calif.
Ciudad de los Angeles
12 August 1847

8. Jonathan D. Stevenson to Richard B. Mason

Head Qts. S. M. Dist. (Califa.)
CIUDAD DE LOS ANGELES
September 21, 1847

SIR,

Pursuant to instructions I called upon Mr. Stearns for the proofs of his Cattle contract, with Lt. Col. Fremont; I have the honor to enclose a copy of my communication to him together with his answer which I have certified to be the Original document handed me by Stearns himself. Very Respectfully Your Obdt. Servt.,

J. D. STEVENSON
Col. Comdg. S. M. Dist.

Col. R. B. Mason
1st U. S. Dragoons
Govr. of California

9. Jonathan D. Stevenson to Abel Stearns

Head Qts. S. M. Dist.
CIUDAD DE LOS ANGELES
September 17th. 1847

SIR,

The mail of this morning brought me a communication from Col. R. B. Mason Govr. of California relative to the Cattle received by you from Col. Frémont; and as he requires further information on the subject, I give you herewith an extract from his communication and request that you will furnish me with an answer at your earliest convenience communicating all the information you possess upon the points referred to by him. Respectfully Your Obdt. Servt.,

J. D. Stevenson
Col. Comdg. S. M. Dist.

A. Stearns Esqr.

Extract
Head Quarters, 10 Mily. Dept.
Monterey, Calif. Sept. 7th. 1847

Sir,

Your Report on the ownership of a lot of Cattle delivered by Dr. E. Celis to Mr. Stearns of Los Angeles in May and July last has also been received together with the original letter of said Stearns to you stating that he holds the cattle referred to for a term of three years, according to agreement with Lieut. Col. Fremont and that he Stearns considers these cattle as the private property of Lieut. Col. Fremont.

If the agreement to which Mr. Stearns refers be in writing, please procure an authenticated copy of it, or if it be a mere verbal agreement witnessed by disinterested persons, then cause Mr. Stearns to furnish you with such evidence as would prove his right to the trust he claims before a competent Court.

Col. Mason considers this agreement between Lieut. Col. Fremont and Mr. Stearns of importance and wishes you to procure the papers, and evidence above referred to and send them here by the return mail. I have the honor to be Your Obdt. Servant,

(Signed) W. T. Sherman
1st Lieut, 3rd Arty.
A. A. A. General

To Col. J. D. Stevenson
7th Regt. N. Y. Vols.
Los Angeles, Cal.

10. Abel Stearns to Jonathan D. Stevenson

Angeles September 20th. 1847

Sir,

I have the honor to acknowledge the receipt of your official note of 17th inst. with an extract of an official letter to you from W. T. Sherman A. A. A. General, requiring from me further information relative to a contract by which I hold a certain lot of Cattle received from Dr. E. Celis for account of Lieut. Col. J. C. Fremont; and whether I have a written contract or a verbal one; if the latter to furnish you with the evidence to prove the right to my trust. In answer to which I have to observe; that I hold the Cattle by verbal Contract; Witness to the same, Mr. Samuel Hensly [Hensley], Capt. in the late California Battalion, to whom I refer you particularly. He resides near Nueva Helvecia [Helvetia], also Midshipman John K. Wilson, and Lieut Arch. H. Gillespie, U. S. Marine, both I think were present and knowing to the contract. As the above named gentlemen are not here, I cannot furnish you with their certificates relative to the contract. Very respectfully your Obt. Servt.

ABEL STEARNS

To Col. J. D. Stevenson
Comdg. S. M. Dist.

I certify the foregoing to be an original document handed me by Abel Stearns on the 20th Inst. as an answer to a note from me dated 17 September 1847 calling upon him for certain information relating to a Cattle contract between himself and Lt. Col. Fremont of the U. S. Army.

Los Angeles, Califa.   J. D. STEVENSON
Sept. 21st. 1847   Col. Comdg. S. M. D.

Monterey October 7th 1847
Having been referred to as a Witness in relation to a contract between Lt. Col. Fremont and Mr. Abel Stearns, I have to state that I have no recollection of being present when the verbal agreement was made, but that I possessed at the time some knowledge of a contract existing what the nature of it was I am now unable to say.

J. K. WILSON
Midn. U. S. N.

LS (DNA-94, LR, M-1348 1847, f/w K-209 1846). Endorsed: "Received, January 27, 1848." "Respectfully laid before the Sec. of War. Jany. 29th. R. Jones, A.G." All enclosures may be found with Mason's covering letter. For enclosures B and F there are also certified copies in Spanish.

JCF was very short of resources for the support of his battalion, and he solicited loans from various individuals. These papers reveal that through Charles W. Flügge, Célis was asked to furnish provisions and cash. In turn, JCF obligated himself and the U.S. government for repayment. Célis delivered the cash immediately without interest, for the term of eight months, and was to deliver cattle as required. When JCF was removed from his command and the California Battalion disbanded, he ordered the cattle delivered to Abel Stearns, who on 1 May acknowledged receipt of 481 head and on 7 July of an additional 119 (making the delivery of the 600 complete), although as early as 26 April JCF had certified that Célis had complied with his part of the contract by delivering the number of cattle specified.

A letter of William T. Sherman to the U.S. military commandant of the Southern District, Jonathan D. Stevenson, reflects the doubts of Colonel Mason that the beef was ever intended for the commissary. Sherman wrote, "It is supposed that a Mr. Lergo supplied the Californian Battalion with Fresh Beef, daily or according to their wants, during the period embraced in the contract *viz* from the 3d. of March 1847 to the time of their discharge in the following month of April. If such be the case, you will please ascertain the fact and report it to these head quarters together with the evidence that supports it, you will likewise cause Mr. Celis to present the receipts of the Commissary, who according to the Contract should have received the cattle, and he must have done so, as Lt. Col. Fremont has certified that the contract has been fulfilled" (Sherman to Stevenson, Santa Barbara, 1 Aug. 1847, DNA-393, 10th Military Department, LS, vol. 1, March–Dec. 1847).

In DNA-393, 10th Military Department, LR, 14-S-1847, which also contains copies of all the documents pertaining to the JCF-Célis contract, is a copy of R. B. Mason's endorsement under date of 13 Nov. 1847 on the contract which David Spence, as agent for Célis, presented to him. It reads as follows: "I decline and refuse to have anything to do concerning this contract, for the reason that I have, in my possession satisfactory evidence that the six hundred head of cattle mentioned herein were never delivered to the commissary of the troops as certified to by Lt. Col. Frémont, and none of them were even slaughtered for the use of said troops, on the contrary, the said cattle, which turn out to be a lot of breeding cows, not beef cattle, were delivered by the contractor, Mr. Celis, subsequent to the date of Col. Frémont's certificate, and subsequent to the discharge of the troops under his command, to a Mr. Stern [Stearns] of the Pueblo de los Angeles, who writes that he holds the said cattle to breed on shares with Col. Frémont, for three years."

JCF justified delivering the cattle to Stearns and giving an early receipt to Célis on the ground that he was attempting to give some financial protection to himself and Célis should the U.S. government follow Kearny's policy of refusing to assume responsibility for the debts incurred during JCF's governorship (Frémont to W. L. Marcy, 19 May 1848, enclosure in Charles M. Conrad to C. F. Smith, 27 Sept. 1852, DNA-92, LR, 1852–54; Frémont to Jacob R. Snyder, 11 Dec. 1849, in *Alta California,* 15 Dec. 1849).

1. Formerly of Jessamine County, Ky., Capt. Samuel J. Hensley (1817–66) had been a trapper in New Mexico before coming to California with Joseph B. Chiles in 1843. He became supercargo of Sutter's launch, participated in the Bear Flag Revolt, and at the time of JCF's contract with Célis was commissary for the California Battalion. Hensley went east with JCF in 1847 to testify at his court-martial. He returned to California in 1848, opened a store at Sacramento in partnership with Pierson B. Reading, and a few years later helped to establish the California Steam Navigation Company, of which he became president (PIONEER REGISTER; GIFFEN [2], 37, 40, 70, 71–72).

2. Stephen Clark Foster (b. 1820), a native of Maine and a Yale graduate, had practiced medicine in Missouri and traded in New Mexico and Sonora before coming to California as an interpreter with the Mormon Battalion. In

the 1850s he played a prominent role in governing Los Angeles and was a state senator from 1850 to 1853 (PIONEER REGISTER).

3. William Tecumseh Sherman (1820–91), destined for fame and high command in the Civil War.

232. Frémont to Albert Gallatin

WASHINGTON CITY October 10th 1847.

MY DEAR SIR,

Your letter of September 15th reached this city during my absence, and since my return, I have been so much oppressed with accumulated business, that I could not find sufficient time for so satisfactory a reply as I had promised myself the pleasure of sending you. Finding that I cannot yet free myself from engagements, and the delay becoming somewhat long, I write to tell you that I am endeavoring to prepare you such a sketch or skeleton map of my routes through the Basin country as will be the best answer to your enquiries.[1] In the meantime, I will answer some of them briefly.

The point of departure on leaving California, is from the Sacramento river. There are several other points at which that great range may be crossed, but a knowledge of these is confined to my own party. You will remember that a river called Mary's had been the object of my search during the expedition of 1843–44. This has been surveyed throughout its entire course in my last journey. Bridger's fork [Bruneau River] must be an affluent to this stream as the Basin waters are entirely separated by a mountain chain from those of the Columbia river. The sketch I propose sending will fully exhibit the geography of this northern part of the basin. I think that you will find our recent survey of considerable interest, as it was particularly directed to a determination of the Basin & the Sierra Nevada. I would be glad to know the limit of the time within which, what information I have will be useful to you.

I am with very high respect and much regard Your very obedient servant,

J. C. FRÉMONT

ALS-JBF, RC (NHi).

1. JCF seems not to have transmitted the sketch map to Gallatin in time for publication in the *Transactions* of the American Ethnological Society

(1848), vol. 2. There Gallatin discusses only JCF's 1845 map. It seems likely that Gallatin eventually received a copy of the 1848 map, which was to accompany JCF's *Memoir*. "You did not let me know whether the tracing of my map, which I told you I could let you have for Mr. Gallatin, would be in time to be of any use," he wrote to John Russell Bartlett. "It is now ready, and if it will be of any use I will immediately send it on hearing from you" (11 July 1848, NIC). In June 1850 Bartlett would replace JCF on the U.S.–Mexican Boundary Commission.

233. Frémont to Roger Jones

Washington City October 11th. 1847

To the Adjutant General.
Sir,

The place which has been designated by the Department for the holding of the Court Martial by which I am to be tried is extremely inconvenient to me and increases the difficulty of my defence as both facts and laws and records can be more easily had in Washington than elsewhere. I therefore respectfully request that a place of trial be named nearer to my means of defence & of counsel.

I also beg leave respectfully to urge upon you the justice & propriety of my being tried on all the allegations in the publications against me, & which have been already filed in your office. These cannot be regarded as anonymous Captain Emory having been mentioned by Col. Benton as the imputed author, and that officer having never denied the charge. In addition to this the Editors of the Picayune, Louisville Journal, St. Louis Republican, and Pittsburg Gazette, all vouch the respectability of their informant, and they are not anonymous.

Considering these publications as being in fact specifications under General Kearny's general charges I trust that you will as a matter of justice to me cause them to be included in the charges already arranged for the decision of the court. I remain with much respect Your most obedient servant.[1]

J. C. Frémont
Lt. Col. U. S. A.

LS, SC (DNA-94, LR, F-234 1847). Endorsed: "Respectfully laid before the Sec. of War. R. Jones, A. G. [See letter to Lt. Col. F. of Septr. 27/47]. Ansd. Octr. 13th. R. J."

1. Later JCF's counsel renewed the application of their client to be tried on certain newspaper publications containing charges against him. They objected to Fort Monroe, 200 miles from Washington, as an "out-of-the-way place" (Benton and William C. Jones to Roger Jones, 25 Oct. 1847, Doc. No. 242).

234. Joseph L. Folsom to William T. Sherman

Quartermaster's Office
SAN FRANCISCO
Octr. 12th. 1847

SIR,

I have the honor to forward the subjoined copies of papers the originals of which are now in my possession for the information of Col. Mason.[1] They were obtained from Mr. Shadden[2] today and the affidavits were put upon the backs of them at my request. I have receipted to him for the originals and have given him certified copies instead of them. I also gave him a certificate setting forth that he was entitled to compensation for keeping the public animals at the rate agreed upon with Col. Fremont up to the time I had them removed from his place. I am Sir Respectfully Your most Obt. Servt.,

J. L. FOLSOM
Capt. Asst. Quartermaster
U. S. Army

Lieut. Wm. T. Sherman
A.A.A. Genl. &c.
Monterey, California

[*Enclosures*]

MONTEREY, CALIFORNIA
May 29th. 1847

Mr. Thos. J. Shadden
SIR,

You will please deliver to Major P. B. Reading all the cattle which I left in your charge and much oblige. Yours Respectfully,

(Signed) J. C. FREMONT
Lieut. Col. U. S. A.

Upon the back of this order is endorsed the following affidavit:

I, Thos. J. Shadden depose and say, that the cattle named in this order are a portion of those for which Colonel J. C. Fremont U. S. Army made an agreement with me for the keeping on account of the United States, and the cattle were the property of the United States.

(Signed) Thos. J. Shadden

Sworn & Subscribed this day Oct. 12th. 1847
(Signed) George Hyde,[3] 1st Alcalde District San Francisco

Received July 22d. 1847 from Thos. J. Shadden Esq. for and on account of Lieut. Col. J. C. Fremont sixty-seven head of cattle counting cows, steers about eighteen months and sucking calves, also twenty-six head of horses & two mules.

(Signed) P. B. Reading

P. S. The above cattle and horses were branded "F".

(Signed) P. B. R.

Upon the back of this receipt is endorsed the following affidavit:

I, Thos. J. Shadden, depose and say that the cattle and horses for which this receipt was given, were a portion of the United States animals for which Colonel J. C. Fremont U. S. Army made an agreement with me for the keeping that the cattle were delivered in pursuance of the written order of Colonel J. C. Fremont attached hereunto, and the horses by virtue of authority contained in a private letter from Colonel J. C. Fremont to P. B. Reading who received both the cattle and horses enumerated within.

(Signed) Thos. J. Shadden

Sworn & Subscribed this Day Oct. 12. 1847
(Signed) George Hyde, 1st Alcalde District San Francisco

I hereby certify that Mr. T. J. Shadden was employed to keep a band of cattle belonging to the United States from the eighth day of October, One thousand and eight hundred and forty six, at twenty-five Dollars per month.

Camp on American Fork   (Signed) J. C. Fremont
June 15th. 1847   Lt. Col. U. S. A.

This is to certify that Mr. T. J. Shadden has kept a band of horses belonging to the United States from the sixth Day of December, One Thousand Eight hundred and forty-six to the fifteenth of this present month, making in all six months and nine days, at fifty dollars per month.

Camp on American Fork   (Signed) J. C. FREMONT
June 15th. 1847   Lt. Col. U. S. A.

LS, RC (DNA-393, 10th Military Department, 299-1847). Endorsed: "Recd. Oct. 17." Capt. Joseph Libbey Folsom (1817–55) was chief of the Quartermaster Department station at San Francisco. Through heavy investment in town lots and by purchase of the Leidesdorff estate in San Francisco, he became one of California's wealthiest men.

1. Folsom had been charged by Col. Richard B. Mason to take possession of all horses and cattle owned by the United States under JCF's control. Folsom soon found that some of the animals pastured by JCF on a farm owned by Thomas J. Shadden had been taken by Pierson B. Reading for private use, and that the manager of JCF's farm on the Joaquin planned to do likewise. JCF's orders about the livestock were written after he was relieved from duty, Mason argued, and hence were issued without authority. He then instructed Folsom to obtain the original orders (or authenticated copies) containing Shadden's endorsements, so that JCF might be charged with the value of the property by the Treasury Department. As these documents indicate, Folsom complied. Details relating to this episode may be found in Folsom to W. T. Sherman, 11 Aug. 1847 and 29 Aug. 1848 (DNA-393, 10th Military Department, F-7-48), and Sherman to Folsom, 13 Aug. 1847 (DNA-393, 10th Military Department, LS, vol. 1, March–Dec. 1847).

2. Thomas J. Shadden had come from Oregon to California in 1843 with the Hastings party. After JCF stopped keeping his own commissary stores at Sutter's Fort, he had the public cattle driven to Shadden's farm in Yolo County and arranged with Sutter to supply beef for the troops (Folsom to Sherman, "Pueblo de San Jose," 11 Aug. 1847, DNA-393, 10th Military Department, F-7-48).

3. A lawyer and former secretary for Commodore Stockton, George Hyde succeeded Edwin Bryant as first alcalde in San Francisco. After his resignation in March 1848 he remained in San Francisco, taking some part in city politics and becoming a real estate broker (GRIVAS, 89, 107, 113, 194, 196).

235. Roger Jones to Frémont

W. D. A. G. O. WASHINGTON. Oct. 13. 1847.

COLONEL:

Your letter of the 11th instant,[1] renewing your application to be tried on matters of allegation published in certain newspapers of the country, and also requesting that the court instituted for your trial on charges preferred by Brig. Genl. Kearney may be ordered to assemble at a place nearer your means of defense and counsel than Fort Monroe, as directed in "General Orders," No. 32 has been laid before the Secretary of War. And with respect to the first request I can only repeat that it is not seen that the usage and practice of the service in the present instance can be departed from. It is a fixed principle of the Military Service that the sufficiency of all matters of charge, should be determined by the commanding General or the superior authority. The matters alluded to in your communication of yesterday, and not embraced in the charges with which you have been furnished by the Judge Advocate, have been considered and are not deemed by the War Department such as can properly be made the subject of additional charges.

The reasons you have offered for changing the place of holding the Court have also been duly weighed; but I am instructed to inform you they are not judged sufficient to overrule the considerations, which led to the selection made in the original order in the case. I am, Colonel, &c.

R. JONES, Adjt. Genl.

Lbk (DNA-94, LS, 24:239).
1. See Doc. No. 233.

236. Frémont to William L. Marcy

WASHINGTON CITY, October 13th. 1847

To the Secretary at War
SIR,

In the execution of my duties as Military Commandant during the war in California and afterwards as civil governor of the Territory I incurred many liabilities, some of which I think it absolutely necessary to bring to your attention. These are:

1. The payment of the volunteers for their services during the war, and for supplies in arms and other necessaries furnished by them.

2. Payment to citizens of that territory of money loaned me by them, and which was required and expended in administration of the government and partial payment of the troops.

The principal amount required for payment of the troops is comprehended in what is due to the volunteer emigrants for services during the insurrection in the southern part of upper California. These men were just arriving on the frontier of the territory and at the first call for their services quitted their families leaving them unprotected and exposed to the inclemencies of a rainy winter, and repaired to my camp, bringing with them arms, ammunition, wagons and money, all of which they freely contributed to the public service. These men returned to their families without money and without clothes and the long delay of payment has consequently created much dissatisfaction.

Paper given to them by properly authorized officers as certificates of service, has been depreciated by officers recently in command and much of it consequently sold at one tenth of its true value. As these public services were rendered promptly & in good faith by all concerned, at a time of imminent danger to the American arms I trust that some measure will be taken properly to recognize them and to redeem the pledges made to the people by myself in my public and private capacity. For this purpose I enclose a brief estimate from the Pay Master of the Battalion.

Amounts of money required for civil and military purposes were at different times and by different individuals loaned to me as the Governor of the Territory acknowledged as such by them. These sums of money are not large, but having been obtained under the high rates usual in that country public interest is suffering by the delay. Those liabilities which require immediate attention, including in the amount drafts on the State Department, will require about forty thousand dollars.

The two subjects which I have here presented for your consideration are causes of much dissatisfaction in the territory, and I have thought it a matter of duty to myself and the people with whom I have been connected as well as to the Government, respectfully to apply for the means of removing it. I have the honor to enclose for your information notices of protests, in the amount of nineteen thousand five hundred dollars of drafts drawn by me upon the Secretary of State, which were yesterday dishonored by Mr. Buchanan.[1] Those are among the drafts to which I have referred in the estimated amount of forty thousand dollars required for urgent liabilities. I am with great respect Your obedient Servant,

J. C. Frémont

Pierson B. Reading to Frémont

Monterey California
May 29th 1847

Sir,

According to your instructions, I have made an estimate of the amount of funds required for the payment of the California Battalion, and find the sum to be Eighty five Thousand four hundred and ninety-four Dollars $85,494. this amount being in the form of Certificates which were issued to Officers and privates in the settlement made by me, at the disbanding of the Battalion, taking at the time the necessary vouchers. Very Respectfully Your Obdt. Servt.,

P. B. Reading
Paymaster
Califa. Battalion
U. S. Troops

Lieut. Col. J. C. Fremont
U. States Army

LS, RC. This letter and its ALS enclosure are enclosures in a letter of Charles M. Conrad, Secretary of War, to C. F. Smith and other members of the Board for the Examination of Claims Contracted in California under Lt. Col. Frémont, 27 Sept. 1852 (DNA-92, LR, 1852–54). Endorsed: "Rec. Oct. 14. '47. Ansd. 15 Oct. 1847." A signed letter, in substance the same as that printed here but dated 8 Oct. 1847, is in the *Annual Publications* of the Historical Society of Southern California, 6 (1903):48–49. Under date of 8 Oct. 1847, it may also be found on pp. 3–4 of *California Claims*, Senate Report 75, 30th Cong., 1st sess., Serial 512. The printed versions do not mention that the protests in the amount of $19,500 had been disallowed by the Secretary of State.

1. These refer to the drafts drawn on Secretary of State Buchanan in favor of Francis Hüttmann and presented by Nanning Koster & Co. of New York City for payment to the Secretary of State, who in turn referred them to the Secretary of War. A number of documents respecting drafts of JCF in favor of Hüttmann are enclosures in Conrad to Smith, 27 Sept. 1852 (DNA-92, LR, 1852–54).

237. Albert Gallatin to Frémont

MY DEAR SIR

Your favor of 10th instant has been very gratifying to me; and nothing can be more satisfactory a reply to my queries than the sketch map which you are kind enough to prepare for me.

The further explanations which I may wish relate to the presumed Badger's [Bridger's] Fork and the St. Mary's [Humboldt] of the desert.

In a manuscript map bearing date 1831, and prepared under the direction of the late General Ashley who communicated it to me, Badger's Fork is laid down as beginning 30 to 40 miles west of the Great Salt Lake, in latitude 31° and running thence nearly due west about three degrees of longitude. He thought that it did empty into the Owyhee, which was a manifest error. If it does exist it must be lost in the sands or terminate in a lake; and it is clear that you should have crossed it on your late return from California. A party sent by Captain Bonneville did, from the western shores of the Great Salt Lake, reach and descend a river which led them to California. It was supposed to have been this Badger's Fork; but I suspect that it was the St. Mary's.

I would wish to have some further information respecting the character of the St. Mary's river. Are there any trees along its banks? Is there any land on its banks that might be rendered fit for cultivation, any spot having the capacity of an intermediary settlement? Wherever water has been found in the deserts of Arabia or Africa, cultivation has taken place and an Oasis has been formed.

Are there any mountains in the desert? Did you meet with any Indians living there, and what were their means of subsistence?

If perchance you should have become possessed of a vocabulary, however limited, of the Eutaws, or of any other Indian tribe whatever, you would greatly oblige me by communicating them to me.

The limit of the time, within which the information you have should be communicated to me, must necessarily be subject to your own convenience: but I am much pressed by the printer. The essay which I am preparing will be inserted in the second volume of the Transactions of the New York [American] Ethnological Society, the whole of which, with the exception of my essay, will be completed at the end of this month. And moreover the essay begins with the geographical part: so that it is really important to me that your communication should reach me as soon as practicable.

Mr. Benton kindly transmitted to me two copies of your work, one of which I forwarded to the distinguished geographer and antiquarian Mr. Jomard[1] of the French Institute. The Ethnological Society of which I am President has acquired some reputation abroad by the first volume of its Transactions: and we correspond with a number of the learned societies and many most distinguished individuals in Germany, France and England. Should you wish to have some more copies of your former work forwarded abroad we will take great pleasure in transmitting them.

I presume that the information which you will communicate to me will be but a prelude to an elaborate report of your late explorations, the sequel of your former work. This abridged communication will be a foretaste of the great work, and the means of calling the attention of the learned European world to your valuable labors. With the same object in view, I would suggest the propriety of describing briefly to me the astronomical and other instruments used by you in your explorations. <*It seems to me that your barometers were not good, and I place more reliance on the heights deduced from the degree of the thermometer at which water boils.*

I do not know why you gave the name of Sevier to Ashley's lake. Ashley was undoubtedly the first discoverer and resident on its banks. The Rio Virgin is identic with the stream called by Ashley, Adam's River.>

Have you acquired any reliable information concerning the Navajos, Moquis or any other cultivating tribe, on the upper waters of the great Colorado of the West?

[*Unsigned*]

Colo. J. C. Fremont
Washington

SC (NHi).
1. Edme François Jomard (1777–1862) was president of the Geographical Society in Paris and author of *Observations on Ancient and Modern Egypt or a Historical and Picturesque Description of the Monuments* (4 vols., 1830).

238. Thomas H. Benton to Frémont

FRANKFORT, KEN. Oct. 14. 1847.

DEAR SIR,

We were delayed two days in closing a contract for the sale of our small tract of land, 300 acres, adjoining the Saw tract, which was only concluded yesterday, and in an hour after we were on the way. The price was $20,100 which was fair enough, but I should have had more payments if we had been able to stay longer, & probably also have sold the main tract, as we wish to transfer all to Missouri.

We leave this place in the morning (Friday) arrive at Cincinnati tomorrow night—leave that Saturday morning for Washington—and expect to be there on Wednesday, or Thursday.

Mrs. B. and all as usual, and love to all. Your affectionally,

THOMAS H. BENTON

ALS, RC (CLSM). Addressed to JCF in Washington.

239. Frémont to an Unidentified Correspondent

WASHINGTON CITY, Oct. 15, 1847

SIR:

Absence from the city and accumulated business prevented an earlier reply to your letters, both of which have been received. In looking over your letters I find it difficult in the brief space of a reply to answer them satisfactorily, but I will try to do so, and you can write again for what may not be clear. I take up your questions in their order, premising that I am favorably impressed with California, in which I have the good fortune to agree with Humboldt and Vancouver. The climate varies much, very much, in different parts of the country, dependent upon its physical features or position in regard to the sea; those localities that are much exposed to the ocean being made during certain seasons of the year cold and unpleasant by heavy fogs and high winds from the northwest. At such places wheat is sometimes subject to be injured by rust. It will strike you in this connection that along the coast country the fogs favor vegetation, supplying the place of rain. In other localities the climate is unsurpassed in its good and pleasant character. In the time of the old missions in latitude 33° and 34°, apples, pears, peaches, pomegranates, plantains, bananas, sugar-cane, and indigo flourished together.

The town of San Francisco, on the coast near the entrance of Francisco Bay, is built on sandy soil, and is subject to the fogs and high winds. The town of St. Josephs [San Jose], on the south-eastern shores of that bay, is at the mouth of a large and very fertile valley, and enjoys a very pleasant climate. Wheat is the staple among the breadstuffs in the country lying around Francisco Bay, and the country around Los Angeles is the corn region. An American who went out with me is planting tobacco in the neighborhood of Santa Barbara. He tells me that it promises well.

Mr. Candroit [Cordua], a German farmer in the Sacramento Valley, told me recently that his average produce was 25 bushels (wheat) to the acre, which he judged would be the average produce of the Sacramento Valley. Agricultural implements are very few and will be much needed. So far, there is not a sufficient number of flouring mills to answer the demand and comfortable houses are nearly impossible to be had. Trade was formerly carried on by barter, articles in which it consisted being few, but money now is beginning to circulate. Cotton and woolen goods may be sold to advantage under any reasonable tariff. Agricultural labors, during the time of the old mission, were always carried on by irrigation, to which the country is admirably adapted. I think that this will always be necessary to secure certain crops in the southern part of Upper California. As a stock country, I do not think California can be equaled, the grasses being numerous and abundant, of superior quality and furnishing subsistence for cattle all the year round.

I feel interested in assisting to form a correct opinion of the value of California, and will be glad to furnish you any information I may possess. I am, very respectfully, yours,

J. C. FREMONT

Printed in New York *Times,* 1 July 1877, from the San Francisco *Bulletin,* 16 June 1877. The letter had been obtained from a resident of San Francisco and published by the *Bulletin* to show the quick growth of San Francisco over a thirty-year period. The California editor noted that San Jose "can hardly be said to be situated on the 'shores of the Bay.'"

240. William L. Marcy to Frémont

War Department
WASHINGTON, October 15, 1847

SIR:

I have received your letter of the 13th instant, accompanied by notices of protests on certain drafts drawn by you, when in California, on the Secretary of State of the United States.

I regret to inform you that I am not aware that any provision has been made for the payment of these claims. There is no appropriation under the control of this Department, out of which payment could be made of these drafts, or even of any part of them in the form in which they are now presented. The services of the members of the California battalion, under existing laws, can only be paid by the paymasters, on rolls regularly made out. In anticipation that troops would be raised in California, an order was issued from this Department for their muster, with a view to payment. The only mode provided to pay accounts for subsistence, quarters, transportation, &c., &c. in California, now authorized by law, is through the officers of the Commissary and Quartermaster's Departments, on vouchers which can be passed by the accounting officers. Any extraordinary expenses which cannot be met by the revenues or collections in California, cannot be paid without special legislation. The same remark is applicable to the expenses of the temporary civil government of that country. This subject will, undoubtedly, be presented to the consideration of Congress, at its approaching session, and means asked to discharge all just claims of this nature on the Government. Very respectfully, your obt. servt.,

W. L. MARCY
Secretary of War.

Lieut. Col. J. C. Fremont, US.A.,
Washington City

P.S. The protests are herewith returned.

Lbk (DNA-107, LS, 28:96). Also in *California Claims*, Senate Report 75, p. 4, 30th Cong., 1st sess., Serial 512.

241. Thomas H. Benton to Roger Jones

WASHINGTON CITY, Oct. 26 [25], 1847

To the Adjutant General,
SIR,

In the month of July last I gave the name of Capt. [Andrew Jackson] Smith, of the 1st Dragoons, as the supposed author of a publication, then communicated, against Lt. Col. Fremont: I am now informed that he is not the author, & therefore, withdraw his name, and substitute that of Major St. George Cooke, of the Second dragoons. Respectfully, Sir, your obedient Servant,

THOMAS H. BENTON

ALS, RC (DNA-94, LR, B-977 1847). Endorsed: "[Make the correction accordingly, as requested by the Honble. Mr. Benton. Capt. Townsend.] RJ. Recd. Octo. 25. R. J."

242. Thomas H. Benton and William C. Jones to Roger Jones

WASHINGTON CITY, Oct. 25, 1847

To the Adjutant General,
SIR,

As counsel for Lt. Col. Frémont in the trial now impending against him at the instance of Brig. General Kearney, we have had, among other things, under consideration, your letters of Sep. 27th. and Oct. 13th.[1] in answer to Lt. Col. Frémont's application in his letter to you of the 17th ult.[2] In considering the reasons for refusing to institute charges on the newspaper publications referred to, *to wit,* that they were anonymous & that it was not the practice of the service to arraign an officer upon charges based upon anonymous newspaper publications. Without objecting to the propriety of this usage, as a general rule, we have to say that, in this case, the publications in question could not be considered as anonymous, the names of two officers of the army having been filed in the War Office in the month of July last by Senator Benton as the supposed writers, one of whom (Capt. Emory, of the Topographical Engineers) was present in the city, the other (Capt. Smith of the First Dragoons) was absent in California. The name of Capt. Smith has since been withdrawn by Senator Benton, as an erroneous supposition with respect to his authorship, but that of Major St. George Cooke, of the Second Dragoons, substituted as the believed author, who is now in the United States, and is a witness summoned on the part of the prosecution.[3] The names of these officers being given to the Department as the supposed authors of part of the publications, they cannot be considered as anonymous, & coming within the rule of the War Department. Others of the publications were from letter writers, assuming an air of semi-officiality, and a knowledge of the contents of unpublished dispatches, and evidently coming from persons in or about the Department, and, therefore, claiming a place in the public mind very much above the character of anonymous publications. Besides, the rule was probably adopted for the benefit of officers, & to prevent them from being harrassed with unfounded accusations. If so, the benefit of the rule has been renounced and waived by Lt. Col. Frémont in the fact of his asking a trial on the said publications. The *matter* of these publications is a further reason for having a trial upon them, for they all relate to the charges on which Lt. Col. Frémont is to be tried, and are public specifications under those charges, greatly prejudicing the public mind against him. We, therefore, insist, that the publications heretofore filed in the War Office, and the two herewith communicated (Appendix A & B) be delivered to the Judge Advocate to frame charges and specifications on every head of misconduct which they allege or insinuate; and give the names of Capt. Emory, Major St. Geo. Cooke, Francis J. Grund, and Samuel Haight, editor of the Pittsburg Gazette, to prove them. If any objection is made for the want of a prosecutor, on this part of the charges, we answer that we apprehend the rule which requires prosecutors was made for the benefit of the accused, & to prevent him from being irresponsibly harrassed—that this benefit is waived & renounced in this case; and, finally, that the Department may order any officer to prosecute, if they deem that formality material.

The undersigned also claim for Lt. Col. Frémont a trial for having commenced hostilities against the Mexican authorities in California without instructions from his Government, & before he had heard of the actual existence of war, & of all his conduct during the war, & especially in all that relates to the raising and marching of the California Battalion, the pardon of Don Jesus Pico, and the Convention, or Capitulation granted to the insurgent Californians under Don Andres Pico. They claim a trial, on these points, as due both to Lt. Col. Frémont, and to the Government. As a military subordinate he can make no report, & has made none, and says that he has not been required by any authority to make one. At the same time, hostilities actually commenced under circumstances, if unexplained, to bring great censure on Lt. Col. Frémont, and also to give colour to the charge of the Mexican Government, that he was sent to California under the colour of a scientific expedition, to excite an insurrection against the Mexican Government while the two Governments were in a state of peace. The witnesses already summoned will be sufficient to clear up these important points, and also to depose to all the facts in relation to the raising and marching the California Battalion, under the orders of Commodore Stockton, the pardon of Don Jesus Pico, & the capitulation granted to the forces under Don Andres Pico; events in themselves of decided effect in the Californian war, of which no report has been made for which Lt. Col. Frémont has been greatly blamed, & which the truth of history, as well as the honor of his own character, and the character of the government, require to be correctly known. They also ask, as proper evidence on this part of the case, a copy of the letters from Mr. O. Larkin, U.S. Consul at Monterey, to the Hon. Secretary of State during the time that the difficulties were growing up between Lt. Col. Frémont and the Military Commandant General, Don Joseph Castro, in the Spring 1846, and which give authentic information on the first & early state of these difficulties.

Besides the publications communicated, there are others injurious to Lt. Col. Frémont in relation to a challenge to Col. Mason to fight a duel, in the month of April last, at Puebla de los Angeles, and afterwards following him to Monterey for that purpose. The good of the service, & the honor of Lt. Col. Frémont, requires this affair to be investigated, which can easily be done upon the testimony of the witness already summoned to attend the trial, although the two best witnesses in the case (Capt. Smith of the First Dragoons and Major Reading of the late California Battalion) are in California.

In looking over the charges & specifications it is seen that the imputed acts of mutiny, disobedience, and disorderly conduct, refer to a period of time when Commodore Stockton and Genl. Kearney

437

were contending for the supreme command in California, and when the decision of that contention, was attempted to be devolved upon Lt. Col. Frémont, as commander of the California Battalion, by General Kearney giving him orders in contradiction of those of Commodore Stockton, which decision Lt. Col. Fremont declined to make, & determined to remain as he and the battalion were, under the command of Commodore Stockton, until his two superiors decided their own contest. Looking upon this to be the correct answer, the undersigned feel it to be their duty to Protest, and do hereby Protest against now trying that question in the person of Lt. Col. Frémont in a charge of mutiny & disobedience of orders and conduct prejudicial to good order—charges going to his life and character—for not obeying the orders of Genl. Kearney. They make this Protest; and reserving to Lt. Col. Frémont all the benefits to be hereafter derived from it, they deem it their duty to prepare for the trial of the charges & specifications as made (which is, in fact, the trial of Commodore Stockton, of the Navy, in the person of Lt. Col. Frémont, of the army,) and for that purpose they claim the benefit of all the defences which Commodore Stockton could himself demand, if personally on trial before a naval Court Martial. Under this sense of duty, and with a full conviction that they cannot do justice to Commodore Stockton, (to whom, happily, a decision against him will be legally nugatory, & may be contradicted by the decision of a naval court martial, while unhappily it will be fatal to Col. Frémont), they ask to be furnished as early as possible with official copies of all orders to Commodore Sloat, (under whom Lt. Col. Frémont first served), also to Commodore Stockton and Commodore Shubrick, and any other naval officers, charging them with military or civil powers in California, also with copies of all their reports in which Lt. Col. Frémont or the California Battalion is mentioned, or referred to; also, copies of all communications from them, or either of them, which shew the nature and extent of powers which they, the said Naval Commanders, actually exercised in California; also copies of the joint Proclamation of Commodore Shubrick & Genl. Kearney, in settling the boundaries of their power in California between themselves; also a copy of General Kearney's Proclamation at the same time; also a copy of the orders to Genl. Kearney to proceed to California, and a copy of the orders, if any, to proceed from California to Mexico; and a copy of the orders, if any, which related to Lt. Col. Frémont's movements in, or from California, & a copy of the orders, if any, by which Genl. Kearney brought home to the United States *the topographical party* formerly under the command of Lt. Col. Frémont, when Brevet Captain of Topographical Engineers. (Note: This request is distinct from the one made by Lt. Col. Frémont on the 17th Sept. last, and answered by the Adjutant General on the 27th of September; that request being for the order which was applicable to Lt. Col. Frémont *and* his party; that is applicable to the party alone, and is not covered by the suppositious authority then suggested by the Adjutant General.)[4]

The undersigned, in looking over the charges and specifications, perceive that there are three sets of charges on the same specifications, so as to give the prosecution three chances against Lt. Col. Frémont on the same point. The first charge is "MUTINY,"—the punishment for which *may* be death, and the conviction for which is *always* infamous. The second charge is for *"Disobedience of the lawful commands of his superior officer,"*—the punishment for which *may* be trivial, and the conviction a title to honor & preferment. The third charge is for *"Conduct to the prejudice of good order and military discipline,"*—which might involve no higher point than a piece of form, of etiquette, or a punctilio. Between the degree of enormity of these three charges the difference is immense & immeasurable; and although in criminal prosecutions at Common Law a man may be indicted for murder and manslaughter on the same act, yet in Courts Martial, which concern the honor as well as the lives of officers, and where proceedings should be direct and simple, and go to convictions on the merits instead of technicalities and punctilios, every charge should have its separate specifications; and where so high a crime as mutiny is charged, no inferior charge should be predicated on the same act. But in this case the proceeding goes further than at Common Law: it goes to *three* different charges, of three degrees of enormity, for the same act, the first charge the highest, the last the lowest in the military code; while an indictment for murder and manslaughter never goes down to a conviction for some petty insult. The undersigned have deemed it their duty to notice, *and at this time,* this three fold prosecution on the same sets of acts, but they are instructed by Lieut. Col. Frémont to go into trial upon the whole—to make no objection to any thing—but to insist to the last upon a full trial—a trial upon the points of accusation against him in all the charges of Genl. Kearney,—in all the subsidary publications,—in all the published letters from Washington City assum-

439

ing the air of semi-officiality; and, in fine, upon all his conduct in California.

The undersigned deem it their duty to object to the place of trial—Fortress Monroe—two hundred miles from Washington, and in an out-of-the-way place, and in a corner—and where they feel they cannot do justice to Lt. Col. Frémont for want of the chances of defence, of law or fact, which might turn up during the .trial. The whole trial is a surprise upon him. He was brought from California without any knowledge that he was to be arrested on the frontier of the United States, and tried on the shores of the Atlantic, for offences charged on the shores of the Pacific. His prosecutor, availing himself of authority & influence and knowing his own secret purpose, brought along with him a train of witnesses, some military, one naval, several in civil life; while, it so happens, that the witnesses, military, naval and civil, which would have been of the highest moment to Lt. Col. Frémont, are left in California, or sent into the Pacific Ocean! The arrest was a surprise upon Col. Frémont. In his amazement, he asked, for what? Instead of informing him, he was referred to the war office for the specifications. Arriving in Washington City, he applied on the 17th of September for these specifications; he was informed in writing that he would get them *"in due time."* On the 4th day of October he received them, with the further notice that he was to be tried in a fort two hundred miles distant. Since that time he has picked up such means of defence as could be found, and discovers something more from day to day, and might, peradventure, find something more during the period of the trial, if tried at a place where people congregate. No one can foresee what may turn up during a trial—what new evidence may be wanting, either original, or rebutting, or explanatory—what points of law may require elucidation—what reference to documents in offices may become necessary—what gentlemen in office, and whose presence is necessary in their offices, may be wanted. All this, in an ordinary case, where there has been ample notice for preparation: how much stronger then in this case, where the arrest & trial is a surprise, the scene of delinquency laid at such a distance, with so many witnesses brought from afar for the prosecution, and none for the defense. Under these circumstances, the undersigned ask that the place of trial may be changed to Washington City. It is the place where Commodore Porter was tried under somewhat similar circumstances, that is to say, for offences charged to have been committed in a distant and foreign land: and the history of his trial shows that he found advantage, both of law & fact, in being tried in the Metropolis, and at the seat of Government of his country. To enable us to do the better justice to Lt. Col. Frémont, we ask that the place of his trial may be changed to this city. Respectfully, Sir, Your obedient Servants,

THOMAS H. BENTON
WM. CAREY JONES

[*Enclosures*]
Appendix, A.
Pittsburg Gazette, May, 1847
California—Trouble in the Camp.

The Pittsburgh Gazette of Monday states:

"A serious quarrel has arisen between Commodore Stockton and Lieut. Col. Freemont, on one side, and Gen. Kearney on the other. Gen. Kearney, it seems, carried out full powers as Governor and Military commander of California, signed by President Polk, and revoking those previously given to Commodore Stockton, who had previously been superceded as Commander of the Naval forces in the Pacific by his senior, Commodore Shubrick. It has been concealed from the American people that previous to the arrival of Gen. Kearney in California our forces had on different occasions met with disgraceful discomfitures. Capt. Mervine of the Navy, in attempting the recapture [of] a small village on the coast, landed according to orders about 200 seamen and marines, without artillery, and was repulsed with the loss of fifteen or twenty killed and wounded, by some 150 Mexican troops, who had two pieces of flying artillery which they managed with great skill; by the bad management of Stockton and Freemont, the Mexicans recaptured several places of which we had at first obtained possession. It was only until Kearney arrived that matters assumed a more favorable aspect, but strange to say, on his presentation of his authority as Governor, *Stockton refused to recognize it, and defied his authority, and claimed for himself that power, and bullied Kearney into submission.* Freemont at first, was disposed to side with Kearney, until some difficulty arose between them in reference to some improper conduct of Col. F., and when Gen. K. refused to substitute Col. Freemont for himself as

Governor, the *latter joined Stockton* who forthwith gave him the appointment. One serious charge against Col. Freemont we learn, is making improper and incorrect reports to the administration for sinister purposes. Gen. Kearney we further understand is only awaiting the arrival of troops to sustain him, and he will then very probably arrest both Stockton and Freemont, as mutineers, and we should not be surprised (if Kearney gets the power) to hear of their trial, and even summary execution, as the most violent feelings of hostility exists according to our correspondent's statements and on which entire reliance may be placed. Why the administration have so sedulously concealed from the public eye these important facts is a grave enquiry."

The Gazette is further informed by its careful Washington correspondent that two cabinet meetings have been held upon this serious subject, without any determination having been agreed upon. Secretary Marcy is said to stand up in defense of Gen. Kearney, while Mr. Secretary Mason upholds Com. Stockton and Col. Freemont. Mr. Walker's ill-health prevents him from taking part in these consultations. The course of the administration in withholding this information from the people whose servants the government officers are, is attributed to fear of offending Col. Benton, father-in-law of Freemont, and Com. Stockton. The sense of duty which should do justice to Gen. Kearney, is of less force that the fear of offending the persons named. Walker was opposed to placing Col. Benton in command of the army as Major General, and were he in the Cabinet consultation, would favor Kearney.

The people will be anxious to learn more of this insubordination and mutiny, and their officers will be compelled to disclose the transactions in full. Perhaps now that the Virginia elections are over, they will venture to give their information publicity.

The Washington Union of Saturday night, states that Gen. Kearney has been authorised, *not ordered,* "to turn over his command to Col. Mason, which was done on his application of last fall to return home, after regulating affairs in California. We presume he is now on his way home, and may be expected some time this summer."

The correspondent of the Journal of Commerce, writing from Washington under date of the 5th inst., says: "The difficulties between Gen. Kearney and Com. Stockton will not be so easily reconciled as I had supposed. Some developments respecting the matter will soon be made."

Appendix, B.
Baltimore Sun, June, 1847

I happen to know that some dispatches have been received on the subject of the difficulties between the Gen. and the Commodore, which have not yet been published, and which have created much difficulty in the cabinet. There is nothing in the difficulty, which cannot, as Lieut. Gray justly remarked in this city, be easily adjusted by the exercise of that degree of mutual forbearance and good feeling which have always characterized the two arms of the service. But there are two things in this difficulty which are calculated to produce ill feeling, and which have no connexion with the service. It is supposed that Gen. Kearney has reason to believe that, through the influence of Col. Benton, Col. Fremont is to be or has been put in command over him.

ALS, RC (DNA-94, LR, F-255 1847). Endorsed: "Received & Respectfully laid before the Sec. of War. Oct. 25th. R. Jones, A. Genl." The Secretary of War immediately sent the communication to the President "agreeably" to his request (W. L. Marcy to Polk, 25 Oct. 1847, DLC—Polk Papers), and the JCF case was the chief business at the cabinet meetings on 26 and 27 Oct. (POLK, 3:205–6).

The letter, the 27 Oct. 1847 reply of the Adjutant General, and Benton's and Jones's rejoinder, also bearing the 27 Oct. date, appeared in the *National Intelligencer,* 6 Nov. 1847. Benton had given the letters to the newspaper so that the public might know the reasons for seeking a change of place for the trial as well as the points on which JCF asked to be heard to obtain a full trial. The correspondence, Benton wrote, will "show that he has been denied a trial on every point on which he asked it, and has been decreed one on the precise point against which his counsel protested; *id est,* upon the point now under trial; and which seems to be the trial of Com. Stockton of the United States navy, now absent from the United States, in the person of Lieut. Col. Fremont, of the United States army, before a General Military Court Martial, now sitting in the Military Arsenal at this city."

William Carey Jones, who was acting with Benton as JCF's legal counsel, was the husband of Eliza Benton, JBF's older sister. Because he was a legal expert on Spanish land titles and a fluent linguist, the federal government appointed him in 1849 a special investigator of California land titles.

By the late 1850s a schism had developed between Jones and the Frémonts, and JBF intimated to Elizabeth Blair Lee that Jones had worn away much of her father's remaining regard for·JCF. "If he [Jones] ever makes the chance, I will get him apart from Liz and 'blow him sky high'—and I know all his vulnerable points" (see letters of 8 March [1857?] and 23 Sept. 1857, NjP—Blair-Lee Papers).

1. See Doc. Nos. 220 and 235.
2. See Doc. No. 214.
3. See Doc. No. 241.
4. In response to these requests, Roger Jones forwarded on 2 Nov. the fol-

lowing documents: (1) Shubrick-Kearny circular of 1 March 1847, which set the boundaries of power in California between them (Doc. No. 150); (2) Kearny's proclamation of 1 March 1847 (Doc. No. 151); (3) Gen. Winfield Scott's letter of 31 May 1846 containing orders for Kearny to march to California; and (4) General Scott's letter of 3 Nov. 1846, by which Kearny was instructed that if he were to find JCF in California, he was not to detain him "against his wishes, a moment longer than the necessities of the service may require" (CT. MARTIAL, 48–50). He noted that there were no orders "especially referring to the *'Topographical party'*" and none directing General Kearny to proceed to Mexico from California. On the following day, however, he sent a copy of the 10 Dec. 1846 letter of the Secretary of War to Kearny, "containing a *suggestion* that he should move from California to Mexico." See the letters of R. Jones to Benton and W. C. Jones, 3 and 10 Nov. 1847 (DNA-94, LS, 24:269–70, 284).

243. Roger Jones to Frémont

W. D. A. G. O. WASHINGTON, Oct. 26, 1847

COLONEL:

I enclose herewith "General Orders," No. 32, dated September 27, 1847 detailing the General Court Martial by Order of the President, for your trial, which you will please to receive in lieu of the copy transmitted with my letter dated the 27th ultimo. Please to return to the Office the copy first received, for which the one now enclosed is the substitute.[1] I am, Colonel, &c.

R. JONES, Adjt. Genl.

Lbk (DNA-94, LS, 24:256). For general orders no. 32, see CT. MARTIAL, 2.
1. For the necessity of a substitute, see Doc. No. 244.

244. Frémont to Roger Jones

C. Street Oct. 26. 1847

SIR,

I herewith return you the paper as requested and accept the substitute sent, and have to say that if, at any time during the trial any errors or omissions should be found, either of form or substance, I agree to their immediate correction. In this case the omission of the

444

word "President" would have vitiated the record, but I would have had it supplied at any moment, as I want no acquittal but on the merits. Respectfully Sir, Your obedient servant,

J. C. Frémont
Lt. Col. Mounted Riflemen

To the Adjt. Genl. Jones

LS, RC (James S. Copley Collection, La Jolla, Calif.).

245. Frémont to Pierson B. Reading

Washington City October 26th. 1847.

My dear Sir,

I write to you in the midst of the serious preparation for a court-martial by which I am to be tried next week, on charges preferred against me by Genl. Kearny. Information of the difficulty in California & allegations against me, with a rumor that I had been arrested had reached this country some time before I arrived. Mr. Emory on his way, & from Havana to Washington had circulated & published in various newspapers, statements scandalously false & infamous against Com. Stockton and myself. These statements were flatly contradicted, and the lie given to Emory in private and public, in conversation & newspapers by Col. Russell, Capt. Jacobs,[1] and other friends. Col. Benton forwarded these publications to the War Dept. requiring that upon these & similar allegations I should be brought before a court martial. Things were in this state when I arrived. I immediately adopted Col. Benton's application to the Department & in a letter to the Adjt. Genl. dated 17th September & published at the time, I applied for a full & speedy trial on all points & all allegations, objecting to nothing & waiving all technicalities. Up to this time the administration has persisted in confining the trial to the narrowest possible bounds, but we still have reason to hope that a full trial will be allowed; and even if that be not obtained, we still expect to be able on the trial to bring out the whole course of my conduct in California. We expect the result of the trial to be a complete justification.

You remember Genl. Kearny's unjust and aggravating conduct to me in California, and how fully he was imitated in it by his officers.

445

The same course was pursued along the whole road until we reached Fort Leavenworth; but I had the gratification to meet in all the great emigration many strong and warm friends. They were using my maps on the road, travelling by them,—and you may judge how gratified I was to find that the[y] found them perfectly correct & could do so.

During all my road in, I was kept entirely in ignorance that there was [an] intention on the part of Genl. K. to arrest, or even prefer charges against me, for you [know] we expected to go immediately to Mexico. We had started from our camp near the Fort, being on our way to Westport, & riding ahead to take leave of the Genl. I was met by an orderly, requesting me to come to him. I did so, and was arrested in the fort. The Genl. telling me that it was for mutiny, disobedience of orders, assumption of powers &c.

The trial is now at hand. Kearny brought with him his tutored and instructed witnesses keeping me in ignorance of his design to arrest me, at the same time that he had written to the United States as early as the 11th & 20th of May, that he intended to do so.[2] I have only such witnesses as chanced to come with me & such as turn up from day to day but I feel satisfied that these will be sufficient to bring defeat & shame upon Genl. Kearny. It is a matter of great regret that you and other friends who know so well the conduct of affairs in California cannot be here. Of Com. Stockton we hear nothing yet, but daily expect him.

In the meantime, I am glad to tell you that I am very generally sustained throughout the country by public opinion. In a very flattering letter signed by a large number of the most respectable citizens of all parties in St. Louis, I was offered a public dinner, which I declined. The city of Charleston in my native state voted me a sword, accompanied by resolutions highly approving my course in California, and previous conduct. Holding that while in a state of arrest on an infamous charge, I ought not and cannot receive my mark of public respect, I am awaiting the result of the trial to receive this gratifying gift from my fellow citizens of my own state. Since my return the ladies of Charleston have added a belt;—I send you a paper containing a notice of this last mark of their continued regard. I will try to send you a paper containing the letter of the 17th Sep. & will send you several others bearing upon the subject. I send you a copy of a letter from Col. Benton to Mr. McCrady, one of my best & warmest friends and will endeavor also to send you a copy of a letter sent yesterday by my counsel to the Adjt. Genl. I must wait another occasion for many things I wish to say to you. My main object is to give you, & through you, our other friends information of the true state of things here.

I hope therefore you will let Mr. Snyder and as far as you can, all the others know, that we do not doubt a victorious issue to this trial. I will write a brief line to Snyder & refer him to you.

Please assure Dr. Isbell[3] and other emigrants and friends who were engaged with us in the war, that we keep their interest steadily in view and that everything will be satisfactorily arra[n]ged for them. Nothing can be done until the meeting of Congress—we are therefore waiting for that, and they may be assured that appropriations will be granted, covering all expenditures, and a public recognition made for their good services. These will all be brought out by the trial. It will be necessary when the time comes that you again resume your office as Pay Master & Major Snyder his as Quartermaster in order to settle the Battalion business, and a farther commission given to you, to audit claims for losses. All your certificates of pay brought in by our party, [*several illegible words*], and by the previous party were immediately paid at St. Louis, by order of the Government.

I send you two letters from your brother, to whom I was able to give gratifying information of you. I will write to you again and as often as opportunity shall offer. I trust that my private business goes on prosperously. I expect to see you next year, in the earlier part. I will endeavor to send you an amount of money to be used for me in California when I next write.

If you can, I would be glad if you would purchase for me our friend Jesus Pico's place on the coast.[4] He offered the half of it to Owens for me for thirteen hundred dollars. At that time I was not willing to buy. Perhaps he will sell the whole of it for two or three thousand dollars. If he should not be willing to sell, perhaps you could buy some other place upon the coast between the Bay and Monterey. Manuel Castro had a place for sale in that locality, which I wished to purchase because it was heavily timbered and this would be an indespensable thing with me. At the foot of Mt. Diavolo [Diablo] on the Bay, there are some places [near] San Landry [Leandro?] that possibly might be purchased. *Las Pulgas* on the bay,[5] between Sanchez' rancho & Santa Clara, was for sale at two thousand dollars. I wanted Larkin to get it for me but for some reason he did not. If it still could be had I should very much like this.

I expect to come to California and trust that you will make one of these purchases for me as I have set my heart upon living at one of these places. I trust that you will not fail to secure one.

As soon as I possibly can arrange my business I will send you money for that purpose; in the meanwhile if this object can be accomplished now I authorize you to draw upon me, and I will see that the drafts be accepted and paid at this place. You may perhaps find some one coming in who may be willing to take the drafts. Now and until we see or hear from each other again I am truly your friend,

J. C. FRÉMONT

LS, RC (C). Directed to Maj. Pierson B. Reading, "at or near San Francisco, Upper California." No enclosures found.

1. In 1846 Richard Taylor Jacob had traveled by horseback to California with William H. Russell and Edwin Bryant. During the march of JCF's battalion south in the winter he had commanded Company H, which had a large Indian contingent. Jacob left California in Jan. 1847 and, as will be noted later, came to Washington for JCF's court-martial and began courting Benton's younger daughter, Sarah. The marriage took place during JCF's trial. Jacob later became lieutenant governor of Kentucky.

2. Kearny had written the Adjutant General on 13 May 1847 that JCF's "conduct in California has been such that I shall be compelled on arriving in Missouri to arrest him, & send him under charges to report to you" (DNA-94, LR, K-238 1847).

3. Dr. James C. Isbel, a physician from Ohio, had served for a short time in the Santa Clara Company while his wife taught the children of American immigrants awaiting the end of the war. Later Isbel carried on a unique and lucrative exchange of beads for gold dust with the Indians and gave financial backing to the cattle enterprise of Thomas, Henry, and Alexander More, the future purchasers of Sespe rancho (PIONEER REGISTER; CLELAND, 84–87).

4. A reference to Pico's Piedra Blanco at San Luis Obispo, which later became a part of Hearst's San Simeon.

5. I.e., on the peninsular side of the bay.

246. Frémont to Jacob R. Snyder

WASHINGTON CITY, Oct. 26th, 1847

MY DEAR SIR,

I have written at length to our friend Major Reading to whom I refer you to a full account of the situation of affairs here. I am pressed by accumulated business and therefore write only to assure you of my continued regard and to say to you that I am not forgetful of you nor of our other friends nor of their interests in California. I have brought our business before the Departments, and it will be laid by them before Congress the session being now near at hand. Appropriations will then be granted for our expenditures and as it will be necessary, I hope it will be satisfactory to you also, to take up your business of the Quartermaster's Dept. and carry it through. It will be proper that you as well as Major Reading should form part of a commission for damages during our war. I will write again by next opportunity and expect to be with you in California in the Spring.

In the meantime I am very truly yours,

J. C. Frémont

Copy (Society of California Pioneers—Jacob Rink Snyder Collection).

247. Frémont to Abel Stearns

Washington City Oct. 26th 1847

My dear Sir,

I write to you under the pressure of accumulated business and in the midst of the serious preparation for a court martial by which I am to be tried on charges preferred by Genl. Kearny. The day appointed for the beginning of the trial is the 2d of November—false and infamous charges made by Lieut. Emory and other agents of Genl. Kearny and published in newspapers from Havana to Washington had been industriously circulated to prejudice the public mind before our arrival. Col. Russell, Capt. Jacobs and other friends immediately gave the lie to Emory & to these publications, in the newspapers and in private society. To these public & private charges of falsehood Lieut. Emory has made no reply. Col. Benton immediately on the appearance of those publications required from the Dept. of War that I should be brought before a court martial on *all* the allegations against me. Genl. Kearny's charges were for mutiny, disobedience of orders, assumption of powers &c. Immediately on my arrival, in a letter to the Adjt. Genl. which was published at the same time, I adopted Col. Bentons application and farther demanded a full & speedy trial upon every & all accusation against me, waiving all form & technicalities.

The administration have been endeavouring to narrow down the trial to Genl. Kearny's charges, but we expect to succeed in obtaining such a trial as will bring before the court all my conduct in California. Col. Benton & my brother in law Mr. Jones are my counsel before the court, & we entertain no doubt of a victorious issue. I will endeavour to send you some papers on this subject & write you more fully when another occasion offers. I have written at length to my friend Major Reading and you may chance to see that letter.

I beg that you will see our friends Senores [C]elis and Cot and assure them that I am keeping their interests steadily in view and that [they] need entertain no uneasiness in regard to their advances. I have already brought their case & that of others to whom we are indebted before the administration in writing, but I think it will be necessary to wait for the session of Congress now near at hand. The Dept. promises to ask an appropriation from Congress & my friends will see that it is granted, and the debts with the interests we have allowed upon them, will be immediately paid. It may be well to say to you that all the certificates which were brought home by my party & the one previous, were immediately paid at St. Louis by order of the Govrnt.

I am obliged to write briefly, and have only written to give yourself & other gentlemen who are connected with me in monied interests, information on which they may rely. Please say the same to Mr. Roland,[1] etc. Com. Stockton is not yet arrived. Please offer my regards & remembrances to Mrs. Stearns & Dona Isidora,[2] with any other of your family who may happen to be with you.

I hope that my horses will be in good riding order next summer when I expect the pleasure of seeing you. I am with very great regard & respect Yours truly,

J. C. Frémont

LS, RC (CSmH—Stearns Papers). Endorsed.
1. John Rowland (ca. 1791–1873), who with William Workman had led an immigrant party from New Mexico to California over the Old Spanish Trail in 1841. They became owners of the 48,000-acre Rancho de la Puente near Mission San Gabriel.
2. Arcadia (Mrs. Abel Stearns) and Ysidora (who later married Cave J. Couts) were daughters of Juan Bandini.

248. Roger Jones to Thomas H. Benton and William C. Jones

W. D., A. G. O., Washington, Oct. 27. 1847

Gentlemen:

Your communication, as the counsel of Lieut. Colonel Frémont, of the 25th instant, has been submitted to the War Department, and I am directed to make the following reply.

With an earnest desire that the proceedings in the case of Lieutenant Colonel Frémont, should be in such a form and so conducted as to secure to him a full and fair trial, the Government will so far as its agency can be properly interposed, do whatever will tend to such a result. But a compliance with your request, in his behalf, to introduce other charges containing matters not embraced in those already prepared, would present embarrassments which would be difficult to surmount, and require a course of action which is believed to be unusual and objectionable.

In urging the incorporation of additional charges on matters stated in the newspaper publications, which if sustained might properly be made a subject of charge for the consideration of the court martial, it is certainly not to be understood that you believe them to be well founded. The Department is not aware that evidence affording a colorable pretext for trying Lieut. Colonel Fremont on such charges, can be produced. It cannot consent to occupy the position of preferring charges which it has no reason to believe can be sustained by proof, nor would it deem it proper, in order, as is suggested, to comply with the forms of proceeding, to direct an officer to act as prosecutor on them. So far, therefore, as relates to the trial, it appears that the encumbering [of] the record with such charges would be useless, not to say improper. If there should be no proof whatever to sustain them, and it is believed the prosecution could produce none, no proof could be required to rebut them; indeed, it is quite certain, none would be heard by the Court to refute what had not been sustained, and on this view of the case, the trial would come back to the same state in which it would be without such additional charges. The issues would be confined to charges and specifications in support of which some material evidence had been offered on the part of the prosecution. What range of defence under them will be the right of Lieut. Col. Fremont to take, is for the Court to determine, but it is

451

not to be doubted that it will be ample for all the purposes of setting his conduct so far as it is called in question, in its true light.

In relation to what took place in California before the commencement of hostilities between the United States and Mexico in which Lieutenant Colonel Frémont acted a prominent part, the Department has not been made acquainted with anything done by him which has given dissatisfaction, and cannot therefore be induced to make it a matter of charge. Indeed, his conduct in this respect was presented to Congress at the last session with no equivocal expressions of approval.[1]

In regard to that part of your communication which represents that the whole trial is a surprise upon Lieut. Colonel Frémont, that the witnesses whose testimony would have been of the highest moment to him, have been left in California, while the prosecutor brought along with him those for the prosecution, and that the charges were not made known to him till the 4th instant, I am directed to assure you that it has not been the wish of the Department to precipitate the trial in this case, and it is anxious to remove all grounds of complaint on this point. Lieutenant Colonel Fremont addressed a communication to this Department on the 13th [17th] day of September in which he urges a speedy trial, and suggested that he would be prepared to meet the charges against him in thirty days. The time for holding the court was fixed at a more distant day than that indicated by him.

Nothing certainly could be further from the views of the Department than to take a course in this matter that should even seemingly be open to the imputation of unfairness towards the accused, or to concur in any procedure that should in anywise withhold from him the amplest means of defence. It will most readily take such steps as may be deemed necessary or proper to obviate all objections of surprise or unfairness, and afford any facility which may be needful for the defence. Should it be made known that Lieutenant Colonel Fremont wishes to obtain the testimony of persons at a distance, an opportunity will be readily given to procure it. For this purpose the meeting of the Court will be deferred, if Lieut. Colonel Frémont should not object to that course. The Department desire to be informed at the earliest period of his views on this subject. If the attendance of officers of the Army or Navy, now absent on distant service, should be desired by him it is suggested that their names be furnished in order that arrangements be made for their return. I am directed to state that the documents and papers specified in your letter or such of them as are to be found in the Department will be furnished as soon as they can be prepared.

The decision on that branch of your letter which asks for the change of place for holding the Court is deferred till it is determined whether for the purpose suggested, the assembling of the Court be postponed. I am Gentlemen &c.

R. JONES
Adjt. Genl.

Lbk (DNA-94, LS, 24:259–60). One of three letters given to Gales and Seaton by Benton and William C. Jones after the beginning of the trial and published in the *National Intelligencer,* 6 Nov. 1847.

1. "No equivocal expressions of approval" appeared in the *National Intelligencer,* 6 Nov. 1847, as "no unequivocal expressions of approval," prompting Roger Jones to ask Benton to have the error corrected (Doc. No. 254). The *National Intelligencer,* 9 Nov. 1847, acknowledged a clerical error in the copy and made the correction.

249. Thomas H. Benton and William C. Jones to Roger Jones

C Street, Oct. 27th. (evening) 1847.

To the Adjutant General,
SIR,

In reply to your communication of this date, just received, we have to state on the part of Lt. Col. Frémont, that he knew all the disadvantages of his position for want of witness from California when he agreed to go into trial upon the testimony then in the United States —that he has had the thirty days which he asked to collect that testimony; and although Commodore Stockton has not yet arrived (whose presence is so essential) yet he wishes no delay, or postponement, and will proceed to trial on the day appointed, with the full determination to bring it to the most rapid conclusion consistent with a full examination of the merits of the case.

With respect to the change of place from Fortress Monroe to this city, we have to say that, further reflection, and the actual *experience* of this day, convinces us that JUSTICE to Lt. Col. Frémont requires the change; and, further, that we fully believe that the trial can be brought to a conclusion in much less *time* in this city than in any place out of it, and especially in a place so distant & so out-of-the-way as Fortress Monroe. Respectfully, Sir, your obedient servants,

THOMAS H. BENTON
WM. CAREY JONES
Of Counsel, &c. &c.

ALS, RC (DNA-94, LR, B-989 1847). Endorsed: "Rec'd October 28 and Respectfully submitted to the Sec. of War. Oct. 28. R. Jones." "Change of place of holding the court ordered. W. L. M[arcy]." "Ansd. Oct. 28. R. Jones."

250. Roger Jones to Thomas H. Benton and William C. Jones

W. D., A. G. O., WASHINGTON, Oct. 28. 1847

GENTLEMEN:

Your note of last evening's date (Oct. 27) has been received and submitted to the Secretary of War.

With respect to the change of the place of the meeting of the General Court Martial, from Fortress Monroe to this City, as requested, I enclose for Colonel Frémont, a copy of Special Order, No. 55,[1] of this day's date, from which it will be seen that the Court by direction of the President, has been ordered to assemble at the Washington Arsenal in this City. I am, Gentlemen &c.

R. JONES
Adjt. Genl.

Lbk (DNA-94, LS, 24:262).
1. See CT. MARTIAL, 2.

251. Frémont to John Torrey

WASHINGTON CITY Nov. 1st. 1847

MY DEAR SIR,

I have been daily promising myself, the pleasure of a long letter to you but accumulated business pressing upon deranged health, has daily diverted me from this and many other attentions to friends whom I have seemed to neglect. Whenever I think of California and plants you come in also, & this subject of frequent thought arising in my mind this morning I write a line before becoming involved in the business of a trial which will occupy all my time and not improve my health. I enclose a little flower, the name of which I should like to know, and which you will remember as being among our California plants in the previous collection. You know that this pleasant work was interrupted in California, but notwithstanding, the collection was good, and agreeably to your suggestion sealed up in air-tight cases. I was obliged to leave them behind in California, but expect them by the first vessel which shall arrive. As soon as I receive them I will put them at your disposition.

I will confess to you that it was matter of great regret to me to loose the F. vermicularis.[1] I hope to hear from you soon, and am Very truly yours,

J. C. Frémont

Dr. John Torrey

ALS-JBF, RC (NNNBG—Torrey Correspondence).
1. Torrey's *Fremontia vermicularis,* now *Sarcobatus vermiculatus.* For Torrey's description of this species, and various references to it, consult *S. vermiculatus* in the index of Vol. 1.

252. Thomas H. Benton and William C. Jones to Roger Jones

C. Street, Washington
Nov. 3, 1847

To the Adjutant General,
Sir,

We acknowledge the receipt, last evening, of your letter of yesterday, with the accompanying papers from the War and Navy Departments, for which we thank you.

We have further to request a copy of the orders, if any, that were addressed or sent to Brig. Gen. Kearney, after information had been received that he had started from Santa Fé to go into California.

Also a copy of Gen. Kearney's reports to the Department, on leaving & subsequent to his leaving Santa Fé. Very respectfully, your obt. servants,

THOMAS H. BENTON
WM. CAREY JONES

ALS, RC (DNA-94, LR, F-260 1847, f/w F-255 1847). Endorsed: "Received, Nov. 4, 1847." "Respectfully laid before the Sec. of War, Nov. 4th. R. Jones." "Ansd. Nov. 4/47 (in part). See letters of Nov. 10 & 15 to Col. Benton & Mr. Jones."

Roger Jones's letter of 10 Nov. 1847 requested that JCF's counsel give the judge advocate access to the communications furnished JCF from the War, State, and Navy departments (DNA-94, LS, 24:284); the letter of 15 Nov. sent copies of Kearny's official dispatches as requested in Benton's and Jones's letter of 3 Nov.

JCF's counsel requested on 5 Nov. "copies of all the orders & instructions to Commodore Stockton, or any other commodore in the Pacific Squadron, which were sent out subsequent to the receipt of information that Gen. Kearny had left Santa Fe to go into California, & prior to the 20th June 1847" (DNA-94, LR, F-266 1847, f/w F-255 1847). On 6 Nov. he requested a copy of the order creating the 9th and 10th Military departments (DNA-94, LR, F-263 1847).

253. Frémont to Henry H. Sibley

WASHINGTON CITY Nov 5. 1847

MY DEAR SIBLEY,

I make you a hasty acknowledgement for the pleasure afforded me by your letter,[1] which I should and ought to have anticipated. My warmest thanks were due to you for your prompt friendship in protecting me from attack and aspersion in my absence. It was like yourself and to have been expected from, but from very few others besides. It brought you and old associations strongly and freshly before my mind. I will send you daily a copy of the Intelligencer, which correctly reports the proceedings of the court before which I am now being tried. You must not entertain any uneasiness on account of Genl. Kearny's evidence as it will be made clear in the end. It may be two months before this (the point of asking him for the governorship) can be explained or shown to be false, but it will be done in the end.[2] Today we have carried the points which command the issues of the case. It may be one, two, or three months before we

456

come to the issue, but we have carried the points which command the field. Very truly your friend,

J. C. FRÉMONT

ALS, RC (MnHi—Sibley Papers).
1. Sibley's letter has not been found.
2. Kearny's testimony of 4 Nov. had depicted JCF as bargaining for the governorship (CT. MARTIAL, 38–39).

254. Roger Jones to Frémont

A. G. O. WASHINGTON, Nov. 6, 1847

DEAR SIR,

In reading the copy of my letter to Hon. T. H. Benton and W. C. Jones, Esq. as counsel for you, dated Oct. 27, 1847, published in this morning's Intelligencer, I notice a trifling error in the use of the word "unequivocal" instead of *equivocal,* in the sentence "Indeed, his conduct, in this respect, was presented to Congress at the last session, &c." In looking at the original, I find it correctly written "equivocal" and am not sure whether the mistake seen in print to-day, originated from a typographical error, or in this office when transcribing the letter sent Colonel Benton. If the latter, do me the favor to have it corrected. I am, dear Sir &c.

R. JONES

Lbk (DNA-94, LS, 24:277–78).

255. Thomas H. Benton and William C. Jones to Roger Jones

WASHINGTON, Nov. 9, 1847

To the Adjutant General,
SIR,

Genl. Kearney having on Monday last testified as follows:

"The charges on which Lieut Col. Frémont is now arraigned are not my charges. I preferred a single charge against Lt. Col. Frémont,

457

The charges on which he is now arraigned have been changed from mine . . . .

"Question [by Lieut. Col. Frémont]. Did you give any information to the person who drew up the seventh specification under the first charge in relation to the cannon?"

"Answer. I did not."

And we having hitherto understood that a trial was refused to Lt. Col. Frémont on any other charges or specifications than those founded on the allegations set forth by Gen. Kearney; we have to inquire, whether any charges or specifications in this case have been preferred & incorporated by any other person than Gen. Kearney, and, if so, by whom? and also to request the original of the charge or charges and specification or specifications furnished to the Department by Gen. Kearney. Very respectfully, your obt. servants,

THOMAS H. BENTON
WM. CAREY JONES
Of counsel for Lt. Col. Fremont

ALS, RC (DNA-94, F-270 1847). Endorsed: "Respectfully laid before the Sec. of War. R. Jones. [See the answer as directed by the Sec. of War. R. Jones, Nov. 11, 1847]." Also in *National Intelligencer,* 15 Nov. 1847. Roger Jones's answer is our Doc. No. 258. The letter of inquiry was prompted by part of Kearny's 8 Nov. testimony (see CT. MARTIAL, 64). As noted in Doc. No. 220, n. 2, Kearny had made a single charge of mutiny.

256. Roger Jones to Frémont

A. G. O. WASHINGTON, Nov. 10. 1847

COLONEL:

Captain Lee,[1] Judge Advocate, having requested copies of all the communications furnished to your counsel thro' this Office, from the War, State, and Navy Departments, and it being impracticable to have duplicate copies prepared at this time, although it is necessary that he should possess them in order to conduct the case understandingly, you are requested to allow him access to them that he may obtain copies of such as he may deem requisite. I am, Colonel, &c.

R. JONES, Adjt. Genl.

Lbk (DNA-94, LS, 24:284).

1. Capt. John Fitzgerald Lee, the judge advocate or prosecuting attorney for the Army in this case, was JCF's age—thirty-four. Lee commanded the Washington Arsenal, but in 1849 he was breveted a major and appointed to the staff of the Judge Advocate of the Army, in which capacity he served until his resignation in 1862. From that date until his death in 1884, he resided on his farm in Prince Georges County, Md.

257. Frémont to Roger Jones

WASHINGTON CITY, Nov. 11th 1847

GENERAL,

Your letter of yesterday in which I am requested to permit to Capt. Lee, the Judge Advocate of the Court, access to the various official papers with which I have been furnished by the Department, was duly received; and I will accordingly inform him they are all at his disposal. Very respectfully Your obedient Servant,

J. C. FRÉMONT
Lt. Col. Mounted Riflemen

To Adjt. Genl. Jones,
Washington City

LS, RC (DNA-94, LR, F-274 1847). Endorsed: "Nov. 12, 1847."

258. Roger Jones to Thomas H. Benton and William C. Jones

W. D., A. G. O., Nov. 11. 1847

GENTLEMEN:

Your letter of the 9th inst. making certain inquiries respecting the charges and specifications, &c. in the case of Lieut Col. Frémont has been submitted to the Secretary of War, and I am directed to inform you that the charges and specifications produced to the Court Martial, now in scssion for his trial, were based upon the facts alleged and officially reported to the Department by General Kearney; and, it is not known or understood that any charge or specification has been introduced, based on facts derived from any other source whatever.

I am also instructed to say, that the original charge and specifications against Lieut. Col. Frémont, presented by General Kearny, and other communications from him or transmitted by him to the Department, were placed in the hands of the Officer selected for Judge Advocate, with the general directions of the Department to put the matters of charge therein contained, in a proper form and shape for trial; and with the further remark, in substance, as it might be a matter of doubt what was the legal designation of the offence which the facts alleged would constitute, they might be, it was presumed, set forth as specifications under more than one general charge.

The original charge and specifications prepared, and filed by Genl. Kearny, are still in the hands of the Judge Advocate, subject to be produced by order of the court, should it deem the production of them proper for any purpose whatever.

The Department would find great difficulty in adopting the conclusion that it could rightfully direct the Judge Advocate as to the particular manner of conducting the proceedings of the court, or as to submitting to, or withholding from, the accused, the papers in his hand. It does not however, perceive any objection the Judge Advocate may have to yield to your request to inspect the original charge and specification prepared by General Kearny. I am, Gentlemen &c.

R. JONES
Adjt. Genl.

Lbk (DNA-94, LS, 24:286–87); also in the *National Intelligencer,* 15 Nov. 1847. On 13 Nov. 1847 Benton and William C. Jones attempted to have this letter and their own of 9 Nov. (Doc. No. 255) read in court, but that body declined to hear them (CT. MARTIAL, 93–94). They continued to press for the *exact* sources of the charges against JCF, even distinguishing between categories of communications made by Kearny (Doc. No. 260).

259. J. J. Abert to Frémont

Bureau of Topogl. Engs.
WASHINGTON November 26. 1847

SIR,

I have duly received your letter of the 25th stating the reasons which will delay the report of your last expedition.[1]

It appears to me that your course of communicating matter of this expedition to Mr. Preuss, is rather irregular. The information you have should first be submitted to the Bureau under which you acted, and then under the customary calls of the Senate, it would be submitted to that body, and be subject to whatever course it might please to direct. Such has been the custom in all other cases, except where the War Department has found it advantageous earlier to bring out information in the form of maps for the use of the Army.[2]

Allow me to call your attention to your Accounts. These delays in their adjustment may prove embarrassing to you. To adjust as far as you have vouchers is a course more advisable to pursue. Respectfully Sir Your Obt. Servt.

J. J. ABERT
Col. Corps T. E.

Lbk (DNA-77, LS, 10:273).
1. JCF's letter was entered in the register when received, but is no longer on file.
2. By a Senate resolution of 2 Feb. 1847, Charles Preuss had been employed to work on maps of the central section of the Rocky Mountains and of Oregon and California, with the understanding that he would incorporate the new additions which JCF's third expedition might produce. When the explorer returned to Washington in the fall of 1847, he seems to have communicated his observations directly to Preuss rather than through the customary channels, bringing this reprimand from Abert. Only one map was drawn, and although it bears the label "Map of Oregon and Upper California," it is really more general, dealing with the Rockies as fully as with the country farther west and embodying the cartographical results of JCF's third expedition. It is Map 5 in the Map Portfolio, published with our Vol. 1.

260. Thomas H. Benton to Roger Jones

WASHINGTON, Dec. 24, 1847

To the Adjutant General:
SIR,

In your letter of 11th November last, you inform us that "the charges & specifications produced to the Court Martial, now in session for the trial of Lt. Col. Frémont, were based upon the facts *alleged & officially reported to the Department* by Genl. Kearney:" also, that "the original charge & specifications against Lt. Col. Frémont presented by Genl. Kearney, & *other communications from him or transmitted by him to the Department,* were placed in the hands of the officer selected for Judge Advocate, with the general directions of the Department to put the *matters of charge therein contained* in a proper form & shape for trial," &c.

We respectfully request now to understand, whether any distinction is intended, in your letter, between *"facts alleged"* by Genl. Kearney, and those "officially reported to the Department" by him; and, if so, to be informed of the nature & extent of those described under the first words. Also, whether any "matters of charge" were incorporated into the Charges and specifications produced before the Court, taken from the "other communications," alluded to as having been placed, in addition to the "original charge & specifications presented by Genl. Kearny," in the hands of the Judge Advocate; and, if so, to be informed which of the matters before the Court were taken from the "original charge & specifications" of Genl. Kearny, and which from his "other communications." Also, whether any thing contained in the "original charge and specifications presented by Genl. Kearney," has been omitted in the Charges & Specifications produced to the Court; or any thing additional inserted in them not contained in the "original" of Gen. Kearney; and, if so, what. Also, whether among the communications placed in the hands of the Judge Advocate, or in any allegations referred to him by the Department, were any upon which Charges or Specifications have *not* been produced to the Court; and, if so, the nature of such communications or allegations. Also, whether charges or offences of any kind whatsoever have been alleged, communicated or reported to the Department by Genl. Kearny, either verbally or in writing, against Lt.

462

Col. Frémont, that are not specifically set forth in the charges & specifications before the Court; and, if so, to be informed what is the nature of such charges or offences, and when & in what shape and manner they were communicated. Also, on what day the "original charge & specifications presented by Genl. Kearny," was filed in the Department. Very respectfully, Your obt. servants,

THOMAS H. BENTON
WM. CAREY JONES
of counsel for Lt. Col. Frémont

ALS, RC (DNA-94, LR, B-1186, f/w M-1299 1847). Endorsed. The letter was laid before the Secretary of War with Jones's opinion written on the back: "An officer on trial has no right to demand information respecting matters of charge, beyond the charge, or charges, and their specifications, to which the prisoner makes his plea, and upon which he may be ordered by the competent authority, to *be tried*. This is a fixed principle, and the immemorial usage of the military service, and it ought to be inviolably observed. There is no instance, as far as I know, of the non-observance of the Rule & the practice. The Adjt. General has no knowledge of the 'other communications' herein referred to—or of any other 'facts alleged' &c. more than may be seen in the matters as originally charged by General Kearny, which bear date September (11th or 13th)."

Secretary of War Marcy gave his directions for a reply on December 30: "All the documents on file in this Department in anywise relating to the matters involved in the trial of Lieut. Colonel Frémont have been, and still are accessible to him and his counsel. The information, as it is applied for by the counsel of Lieut. Colonel Fremont, is wanted, I presume, for the purposes of the trial, and all beyond what these documents furnish, so far as it is within the knowledge of any one here, would, it seems to me, come out, more properly, as testimony than in a correspondence with the counsel of Lieut. Colonel Frémont. You will suggest this as my view of the subject, in your reply to the letter referred to me, and at the same time give the assurance that all documents in the Department, having any bearing on the matter before the court, will be readily submitted to the inspections of Lieut. Colonel Frémont or his counsel, and copies of such as they may indicate will be furnished. Such as have been passed over to the Judge Advocate and are retained by him for the purpose of the trial, cannot be properly ordered to be restored to the files of the Department until the close of the proceedings of the Court, but while with the Judge Advocate, it is presumed that Lieut. Colonel Frémont can have such use of them as may be required for his defence" (Marcy to Jones, 30 Dec. 1847, DNA-94, LR, M-1299 1847). By direct quotation, Roger Jones communicated these views to JCF's counsel on the same day.

261. Thomas H. Benton to Roger Jones

C Street, Dec. 29. 1847

Sir,

I have the honor to request that you will inform me who were the officers of the U. S. Army who were at Fort Leavenworth on the day of the arrest of Lt. Col. Fremont at that place? also, where they are now? It would also, be a further favor, and save a search of the army register, if you would inform me whether any of the said officers had been educated at the public expense, at West Point. Very respectfully, Sir, Your obedient servant.

THOMAS H. BENTON

ALS, RC (DNA-94, LR, F-323 1847). To this request, Roger Jones replied that the officers were Lieut. Col. Clifton Wharton, 1st Dragoons, commander of the post; Maj. Nathan Boone, 1st Dragoons; Bvt. Maj. John M. Scott, 1st Infantry; Lieut. William Edgar Prince, 1st Infantry; Capt. Langdon Cheves Easton, assistant quartermaster; assistant surgeon W. S. King; and Rev. Leander Ker, chaplain. He added that he did not know if any were absent on the day of arrest. Furthermore, he stated that the precise day of JCF's arrest was unknown, though it was believed to be about 20 Aug. Actually it was 22 Aug. All the officers were still at Fort Leavenworth at the time of Benton's inquiry except Prince, who had been transferred to Santa Fe, and Dr. King, who was on sick leave in Philadelphia. Of the seven, only two—Scott and Easton—were educated at West Point (Jones to Benton, Washington, 31 Dec. 1847, Lbk, DNA-94, LS, 24:372).

262. Thomas H. Benton and William C. Jones to Roger Jones

WASHINGTON, 6 Jan. 1848

To The Adjutant General,
Sir,

We request copies of the following papers, for use in the trial of Lieut. Col. Fremont: 1st the letter from the State Department to Consul Larkin, Monterey, California, taken out by Commodore Stockton, & mentioned in the sealed instructions with which Commodore S. sailed from the United States, in October, 1845; 2d.

the instructions, if any, sent to Consul Larkin, in the winter or Spring of 1846, by Lieut. Gillespie, of the Marines; 3d. the letter or report, if any, from Commodore Sloat, of July, 1846, which led to a letter of recall to that officer; 4th. the letter of recall to Commodore Sloat, sent out in August, or September, 1846, & subsequently returned to the Department, on account of the messenger by whom it was sent meeting Comm. Sloat on his return; 5th. the letter or order referred to in the margin of the recorded copy of the sealed instructions to Commodore Stockton, of October, 1845, which reference will be found in the letter or order book of the Navy Department. Very respectfully, Your obt. servants,

THOMAS H. BENTON
WM. CAREY JONES
of counsel for Lt. Col. Frémont

ALS, RC (DNA-45, Executive Letters, Jan.–June 1848). First endorsement: A routine summary of contents of letter. Second endorsement: "Respectfully submitted to the Secretary of War. The papers called for are all, probably, in the Departments of State and of the Navy to whom it is thought this application should have been addressed; and it is, therefore, respectfully recommended that the Heads of these departments be requested to communicate directly with the counsel of Lt. Col. Fremont on the subject to which it relates. R. Jones, Adjt. Gen. Jany. 8/48." Third endorsement: "Recommendation of Adjt. Genl. approved. It will be proper to notify the counsel of Lt. Col. Fremont that the papers referred to are in the Navy & State Dept. & that his application has been referred to those Depts. W. L. M. 10 Jany. 48." Fourth endorsement: "Respectfully referred to the State & Navy Departments. War Dept. Jany. 10. 1848." Fifth endorsement: "Recd. at Navy Dept. Jan. 13. 1848." On 8 Jan. Roger Jones replied to Benton and William C. Jones that the information desired was believed to be in the files of the State and Navy departments exclusively (DNA-94, LS, 24:384).

Although many requests of JCF's legal counsel for copies of dispatches and documents are not reprinted here, this one is included because it clearly indicates that Benton suspected Larkin of having special instructions on California affairs. Gillespie's deposition before the subcommittee of the Senate Military Affairs Committee later in the month disclosed that he communicated to JCF the context of the State Department's 17 Oct. 1845 instructions to Larkin (Senate Report 75, pp. 25–33, 30th Cong., 1st sess., Serial 512), although it may not have been until mid-February that Benton actually saw a copy of the instructions (see Benton to Buchanan, 18 Feb. 1848, Doc. No. 267). In view of these facts, it is difficult to understand why both JCF and JBF denied in 1884 to Josiah Royce, American historian and philosopher, that JCF knew of Larkin's instructions and his appointment as a confidential agent. JBF found "absurd" and "impossible" the idea that Larkin, "prodigiously vain" and "garrulus," had been a secret agent (see Royce to H. L. Oak, 9 Dec. 1884, 1 Jan., 14 March, 14 April, 8 Aug. 1885, ROYCE [2], 141–45, 145–56, 151–53, 154–57, 170–74). It is not surprising that Royce concluded that JCF had "lied, lied unmistakably, unmitigatedly, hopelessly." In an article written and edited by JBF from her husband's notes and published after his death, the Frémonts admit that Gillespie acquainted JCF with Buchanan's instructions to Larkin. But they maintain that a conciliatory policy was no longer practicable, "as actual war was inevitable and immediate; moreover, it was in conflict with our [JCF's and Gillespie's] own instructions" (FREMONT [1]).

263. Frémont's Petition to Congress

[27 Jan. 1848]

To the Senate and House of Representatives of the United State of America in Congress assembled:

The petition of John Charles Frémont, a citizen of the United States, Respectfully shows:

That, in June of the year 1846, being then a brevet captain of topographical engineers in the service of the United States, and employed as such in California, he engaged in military operations with the people of the country for the establishment of the independence of California, before the existence of war between the United States and Mexico was known, and was successful in said undertaking; the independence of California being proclaimed at Sonoma on the 5th day of July, and the Mexican forces routed and dispersed. That immediately on hearing of the war between the United States and Mexico, the flag of independence was pulled down and that of the United States ran up in its place, and under this flag military service was rendered to the United States until the conquest was complete, and supplies obtained from the people mostly on credit of certificates given for them. That, after the conquest, a temporary government was formed; the expenses of which, like those incurred for military operations, are mostly yet unpaid, and should be paid by the United States, to whom all the benefits of the conquest of California has accrued.

That in the month of October last, this memorialist, by a letter of that date, brought the payment of these claims to the notice of the Secretary of War, whose answer of the 15th of the same month, also herewith shown, stated the inability of the department to pay them in the then existing state of the laws on the subject, and suggested the remedy of *"special legislation."* For that remedy this memorialist now applies, and for the sake of justice to the United States and the claimants, he asks that a committee may be allowed to investigate the nature and general amount of the claims, which can easily be done, as there are, at this time, in Washington city several officers of the army and navy, and many citizens of California, well acquainted with the nature of these claims, and entirely disinterested, and who can give valuable information to the government.

Your memorialist states that he himself has knowledge of almost every transaction on which any just claim can be founded; that most of them accrued under his direction; and that he was careful to have certificates given, both for the safety of the government and the claimant; and that he always employed responsible men, who are ready and able, before a proper commission, to verify every just claim and to detect every false one.

Your memorialist deems it due to justice, both to the United States and to the claimants, to have these claims audited and allowed by a commission in California, and paid there by the proper officers of the pay, quartermaster, and commissary department; and that no payments ought to be made at this place, except to claimants in their own proper person. To do otherwise would be to throw the claims into the hands of speculators, to the double injury both of the United States and the claimant.

Your memorialist believes that half a million of dollars would pay all the just claims in California, of every kind, and defray all the expenses of a commission to verify them, and he could now give a general estimate of amounts, under the different heads, to justify that opinion, but deems it better to have testimony taken upon the subject before a committee of Congress, or of either House, which can now be readily done.

Your memorialist asks for this investigation as an act of justice to himself, as well as for the security of the United States and justice to the people who have given their services and property to the government, in order that his name may not be made a cover for false claims, and accounts proved against the government which he could either disprove himself, or point out those who could.

The memorialist avers that the people of California served the United States faithfully and patriotically, and deserve to be fairly and promptly paid for their services, sacrifices, and supplies, and he deems it his sacred duty (independently of his personal liabilities on account of the government) to bring their case fully before Congress, and use his best endeavours not only to have them paid, but paid in a way that will save their claims from passing for trifles into the hands of agents and speculators.

Your memorialist, feeling his own reputation concerned in the settlement of the California claims, as well as the interest of the United States and the just claimants, prays that the committee which may be charged with this memorial, may be allowed to summon the necessary witnesses, administer oaths to them, and take their testimony in writing, and report it to the House to which it may belong, for its consideration and preservation.

And your memorialist, as in duty bound, will every pray, &c.

JOHN CHARLES FRÉMONT.

Printed in *California Claims,* Senate Report 75, pp. 1–3, 30th Cong., 1st sess., Serial 512. Benton presented JCF's petition to the Senate on 27 Jan. 1848 and saw it referred to the Military Affairs Committee (*Congressional Globe,* 27 Jan. 1848, 30th Cong., 1st sess., p. 261), which on 1 Feb. was authorized to take testimony and summon witnesses.

264. John F. Lee to Roger Jones

WASHINGTON. February 1. 1848

To the Adjutant General of the Army
SIR.

I submit herewith the proceedings of the general court martial in the case of Lt. Col. Fremont, which adjourned without day, yesterday.[1] Respectfully Yr. Obt. Servt.

J. F. LEE
Judge Advocate

ALS, RC (DNA-94, LR, L-31 1848). Endorsed: "The Proceedings Respectfully Laid before the Sec. of War as soon as Recd. R. Jones. Feb. 1. 1848." The court had found JCF guilty on all charges and specifications and had sentenced him to be dismissed from the Army. But because of his distinguished public service and the peculiar circumstances of the case, seven of the thirteen members recommended him to the clemency of the president. Four of the seven noted that under the circumstances, more experienced officers than JCF might have had difficulty deciding whether Stockton or Kearny was in lawful command in California.

The Secretary of War immediately transmitted the proceedings to the president, who, after reading the record and discussing the case with his cabinet, concluded that the facts proved did not constitute the military crime of mutiny. But he did believe that the charges of disobedience to the lawful commands of a superior officer and conduct to the prejudice of good order and military discipline had been sustained by proofs. He approved the sentence of the court but decided to remit the penalty of dismissal from the service, instructing the Secretary of War to have JCF return to duty.

1. The manuscript record of the court-martial proceedings may be found in DNA-153, EE-575. The printed record, plus JCF's long defense, is Senate Exec. Doc. 33, 30th Cong., 1st sess., Serial 507, and has been republished (with added notes) as a supplement to this volume of *The Expeditions of John Charles Frémont*. CT. MARTIAL citations, then, may be found either in the serial set or in the supplementary volume.

It was Benton who was primarily responsible for the publication of the court-martial proceedings. As a result of his motion, the Senate by a resolution on 29 Feb. called upon the president to transmit a copy of the proceedings. He complied on 7 April, and on 12 April the Senate ordered 3,000 "extra copies" printed (*Congressional Globe*, 28 and 29 Feb., 7 and 12 April 1848, 30th Cong., 1st sess., pp. 397, 403, 593, 623). This procedure and this number seem not to have been unusual, for less than six months later the Senate ordered 3,000 "extra copies" of the proceedings of the court-martial of Gen. Gideon J. Pillow, a friend of President Polk's (*ibid.*, 3 Aug. 1848, p. 1030).

265. Frémont's Deposition

[5 Feb. 1848]

This deponent, in conformity to the intimation of the committee, will consider the California claims under two divisions, those accruing under the first movement for independence, before the war with Mexico was known in California, and those arising after the flag of the United States was raised. It is very proper so to consider them; for although the United States, as receiving all the fruits of the movement for independence, is as justly bound to pay the expenses of that movement as of the operations afterwards carried on under her own flag, yet the first movement, having been without expressed authority from the United States, and revolutionary in its character, it is entirely proper, as intimated by the committee, that the nature and origin of that movement should be known.

The movement for independence was one of self defence on the part of the American settlers in that part of California, and of the topographical party in the service of the United States, of which this deponent then had the command.

This deponent, with a topographical party, had left the United States in the spring of 1845 on his third expedition of exploration, and to avoid difficulties with the Mexican authorities in California, left that province for Oregon early in the spring of 1846, and in the beginning of May had reached the north end of the great Tlamath lake, which lake is cut by the parallel of 42°, so that he was then in Oregon. His progress further north was then barred by hostile Indians and impassable snowy mountains, and he was meditating some change in his route, when, late in the evening of the 8th of May, two horsemen came up to our camp. One was Samuel Neal, formerly of my topographical party. He informed me that a United States officer was on my trail, with despatches for me, whom he had left two days behind with a small escort, but doubted whether he would ever reach me on account of the dangers from the Indians. On the morning of the 9th, I took nine men, four of them Delaware Indians, travelled down the west side of the lake about sixty miles, and met the party that evening.

That officer was Lieutenant Gillespie, of the marines.

He brought me a letter of introduction from the Secretary of State, Mr. Buchanan, and letters and papers from Senator Benton and his family. The letter from the Secretary was directed to me in my private or citizen capacity, and, although importing nothing beyond the introduction, accredited the bearer to me as coming from the Secretary of State, and, in connexion with the circumstances and place of its delivery, indicated a purpose in sending it which was intelligibly explained to me by the accompanying letter from Senator Benton, and by communications from Lieutenant Gillespie. This officer informed me that he had been directed by the Secretary of State to find me, and to acquaint me with his instructions, which had for their principal objects to ascertain the disposition of the California people, to conciliate their feelings in favor of the United States, and to find out, with a design of counteracting, the designs of the British government upon that country.

These communications, and the dangers of my position, (three men were killed in our camp the night Lieutenant Gillespie delivered his letters,) induced me, after returning to my party at the north end of the lake, to turn back to the valley of the Sacramento. Arrived there, information was received that Gen. Castro was then raising forces and exciting the Indians both against the settlers and

the small party under the command of this deponent, upon the unfounded pretext of an intended insurrection by them against the
Mexican government in California. Upon his own view of the dangers of their situation, and the earnest applications of the settlers,
this deponent joined them with his party, and, (what they deemed
of great moment,) his name as an American officer, in the month of
June, 1846, and by the 5th day of July the movement was so far successful that a declaration of independence was made on that day at
SONOMA, and the whole country north of the Bay of San Francisco,
being freed from Mexican power, this deponent, at the head of 160
mounted men, principally American settlers, sat out to go round by
the head of that bay to attack Gen. Castro on the south side of the
bay. While proceeding against Gen. Castro, authentic information
was received that, on the 7th of July, Commodore Sloat had taken
possession of Monterey, and hoisted the American flag; upon which
the flag of independence was immediately hauled down, and that of
the United States ran up; and under the flag of the United States
all subsequent operations were carried on.

I came down to Monterey with my command, upon the request
of Commodore Sloat, to co-operate with him; and immediately on
my arrival waited upon him, in company with Lieutenant Gillespie,
on board the frigate Savannah. Commodore Sloat appeared uneasy
at the great responsibility he had assumed. He informed me, that he
had applied to Lieutenant Gillespie, whom he knew to be an agent
of the government, for his authority, but that he had declined to give
it. He then inquired to know under what instructions I had acted in
taking up arms against the Mexican authorities. I informed him,
that I had acted solely on my own responsibility, and without any
authority from the government to justify hostilities. Commodore
Sloat appeared greatly disturbed with this information, and gave me
distinctly to understand that in raising the flag at Monterey, he had
acted upon the faith of our operations in the north. Commodore
Sloat soon relinquished the command to Commodore Stockton,
who determined to prosecute hostilities to the complete conquest
of California. He proposed that Lieutenant Gillespie and myself
should serve under him, with all the force we could get; which
we agreed to, our men doing the same, as Commodore Stockton
so fully testified before the court martial; and from that time forward, all my operations were carried on under the orders of Com-

modore Stockton, or by virtue of commissions bestowed by him. I was appointed by him major of the California battalion, afterwards military commandant of California, and afterwards governor and commander-in-chief in California; and under all these appointments expenses were incurred, which remain to be paid.

Commodore Stockton reported to the government all these appointments that he gave me, and our success in conquering the remainder of California in the summer of 1846, and suppressing the insurrection during the winter, which broke out in the south in the month of September; he also gave an account of it before the court martial. Commodore Sloat reported also my coming down to Monterey, and our success in freeing the northern part of California from Mexican power, and the retreat of General Castro towards the south, flying, as he correctly said, before Frémont.

The fruits of the revolutionary movement thus passed to the United States, and have remained with her ever since. These fruits were very considerable. Besides the peaceable possession of all the northern part of California, and the actual force in the field under the independent flag, which immediately went into service under the United States, there is good reason to believe, and evidence now at hand to sustain that belief, that the revolutionary movement prevented a design of the Californians to put their country under the flag of the British, and also prevented the completion of the colonization grant of three thousand square leagues to Macnamara, who was brought to California in the British sloop of war Juno, in the month of June, 1846. Admiral Seymour, in the Collingwood, of 80 guns, arrived at Monterey on the 16th of July. Macnamara was on board the Collingwood when I arrived at Monterey on the 19th, and was carried away in that vessel. The taking possession of that place on the 7th had anticipated him, and the revolutionary movement had checked the designs of the Californians to place the country under British protection; and also prevented the fulfilment of the great grant to Macnamara, the original papers of which I now have here, to be shown the committee and to be delivered up to the government.[1] Testimony now here, or near at hand, can be had to these points, namely; Captain Gillespie, Messrs. Childs [Chiles] and Hensley, Lieutenant Minor, of the navy, at Fredericksburg, Virginia, and the reports of the United States consul at Monterey, Mr. Larkin.

This deponent now states the general nature and probable amount of the claims arising under these operations, which he estimates in round numbers as follows:

From 3,000 to 4,000 horses, averaging thirty dollars each, say	$120,000
3,000 head of cattle, averaging $10, say	30,000
1,000 saddles, bridles, spurs, and horse equipments, averaging $60	60,000
400 rifles, at $30 each	12,000
Drafts protested and obligations, including damages and interests, say	50,000
Claims for provisions taken, and damages at *San Pedro* and *Los Angeles,* examined and allowed by a commission before I left California	29,584
Provisions and supplies, to wit: flour, grain, coffee, sugar, vegetables, and other small items, to wit: sheep, wagons, gears, damage to ranchos, say	100,000
Services of the California battalion, say	100,000

These are mere conjectural estimates made from general knowledge, not pretending to the accuracy of estimates upon data.

The above expenses were for near about one year of time, and almost every thing obtained was without money; the whole amount of which furnished to me by Commodore Stockton, from naval funds, was $20,004, (of which $10,004 on a requisition for $20,004,) and $2,199 in funds and stores, from Captain Montgomery, of the Portsmouth sloop-of-war. For a part of the supplies certificates or receipts were given; this was when the supplies were obtained from friends, or from inhabitants of the country who gave up what was wanted for carrying on the war. Other parts were taken from the enemy, or from the insurgent or inimical population. I know almost every transaction myself, or I know those who do know them, so that I would be able to verify, or have verified every just account, and be able to detect every unjust one.

The above estimate includes claims not arising under my command, but is intended to provide for all, whether arising from the immediate orders of Commodore Stockton, or from his command through others, or from Captain Mervine, Captain Montgomery, and other naval or military officers engaged in the conquest of California. About half a million of dollars is my general estimate of the amount required, but I think $600,000 should be appropriated to cover unforeseen items, or errors in the estimate. That sum would be very small for the services rendered, as the naval forces, and the inhabitants of the country and the California battalion, conquered the country for the United States before the New York regiment and other troops, destined to make the conquest, arrived there.

I offer, as corroborating testimony, the following letter of Mr. Thomas O. Larkin, the United States consul at Monterey, dated May 30, 1847, addressed to General Kearny on the eve of his departure from that place, and intended to be shown to the President, and to make known to him the merit of the California battalion and the inhabitants of California, in carrying on the war upon their own means, and at great sacrifices, and the urgent necessity for paying their claims.[2] The letter I offer is a copy from the original, given to me by Mr. Larkin himself, and was by him made known at the time to Captain Gillespie as well as to myself. I believe it to be substantially true, and offer it as a corroboration of my statement.

J. C. FRÉMONT.
Sworn to and subscribed before me, this 28th February, 1848.
LEW CASS.

Question to Colonel Frémont

Did you know, or understand from credible report, that the Californian authorities were granting or selling the national domain or the missions, and on what terms—and what effect, if any, the revolutionary movement had in stopping these grants or sales?

I did understand from credible report that the Californian authorities were granting and selling the missions and other public domains. In some cases these lands were so conveyed simply as grants, in others as reward for services rendered to the government, and in others for amounts of money that had been advanced, or were to be paid to the government. I understood that in this way nearly all the missions south of San Louis Obispo, the mission of San Raphael in Sonoma, and some of the large islands on the coast were granted. I understood that many of these grants were hastily made, without the usual legal forms, and wanting the usual formalities, and I understood from citizens of the country, such as Don Abel Stearns, of the Pueblo de los Angeles, that these mission grants were illegally made, and ought not to be considered valid. I saw in the public archives deeds and titles of some of the lands which were so conveyed away by the government of the territory. Among them were the following, viz:

1. The *Mission of San Gabriel,* granted on the 8th of June, 1846, to Julian [William] Workman and Hugo Reid, (English subjects.)

2. The *Mission of San Rafael,* to Julian Workman and Francisco Plinio Temple, on the 8th of June, 1846.

3. *The Island of San Clemente,* granted about the middle of May, 1846, to Julian Workman and Andres Pico.

4. *Bird Island,* granted on the 3d of June, 1846, to Julian Workman.

6. *San Mateo,* (part of the Mission of Dolores,) granted in the month of May to Cayetano Arenas.

7. *Mission of San Luis Rey,* granted (I believe) in the month of June, 1846, to Señor Cot.

I submit the following extract from a deed given by Governor Pico under date of June 8th, 1846, to Julian Workman and Hugo Reid, of the Mission of San Gabriel. A copy of the deed is contained in a letter now in my possession from Mr. Reid to Commodore Stockton. The words of Governor Pico are:

"Authorized beforehand by the most excellent assembly of the department to dispose of the missions for the payment of their debts, and avoiding of the total ruin of them, as well as to proportion resources that may serve for the general defence in case of a foreign invasion, which according to recent dates is not far off," etc., etc., etc.

The facts above narrated, with many attending circumstances, led me to believe that the authorities of California designed to create as large as possible a British interest in the country, or in other words, to convert, wherever it could be done, public or Mexican property in California into British property. These things were mostly done hurriedly, and mostly at the same fixed period of time, and taken in connexion with my collision with the authorities in March, '46, and the declaration of the same authorities that I had come into the country to excite a revolt, and the disposition shown by the American settlers in offering to aid me, and the consequent proceedings against them, further led me to believe that the action of the authorities was influenced by apprehension of danger from the Americans. I believe that the action of the authorities in the grant to Macnamara was precip[it]ated by the revolution in the north.

J. C. FRÉMONT.

Printed in *California Claims,* Senate Report 75, pp. 12–17, 30th Cong., 1st sess., Serial 512. On 5 Feb. 1848 JCF read this written deposition to the subcommittee charged by the Senate Military Affairs Committee with taking and reporting back to it testimony relating to the California Claims. Members of the three-man subcommittee included Benton, Thomas J. Rusk of Texas, and John J. Crittenden of Kentucky, who frequently did not attend. Late in February the Senate received the favorable report of the Military Affairs Committee and ordered 20,000 copies printed.

1. Between 1837 and 1846 there were a number of proposals to compensate British holders of Mexican bonds for their losses by granting them land in California. One such scheme was that of Eugene McNamara, a young Irish priest who in Mexico City in 1844 advocated settling thousands of Irish Catholics in California. President José Joaquín Herrera approved, but his successor objected, and McNamara was advised to go to California and submit his project to departmental authorities there (ENGELSON, 144). He did so, and at Santa Barbara on 4 July 1846, Pío Pico signed a grant which would have permitted the settlement of 3,000 families in the lower San Joaquin Valley. Possibly the date may have been fixed to antedate the raising of the American flag at Monterey on 7 July, but in any event the United States never recognized the grant. To the State Department JCF claimed that the revolutionary movement had frustrated the design of the Californians to put their country under British protection (see Doc. No. 271). His inveterate enemy, Emory, scoffingly termed the whole McNamara business "a perfect humbug" (Emory to Jefferson Davis, 14 May 1848, ICHi). The documents relating to the grant are printed in English and Spanish in *California Claims,* pp. 19–25, 77–83.

2. Larkin's letter is not reprinted here. It may be found in *ibid.,* 17–18, and under date of 29 May in LARKIN, 6:177–78.

266. Frémont to Harris Wilson

WASHINGTON CITY, Feby 8th 1848

SIR,

I received your letter of December 16th in relation to a draft drawn by me upon Robt. Campbell, in favor of Saml. Neal, for 149.37/100 and which draft has been lost.

Constant occupation growing out of the late Court Martial, obliged me to lay my correspondence almost wholly aside; & I beg you to receive this as an apology for an apparent neglect of your letter. Since the loss of the draft I have frequently seen Mr. Neal in California. I *think* but am not sure, that I there renewed the draft; I will endeavor to ascertain the fact, so as to satisfy myself of the propriety of paying the draft now. As you say that the holders are poor men, and I know Neal to be an honest one I believe the best course would be to pay the draft. In that case I will write to you in a few days, & will [expect] you to give me such a receipt as will secure one against being obliged to pay it over again. I am very respectfully Your Obdt. Servt.

J. C. Frémont

Harris Wilson Esq.
77 Murray St.
N. Y.

ALS-JBF, RC (MoSHi—Robert Campbell Papers).

267. Thomas H. Benton to James Buchanan

Senate Chamber, Friday
[18 Feb. 1848]

Dear Sir,

Genl Cass has shewn me your note, & the draft of the letter to Mr. O. Larkin. I have authorized him to speak for me in his interview with you this evening.[1]

I do not think it necessary, nor desirable, to publish the instructions, nor in fact, any part of them. The depositions of Fremont & Gillespie are brief, and general, and only go to the general point of observing & counteracting foreign designs in California & conciliating the people towards ourselves.[2] No authority for hostilities is claimed under them; and, as they stand, they only shew the natural and proper desire of the government to frustrate the prejudicial designs of foreigners in California which designs were found to be far more dangerous than known of here, and requiring a remedy of a much stronger kind than the government contemplated; and, fortunately, we have the full proof now here to shew the danger of the designs which were then on foot, and the necessity for the strong remedy which was applied. Yours respectfully,

Thomas H. Benton

ALS, RC (PHi—Buchanan Papers). Endorsed.
1. A few months after this evening interview with Buchanan, Lewis Cass

477

(1782–1866), chairman of the Senate Military Affairs Committee and senator from Michigan, became the Democratic party's nominee for the presidency. He received only token support from Benton (CHAMBERS, 333–37). But his defeat did not end his political career; he was re-elected to the Senate in 1851 and in 1857 became Secretary of State.

2. For JCF's deposition, see Doc. No. 265. Gillespie's, printed in the same Senate committee report as JCF's (pp. 25–33), is similar to that of the former commander of the California Battalion. It does assert that Buchanan had directed him to show JCF a duplicate of the confidential Oct. 1845 dispatch to Larkin.

268. Frémont to Roger Jones

WASHINGTON CITY,
C. Street, Feby 19th 1848

To the Adjutant General,
SIR,

I have this moment received the general order, No. 7 (dated the 17th instant)[1] making known to me the final decision in the proceedings of the general court martial before which I have been tried, and hereby send in my resignation of Lieutenant Colonel in the Army of the United States.

In doing this I take the occasion to say that my reason for resigning is, that I do not feel conscious of having done any thing to merit the finding of the court; and this being the case, I cannot, by accepting the clemency of the President, admit the justice of the decision against me. Very respectfully, Sir, your obedt. servt.

J. C. FRÉMONT

ALS, RC (DNA-94, ACP File). Endorsed: "Rec'd 1/4 past 3 P.M. Feby 19th 1848. Respectfully laid before the Sec. of War. R. Jones." On the same day the Secretary of War submitted JCF's resignation to the president, but there was a delay in its acceptance, and an impatient JCF would write again to the Adjutant General.

1. The twenty-eight-page printed copy of general orders no. 7, signed by Roger Jones, Adjutant General, and dated 17 Feb. 1848, is not reprinted here but is in DNA-92, Consolidated Correspondence File, John C. Fremont. It enumerates the charges and specifications upon which JCF was tried, sets forth the findings and sentence of the court, and implements the wishes of the president with the following order: "Lieut. Col. Fremont of the Mounted Rifle Regiment is accordingly released from arrest, and will join his Regiment in Mexico. The General Court Martial of which Brevet Brigadier General

George M. Brooke is President, is hereby dissolved." All the information and documents contained in general orders no. 7 are in various places in CT. MARTIAL. See particularly pp. 4–27 for the charges and specifications, pp. 337–39 for the findings and sentence of the court, and pp. 340–41 for the president's decisions and orders in the case.

269. Frémont to John Torrey

WASHINGTON CITY, February 24th. 1848

MY DEAR SIR,

I am about sending to California a number of seeds, and would like to have your opinion as to whether they should be simply in paper envelopes, or soldered up in tin boxes. I am also sending slips of vines & would like to know from you the best way of preserving them during the long sea voyage. May I ask for an early answer, as the vessel leaves shortly for California. Very truly yours,

J. C. FRÉMONT

ALS-JBF, RC (NNNBG—Torrey Correspondence).

270. Frémont to John Torrey

WASHINGTON CITY Feby. 24th 1848

MY DEAR SIR,

I had just sent you a little enquiry about some seeds I wished to take to California, when I received your kind letter of yesterday. When I resigned my commission of Lt. Col. of Cavalry, I gave up also my commission in the Topl. Engineers, which had in fact been vacated by my acceptance of the former. I have therefore entirely withdrawn from the public service, but I am deeply gratified with being able to say to you that our work will still go on, and that I even hope to be able to give it a greater extent and beauty than we had before anticipated. This, although only a hope at present, will, I have great reason to believe be verified, and in the mean time I am permitted to assure you, that there will be no interruption in working up the materials that we have already collected. So soon as I obtain more certain knowledge, I will write to you again and in the mean time I would be glad to know at what time you propose visiting this city.

I thank you sincerely and earnestly for the expression of your sympathy. Throughout this business I have tasked my judgement to do what was right, and it will be a high gratification to know that my friends approve my conduct.

A short time since I petitioned Congress to pay the debts accruing from our operations in California and the Military Committee have been occupied in examining the subject. They have reported the bill, and the result of their examination to the Senate which has ordered 20,000 extra copies to be printed. I will send you one.

Mr. Benton & the family join in regards to you. With much regard I am Yours very truly,

J. C. Frémont

Dr. John Torrey,
New York

ALS-JBF, RC (NNNBG—Torrey Correspondence).

271. Frémont to James Buchanan

C. Street, March 1. 1848

To the Hon. Secretary of State
Sir,

I enclose you the original papers in the Spanish language in relation to the Macnamara grant of land in Upper California, taken by me from the government archives in Los Angeles when I was Governor of California under the appointment of Commodore Stockton.

I also enclose a copy of the depositions taken before the military committee of the Senate, in relation to claims growing out of military operations in California, at pages 19 to 25 of which is an English translation of said papers, and in the appendix to which there is a copy in Spanish.

In the depositions of myself, Capt. Gillespie, Capt. Hensley, Capt. Owens, Lieut. Loker, may be seen the consequences which resulted from my turning back to the valley of the Sacramento from the great Tlamath lake, and which return, and subsequent operations with the American settlers in California, were influenced by the letters from yourself and Col. Benton which Capt. Gillespie brought me and the communications which he made me. These depositions may be considered as a *report* of those operations, influenced, but not commanded by the communications from the department of State through Capt. Gillespie, and which I have not felt myself authorized to make in any other form. Respectfully Your Obedient Servant,

J. C. FRÉMONT

ALS, RC (DNA-59, Miscellaneous Letters Received, Jan.–March 1848). Endorsed: "Recd. 2 March 1848." With this letter are enclosed the original Spanish documents relating to the McNamara grant. For these, see *California Claims,* Senate Report 75, pp. 77–83, 30th Cong., 1st sess., Serial 512, a copy of which JCF also submitted to Buchanan (see Doc. No. 265 and notes).

272. Frémont to John Torrey

WASHINGTON CITY, March 2d. 1848

MY DEAR SIR,

I have replied fully to yours of the 28th ultimo, directing to New York, but send this to Princeton, fearing you may have already left the former place. I shall leave this city in the course of next month for the Missouri frontier,[1] thence to California with an exploring party, taking a direct route to the bay of San Francisco. I have no thought of abandoning our intended work, and will immediately endeavor to obtain necessary means. Please let me know the amount we shall probably need both for what we are now indebted and for future operations. I am very glad to know that you did not undertake the collections of the Exploring Expedition. I suppose that my other note will reach you shortly after this, if not before. Please let me hear as soon as possible, as now we must move fast to be out early in the Spring. Very truly yours,

J. C. FRÉMONT

Dr. John Torrey,
Princeton.

ALS, RC (James S. Copley Collection, La Jolla, Calif.).
1. JCF did not leave Washington until early September.

273. James Buchanan to Frémont

Department of State
WASHINGTON, 2 March 1848

Col. J. C. Fremont
SIR:

I have received your note of yesterday, with the original papers in
the Spanish language, in relation to the Macnamara grant of land
in Upper California, taken by you from the Government archives in
Los Angeles whilst you were Governor of California, together with
a copy of the depositions taken before the military committee of the
Senate, in relation to claims growing out of military operations in
California, &c. &c.

These documents, so important for the Government, and bearing
such conclusive testimony to the valuable services which you have
rendered your country in that distant region, shall be carefully preserved in the archives of the Department. I am, &c.

JAMES BUCHANAN

Copy (DNA-59, Domestic Letters Sent, 36:383–85).

274. Frémont to Lewis J. Cist

WASHINGTON CITY, March 3d. 1848

SIR,

I make you at a late date my acknowledgements for the gratifying
terms of your note, and offer you as an apology the entire occupation
of my time by the recent court martial, which obliged me wholly to
lay aside my correspondence.

I sent you some time since a copy of my defence,[1] and accompany

this with a copy of a report from the military committee of the Senate, which I hope will have interest for you. Respectfully,

J. C. FRÉMONT

L. J. Cist, Esqre.
Cincinnati, Ohio

ALS, RC (IU). Lewis J. Cist (1818–85) of Cincinnati, son of the publisher
of *Cist's Advertiser,* was a bank clerk and a literary contributor to various
periodicals throughout the country. After his marriage in St. Louis in 1850,
he was affiliated with Missouri financial institutions until 1870, when he returned to Cincinnati.

1. JCF's defense, which constitutes Appendix 4 of CT. MARTIAL, was also
issued separately as a seventy-eight-page pamphlet under the title *Defence
of Lt. Col. Fremont before the Court Martial* (Washington, D.C., 1848).

275. Frémont to James Buchanan

C Street, March 7. 1848

To the Hon. Mr. Buchanan,
SIR,

I have to make you many thanks for the kind interest which you
have manifested in my behalf, and would take great pleasure in conforming my conduct to your opinion, if it was possible. But it is not
possible. I feel the sentence of the court martial against me to be unjust; and while that feeling remains I can never, by any act or word
whatever, even by the remotest implication, admit or seem to admit,
its justice. Very respectfully, Sir, Your Obt. Servant,

J. C. FRÉMONT

ALS, RC (PHi—Buchanan Papers). Endorsed.

276. Frémont to John Torrey

WASHINGTON CITY, March 12. 1848

MY DEAR SIR,

I have received both your letters of the 8th. and 9th.,[1] and feel
pleasure in making a satisfactory reply. I have good reasons for be-

lieving that I shall receive aid from the government in carrying on the work, and am now making my arrangements in that expectation.[2] Perhaps you will be able to give me the approximate amount which we shall require for our botany, as I should like to include it in the general estimate. Although [David] Douglas, [Thomas] Nuttall, & [William] Gambel[3] have done a great deal yet I am persuaded that much remains to be done, and that such an expedition as I now propose to make would collect rich material for the work.

Perhaps we could safely base our estimate on eighty quarto or a hundred and fifty octave plates.

Mr. [Richard H.] Kern. of Philadelphia, a brother of the artist who accompanied the last expedition, will go with me on this, and from what I have seen of his work you may anticipate beautiful drawings.

I should have been glad to have some little conversation with Mr. Nuttall before going out. Is he likely to come this way? If you can do so conveniently please procure me a copy of his Gambel memoir when it comes out.[4] Dr. Wislizenus' book is not yet published, but so soon as it is I will send the catalogues.[5] I enclose you a draft for Mr. Endicott[6] and a bill made out in proper form. The Departments here are fond of giving trouble and require every thing their own way. I think the charges are quite moderate and the work appears to me extremely good. I like very much your idea of importing an artist. I have always understood that while we fairly compete with Europeans in work on steel, they far excel us in lithography. It has been however suggested to me that this may be partly owing to the fact that we print on muslin paper, and they on linen; the latter being much the best. I think it would be best to purchase the stones from Mr. Endicott.

I regret to know that you will not be able to visit Washington again, and must try to get along in stead by frequent letters. It would be a very agreeable thing indeed to my wife if your daughter could carry out her inclination, and make a visit with her to California. Steam will soon make all this easy. But Mrs. Frémont will write for herself and continue as well as she can on paper an acquaintance that she would have had much pleasure in making personally.

I have to thank you for the pamphlet sent me, and will be grateful for any aid of the kind that may occur to you.

Mr. Endicott can sign the bill and send it to me under cover to Mr. Benton. Have you tried the effect of drawing the plants with crayon? I believe that greater depth of shade and finer effect are so obtained, but I suppose you think these less important than the clearness of outline in Mr. Endicott's present style. Very truly yours,

J. C. FRÉMONT

ALS, RC (NNNBG—Torrey Correspondence).

1. Not found.

2. JCF hoped that the federal government would subsidize another year of exploration before writing a report similar to those of his 1842 and 1843–44 expeditions. He was preparing a *Geographical Memoir* "in illustration" of a map of Oregon and California, which Preuss was drawing, but he considered it a preliminary sketch and only partial fulfillment of the Senate order of 2 Feb. 1847 calling for the construction of two maps—one of the central section of the Rocky Mountains and one of Oregon and Upper California. But additional geographical labors were required for their completion.

The question of continued public support came before the Senate in July 1848, when Senator Sidney Breese of Illinois offered a resolution to name a select committee of five to consider publishing the results of the third expedition "and also to inquire into the expediency of providing for the continuation and completion" of JCF's surveys, "with a view to develop the geographical character of the country, and the practicality of establishing railroads or other communications between the valley of the Mississippi and the Pacific Ocean." Ultimately the committee, headed by Breese, reported favorably, recommending that $30,000 be appropriated for JCF's projected surveys and explorations, and on 5 Aug. 1848 by an 18-to-16 vote the Senate approved that sum in an amendment to the civil and diplomatic appropriation bill. The House rejected it 128 to 29 on 10 Aug., shortly before Congress adjourned (Senate Committee Report 226, 30th Cong., 1st sess., Serial 512; *Congressional Globe*, 5 and 10 Aug. 1848, 30th Cong., 1st sess.). JCF was then forced to seek private financing for his fourth expedition.

3. William Gambel (1821–49), naturalist, ornithologist, and botanist, had collected specimens in the southern Rocky Mountains and around Los Angeles in 1843. He became assistant curator of the Academy of Natural Sciences in Philadelphia in 1847, received a medical degree in 1848, and in 1849 made a perilous winter crossing of the Humboldt Sink and Sierra Nevada, only to die of typhoid fever in a mining camp in Plumas County, Calif. (EWAN, 213).

4. Thomas Nuttall (1786–1859), naturalist, botanist, and ornithologist (see our Vol. 1, p. 134n). His memoir upon Gambel's Rocky Mountain and California collections appeared first in the *Journal* of the Academy of Natural Sciences of Philadelphia, n.s., 1 (1848):149–89.

5. Friedrich Adolph Wislizenus's *Memoir of a Tour to Northern Mexico, Connected with Col. Doniphan's Expedition, in 1846 and 1847* was printed later in the year as Senate Misc. Doc. 26, 30th Cong., 1st sess., Serial 511, and received high praise from Alexander von Humboldt.

6. The Mr. Endicott was George Endicott, a New York engraver who was to die a bit later in the year. He and his brother, William, were being paid for engravings they had made in 1845 for the botanical illustration of JCF's second report (see Vol. 1, p. 392n).

277. Frémont to Roger Jones

C Street, March 14, 1848

To the Adjt. Genl.
SIR,

I have not yet had the honor to receive any reply to my letter of resignation of the 17th [19th] ultimo, and as the President's acceptance is necessary to give legal effect to that act, I have to request that, at some convenient opportunity, you will take the trouble to obtain the reply, and make it known to me. Respectfully, Sir, your obedient servant,

J. C. FRÉMONT

ALS, RC (DNA-94, ACP File). First endorsement: "Respectfully laid before the Sec. of War. R. Jones. March 14." The War Department sent the letter on to the president, and the second endorsement reads "The Secretary of War will accept Lieut. Col. Fremont's Resignation March 14th. 1848:— J. K. P." A note states that a letter was sent to JCF, 15 March 1848.

278. William G. Freeman to Frémont

A. G. O. WASHINGTON, March 15, 1848

SIR:

Your resignation has been accepted by the President of the United States, to take effect this day. I am sir &c.

W. G. FREEMAN, A. A. G.

Lbk (DNA-94, LS, 24:517). Copies of the letter were sent to the Paymaster General and to the commanding officer of the Regiment of Mounted Riflemen, Mexico City.

Appendix

Roster of 1845–47 Expedition[1]

Hired in the East or on the Missouri Frontier	Discharged before Reaching California	Paid in St. Louis or Washington	Paid in California	Discharged in California but Paid Elsewhere
*Archambeault, Auguste				—
*Beauchamp, David	—		—	
Boulgard, Joseph			—	
*Breckenridge, Thomas E.		—		
Calloway, William			—	
*Charley (Delaware)			—	
Connor, James (Delaware)			—	
*Cosgrave, Anthony		—		
Crane (Delaware) killed				
*Davis, Jerome C.		—		
Denny (Indian) killed				
*Desnoyes, François				—
Detaile, François		—		
*Dodson, Jacob[2]		—		
Everett, Solomon (Delaware) *or simply* Solomon			—	
Fabbol				
*Ferguson, Josiah C.		—		
*Findlay, William		—		
*Godey, Alexander		—		
*Gregorio (California Indian)				
*Hamilton, Aaron		—		
*Hudspeth, Benjamin M.		—		
*Hughes, William		—		
Joyat, John	—		—	
*Juan (California Indian)				
*Kern, Edward M.		—		
*King, Henry		—		
Lajeunesse, Basil killed				
Lapierre, Louis			—	
Lowitch, Dickey (Delaware?)				—
*Martin, Thomas S.		—		
*Maxwell, Lucien B.[3]			—	
*Mercure, Henry		—		
*Moore, Risdon		—		
*Morin, Antoine				
*Perkins, William (Chinook Indian)			—	
*Proue, Raphael		—		
*Russell, R. Eugene		—		
*Sagundai, James (Delaware)			—	
Savage, L. W.			—	

Hired in the East or on the Missouri Frontier	Discharged before Reaching California	Paid in St. Louis or Washington	Paid in California	Discharged in California but Paid Elsewhere
*Schreiber, Charles	—			
Skirkett, Bob (Delaware)		—		
on vouchers as Job S. Ricketts				
*Stepp, Joseph	—			
Swanuck, James (Delaware)		—		
*Talbot, Theodore	—			
Taplin, Charles		—		
*Tison, François	—			
*Wetowka (Delaware)				
*White, James T.	—			
*Whitton, Jesse W.				—
*Wise, Marion	—			

Hired in Mexican Territory

Bihil, José				—
Caramillo, Pablo		—		
*Carson, Christopher		—		
*Fernandez, Andreas				—
*Luna, Jesús				—
*Owens, Richard	—			
*Ruiz, Manuel				—
*Scott, John	—			
Walker, Joseph R.		—		
Williams, William S.	—			

Hired in California

*Barrett, James	—			
*Bercier, Francis		—		
*Davenport, Alfred	—			
Gallego, Jesús M.		—		
*Hicks, William		—		
*Jackson, James		—		
*Laframboise, John	—			
*Loker, William N.[4]	—			
*Manuel (Indian)	—			
*Myers, John J.		—		
*Roberts, John M.	—			
Sipp, James		—		
*Taman, Ignace		—		
*Tinkey, David		—		
*Vinsonhaler, Lorenzo D.	—			

Place of Recruitment Unknown

Serfacio[5]				

1. This roster is compiled from letters, financial vouchers, the *Memoirs,* Doc. No. 5, and ROGERS [3] and includes *voyageurs,* hunters, guides, and even mule drivers. It does not include the men who became a part of Lieutenant Abert's command at Bent's Fort but does include those who were recruited in California. At his court-martial JCF stated that he entered California with sixty-two men, but the names of only sixty-one, including Joyat, Beauchamp, and Serfacio, have been ascertained.

Because of the many variants in the terms of enlistment, it has been necessary to establish broad categories within the roster, and none indicates accurately the lengths of service. A few examples, however, will show the many possibilities. Joseph R. Walker was discharged on 4 March 1846 before the JCF-Castro confrontation; Myers, who had been hired on 1 April 1846, was discharged on 18 June 1847; and Vinsonhaler was not hired until 20 April 1847.

The precise details of many services are unknown, and in some cases it has been impossible to determine the place of discharge. This is true for Fabbol, whose name appears only in Doc. No. 5, and for Gregorio and Juan, two Sierra Indian boys whose names appear on the muster rolls of the California Battalion. The boys had come east with JCF in 1844, returned to California with him in 1845, and presumably accompanied him east again in 1847, since they were members of his disastrous 1848 expedition.

Sometimes it has been impossible to ascertain if men actually left the expedition when their services were terminated. Joyat and Beauchamp were paid for services from 3 June to 6 Sept. and 26 Oct. respectively, when the expedition was still many miles from California, but the place of payment is given as William Fisher's Laguna farm near San Jose on 19 Feb. 1846. Bihil, Fernandez, Luna, and Ruiz were paid for services to 5 Oct. 1846, but the payments were made at Taos on 15 April 1847 by Theodore Talbot and are a clear indication that these *voyageurs* accompanied the Carson-Beale-Talbot party east as far as Taos.

An asterisk (*) before a name indicates that the man became or had been a member of the California Battalion.

2. Being a free black, Dodson could not lawfully enroll as a volunteer, but he did serve as a private and later petitioned Congress for the pay, bounty land, and travel allowances to which a California volunteer was entitled (Senate Report 403, 33rd Cong., 2nd sess., Serial 775).

3. Although not listed on the rosters of California volunteers (ROGERS [3]), Maxwell seems to have served. Stockton appointed him a second lieutenant on 23 July 1846, and two days later Talbot noted in a letter to his sister Mary that Carson, Owens, and Maxwell were lieutenants in his company (DNA-45, Entry 395 [E-20-A], Letterbook of Robert F. Stockton, 1846–47; DLC—Talbot Papers).

4. Loker is not usually considered to have been a member of JCF's expedition, but on 24 Aug. 1848 J. J. Abert requested that the Third Auditor pay Loker for "services rendered by him in the expedition to Oregon & California" out of the appropriation "for arrearages of the Military and Geographical Surveys West of the Mississippi" (DNA-77, LS, 10:462–63). These services may have been limited to transporting the records of the expedition from St. Louis to Washington.

5. Abert's letter to Peter Hagner indicates that Serfacio, a mule driver, died on the expedition, but it gives no place or date (1 March 1849, DNA-77, LS, 11:133–34).

BIBLIOGRAPHY

ABELOE Hoover, Mildred B., and Hero E. and Ethel Grace Rensch. *Historic Spots in California*. Revised by William N. Abeloe. 3rd ed. Stanford, Calif., 1966.

ABERT [1] Abert, Lieut. James W. *Journal of . . . from Bent's Fort to St. Louis, in 1845*. Senate Exec. Doc. 438, 29th Cong., 1st sess., Washington, D.C., 1846, [Serial 477].

ABERT [2] Galvin, John, ed. *Through the Country of the Comanche Indians in the Fall of the Year 1845: The Journal of a U.S. Army Expedition Led by Lieutenant James W. Abert*. San Francisco, 1970.

AMES [1] Ames, George Walcott, Jr. "Gillespie and the Conquest of California," *California Historical Society Quarterly*, 17 (June, Sept., Dec. 1938) :123–40, 271–84, 325–50.

AMES [2] ———. "Horse Marines: California in 1846," *California Historical Society Quarterly*, 18 (March 1939) :72–84.

AMES & HUSSEY Ames, George W., and John A. Hussey. "Preparations to Meet the Walla Walla Invasion," *California Historical Society Quarterly*, 21 (March 1942) :9–21.

ANDERSON Morgan, Dale L., and Eleanor T. Harris, eds. *The Rocky Mountain Journals of William Marshall Anderson: The West in 1834*. San Marino, Calif., 1967.

ANDREWS [1] Andrews, Thomas F. "The Ambitions of Lansford W. Hastings: A Study in Western Myth-Making," *Pacific Historical Review*, 39 (Nov. 1970) :473–91.

ANDREWS [2] ———. "The Controversial Hastings Overland Guide: A Reassessment," *Pacific Historical Review*, 37 (Feb. 1968) :21–34.

BAILEY Bailey, Paul. *Sam Brannan and the California Mormons*. Los Angeles, 1959.

BANCROFT Bancroft, Hubert H. *History of California*. 7 vols. San Francisco, 1884–90.

BAUER Bauer, K. Jack. *Surfboats and Horse Marines: U.S. Naval Operations in the Mexican War, 1846–48*. Annapolis, Md., 1969.

BEAN Bean, Walton. *California: An Interpretive History*. New York, 1968.

BENTON [1] Benton, Thomas H. *Thirty Years' View.* . . . 2 vols. New York, 1854–57.

BENTON [2] ———. *Thrilling Sketch of the Life of Col. J. C. Fremont . . . with an Account of His Expedition to Oregon and California, across the Rocky Mountains, and Discovery of the Great Gold Mines.* London, [1850].

BIGELOW Bigelow, John. *Memoir of the Life and Public Services of John Charles Fremont.* . . . New York, 1856.

BIOG. DIR. CONG. *Biographical Directory of the American Congress.* Washington, D.C., 1961.

BOLTON Bolton, Herbert E. "Pageant in the Wilderness: The Story of the Escalante Expedition to the Interior Basin, 1776," *Utah Historical Quarterly,* 18 (1950) :1–265.

BONSAL Bonsal, Stephen. *Edward Fitzgerald Beale: A Pioneer in the Path of Empire, 1822–1903.* New York, 1912.

BRANDON Brandon, William E. *The Men and the Mountain: Frémont's Fourth Expedition.* New York, 1955.

BRYANT Bryant, Edwin. *What I Saw in California.* New York, 1849.

CAL. HIS. SOC. DOCS. "Documentary," *California Historical Society Quarterly,* 1 (July, Oct. 1922, Jan. 1923) :72–95, 178–91, 286–95; 2 (April, July, Oct. 1923, Jan. 1924) :69–74, 161–72, 246–51, 350–62; 3 (April, July, Oct. 1924) :84–88, 178–90, 270–89; 4 (March, Dec. 1925) :81–87, 374–91; 5 (March, Sept. 1926) :184–95, 296–310; 6 (March, June, Sept., Dec. 1927) :77–90, 181–91, 265–80, 364–74; 7 (March 1928) : 79–85; 8 (March 1929) :71–77; 9 (March 1930) :81–86.

CAMP Camp, Charles L. "The Chronicles of George C. Yount, California Pioneer of 1826," *California Historical Society Quarterly,* 2 (April 1923) :3–66.

CARSON Carter, Harvey L. *"Dear Old Kit": The Historical Christopher Carson with a New Edition of the Carson Memoirs.* Norman, Okla., 1968.

CARTER [1] Carter, Harvey L. "Dick Owens," in *The Mountain Men and the Fur Trade of the Far West,* ed. by LeRoy R. Hafen. 8 vols. to date. Glendale, Calif., 1965—. 5:283–90.

CARTER [2] ———. "Jim Swanock and the Delawares," in *The Mountain Men and the Fur Trade of the Far West,* ed. by LeRoy R. Hafen. 8 vols. to date. Glendale, Calif., 1965—. 7:293–300.

CARTER [3] ———. "John L. Hatcher," in *The Mountain Men and the Fur Trade of the Far West,* ed. by LeRoy R. Hafen. 8 vols. to date. Glendale, Calif., 1965—. 4:125–36.

CASSIN Cassin, John. *Illustrations of the Birds of California, Texas, Oregon, British and Russian America.* Philadelphia, 1856.

CHAMBERS Chambers, William N. *Old Bullion Benton, Senator from the New West: Thomas Hart Benton, 1782–1858.* Boston, 1956.

CLARKE Clarke, Dwight L. *Stephen Watts Kearny, Soldier of the West.* Norman, Okla., 1961.

CLELAND Cleland, Robert G. *The Place Called Sespe: The History of a California Ranch.* San Marino, Calif., 1957.

CLYMAN Camp, Charles L., ed. *1792–1881 James Clyman Frontiersman: The Adventures of a Trapper and Covered-Wagon Emigrant as Told in His Own Reminiscences and Diaries.* Portland, Ore., 1960.

COLTON Colton, Walter. *Three Years in California.* New York, 1850.

COOKE Cooke, Philip St. George. *The Conquest of New Mexico and California: An Historical and Personal Narrative.* New York, 1878. Reprinted, Chicago, 1964.

I. COOPER Cooper, Isaac. "The Plains, Being a Collection of Veracious Memoranda, Taken during the Expedition of Exploration in the Year 1845, from the Western Settlements of Missouri to the Mexican Border, and from Bent's Fort on the Arkansas to Fort Gibson, via South Fork of Canadian—North Mexico and North Western Texas. By François Des Montaignes (pseud.) of St. Louis," *Western Journal and Civilian* (St. Louis) (1852–53, 1856). 9:71–73, 146–48, 221–22, 290–93, 366–68, 433–36; 10:69–73, 149–52, 222–26, 295–301, 370–75, 441–45; 15:364–70.

J. F. COOPER Beard, James Franklin, ed. *The Letters of James Fenimore Cooper.* 6 vols. Cambridge, Mass., 1960–68.

CT. MARTIAL *Message of the President of the United States, Communicating the Proceedings of the Court Martial in the Trial of Lieutenant Colonel Frémont,* Senate Exec. Doc. 33, 30th Cong., 1st sess., Washington, D.C., 1848, [Serial 507].

R. E. COWAN Cowan, Robert E. "The Leidesdorff-Folsom Estate: A Forgotten Chapter in the Romantic History of Early San Francisco," *California Historical Society Quarterly,* 7 (June 1928):105–11.

R. G. COWAN Cowan, Robert G. *Ranchos of California: A List of Spanish Concessions, 1775–1822 and Mexican Grants, 1822–1846.* Fresno, Calif., 1956.

CRAMPTON Crampton, C. Gregory. "The Opening of the Mariposa Mining Region, 1849–1859, with Particular Reference to the Mexican Land Grant of John Charles Frémont." Ph.D. dissertation, University of California, Berkeley, 1941.

CULLUM Cullum, George W. *Biographical Register of the Officers and Graduates of the U.S. Military Academy . . . 1802 to 1890.* 3rd ed. 3 vols. Boston, 1891. Supplementary vols. under various editors to 1950.

CUTTS   Cutts, James Madison. *History of the Conquest of California and New Mexico by the Forces of the U.S. in the Years 1846 and 1847.* Philadelphia, 1847.

DAKIN   Dakin, Susanna B. *The Lives of William Hartnell.* Stanford, Calif., 1949.

DELLENBAUGH   Dellenbaugh, Frederick S. *Frémont and '49.* New York, 1914.

DE VOTO   DeVoto, Bernard. *The Year of Decision: 1846.* Boston, 1943.

DAB   *Dictionary of American Biography.* 22 vols. New York, 1928–58.

DNB   *Dictionary of National Biography.* 27 vols. London, 1908–59.

DILLON   Dillon, Richard. *Fool's Gold: The Decline and Fall of Captain John Sutter of California.* New York, 1967.

DOFFLEMYER   Dofflemyer, William. "Juan Flaco: The Paul Revere of California," *Pacific Historian,* 13 (Fall 1969) :10–21.

DOWNEY   Downey, Joseph T. *The Cruise of the Portsmouth: A Sailor's View of the Naval Conquest of California, 1845–1847.* Ed. by Howard R. Lamar. New Haven, Conn., 1958.

DRURY   Drury, Clifford M. "Walter Colton, Chaplain and Alcalde," *California Historical Society Quarterly,* 35 (June 1956) :97–117.

DU PONT   DuPont, Samuel Francis. *Extracts from Private Journal-Letters of Captain S. F. DuPont, While in Command of the "Cyane," during the War with Mexico, 1846–1848.* Prepared by S. M. DuPont. Wilmington, Del., 1885.

DUVALL   Rogers, Fred Blackburn, ed. *A Navy Surgeon in California 1846–1847: The Journal of Marius Duvall.* San Francisco, 1957.

ELLISON   Ellison, William H. "San Juan to Cahuenga: The Experiences of Frémont's Battalion," *Pacific Historical Review,* 27 (Aug. 1958): 245–61.

ENGELSON   Engelson, Lester G. "Proposals for the Colonization of California by England," *California Historical Society Quarterly,* 18 (June 1939) :136–48.

EWAN   Ewan, Joseph. *Rocky Mountain Naturalists.* Denver, Colo., 1950.

FARQUHAR   Farquhar, Francis P. "Frémont in the Sierra Nevada," *Sierra Club Bulletin,* 15 (Feb. 1930) :74–95.

FLETCHER   Fletcher, F. N. *Early Nevada: The Period of Exploration, 1776–1848.* Reno, Nev., 1929.

FRÉMONT [1]   Frémont, John C. "The Conquest of California," *Century,* n.s., 19 (1890–91) :917–28.

FRÉMONT [2]   ———. *Defence of Lt. Col. Frémont before the Court Martial.* Washington, D.C., 1848.

FRÉMONT [3]   ———. *Geographical Memoir upon Upper California, in Illustration of His Map of Oregon and California.* Senate Misc.

Doc. 148, 30th Cong., 1st sess., Washington, D.C., 1848, [Serial 511].
See also MEMOIRS.

GARNER   Garner, William Robert. *Letters from California, 1846–1847*. Ed.
by Donald Munro Craig. Berkeley, Calif., 1970.

GARRARD   Garrard, Lewis H. *Wah-To-Yah and the Taos Trail*. Cincinnati, 1850.

GIFFEN [1]   Giffen, Helen S. "The California Battalion's Route to Los
Angeles," *Journal of the West*, 5 (April 1966) :207–24.

GIFFEN [2]   ———. *Trail-Blazing Pioneer: Colonel Joseph Ballinger
Chiles*. San Francisco, 1969.

GLEASON   Gleason, Duncan, ed. "James Henry Gleason: Pioneer Journal
and Letters, 1841–1856," *Historical Society of Southern California
Quarterly*, 31 (March and June 1949) :9–52.

GRIFFIN [1]   Ames, George Walcott, Jr., ed. "A Doctor Comes to California—The Diary of John S. Griffin, Assistant Surgeon with
Kearny's Dragoons, 1846–47," *California Historical Society Quarterly*, 21 (Sept., Dec. 1942) :193–224, 333–57; 22 (March 1943) :41–66.

GRIFFIN [2]   Warren, Viola L., ed. "Dr. John S. Griffin's Mail, 1846–53,"
California Historical Society Quarterly, 33 (June, Sept. 1954) :97–
124, 249–70; 34 (March 1955) :21–39.

GRIVAS   Grivas, Theodore. *Military Governments in California, 1846–1850*.
Glendale, Calif., 1963.

GUDDE   Gudde, Erwin G. *California Place Names: The Origin and Ety-
mology of Current Geographical Names*. 3rd ed. Berkeley, Calif.,
1969.

HAFEN & HAFEN   Hafen, LeRoy R., and Ann W. Hafen, eds. *Frémont's
Fourth Expedition: A Documentary Account of the Disaster of
1848–49*. Glendale, Calif., 1960.

HAINES   Haines, Francis D. "Tom Hill—Delaware Scout," *California
Historical Society Quarterly*, 25 (June 1946) :139–48.

HAMMOND & MORGAN   Hammond, George P., and Dale L. Morgan. *Captain Charles M. Weber. Pioneer of the San Joaquin and Founder
of Stockton, California, with a Description of His Papers, Maps,
Books, Pictures and Memorabilia Now in the Bancroft Library*.
Berkeley, Calif., 1966.

HARLAN   Harlan, Jacob W. *California '46 to '88*. San Francisco, 1888.

HAWGOOD [1]   Hawgood, John A., ed. *First and Last Consul: Thomas
Oliver Larkin*. 2nd ed. Palo Alto, Calif., 1970.

HAWGOOD [2]   Hawgood, John A. "John C. Frémont and the Bear Flag
Revolution: A Reappraisal," *Southern California Quarterly*, 44
(June 1962) :67–96.

HEILMAN & LEVIN   Heilman, Grace E., and Bernard S. Levin. *Calendar* of *Joel R. Poinsett Papers in the Henry D. Gilpin Collection.* Philadelphia, 1941.

HEITMAN   Heitman, Francis B. *Historical Register and Dictionary of the United States Army.* 2 vols. Washington, D.C., 1903. Reprinted, Urbana, Ill., 1965.

HEIZER   Heizer, Robert Fleming. "Walla Walla Indian Expeditions to the Sacramento Valley," *California Historical Society Quarterly,* 21 (March 1942):1–7.

HEYMAN   Heyman, Max L. *Prudent Soldier: A Biography of Major General E. R. S. Canby (1817–1873).* Glendale, Calif., 1959.

HUSSEY [1]   Hussey, John A. "Identification of the Author of 'The Farthest West' Letters from California, 1846," *California Historical Society Quarterly,* 16 (Sept. 1937):209–15.

HUSSEY [2]   ———. "New Light upon Talbot H. Green," *California Historical Society Quarterly,* 18 (March 1939):32–63.

HUSSEY [3]   ———. "The Origin of the Gillespie Mission," *California Historical Society Quarterly,* 19 (March 1940):43–58.

IDE [1]   Ide, Simeon. *A Biographical Sketch of the Life of William B. Ide.* . . . Claremont, N.H., 1880. Reprinted with *Who Conquered California? . . . History of the Conquest of California, in June, 1846 by the "Bear Flag Party."* Glorieta, N.Mex., 1967.

IDE [2]   ———. *Who Conquered California? . . . History of the Conquest of California, in June, 1846 by the "Bear Flag Party."* Claremont, N.H., 1880. Reprinted with *A Biographical Sketch of the Life of William B. Ide.* Glorieta, N.Mex., 1967.

JOHNSON [1]   Johnson, Kenneth M. *The Frémont Court Martial.* Los Angeles, 1968.

JOHNSON [2]   ———. *The New Almaden Quicksilver Mine, with an Account of the Land Claims Involving the Mine and Its Role in California History.* Georgetown, Calif., 1963.

E. C. KEMBLE   Rogers, Fred B., ed. *A Kemble Reader: Stories of California, 1846–1848, by Edward Cleveland Kemble, Early California Journalist.* San Francisco, 1963.

J. H. KEMBLE   Kemble, John H. "The First Sea Vessel to Navigate San Francisco Bay," *California Historical Society Quarterly,* 14 (June 1935):143–46.

KERN   Kern, Edward M. "Artist's Journal of a Pioneer Trip," *Life,* 46 (April 1959):95–104.

KORNS   Korns, J. Roderic, ed. "West from Fort Bridger: The Pioneering of the Immigrant Trails across Utah, 1846–1850," *Utah Historical Quarterly,* 19 (1951):1–297.

LARKIN   Hammond, George P., ed. *The Larkin Papers: Personal, Business, and Official Correspondence of Thomas Oliver Larkin, Mer-*

chant and United States Consul in California. 10 vols. Berkeley, Calif., 1951–64.

LAYNE   Layne, J. Gregg. Annals of Los Angeles . . . 1769–1861. San Francisco, 1935.

LYMAN   Lyman, George D. John Marsh, Pioneer. New York, 1931.

MC ARTHUR   McArthur, Lewis A. Oregon Geographical Names. 3rd ed. Portland, Ore., 1952.

MACK   Mack, Effie Mona. Nevada: A History of the State from the Earliest Times through the Civil War. Glendale, Calif., 1936.

MC KELVEY   McKelvey, Susan D. Botanical Exploration of the Trans-Mississippi West, 1790–1850. Jamaica Plain, Mass., 1955.

MC KITTRICK   McKittrick, Myrtle M. Vallejo, Son of California. Portland, Ore., 1944.

MC LANE   Monaghan, Jay, ed. The Private Journal of Louis McLane, U.S.N. 1844–1848. Los Angeles, 1971.

MALONEY   Maloney, Alice B. "A Botanist on the Road to Yerba Buena," California Historical Society Quarterly, 24 (Dec. 1945):321–25.

MARTI   Marti, Werner H. Messenger of Destiny: The California Adventures, 1846–1847 of Archibald Gillespie. San Francisco, 1961.

MEMOIRS   Frémont, John Charles. Memoirs of My Life . . . Including in the Narrative Five Journeys of Western Exploration during the Years 1842, 1843–4, 1845–7, 1848–9, 1853–4. Together with a Sketch of the Life of Senator Benton in Connection with Western Expansion by Jessie Benton Frémont. Only vol. 1 published. Chicago, 1887.

MORGAN   Morgan, Dale L. Overland in 1846: Diaries and Letters of the California-Oregon Trail. 2 vols. Georgetown, Calif., 1963.

MURRAY   Murray, Keith A. The Modocs and Their War. Norman, Okla., 1959.

NASATIR   Nasatir, Abraham P., ed. "The French Consulate in California, 1843–1856," California Historical Society Quarterly, 11 (Sept., Dec. 1932):195–223, 339–57; 12 (March, June, Dec. 1933):35–64, 155–72, 331–57; 13 (March, June, Sept., Dec. 1934):56–79, 159–75, 262–80, 355–85.

NAVAL SHIPS   U.S. Naval History Division. Dictionary of American Naval Fighting Ships. 5 vols. to date. Washington, D.C., 1959—.

NEVINS   Nevins, Allan. Frémont: Pathmarker of the West. New York, 1955.

NEVINS & MORGAN   Nevins, Allan, and Dale L. Morgan, eds. Geographical Memoir upon Upper California in Illustration of His Map of Oregon and California by John Charles Frémont. Reprinted from the 1848 ed. San Francisco, 1964.

NEW HELVETIA DIARY   New Helvetia Diary: A Record of Events Kept by

John A. Sutter and His Clerks at New Helvetia, California, from September 9, 1845 to May 25, 1848. San Francisco, 1939.

NUNIS [1]   Nunis, Doyce B., Jr. "Michel Laframboise," in *The Mountain Men and the Fur Trade of the Far West,* ed. by LeRoy R. Hafen. 8 vols. to date. Glendale, Calif., 1965—. 5:145–78.

NUNIS [2]   ———, ed. "Six New Larkin Letters," *Southern California Quarterly,* 49 (March 1967):65–103.

OGDEN   Davies, K. G., A. M. Johnson, and Dorothy O. Johansen, eds. *Peter Skene Ogden's Snake Country Journal, 1826–27.* Hudson's Bay Record Society, vol. 13. London, 1961.

OUTLAND   Outland, Charles F. "Frémont Slept Where?" *Journal of the West* (July 1966):410–16.

PHELPS   Phelps, William D. *Fore and Aft, or Leaves from the Life of an Old Sailor.* Boston, 1871.

PHILLIPS   Phillips, Catherine Coffin. *Jessie Benton Frémont: A Woman Who Made History.* San Francisco, 1935.

PIONEER REGISTER   Bancroft, Hubert Howe. *Register of Pioneer Inhabitants of California, 1542–1848.* Reprinted from vols. 2–5 of *History of California,* published in 1885 and 1886. Los Angeles, 1964.

POLK   Quaife, M. M., ed. *The Diary of James K. Polk during His Presidency, 1845 to 1849.* 4 vols. Chicago, 1910.

POSNER   Posner, Russell M. "A British Consular Agent in California: The Reports of James A. Forbes, 1843–1846," *Southern California Quarterly,* 53 (June 1971):101–12.

POURADE   Pourade, Richard F. *The History of San Diego.* 6 vols. San Diego, 1960–67.

PRICE   Price, Glenn W. *Origins of the War with Mexico: The Polk-Stockton Intrigue.* Austin, Tex., 1967.

RADCLIFFE   Radcliffe, Zoe Green. "Robert Baylor Semple," *California Historical Society Quarterly,* 6 (June 1927):130–58.

REVERE   Revere, Joseph Warren. *A Tour of Duty in California: Including a Description of the Gold Region: An Account of the Voyage around Cape Horn; with Notices of Lower California, the Gulf and Pacific Coasts, and the Principal Events Attending the Conquest of the California.* Ed. by Joseph N. Balestier. New York, 1849.

RIEDER   Rieder, Roland C. "Pedro Carrillo and the Los Angeles Land Office," *Pacific Historian,* 6 (Nov. 1962):179–80.

RINGLER   Ringler, Donald P. "Mary Austin: Kern County Days, 1888–1892," *Southern California Historical Society Quarterly,* 45 (March 1963):25–63.

ROBINSON   Robinson, Fayette. *An Account of the Organization of the Army of the United States; with Biographies of Distinguished Officers of All Grades.* 2 vols. Philadelphia, 1848.

498

ROGERS [1]   Rogers, Fred B. "Bear Flag Lieutenant: The Life Story of Henry L. Ford," *California Historical Society Quarterly,* 29 (June, Sept., Dec. 1950) :129–38, 261–78, 333–44; 30 (March, June 1951): 49–63, 157–75.

ROGERS [2]   ———. *Montgomery and the Portsmouth.* San Francisco, 1958.

ROGERS [3]   ———. "Rosters of California Volunteers in the Service of the United States, 1846–1847," *Publication* of the Society of California Pioneers (1950) :17–28; (1951) :25.

ROGERS [4]   ———. *William Brown Ide: Bear Flagger.* San Francisco, 1962.

ROLLE [1]   Rolle, Andrew F. *An American in California: The Biography of William Heath Davis, 1822–1909.* San Marino, Calif., 1956.

ROLLE [2]   ———. "Wagon Pass Rancho Withers Away: La Ballona, 1821–1952," *Southern California Historical Society Quarterly,* 34 (June 1952) :147–58.

ROYCE [1]   Royce, Josiah. *California from the Conquest in 1846 to the Second Vigilance Committee in San Francisco: A Study of American Character.* Boston, 1886.

ROYCE [2]   Clendenning, John, ed. *The Letters of Josiah Royce.* Chicago, 1970.

SERVÍN   Servín, Manuel P. "The Secularization of the California Missions: A Reappraisal," *Southern California Quarterly,* 47 (June 1965) :133–49.

SIMPSON   Simpson, Capt. J. H. *Report of Explorations across the Great Basin of the Territory of Utah for a Direct Wagon-Route from Camp Floyd to Genoa, in Carson Valley, in 1859. . . .* Washington, D.C., 1876.

SNYDER CALENDAR   Works Projects Administration, Northern California Historical Records Survey. *Calendar of the Major Jacob Rink Snyder Collection of the Society of California Pioneers.* San Francisco, 1940.

STEGER   Steger, Gertrude A., ed. "A Chronology of the Life of Pierson Barton Reading," *California Historical Society Quarterly,* 22 (Dec. 1943) :365–71.

STENBERG   Stenberg, Richard R. "Polk and Frémont, 1845–1846," *Pacific Historical Review,* 7 (1938) :211–27.

STERN   Stern, Theodore. "The Klamath Indians and the Treaty of 1864," *Oregon Historical Quarterly,* 57 (Sept. 1956) :229–73.

STOCKTON   [Bayard, Samuel J.] *A Sketch of the Life of Com. Robert F. Stockton; with an Appendix, Comprising His Correspondence with the Navy Department respecting His Conquest of California; and Extracts from the Defence of Col. J. C. Fremont. . . .* New York, 1856.

STOWELL Thorne, Marco G., ed. "Bound for the Land of Canaan, Ho! The Diary of Levi Stowell," *California Historical Society Quarterly,* 27 (March, June, Sept., Dec. 1948):33–50, 157–64, 259–66, 361–70; 28 (March 1949):57–68.

STREETER Streeter, William A. "Recollections of Historical Events in California, 1843–1878," *California Historical Society Quarterly,* 18 (March, June, Sept. 1939):64–79, 157–79, 254–78.

SWARTZLOW Swartzlow, Ruby Johnson. "Peter Lassen, Northern California's Trail-Blazer," *California Historical Society Quarterly,* 18 (Dec. 1939):291–314.

TAYS [1] Tays, George. "Captain Andrew Castillero, Diplomat," *California Historical Society Quarterly,* 14 (Sept. 1935):230–68.

TAYS [2] ———. "Frémont Had No Secret Instructions," *Pacific Historical Review,* 9 (June 1940):157–71.

TAYS [3] ———. "Mariano Guadalupe Vallejo and Sonoma—A Biography and a History," *California Historical Society Quarterly,* 16 (June, Sept., Dec. 1937):99–121, 216–55, 348–72; 17 (March, June, Sept. 1938):50–73, 141–67, 219–42.

TURNER Clarke, Dwight L., ed. *The Original Journal of Henry Smith Turner with Stephen Watts Kearny to New Mexico and California, 1846–1847.* Norman, Okla., 1967.

TWITCHELL Twitchell, R. E. *The Leading Facts of New Mexican History.* 2 vols. Cedar Rapids, Iowa, 1912.

TYLER Tyler, Sergeant Daniel. *A Concise History of the Mormon Battalion in the Mexican War, 1846–1847.* N.p., 1881. Reprinted, Chicago, 1964.

UPHAM Upham, Charles Wentworth. *Life, Explorations and Public Services of John Charles Fremont.* Boston, 1856.

WATSON Watson, Douglas S. *West Wind: The Life Story of Joseph R. Walker.* Los Angeles, 1934.

WAUGH Waugh, Alfred S. *Travels in Search of the Elephant: The Wanderings of Alfred S. Waugh, Artist, in Louisiana, Missouri and Santa Fé, in 1845–1846.* Ed. by John F. McDermott. St. Louis, 1951.

WEBER Weber, David J. "John Rowland," in *The Mountain Men and the Fur Trade of the Far West,* ed. by LeRoy R. Hafen. 8 vols. to date. Glendale, Calif., 1965—. 4:125–36.

C. I. WHEAT Wheat, Carl I. *Mapping the Transmississippi West, 1540–1861.* 5 vols. San Francisco, 1957–63.

F. M. WHEAT Wheat, Francis M. "Senator Benton Lays His Plans—Some Newly Discovered Material on the Frémont Court-Martial," *California Historical Society Quarterly,* 13 (June 1934):150–54.

WHITWELL Whitwell, Gertrude Howard. "William Davis Merry Howard," *California Historical Society Quarterly,* 27 (June, Sept., Dec. 1948):105–12, 249–55, 319–32.

WILSON   Woodward, Arthur, ed. "Benjamin Davis Wilson's Observations on Early Days in California and New Mexico," *Publications of the Historical Society of Southern California*, 16 (1934) :74–150.

WILTSEE [1]   Wiltsee, Ernest A. "The British Vice-Consul in California and the Events of 1846," *California Historical Society Quarterly*, 10 (June 1931) :99–128.

WILTSEE [2]   ———. *The Truth about Frémont: An Inquiry*. San Francisco, 1936.

WOODWARD   Woodward, Arthur. "Lances at San Pascual," *California Historical Society Quarterly*, 25 (Dec. 1946) :289–308; 26 (March 1947) :21–62.

WORK   Maloney, Alice B., ed. "Fur Brigade to the Bonaventura: John Work's California Expedition of 1832–33 for the Hudson's Bay Company," *California Historical Society Quarterly*, 22 (Sept., Dec. 1943) :193–222, 323–48; 23 (March, June 1944) :19–40, 123–46.

WRIGHT   Wright, Doris M. "A Yankee in Mexican California." Ph.D. dissertation, Claremont Graduate School, 1954.

YOUNG   Young, Otis E. *The West of Philip St. George Cooke, 1809–1895*. Glendale, Calif., 1955.

ZOLLINGER   Zollinger, J. Peter. *Sutter: The Man and His Empire*. Gloucester, Mass., 1967.

INDEX

The following abbreviations are used: JCF for John Charles Frémont; JBF for Jessie Benton Frémont. The Appendix is not indexed.

Beaumont, William (physician), xliv
Belden, Josiah, 154n
Bell, Alexander, 326
Belty, William, 333
Bent, William, 10n
Benton, John Randolph, 370, 371n
Benton, Thomas Hart: and Polk, xxvii, 185n, 380–81; and 1845 letter to JCF, xxvii, xxxi, 470; seeks compensation for JCF, xxxii; on Kearny and Biddle, xxxviii, xliii, 351n, 353n; and newspaper charges against JCF, xxxix, 364–65, 379–80, 435–36, 441–43; requests JCF's court-martial, xxxix-xl, 365, 376, 380–81; JCF visits in Kentucky, 8n; JCF writes to, 123; and Sally McDowell's case, 141, 143n; advises JCF on trial, 400–401, 403–4, 405–6; to act as JCF's counsel, 405; sells Kentucky property, 432; charges Cooke, 435, 436; defense strategy for JCF, 435–43
—letters: to R. Jones, 364–66, 375, 435, 435–36, 453–54, 455–56, 457–58, 462–63, 464, 464–65; to JCF, 370, 400–401, 403–4, 405–6, 432; to miscellaneous, 379–80, 380–81, 477
—letters: from JCF, 137–39, 181–85, 281–84; from R. Jones, 376–77, 451–53, 454, 459–60
Benton, Mrs. Thomas Hart, 5, 148, 432
Biddle, James: and Mason, xxxviii; mentioned, xliii, 297n; at Monterey, 335; and Stockton, 343; identified, 344n; part in Mason-JCF quarrel, 352–53; to sail east, 354
Bidwell, John: goes to Sonoma, 162n; and military operations at San Diego, 231n
Big Smoky Valley, 45n
Big Valley, 98, 99
Bird Island. See Alcatraz Island
Black, John (consul), 141
Blackburn, William, 229
Blacks Fork, 44n
Bonsell, Jacob, 333
Boone, Nathan, 464n
Bowen, Tom, 203; identified, 204n
Branch, Francis Z., 391; identified, 392n
Brandywine (vessel), 126n
Brannan, Samuel, 221, 404n; identified, 222n
Brant, Joshua B., xliii

Breckenridge, Thomas E.: and gold, 40; recounts Indian massacre, 124n; claim of, 287, 288, 291n
Brennard, 231n
Bridger's Fork. See Bruneau River
Briggs, Francis, 287, 288–89
Brock, Hiram, 333
Brockman, Israel, 322
Brooke, George M., 478n–479n
Brooklyn (vessel), 195n
Brown, Lt., 404n
Brown, Mr., 403, 404n
Brown, John (Juan Flaco), 205n, 324, 343, 349, 350; identified, 324n
Brown, William (witness), 404n
Bruneau River, 382, 422, 430
Bryant, Edwin: identified, 239n; on California Battalion, 240n; due bill to, 329n; to be summoned as a witness, 403
Buchanan, James: mentioned, xxi, 123, 138; and instructions to Larkin, xxii, 126n–127n, 477; and Benton, xxxii; on Kearny, xxxvi; and letter on Gillespie, 127n, 470; letters from JCF, 292–94, 480–81, 483; letters to JCF, 362–63, 482; dishonors JCF's drafts, 428; letter from Benton, 477; on JCF's services, 482
Buchet [?], Luis, 326
Buffalo, 15, 16
Buffalo Creek. See Washita
Buffalo-fish, 16
Bur-clover (Medicago hispida), 32
Burgess, Thomas H., xxxivn
Burrass, Charles D.: sent to Sutter's, 210, 212; identified, 211n; killed, 230n–231n
Buteo regalis, 62n
Butte Creek, 88
Buzzell, Joseph W., 299n

Cahuenga, Treaty of: armistice, 251; Kearny on armistice, 252; provisions, 253–54; additional article, 259; mentioned by Benton, 437
Calaveras River (Creek), 31, 60
Caldwell, C. F., 216
California: American fear of British occupation, xxi, 3–4; tallow and hide trade, xxi; number of Americans (1846), xxi

California Battalion: at Monterey, xxxiv; Stockton's "memoranda" on, 174; JCF to command, 177; muster rolls of, 177n; Stockton authorizes increase in size of, 192–93; march from Monterey to Los Angeles, 234–39; size after reorganization, 235; and officer accounts, 306; pay of volunteers, 306–7; at San Gabriel, 311n; men refuse Kearny's muster, 311n; JCF's orders to Owens re, 320–21; list of unexpired services in, 333; terms of JCF's contract with volunteers in, 334; transfer of property of, 342; amount needed to pay, 429

California claims, xliv–xlvi, 427–29, 447, 449, 450; in U.S. Senate, xlv; JCF's memorial on, 466–68

Californian (Monterey and San Francisco): on claims, xliv–xlv; on Stockton-Kearny command, 344n

Californios: way of life, xxi–xxii; Stockton on subservience of, 194

Callao (bark), 329n

Calocedrus decurrens (incense cedar), JCF refers to as "white cedar," 29, 122

Campbell, Archibald, 8n

Campbell, Robert, 9n, 12; as JCF's agent, 362n; seeks to learn authorship of newspaper charges against JCF, 365

Canadian River, 8, 12

Canby, E. R. S., 99; identified, 125n

Carpenter, Lemuel, 326

Carrillo, José Antonio: and Treaty of Cahuenga, 253, 254; identified, 255n

Carrillo, Julio, 173, 174n

Carrillo, Pedro C., 33; identified, 45n; meets JCF, 238; on JCF's popularity, 283; at Santa Barbara, 305

Carson, Christopher: joins 1845 expedition, xxiv, 13; and Kearny, xxiv, xli, 196n, 269n; crosses Salt Desert, 20; and old Indian woman, 25; mentioned, 47; meets Talbot's party, 60; in Oregon, 108, 112, 113, 116, 117, 118; shoots Klamath, 121; recounts Indian massacre, 124n; and killing of de Haros, 186n–187n; express for JCF, 195, 196n; interview with Polk, 361n–362n; and lieutenancy, 363

Carson Lake, 51–52

Carson River, 52

Carter, G. S., 322n

Cascade Range, 90, 95, 97, 103; JCF to examine, xxiii

Cash, James, 231n

Cass, Lewis: and California claims, xlv; interview with Buchanan, 477

Cassin, John (ornithologist), 62n

Castillero, Andres, 46n

Castillo de San Joaquin (Fort Point), 163n

Castro, Angel, 70n

Castro, José: and JCF, xxvi, 64, 67n–68n, 74–85, 123n, 152, 181–85; quoted by Larkin, xxvii–xxviii; flees to Sonora, xxxiii, 191n; identified, 67n; letters from, 74–75; letters to, 76; proclamations of, 81, 85, 157, 158n–159n; at San Juan Bautista, 82, 85; motives of, 123n; at Santa Clara, 153n, 155, 160; and Sloat, 169, 170n, 172–73; at Los Angeles, 185, 188–89; and Stockton, 190n–191n; buries guns, 191n; mentioned by Benton, 437; and charge of inciting Indians, 470

Castro, Manuel de Jesús: identified, 67n; letters from, 75, 77; letters to, 76; referred to as "Emanuel" by Montgomery, 157; re American emigrants and land titles, 185n–186n; and revolt, 232; place for sale, 447

Célis, Eulogio de: letters to, 273; identified, 273n; in list of names, 326; contract with JCF, 407–21; mentioned by JCF, 451

Chambers, A. B., 365–66

Charleston, S.C., 446

Charley. *See* Schreiber, Charles

Chauchiles. *See* Chowchilla River

Chavez, Julian, 326

Cheyennes, 6

Childs, Ebenezer Larkin, 141, 142

Chiles, Joseph B., 55

Chinook, William (William Perkins), 5, 8n, 9n, 287, 290,

Chowchilla River, 37

Cist, Lewis J.: letter to, 482–83; identified, 483n

City Creek, 19

Cloud, Jeremiah H., 312

Clyman, James, 44n; letter to, 131; identified, 131n–132n

Coast Range, 91

Coats, George, 216
Colchester, Charles Abbot, Lord, 150, 151n
Collingwood (British man-of-war), 184–85, 187n
Colorado River, 16, 43n
Colton, Walter: on conquest of California, xxxv; alcalde, 298, 402; identified, 300n
Columbus (ship), 241n, 297n
Congress (frigate): and Stockton, 127n; mentioned, 154n; expected at Monterey, 157, 169, 170n: at Monterey, 176n; sails south, 210n
Conner Spring, 45n
Connor, James, 10n, 60
Conway, Frederick Rector, 379–80
Cooke, Philip St. George: commander of southern military district, xxxvii, 312; on JCF's express, 196n; on poverty of officials, 286n; on Russell, 305n–306n; identified, 312n; letter from, 320; letter to, 323; present at JCF-Mason interviews, 332n; ordered east with Kearny, 359; and newspaper charges against JCF, 366n, 435, 436; and orders for Mexico, 388n
Cooper, Isaac, 9n, 10n
Cooper, James Fenimore, 304n
Cordua, Theodor, 87; grows wheat, 433
Cosgrave, Anthony, 206; identified, 207n
Cosumnes River, 31, 36; Arce's horses captured on, 182
Cot, Antonio José: letter to, 285–86; and loan to JCF, 285–86, 369; identified, 286n; mentioned by JCF, 451; and land grant, 475
Cyane (sloop-of-war): at Monterey, xxxi, 157, 169, 170n; carries Gillespie to California, 126n; mentioned, 161; at San Diego, 188n
Cypress (JCF's *taxodium*). See *Sequoia sempervirens*

Dague, Théophile, 397n, 398, 399n
Dana, William Goodwin, 240n, 392n
Davidge, Mr. (Senate clerk), xliii
Davidson, John Wynn: to receive battalion's public property, 335; investigates JCF-Célis contract, 411, 413–14
Davis, Charles Augustus, 150, 151n
Davis, William Heath, 215n
Deer Creek, 89, 94, 95

Delaware Charley: and 1845 expedition, 10n, 36; breaks nose, 95–96
Delaware Indians: join 1845 expedition, 5–6; meet JCF at Bent's Fort, 10n; and Great Basin Indians, 23–25; and Horse-thief Indians, 34–35; in mourning, 114–16; blamed for death of de Haros, 187n; find Castro's guns, 191n
Denny (Indian), 12, 113
Denny, Mr. *See* Dana, William Goodwin
Deschutes (Fall) River, 53
DeVoto, Bernard: on JCF, xix
Díaz, Manuel: identified, 67n; mentioned, 82n; letter to, 84
Digger Indians, 50
Dobenbliss, John, 329n
Dobson, Mr., 326
Dodge, John Wood, 364n
Dodson, Jacob (JCF's black servant), 5, 8n, 9n, 33; in Oregon, 119, 121; and relatives, 150; on ride with JCF, 330n; carries letter to Stearns, 353, 356
Donner party, xxxix, 44n
Donner Pass, xxv, 45n
Douglas, David, 73, 484; identified, 74n
Duchesne River, 43n
Due bills, 329n
DuPont, Samuel F.: and *Cyane*, 178n; letter to, 187; on Castro's retreat, 191n
Durand, St. Vrain, 290n
Duvall, Marius: naval surgeon, 153n; on death of de Haros, 186n; on JCF's popularity, 325n

Easton, Langdon Cheves, 464n
Elk branch of the Canadian. *See* Red Deer Creek
Emigrant road, 49, 62n
Emory, William H.: journal of, xxxivn; and JCF, xxxivn, xxxix, xl; on Gillespie, xlv; delivers Kearny's order to JCF, 265; identified, 266n; and newspaper charges against JCF, 365, 400, 423, 436, 445, 449; to be witness, 390n; on JCF's use of McNamara's scheme, 476n
Endicott, George (engraver), 484, 485
Endicott, William (engraver), 485n
Erie (sloop), xlvi, 169, 170n; expected to bring funds, 285
Erodium circutarium, 19, 32, 41
Escalante, Silvestre Vélez de, 17–18, 43n

507

Frémont, John Charles (*cont.*)

xlivn; and California claims, xliv–xlvi, 427–29, 466–68, 473–74; and *Geographical Memoir,* xlvi; appearance and character, xvli–xlvii; organizes 1845 expedition, 9n, 10n; divides party at Mound Springs, 23; route across Great Basin, 23–27; at Walker Lake, 27, 52; to Sutter's Fort, 28–30; searches for Talbot's party, 31–42; goes to Yerba Buena, 42; visits quicksilver mine, 42; intends to improve road to Oregon, 47; moves toward Santa Cruz, 70–73; and stolen animals, 70n; and controversy with Castro, 74–85, 123n, 181–85; moves to Sacramento Valley, 86–90; at Lassen's, 89–90, 94–95, 123, 124n; in Oregon, 102–22; and Gillespie, 108–11, 181–85; and 1845 letter from Benton, 110; returns to California, 123, 128n; and part in Indian massacre, 124n–125n; and Flügge, 128–29; and intentions to go east, 129–30, 132–33, 138–39, 152, 160, 185; needs money or supplies, 130n, 139–40, 181–82, 199–200, 220–22, 284–85, 292–94, 296; refuses to add to party, 130n, 131; recounts Oregon and California events to Benton, 138, 181–85; and aid from Montgomery, 146–47; mother of, 148; promotion of, 148, 149, 159; at Sonoma, 162, 163n–164n; organizes battalion, 162, 164n, 184; at San Rafael, 162n, 163n; and Torre, 163n; spikes cannon, 163n, 183; on prisoners at Sutter's Fort, 173, 174n; and Sloat, 176n–177n; to San Diego, 178; on death of de Haros, 187n; and occupation of Los Angeles, 191n; appointed military commandant, 200; and property interests of, 203–4, 297–99, 447–48; and brand of exploring party, 206, 207n; and difficulties with French subjects, 216–20, 396–99, 400–401; and battalion's southern march, 234–39; and Treaty of Cahuenga, 253–55; appointed governor, 267; and actions as governor, 273–76, 277–80, 285–86, 291–92, 317, 319; writes Benton re controversy with Kearny, 281–84; briefs Shubrick, 295–96; hopes for confirmation as governor, 309n; and permission to leave California, 310,

363; ordered east with Kearny, 359; arrest of, 375; re his role in California, 377–78, 465n–466n, 469–75; desires a speedy trial, 383, 452, 453; charges and specifications against, 383–85, 393, 394n, 439, 459–60, 462–63; visits South Carolina, 386; and contract with Célis, 407–21; re his arrest and approaching trial, 445–47; re botanical collection, 455, 479–80; delays report, 461; on import of communications brought by Gillespie, 480–81; and fourth expedition plans, 481, 483–84, 485n

—letters: to miscellaneous, 11–12, 46–48, 68–70, 129–30, 131, 187, 211–12, 216–17, 229, 248, 249, 271–72, 273, 274, 276, 278–79, 280, 285–86, 291–92, 295–97, 300–301, 307, 320–21, 327, 360, 422, 432–33, 448–49, 456–57, 476–77, 482–83; to Larkin, 73, 81–82, 137, 203–4; to Leidesdorff, 132–33, 180, 208; to Benton, 137–39, 181–85, 281–84; to Gillespie, 139–40, 180, 200–203, 306–7, 318; to Montgomery, 151–53, 162–63, 210, 220–21; to Kern, 173, 206, 207, 209, 214, 229–30; to Reading, 201–2, 277, 278, 306, 316, 445–48; to Mervine, 225–26, 227, 233; to Kearny, 257–58, 268–69, 366–68; to Stearns, 273, 353–54, 449–50; to Buchanan, 292–94, 480–81, 483; to Mason, 332–33, 336–37, 338–39, 340, 341–42, 345–46, 348, 349, 354–56; to R. Jones, 383–85, 386–87, 394–96, 423, 444, 459, 478, 486; to Marcy, 397–98, 401, 427–29; to Torrey, 454–55, 479–80, 481, 483–85

—letters: from miscellaneous, 74–75, 128–29, 147–50, 168–70, 170–72, 265–66, 277, 284–85, 302–3, 304–5, 308, 320, 326, 356–57, 358, 362–63, 364, 377–78, 381–82, 391–92, 430–31, 482, 486; from Larkin, 74, 78–79, 83, 140–42, 165–66, 172, 179, 324, 325; from Montgomery, 143–45, 146–47, 155–57, 160–61, 166–68, 212–13, 214–15, 215–16, 223, 280–81; from Stockton, 174, 177, 178, 188–89, 190, 192–93, 196–98, 198–99, 199–200, 204–5, 206, 208, 247, 249–50, 272, 305–6; from Mervine, 226, 228, 232; from Kearny, 250, 252, 255, 257, 268, 310, 331, 350–51, 368–69; from Mason, 332, 334–35, 337, 338,

339, 340–41, 345, 347, 348, 351–52, 357; from J. J. Abert, 360–61, 406, 407, 461; from Benton, 370, 400–401, 403–4, 405–6, 432; from R. Jones, 393, 426–27, 444, 457, 458; from Marcy, 396–97, 402, 434

Frémont, Lily, 148, 149; Benton on, 370

Fremontia vermicularis. See Sarcobatus vermiculatus

Fremont Peak, 123n

Gabilan Mountains, xxvi

Gabilan Peak. *See* Fremont Peak

Gallatin, Albert, 150, 151n; letters from, 380–81, 430–31; seeks information on geography and Indians, 381–82; letters to, 386, 422

Gambel, William, 484; identified, 485

Gard, Charles, 333

Gard, John, 333

Garfias, Manuel, 234n

Garner, William, xlvn; witness, 298, 401; identified, 300n

Gaviota Pass, 241n

Geddes, Paul. *See* Green, Talbot H.

Gendreau, François: in charge of *caballada,* 173; and Walla Wallas, 174n, 209; and Battle of Natividad, 230, 231n

Geographical Memoir, xlvi; preparation of, 485n

Giffin, John S., xxxv

Gila River, xxiii

Giles, Joel, 68n

Gillespie, Archibald H.: and mission, xxvii–xxx, 4–5; and testimony in Senate, xxxii, 465n, 480; to be secretary, xxxiii, 192, 194; and rebellion at Los Angeles, xxxiii, 205n–206n; and Kearny, xli; and California claims, xlv; in Oregon, 108–23; on Castro's motives, 123n; identified, 126n–127n; at Sutter's Fort, 127n; at Lassen's, 127n, mentioned, 138, 142; obtains supplies for JCF, 140n, 153n, 181; seeks news on Stockton and ships, 145n; on Phelps' service, 164n; made adjutant in battalion, 164n; and battalion, 174; and Sloat, 176n–177n; JCF comments on role of, 183–85; on death of de Haros, 187n; stationed at Los Angeles, 193; appointed major, 266n; on JCF and Kearny, 309n–310n; ordered to Washington, 312; re-

putedly a witness to JCF-Célis contract, 408, 421

—letters: from JCF, 139–40, 180, 202–3, 306–7, 318; from Stockton, 343–44, 349, 350

Gleason, James H., 154n

Godey, Alexander: carries Kearny's plea for aid, xxxivn; joins 1845 expedition, 5; JCF describes, 13–14; fights Indians, 37; mentioned, 60, 379n; courier for JCF, 74; in Oregon, 108, 112, 113; on death of de Haros, 186n–187n; at Las Mariposas, 299n

Gold: JCF's men notice, 40

Golden Gate, 163n; JCF names, 46n

Gómez, José Joaquín, 63, 82; identified, 65n; Larkin captured at rancho of, 232n

Grand River. *See* Colorado River

Grantsville, Utah, 44n

Gray, Andrew V. F., 243n

Grayback Mountain, 44n

Grayson, William John, 150; identified, 151n

Great Basin: JCF's 1845 route across, 23–27, 45n; Indians of, 26–27; JCF describes, 46–47

Great Britain: and Oregon, xx; and California, xxi, 3–4, 472, 475; "Little England" policy of, xxi; JCF's fear of, 138

Great Salt Lake: JCF mans shores of, xxiv; JCF describes, 17–19

Green, Talbot H., 324; identified, 324n; supplies Topographical party, 360

Green River, 43n

Gregorio (Indian boy), 5

Grigsby, John: captain, 164n, 216; at Sonoma, 184; identified, 187; letter from, 277; resigns commission, 277

Grimes, Eliab, 30, 86; identified, 123n

Grund, Francis J., 436

Guerra, Francisco de la, 33; identified, 45n

Guerra, Pablo de la, 190n

Haight, Samuel, 436

Hall, Ann B.: illness of, 385; death of, 387n

Hall, Willard P.: letter to, 300–301; identified, 301n–302n; to be summoned as witness, 403

Halleck, Henry Wager, 359

Hamilton, Aaron, 45n
Hamilton's Creek, 30
Hamley, George W., 238
Hannah (brig), 67n, 78
Hardscrabble, 43n
Harlan, Jacob W.: fences land, 204n; on JCF-Mason quarrel, 348n
Harlan-Young party, 44n
Harmer, Richard M., 392n
Haro, Francisco de, 163n; killed by JCF men, 183, 186n–187n
Haro, Ramón de, 163n; killed by JCF men, 183, 186n–187n
Harrison, Ben (black servant), 127n
Harrison Pass, 45n
Hartnell, William E. P.: JCF camps at rancho of, xxvi, 72; identified 72n; mentioned, 73; as translator and interpreter, 82n, 141n, 401
Hastings, Lansford W.: identified, 44n; and *Guide,* 73, 74n; recruits at San Jose, 212–13, 220; joins JCF, 228n
Hastings Cutoff, 21, 44n
Hatcher, John L., 8; identified, 10n–11n
Hays, James, 231n
Helianthus, 19
Henderson, Andrew A., 155, 158n; at Sutter's Fort, 160; at Sonoma, 162, 163n
Hensley, Samuel J.: and California claims, xlv; reputedly a witness to JCF-Célis contract, 408, 420; identified, 421; deposition of mentioned, 480
Herald of Religious Liberty: on JCF-Kearny reconciliation, xliii
Hill, Tom, 229n
Hinckley, William S.: visits New Almaden with JCF, 42; identified, 46n; partner of Leese, 154n; death of, 163n
Hoit, John, 329n
Hood, Washington, 126n
Hooker, Joseph, xliiin
Hopi (Moqui), 431
Horse chestnut, 122–23
Horse-thief Indians. *See* Mission Indians
Howard, William Davis Merry: reports no horses in southern California, 211; identified, 212n; protests Weber's methods, 234n; on JCF's reluctance to obey Kearny, 309n
Hoyt, Amasa, 216
Hudson's Bay Company: post on Ump-

qua, 113, 123, 128n; trapping parties of, 125n
Hudspeth, Benjamin, 56
Hudspeth, James M., 44n
Hugh's Creek. *See* Jordan River
Hull, Joseph B.: governor of northern district, 223, 224n; mentioned, 232; at San Pedro, 335
Humboldt, Alexander von: map of New Spain, 17–18
Humboldt River, 22, 45n, 49, 430; Kern's description of, 50–51
Hunter, Benjamin F., 146, 151, 152, 153n, 155, 157; identified, 147n
Hunter, Jesse D., 337
Hussey, John A., xxviin
Hüttmann, Francis: and custom house duties, 328, 329n; and JCF's drafts, 429n
Hyde, George: alcalde, 425; identified, 426n

Ide, William B.: leads Bear Flaggers, xxix; on JCF's role in revolt, 154n–155n; sends Todd to Montgomery, 158n
Indians: Klamath, xxi, 103, 106–7, 128n, 138; JCF encounters Cheyenne, 6; of Great Basin, 26–27; acorn cribs of, 29, 33, 87; Cosumnes, 31; Mission, 34–36, 45n; Shoshoni, 49; Digger, 50; of Walker Lake region, 53; massacre of, 124n; Sutter's expedition against, 125n; Modoc, 99, 128n; Walla Walla, 174n, 230, 231n; JCF accuses Castro of inciting, 182; in California Battalion, 235; "Tularie," 302; Navajo, 431; Moqui (Hopi), 431
Isbel, James C., 447; identified, 448n

Jacob, Richard Taylor: commands Indians, 235, 239n; defends JCF, 445, 449
Jesus, José (Siyakum chief), 302n
Johnson, Mr., 350
Johnson, J. W., 333
Johnston, Abraham R., xxxivn
Jomard, Edme François, 431
Jones, Roger: on arrest of JCF, 376–77; writes that JCF cannot be tried on newspaper charges, 451–52; indicates that JCF may delay trial, 452
—letters: to Benton, 376–77; to JCF,

Marshall, Henry, 231n
Martin, Thomas S., 124n
Martínez, Ignacio, 203n
Mary's River. *See* Humboldt River
Mason, Richard B.: and quarrel with JCF, xxxviii, 346–53, 346n, 353n, 354–56, 357; on JCF's financial transactions, xlv–xlvi, 369–70, 407–9, 421n; seeks information on death of de Haros, 186n; present at JCF-Kearny interview, 300n; on JCF's reception of Shubrick's order, 310n; identified, 330n; reaches Los Angeles and carries out Kearny's orders, 332, 333–42; charges JCF with disobedience and delay, 338; governor, 359
—letters: to JCF, 332, 337, 338, 339, 340–41, 345, 347, 348, 351–52, 357; to R. Jones, 369–70, 407–20
—letters: from Kearny, 330; from JCF, 332–33, 336–37, 338–39, 340, 341–42, 345–46, 348, 349, 354–56
Maxwell, Lucien B.: crosses Salt Desert, 20; encounter with Horse-thief Indians, 34–35; scalps Klamath, 120
Mellus, Henry, 123n; has rifle powder, 215; identified, 215n; protests Weber's methods, 234n
Merced River, 34, 36
Merritt, Ezekiel: captures Arce's horses, xxix; and Bear Flag Revolt, 153, 154n; and recapture of San Diego, 230, 231n–232n
Mervine, William: and *Cyane,* xxxi, 161; to aid Gillespie, xxxiii, 205n, 224n; and *Savannah,* xxxiii, 178n, 205n; at Monterey to assist JCF, 224; effects of defeat of, 250
—letters: to JCF, 226, 228, 232
—letters: from JCF, 225–26, 227, 233
Mexico: war with, xxix, 193n; possibilities of war with, 3–4
Micheltorena, Manuel, xxii
Miera y Pacheco, Bernardo de, 43n
Miller, William D., 226, 329n
Minor, George: and recapture of San Diego, 232n; on Stockton-Kearny command, 344n
Mission Indians, 34–36
Missions: San Juan Capistrano, xxxv; San Fernando, xxxv, 239, 241n, 251; secularized, 45n; San Jose, 60–61, 203,

204n; San Juan Bautista, 82, 85, 141, 176n; San Francisco Solano, 154n; San Rafael, 163n, 475; San Buenaventura, 239n; San Miguel, 240n; San Luis Obispo, 240n; San Luis Rey, 245, 306n, 475; Dolores, 475; San Gabriel, 475
Missouri *Republican* (St. Louis): and accusations against JCF, 364, 365, 379–80, 423; on military orders of Turner and Cooke, 388, 390n
Missroon, John S., 173n
Modocs, 99, 128n
Moerenhout, Jacob Antoine: difficulties with JCF, 216–20, 398, 399n; letter to, 216–17; identified, 217n–218n
Mojave Desert, 62n
Mokelumne River, 31, 36
Molalla War, 128n
Monitor Range, 45n
Montgomery, John B.: at Monterey, xxvii; identified, 145n; and Gillespie and JCF, 140n, 145n–146n, 146; offers to aid JCF, 146–47; and Bear Flaggers, 155–57; and Castro, 157, 158n, 160; on Semple's party, 163n; and Sloat, 164–65; raises flag at Yerba Buena, 166; mentioned, 181, 183; congratulates JCF on promotion, 213; arms recruits, 215–16; forwards munitions to JCF, 222n
—letters: to JCF, 143–45, 146–47, 151–53, 155–57, 160–61, 166–68, 212–13, 214–15, 215–16, 223, 280–81
—letters: from JCF, 162–63, 210, 220–21; from Sloat, 164–65
Montgomery, John E., 224n
Montgomery, William H., 224n
Moqui. *See* Hopi
Mormon Battalion: arrival in California, xxxvi–xxxvii
Mormons: arrive at San Francisco, 194, 195n; Stockton's attitude toward, 194, 195n–196n
Morris Basin, 44n
Moscow (bark), 74n, 163n
Moulton, Elijah, 287, 289, 290n
Mound Springs, xxv, 44n, 48
Mount Diablo, 447
Mount Linn, 91, 125n
Mount Shasta, 91, 92–93, 103, 125n

Poinsett, Joel R.: on JCF's court-martial, xl; mentioned by JBF, 150

Polk, James K.: foreign policy of, xx–xxi; and Gillespie, xxvii, 109; and Gillespie and JCF, xxix; and JCF's court-martial, xl; letters to, 193–95, 380–81, 388; remits JCF's penalty, 468n, 469n; accepts JCF's resignation, 486

Poppies, California (*Eschscholtzia californica*), 86, 92, 94. JCF's three-leaved Mariposas poppy: *see* Mariposa lily

Portsmouth (sloop): at Monterey, xxvii, 170n; at Sausalito, 140n, 145n, 153; at Yerba Buena, 162n

Preuss, Charles, xxxix; cartographic work of, xlvi, 461, 485n; not on 1845 expedition, 6; mentioned by JBF, 148; and Las Mariposas, 299n

Price, Glenn W., xxix

Primavera (brig), 319

Prince, William Edgar, 464n

Provo River, 16, 43n

Prudon [?], Mr., 326

Prudon, Victor, 154n, 155; prisoner at Sutter's Fort, 173, 173n–174n, 182

Pryor, Nathaniel Miguel: in a list of names, 326; due bill to, 329n; Mason at house of, 332

Purgatoire. *See* Purgatory River

Purgatory River, 8, 11, 13n

Quercus kelloggii, 122
Quercus lobata (Valley Oak), 29, 32
Quercus longiglanda. See Q. lobata
Quercus wislinzènii, 29, 32

Radford, John D., xliii

Radford, William, xlii; influence on Rowan, 344n

Ranchos: Warner's, xxxiv; Laguna Seca, 62n; San Pedro, 65n; Verjeles, 65n; San Jose del Valle, 65n; Las Mariposas, 67n; Alisal, 72n; Esquon, 88; Buenaventura, 124n; Petaluma, 154n; Barranca Colorado, 154n; Los Cerritos, 189n, 190; Los Alamitos, 189n; Santa Margarita, 191n; Pinole, 203, 204n; Brentwood, 209n; Natividad, 229n; Tinaquaic, 240n; Nipomo, 240n; Piedra Blanca, 240n; Las Pulgas, 447

Reading, Pierson B.: and possibility of appointment to California Claims Commission, xlv, 447, 448; Indians burn house of, 124n; identified, 203n; and JCF's *caballada,* 202; and Treaty of Cahuenga, 253, 254; authorized to issue due bills, 277; and JCF's Las Mariposas, 299n; to negotiate loans, 316; part of in JCF-Mason quarrel, 346, 358; and receipt of public chattels, 425, 426n; estimates amount needed to pay California Battalion, 429; mentioned by Benton, 437

—letter: to JCF, 358

—letters: from JCF, 201–2, 277, 278, 306, 316, 445–48

Red Bank Creek, 91

Red Deer Creek, 13n

Redlum Spring, 44n

Redwood. See *Sequoia sempervirens*

Reed, B. A., 333

Rees, James, 333

Reid, Hugo, 475

Requena, Manuel, 322n

Revere, Joseph W., 155, 157n, 160

Rhett, Robert Barnwell, 125n

Rheusaw, Hiram, 329n

Richardson, William A., 163n

Ricketts, Job S. *See* Skirkett, Bob

Ridley, Robert, 163n, 173n, 174n

Rincon, 238; and use of *Julia Ann,* 248, 249

Roberts, J. M., 333

Robidoux, Louis, 326

Rosa, José de la, 158n

Round Valley. *See* Big Valley

Rowan, Stephen Clegg: and Kearny, 282; identified, 284n; on Stockton-Kearny command, 344n

Rowland, John, 450

Royal Gorge, 15

Royce, Josiah, xix, 67n, 465n–466n

Ruby Mountains, 62n

Ruby Valley, 45n

Ruiz, Bernarda, 237–38

Russell, R. Eugene, 153n; claim of, 287, 288, 290n, 291n; with Carson and Talbot, 361n

Russell, William H.: on Stockton-Kearny dispute, xxxv–xxxvi, 258n; secretary of state, xxxvii; and return east, xxxix; circulates petition on JCF,

Russell, William H. (cont.)
xlvn; party of to California, 44n;
identified, 214n; and Treaty of Cahuenga, 253, 254; and pay of, 278;
represents JCF at party, 305, 306n;
letters from, 323, 328; on battalion and
rumors of resurrection, 323; defends
JCF, 445, 449

Sacramento (JCF's horse), 5, 9n, 118–19
Sacramento River, 89, 92
Sacramento Valley, 92
Sagundai, James: and 1845 expedition,
6; identified, 10n; spring named after,
25; scalps Klamath Indian, 113; re-
venge on Klamaths, 114–16
Sagundai's Spring, 25
St. Johns. See Missions: San Juan Bau-
tista; San Juan Capistrano
St. Louis, Mo.: offers public dinner to
JCF, 377–78, 446
St. Mary's. See Humboldt River
St. Vrain, Cerán de Hault de Lassus de,
10n
Salinas River, 72, 392; JCF encamped
on, 76
Salmon Trout River. See Truckee River
Salt Desert, xxiv
Salt Lake City, Utah, 43n
Sanchez, Francisco, 63; identified, 65n
Sanchez, Tomás A., 274; in list of
names, 326
San Clemente Island, 475
Sanderson, George B., 359
San Diego, Calif.: JCF at, xxxiii; Kearny
at, xxxv; Stockton at, xxxv; recap-
tured by Americans, 230, 231n–232n
San Francisco (Yerba Buena), 140n, 433
San Joaquin River, 34, 38, 60
San Joaquin Valley: JCF's 1845 route
through, 31–34; JCF withdraws from
Gabilans to, 86
San Jose (mission). See Missions: San
Jose
San Jose, Calif., 60–61, 433; JCF ex-
pected at, 172
San Juan Bautista, xxvi
San Marcos Pass, 241n
San Mateo, Calif., 475
San Pasqual: and Kearny's defeat, xxxiv,
243n; cannon lost at, xl–xli

San Pedro: Congress to sail for, 178;
Congress at, 188
Santa Barbara: captured by Stockton,
189n; JCF reoccupies, 237–38
Santa Cruz, 70–72
Santa Fe Trail, 10n
Santa Ynez Mountains, 237
Sarcobatus vermiculatus, 455n
Sausalito: Portsmouth at, 145n, 146n;
JCF at, 163n
Savannah (frigate): at Monterey, 169,
170n; under command of Mervine,
224
Schenck, James F., 191n
Schreiber, Charles: cook for Talbot's
party, 55; claim of, 287, 289; identi-
fied, 290n
Scott, John M., 464n
Scott, Winfield, xxxvii, 309n
Sears, John, 186n
Secret Pass, 62n
Selden, Edward A.: commands Julia
Ann, 238, 241n; letter to, 248; to aid
JCF, 248, 249
Semple, Robert: takes Ridley prisoner,
163n; editor of Californian, 344n
Sequoia sempervirens (JCF's cypress),
71
Sevier River, 431
Seymour, George F., 184, 187n
Shadden, Thomas J., 424–26
Shannon, Wilson, 142n
Sherman, William T.: re JCF-Célis con-
tract, 419, 421n; letter to, 424–26
Shoshoni: Talbot's party meet, 49
Shubrick, Henry Hastings: letter to,
456–57
Shubrick, W. Brandford: and Kearny,
xxxvii, 303; letter to, 295–97; identi-
fied, 297n; letters from, 302–3, 308;
on Stockton's appointment of JCF as
governor, 303n–304n; and orders re
naval officers, 308; issues circular with
Kearny, 313; to command Pacific
Squadron again, 354; mentioned by
Benton, 406, 438
Sierra Nevada: JCF to examine, xxiii;
JCF's 1845 crossing of, 47; Kern's de-
scription of, 54; and Cascade range,
97
Sigler, Levi: with Gillespie, 109, 127n
Simpson, James Hervey, 61n

Sitka (steamer), 65n
Skirkett, Bob, 10n
Skull Valley, 20, 44n
Sloat, John Drake: instructions of, xxii, 127n; slow to seize California, xxx–xxxi; and JCF, xxxii; mentioned, 109, 145n, 406, 438; expected at Monterey, 161; letters from, 164–65, 168–70; to raise flag, 164, 165n; proclamation of, 165n; "summons" to Castro, 164, 165n; desires JCF's cooperation, 165, 166, 168, 169, 172–73, 184; and Castro, 169, 170n; and Stockton, 177n, 185; sails home on *Levant*, 185; owner of San Francisco lots, 204n; unhappy with JCF and Gillespie, 343–44, 471; and 1846 letter of recall, 465
Smith, Andrew Jackson: identified, 279; as Mason's friend, 358; and newspaper charges against JCF, 365, 366n; not author of "Justice" letter, 435, 436
Smith, C. H., 333
Smith, George, 216
Smith, Jedediah S., 126n, 382n
Snyder, Jacob Rink: quartermaster of Battalion, 287–90 *passim;* identified, 291n; letter from, 302; letters to, 307, 448–49; appointed superintendent of Mission San Gabriel, 307; due bill to, 329n; possibility of appointment to California Claims Commission, 447, 448
Soberanes, Mariano, 240n
Socorro, N.Mex., xxxiv
Sonoma, Calif.: capture of, xxix, 152, 153n, 154n, 182; arms at, 158n; boat sent to for JCF, 206
Spear, Nathan, 154n
Speiden, William, 199, 200n; letter from, 284–85; on Stockton-Kearny command, 344n
Spitler, J. D., 333
Stanley, Larkin, 322
Stansbury Mountains, 44n
Stearns, Abel: Larkin's correspondent, 82n, 176n, 179n; owner of Los Alamitos, 189n; letters to, 273, 353–54, 449–50; in list of names, 326; on needs of California, 356–57; letter from, 356–57; and part in JCF-Célis contract, 408–21 *passim;* on illegal land grants, 474

Stearns, Mrs. Abel (Arcadia Bandini), 450
Steinbach Canyon, 123n
Stenberg, Richard, xxix
Stenner, William, 319
Stephens, John Lloyd, 150; identified, 151n
Stepp, Joseph: identified, 80n; with Gillespie, 108, 127n; in Oregon, 112, 118, 121; gives Larkin's letters to Castro, 141
Stepperfeldt. *See* Stepp, Joseph
Sterling (vessel), xxxiii, 159n, 180, 208n, 210n
Stevens, John, 287, 289
Stevenson, Jonathan D., xlv; at Los Angeles, 351n; investigates JCF-Célis contract, 411, 413–14, 415–20
Stockton, Robert Field: mentioned, xxviii, 154n, 453, 465; controversy with Kearny, xxxii–xlii, 241–47, 263–71, 305; commissions Battalion officers, xxxiii, 471–72; and plans to invade Mexico, xxxiii, 192–93, 204–5; *rapprochement* with Kearny, xlii; Gillespie inquires about arrival of, 145n; and organization of Battalion, 174, 177n; identified, 176n; as Sloat's successor, 185; at San Pedro, 188, 189n; and Castro, 190n–191n; plans to appoint JCF governor, 192, 194; on conquest of California, 193–95; orders seizure of archives, 198; appoints JCF military commandant, 200; owner of San Francisco real estate, 204n; summons JCF to help quash rebellion, 205n; at San Diego, 224; advises JCF on military tactics, 247, 249–50; on Treaty of Cahuenga, 255n; appoints JCF governor, 267; leaves Los Angeles, 272n; and anger over newspaper accounts, 343, 344n; urges Gillespie to reconcile JCF and Mason, 349; Benton insists that JCF's trial is really the trial of, 437–38
—letters: to JCF, 174, 177, 178, 188–89, 190, 192–93, 196–98, 198–99, 199–200, 204–5, 206, 208, 247, 249–50, 272, 305–6; to Polk, 193–95; to Kearny, 243–45, 246, 264; to Gillespie, 343–44, 349, 350

—letters: from JCF, 211–12, 249; from Kearny, 241–43, 246, 252, 263, 270–71

Stokes, Edward: carries Kearny's message to Stockton, xxxiv, 224n

Stonington (whaler), 231n, 238

Streeter, William A., 240n

Sunflower. See *Helianthus*

Suñol, Antonio María, 63; identified, 65n

Sutter Buttes, 153n

Sutter, John Augustus: and JCF, 30–31, 154n; expedition against Indians, 125n; joins Bear Flaggers, 157, 158n

Sutter's Fort: JCF reaches (1845), xxv, 30–31; JCF returns to after conflict with Castro, 86; flag raised at, 168n, 170–72

Swanok. See Swanuck, James

Swanuck, James: and 1845 expedition, 6; identified, 10n; revenge on Klamaths, 114–16

Swift, Granville P.: captain, 164n; and killing of de Haros, 186n; at Monterey, 199n

Swords, Thomas B.: buries Donner remains, xxxix; on Battle of San Pasqual, 243n; ordered to Monterey, 312; identified, 312n; ordered east with Kearny, 359

Sycamore. See *Platanus racemosa*

Tahkaibuhl, 10n

Talbot, Theodore: commands 1845 detachment, xxv, 22, 27, 45n, 47; joins 1845 expedition, 6; on selection of expedition men, 9n; at Fort Leavenworth, 9n; at Bent's Fort, 10n; route into California, 48–61; on JCF, 67n; on Castro's motives, 123n; at San Francisco, 124n; on death of de Haros, 186n; rejoins JCF at Monterey, 230, 234n; claim of, 287, 290n; as courier, 294, 295n; and trip east, 360, 361n

Tasso (bark): Montgomery sends munitions by, 214, 215n

Taxodium (JCF's cypress). See *Sequoia sempervirens*

Taylor, Zachary: and Mexican War, 193n; brevet mentioned, 214; JCF desires to join, 368n

Tays, George, xxx

Temple, Francis Pliny F., 189n; sells Al-

catraz Island, 317; in a list of names, 326; land grant of, 475

Temple, John: identified, 189n; lends money to JCF, 279; in a list of names, 326

Temple's Farm. See Ranchos: Los Cerritos

Third expedition: JCF on scope of, 3–4; route of, 6–7, 10n, 14–16, 19–31, 43n, 45n. See also Topographical party

Thomas, Francis, 141, 143n

Thompson, Bluford K.: in Battle of Natividad, 229–30; identified, 231n

Thorne, William (Billy the Cooper), 230, 231n

Thuya gigantea. See *Calocedrus decurrens*

Timpanogos. See Provo River

Tisdale, John B. (artist), 9n

Todd, William L., 158n

Toiyabe Mountains, 45n

Topographical party: Kearny's and Mason's orders re, 331, 340, 341; and supplies, 360; August 1847 number, 375

Toquima Range, 45n

Torre, Joaquín de la: at Olompali, 162n; and JCF, 163n; escapes, 183; identified, 272n

Torrey, John, xix, xxxn; and JCF's plants, xlvi; letters from JCF, 454–55, 479–80, 481, 483–85

Torrey River. See Williamson River

Trinity River, 90

Truckee River, 28, 62n

Tularé Lake Fork. See Kings River

Tulareños ("Tularie" Indians), 302

Tule Lake, 99

Tuolumne River, 32, 33, 36, 86

Turner, Henry Smith, 243; identified, 245n; on Stockton-Kearny-JCF feud, 270n; sent south with orders for JCF, 310n, 311n; on Kearny, JCF, and Benton, 311n; returns to Monterey, 323n; ordered east with Kearny, 359; to be witness, 390n

Turner, Mrs. Henry S. (Julia), 311n

Tyler, John, 8n

Uinta River, 43n

Umpqua River, 90; Hudson's Bay Company's post on, 113, 123, 128n, 138

U.S. Navy: strength off California, 169, 170n
Upper Klamath Lake, 95, 103; JCF at, 181
Utah Lake, 43n
Ute Pass, 15

Vallejo, Mariano G., xxvii; imprisonment of, 152, 154n, 155, 170–74 *passim,* 182; identified, 154n; plea to Montgomery, 158n; letters to JCF, 170–72, 304–5; letter from JCF, 276; appointed councilor, 276
Vallejo, Rosalia (Mrs. Jacob Leese), 154n
Vallejo, Salvador, 154n, 155; imprisonment of, 173, 174n, 182
Vandalia (vessel): Gillespie embarks on, xxxiii, 205n; JCF meets, 210n, 211
Vignes, Jean Luis, 326
Villavicencio, Javaela (wife of José de Jesús Pico), 236, 240n
Vincent, George W., 180; at Santa Barbara, 208
Vinsonhaler (Vincenthaler), Lorenzo D., 333
Viola chrysantha, See Viola douglasii
Viola douglasii, 41

Walker, Joseph Reddeford: joins 1845 expedition, xxiv, 20, 44n; guides Talbot, xxv, 23, 28, 47, 49; early explorations of, 50, 51, 55; and Chiles, 56; waits for JCF on Kern River, 61; battles with Indians, 50, 62n
Walker Lake, 23; JCF's party at, 27; Kern's description of, 52, 53–54
Walla Walla Indians, 174n; in Battle of Natividad, 230, 231n
Warner, William Horace, 359; to receive JCF's instruments, 361
Warren (sloop): and *Julia Ann,* 221, 222n; brought no money, 227; to transport discharged volunteers, 335, 336, 337, 338
Wasatch Mountains, 18, 43n, 44n
Washington *Union:* publishes JCF's 17 Sept. 1847 letter, 386, 387n
Washita, 8, 13n

Watmough, James H., 146, 153n, 168; identified, 147n
Watson, J. M., 308n
Waugh, Alfred S. (artist): describes JCF, xlvi–xlvii; JCF refuses to take on expedition, 9n
Weber, Charles M., 220; identified, 222n; and JCF, 225–26, 227, 228n, 229, 233, 234n; and Hastings, 227, 228n; and Montgomery, 228n; letter to, 229; opposition to, 233, 234n
Webster, Daniel, 149
Welsh, William, 203, 204n
Western Expositor (Independence, Mo.): on JCF's 1845 expedition, xxiii
West Point, 464n
Wetowka (Wetowa), 10n, 60, 120
Wharton, Clifton, 375, 464n
White, James T., 56
White Deer Creek, 13n
White River, 62n
Whitton, Jesse W., 21, 44n
Whitton Spring. *See* Mound Springs
Wilcox, Frank, 216
Wilkes, Charles, 126n
Williams, Isaac, 203n
Williams, William Sherley, xxiv, 43n
"Williams Fishery," 16
Williamson River, 103, 120
Wilson, Benjamin Davis: at Cajon Pass, 202–3; identified, 203n; capture of, 203n; on JCF, 258n; in list of names, 326; mentioned, 327
Wilson, Harris: letter to, 476–77
Wilson, John K.: letter to, 280; mentioned, 321n; and knowledge of JCF-Célis contract, 408, 420
Wiltsee, Ernest, xxx
Wislizenus, Friedrich Adolph, 484, 485n
Wolfskill, William, 326
Work, John, 125n–126n
Workman, William: letter to, 327; identified, 327n–328n; and land grants, 475
Wrighter, Benjamin, 333

Yount, George C., 132n
Yuba River, 87

Zeilin, Jacob, 344n